Second Chance

Louis Auchincloss

by Louis Auchincloss

Second Chance

TALES OF TWO GENERATIONS

❀❀❀❀

Louis Auchincloss

Houghton Mifflin Company · Boston

1970

"Black Shylock" and "The Sacrifice"
originally appeared in PLAYBOY *Magazine;*
"The Waiver," in *Cosmopolitan;*
"The Cathedral Builder," in *McCall's;*
"Days of Wrath," in *Redbook;*
and "Suttee,"
in *The Virginia Quarterly.*

First Printing   w

Library of Congress Catalog Card Number: 77-108306

Printed in the United States of America

For Adele
This, and all my work

Contents

Black Shylock

FRANCIS DOWS did not go along with the generally accepted principle of our century that a teacher has a moral obligation to like his pupils. Affection was not necessary to the training of tigers, seals or even of dogs, so why should it be to the instruction of such brutes as made up the eighth grade English class at St. Christopher's? Of course, he had to be careful to avoid being caught, by parents or even by the boys themselves, in any open display of animosity. It was a kind of parlor game, and one that the latter, God bless them, thoroughly enjoyed. They were always doing their exuberant, whooping best to drive him into open country.

The boys of St. Christopher's exuded the peculiar confidence of Manhattan's upper middle class, rejoicing belligerently in being thoroughly abreast of all modern currents. They were "up" on everything, from the destruction of the ecology to the building of antiballistic missile sites, and their ideas of integration, urban renewal and world disarmament were fashionably liberal. Sometimes Francis felt that he was being answered by thirty shrill voices from the *New York Times'* editorial page. It was a world that he had known only too well through his ex-wife's family. Indeed, his own son was in the eighth grade, a situation which the boy, considering his abominable grades, owed more to his maternal grandsire's position as chairman of St. Christopher's trustees than to his father's being a poor pedagogue.

Standing, on a November morning, by the door to his classroom in the five minute break between classes, Francis assumed the pose of storklike immobility that he felt to suit his tall, pole-like, darkly-tweeded figure and pretended to be oblivious of the din of the corridor. The eighth poured by him into the class-room, shouting, laughing, whistling. Francis ignored them, even when they greeted him loudly by name, as a long-incarcerated creature in a zoo might ignore the hustling crowd beyond its bars. His aloofness was not resented. He even enjoyed a certain bleak popularity with the older boys as a "character," whose reputation for sardonic sarcasm gave a mild status to those whom he deigned to notice. It was a mark of sophistication to be singled out as a target by Mr. Dows.

As the second bell sounded, and as Francis turned to enter his classroom, he spotted, peering up over the landing of the stair-way and apparently waiting for him to disappear, the pale, round countenance of Mr. Tomkins, the headmaster, and the redder one, under red-gray hair and over a blue collar, of his former wife's father, Leo Wright. The headmaster was taking his chairman on the monthly tour and obviously hoped to avoid a confrontation with the detested "ex." Chuckling, Francis strode over to them.

"Good morning, Headmaster. Good morning, Mr. Chair-man. I trust you are well? I trust Mrs. Wright is well? I trust all your family are well?"

"Just fine, thank you, Dows," Leo Wright grumbled. "Just fine."

"Would you do me the honor of visiting my class? I think you might find a bit of amusement in it. We shall be discussing *The Merchant of Venice,* which the eighth grade is acting for Christ-mas. I had so hoped that your grandson, Daniel, might play Gobbo, but Mr. Tomkins seems to feel that it would be difficult for him to be directed by his own father. Do you agree, sir?"

Mr. Wright gave a glance of appeal to the headmaster. Mr. Tomkins, normally a gentle, preoccupied man, could be surprisingly forceful under direct attack.

"It is hardly the time, Dows, to go into family matters," Mr. Tomkins reproved him. "Nor is Mr. Wright here this morning for his amusement. May I remind you that your class is waiting for you?"

"Thank you, Headmaster." It was another of Francis' little needling habits to address Mr. Tomkins in the English style. "I shall be with them anon. Good day, Mr. Wright. Please give my best wishes to Mrs. Wright. And to Mrs. Wright Dows."

And with a simpering smile as a final insult, he returned to his classroom, noting with satisfaction as he closed the door that the little encounter had been overheard and enjoyed by all.

"I was so hoping," he announced to the class, "that my former father-in-law, the august chairman of St. Christopher's board, would be able to visit us for a few minutes, but, alas, he is too busy. His time is precious. Your classmate's grandfather has a great name in the paper book industry. He brings Shakespeare to the unwashed multitudes. To the poor and lowly. To the slums and ghettos." Here Francis paused, as if lost in admiration. "In due time he will no doubt bring Shakespeare to the moon!"

He directed a smile at his son Daniel seated in the back row, but the boy did not return it. This did not have to mean any resentment on Daniel's part. He was very saving in his responses. He seemed to accept the situation, the reverse of his classmates', that he should see his father at school and not at home. He was a fat, moon-faced boy with small distrustful eyes. He did badly in his studies only because he was lazy. One could tell by the sharpness of the wisecracking with which he dominated his more successful contemporaries that he had a store of unused intelligence. He liked to loiter in corners, in playgrounds, in drugstores, and impress other boys with his knowledge of sex. For adults, as for schoolwork, he had no use, barely even contempt. It was as if he were simply waiting for the inevitable enfranchisement of time.

Francis pulled out his pocket watch and held it down to his navel as he examined it. "I shall ask you to write a theme this morning. Do you consider that Jessica was morally justified in stealing her father's ducats when she eloped with Lorenzo? Ten minutes."

Ignoring the groan that always went up at the announcement of a theme, he took his seat as they turned to their pads. He needed a moment to savor the little scene in the corridor. For six years now, ever since Arabella had flown to Juárez for their divorce, his keenest satisfaction had been in *not* resigning from St. Christopher's faculty. Word had been privately conveyed to him that if he would give up a position, originally obtained only through the grace of his father-in-law, the latter could be counted on to secure him a better one, at a larger salary, at Buckley or St. Bernard's. But Francis had retorted that St. Christopher's suited him down to the ground and that he liked being able to see his son Danny on weekdays as well as on the meager Saturday afternoon visits stipulated in the separation agreement drawn up by Mr. Wright's expensive counsel. Oh, he had them! They could never remove poor Danny from a school where his bad record was covered by his grandfather's favor, and they could never remove *him*, the wretched father, without seeming to act for the most invidious of reasons.

"Hand in your papers," he told the class, precisely at the expiration of the given time, "and let us proceed to the day's topic. We shall not discuss Jessica until I have read what you have to say. Personally, I think she was a bitch." He paused for a moment, as the room tittered. "I see that expression of 'Good, I guessed right!' on some of your faces. But most of you must surely know by now that your grades are not advanced by the coincidence (if it *is* a coincidence) of your happening to agree with me."

The tittering ceased, and Francis turned to the subject of the morning.

"We do not know how Shylock was portrayed in Shakespeare's day, but it seems probable, by comparison with Marlowe's *Jew of Malta,* that he was depicted as the blackest kind of villain. Certainly this interpretation prevailed in the next two centuries. It was not until the nineteenth that great actors, particularly Sir Henry Irving, began to enjoy playing him as a sympathetic, even a noble character. Today, in some quarters, there has been a reaction against this so-called 'sentimentalization' of Shylock. How about you, Burrows? How would you play him?"

"Well, I think, sir, you could do it both ways. Shylock is certainly a villain to plot against Antonio, but then Antonio shouldn't have spat on his gabardine."

"I've always found it a bit difficult to picture Antonio doing that," Francis observed judiciously. "It doesn't seem quite like him."

"But Shylock says he does."

"Perhaps he was speaking figuratively. Anyway, Antonio certainly sneers at him, which may be just as bad. How would you do Shylock, Gates?"

"I think I'd make him pathetic, sir. After all, he loved his daughter, and she betrayed him."

"*Did* he love Jessica? In what line of the text does he reveal that to you?"

"Well, I can't point to the exact line, sir, but the general impression . . ."

"I have nothing to do with your general impressions, Gates. How about you, Pitney?"

"Well, sir, I think I agree with Burrows."

Francis was disappointed as he went through the class. After all, at least a fifth of them were Jewish, though none came of orthodox families. He found it difficult to believe that the question of persecution would not, sooner or later, find its way into the discussion. But after ten minutes of chatter, he had to give up indirection.

"What about playing Shylock as the hero and spokesman of a persecuted race?" he demanded. "What would you say to that, Levy?"

"He wasn't persecuted, sir. He was disliked. I asked my father about it. He said we Jews were all right as long as we were only disliked. We can rule the world as long as we're only disliked."

"But Jews were more than just disliked in Shakespeare's time," Francis protested. "They were actively persecuted in many places. I wonder if their plight was not comparable to that of the Negro in our own time. Mightn't *that* be the way to play *The Merchant* today? With Shylock a Negro?"

The class murmured in surprise.

"But the text doesn't justify that!" Levy pointed out, shocked. "Everyone would think you had mixed it up with *Othello*."

"Works of art are like constitutions," Francis retorted. "They need to be constantly reinterpreted. We don't have to be confined to what Shakespeare subjectively intended. Burrows, you're going to be Shylock. How about doing it in blackface?"

"Oh, Mr. Dows, you're kidding!"

"I'm not, truly. I suggest it's the only way to make him the hero."

"The hero! But, sir, he wants to *kill* Antonio. He wants to cut his heart out with a knife. He wants to do it himself, too!"

"Yes, but *why* does he want to do it?"

"Because Antonio has been snooty to him."

"Exactly. Because he has spat upon him! Figuratively or not."

"But, sir, you don't cut a man's heart out for that."

"It's just what you *do* do!"

The last comment came from the back bench and was uttered in a kind of bark. To everyone's surprise the utterer was Daniel Dows. Daniel had never before voluntarily contributed to a class discussion, which had been set down to his natural embarrassment at having his father in charge. Similarly, he had refused any part in the class plays and could only be used to paint scenery. But now he seemed involved. He glared about the room as if his own integrity had been called in question.

"Thank you, Daniel," Francis replied. "I'm glad that the Dows think alike. Nobody is going to spit on *our* gabardines, are they?"

Daniel at this immediately lost interest. He shrugged and drew a large circle on the pad before him.

"Seriously, boys," Francis continued, "I suggest that Daniel and I are the only ones here in tune with the times. The greatest crime in the world we live in — perhaps the only one that young people still take seriously — is to insult a man because of his race. Now what does Antonio do but just that? He struts about the Rialto in his languid way, sneering at Jews and expectorating on their gabardines. For this he has deserved the humiliating death from which he is only spared by the tricky casuistry of Portia, a typical establishment lawyer. But the fact that Shylock goes down to defeat before white power cannot lessen the splendor of his ideal!"

The room looked at him doubtfully. They never knew whether he was joking or not, but like good bourgeois they also knew that it did not much matter.

"It would be an awfully funny *Merchant*," Burrows observed.

"It would be an awfully novel one," Francis returned, "and I can assure you that it would not be soon forgotten. What do you say we try it?"

This was followed by an outburst of questions.

"Would we change the text to make Shylock really black?"

"Would a Negro be apt to be a moneylender?"

"How about Jessica? What color would she be?"

"And Tubal?"

Francis held up his hands for silence as the questions proliferated. "We would not change a word of the text. The Jews in Venice would be black, that's all. Tubal would certainly be black. Jessica could be very light, for in the play she abandons her Jewish faith. But the real change would be in the Venetians. In the trial scene they would become a howling, lynching mob, out for Shylock's blood!"

The boys who were cast as Gratiano and Bassanio began to see possibilities in this, and enthusiasm gradually permeated the class. As Francis had foreseen, it was the idea of secrecy that most appealed to them, the prospect of confounding the Yuletime audience of their unwary parents with a shocking interpretation of the bard. By the end of the hour they were so excited that they were talking among each other, threatening corporal chastisement on any member who "leaked" the plan.

Afterwards, as he neatly erased from the blackboard the suggested chronology of Shakespeare's plays that he had as neatly chalked there for his own diversion, Francis considered with gratification the continuing frustration of Messrs. Tomkins and Wright. For how could they possibly object to his black Shylock? Was it not "relevant," as the young people said? Was it not just about as relevant as a production could be? Was it not precisely the kind of thing that his ex-father-in-law *pretended* to believe in?

He had met his wife while he had been working for this brisk, bustling, jovial, red-faced, red-tied, blue-shirted reissuer of classics and smut. Arabella and her brothers had been bigger, paler, milder reproductions of the busy sire whom they had wholly admired and almost invariably obeyed. Indeed, so far as Francis could make out, the only expression of filial independence in the life of his bland, blond spouse had been her surprising and bitterly contested election of himself. For Leo Wright, however strong a partisan of the struggling writer, had no desire for one in his own family. A writer to marry a Wright had first to make his mark, had first to qualify with a signed photograph in the gallery of celebrities that constituted the great man's office. It had been Arabella's single error to have believed that she had outguessed her progenitor in respect to Francis' capacity to join this gallery.

Oh, the Wrights had all tried, yes, but it had been worse than if they hadn't. Stuck with Francis Dows, they had attempted to make something of him, and in so doing they had revealed the full horror of their Philistinism. They had got hold of his poor, pale manuscripts and had belabored him with suggestions: that he should put in more sex or more violence, that he should use more images or more literary conundrums, that he should be obscurer or simpler, more lucid or more problematical. The only short story that he had published after his marriage, a brief sylvan fantasy of childhood memories of the Adirondacks, had been greeted with snorts of derision. "Writing for yourself in that way," his father-in-law had reproached him, "is a form of masturbation." Francis had retorted that publishing as the Wrights did it was a form of rape. This crack had resulted in his transfer to St. Christopher's.

Standing up to the assembled Wrights would have been all very well, might indeed have provided the justification of a lifetime — or part of one, anyway — had Arabella only learned her proper role. She belonged with her family — what could have been more blatantly obvious? Yet she had had the poor taste to cling tenaciously to her conjugal duties, to try with a foolish pathos to reconcile her family and husband, to quench the scorn of one and to deflect the irritability of the other. It exasperated Francis that, even agreeing with the Wright estimate of his incapacity as she could never quite help herself from doing, his wife should still want him. Arabella's husband might not be much, her blurry gaze seemed to concede to her impatient father, but might she not for that very reason be allowed to keep him for her own? There were moments when Francis, trying to prove to her what her mistake had been, was made to feel as if he were pounding with an oar on the desperate fingers that clutched the gunwale of a lifeboat. God, what a position to be in! There was no end to the malefactions of the Wrights. Even when he was most their victim, they went on as if *he* were the monster!

Arabella had given in at last. She had returned to her family with her son; she had gone to Mexico under the orders of her father's attorney. Back in the Wright camp she had resumed her filial, pre-Dows submissiveness. Nothing now interfered with the bristling wall of Philistia by which Francis felt himself encircled. The war would be open and clean and without quarter.

He could represent the soul of man against the spirit incarnate of vulgarity. He could fight the enemy from within its own citadel.

*

The rehearsals of *The Merchant of Venice* were almost as exciting as Francis had hoped. The boys developed an unprecedented enthusiasm. It exhilarated their director to observe with what high spirits and facility they converted themselves, under his interpretation, into a wolf pack. The boy who played Antonio, in his first scene with Shylock, was quite marvelously mocking. When he said, "The Hebrew will turn Christian: he grows kind," he did it in a pretended aside to Bassanio, but raised his voice so that poor Shylock would be bound to hear. Then he and Bassanio burst into wild shrieks of insanely insulting laughter. Salanio and Salarino continued the baiting in the same spirit, and Francis was almost ready to wager that by the time of the trial scene the audience would have been antagonized to the point of wanting a pound of Portia's flesh.

And then, only three days before the Christmas performance, Burrows, who played Shylock, came down with the mumps. For forty-eight hours Francis worked desperately with one and then another substitute, but it was hopeless. They simply could not learn the part in the time left. Francis locked himself in his classroom for fifteen minutes of contemplation. Was it, as his pounding heart told him, the chance of his lifetime? Then he walked down the corridor to the headmaster's office and announced that he would have to act Shylock himself or cancel the play.

"But *can* you?" Mr. Tomkins asked in astonishment. "Can you learn the part overnight?"

"I know it already," Francis replied, with a touch of superiority. "I shall simply have to run it over by myself and rent my costume. But for that I shall need all tomorrow morning off. Can you get someone to take my classes?"

"Certainly, my dear fellow. I'll take them myself!"

"Then I shall be here at two. The curtain's at two-thirty. Everything else is ready."

Francis made himself up the following afternoon in a closet off the stage. He allowed nobody to see him until the curtains had actually parted, and he could hear Antonio, in the opening line, wondering why he was so sad. Then he walked to the wings and awaited his cue.

There was a gasp from the dark void beyond the footlights as the tall black figure in flowing robes of sky blue strode out upon the stage followed by a gesticulating Bassanio. Folding his arms, towering ominously and silently over Antonio's friend, the Shylock of Francis Dows gazed contemptuously about at a white man's Venice. He allowed the would-be borrower to gesticulate for a minute before he responded, with a rich low gravity of tone: "Three thousand ducats; well." He maintained this air of aloofness right up to his first aside, and then, stepping to the footlights and removing himself abruptly from the world of Bassanio and Antonio, he shouted in a fit of fury, directly into that section of the audience where he knew Leo Wright was sitting: "I hate him for he is a Christian!"

In the negotiation of the contract he never fawned hypocritically, never whined and bowed, as he had seen so many Shylocks do. He pointed out, in measured tones, with haughty demeanor, the wrongs that Jews habitually received of Venetians and contrasted these with the good that he ostensibly offered to Antonio, throwing off the implied question, with a magnificent shrug of his shoulders, of which, under the circumstances, was the superior race.

As the audience recovered from the first shock of his costume

and black face, it became silent as a school audience hardly ever
was. When Shylock went off-stage, the applause was tumultuous.

Francis, exulting in the wings, thinking with feverish rapidity, decided on a new version of the scene with Tubal. This had
posed the biggest problem for his heroic interpretation, for in it
Shylock seems irretrievably avaricious. But he would play it
now as if the stolen ducats represented to Shylock the indispensable weapons of a persecuted race. When he came on stage, he
was bent over, groaning, clasping his hand to his side as if in
despair at the thought of an empty scabbard. And his contempt
for Jessica was total, monumental. She had written herself out
of the tribe; she had ceased to exist for him. The money that he
was spending in her pursuit was only to recover the ducats, ducats that would be vital to his war against the hated Christian.

The trial scene was the perfect climax to his interpretation.
Never had he dreamed that the eighth grade could rise to such
histrionics. As he stood in the center of the court, drawing himself up to his gauntest, his grimmest, running his finger gently
over the bared blade of his knife, the boys who played the Venetian riffraff howled about him, screaming anti-Semitic insults,
and were pushed back by supposed marshals of the court. Francis, aware of the tenseness of his audience, wondered if he had
not become the incarnation of the spirit of old Africa demanding the flesh of Simon Legree!

The boy who played Portia almost stole the scene from him.
He was cute, giggling, tricky. It was as if all the principal characters were in on the plot, drawing it out only to intensify the
ultimate humiliation of the Jew. But Francis had everyone's attention back at the end. When he broke, he broke rapidly,
bending over as if stricken by a hideous stomachache and fairly
screamed in his agony. Then, limping slowly, his hands on the

shoulders of two tiny marshals, he hobbled off stage, as if to desired extinction, while the mob howled in victory.

When he appeared to take his curtain call, the whole room rose. It was a day without precedent. His ex-father-in-law came backstage to shake his hand.

"It was a fantastic experience, Francis," he said in a tone that his ex-son-in-law remembered as the one that he reserved for his most important authors. "I take a personal pride in the whole thing because I always maintained that you had a first-class talent. Only we didn't know exactly what it consisted of. Now, of course, it's clear. You're a great interpreter! You have the gift of putting Shakespeare across so that he's almost frighteningly alive. I don't say that you should necessarily go on the stage. But maybe we should arrange for a series of Shakespeare readings or recordings. I don't know. We'll have to see. We'll have to look into things. God bless you, my boy!"

When Leo Wright had left, Mr. Tomkins came in to add his felicitations.

"I've brought someone else to see you, Francis," he said, and Francis turned around to see his son.

"You were good, Dad."

Francis stared intently at that impassive face. Then, with only half an idea of embarrassing the hovering headmaster, he threw his arms around the boy's neck. Mr. Tomkins fled.

"Oh, Danny, do you really think so?"

Danny pulled away roughly from his father's embrace. "I said I did, didn't I? You don't have to make a production of it."

Francis stood up straight at this, again the teacher, a bit wilted, of the eighth grade. "I'm sorry. I must have been carried away. I guess that's what acting does to a man. And a very good reason why gentlemen should not become actors. But your approval means something to me, Daniel. I've only had its reverse. I've only been conscious of you sitting there, in the back of the classroom, sneering."

"I don't sneer at you."

"Oh, come off it. You know you do!"

"I don't. You're a good teacher. You're a good actor, too. Ma says you could have been a real actor."

"*Does* she? I didn't think she ever mentioned me."

"Oh, she talks about you all the time. She's always asking about you. You could have her back, you know. You wouldn't even have to whistle."

Was it possible? Was it conceivable that life could be that simple? That all he had to do was whistle, and a loving, rich wife would be his? For a moment Francis felt like one who has been awakened from a deep sleep by the sudden rattle of a shade snapped up. He turned away, writhing inwardly, burrowing his face into an imagined pillow to shut out the hard, garish light of a world that refused to let him be a rebel and martyr.

"No, Danny, I can't do that. I can't put the clock back. I never fitted into your grandfather's family, and even if divorce is wrong, remarriage doesn't make it right. And I'm not going to stay on at St. Christopher's, either. Because I've discovered something. I've discovered I'm a fraud and a phony. I've cultivated the art of protest without having anything to protest about. I've been playing parlor games in a world that's serious. But at least I know now what a man can do. A man with a cause."

But even as he talked he felt his elation draining away. He was not going to be a man with a cause. Not at forty, anyway. The human mind was made up of habit as the body was of water. And as the vision of his indefinite continuance as a self-

dramatized rebel, a poser before boys, jumped back into his
mind, like an old, hated slide stuck in a projecting machine, he
felt nausea in his throat.

"Daniel, help me!" he appealed. "Help me! I can't stay
here!"

The boy turned and walked deliberately to the lectern. It was
the headmaster's, kept in that room while the stage was in use,
and it supported the great school Bible from which the lesson
was read at prayers. As Francis watched, paralyzed, his son
opened the heavy volume, grasped a full handful of pages and
ripped them out. Tossing them to the floor at his father's feet,
he stated in his flat tone, "You told the class that if a man spat on
you, you should cut his heart out."

Francis, awed, knew that he was looking into the eggy eyes of
a delinquent. He would have to find a cause, and a good one, to
make up for what he had done to him.

The Cathedral Builder

HENRY ADAMS said that the archangel loved heights; it was why he had perched on the dizzying pinnacle of Mont Saint Michel. He might have perched high, too, over Manhattan, had the spire of Saint Matthew's ever been completed and had he been able to take his proper place, his trumpet to his lips, at an elevation of three hundred feet over the hilltop double block that looked down, on the west to Central Park, on the east to the East River, on the south to Park Avenue and on the north directly into Harlem. But Saint Matthew's Cathedral had never been completed, and it stood without transepts, without towers or spire, with naked ribs over its crossing, a vast French Gothic monster, huddled miserably on its hill, as if hacked and slashed by sadistic giant enemies and left to die, a sad reminder of the difference between Protestant Episcopal ambition in 1900 and its actuality sixty years later.

It had been nothing to me before I had met old John Lancaster. I had a small apartment a few blocks south and had to pass it on my way to the subway, and I had once attended a wedding in its vast and rather awe-inspiring nave. I had tended to go along with the conventional sneers to which the edifice was always subject: that it was absurdly derivative, hopelessly out of touch with our times, that it was the queen of anachronisms, a futile and desperate effort to capture, with twentieth-century money and twentieth-century engineering, a few warm sparks from the vibrant flame of the Gothic age of faith.

But to old John — he was eighty-nine when I met him —

Saint Matthew's was simply the most beautiful church in the
world, and he had seen the great French cathedrals. He would
point out details of the statues in the porches, of the figures on
the bronze doors and argue that twelfth-century workmen had
not had the tools to accomplish what we were able to accomplish
today. Every Sunday he and his wife would sit under the window of the temptation in the wilderness that his father had
given, and John would ponder the problem of the unfinished
cathedral in his heart. The first time that I had been summoned
to his office in Everett & Dunton, my eye had at once taken in
the architect's print of the completed church over his desk.

"Is that meant to be Saint Matthew's, sir?" I had exclaimed in
surprise. "Oh, if it could only look like that!"

He had slapped his black-veined, brown hand on the crackling copies of an old trust accounting and exclaimed, "It will,
young man. It will! How long do you think it took to build
Reims?"

But even three years later, sitting at old John's funeral service
in the narthex under the great north tower which had been his
first love, I still could not believe it. For who else had his faith
in the cathedral? Who even wanted to have it? From the back
row of folding chairs brought out there for the service, my eyes
traveled up and around the clerestory that rose a hundred and
fifty feet from the floor stones and I made out two of the upper
windows. One was in shimmering deep-sea blue, Christ on the
waters; the other mixed the same blue with scarlet for the
moneychangers in the temple. It *was* — at least inside and on a
wintry morning, somber except for the sudden blinding beams
when the sun, emerging from behind a cloud, enkindled the
high windows — a beautiful church. One could not see the
spineless crossing, the uncovered ribs, the stubby front. Every-

thing — at least everything I could see from my folding chair — seemed awesome and austere.

And then I realized with a start that I had changed my conception of it. Always hitherto I had seen the cathedral with my own eyes. This had ceased. It was not simply that, hurrying to the early service, I had missed breakfast and was imagining things on an empty stomach. I was actually seeing the cathedral through John Lancaster's eyes — seeing it, I mean, with all his bias, just as I had previously seen it through my own and those of others. In a blaze of revelation aided by the sun's return, I understood at last what it had been to him, or even possibly what it now was to him. It was heaven! As it had once been the symbol of the Kingdom of God on earth, now perhaps, for him at least, it was that kingdom itself. I stretched my neck to see all the way down the giant nave to the altar encircled by its eight monumental marble pillars linked by Romanesque arches, and I tried to picture John Lancaster's God there, tall, with steely gray hair, robed in glistening white, raising the communion cup to the cross as in mellifluous tones he uttered the beautiful Jacobean words of the prayer book.

For there was no question that John's God would be white, Anglo-Saxon, genteel and of the Protestant Episcopal persuasion. John believed that his deity had been apologized for too much by defective servants in recent decades of chaos. Now the deity was supreme again, and ranged below him I could almost make out his lesser priests, subservient at last, repeating their respectful responses, a fat Irish monsignor, a bearded rabbi and a Negro Baptist preacher reminiscent of "De Lawd" in *The Green Pastures*. I felt a faint shudder, as used to come over me in reading descriptions of hellfire. Suppose it were *true?* Suppose I, too, were dead and gone to heaven, his heaven, to sing everlastingly under the vaulted clerestory of Saint Matthew's to the Holy Trinity? I closed my eyes and remade the image of the stunted exterior. No, the cathedral was not finished and never would be. I welcomed chaos again.

2

Everett & Dunton, where I had first met John, was a small, ancient law firm on William Street lucratively but unobtrusively engaged in an estate and trust practice. The four partners made large incomes and pretended they didn't; the half dozen underpaid clerks fell into two categories, depending on their age: those who were sullenly resigned to their fate and those who spent their lunch hours hunting a better job. I was among the latter. The clients were either dead or so interwound with one of our estates that it was cheaper to put up with our slow service than go elsewhere. We were a small forgotten pocket, a backwater, a fossil imbedded in the vast structure of the law. There are thousands such.

John Lancaster was a member of the bar, but he was neither a partner nor an associate of the firm. He rented the dingy little office with the roll-top desk and the architect's drawing of the finished cathedral under an arrangement with the firm that went back so far that even the older partners had lost track of its origin. In his jumbled downtown life, which seemed to consist of a vague insurance business and some oddly unprofitable fiduciary positions, Mr. Lancaster helped himself to law clerks and stenographers with a liberality that was countenanced by my bosses in the long sustained faith — reputedly based on nothing but legend — that he was a millionaire and that they would ultimately handle his estate.

We clerks liked the jaunty, cocky, dapper little man, with his

breezy formulas for every occasion, who would pause in our
doorways to tell us jokes, always clean, that might have been
garnered from the files of the New-York Historical Society. He
seemed a benevolent apparition from the preceding century,
with a rich flavor of Dickens, a Scrooge redeemed on his way to
buy a turkey for the Cratchits, a chromolithograph from a Victorian novel in our drab back offices. His laughs and exclama-
tions were loud, crackledy and automatic. The way he briskly
rubbed his hands in cold weather and his brow in hot seemed
dictated by the calendar rather than the thermometer. He
bobbed about the office like a Punch — one almost expected
him to take a swat at people with a stick held between his arms.
We loved to think that he would prove a splendid fraud and die
a pauper.

If he were rich, it was certainly not evidenced by his style of
living. He and his old wife, childless, had never moved from the
bleak, comfortless apartment that they had purchased at the
turn of the century on Riverside Drive (then showing prospects,
later doomed, of becoming fashionable) or added a single
picture to the collection of egregious fakes of Flemish and Italian masters that John's grandfather had purchased on a "grand
tour" in the 1830s. Mr. Lancaster had perhaps seemed well-to-
do as a young man; as an old one he might have been disguising
poverty quite as easily as wealth. He tipped the elevator man a
dollar at Christmas and returned his charity appeals to their so-
licitors bearing the legend of his special stamp: "I regret that
increased taxation makes it impossible for me to support your
worthy cause."

I have always had a cult of the near past, the past of my parents and grandparents, and I made a point, whenever I was doing a job for Mr. Lancaster, of drawing him into a discussion of
New York in the nineties. It took me some time to discover that

he never told me anything that I could not have found in one of those big popular illustrated books called *New York Yesterday* or *Treasures of Our Past.* Mr. Lancaster's memories seemed to be made up of famous headlines. And besides, unlike many octogenarians, he had an intense interest in the present. It was not that he approved of anything that was going on. On the contrary, he disapproved, very decidedly, of everything, but never in a whiny, cantankerous, old man's way. The troubles of the modern world seemed to strike him as not only richly deserved but as faintly hilarious. He would pause at my door every morning to chortle over a strike, a political scandal, a riot.

"Keep it up, keep it up!" he would exclaim, as if in some vague fashion I had been the engineer of the day's crisis. "When more than half the population is on welfare, will the minority be allowed to strike? Or would that be an unfair labor practice? Eh, Jerry? Eh, what?"

He had cultivated disapproval until his mind had become a kind of rock garden of fixed but complacently expressed hostilities. There was no hate in his animadversions. Indeed, there seemed to be very little of the juice of human emotion left in him. He sought me out and lunched with me occasionally in a cafeteria (Dutch treat) but only because I listened.

His passion for Saint Matthew's Cathedral was, I suspect, the one true passion of his life. His father had been a member of the original fund-raising board, and Bishop Hilton, the church's Pope Julius II, had been a cousin. Mr. Lancaster loved to fulminate against the "Laodicean" Episcopalians of our day who no longer even tried to raise the funds needed to finish the edifice conceived by their braver and more idealistic predecessors. When I once suggested that my contemporaries might not find the completion of a giant Gothic cathedral the solution to what they deemed the important problems of the day, he stood

with a raised hand and forefinger in my doorway like a denunci-
atory prophet.

"And what is more important than the House of God? Oh, I
know, they say it's not the right kind of house. You hear a lot of
tommyrot about its being derivative. Of course, it's derivative!
If French Gothic is the right style for cathedrals, why should it
be confined to France? Or to the twelfth century? Eh? Isn't
your White House derivative? Isn't Monticello? Aren't the
greatest English country houses Palladian? How do we know
that the Parthenon wasn't copied from some older temple? I tell
you what, young fellow. We must go back, way back, to find our
faith again. Do you expect to find it in the Museum of Modern
Art? God help you!"

When I was bold enough to ask him if he would take me on a
tour of the cathedral and show me why I should believe in it, he
was so pleased that he did an unprecedented thing. He invited
me to his home for lunch the following Sunday.

<h1 style="text-align:center">3</h1>

I had thought that I knew enough about Mrs. Lancaster from
the financial starvation that she must have had to put up with to
be justified in picturing her as a mild, resigned, rather blurred
little lady. But, as it turned out, she was not that at all. She was
a brisk, talkative, sensible, white-haired, red-faced old girl who
monopolized me as if I had been her friend and paid no attention to her husband or to the ancient crone who served our indifferent meal. In fact, she seemed as alien to the whole
apartment with its glass cases of cracked nineteenth-century
porcelain shepherds and courtiers, its elaborate, rotting Victorian furniture, its ghastly paintings, as if she were a guest and
stranger like myself. I soon made out that she loved movies, de-

tective stories and cards. She and Mr. Lancaster seemed to live
together without quarrels and without intimacy.

"John says he's going to take you on a tour of the cathedral,"
she observed toward the end of our meal. "I'm afraid I have a
bridge engagement, but anyway I shan't be missed. The cathedral is John's mistress, you know." She exchanged perfunctory
smiles with her husband down the table. Obviously, it was an
old, old joke. Looking at him, however, she was reminded of
something. "Oh, I didn't tell you, did I, John, the funny thing I
saw during the sermon this morning?"

"No, m'luv."

"I happened to be looking at the tomb of Bishop Hilton."
She turned to me to explain. "It's in the north aisle, under the
window. There's a marble effigy of the old man, laid out in his
robes and miter. His aquiline nose rises like a great mountain
peak over a snowy plain! Well, while I was gazing at it, a small
Negro boy scrambled up on the tomb and *grabbed* that marble
nose. It was really too funny, too absurd."

I had seen John Lancaster excited, but I had never seen him
angry. He turned to an alarming shade of red. "I'm glad you
find it so amusing, Justine!" he shouted at her. "You could
probably cackle at the sight of your own house on fire. The boy
does that because he has no respect for God or his cathedral.
And *why* does he have no respect? Because God cannot finish
it! It stands there as a symbol of his powerlessness! Young people despise weakness. They despise it in man, and they despise it
in God. And they're quite right, too!"

Mrs. Lancaster was completely unperturbed by his outburst.
Indeed, I suspected that she enjoyed it. "Oh, John, you take it
all so seriously. That boy would have tweaked the bishop's nose
just as much in a finished cathedral. It's *where* it is, that's the
trouble. They built it too far uptown."

"God isn't uptown or downtown," her husband grumbled, and they dropped the subject.

Mr. Lancaster was preoccupied for the rest of our meal and even preoccupied on our tour of the cathedral. He hardly looked up as we trudged down the aisles and circled the chapels in the apse. He pointed up to windows and nodded at bays, but he explained nothing and answered my questions in monosyllables. When we paused before the recently desecrated tomb of Bishop Hilton, he seemed very pensive. Obviously, his wife's anecdote had deeply disturbed him. Only afterwards, resting on a bench in the garth to enjoy the early spring air, did he resume communication.

"You must have observed, young man, that I have treated you with more familiarity than the other clerks in the office."

"You have been very kind, sir."

"Would you like to know why?"

"I suppose you find my work satisfactory."

Mr. Lancaster smiled with a sudden foxiness. "That's very true. But there is something more. I want you to know *me*. I want a smart youthful witness to be able to testify, if necessary, that I am perfectly sane."

I stared. "Has anyone doubted it?"

"Not yet. But they may, when they hear my plan." He put his bony fingers on my knee and gave it a painful twitch. As I stifled an involuntary exclamation of discomfort, he hissed in my ear, "I'm going to finish the cathedral!"

I was surprised at the keenness of my immediate disappointment. I had become fonder of the old boy than I had realized, and I hated the idea that he might, after all, be senile. "And how do you propose to do that?"

"By spending my fortune." He sat back now, still watching me, and complacently crossed his arms.

I glanced up at the wall of the uncompleted south transept. "Have you enough? Has anyone?"

"Young man, you will go with me to my vault tomorrow and count securities!"

4

John and I sat in the bare windowless chamber of the safe-deposit company, counting the piles of crisp, crackling stock certificates that we had removed from the big metal box on the table. Picking up paper after paper, engraved with the legend "one thousand shares" under pictures of factories, of tractors, of trains, of vessels, of forests, lakes and rivers, of eagles and buffalo, feeling the wealth of America snapping through my fingers, I reflected that to a modern miser this might be an adequate substitute for the chink of hoarded gold. When we had finished, I made a rough tabulation and then carefully checked the market prices in my morning *Times*. If there had been a question, it was all gone now. John's holdings in only thirty-six companies came to an aggregate value of more than twenty millions.

His expression as he watched me was almost beatific. He grabbed the pad on which I had jotted my final figure and, holding it close to his now tender eyes, nodded his head several times and uttered a dry little chuckle. The close atmosphere of the tiny room made me think of a tomb. I might have been an Egyptian slave, buried with his master and his master's treasure. What were those clean bare gray walls but the walls of John Lancaster's life, protecting, uselessly, his useless wealth?

"Well, there we are," I said, shrugging as I threw down my pencil. "You have convinced me, although I was perfectly happy to take your word. And if you propose to give this money away, is it for me to complain? I'm not one of your heirs."

"Oh, I have none! Or so distant as to be almost untraceable. I'm the last of four old New York lines, and Justine has her own money. So there's no reason, is there, that I should not put a lifetime's scheme into immediate execution?"

"A lifetime's? How could it be?"

"Well, not quite a lifetime's, of course. I could hardly have planned to finish a cathedral before it was begun, could I?" Old John seemed to derive an actual warmth from the presence of those little heaps of securities. He reached his long, thin fingers toward them as toward a fire. "But the cathedral began abuilding seventy years ago, my boy. That's quite a hunk even of my life."

"And you planned this back *then?*"

"Well, the idea formed itself very slowly. I hoped at first that Mrs. Lancaster and I would have a family. It was many years before I abandoned all hope of that. And then, of course, I had to make the money. Or, rather, help the money to make itself. What you see before you, young fellow, represents the fruit of sixty-five years of investing and reinvesting! Do you know what my original inheritance amounted to?"

"What?" I asked, still a bit dazed.

"Slightly under four hundred thousand dollars. And I have never spent a single penny of the principal or income! I set it aside for growth, and, ever since, I have lived on what I earned."

I reflected that Mrs. Lancaster was fortunate to have enjoyed her own money. But what appalled me most was the boldness of the old man's justification of all the decades of his miserliness. He was not hoarding, not he. He was guarding his chest for God!

"But why, sir, have you waited until now?"

He gave me a sharp glance. "You think I took quite a chance, do you? I took none at all. For the past thirty years my will has bequeathed my residuary estate to the building fund of the cathedral."

I started now, under his instantly jealous eye, to replace the securities in the box. My mind was filled with questions that there was no point putting to him. He would have no better idea than I of the psychological origin of his avarice, or of what shattering childhood episode or condition had prompted him to build this hidden fortress of securities against an imagined terror. But the great question was not why he had done it or even what excuse he had manufactured for it, but how he had managed to decide to turn that excuse into reality. I could entirely see that a miser might convince himself that he was saving his gold to build a church, but how could he break out of the vice of his habit — particularly at eighty-nine — to *do* it?

"I should have thought that, much earlier, you would have wanted the pleasure of seeing a dream become a fact," I ventured.

"I always knew that I should have a sign when the proper time had come."

"And that was the boy tweaking the bishop's nose?"

The door opened, and the attendant for whom I had rung entered to take the box. Mr. Lancaster rose quickly to follow him to the vault. Obviously he would have to see the precious box restored with his own eyes. But even on so solemn a task he seemed to retain some of his new gleeful, Puckish mood. He turned to wink at me.

"I think the disgraceful episode to which you refer," he half whispered, "was a sign, if anything, that I was overdue!"

5

Bishop Sherwood, who knew Mr. Lancaster well, had some difficulty taking in the project. He had a charming, melancholy gray face and a charming soft voice. At first he thought we were talking about the new plan of the trustees to finish the cathedral on an "as is" basis, simply covering over the exposed portions of the skeleton to turn it into a modern Gothic box. Mr. Lancaster was highly contemptuous of this idea.

"Let me tell you at once, Bishop, that I shouldn't care to contribute a nickel of my money to that shameful abortion! No, sir, I am talking about completing the cathedral on the *old* plan. I have seen the estimate, and I am prepared to pay. If you don't believe I have the money, ask young Haskins here."

The bishop looked slowly from Mr. Lancaster to me and then nodded. He had lived too long among the rich not to know that the maddest schemes were often based on the plainest realities.

"You will forgive me, Mr. Lancaster, I trust, for my slowness in grasping the princely quality of your proposition. Of course, I shall assemble my board immediately to tell them the great news." Here the bishop stared down for several seconds at the spotless white blotter on the vast uncluttered surface of his desk. "But let me be bold enough to ask you one thing. Are you absolutely convinced that you wish this splendid generosity to be expressed entirely in bricks and mortar?"

Mr. Lancaster's eyelids drooped to give him the languid expression that I knew signified suspicion. "What do you mean? Is there some other material that you propose to build the cathedral with?"

"Well, of course, you and I, sir, love the cathedral, but I suppose we can still face the fact that its size — and even its site —

may not be wholly suitable to the troubled world in which we live. I cannot help wondering if the expenditure of so vast a sum on an edifice, at the very gate, so to speak, of Harlem, where so much real poverty exists, may not bring down upon our heads the anger of that community. Perhaps if we could issue a press release to show that for every dollar spent on the cathedral, another would be spent on parish houses or church schools or missions . . ."

"That is perfectly acceptable, provided you get those other dollars from other donors," Mr. Lancaster interrupted in a metallic tone. "*My* money must go entirely for construction. However, that need not embarrass you. You may publish to the world that you were faced with the alternative of taking my money for the cathedral or not taking it at all. I can hardly believe that under those circumstances anyone would criticize you."

"Only those who do not read the newspapers."

"Really, Bishop!" Mr. Lancaster now rose to his feet, and his voice quavered. "Can you not leave the construction of God's house to God? How do you know he has not sent me?"

The bishop, too, rose, genuinely distressed. "I am sure he did, Mr. Lancaster. But maybe also he sent *me* to make these suggestions. However, it goes without saying that I shall lay your proposal before my board this week."

If Mr. Lancaster was a bit deflated by the bishop's reaction, he was more so by his wife's. We went to his home for tea immediately afterwards, and he told her the plan.

"You don't seem surprised," he muttered, as she continued, imperturbably, to busy herself with applications of cream and sugar.

"I'm not in the least surprised. Do you think I've been unaware of your obsession?"

"And you don't mind about the money?"

"Why should I? I can always live on my own. Granted, it's not much, but I don't need much. I'm like you, John. I don't really care about money."

"*I* don't care about money? Why, over the years I've nursed it like a baby. I've nurtured it and made it grow. I've even . . ."

"Nonsense! You've hoarded it, that's all."

Mr. Lancaster became very dry at this. "Are you implying, Justine, that I have not treated you right?"

"Of course not. I've had everything I've wanted, just as you've had everything you've wanted. The point is that neither of us have wanted very much. We'd have been just as rich with one million as twenty. You've worked and fussed all your life over that money. Now I'm glad you're going to let it work and fuss over you."

"But that's just what I'm *not* going to do, Justine. You don't seem to understand. This is charity!"

"Precisely. And charity begins at home."

Which was all Mrs. Lancaster had to say on the subject. I could see that old John was disappointed. Perhaps he had looked forward to shocking her, the eternally unshockable. But, on the other hand, was it not a carte blanche beyond his wildest expectations? How many wives, even at her age, even with her means, would have kissed good-bye so easily to so great a fortune? When I saw him turn his attention now to his tea and drink it noisily, I realized that he was not going to push his luck with Justine any further.

6

Nobody but I foresaw the disasters of the next two years, because nobody but I understood how imperative it was to John

that the cathedral be completed in his lifetime. It was not
enough that he should guarantee its construction; he had to see
it in all its final glory. Against this goal there were two grave
impediments: the rapid rise of building costs and his own great
age. Only two months after the festive dinner given by the
trustees in John's honor, I began to suspect that big as his fortune then seemed, it was not going to be nearly big enough.

And then the church authorities were so slow. There had
been no construction done on the cathedral for a quarter of a
century, and the inertia that had set in took months to dispel. It
was fully a year from the date of John's pledge before the
scaffoldings for the north tower were up, and by that time John
himself had become quite agonizingly conscious of the problem.
He had a new estimate made of construction costs and found
that he was already short by six million. He appeared ashen-
faced at the door of my little office to announce the catastrophe.

"The spire over the crossing must go!" he almost sobbed.
"That is all there is to it. It must go, my beautiful, beautiful
spire! Oh, God, that you should be so served, and by your own
priests! By your own priests!"

We went together uptown in a taxi (he had become suddenly
quite careless of expense) to meet the architect in the bishop's
office. Neither of these gentlemen seemed at first to sense the
dimensions of the tragedy. Why could the question of the spire
not simply be left to the future? The Lord had sent one John
Lancaster. Might he not provide another?

John's voice rose shrilly in reply: "But I must see the cathedral finished! Can't you understand that? The roof of the
crossing cannot be left an eyesore as it is now."

The bishop and the architect became very grave at this. If, at
some time in the future, the money for the spire were ever

raised, the expense of erecting it would be greatly increased if the roof over the crossing and transepts had been completed.

"But you never *will* get the money for the spire!" John almost shouted at them. "And my pledge calls for completion of the edifice. Read it!"

It was decided that no action could be taken without another meeting of the board, and when, at that meeting, the resolution to complete the cathedral without the spire was carried by only one vote, John realized that he would need more help in the future. He went to the partners of the firm and offered to pay my salary if I would work for him exclusively. They agreed. Their bedazzlement at the revelation of his fortune had been equalled only by their dismay at his announced determination to dispose of it in his lifetime, but no doubt they had calculated that he might die with some of it unspent and that it might still be profitable to be his executor. As for myself, I agreed for the simple reason that I was now in so deep with old John that it seemed impossible ever to pull out.

The next year and a half was a strange, terrible time in my life. My intimate connection with his enterprise seemed to sever me, not only from my own identity, but from the rest of life itself. I lived in a feverish dream, working for an end in which I had neither faith nor enthusiasm, trapped in an old man's mania. John expected me to act as his scourge in driving architects, contractors and divines to a frenzy of speed. Usually, I failed. Occasionally, I saved a month, sometimes two. Slowly — oh, so slowly — the great north tower began to rise.

But John seemed to age with its construction. He came hardly at all to the office now, but spent his mornings at the cathedral, sitting on a bench, a black cloak huddled over his shoulders, staring up at the scaffolding. The lines under his opaque gray eyes and at the corners of his lips had become dark trenches, and the skin of his neck and hands was as brown and spotted as ancient leather. Sometimes he was so still for so long that he might have been the sculpted figure of some old, shriveled martyr waiting to be hoisted to its niche in the porch over one of the main doors. A mocking press sent photographers to snap him, but he did not even notice them. He lived for his race with time.

I thought in contrast of the complacent patrons painted into medieval religious pictures. John seemed more a victim than a patron; it was as if the great dark cathedral above him had lured him into its shadow and was waiting, remorselessly, to crush him to dust by the mere suggestion of its countless stones. John, seeking for heaven, seemed to have stumbled among the damned. His frozen features, expressing anxiety and despair, might have been a detail in the last judgment of some old Florentine master.

Why had it had to happen? Why after eighty-nine years of living by the rule of each day, why after so many decades of being clean and clear and brisk and neat, why after the precarious happiness of his small but durable heap of aphorisms, had this little old gentleman come to this sorry fate? Was his a face for such an agony? Why should the sufferings of a Michelangelo have been stuffed into the pelt of poor John?

The north transept had to be abandoned; then two of the apse chapels; then the roof of the crossing — at least as planned. And finally the plans for the south tower, the twin of what was now being built, was in danger.

On a chilly fall afternoon, as I was urging him, one arm about his shoulders, to go home and get away from the darkening sky and now biting wind, I felt him suddenly go limp, and I hoped for a moment that he had died. I even found a second to pray that he had. But then he straightened up, opened his eyes and glared at me.

"It's all up, Jerry. Of course, you've seen it all along. The money will do for the tower and the south transept. All I shall have accomplished will be to have made the cathedral look more ridiculous than it already does. May God forgive me."

"It's not so," I protested bitterly. "Now you've made the start, other rich men will come forward. You'll see."

"No, Jerry. The show is over. You will prepare a letter for my signature authorizing the cathedral authorities to use the balance of the pledged fund for their general purposes. There is no reason that I should bind them to throw good money after bad."

I did not even wait for the following morning. We went into the cathedral then and there and sat in two chairs at the end of the nave while I wrote out the letter on a piece of blank stationery that I found in my briefcase. John signed it, and I took him home in a taxi. We said nothing all the way, but when I helped him out at his apartment house, he pressed my hand with his cold, bony fingers. I think we both realized that we had awakened from a mad dream.

7

It was a bit of a shock to me to find, after the funeral, that I alone was to go in the limousine with Mrs. Lancaster in the tiny cortege that proceeded to Woodlawn Cemetery. But, of course, who else was there? It was cold, and we shared the blanket over our knees. Mrs. Lancaster was entirely in character: no tear glistened in her eyes; no throb altered her usual tone of voice. We might have been going to a matinee.

"I had quite a time with the bishop," she told me. "He wanted to eulogize John and tell the story of the tower. But everyone there knew it. And in death I find that I lean toward Rome. No flowers, no special prayers, no laudations. Corpses are all equal. If there's a God, he knows what you've done. If there isn't, why prate about it?"

"I felt that Mr. Lancaster was there," I ventured, after a moment of hesitation. "I mean, actually there in the cathedral. I felt that was what heaven might be for him."

Mrs. Lancaster, however, had little inclination for this kind of speculation. She gave me a brief, faintly pitying glance. "If it's ever finished, you mean. The way it is now, it's more like purgatory."

"I wish he could have thought at the end that there was at least some hope."

"What had John ever done for God or man to deserve the blessing of such a hope as that?"

I was taken aback by the sharpness of her tone. "Do you count all he did to build that tower nothing?"

"I don't know what you mean by nothing. It was his pleasure. His hobby, if you will."

"Nothing more?"

"Well, *what* more?"

I knew, of course, that she was right, but it seemed indecent, on the way to the interment, to maintain such rigid fair-mindedness.

"But he suffered, Mrs. Lancaster, he *suffered!*" I exclaimed. "I haven't been with him through this last year without being aware of his agony. If he hadn't been so old, I would have said it had killed him."

"Well, something has to do that, at ninety-one," she retorted. "I see you think me a heartless old bag, and perhaps I am.

Being married to John Lancaster for sixty-one years didn't exactly help. In the beginning I used to try to get through the wall of his dry little jokes and expletives, all his steely little habits, but time taught me that it was hopeless."

I felt that so many things were in pieces that I didn't care what else I tossed to the floor. "Then you didn't even love him. He didn't even have that."

"I don't know if John and I had love. We had a bond. I daresay it's as much as many people have. You may have more one day. I hope so. You're full of sentiment, which is nice. Don't marry a girl like John, that's all. It shouldn't be hard. I can't imagine there are very many of them."

Mrs. Lancaster seemed to realize now that she had shocked me. She wanted to make up. It was all wrong that she, the bereaved, should be the consoler, but so it was.

"I'll tell you another thing, Jerry," she continued in a placating tone. "The last two years have been the best."

"You mean for you?"

"Not at all. I mean for him."

"How do you make that out?"

Her snort was magnificent, as she seemed to cross me off for the last time. "Because he *lived,* my poor friend! Can't you see that, you who love clichés?"

Well, there was certainly nothing left that I could say to *that.* If she chose to believe that the privilege of living consisted of futile suffering, if it gave her some weird consolation to think that her own life at the card table had been a lesser thing than her husband's, something further from the central pulse of man's existence than old John's sobbing over his unfinished church, I was not going to deprive her of it. What depths of cynicism underlay her sentimentality! But I had to do some thinking about myself. I had to get out from under the little pile of symbols that John's death had brought crashing down upon my head.

"He liked to believe, poor man, that he had been divinely inspired," she continued. "Like Joan of Arc. Those people have their compensations."

"I'm sure they must enjoy the flames," I said bitterly, and then, at last, the poor old girl was silent.

I had my image now, such as it was, the image that would have to be *my* comfort. It was a photographic mental picture of the north tower, handsome but cold, dull, uninspiring, yet nonetheless impressive in its sheer size and in the obvious expensiveness of the workmanship that had gone into it. I saw all of its ineradicable modernity, and yet behind that I could still make out some hint of the long past age of which it was so determined to be the nostalgic expression. And perched on a balustrade, a fist under his chin, hook-nosed, elfin, with eyes staring vacantly into space, ugly but by no means detestable, a non-soul neither in bliss nor in purgatory, not a bishop nor even a communicant, but there, indisputably there as long as the tower should stand — and one was not sure how long that would be — was the gargoyle which was already too much a gargoyle to more than suggest my late friend.

The Waiver

When Julie Leinsdorf had moved into her small, expensive new apartment on Central Park South, with its splendid but not quite compensating view of the great green oblong of Central Park, she had been warned by a friend to convert the spare bedroom as promptly as possible into a library.

"Or any other kind of stiff inhospitable chamber," the friend had added, "so long as it can't be slept in. A guest room in this city is the height of folly. The first thing you know you'll be putting up friends of friends."

But Julie had had more confidence in her own powers of refusal. She wanted a bed for an occasional visitor, particularly for her son Bobbie when he came on from Hollywood. She did not need a library as her few books, all sets, went very prettily in the living room with the dining alcove, amid her bibelots and French period furniture, on either side of her portrait, done only ten years back (or so she allowed her friends to pretend to think) with the long red hair, the long ivory arms and tapering fingers, the long, haunting pale oval face. It was absurd, paying what she had to pay for the protection of a doorman and a smitch of view, not to be able to offer a night's shelter to a friend.

It was thus that she had been saddled, first with Jane Doyle and then with Sally. Her daughter Karen, mother of both, who lived in White Plains (if, as Julie always said, one could call that living) had made such a scene about the burden of Jane's city rent while Jane was taking courses at Columbia, that Julie had finally succumbed and invited the girl to spend the winter with her. It had been a ghastly failure. Jane, big, dark and flat voiced, had been interested only in "restructuring" society and had obviously regarded her grandmother as the kind of parasitic anachronism that had betrayed their sex through the ages to the contempt of all serious revolutionaries. Jane had been twice arrested in six months for illegal protests, and Julie had been spared the ultimate pain of evicting her by the girl's own decision to go to Washington to work in the poverty program.

But Jane had been promptly followed by Sally. Sally, it was true, was a good deal more Julie's idea of a granddaughter, having even a smattering of Julie's old beauty: the oval face, the luxuriant hair (though long and straight, and blond), the wide eyes with the steady gaze, and she had also more fitting ideas of a woman's role in life, being a model and not a rebel, but she took even less interest in her grandmother than had Jane. Jane at least had cared enough to disapprove; Sally seemed entirely intent on herself and the handful of moody, hirsute boys who came to the apartment to listen to records in her room. Her answers to Julie's timid questions were usually that they were "irrelevant" or "unmeaningful." Asked once directly if she was "happy," she had replied, "My friends don't think in those terms."

Karen Doyle, mother of these Gracchae, came in from White Plains once a week and always lunched with Julie. Who else, her mother would ask herself fretfully, would have paid for her meal? It was hard to believe, with that big, white, staring, watery-eyed face, with that sullen chin and those immense hips — like the hips of lower-class women who lived on starch — that Karen was only forty-two. Small wonder Bill Doyle was always away on business trips! Small wonder that if he *did* earn any money, he didn't choose to spend it on his wife and children!

"I don't understand either of your daughters," Julie grumbled to Karen on the latter's first visit after Sally's answer to the "happy" question. "I don't understand their whole generation. What do they want out of life, anyway?"

"Well, certainly Jane and Sally want different things. Jane wants to do the world over, and Sally wants it in her stocking for Christmas."

"I wonder if it doesn't come down to the same thing. It's always *themselves* in relation to everything else. Why are they so egocentric? And why must they take it so completely for granted that all older people are dunces? I suppose it's the affluent life of the suburbs that one keeps reading about. With the father off on business trips and the mother playing bridge or drinking martinis . . ."

"I *don't* play bridge!" Karen retorted indignantly. "I can't afford to lose. And as for martinis, most of the time I have to settle for beer." She turned a light pink as she caught her mother's expressive glance at her hips. "And poor Bill doesn't take any more business trips than he has to to hold his job!"

"You needn't take it all so personally," Julie reproached her in a gentle tone, wondering how any woman dared to let herself sound as unattractive as Karen did.

"You meant it personally, Ma, and you know it!"

"No, no, I was thinking on a much broader level. You never give me credit for that, Karen, but I do sometimes. I was thinking that we all seemed to be caught up in this thing. We women, I mean. Jane caring only for revolutions and Sally for men and I . . . well, and I worrying whether the pink of that divan isn't perhaps just a shade too pink." Julie here smiled the "candid" smile that usually disarmed her interlocutor. Of course, she knew that Karen was totally immune to it. "We twentieth-century women find our lives over too soon. We burn ourselves out. We love too young. We marry too young. We have our children too young. And then, suddenly, they're grown up and burning themselves out, and we have nothing to do but shake our heads and watch them make the same old mistakes."

"I have plenty to do!" Karen retorted. "I'm on the library board. I'm district secretary for the community fund. And Bill and I take drawing lessons at night because his boss says everyone ought to have a hobby!"

"Darling, if you *will* be so personal, there's no point our discussing anything."

"Oh, Mother, you make me sick. You say Sally cares about men. What the hell do you think you ever cared about? What is all you care about *now?* I hate to think what would happen to me if Bertie Cram and I fell overboard, and you had only one life belt to throw!"

"I don't happen to be a modern parent, Karen. I will not tolerate being spoken to in that vulgar way."

"Oh, shit."

Julie reflected, when Karen had gone, that she really hardly liked her anymore. Surely not many mothers could have as little satisfaction as she from their children. Karen was the embittered consort of a man who was always just about to fail in business but never quite did, and Bobbie, though a moderate success as a screenwriter, was a militant pansy and, like so many such, inclined to be biting and sarcastic to his mother. Was it any wonder that she preferred the company of Bertie Cram to any of what her lawyer, Mr. Pryor, liked to describe as her "issue"?

Of course, there was no point even arguing with Karen on the subject of men. Karen, like all frumps, could not conceive that a woman who had been married four times could ever have cared about anything but sex. She could never have been persuaded that to brand her mother as a "four time loser" was to take much too seriously three out of the four ceremonies in which Julie had become a bride.

Yet one had only to examine them fairly, which nobody ever did. Her first marriage, to Hank Leinsdorf, had been the "real" one. It had had love and youth and children in it, and it had lasted, after all, for twenty years. Had it been her fault that Hank had become an alcoholic and divorce a practical necessity? Then there had been the ridiculous "rebound" marriage to Ted, a compulsive philanderer, which had lasted less than two years, followed by the dreadful decade that she had spent shackled to Brent, the Pasadena hairdresser with sexy eyes who had evaded Mr. Pryor's every effort for a valid divorce until finally bribed with a shocking sum. And, lastly, there had been the sentimental farce of her remarriage to Hank Leinsdorf on the mistaken theory that he had been cured. Rationally reviewed, did it not boil down to a single marriage, ruined by drink, and the predictable consequences to a lonely and desperate woman?

And take Bertie Cram. Was he not in the same boat? He had been married for half his adult life to the mother of his four children who had left him, for no reason at all, during the nervous crackup that had accompanied her change of life. Since then he had done what any normal, healthy, humiliated man might be expected to do: he had married and divorced a couple of absolute *whores* who had fleeced him of his last cent. But now, at sixty-five (which was her age, too, though nobody would have guessed it except for the brutal fact of Karen) he was a respectable, attractive, hard-working man trying to come back as a customer's man in a brokerage house where the youngest partner was half his age. It was not easy, and Bert carried it off with style. But once the world started sneering, it seemed, it never stopped. Even Karen, who always needed help, financial as well as emotional, felt entitled to sneer.

Bert and Julie met at least every other day. Half the time, to save his pride, they dined in her apartment or in the restaurant on the ground floor of her building in which she could sign the check on the theory that it was an extension of her home. On other occasions he took her to parties given by his friends, who seemed to be many and prosperous. But Julie was always very strict about the proprieties. Bert was never allowed in her apartment after midnight, nor would she go to the apartment of any of his married friends unless the wife had written or telephoned to invite her. She maintained that the more a woman had been married, the more careful she had to be.

What existed between them might have been described as a unilateral engagement. Julie liked to have it tacitly understood that he was committed, but that she was not. He had proposed, and she regarded his promise as binding, although not accepted. He was to be respectfully, never importunately ardent; she was to be cool, tolerant, the least bit sad about the whole thing. His hope was to be of the slenderest. It was even permissible for his friends to think of her as "cruel."

On the very evening of Karen's stormy departure, however, and as if to prove that the world that day was in conspiracy to destroy the gentle diversions of Julie Leinsdorf, Bertie Cram presented her with an ultimatum. Sitting at their regular table in the downstairs restaurant, he suddenly announced that his situation was becoming ridiculous.

"My friends call me the languishing Lothario," he pointed out. "They say I'm tied to your apron strings."

"I'm glad they think of me as wearing an apron."

"Now, Julie, don't take it that way. Every gal I know is madly jealous of your looks and figure, not even to mention your clothes. Emmy Starr was saying just the other day that you reminded her of Jeannette MacDonald in 'The Love Parade.' If I told her you had two grown-up granddaughters, she'd drop dead!"

Julie wondered if it might not have been for her preservation that the gods had made her different from other women in one respect: she was at her most levelheaded in the presence of a man. When she was away from Bert, she tended to see him in the light of a hero, as sincere and brave and manly in a world that had treated him badly, but with him she was alert to his least aspect of shabbiness. The Bert beside her now fell just short of what he seemed to be when absent, of what she most needed him to be, of what indeed he would *have* to be if she were ever to be Mrs. Cram. For all his straight steely hair, firm nose, unwavering gray eyes and stalwart figure, for all his effort in tweeds and pipe to seem a "man of distinction," there was something in his cryptically steady gaze of the apprehension of a blow, of the air of a man who has been downed once and would not find it at all impossible to be downed again.

"And how long do you give me to make up my mind?" she inquired.

"You make me sound so unreasonable, Julie! I'm simply asking you to do me the honor of taking my offer seriously. I'm not saying, if you don't, that I'll stop seeing you next week or next month or even next year. I'm only saying that we can't go on like this forever."

"We're not going to live forever, Bert. I'm not anyway."

"Please, dearest! Be nice."

Julie looked quickly up to see if the waitress was near enough

to have heard his "dearest" and frowned irritably upon finding
that she was. Really, the whole thing was too tacky. Why on
earth should he be so anxious to marry her unless he needed the
money? It was no fortune, heaven knew — she had to invade
her principal heavily each year — but it might seem one to a
pauper. And even if she exempted him from being mercenary
for himself, might he not want to marry her for his children's
sake? Might he not even deem it his duty? Wouldn't that make
it worse? She shuddered at the idea of his big, brassy daughters
moving in with her, rearranging her things, cadging small
loans.

"Where would you propose that we be married?" she asked
when the waitress had moved off. "By a justice of the peace?"

"Oh, better than that, honey. Much better. Judge Davis, of
the Appellate Division, would be glad to do it. He's an old
friend of mine. We could have a little reception in his chambers
afterwards with champagne and everything."

"But wouldn't we have to go to one of those awful clerks in
City Hall and have our divorce records checked? Oh, Bert, I
can't go through that again! Think of it, *seven* of them between
us! Oh, no, it's too degrading."

"I'll slip the man ten bucks, and he won't say a word."

"Well, I'll think it over," she said dolefully. "That's all I can
promise you."

Upstairs, alone in her apartment, she was wretchedly nervous
and upset. She yearned for someone to talk to, even Sally, and
when she heard her key in the front door, she jumped up in
excitement.

"Hi, Gran."

For once, happily, the girl was alone. Her pale face wore its
customary air of expressionlessness, but when Julie asked her to
have a nightcap, she shrugged with a shade less indifference than

usual and allowed her body to drop heavily on the fragile sofa. Then she pushed her hair out of her eyes.

"I don't use alcohol."

Julie was careful not to take up the question of what she used instead. "I need your advice. I'm thinking of getting married again. To Mr. Cram."

Sally stared. For the first time since she had moved into the apartment she seemed to take Julie in as a person having an existence independent of Sally Doyle's. But the process was not necessarily a complimentary one. "You? Married?"

"Well, I have been before, you know."

"Yes, but not for ages."

"I don't know what you mean by ages. Or where you young people get your ideas about life!" Julie was surprised at the pitch of her own irritation. It must have come from the state of her nerves. "I don't know why you have to assume that all the world but yourselves are decrepit. And even if we are, we still have the same feelings you do. Why, I feel more things for Bert Cram than I even felt for your grandfather. So there! You think you know everything, but you're really as ignorant as a goose!"

Sally considered this without the least show of resentment. Then she nodded. "Perhaps I am. I never thought of it that way. Perhaps it's Mother. She's always talking about how old *she* is. It could be her hysterectomy."

"I wouldn't be at all surprised," Julie agreed with an instant rush of sympathy. All her irritation vanished as she tossed Karen on the suddenly glowing coals of this new relationship. "Not in the least bit. Your mother's one of those women who like to forget they're women. At forty-two! Imagine. Except I suppose even that seems old to you. But it's not, my girl. Far from it! I've never had that operation, and I'm still very much a woman, thank you!"

"Do you sleep with Mr. Cram?"

Julie quailed. It seemed a very odd question for a grand-daughter to be asking. But she tried to rise to it. "No."

"Why not, if you feel that way?"

"Because he wouldn't respect me."

"Oh, Gran!"

"He wouldn't, Sally. He's not like the boys of your generation. Believe me, I know."

"The forms mean that much?"

"The forms mean that much to some people."

"It's fantastic!" Sally threw her head back and stared at the ceiling. "Here you and I, according to what you've just said, are in the same boat. On the same cruise, the same trip, if you want to put it that way. Under the same moon and the same stars. You see it, you say you feel it, but you still care what labels are fastened to your luggage, way down in the hold!"

"Maybe that's the generation gap."

"Maybe." Sally smiled for the first time in her visit to Central Park South as if she were actually amused. Then she yawned and got to her feet. "At any rate I suggest that the first thing we do is get one of those labels. Obviously, you and Mr. Cram had better be married as soon as possible."

"Oh, darling, do you really think so?"

"Don't you?"

Julie jumped up and peered anxiously into the girl's clear, sober eyes, searching hard for reassurance. "Maybe I do, Sally. Maybe I have, all along. Maybe I just needed you to straighten me out. Perhaps you young people know a thing or two we don't."

Sally now attached herself to her grandmother. She seemed determined to see her through. She insisted on calling her "Julie" and dropping the outmoded "Gran"; she took her to new dress shops and raised her hemline above the knees; she joined her and Bert, with one of her less obnoxious boy friends, on two occasions for dinner, and, after the second, insisted that they all go down to the East Village to a psychedelic nightclub. Julie had been rather frightened by the deafening music and the violent dancing, but Bert had obviously loved it, and she had supposed that she should be grateful to Sally. The latter at least had brought her to the point of consulting her lawyer.

Mr. Pryor, a big-nosed, bold-eyed, bald man who made appalling jokes and did all the laughing at them, had represented Julie on her last two divorces. Being afraid of him, she dared not go to anyone else. Yet his obvious sharing of all her doubts about Bert did little to ease her state of mind. His green eyes positively shimmered with hostility to the proposed mate as he laid down the necessary preliminaries to any legal union. First and foremost, Bert would have to sign away any and all rights that the law might give him to share in Julie's estate. He would have to "waive."

"I'm not sure he'll do that, Sam. He's very proud."

"Oh, he'll do it all right," Pryor retorted drily. "He won't show his hand by refusing. He'll hope to charm you into leaving him everything by will. I know these 'gentlemen,' Julie. Give me a few days to investigate, and then we'll have him down here."

But when that day came and Julie was sitting again in Pryor's office, nervously watching him and Bert face each other across the former's wide bare desk, she was not at all sure that Bert would back down. He looked very wary. Indeed, she had never seen him so still or so intense. Even Pryor seemed less confident. The jokes were more numerous than usual.

"I guess if there was ever a case of two being company and three a crowd, you think it's right now, eh what, Mr. Cram? But

I don't want you to put any of the blame of this meeting, or of the suggestion that I'm going to make, on our fair friend here. *I'm* the one and only big bad wolf in this fairy tale. Not, I trust, that there are any fairies in it. Our problem seems quite the opposite." Here his stertorous laughter stunned Julie like the music in Sally's nightclub.

"Please, Mr. Pryor, come to the point."

Never had Bert sounded more dignified, more manly.

"Very well then, Mr. Cram. Very well. If you like the service speedy, the service shall be speedy. We like to please our customers. I want to point out that you and Mrs. Leinsdorf each have your own posterity and, presumably, your own property. Under the circumstances it is only natural, indeed it is essential, that in uniting your destinies you should first exclude any property of Mrs. Leinsdorf's from the normal operation of matrimonial claims."

"I should never dream of interfering with Mrs. Leinsdorf's disposition of her own property. Is that what you're getting at, Mr. Pryor?"

"It is, sir. It is precisely that. In fact you've struck that little old nail smack in the middle of its little old head. All I want you to do now is to implement your intention by a short but effective legal instrument. Isn't that the neat and tidy way to do things?"

"Perhaps it is, sir. But it's not mine. As I say, I should never contest Mrs. Leinsdorf's will. I should never assert the least claim against her estate. But neither, on the other hand, will I agree *not* to do such things."

"Why not, Mr. Cram?" Here Mr. Pryor allowed himself what was almost a wink in Julie's direction.

"Because, sir, a gentleman scorns to promise that he will be a gentleman. If Mrs. Leinsdorf does not trust me enough for that, she does not trust me enough to marry me. Good day, Mr. Pryor." Bert rose and made a stiff little bow to Julie. "I leave you, my dear, in the tender hands of your watchful counsel. My part in this conference is obviously concluded. I do not wish to influence your decision by remaining. You will know where to reach me if you desire."

Julie was so bewildered and upset that she could not even say good-bye. But as soon as the door was closed behind Bert, Mr. Pryor abandoned his smiles and jokes.

"I'm afraid he's smarter than I thought, Julie. He's gambling for higher stakes. You may have to give him up."

"You're not very complimentary, Sam. Do you assume that no man would marry me except for money?"

"Not any man. *That* man."

"But he's risking the marriage! If he's so mercenary, why wouldn't he sign the waiver, as you said the other day, and marry me in the *hope* that I'd leave him something? I would, too!"

"For a very good reason. Once you were married to him, you'd know the jam he's in, and once you knew *that*, you wouldn't leave him a nickel."

"What jam? I know he has no money."

"But you don't know that he has obligations. Family obligations. One of his daughters, Ethel, has just discovered that her husband has a swollen heart and can never work again. The other, Miriam, is about to be divorced for her affair with an elevator man in her apartment house. They'll both be swinging around his neck, *with* their children. Need I tell you whose neck they'll be transferred to?"

"Not mine! I won't give them a penny! I'll tell Bert that, too. He'll understand."

"But without that waiver he'd have the right to a third of

your estate on your demise. And I'd be mighty careful what I ate or drank if I were *his* wife under those circumstances."

Julie stared at the horrible man in panic. "But that won't be!" she cried, as if he were slowly advancing toward her with a deadly weapon. "That won't be, because I'll never marry him! Not unless he signs that waiver, anyway!"

"Would you marry him *then?* Knowing what you know now? Knowing what he hasn't told you? Knowing what he wasn't *going* to tell you?"

Julie covered her face with her hands and sobbed. "What shall I do, Sam? For God's sake tell me, what shall I do?"

"Go on a cruise, Julie," the voice came back at her, still firm but gentler now. "Go on a cruise in the Caribbean. Take Karen. She's tired and frazzled with suburban life. She'll be only too happy to go with you. You two ought to find a lot in common now. Oh, I know you've had your quarrels. A family lawyer has to know these things. She and I have talked about Cram, and we're a hundred percent agreed. You two should go off together now, away from the slush and sleet, and forget everything but the sea and the card table. Leave Mr. Cram to yours truly. I'll write him a very polite but a very conclusive letter. Don't worry. I won't say a word about his family problems."

Karen responded eagerly to the idea of the cruise. In fact, she took over all the plans and arrangements with so firm a hand that only three days after the suggestion had been made she and Julie were seated in the crowded foyer of the S.S. *Britannic* amid noisome going away parties, drinking the half bottle of champagne that Bill Doyle (who had seemed very pleased at his wife's good luck) had sent them. Julie decided that she had never felt so depressed in her life. She had neither seen nor talked to Bert since he had walked out of Pryor's office, and she was bleakly determined to face the fact that she had ruined her life. Karen looked more than usually on the defensive in a new and unbecoming green box hat.

"The only thing worse than being seen off is not being seen off," Julie grumbled.

"Sally said she was coming."

"Oh, the promises of *that* age." Julie waved her hand wearily to dismiss them. "Why should she come, anyway? She thinks I've made a fool of myself, and she's probably right."

"Now, Mother."

"She *is*, Karen. Why should I care what you all say about Bert's being after my money? Is he any more after it than you and Bill are?"

"That's a nasty thing to say, right at the beginning of what's supposed to be our happy reunion together. And even if it were true, I have some claim to that money. Daddy made it."

"He did not! More than half of it came from *my* father."

"Oh, Mother, let's not be sordid. Bert Cram's no good, and you know it. Let's try to forget him. Maybe we'll meet a nice man on the cruise."

"Really, Karen, you're getting too common. They're all gigolos. Besides, the way I feel right now, I expect to expire in my cabin."

"Fortunately they carry coffins aboard. Just in case."

"Thanks! What a gay start we're having. Oh, thank heaven, there's Sally now."

Sally, in a very short bright red skirt, a satchel swinging from her shoulder, was crossing the foyer in her loping stride. "Could I speak to Julie alone?" she asked her mother abruptly.

"I hate your calling your grandmother 'Julie,'" Karen protested, but she got up. "Don't be too long. I want to say goodbye to you myself, dear."

Sally ignored her, saying nothing until she had gone. "Julie, he's here," she then said quickly. "You've got to get off this crazy ship. You've got to get off this crazy ship and marry him."

"Sally, I can't! He'd eat me out of house and home. He'd fleece me for his ghastly daughters!" Julie's voice suddenly died on her, and as she waited for it to come back, she was frightened by the violent pounding of her heart. "Why do you act for him?" she cried in anguish. "Why do you want to do me in? What has he given you?"

"Don't be idiotic, Julie. I want you to be happy. I want you *both* to be happy. For once, anyway, in your tragic, wasted lives. What does it matter if he needs your money? What could you do better with it than help him?"

Julie stared at the girl. "And what would become of *me* then? What would he do to me when it was gone?"

"Well, wouldn't it be interesting to find out? Come, I'll show you where he is!"

Julie allowed herself to be dragged out on deck and dazedly followed Sally's pointing finger to a spot in the crowd on the pier. Bert was standing by a bollard, smoking. As she watched, he tossed his cigarette down on the oily water. He seemed assured, relaxed, perhaps too relaxed, certainly too assured. Then he looked up, suddenly, as if feeling her eyes upon him, and smiled and waved. Julie waved feebly back.

"Come on, Julie, get off the boat," Sally hissed in her ear. "I'll tell Mother. She can take the cruise alone. She'll be all right."

Julie could not take her eyes off Bert. As always, when she saw him, she saw him clearly. He was not in the least sinister, after all. He would never kill her, or even hurt her. He wanted her money, of course, and if he ever got his hands on it, he would spend it, as he had spent his own. But having spent it, he would not leave her. He would even try to support her, as a recompense. He was only doing for his daughters what he felt he had to do for them. And so discreet, so quiet, so gentlemanly a husband would he be that she would not be able to keep her purse shut. Suddenly she sobbed. It would never do. It was the best that she was offered, but it still would never do. The only thing that terrified her now was that she might still give in.

"No!" she cried to Sally. "Life is bad, but it's not that bad. I'm a poor creature, but I have a little money and a few nice things and just enough fortitude to know that at my age that's more than a man. More than *that* man, anyway."

"Julie!" Sally's voice had a sudden righteous lilt. "Is that what it all boils down to, after all? Your absurd illusion of security? What has it ever done for you, I'd like to know, your poor smitch of a rag of security? Your pathetic little handful of stocks and bonds and your sacred chastity belt of divorce decrees? When will you *live?*"

Julie looked sadly down to the wharf and took in for the last time her "life." She gave him a final wave.

"Wait till you're my age, dear," she said as she turned away. "You'll learn what those things are worth."

"Never!" the girl cried.

"Oh, yes, you will."

"Never!" she cried again, this time with passion.

Through the loud-speaker system now came the warning: "All ashore who are going ashore." Watching Sally's back as the girl walked to the gangway, Julie thought with dismay that the cruise would last only three weeks and then she would be home with the job to be done all over again. With Bert, probably, or with someone worse. No, with Bert. Always with Bert. Putting her hands to her eyes, she thought almost with relief of those coffins down in the hold.

The Prince and
the Pauper

BROOKS CLARKSON knew at once when his wife had gone too far. For years he had waited for the moment, knowing that he would recognize his doom when it fell. And, what was more, he was convinced that the other guests at that little Saturday night party in Glenville, all contemporaries, all weekday commuters like himself, had recognized it at the same time. That might have seemed curious to some. Was it so unusual for one of his crowd, on Long Island's not notedly puritan north shore, to get roaring drunk on Saturday night? If Fanny Clarkson, so gay, so fée, such a bewitching little wisp of a blond doll, kicked off her slippers, stripped to the waist and sang an obscene song, wasn't it the natural release of any poor female after a week of suburban coping? Doomed? Brooks Clarkson doomed? Doomed at thirty-nine, when one was as handsome as he, a partner, like his father before him, in the Broad Street firm of Emmons, Taylor & Clarkson, with a beautiful house in Glenville, a beautiful wife and three beautiful daughters? Yes! Certainly!

Fanny, like Eve, had first tasted of the apple, but he, like Adam, had readily followed. For years now they had been going to bed half sozzled. It was such a simple way to cloud over the beady eyes of the world: the eyes of his law partners who suspected that his smooth talk and high connections covered a deficiency in aptitude, the eyes of his fellow trustees of the Glenville Library, the Glenville Museum, the Glenville Art Society, who suspected that he used his civic positions as a cover for his spiritual emptiness, the eyes of Fanny herself who suspected that he was only half a man. Oh, blessed sin, blessed whiskey! But, of course, he and she were bound to drink more and more, and people were bound to get sicker and sicker of them. And that, in the long run, would provide a kind of dim solution.

Brooks had a theory of what was wrong with him. He had never divulged it to a living soul, not even to Fanny, and he never would, but he hugged it to his heart. It was a conceited, odious little theory, but it did not have to be either conceited or odious if no one knew. It was simply that he was different from other people. He was different from his clients, his partners, his Glenville friends, his cousins, even his brothers and sisters. He was different because he was an aristocrat, the last of his breed.

It was not, obviously, considering those who were *not* aristocrats, a mere question of birth or money or position. These things were only the outward and dispensable signs. It was a question of soul, and questions of soul could never be hidden. Somehow he stank of it, somehow it exuded from him, and, inevitably, like some bleeding creature in the ocean, he was bound to attract the notice of carnivorous neighbors. For his fellow Americans might worship wealth and admire arrogance; they might be dazzled by power and taken in by strutting, but they would never pardon an aristocrat. They could never forgive a man who conceived it his duty and privilege to serve his social inferiors. They would never forgive *noblesse oblige*.

And now the farce was almost over. Now the last invitations in Glenville would cease. Now his partners would meet secretly without him to discuss steps to be taken. Now he had been summoned, so to speak, before the Committee of Public Safety, and everyone knew how *that* had to end. There would be a brief incarceration; there would be the travesty of a trial; there would be the ride in the rumbling cart through narrow, jeering streets and finally the relief of turning into the big sun-bathed square and seeing ahead, soaring over the upturned faces of the vulgar and curious, the tall narrow instrument that guaranteed his swift release.

Fanny could not suspect all this, but she suspected something. She gazed at him darkly over the rim of her cocktail glass the next day, a Sunday, when they were alone before lunch. Brooks stood with his back to her at the bar table, slowly mixing his own, feeling the intensity of her gaze.

"Why do you give me this drink, darling?" she asked in her high, bright tone. "Shouldn't I be punished?"

"Punished? For what?"

"For disgracing you. For behaving in a way that would have convinced your late sainted grandmother that I was the Whore of Babylon. Don't minimize it, Brooks. Be angry. Don't you see, I want to be punished?"

"You were a bit gay. Why not? Is that a crime? Remember what Sylvia Fales did last week."

"Ah, but she's not a Clarkson."

"She's married to my cousin, isn't she?"

"Somehow it's different. Anyone can do anything but a Clarkson. As a matter of fact, any Clarkson can do anything but a *Brooks* Clarkson. Tell me the secret, honey. Why do you bear the sins of the world alone? I pine to know."

"There's no secret, Fanny." He turned and brought the shaker over to fill the empty glass that she held out to him. "You're imagining things. All I want is to have you enjoy yourself. All I want is to have you be happy."

"Even if I'm a happy lush?" She took a deep sip from her refilled glass. "Even if I make an ass of myself again next Saturday night?" Her luminous, faintly feverish eyes followed him about the room. "Sometimes I think you'd be glad if I went to pieces. To get it over with, once and for all."

"Fanny!" he cried, "how can you say anything so horrible? Don't you know I want the world for you?"

"Oh, your world!" She laughed desperately. "What do I want with your world, Brooks? What could I possibly do with it? Does it even exist?"

Brooks never had anything to say to this kind of comment, and when he had finished his drink, he quickly poured himself another. Not until the third, however, did he begin to sense the tingle in the ears, the prickle in the chest, the glow about the heart, that accompanied the gradual cessation of pain. With gin they would get through until the guillotine.

2

Brooks had no real friends, but, as appropriate for an aristocrat, he had a protégé. Patronage was a function of his class, and he took it seriously. He made himself responsible for Benny Galenti, whose position in life he saw as the inverse of his own. If this were so, the ultimate outcome had to be as happy for Benny as it should be sad for himself.

Benny started in Emmons, Taylor & Clarkson as an office boy. He was the son of Italian immigrants on the Lower East Side, and his original ambition had been to be a lawyer. He had a slight, tight physical build, thick shiny black hair and blue, staring eyes, slightly misted, as if the sunny Sicilian sky of his family's origin had been diluted with the smog of a new world. Like many second-generation Italians, he had lost the color and excitability of the first. He was careful, methodical, almost Nordic. He had gone to night college and completed one year at law school when the disaster of his fiancée's pregnancy had necessitated their marriage and the permanent abandonment of law.

Brooks had been attracted to him from the day when Benny,

intuitively sensing the junior partner's need to befriend an inferior, had walked into his office and asked for a loan. His wife, it seemed, was having a second child, who would be an "Irish twin" of the first. Brooks at once advanced the money, which was promptly repaid, and later made many other loans, which enjoyed the same happy fate. Benny, eased of his burdens, shot ahead in the firm. He seemed pushed by a demoniac energy that might have been designed to prove that he was as good as any lawyer. When he finally achieved the post of office manager, petted by the partners and feared by the clerks, Brooks was especially gratified. If he was the soft old past, Benny was the ruthless future.

But there was one thing on which he had not counted: Benny's gratitude. Brooks was considerably disconcerted to find that his protégé was determined not to let him go to the devil with impunity. Benny would come to his office, close the door and subject his benefactor to endless sermons.

"You've got to kick the booze, Brooks, and you've got to watch your office hours. Do you think your partners don't know just how many Fridays you've taken off this past year? And just how many days you've wandered in at noon? Do you think they don't know about that bottle of bourbon in your desk? Quit kidding yourself! They know all those things and many more. They're planning right now to cut your percentage by a full half! Mr. Emmons is claiming your biggest estate, Carey, as his client. He says you've let him do all the work too long."

"But Gus Carey was my own great-uncle," Brooks exclaimed, raising his hands in mock dismay. "What are we old families coming to?"

"A fat lot they care about that! Old family connections, old school ties, those things are great, so long as they're kept current. But you're slipping behind, Brooks. Catch up!"

"I wonder if these trends are reversible," Brooks speculated with a yawn, jabbing his blotter with a paper cutter. "The social scene, like the human body, seems to have to change its cells. We Clarksons used to have a fleet of clipper ships in the China trade. White sails speeding across the broad Pacific! Where were the Galentis then, I wonder. One family declines, another rises. It's rather beautiful, really."

"Who's rising?"

"You are, Benny. You've only just started."

"Brooks, you're getting to be a bore on that subject. Maybe I could have had a future once. If I hadn't married so young. Or been a member of a church that didn't ban birth control. But as it is, my friend, Benny Galenti has gone quite as far as Benny Galenti's ever going. Why, I can't even afford to move to a decent neighborhood! You talk to Teresa and see what a big success *she* thinks I am!"

"Can't you get a mortgage?" Brooks always seized any chance to get the subject away from his own drinking. "Or would you rather finance it privately? I'm perfectly willing to stake you to a move to the suburbs. Why haven't you asked me?"

Benny seemed suddenly embarrassed. Was it, Brooks wondered, because he had planned the conversation this way? If he had, it would be only natural. What was the good of a Brooks Clarkson except to help a Benny Galenti?

"No, no, Brooks. You've done too much for me anyway, and, besides, you're going to need all your money if you keep on this way. How do you expect to live when . . . ?"

"Why don't you move to Glenville?" Brooks interrupted in a sudden inspiration. "You could have the old superintendent's cottage on our place. It's a shingle horror, but it's got plenty of room. We could fix it over for you. I was going to have to do that, anyway."

Benny's stare might even have meant that he had considered this, too. "What about my kids? Where would they go to school? We can't afford your private academies."

"Do you think everyone in Glenville is rich?" Oh, he had shut him up now! The terrible sermon was over. "We have one of the best high schools on Long Island. It would solve your vacation problem. You wouldn't have to take your family to the beach."

Benny's expression of embarrassment and gratitude was moving on a face that was usually so noncommittal. "I couldn't accept it, Brooks. You know that. Why, you could rent that cottage for a fortune these days!"

"Ah, but I won't!" Brooks cried, elated at the realization that his inspiration was actually going to work! Teresa, he suddenly saw, would make Benny accept, even if he balked now. "I can't have anyone that close to me who isn't absolutely congenial. And I'm very fussy! If you don't take it, it stays vacant. So there!"

3

Fanny was upset when Brooks told her that night of his offer of the cottage. She had always been jealous of his admiration of Benny.

"You mean we'll have those Galenti children all over the place! How many are there now? Six? Why, Brooks, we won't be able to call our home our own!"

"You'll find that Teresa has total control of her children. You'll never even know they're there. Besides, this will help me at the office."

"Are you crazy? Is Benny Galenti anything more than a glorified office boy? How can he help *you* at the office?"

"Benny is a very good friend to have," he said stubbornly.

"Why not give him *our* house then? And we can move into the cottage!"

"Don't be difficult, Fan. I know what I'm doing. It will all work out for the best."

"Will it? Best for whom? For us? Will we absorb by osmosis some of the vigor of the proletariats who squat at our doorstep? Is that the idea?" Fanny was inclined to be dramatic after her second drink. After the third she became playful, after the fourth self-pitying, after the fifth despondent. Now she was still in high, if rapidly souring, spirits. "Perhaps the virtue of this brave new world will inoculate our old stock so that we *shall* relish of it! Perhaps Fanny Clarkson will learn to be a model of sobriety, and Brooks, at last, will be at ease with the lower orders! Perhaps our daughters will be saved from dissolute Prince Charmings by sturdy bricklayers!"

"Please, Fan. You know I can't bear that kind of talk."

"Well, don't despair. I shall learn my good manners from Mrs. Galenti!"

Brooks feared that she would not even *show* good manners to Teresa Galenti, but even he was not prepared for the terrible scene that took place, six months later, when Benny and his wife, after settling themselves and their children in the now spotless and repainted cottage, paid their first call at the big house. Benny was in a blue suit, and Teresa, a small, firm, hard-eyed woman with the blackest hair anyone had ever seen, was wearing a red dress with a red hat that was too big. Fanny, despite all Brooks' advance warnings of the call, was dressed in a negligee that had two coffee spots on the front.

Brooks saw his house, his wife, himself, through the dark, darting eyes of Teresa Galenti. He noted the faded curtains, the cigarette holes on the sofa, the children's school books piled on the floor. He heard his daughter Anne's violent stamping on the stairway and winced as she slammed through the living room without pausing to greet the guests. Fanny, reclining languidly on a chaise longue, was in her "literary" stage of inebriation, where most of her references were to books.

"What must you think of the state of things in this house, Mrs. Galenti? Oh, you must be shocked, don't deny it! Those curtains should have been changed a year ago. How you stare! Or how you *would* stare if your manners weren't so good. I haven't intruded on you yet in the cottage, but I confess I've walked by and peeked in the living room window. How neat and trim and freshly painted it all is! Oh, it puts us quite to shame up here in our Cherry Orchard!"

"I think of you as very fortunate indeed in having such a charming home," Teresa Galenti replied firmly.

"Do you? How charming of you. Isn't it charming of Mrs. Galenti to say that about our 'charming home,' Brooks? But perhaps I may be allowed to console myself with another comparison. Your cottage, Mrs. Galenti, is orderly, serene, peaceful. But up here on the hill we're Wuthering Heights! Uncomfortable, if you like, unpainted, if you will, unadorned. Yet we still clutch to our remnant of soul. Or do you think I flatter myself, Mrs. Galenti?"

"It must be nice to have read so many books." Teresa's tone was perfect. She knew that she was being insulted and that she could not strike back. But she did not whine; she did not crawl; she did not scratch. Her contempt was as high and cold as the wind on Wuthering Heights.

Brooks was suddenly furious. He could have forgiven Fanny anything but an attack on Benny's wife. Now the cruelty of his revenge was in proportion to her long immunity. "I don't know why Fanny has to delve so deeply into the literary past for comparisons to our house," he said bitterly to the Galentis. "I should think modern writers had examples enough. What about *Tobacco Road?*"

Fanny turned on her husband, her eyes vibrant with the shock received. "Oh, Brooks, how *could* you!" she cried, and, clapping her hand to her mouth, she jumped up and ran sobbing from the room.

Benny rose and walked over to his wife. "Come on, Tessie. It looks like we've picked the wrong day to call."

Brooks followed them to the door, muttering apologies, but Benny was very short with him. Brooks understood. It was not so much Fanny's scene that Benny minded. It was the scene he would have to face from Teresa when they got home.

That night Brooks got very drunk, and the next day he did not go to the office. The following night he got drunk again, but on the morning after Benny called at the house and insisted on driving him to town. All the way in he lectured him.

"You've got to pull yourself together, Brooks. I won't mince words. The gossip is all over the office that you're going to resign. Mr. Emmons is spreading it. Teresa thinks your case is hopeless. She says I'm wasting my time."

Brooks, holding his head still to diminish the throb of his hangover, thought how much easier it would be for them both if Benny would only conform to the role that destiny had assigned to him. If he would only concentrate on moving forward and upward, without looking back at those who slipped! Life might be almost endurable if people would stick to their parts and not keep ab-libbing sentimental clichés into a script that was beautifully hard and true. What was intolerable was this constant stopping of the show and turning on the lights, this endless inquiring of "Where are we *now?*" But how could he stop Benny?

"A man has just so much energy," he said at last. "Keep yours for those six young Galentis, will you?"

"I can do my job and still look after you, Brooks. How much energy do you think it takes to be an office manager?"

"You should save it for the future, then."

"Whose future, for God's sake? Where do you get this crazy idea that I'm going places? A man doesn't go places from my job. In a capitalist world he's got to have capital. You know that. You're just trying to get me off the subject. I've got a plan that you're not going to like, but it can't be helped. I want to put you in the sanatorium at Brunswick and get you dried out. I . . ."

"Benny, listen to me!" Brooks interrupted excitedly. Oh, he saw his way now! "About this capitalist world. What about the new duplicating machine you talked us into putting in the back office? Didn't you say it was some kind of miracle?"

"The Xerox? Of course, it is."

"What's Xerox stock selling at now?"

"Around a hundred."

"Well, go buy it, man! Isn't that your fortune? Buy Xerox!"

"I have bought Xerox. I've got a hundred shares. But even at that I had to borrow at the bank and dip into the children's college fund. If Teresa knew how much, she'd clip my ears back!"

"Buy a thousand! Go ahead. I'll stake you to it!'"

"Jesus, Brooks, do you mean it?"

As Benny gripped the wheel on top, both hands together, and stared tensely ahead down the parkway, Brooks had a sudden suspicion, despite all Benny's kindness and his conscience, that he had foreseen from the beginning of their drive, not only that this offer would be made, but that it would be accepted. What of it? There would be no further talk now of "drying out."

4

In the four years that followed the date of this conversation the face of Glenville was lifted — or dropped — depending on one's point of view. The last line of the old estates was broken, and housing developments proliferated in their debris. Destruction was not confined to the works of man. Hills were leveled, ponds drained, streams deflected from their course. A person who had been away for six months could hardly find his way about; he would discover a supermarket where there had been a meadow, a golf course where there had been a thick wood. The Glenville Country Club, lying across the route of the new parkway, was condemned, and the members were obliged to buy a new site and to plan a new clubhouse. To meet the great expenses of this project the governors decided to enlarge their membership, and it was to induce Benny Galenti to join that Byron Fales, the club president, called on him and Teresa one weekday night after dinner.

"You've got a fine place here, Benny," Fales told him when Teresa had brought him his whiskey. "Such a relief after all the modern junk you see. I like a window to be a window and a door a door. And, God damn it, I still like a bathroom to be a bathroom."

Benny watched his guest taking in, piece by piece, the furniture which Teresa had bought at Sloane's in Manhasset. But Fales was not sarcastic like his cousin Brooks Clarkson. His expression of admiration was perfectly genuine.

"What did the whole thing cost you?" he continued, in his blunt manner. "No, don't tell me, let me guess. Do you ever watch 'The Price Is Right' on TV? I bet the whole works cost you — with the furniture — a hundred and seventy-five g's."

Benny laughed. "It's a good guess."

"You could have afforded more, of course. I've noticed the guys with new fortunes these days are usually conservative spenders."

"We have everything we need, Mr. Fales," Teresa said in a slightly sharp tone. It amused Benny that for all her passion to get in with the Fales and their group, she could never wholly control her hot temper. "We have our home and two cars and all the children in private schools. What more do we need to be happy? A Renoir?"

Byron Fales laughed easily. His self-confidence was sublime. He was a Fales, and he had made as much money as Benny in Xerox. His cousin Brooks had told him, late one Saturday night at the club, four years before, in 1962, of his loan to Benny for the thousand shares, and he had been much struck. The following Monday he had purchased a thousand shares for his own account. Did he care that he was stout of girth and coarse of manner, that neither his conversation nor his demeanor suggested the expensive private education, lavished upon him in childhood, that people like the Galentis now sought for their own offspring? Why should he? He knew that all they wanted was the opportunity to bring up their sons to be like Byron Fales.

"A Renoir? I don't know if you're talking about a car or a picture, as the Texas oil tycoon is supposed to have said. But is that right? Are all the kids in the Horton School now? I thought Giulia was still in Glenville High."

"No, she's in Horton, too," Teresa said with satisfaction. "Fortunately, there was a vacancy last month."

"Fortunately, Tessie?" Benny asked drily.

"Well, fortunately for Giulia, I mean."

Fales looked shrewdly from Benny to his wife. "What was the vacancy? Oh, yes, that was the Clarkson kid, wasn't it? Anne.

Jesus, can you beat that! Fifteen and taking pot! But what can you expect with parents like hers? Brooks is my cousin and all that, but they've certainly let themselves go. Have you been by their house recently? It looks as if they were hanging washing out the window! The new people on that road have complained they're depreciating the neighborhood."

"Brooks Clarkson depreciating the neighborhood!" Benny exclaimed with a scornful laugh.

"Well, why not, Benny?" Teresa demanded indignantly. "Mr. Fales is quite right, and they're his cousins! You've got a fixation on Brooks Clarkson, that's your trouble. A drunk's a drunk, no matter how blue his blood. Isn't that so, Mr. Fales? Why, do you know he shoots holes in his ceiling at night, lying on the floor? He's going to kill somebody one of these days. And his girls are nothing but tramps. People won't even have them as baby sitters!"

"Shut up, Tessie!"

"She's right, Benny," Fales intervened authoritatively. "She's absolutely right. Ever since he got kicked out of his law firm, he's been going downhill like a crazy wagon. If it weren't for that last little trust my uncle set up, he'd be on relief."

"What's that to me?" Benny cried. "I owe him everything!"

"That's ridiculous. But I didn't come here tonight to talk about my disreputable relatives. I came to talk about the new clubhouse. We want you to join, Benny."

Benny caught the instantly earnest look in Teresa's eye, her quick small gesture of appeal, and he turned away to hide his mortification. "You must need the money awfully bad," he muttered. "What's the tariff?"

"Now that's no attitude to take," Fales reproached him. "I'd expect you to take ten thousand of the new club bonds. Sure. That's what I'm expecting of *all* the new members. I'm taking twenty myself, in case you're interested. But that's not the point. I can get any number of new members for that price. People are lining up around here to get into the Glenville Country Club. The point is that we want people like you."

"Why? Because my parents were first generation Italian immigrants? Because I'm a graduate of C.C.N.Y.? Because Teresa and I are Roman Catholics? Or mackerel snatchers, as you probably call us!"

"Benny!"

"Don't worry, Mrs. Galenti," Fales reassured her. "He's not going to get my goat, no matter how hard he tries. I'll tell you why we want you, Benny. We want you because you and your family are decent people, and that's a breed that's getting kind of rare in Nassau County. We want you because you believe in things. Because you believe in your own marriage, for example. Because you believe in bringing up your children properly. I'll bet none of *your* kids go in for dope. We want you because you're the kind of people who still take pride in the American flag and aren't ashamed to admit it. So there! Call me a Fourth of July windbag. Go ahead!"

"You're a Fourth of July windbag!"

"Oh, Benny," his wife cried. "Must you throw away every favor that comes our way? Why do you do it? To spite me?"

"What have I thrown away? Have I thrown away this house or your clothes or our private schools or any of my fabulous Xerox stock?" Benny got up and paced the room angrily. "What have I done since I made my lucky strike but look down in my stupid lap as it filled with treasures?"

"Lucky?" Fales broke in. "You call it luck to take the calculated risk that *you* took? To sell everything you had, to borrow every cent you could and put it all in one stock? That took guts, man!"

"It took despair," Benny retorted sullenly. "Oh, all right, so it took a bit of nerve, yes. But why should a bit of nerve be rewarded so extravagantly? Why should it make me a fat cat, a sleek citizen, a gentleman of clubs, a friend of Byron Fales, a pillar of the community! A man ought to work his way up the ladder, rung by rung. He ought to have to save, pinch and scrape. Then there'd be some kind of substance to him when he got to the top!"

"But we *did* all those things, Benny," Teresa pleaded. "Didn't we learn everything the hard way? The only thing that ever came fast was the Xerox!"

"But all that pinching and scraping didn't *contribute!*" Benny protested, beginning to feel that he was making a fool of himself, but unwilling to yield on what he deeply felt must be a matter of some kind of principle. "I was nobody till I had my lucky day. I might as well have made it in Las Vegas!"

"We stockbrokers don't care for that kind of comparison," Fales retorted, with a wink at Teresa. "But let us agree to disagree. With me Xerox was sheer financial acumen; with Benny it was dumb luck. But do please, Mrs. Galenti, bring your lucky husband to the club dance on Saturday night. Dine with us first at eight. I'll have a nice little party, and I think we'll persuade Benny that we want you both for your *beaux yeux* and not your market portfolios."

"Oh, Mr. Fales, I promise you!" Teresa exclaimed, with clasped hands. She might have been a schoolgirl whose head had just been patted by the principal.

"Benny," she began imploringly, after Fales had left, "tell me you're not going to spoil this for me and the kids!"

"I can't talk about it till I've seen Brooks."

"That rotten rum pot, that . . ."

"Oh, shut up, Tessie!"

Ten minutes later he drove alone to the Clarksons'. In the moonlight he could make out the ragged countenance of the old place: the choked, unweeded garden plots by the gravel drive, the broken windowpanes in the garage, the peeling paint, as he approached it, on the front door. Brooks opened it, drink in hand, and bowed sardonically.

"If it's not the Caesar of Xerox! The duke of duplication! Come in, Caesar. Come in, Duke. Fanny has gone to bed, and I was just yearning for someone to drink a nightcap with. Of course, I had not aspired so high as yourself, but if you will only 'condescend,' as the immortal Mr. Collins would have put it, we may still salvage a bit of the moonlight."

Benny sat in the chair and drank silently as Brooks went on in this mocking strain. There was no interrupting him, no shifting of his mind to serious topics. Brooks was reaching the final stage of his decline: a maudlin monologism. To Benny it was more terrible than it had been at any of the worst moments of the past four years. What Brooks had been destroying up until that night had been his career, his family, himself. Now he was destroying his romance.

"I came to ask your opinion," Benny interrupted at last. "I came to ask if you think I'd be doing a cruel thing to Tessie and the kids if I turned down your cousin's invitation to join the Glenville Club."

Brooks stared at him for a moment and then rose. He looked almost handsome again as he reached down to throw some kindling wood on the dying fire. "You'd be doing a cruel thing to *me*," he said with surprising lucidity. "What else do you think I've lived for but to see you in that club? Isn't it the last delicious twist of a crazy world? Please, Benny, you can't deny an old friend a laugh like that! Did you know they threw me and Fanny out?"

"What else could they do? You wouldn't resign and you wouldn't pay your dues!"

"Ah, but that was just the excuse. There have been plenty of examples of the board's looking the other way when *desirable* members defaulted on their dues. But one Saturday night, at the weekend dance, a rather grotesque little incident occurred. Fanny and I had made a wager that I could use the ladies' room and she the men's, on the stroke of midnight, without anyone's noticing, and . . ."

Benny could hear no more. He needed all his concentration to arrest his tears. He was rarely emotional, but when it happened, it could be very bad. He was apt not only to weep but to sob. For a moment he closed his eyes and saw before him the old portrait — or self-portrait — of Brooks Clarkson, of the ancient Clarksons, with his fine triangle of long wavy hair retreating from a noble forehead, a figure that would have dignified the bridge of a clipper ship in fine old days of China trade or the pulpit of Grace Church, robed in shimmering white, or the back of a sweating pony on the polo field at Meadowbrook. But the decline of the dream and the decline of Brooks Clarkson had now fused into the shabby sight that confronted Benny's reopened eyes. Brooks was not passing from the scene as a beautiful memento of a day that could not coexist with the Xerox machines that duplicated to infinity the jargon of a world of irretrievable vulgarity. He was perishing as something too vulgar himself to be duplicated.

"I *shall* join the club," Benny announced, as he rose to leave. "And you shall have your long awaited giggle. I can only hope that the irony of the situation will be all that you have so eagerly anticipated."

The last Saturday night party at the old clubhouse was an affair of almost frenzied nostalgia, but Byron Fales, after the orchestra drums had rumbled for silence, struck the note of the future by toasting a model of the new clubhouse, an ingenious combination of modern and Georgian styles designed to conciliate all tastes, as it was borne in by four waiters, in a blaze of candles, and placed on a table in the middle of the dance floor. The tumultuous applause that followed allowed the members to fold their regrets, like wet umbrellas, on the advent of sunny skies. It was widely agreed that Byron Fales had been, as always, perfect.

At his table, Teresa Galenti seemed perfectly happy. Benny noticed that she did not have much to say to either of her neighbors, or they to her, but obviously this did not matter. She was a seraph in heaven, and as long as seraphs were destined to sing everlastingly, it could hardly matter if they took an occasional night off. But he could not join her because Byron Fales, the star of the evening, chose to monopolize him. Perhaps Fales was sufficiently arrogant to enjoy the anomaly, at the old clubhouse's final party, of devoting his time to a new member.

When Benny had drunk double his normal quota of Scotches, he dared at last to bring up the topic that had been on his mind all evening. He asked if it might be possible to restore the Clarksons to membership if he paid up their delinquent dues.

"The offer does you credit," Fales replied, knitting his brow, "but I'm afraid there's not a chance. Brooks has made his bed, or rather unmade it, and I'm afraid he'll have to toss on the bare mattress. After that last trick that he and Fanny pulled, the board wouldn't want them back, even if they were on the wagon."

"Is there no way to help them, then? Must we just let them go?"

"They've gone, fella. Ask any newcomer what 'Clarkson' stands for in Glenville today, and he'll tell you: booze. Brooks and Fanny are suffering from an incurable disease: decadence."

"But how can you say that?" Benny cried in astonishment. "You, of all people! Isn't he your own cousin?"

"My mother was a Clarkson, it's true. She was Brooks' aunt. But there's never been anything wrong with the Clarksons. Brooks' mother was a Fortescue, and we know about *them*." Fales rolled his eyes and tapped his temple with his forefinger. "Still, I can't believe it's only a matter of genetics. The individual may degenerate, even though the family's sound. You find the same kind of rot in poor whites in the South. You find it among the red Indians. Once it starts, no surgery can stop it. All you can do is make the patient as comfortable as possible."

"By pushing another drink his way?"

"Allow me to push one yours."

Benny watched grimly as those thick, facile hands busied themselves with the bottles and glasses massed in the center of the table. "Make me comfortable, by all means. But there's still something I don't see. How can Brooks be decadent and creative at the same time?"

"What do you suggest he has created?"

"Me!"

"Oh, come off it, Benny. Just because he loaned you some dough in a tight spot doesn't mean . . ."

"Now listen to me, Byron. It was Brooks who singled me out of the office boys in his firm and pushed me ahead. It was Brooks who sold me to his partners as office manager. It was Brooks who got me to move to Glenville and loaned me the money to buy Xerox. It was Brooks. . . ."

"Well, if he's so damn creative, why didn't he buy Xerox himself?"

"Because that isn't his way."

"He could have, couldn't he?"

"I suppose."

"But he'd rather watch, is that it? He'd rather sit back and gaze into his man-making machine? Do you know that you've just proved the very point you were trying to rebut? You've described the most decadent creature that ever drew a fetid breath!"

Benny broke off the conversation and went to look for Teresa who was dancing. Whether Fales was right or Fales was wrong, all that he, Benny, could do now was to put on, as gracefully as possible, the emerald snake's skin that Brooks had shed for him. It might be instructive, at the least, and perhaps of some future utility, to contemplate the affluent festivity of the evening where Xerox was the bridge between the new riches of the Galentis and the renewed riches of the Faleses, and to consider that the switch of rungs between the Clarksons and the Galentis on the Glenville social ladder had taken just four years. But then Brooks had always known the quickest way to do things.

Red Light

THE NARRATOR of a short story, the "I" character, should not be a principal in the action, but an observer, preferably a social subordinate, some old retainer or dependent aunt, some person whose constant presence is easily explainable and whose personality is too dim to distract attention from the principals. She — for I am a she — should not have obtrusive emotions, except that she may, for pathetic or comic effect, experience an unrequited passion for the hero. On that score I would no longer qualify for my present task of narration. I have been out of love with Frank Lyons these twenty years.

He would not believe this, nor would his wife. He might even fire me if he discovered it. For what is more expected of the stout, old-maid secretary (that "treasure" who really "runs" the office) than that she should be in love with her boss? Ah, yes, the Lyonses, too, have read their fiction. For me *not* to be in love with Frank would imply some disillusionment, some active revulsion from the image of himself that all the employees of his publishing house are supposed to share. Indeed it does.

Lily Lyons, absurdly pretty and girllike at sixty, put the case to me one night at cocktails (I am frequently asked to their home) when she leaned over and murmured soothingly, "You and I must look after him, Celia. We have got him this far. We must see him through. Sometimes I think he depends on you more than anyone. Really!"

It is a commonplace that no man is a hero to his valet, but after a lifetime of listening to valets (or secretaries, which comes to the same thing) I sometimes wonder if any man is a hero to anyone else. But I am not as other secretaries. I have a distrust of masters — even of beloved masters — which is a part of my heritage. "Miss Celia Robinson" may not sound like the descendant of Red Indians, but she is. One of my ancestors was captured as a child in Albany by the Iroquois and reared as a brave. By the time his grandson had been recovered, all war paint and feathers, all grunts and yells, some sixty years later, the family had undergone a considerable change. The Robinsons, in the male line, had gone from white to red, and they were to go from red to white again. Observe my high cheekbones, my chalky white complexion, my smooth brow and lined cheeks, and you will detect in the large, grizzled virgin the stamp of a warrior race that knows it has been "had."

No, Frank Lyons is no hero to me. Even in the old days of my "unrequited" love, he wasn't, though I never let him know this. His craving for adulation was, and is, too great. And the funny thing about it is that it goes hand in hand with a deep suspicion of flattery and a fear that people somehow regard him as a fraud, which is ridiculous, because the public doesn't suspect him at all — is quite taken in — and why should he care that someone like myself sees the truth behind the act when my very job, so to speak, is to make him up? It is as if some great actress complained that her dresser knew that she wore a wig. What else is a dresser for?

Really, Frank should take more pride in his own histrionic genius. Nobody could possibly look, or play the part of, the great publisher better than he does. He has that long gaunt thoughtful face, with hardly a wrinkle, and that wonderful crown of thick gray hair. His eyes are gray, and they look at you in a distant, but not unfriendly way, as though to suggest that he has taken in what you are saying, but that it has transported him

to realms of higher thought. You are flattered, but he is thinking of his golf score. He has the other accouterments, too, the
tall rangy figure, the ever-clasped pipe, the splendid, informal
clothes, the Adlai Stevenson political principles. He has commodious, comfortable, Victorian-style homes in town and country and a brilliant collection of friends, drawn from the social
and political worlds, in which his great authors, one at a time,
delight to be dipped. Oh, yes, he knows that writers don't go to
the Lyons' den to meet other writers!

When I became his secretary in 1936, I promptly, but very
discreetly, fell in love with him. To hear him talk of Heming-
way and Fitzgerald, for he had represented his father in Europe
in the early twenties and had known the "lost" generation, to
take letters to senators and presidents, to bask in the gentle
courtesy that he never lost, to appreciate his constant equanimity, his seeming inability to be impressed by anything about the
great but the best things that had made them so, was almost
enough to compensate me for the obvious fact that he saw as
much sex in me as in his coat rack. Romance? My silly, roomy,
impressionable heart had to make the best it could out of its
unilateral passion. And what more could I possibly have asked
for — seeing what *I* was and he was — than the friendship and
confidence that he fairly lavished upon me, asking me for weekends and dinner parties and seeking my advice, not only in his
manifold family problems (he and Lily had many difficult children) but actually (joy of joys!) in the selection of books to be
published? What was all that but a literary secretary's dream of
heaven?

But it was all — romance, hero worship, dreamland — to be
vitiated by one incredible little fact. Once I had grasped this
little truth, once the dimly conceived, oft-rejected, but always
returning perverse suspicion had grown ineluctably into a huge,

sullen conviction — everything else fell into line. For why should Frank have put on an act unless he had something to conceal? Something potentially ruinous to his reputation? Something as ruinous as my unbelievable discovery? Something as simple and as shocking as the dismal fact that he didn't like books!

I have tried to be understanding about Frank. I still try. I know that he felt it was an obligation to his widowed mother and sisters to safeguard the threatened family business when his father died. I know that he had yearned for a diplomatic career and that he gave it up without a protest. I know that Frank Lyons & Son has flourished under his guidance and that many old editors and employees have lived in moderate affluence who might otherwise have been selling apples in the Great Depression. I know, in short, that Frank is considered one of the great publishers of our age. But I don't care. I could have tolerated better any of the other vices that afflict publishers: penuriousness, distrustfulness, jealousy of authors. I would have preferred an editor who starved and cheated his writers to one who was bored by them.

Yet to keep everything straight in the distressing parable that I feel compelled to relate, I should now set down that, although I am not and have not for years been in love with Frank Lyons, I have more recently (and with like secrecy and futility) been in love with Judson Bross, the *jeune premier*, if not the hero, of my tale. Perhaps this requalifies me to be the "narrator."

What did I care that Judson Bross was thirty years my junior? Was he not a wide-eyed, pale, passionate young man, crazy about girls and books and life? Does mere age protect my poor sex from such? Lily Lyons would have said (probably *did* say) that poor old Celia had lost her head over that young man and wanted to mother him to death. Mother him? I wanted to sleep with him! But this grotesque fact, like all important facts about myself, I have been wise enough hitherto to impart to no one.

Judson Bross came to us from Schenectady, from Hamilton College, from various advertising jobs, from nebulous middle-class parents who appeared to have been lost, without a trace. I had thought from his pallor and intensity that he might be a poet, or at least that he might have the soul of one, but by the time I had discovered that he was unendowed with even a grain of taste or discrimination, it made no difference. I had been conquered. He was brash, noisy and pushing, but he was also frank, trusting and affectionate. He adopted us all at Lyons as if he had no other family, no prior ties. I imagined that he was like a poodle: utterly loyal to one master until that master died or failed him, but thereafter perfectly ready to transfer his affections. I never could nail down his past. He seemed to know everybody and nobody in the literary world, to be at once astonishingly sophisticated and astoundingly naive. But what was most surprising of all was that, despite his ambitiousness, he was never on the make. I learned this early in our relationship.

When he first came banging into my office and asked me to lunch, I took for granted that he meant to use me as an access to Frank Lyons. Why else would a young man want to share his midday meal with a walrus? But then I noticed that he did not in the least object to banging into Frank's office on his own. He had no need of accessories. When I apologized frankly for my misapprehension, he stared at me with opaque eyes and gave a disconcerting whoop of laughter.

"What a cynic you are, Celia!" Judd's use of my first name, I might add, was not by solicitation. "If I go out to lunch with Mr. Lyons' secretary, it must be to make her or to make Lyons!"

"I take the world as I've found it, Mr. Bross."

"Then there's no such thing as true friendship?"

"Between an old maid and a handsome young man? No."

"What an arid philosophy! How do you know what goes into my liking you? Why should I? Because you're so gruff and yet so soft? Because you've got that proverbial big heart behind that fierce manner? Because of the office legend that you're a Sioux squaw? Because you're Frank's secretary? Because I'm looking for a mother? I don't know. I've never been analyzed."

"I'm glad I don't have *that* job."

"Let me give you another motive, then. A selfish one, of course. I wouldn't insult your cynical heart by offering a sentimental one. Suppose we put it that when I'm cultivating you, I'm cultivating the real head of the firm?"

"*Me?*"

"*Cherchez la femme!*"

"Well, if you think I play Madame de Pompadour to Frank's Louis XV, you're in a bad way, my friend."

"I don't suggest he's in love with your body, Celia!"

"My brain, no doubt."

"No, your character!"

Well, there was more than a grain of truth in that. Frank could see everybody's point of view because he lacked one of his own. I was impressed that this impertinent young man should have flared the secret of my influence: that I helped the boss to make up his mind. So often in life the making of a choice is more important than the choice itself, and how could Frank choose when he didn't really care, when he didn't, if the truth be told, always quite understand why a choice should be made at all?

After this, I accepted Judd's offer of friendship. He came to have supper with me in my little apartment, studied my collection of authors' letters ("filched," as he impudently insisted, despite their being addressed to me, from the Lyons' files), drank up my brandy and gossiped until the tiny hours about the office. If, as I have indicated, he was never confidential about his own past, it was, I began to see, because it had ceased to exist for him. Certainly he was specific enough about his present. He told me, as if I had been a fellow bachelor, which girls in the office slept around and which he had slept with. I was a bit disgusted, but I was more than a bit intrigued. At any rate I did not ask him to stop.

Judd was in Fiction, and he had a list of his own authors, mostly young men and women employed as writers or models by advertising firms or as actors by television studios, who composed "serious" fiction in their spare time. Thirty years before they might have been poets in Greenwich Village; today they were a blend between Bohemia and Main Street. But then Bohemia and Main Street had ceased to exist. Judd seemed more of a pusher than an editor; he acted almost as an agent in trying to sell his friends' wares to Lyons. Yet his faith in them was entirely sincere. We had an argument over the manuscript of a novel about a happily married woman who had to become a prostitute to support her invalid husband. The moral crisis of the book, which was entitled *Red Light,* arose from the fact that she found that she enjoyed her new trade. The author of this mishmash was a young woman in the East Village called Shirley Tyng.

"It's obscene," I insisted.

"What do you mean by that?" Judd demanded.

"It's dirty for the sake of being dirty."

"Like *Nana?* Like *Sons and Lovers?*"

"Certainly not. Those books are serious. Your friend is only trying to write a best seller. She is aiming at titillating the public by appealing to current sexual fantasies. It's not real."

"Aren't current sexual fantasies real?"

"Let me put it this way. It's like all those academic Victorian paintings. The ones that show naked women at Roman banquets or slave markets. They're obscene because they're not really nudes. They have alabaster skins and no pubic hair. They're fantasies, don't you see?"

"Is *that* the distinction?" Judd demanded. "High-class literature shows pubic hair, and pulp doesn't? Why is pubic hair so important? Aren't both kinds of writing erogenous? Aren't both designed to excite and arouse? You're kidding yourself, Celia, if you think anybody writes about sex without appealing to sex. The only fair way to judge them is by how they succeed. Some men want an alabaster Victorian nude with hair only on the head. Fine! Others may want a gal with sagging bosoms and bushy armpits and a giant fanny by Degas. Fine! Why should one sneer at the other? I'm a democrat in these matters. Shirley Tyng brings me a breath of fresh hair!"

I did not go on with this. I was stupefied. Judd believed only in market. He never tired of pointing out that Shakespeare, Balzac, Dickens and Tolstoy had all been popular in their lifetimes. Obscure poets, abstract painters, plotless playwrights he cheerfully classified as "closet artists" and did not hesitate to rate *Gone with the Wind* a great American novel. What was unique about Judd was not so much his opinions as his conviction that they were universally held. I could never persuade him that any theatergoer who preferred Samuel Becket to George Kaufman, any lover of painting who favored Rothko over Andrew Wyeth, any reader of poetry who turned to Pound and away from Alfred Noyes was anything but a snob and a hypocrite.

Frank Lyons' reaction to *Red Light* was cautious. When I came in that morning for dictation, he walked to the door and closed it. "This is quite a book your friend Judd has come up with. This one of Shirley Tyng's."

That Judd should be described as "my friend" meant simply that Frank was still undecided as to whether or not he should be his.

"It's a pity it can't come out under the Lyons banner," I observed. "It would make you a fortune."

"You're satisfied that we shouldn't do it?"

"Not unless you're after a Pulitzer for pornography!"

"It's so clear to you, then, that it *is* pornography?"

It was suddenly in front of my face, right there in the odd hand of cards that he was dealing, that *I* should be the one to decide the fate of *Red Light*. I took refuge for a moment in coughing, wondering if I had ever been really tempted before. All my life, if seemed, I had ladled out my integrity in great doses to an unseeking world. But now it was different. Now the Devil was urging me to kick over my standards for the sake of a young man on whom I foolishly doted. And what did I do? I hardly hesitated a minute!

"Of course, it's never been clear what's pornographic and what's not," I hedged. "Even the Supreme Court doesn't know. All you can be sure of is that *Red Light* is strong stuff. I guess what I really mean is that I didn't think we'd have the guts to do it."

Frank's smile was just a flicker. "Don't you think I have guts, Celia?"

"You'd think I'd know you after thirty years, wouldn't you? But you never cease to surprise me, Frank. It seems I must take off my hat to you once again. To think of publishing a novel like that at *your* stage of life — when you have everything to lose and nothing to gain — in reputation, that is — well, I guess that takes real guts."

Frank's smile widened into the one that told you that he understood that you were flattering him but that he still loved you for caring. He would file it away as evidence of your affection if not of your truthfulness. But I knew, when he took it out of the drawer again, he might forget its classification.

"I don't see why Mailer and Roth should have a monopoly on this sort of thing," he said. "There ought to be a little spot for Shirley Tyng on that darkening Parnassus. And I'm darned if I'm not going to have a stab at putting her there!"

Thus I was swept into the court of Miss Tyng. When Judd heard what I had done, he obliterated from his mind all of my earlier comments and rushed me out to lunch with his friend, introducing me, with characteristic enthusiasm, as one of her most "ardent champions." But I was no more impressed with Shirley Tyng than I had been with her fiction. She was pretty enough, in a slovenly fashion, with long inky hair and brown skin, but like her plots, she was dirty. I could not see how a man as clean as Judd could put up with that. And then her conceit was monumental. She talked in a flat, dry tone about herself and what her "work" meant to her interlocutor, becoming silent and detached if the conversation veered, for the smallest interval, from the subject of Shirley Tyng. She had apparently subdued the little group that surrounded her in the East Village to a servile respect for her "genius." I knew from the candid Judd that he was, as they say in Paris, *au mieux* with her, but it was obvious what armies had preceded him. I tried to assuage my jealousy by picturing how badly she would fit in at Lily Lyons' parties.

But there was to be no satisfaction for me there, either. *Red Light* enjoyed so enormous a sale that Lily Lyons minded the charmlessness of her new guest of honor as she might have minded the size and hairiness of King Kong. She had a celebrity, and Lily was born to cope with celebrities. I could only clench my teeth as she and Frank went to work, in true American fashion, to convince themselves and the world that they loved their new star for her human attributes alone. Shirley's very body odor became an emanation of her honesty.

At least I had the satisfaction of the reviews. Nobody could take these from me. The success of *Red Light* was purely financial, and the critics were as savage as even a fellow novelist could have wished. It was surprising how much attention Shirley got. Judd excerpted some of the shrillest passages about "filth" and "decadence" and ran them as ads. Perfectly genuinely, he considered them a form of inverted praise. I decided that silence was my only role until the terrible but not unexpected day when he took me out to lunch to tell me that he and his famous author were going to be married. Then my world fell apart, and I lost my head.

"That bitch!" I cried. "You can't do it!"

"Celia, you're a jealous old bag," he retorted hotly. "You want me all to yourself."

"I don't want to share you with her, that's for sure." As I stared back at his baffled, pained countenance I could hardly endure the bleakness of my sense of his victimization. It was not that he would never recover from his inevitable abandonment by his chosen spouse. It was that men who were cast off by that kind of psychotically self-centered bitch always had a funny, special stink of something like failure to them afterwards. "Can't you *see* it won't work?" I pleaded. "Shirley may be all very well as a friend or mistress or whatever you call it today. But not as a wife, dear boy. Never as a wife. Girls like that have no business marrying. They ought to be prevented by law!"

"They have as much right as men like me."

"Oh, no, they don't. Believe me, Judd. You know nothing in the world about them. You may have done a lot of sleeping around, but that's natural for a man. Basically you want to settle down with some sweet little thing and be beautifully faithful except for that brief week in August when she takes the children to the Cape. Oh, I know you like a book!"

"A book by Marquand, it would seem."

"Well, not one by Shirley Tyng!"

"Obviously, this is a subject on which we're never going to agree. Let's make a treaty to stay off it."

I shook my head, closing my eyes so that I could not see his unhappiness or his appeal. "No, Judd, I can't. I don't want to be that close to you anymore. I don't want a front row seat to your disaster. I couldn't bear it!"

After this he became very cool, very clipped in tone, and for the rest of our lunch we discussed nervously the memoirs of a famous party-giver which Frank Lyons had just acquired. In it she explained her method of launching social climbers and listed her fees. Judd thought its sales might rival those of *Red Light*. We were both very glad to get back to the office.

In the year that followed Judd rose on the roster of Frank Lyons & Son until he was one of the most talked-of editors in town. When Shirley submitted her second novel, about a necrophiliac, the fiction editor resigned in disgust, and Judd was promoted to his place. The man responsible was not Frank, but the chairman of our directors, a Wall Street lawyer known for his enthusiasm for "wider markets." If Judd had dropped in popularity with his fellow editors, he had become the hero of the boardroom. But only the sourest and most envious of his new inferiors could really dislike him for it. He was so sure of the rightness of his theories that he was always charming to those who disagreed. Having no malice in his nature, he could never quite believe that it existed in others'. Envy to him was only a thing people talked about — like taste and art.

I must have been the only person in the office who disapproved of Judd as an editor and still prayed for his success. The reason that I prayed was that, unlike the others, I could see that his position was precarious. It depended on three individuals: his wife, Frank Lyons and the board chairman, and of these three, at least two were of dubious loyalty. Everyone knew about Shirley — how she had returned after only six months to her "bachelor habits" — but I alone suspected Frank Lyons.

"Have you read this new novel of Shirley's?" Frank asked me one evening late, when most of the staff had gone.

"No. Nor do I intend to."

"I thought Judd was such a protégé of yours."

"He's gotten too big to be the protégé of an old secretary. Anyway, I detest his wife, and I won't read her books."

Frank raised his eyebrows. "Jealous, Celia? At *your* age?"

"That's one of my few prerogatives."

"Very well." Slowly, carefully, in editor's fashion, he filled his pipe. "But I need your advice, Celia. I need your point of view about what Judd Bross is doing to the firm."

"You mean what Shirley is doing to it?"

"Well, isn't it pretty much the same thing? He has pushed her books. He has made her name. He must take the responsibility for the change in our image."

This struck me as pretty cool. "Your image!" I exclaimed. "And whose fault is that, I'd like to know? Whose decision was it to publish *Red Light?*"

"Your questions are perfectly fair," Frank conceded calmly. "I'm not trying to duck my responsibility. I'm simply asking myself where we go from here. I admit I'm not an infallible judge of fiction. I foresaw that people would find the book shocking. I did not count on their finding it trash."

"Then you're just like Judd! He didn't either. He thinks it's a great novel!"

Frank turned away to the window. The small, latent smile that habitually adorned his handsome face had for once disappeared. It was the only sign that he ever gave that one had gone too far. I felt nervous, for my position at Frank Lyons & Son was just about my whole life, but then the need to say what I had just said had been pressing. Frank *was* just like Judd. Having no real taste, no essential feeling for literature, he was ultimately at the mercy of a profit-and-loss statement. For if one book was pretty well worth another, what other criterion of choice was left to the publisher? Yet Frank perfectly saw at the same time that one could not always take the short view, that the biggest financial asset of his firm was his good name and that if he threw that away for a golden egg, he would be as big a goose as the one he slaughtered. He must have seen Judd as a clown walking behind him, aping his gait, repeating his gestures to the noisy delight of the crowd, yet who could be counted on, no matter how abruptly his victim whirled about, to freeze into an attitude of compliance. What did such an act become but the pantomime of *two* clowns? The one who was mocked and the one who mocked were equally hilarious.

When he turned back to dismiss me with a nod, I knew definitely that I had gone too far. For the the next two months he never mentioned Judd once, and it was obvious that a crisis was imminent. As usual, I worried alone. Everybody else assumed that he adored Judd. His sons, Frank Junior and Timmy, both junior editors, were distinctly jealous. Their father had always been an amateur student of Roman history, and who did not know that the emperors had notoriously preferred adopted sons to their own? This kind of talk seemed to receive its ultimate confirmation when announcement was made in the press that the ancient and distinguished house of Frank Lyons & Son would merge with that new titan, Simon Periodicals, and that

the combined enterprise, despite Simon's vast superiority of capital, would be known as "Lyons & Simon," the older name coming first. It was flashed about the office that Shirley Tyng was a
friend of the Simons' and that Judd had been the architect of
the merger. If this were the case, I had worried in vain. But I
still dared not believe it.

Frank and Lily Lyons gave a supper dance at their double
brownstone house on Lexington Avenue to celebrate the
merger. Lily did such parties charmingly. She believed in the
mixture of ages, and she believed in family, and her children
and nephews and nieces made a handsome, homogeneous group
in the quaint, polished, colorful Victorian interior to pull any
gathering together. They would dart out to corners of the big
parlor where Lily's eye had perceived a dry-up of talk and, having revived the parching group with the liquid of their bright,
youthful, interrogative charm, they would report back to their
mistress. I, as an old acquaintance, was allowed to fend for myself.

That night was difficult, for the Simon people were not a so-
ciable lot and Lily was obliged to bolster her evening with
stunts. The junior editors and relatives did these fairly well, but
they were always the same, which was a bit tedious for the per-
ennial guest. Lily sang German songs; two boys in public relations played a piano duet; Frank did a monologue depicting
Henry James lost in the London Underground; a young secretary danced the hula. But there was a novelty at the Simon
party which was very far from being an improvement. The new
performer was Judd.

It was obvious that Lily had not put him on the program, but
he insisted. After she had twice ignored him, he walked to the
center of the dance floor, where the others had performed, raised
his hands for attention and began. It was supposedly a humor-

ous narration, without topic or connection, a mere string of wisecracks in the style that Bob Hope had made a feature of nightclub entertainment. Judd turned his head back and forth, covering the audience, a fixed little half smile on his face, pausing after each anecdote or joke for the laughter that did not come. It was horrible. So far as I can bring myself to piece it together, it went something like this:

"Frank was telling me that our lady authors have come a long way from Jane Austen. When he was pouring one a scotch and soda and asked her to say 'when' she replied, 'Right after this drink.' The other day, when I was flying to London, I hadn't buckled my seat belt before the lady next to me whispered, 'My husband's impotent.' In the old Cunard days you wouldn't have got that till the third night out. Shirley has a good one about life on rockets. Shirley, by the way, is my wife and all a man could ask for. Her cooking is out of this world. Way out . . ."

Lily could stand it no longer. She strode on to the dance floor and firmly took the amplifier from his hands.

"Thank you, Judd," she said crisply. "I know we'd all like to hear more, but while we have this music (we must remember overtime!) we had better take advantage of it. Ladies and Gentlemen, shall we dance?"

Judd came over to join me in my corner. It was the first time in months that we had been together, but he made it as natural as if there had never been a breach between us. He was holding a very dark drink which was obviously not his first, and I knew at once that he was as dear to me and as attractive as ever, even if he was stouter and balder, even if his opaque, brooding eyes had lost some of their bright intensity.

"I hope you're proud of yourself," I muttered.

"I did it on purpose!" he exclaimed, and I realized that he was angry. It also came over me that I had never seen him really angry before. Excited, bewildered, passionate, but not angry. "I wanted to make them see that I, too, could be part of their cheap vaudeville act!"

"Well, that's certainly what you turned it into."

"That's what it always has been, Celia! *You* ought to see that. You of all people! That's why they all hate me so. Until I came along they could publish all the junk they pleased and stand up at parties and wiggle their asses and think they were the cat's meow. Well, they can't kid themselves when Judd Bross is around! Because I'm a kind of crazy fun-house mirror where they can see their silly selves as they are!"

Silently I took his drink from him and gave myself a swallow. Then I returned it. How must this poor young man have suffered to learn such terrible truths! "Whom do you include in 'them'?" I asked. "Not Shirley, I suppose?"

His mouth curled into a very nasty sneer. "You haven't heard about Shirley? She's taken our merger very seriously indeed. She's been sleeping with Andy Simon."

"Oh, my poor boy!" I would have put my arms around him, but it would have distracted the room and stopped our talk. "Leave her and call it good riddance. There's no law that says a man has to feel humiliated. Besides, that's Shirley's nature. It has nothing to do with you."

"I shall most certainly leave her," he agreed emphatically, "and I shall most certainly *not* feel humiliated. But a man has to know when he's been royally screwed or else he's an idiot. Shirley is only part of what's happened to me. She's just a bitch that runs with the pack. But do you know what the pack has done? Do you know what your sainted boss has cooked up for me?"

"No! On my honor, no!"

He observed me closely for a moment and then nodded. "I

suppose he wouldn't have dared tell *you*. He'd have been ashamed, if nothing else. But here it is. After the merger I'm to be relieved of my editorial duties and shuffled off to their paperback department!"

I stared, incredulous. "But that's a very important department," I murmured. "Why are you so sure it's a demotion?"

"Celia, you know it is as well as I do. They want me out. Now that Andy Simon and his chain of dirty rags are going to be cleaned up by the merger, he doesn't want to be retarnished with the likes of me. He hasn't become a Lyons in order to have Judd Bross slung around his neck to remind him of the stink of his own past! And now that Frank has all the capital of Simon at his disposal, he can flush poor old Judd and his embarrassing best sellers! And Shirley? Oh, she's going higher brow than any of them! It's a mutual admiration society. And nobody could enjoy the wedding feast of Old Name and New Money with *me* around to remind them of what they are!"

I looked at him sadly, hating myself for recognizing that defeat and bitterness had made him almost unattractive. Judd's highly precarious charm depended on naiveté, on high spirits, on success. "What will you do?"

"Quit. Quit and start my own firm. I can do it, too. Oh, Celia, I promise you they'll be sorry. Come with me, will you? Between us, we can lick the world!"

With tears in my eyes, I slowly shook my head. I felt that Judd might be a success, that very possibly Frank would be sorry, but I was still not even tempted. For one thing, I was too old. And in this scary world of mergers and amalgamations, of thrills and obscenities, of art and burlesque, I could only hope to eke out the remnants of my poor career by working for a man who at least *looked* like a publisher.

Days of Wrath

It HAD long been Barclay Dodge's observation, as a "family lawyer," that most members of his social group did not have to wait for an afterlife to receive their due share of heaven or hell. They got it right here. The rule, of course, was not of general application. He conceded that the bulk of humanity were doomed at birth to poverty, starvation and disease. But with his own kind of people, particularly with his own clients, he was repeatedly struck at the justice of their earthly fates.

Take Bill Underhill, who had abandoned the faithful mother of his five children. Had he not been fleeced of his fortune and cuckolded by her successor in precisely the way that an Old Testament Jehovah might have decreed? And take Mrs. Averhill who had refused to give a penny of her vast income to needy nieces. What had they done, when she had lost her mind, but stuff her in a nursing home and leave her to die alone and unvisited? Dodge's files read like a collection of morality tales, where the extravagant were bereft of their money and the dissolute of hope. On the other hand, as in a set of eighteenth-century prints, the prudent were seen to prosper, the loving to be loved, the industrious to succeed.

Oh, it did not always work out so — naturally not — even with the most privileged. But the point was, in a world supposedly governed by chance, how many times it *did*. And it was this that made the observer of the rule turn to an accounting of his own good and bad deeds to explain the chaos of his marriage.

What could he have done, besides remaining a bachelor for the first fifty years of his life, to deserve such hell?

He thought he could make out how he had earned most of his awards and penalties *up* to his marriage. Because he had eaten and drunk in moderation and taken scrupulous care of his body, he had the build of a man of thirty. Because he had worked devotedly for his clients and saved them large sums by expert tax planning, he was prosperous. Because he had served faithfully on the boards of New York's cultural institutions, he was widely esteemed. On the other hand, because he had not played with passion, he had a constant sense of being unfinished; because he had not married, he was lonely; because he had never really engaged with life, he knew the bleakness of the sidelines. It was all fair enough, but it all antedated the catastrophic day when he had taken Lily Poole to that horrid little lavender chamber of denominationless marriages in the Municipal Building. He might far better have climbed into the family vault at Woodlawn.

He had met her, as he met all his women friends, at a dinner party. She had long black hair that she kept nervously pushing back, pale skin and large, roving, tense, worried black eyes that could be suddenly brilliant with silent laughter. She had an odd, scattered beauty that suited her swiftly varying moods, her lapses from total attention to total indifference, her instant sympathy for other humans, her quick indignation at the mere hint of injustice. And her life seemed as disorganized as her manner. She was divorced from a husband with whom she seemed to be still on the friendliest terms; she had two daughters of college age whose custody was with her but who resided with Mr. Poole. Dodge made out that she spent much of her time visiting.

"So few of our generation appreciate the unwed state!" she

exclaimed, when she discovered he was a bachelor. "They must be afraid of it. Afraid to be poets, that's what it amounts to. For can you imagine a poet married, Mr. Dodge? A true poet? Can you conceive of a *Mrs. Keats?*"

Dodge murmured something about the Brownings.

"Neither of them wrote a good line after they were married!" she retorted recklessly. "And look at Shakespeare. He could only save himself by fleeing to London to get away from the wife they forced on him. Shelley and Byron made farces of their nuptial vows. Oh, yes, a poet must live alone. What do we Americans, with our compulsive marrying, know of poetry? And, do you know, we're getting *worse?* That's all the young can think about: getting married. They do it younger and younger, clinging together in panic to ward off loneliness and 'identity' crises. Ugh! It disgusts me. Thank heavens for a man like you."

"But I'm not a poet."

"How do you know? It's not a mere question of rhymes and jingles. It's a question of soul!"

So it had started, and in a month's time they were inseparable. Never had Dodge been treated in the fashion that Lily Poole treated him. He had known what it was to have women try to marry him, even to have women try to seduce him, but he had never had a beautiful woman want him simply as her friend — ultimately her best friend. No matter how often he took her out, no matter how many theaters and operas they attended, she never seemed to expect the least advance. She was always the same, warm, funny, sympathetic, at once intimate and impersonal. She liked, when she was amused, to throw back her head and howl with laughter. She had had love affairs, of which she told him in the most natural possible fashion, but always without appearing to expect any such thing of him. How did she make him feel at once so special and so much a man? Finally, fatally, he asked her.

"Why, honey, I figured love wasn't your line," she replied in her easiest tone. "At least not with me. You may be Romeo himself with all other girls. But must that disturb us? I delight in our friendship."

That night while Dodge was brushing his teeth, he suddenly threw his toothbrush at his own reflection.

"You great goon!" he shouted aloud. "What in the name of Blackstone do you think you are but a poor lonely frustrated male who yearns for a mate? Don't you see that beautiful creature likes you? Grab her, you idiot! It's a miraculous last chance!"

He telephoned Lily that same night and proposed to her. She seemed totally astonished.

"But, honey, you don't want to take on the likes of me. Your life is so neat and well ordered, and I'm always broke and disorganized. Not to mention two great hulking daughters who would probably turn you into a grandfather in a year's time!"

"I'm crazy about your daughters," he interrupted, which was perfectly true. They were big, as she said, and totally lacking in charm, but they were frank and friendly. "And I'd adore to be a grandfather."

"Marry one of them, then, and be a daddy. I've had that operation, you know."

"Oh, Lily, you know I just want you!"

"Honey, you don't know what you're getting into."

"I'll take that chance."

"Well, we'd both better sleep on it."

Dodge was in ecstasy that she had not turned him down. Inexperienced as he was in such matters, he sensed that a non-refusal meant that she would take him, and indeed, the very next morning, she did.

The only person with whom he had trouble was his mother. She had originally wanted him to marry, but in recent years had decided that he never would, and now she resented the overturn of her habit of owning him, into which she felt he had lulled her. Mrs. Dodge was still pretty at seventy-five; she dressed well and was adept at cards, but the fears of old age had begun to make her querulous and petulant.

"I shall continue to take care of all your business affairs," Dodge assured her on the visit when he broke the news. "And I'll drop in every evening on my way home. You're not going to be neglected, Ma. And you're not going to convince me that a married man can't still be a good son."

"It's not that, dear. It's not that at all. I'm surprised that you think me so egotistical. No, believe me, I'm only considering your happiness."

"Which, I take it, you don't believe is assured with Lily."

"Let's put it that it's chancy. She's a charming woman, I know, but what do bachelors of fifty know of charming women *after* they have become wives?"

"What do *you?*"

"I?"

Barclay Dodge's smile became strained. "I mean, Mother dear, do you know something about Lily that I *don't?*"

For a moment it was as if something strange had taken the old place of the mother-son relationship, as if each had retreated to the central pale of his or her sex and now stared out distrustfully, almost antagonistically, at the other over a no man's — and no woman's — land. Was there some atavistic loyalty of female to female that prevailed, at times like this, over the maternal bond? At least when that maternal bond had been strained by a half century of wear?

"Not in the least," Mrs. Dodge responded at last. "I hear only pleasant things about Lily. Maybe at parties she has a drink more than she should, but that's true of half the girls of your generation. I suppose the men don't mind. And maybe she's what would have been considered 'fast' in my day, but isn't that a compliment in yours? No, all I'm worried about is *you*. Can you handle her?"

"Mother, the mere fact that I haven't been married doesn't mean I know nothing about women. It might interest you to know that . . ."

"Don't tell me about your affairs, Barclay. I don't want to hear. American girls cannot be understood in affairs. That's just play-acting."

"What do you think Lily will do to me after we're married, Ma?"

"I don't *know*, dear boy. That's the point!"

Dodge broke off the conversation. He found that he was suddenly trembling with anger. That his own mother should so downgrade him as to think him incapable of satisfying a high-spirited woman was a deep humiliation. What could a man count on if he could not count on his mother's admiration? The ground shook under him. He could only hope to persuade Lily to advance their wedding date. The vacuum that Mrs. Dodge had created had to be filled at once.

Such were the relevant facts, but did they add up to damnation? Only a month after the wedding, at a dinner party given in his and Lily's honor by the senior partner of his firm, she had slid under the table and passed out. It turned out that she had been drinking all afternoon. The next day Dodge learned from her doctor that for ten years she had suffered from intermittent, violent fits of compulsive drinking. There seemed no prospect of an early or even an ultimate cure, as Lily showed no desire for one and refused to discuss her ailment. It was a dim augury.

The fits came at irregular intervals. In the interim Lily would be as charming as she had been before their marriage, but this charm was quite nullified now by his apprehension. When she was gay, he trembled that she would be gayer; when she laughed, he dreaded her hysteria. It sometimes seemed to him that she, too, lived in dread, that she was being warmer and kinder to him than the occasion strictly required because she knew all that he would have to suffer thereafter. Did she love him? He hadn't the least idea. There was an almost terrifying impersonality in her very demonstrativeness. It increased with the number of witnesses, as if she could at least do *that* for him, as if she could at least pull herself together to show the world that she regarded him as her man.

And even her demonstrativeness could be embarrassing. If he spoke at a banquet, he would feel her proud, brimming eyes fixed upon him in mute admiration and would hear her clapping loudest of all. If the conversation at a party fell on a topic of which he had the smallest special knowledge, she would cry him up noisily as an authority. And when her daughters were visiting, she would shrilly insist that they treat him with the strictest respect. If he remonstrated, she would chide him: "No, no, dearest, you're my husband and their true father. You're our leader — don't forget. A man must never allow himself to be taken for granted!"

He would know, when he recognized a certain detachment in her eye, a certain vagary in her gestures, as if she were concentrating on some inner problem that had temporarily made the external world seem trivial or irrelevant, that he was in for a fit.

She would seem hardly to know him. Dodge had read that crocodiles going across land in instinctive search of water lost all awareness of anything but their own forward motion, so that one could kick them or jump on them without their taking notice. Lily would be like that. She would go from party to party, whether or not she had been invited, whether or not Dodge accompanied her. She was like a woman in a trance.

Sometimes she would meet a man who took advantage of her preoccupation, and then she might not come home till the next day. The generosity of her nature in these periods extended to the loan of her body, and she gave it away more where she seemed to guess it to be needed than where she cared to bestow it. Dodge learned, when Lily started these bouts, to fear, more than the society lecher, the inconsolable widower who yearned for consolation or the neurotic bachelor who doubted his own virility. Lily was Browning's last duchess with the vicious twist that not only her smile but herself "went everywhere." When she emerged from her strange obsessions, she would never apologize or try to explain. She apparently expected her husband to understand that she was made differently from other wives, and if he didn't . . . well, what did it matter? She could not change herself, and if the situation was too much for him, he could always leave.

It was this last attitude that was almost unendurable to Dodge. He could have put up with the embarrassment of her drunkenness, with the humiliation of his cuckoldom, if Lily, on recovering her senses, had just once asked his pardon. But she never did. He was only another of the men who had needed her, and she had given him only what she had given them. She herself was never jealous, never suspicious, never even irritable. She shrugged her shoulders at a world of jealous men as if to say, "All right, all right, that's the way you are, poor darlings, but, say what you will, it takes all types to make a world. Some love like the swan, some like the cuckoo bird. If you want to play with swans, play with swans. Who asked you to seek me out in the aviary?"

His mother made a bad situation a good deal worse. She saw to it that nobody was in ignorance of what her only son had to endure. Despite her seeming sympathy to Lily before the marriage, she now denounced her to the world as a tramp. Sometimes it seemed to Dodge that the ultimate refinement of his hell was that as his wife moved into the present of permitted promiscuity, his mother retreated to a past of unqualified Mrs. Grundyism. Surely, he had the worst of both worlds.

What had he done to have merited the shame aroused by the condescending smile of his old-maid secretary when he told her that he was going home early because his wife was ill? What wickedness could have been great enough to justify the tearing to shreds of his sense of decorum when Lily hiccupped at a party or when he knew that her dinner partner was pinching her under the table? His mother gave him one answer.

"When you proposed to Lily, you weren't really thinking of her. You were thinking of yourself. You had it all figured out that you were going to make up for lost time and produce a ready-made family that was as good, if not better, than the ones your friends had spent twenty years raising up. You thought you were going to avoid babies' bottles and diapers and all the trials of adolescence, and suddenly parade before the world with a beautiful spouse and grown-up children! Well, look at you!"

"Look indeed," Dodge murmured in a low, grave tone. "The gremlin assigned to deal out my punishment was a master of his trade."

His mother changed her tone at this. "But I don't mean you *deserved* it, darling! No man could deserve a fate like Lily. Nor could any man have suffered it more patiently. You've been a saint, my poor boy, and everyone knows it. But don't think it's going to last forever. It's *not.*"

Dodge stared with astonishment and alarm into the suddenly malevolent eyes of his old parent. "What on earth do you mean by that?"

"Lily's alcoholism was not the only thing you didn't know about her when you married her."

Dodge jumped up in horror, feeling that his mother had turned into a witch. "Of course, I knew! How would I not know? She'd had a breast operation, but they got it all out!"

"Did they?" Mrs. Dodge's face was as gray and flat as a stone. "Ask her."

"Mother, for God's sake!"

"She failed her last checkup. My hairdresser told me so. Lily came in tight for a permanent and blabbed the whole thing!"

"So you've *known?* How long have you known?"

"Oh, a month maybe." She rose now, frightened at the look in his eyes, and tried to put her arms around him. "Oh, Barclay darling, try not to take it that way! It may be all for the best. Lily's a poor, tormented creature. There's no real future for her, anyway . . ."

"Fiend!" he cried, and, pushing her brutally from him, he ran from the room.

Lily must have been keeping up her courage by turning her back to the gravity of her illness, for she collapsed when Dodge told her that he knew. For two days she disappeared altogether, and was finally discovered by a detective, drunk and unconscious, in the apartment of a taxi driver. At the hospital, still in a very apathetic state, she at last consented to the second and much more drastic operation that her doctor now recommended.

It was too late. All that he could do for Lily afterwards was to keep her "as comfortable as possible," which was not very comfortable. But the real agony for Dodge was less in his wife's pain than in her panic. He had thought that Lily was a woman of spunk and spirit, that, for all her indulgences, she would go out with style. But the very reverse proved to be true. Lily's drinking must have had to cover unbearable fears, and now, faced with death, she disintegrated in a way that was hideous to contemplate. She could not bear to have him away from her side. She would cling on to his hand by the hour and then struggle to a sitting position, fling her arms about his neck, and shriek in agony.

"Oh, Barclay, Barclay, dearest, save me, can't you *save* me! Don't let me go away to where it's all cold and dark and nothing. Isn't there some wonder drug? Oh, you don't care! Of course, why should you? I've given you a terrible time. Now you'll be able to go back to your nice, comfortable bachelor habits. Didn't I always *tell* you you shouldn't marry? But think of *me*, Barclay, all dead, dead, dead. Oh, Barclay, save me!"

"I love you, dearest. I've never loved anyone as I've loved you."

"You lie. You know you lie. You want to comfort me because you can't save me. Oh, save me, Barclay, save me!"

One afternoon when she was briefly and blessedly unconscious Dodge went to the hospital chapel. Sitting alone among the memorial plaques, contemplating the image of Saint Luke in the altar window, he asked himself what he could have done *this* time to deserve such appalling pain. He consciously relaxed his whole body, starting from his feet, and then likened his mind to a piece of white paper, placing in the center of it the soul of Barclay Dodge as it might have existed at the very moment after his mother had informed him of Lily's cancer.

Why had he pushed the old woman off with such fury? Why

had he called her a fiend? Had it been, as he supposed, because
her delay in telling him might have fatally postponed Lily's
operation? Or was it because he had been angered to be told at
all? Because he had divined in a flash that now he would have to
press for an operation that might still save her? Oh, indeed,
there had been *two* fiends in that room! For wasn't Lily's
present condition and condemnation precisely what his
subconscious mind must have been painting for two years? How
could his freedom and pride be recovered but by a death agony
for Lily so appalling as to make people ashamed even to remember that she had been a drunk and a whore?

Could sin be heavier? He sank to his knees and prayed fervently to be forgiven. When he arose, ten minutes later, he felt
that his heart was lighter, and he returned to Lily's room, prepared for any ordeal. But his resolution was not to be needed.
At the door he met the doctor, who whispered that it was almost
over. Going to the bed, Dodge took her hand and kissed it. Lily
recovered consciousness briefly, but she showed none of her
former agony. Just before she expired, he thought that she had
smiled at him.

He had dreaded the presence of his mother in the front pew
with him at Lily's service, but her conduct was perfect. Not by
so much as a glance or a sigh did she make the least allusion to
her son's deliverance, nor did she mutter a syllable of false con-
dolence. When they returned from the interment she simply
pressed his hand and expressed the hope that he would continue
to call upon her as usual.

"Whom else do I have but you, Ma?" had been his only retort.

Little by little, he resumed the life that he had led before his
marriage. He took up again his ancient role of extra man and

dined out on more nights than he didn't. Mourning was no longer expected of the bereaved, nor did he mourn. People welcomed him back to his old role with an enthusiasm that showed how much he had been missed, that showed, indeed, that his contribution had never been really appreciated until removed. And yet what did it all mean to him? Nothing at all. He missed Lily so dreadfully that at night he would cry out in the dark.

He felt that now at last he must be touching the nadir of his sufferings. His loneliness was so appalling that he felt, for the first time in his very rational life, that suicide might one day become a solution to be seriously considered. Yet why should he grieve so sorely for Lily, with her drinking and her adulteries? Was it because she had filled a fundamental need, long neglected, within him? Or because he had earned still another punishment?

On a brilliant June afternoon, six months after Lily's burial, as Dodge stood alone in the cemetery before the impassive brooding angel, just finished, that he had commissioned for her tomb, an artifact that seemed quite happily to unite the demonstrative grief of the last century with the half-embarrassed sorrow of our own, he received his answer. His loneliness and desolation were entirely merited. Had he not at parties, joining in but just so faintly holding back "with one auspicious and one dropping eye," meant to impress upon his friends that, whatever had been the demerits of his late wife, his own overwhelming love had lifted him to a dazzling emotional altitude that far exceeded what any of them had achieved? Had he not been telling them: "You see now, don't you, that Barclay Dodge has not, as you foolishly supposed, missed anything in life? You see now that his heart, which you thought did not really exist, was the greatest part of him?"

Second Chance

He walked away from the grave, chastened, the old Barclay Dodge again. Thereafter, when friends asked him about Lily, he did not look away as if the subject were too painful. He told them frankly that she was better off dead.

The Prison Window

"You always forget, Aileen, that we're not an art institute. Perhaps it would be more fun if we were, but we're not. The Museum of Colonial America, as its name implies, exists for a very specific purpose. We're a history museum. That doesn't mean, of course, that there aren't a great many ways of accomplishing that purpose, such as awakening the young to a proper sense of their heritage and revitalizing the old forms of communication . . ."

"I know, I know," Aileen Post interrupted. It was not the thing to do for a curator to interrupt the director, but when the curator was middle-aged and female and the director male and very young, exceptions had to be admitted. "I know all the jargon. I realize that we have to be 'relevant' and 'swinging' and 'up to the minute.' I understand very clearly that we have to be everything on God's earth but simply beautiful!"

"History is not always beautiful, Aileen."

"Oh, Tony! Don't be sententious. Save it for the trustees. You know what I mean. The *illustrations* of history should be beautiful! We can read about the horrors. We don't have to look at them. Why should there be any but lovely things in my gallery? Why should I have to put *that* in the same room with the Bogardus tankard and the Copley portrait of Lillian van Rensselaer?"

Here she pointed a scornful finger at an ancient rusted piece of iron grillwork that might have fitted into a small window space, two feet by two, which lay on a pillow of yellow velvet on the table by Tony Side's desk.

"Because it's a sacred relic," Tony replied, with the half-mocking smile that, as a modern director, he was careful to assume in discussing serious topics. "Because tradition has it that it covered a window on the ground floor of the Ludlow House in Barclay Street. During the Revolution it was the sole outlet to a large, dark storage room in which Yankee prisoners were miserably and sometimes fatally confined."

If the distressed virgin curator of beautiful things suggested too much the past, her superior was almost too redolent of the present and future. He had long chestnut locks — as long as his trustees would tolerate, perhaps half an inch longer — that fell oddly about a pale, hawklike face and greenish eyes that fixed his interlocutor with the expression of being able to take in any enormity. Tony twisted his long arms in a curious ravel and nodded his head repeatedly as if to say, "Ah, yes, keep on, keep going. I'm way ahead of you, *way* ahead!" It might have been the point of his act to be both emperor and clown.

"It's not that I haven't any feeling for those poor wretches," Aileen protested, her face clouding as it always did at the thought of pain. "God knows, it isn't that. But must their agony be commemorated in *my* gallery? It isn't as if there weren't memorials enough everywhere to dead patriots."

Aileen herself might have been an academic painting of a martyr. One could imagine viewing the long, gray, osseous face and those large, gray, desperately staring eyes raised heavenward, through the smoke of a heretic's pyre. It seemed a wasteful fate that had cast her, tall and bony, with neatly set hair and black dresses, in the role of priestess of antiques.

"Your concept of history is too limited, too snobbish," Tony warned her. "It's odd, for you're completely unsnobbish yourself. But be objective for once and take a new look at your eighteenth century. Aileen Post's eighteenth century. Isn't it all tankards and silverware and splendid portraits and mahogany furniture? Doesn't it boil down to the interior decoration of the rich? Where are your butchers and grocers? Where are your beggars? Where are your slaves?"

"But you shouldn't judge beautiful artifacts by their owners!" Aileen exclaimed with passion. "They represent the aspirations of the age! The way the spire of a Gothic cathedral represents the thrust of man's soul toward heaven! What is history but the story of his reaching? Do you want a museum to show the whips and manacles, the starvation, the failure? Leave that to Madame Tussaud and the printed record. I want the person who comes into my gallery to breathe in the inspiration of the past!"

"Tut, tut, Aileen," Tony warned her, wagging a finger. "You're playing with nemesis. In your books the rich and mighty enjoy not only the delights of this world but the respect of posterity. What is left for the wretched but that pie in the sky they no longer believe in? Watch out! Those wretched can be very determined. They want their bit of the here and now."

"Who? The dead? The dead poor?"

"Why not?" Tony smiled broadly. "Aren't I helping them right now? By setting up the prison window in the very center of your gallery?" He got up and made her a little bow. "Those are orders, my dear."

Aileen left the room without another word. She knew that, mock bow or no, his orders were to be obeyed. Tony Side, under his perpetual smile, was a very serious young man who had no idea of staying in the Colonial Museum for more than a few years. It was too obvious that he was headed for greater things. He would keep his name before the eyes of other institutes — and particularly before the eyes of their trustees — by arranging shows that need have only slender ties to the colonial era. Already he had achieved a considerable success with a gaudy display of eighteenth-century balloons and primitive flying machines against a background of blown-up photographs of Cape Canaveral. It had even been written up in *Life*.

Traversing the Ludlow Gallery of decorative arts on her way back to her office, Aileen noted bitterly that there were only two people in it. Two visitors on a Saturday morning in the middle of the biggest city of the nation! It spoke little for the much touted "cultural revival." Aileen scorned the huge, mute, unthinking crowds that pushed by the high-priced masterpieces of the Metropolitan and the shaggy youths and pert-eyed, trousered girls who gawked at abstracts in the Whitney and the Modern. She told her friends at the Cosmopolitan Club that beauty was obsolete and fashion despot. She nodded grimly when they laughed at her. They would live to see their idols perish as hers was perishing.

When she had first come to the Colonial Museum, twenty-five years before, it had seemed a symbol of permanence in an ever-changing city. The great memorial plaques in the front hall, the names of benefactors carved in stone, the portraits of former presidents and directors had heralded one into the glittering collection as a released soul might be heralded into perpetual bliss. The institution had seemed to rise above its paucity of visitors; its dignity had waxed with its noble and solemn emptiness. The solitary wanderer was rewarded by the rich sustaining silence in which he found himself embraced. It was as if the museum, with its high task of preserving beauty for eternity, could afford the luxury of being capriciously choosy as its votaries.

But now all that was over. Modern New York had repudiated the concept of permanence. No grave, no shrine, no cache of riches was any longer safe. No quantity of carved names on marble, no number of "irrevocable" trust instruments drawn up by long dead legal luminaries, no assemblage of conditions, prayers, engraved stipulations or printed supplications could arrest the erosion of endowments or the increase of costs. The "dead hand" of the past became as light as dust when the money it once represented had slipped away. Aileen found herself faced with the probability that she might survive her own selected tomb.

It was unthinkable. The treasures of the Ludlow Gallery were like so many members of her family. At least a third of them had come to the museum as a direct result of her own detective work and solicitations. The great Beekman breakfront she had discovered in a storage house; the tea service of Governor Winthrop had been redeemed at a sheriff's sale; the Benjamin Wests of the Jarvis family had come as one man's tribute to the "ardor and faith" of Aileen Post. She could smell out eighteenth-century artifacts through stone walls; she could track them down in the dreariest and most massive accumulations of Victorians. How she pitied people who spoke of her misguided adoration of the inanimate! As if a Copley portrait could be dead! As if a coffee urn from Westover could be without life! Only ugliness was dead, and it was Aileen's passionate faith that it should never be resurrected.

Certainly nothing seemed deader than the iron window. Tony, who for all his vulgarisms was a gentleman at heart, had allowed her to choose its site in the gallery, but she knew that he would correct her if she tried to hide it. She had placed it finally, framed in dark polished mahogany, upright, in a glass case, in front of the Wollaston portrait of Valerian Ludlow, the owner of the house from which it had come. Certainly it was conspicuous enough there, in the very center of the gallery. Peering through it, on his first inspection, Tony was pleased.

"It makes it look as if old Ludlow were behind bars," he pointed out with a chuckle. "Very likely he deserved to be."

Aileen at first tried not to see the window when she passed through the gallery. She would keep her eyes averted and quicken her pace as she approached the hated object. But she found that this made it worse. What good was it to banish it from her vision if she only succeeded in summoning it to fill her mind? Somehow she would have to make her peace with it, before it became an obsession.

She then adopted the practice, each time that she had to pass it, of making herself pause to look at it, or really to look through it, for there was nothing to see but its rusted blackness. She observed that one side was slightly more rugged than the other and had probably been the external side, facing on Barclay Street. Gazing through it, as if from inside the Ludlow house, she tried to imagine that thoroughfare as it must have appeared to an incarcerated patriot. Then she would walk around the grille and peer in, as if from the street, to visualize, with a shudder, the dark, fetid hole where the prisoners might have been penned. Sometimes visitors in the gallery would stop to watch her, and, when she had finished, take her place to stare through the window to see what she had been noting. Aileen, amused, became almost reconciled to her new "artifact."

One morning, however, when she was alone in the gallery and looking through the grille from the "prison cell" side she had a curious and rather frightening experience. Ordinarily, she had not looked through the bars *at* anything in particular, but rather at her imagined reconstruction of an eighteenth-century street. That day when she happened to glance at the portrait of Valerian Ludlow, it struck her that he would have often passed that barred cellar window, in his own house, on the way to his own front door, and she attempted to picture him as he might have appeared striding by, viewed at knee height. The portrait helped her by showing him full length, standing by an open window, looking out to a sea on which floated two little vessels, presumably his own, with wind-puffed sails. The expression on his round face (the cheeks seemed to repeat the puffed sails) was one of mercantile complacency. Mr. Ludlow had obviously been one of the blessed of earth.

But now Aileen seemed to see something in his countenance that she had not noticed before. The eyes, instead of being merely opaque, either because of the artist's inadequacy or the subject's lack of expression, had a hard, black glitter. They changed the whole aspect of the portrait from one of seemingly harmless self-satisfaction to one of almost sinister acquisitiveness. At the same time the quality of the paint seemed to have lost its richness and glow. Mr. Ludlow's red velvet coat now had a shabby look, and the sea on which his vessels bobbed was brown rather than a lustrous green. Yet these changes, instead of making the whole picture more trenchant, more interesting, as they might have, seemed instead to push it back into an earlier era of clumsy primitives. Ludlow was now not only disagreeable; he was badly painted. Was his new degradation of character simply the artist's error? Had he come out mean, in the way of a clown drawn by a child? Or was Aileen seeing the real Ludlow for the first time?

Walking now quickly around the grilled window, with a conscious effort of will — for she was distinctly frightened — she turned suddenly and looked through it from the other side. She gave a little cry and then stopped her own mouth, for the sensation that had abruptly appalled her had as abruptly ceased. She had, for two seconds, stared into an absolute blackness, and at the same time her nostrils had been filled with a suffocating stench. Now she smelled nothing, and she was looking once more through the window toward the great glass case that housed the tankard collection.

Badly shaken, she returned to her office to go back to work on her article for the museum magazine on Dutch silver. But she was clear now that she would have to deal strongly with this preoccupation. In future she would walk by the window, not with consciously averted eye, not with undue attention, but simply taking it in casually, as she might take in any other exhibit. She would not flatter it with her fear or with her disdain. She would treat it, if its emanations compelled her to pause, with an icy disapproval, as she might treat a snoopy guard, set there by a jealous director to catch her out in something wrong.

By staying away from the window, she avoided any repetition of the shock of the sinister Ludlow and the black pit (figments, she assured herself, of her overcharged imagination), but she was not sure that she had eliminated all of the window's influence. She still had a sense, whenever she passed it, of some small, crouching, indistinguishable creature, some huge insect or tiny rodent, humped there by its base. And whenever she had to work near it, in the center of the gallery, she was conscious of something in the air, an aroma or maybe just a thickening of the atmosphere, that at once depressed her. If she looked about at the treasures of the gallery from any spot in the immediate circumference of the window, they appeared unaccountably drab. The silver seemed to thicken and tarnish and to lose the special elegance of its century. Bowls, plates, urns suddenly resembled the kind of ugly testimonials given to railroad presidents in the era following the Civil War. The beautiful carved wooden lady of victory that had once adorned the prow of a clipper ship might have been a widening, middle-aging nursemaid in Cen-

tral Park. And the portraits, *all* the portraits, not only Valerian
Ludlow's, seemed to have hardened into so many dusty merchants and merchants' wives as might have choked the wall of
the Chamber of Commerce.

Sometimes she would watch visitors furtively from the door of
her office to see, when they were standing near the prison window, if they noticed what she had noticed, but if they did, they
showed no sign of it. Yet how could she be sure, if the things
actually had changed, that they would notice it? Perhaps what
she saw, under the malign influence of whatever the squatting
creature was, was simply *their* vision of beautiful things. Perhaps that was the mystic significance of the window: that, peering through it, one saw art as it appeared to the Philistine!
Aileen's mind had become a sea of hateful speculations.

One afternoon, at her desk, she looked up and gave a start to
see an old lady standing before her. She had not heard anyone
come in. It took her two or three seconds before she realized
that she knew who it was. It was Mrs. Ada Ludlow Sherry, one
of those "old New Yorkers" who made life for the curators both
difficult and possible. She gave money and she gave things, but
her gifts were hardly a *quid pro quo* for her almost daily interference. She was small and bent but very strong, and her skin,
enamellike, and her hair, falsely red, gave the impression of having been preserved by a dipping in some hardening unguent.
Her agate eyes snapped at Aileen.

"Are you aware, Miss Post, that an atrocious act of vandalism
has been committed in your gallery?"

"Oh, no!"

"Some villain has poked a hole in my great-great-grandfather!
Don't you ever check up on your portraits? There's a ghastly,
gaping rip where his left eye was!"

"In Valerian Ludlow!" Aileen jumped up and ran into the

gallery to the Wollaston painting. Sure enough, old Ludlow blinked at her with one black eye and one blue, the latter being the color of the wall on which he was hung. Aileen gave a little scream of panic.

"This was done within the hour!" she cried. "He had both eyes when I last went by!"

Tony Side was summoned, the alarm was rung and all guards were questioned. Nothing was discovered, and after an hour of futile excitement Aileen was back again at her desk, depleted and scared, with the irate Mrs. Sherry, who refused now to depart. Aileen felt nothing but antipathy as she listened to the old lady's animadversions. Obviously, Mrs. Sherry cared far more for the grudge than for the grievance. She had none of Aileen's nausea at the damage to a beautiful object or her despair for the soul of the perpetrator.

"Some black boy, of course," Mrs. Sherry was grumbling. "Unless it was a Puerto Rican. They're always prating about the hard times they've had, always griping about how they've been deprived of education and opportunities. Is *this* what they want opportunities for? I'd like to see the cat-o'-nine-tails brought back. I'd like to see these boys lashed before the public in Times Square! What do they exist for but to tear our world apart? They don't care that they have nothing to put in its place! It's revenge, pure and simple."

"Revenge," Aileen murmured thoughtfully, glancing apprehensively through the doorway toward the iron grille. Could it be the revenge of a Yankee prisoner of war? But why? Revenge against whom?

"Everybody's too soft and sentimental with them," Mrs. Sherry continued. "If it *is* softness. If it isn't just cowardice, as I suspect it is. Where have our guts gone to, Miss Post? Where are our men, that we are exposed to all this? I tell you one thing, young lady. Nobody would have poked an eye out of Valerian Ludlow's portrait in his day!"

"What would he have done?"

"Don't you know what he would have done? Haven't you read his journal? *He* knew how to handle insubordinates!"

As Aileen watched the terrible old woman, she had just for a second the same eerie sense of blackness that she had experienced in peering through the iron grille. Then, as it passed, she felt a sudden, odd detachment from the immediate scene. She found herself observing Mrs. Sherry as if the latter had been a monologist performing at a private party. She noted the protuberance of the front molars and the drops of saliva at the corners of the thin lips. She marked how the almost transparent, onion-skin eyelids snapped up and down and how hatefully dark were the merciless eyes. Except for the teeth Mrs. Sherry might have been a bird, a big, dark bird of rich, subdued colors whose feathers only made more horrible its dark face and beak, a condor tearing at a carcass. Both of Aileen's hands went to her lips in horror as she saw her world in a sudden new light. The feathers, the feathers alone, were art. The head, the beak, the glazed eyes, the talons were — man!

"Oh, be quiet! Be quiet, please!"

Mrs. Sherry stared down at Aileen incredulously. "I beg your pardon?"

When Aileen, stunned, gathered that she must have actually uttered her reproach aloud, she desperately summoned up the courage to go on. "You're saying the most dreadful things, and you have no business to. You don't know who damaged that portrait. You have no idea. It might have been a guard. It might have been me. It might have been you, yourself!" Aileen rose as if propelled by two strong hands clutching her elbows, and she spoke with a passionate urgency, a wondering, bemused

prisoner of her own new flow of eloquence. "How do I know
that you're not just trying to get someone in trouble? Or a
whole race of people in trouble? How do I know what mad,
twisted motives you may have? Look at your umbrella. You
might have done it with *that!* But, my God, there's something
sticking to it!" She seized the umbrella and rushed out into the
gallery crying, "Guard! Guard!" When the bewildered man
hurried up to her she shouted, "I've got her! The vandal! She
did it with this! Look!"

Here she held the umbrella up to the portrait, the tip toward
the hole. Then she lowered it slowly, dumbly, apologetically,
looking shamefaced at the shamefaced guard. For the round tip
of the umbrella had a thick rubber cover. Mrs. Sherry must
have made it do double duty as a walking stick. Pushed into a
canvas, it would have made a much bigger hole than the one in
Valerian Ludlow's left eye.

"And now, Miss Post, will you be so good as to return my
property? And let me ask this gentleman to conduct me to the
director of this institution that I may complain of your insane
behavior?"

Mrs. Sherry was so carried away that, turning from the
stricken Aileen after she had snatched back her umbrella, she
made the mistake of taking the guard's arm. Her exit was comic
rather than magnificent. But nothing could console Aileen.

Tony, when he came, was very kind. He said that the vandalism had obviously unnerved her. He regretted that so important
a member of the museum as Mrs. Sherry should have been insulted, but he hoped that she could be placated. He suggested
that Aileen would do well to take a few days off and get a good
rest.

"No, I'm all right, I really am," she insisted in a stony voice.
"I promise, you won't have to worry about me."

When Tony had left, obviously much concerned about her, Aileen sat for ten minutes, absolutely still. Then she rose and strode with a new resolution to the middle of the gallery. As she leaned slowly down and stared into the hated window, she whispered hoarsely:

"Who are you, in there? Why have you come back to haunt us? Are you the spirit of some poor boy who died in that black chamber?" As she listened, she felt her first impulse of sympathy for whatever might be behind those bars. She had a vision of a thin, undernourished face, that of some nineteen-year-old Yankee boy, with long light hair and eyes liquid with homesickness, pressed up against the bars. "Were you left behind in General Washington's retreat? Was that how the British caught you? But why do you hate the Ludlows? Wasn't their house requisitioned by the governor? Was that their fault?" In the silence, as she listened intently, she had again that eerie sense of a close malevolence. "Or do you know something about them that we don't know? Was Valerian Ludlow a secret Tory? Was he a traitor?"

The blackness that she imagined behind the bars seemed now to lift, and her eyes fell upon the great portrait in the corner of the gallery of General Cornwallis, his hand on a globe on which the eastern shoreline of the thirteen colonies was clearly visible. Aileen straightened up and returned to her office. There would be no further revelations that day.

The following morning she was greeted by the doorman with the news: "There's been another of them vandals in your gallery, Miss Post." When she arrived at her floor, breathless, after running up two flights, she found Tony and three guards standing before the glass case of the silver tankards. He silently pointed to something as she hurried to his side. On the top tray one of the tankards lay toppled over. Its cover had been wrenched off the hinges and had fallen to the bottom of the case. The coat of arms had been gashed several times by a heavy instrument, possibly a stone. She did not have to look twice to recognize the Ludlow crest.

"Nobody's to touch it until the detective from the police department comes," Tony explained. "This is a weird one. The glass, you see, has not been removed." He put his arm around Aileen's shoulders and led her out of earshot of the guards. "It had to be an inside job," he told her. "Whoever did it must have got the key to the case from your office. But we've checked, and your key case is locked. He may have slipped into your office one day when it was open, taken the key, had it duplicated and put it back. It might have been the same guy who used your umbrella to poke the hole in the Ludlow portrait while you were out to lunch."

"*My* umbrella!"

"Well, I didn't want to upset you, but we found a smitch of canvas by the rack in your office where you keep your pink umbrella. It has to be some nut, of course, with some fantastic grudge against the Ludlow family."

"Oh, you've put that together, have you?" she murmured. "You've recognized the Ludlow tankard?"

"My dear Aileen. Even though I'm a museum director, I'm not a complete nincompoop."

Aileen was seized with a fit of violent trembling. She felt the same fierce prosecuting excitement that she had experienced when she had denounced Mrs. Sherry to the guard. Pulling Tony further away down the gallery, she whispered desperately, "Maybe *I* did it! Maybe I poked the hole in the portrait and then tried to throw the blame on Mrs. Sherry! Maybe I came here last night and let myself into the gallery and scraped the tankard!"

Tony's little smile never failed him, but she could tell by the way it seemed just to flicker that he did not wholly dismiss the theory. "But assuming all this, my dear, what on earth would be your motive?"

"I had no motive."

"Then why would you do it?"

"Because I'm the instrument of a fiend! The fiend that you brought in when you made me take *that!*"

Tony took in the little barred window, and at last even his smile ceased. "I said before that you needed a rest," he replied in his kindest tone. "This time I insist upon it. I want you to take three weeks off, and I want you to see a doctor."

Aileen was surprised and heartened by her own reaction to this disaster. Instead of crumpling before circumstance, she discovered that her spirit was strong and her emotional state serene. When Tony told her that the police detective had said that the force used in rubbing the stone or other substance against the crest of the Ludlow tankard had been greater than that of a woman, she had merely nodded and taken her dignified leave of him. She had recovered faith in her own sanity and did not need the confirmation of a cop. She had promised that she would consult a psychiatrist, but she was already resolved that she would not. There was no use in a confrontation between the world of medicine and the occult. It could result only in her commitment to a lunatic asylum.

She was grateful for the solitude of her enforced vacation and of the time that it afforded her to deal with her ghostly opponent. For she knew now that she had one. No human being could help her. It was her grim and lonely task to track down and outwit the sinister spirit that was seeking to destroy her gallery.

She spent her days in the library of the New-York Historical Society, reading everything that there was to be read on the history of the Ludlow family. The material was rich. She found considerable evidence of a curious effeminate streak in the Ludlow males of the eighteenth century. The first Ludlow in New York, a royal governor, had insisted on wearing woman's robes while presiding at the council, on the theory that he thus more appropriately represented his sovereign, Queen Anne. A generation later, his son had been criticized for making his more muscular African slaves wait on table half-naked, and this son's son, in turn, incurred the resentment of society by keeping exotic birds, expensively imported from Rio, loose in the house where they pecked his guests. The wives of all these gentlemen, on the other hand, had been big, blocky, plainly dressed women, such as one might expect in a community that was still, after all, almost the frontier.

Aileen, like many old-maid scholars, was as sophisticated about the past as she was timid about the present, and she perfectly understood that there might have been a streak of cruelty, or even sadism, in such eccentrics as the male Ludlows. But nowhere could she find the slightest evidence that any of them had been guilty of any public or private injustice, and the record of Valerian Ludlow in the Revolution seemed to repudiate the least imputation of Toryism. She had come almost to the end of her documents when a librarian asked her if she would like to see the microfilm of the manuscript of Valerian Ludlow's journal.

"I should like to look at it, of course," she replied. "I've read it so often in print, I know it almost by heart."

"You mean the DeLancey Tyler edition."

"Well, yes. Isn't that the only one? It's supposed to be complete."

"Supposed to be."

Aileen looked more closely at the young man. "You mean it isn't?"

He shrugged. "Tyler was a great-grandson of the journalist. He published his book in 1900. You know how prudish people were in those days."

Aileen knew by the bound of her heart that her search was over. She spent the next two days tensely reading the diary of Valerian Ludlow on the microfilm machine. The librarian had been quite right. There were substantial sections omitted in the Tyler edition. Ludlow had been a vain and easily offended gentleman of exquisite tastes and domineering manner. He had entered in the journal every slight that he had imagined himself to have received, and he had carefully recorded every punishment meted out to a servant. His descendant and editor had left in all his purchases of artifacts, all his recorded dealings with architects and decorators, all his conversations with the great, but he had carefully suppressed the invidious details of the correction of his staff and family. Aileen read breathlessly as she cranked the machine, turning the pages of the neat, flowing, somehow merciless handwriting. The realization that she was on the threshold of her revelation was actually painful.

She found at last this entry, dated July 30, 1747:

I have neglected my journal for a week because of a disturbing episode which, through God's grace, has now ended happily for most but not all. A group of slaves last Tuesday seized a farm on Lydecker Street and held it against the bailiff and his men for twenty-four hours. What the purpose of these ignorant fellows was we do not know, and they all fled. One constable, however, was killed when his own rifle blew up in his face. Public feeling has been very passionate, and on Thursday morning a large mob called here to demand my Rolfe. I met the leaders at the doorstep, and, I must say, they were very civil. They explained their reasons for believing that Rolfe had been the leading insurrectionist. I found these reasons convincing, the more so as I had had to confine Rolfe to the storeroom only that morning for insubordination. I delivered him up for what I understood was to be a trial, but I doubt that he had one. What is sure is that the mob burnt him alive in Bowling Green. It was a slow fire, and they say the poor fellow's bellows could be heard for six hours. I have discussed this unfortunate matter with Attorney Reynolds, and he advises me that if no trial occurred, I may be able to demand the price of Rolfe from the City Council, as he was taken under a show of authority.

Aileen turned from the machine with a gasp and rocked to and fro in her agony. For minutes she writhed as if she had been that wretched creature on the fire. How could flesh endure it? Six *hours?* The tears came at last to her eyes as she gave herself up to the relief of hating mankind. Mankind? Could she hate Rolfe, too, bellowing hour after hour, bound over a small flame like a sausage? Could she hate the man who must have listened, agonized, at that storeroom window while his master negotiated with the mob? Oh, God, God! But there was no God. There was only beauty, and whatever commiseration she felt for Rolfe she had to prevent him from destroying that. She jumped up as she came out of her daze. If she were only in time!

When her taxi arrived at the museum she fled up the steps and jammed her way through the revolving door.

"Is everything all right, Tom?" she asked the doorman.

"Never a dull moment these days, Miss Post. We had quite a scare an hour ago in your gallery. There was some defective wiring in the broom closet that started a small fire. We've had the chief and hook and ladder and all. Some excitement! But it's all out now."

She bounded up the two flights to her office and fumbled crazily among her keys until she found the one for the prison window's case. Then she sped down the gallery and opened it. She paused for just a moment as she faced the hated bars, and murmuring, "Forgive me, Rolfe," she picked them up and bore them to the window over the courtyard. Looking down to be sure there was no one beneath, she shoved them out, closing her eyes as she heard the clangor of the smashing to a hundred pieces.

For a moment she felt as if someone were pulling her over the sill, dragging her after it. With a violent effort she bounded back and stared about her. She was alone, perfectly alone, although below she could hear the shouts of the alarmed guards. In a moment they would come up, and all would be over. She would lose the job that was simply her whole life. As the inky depression began to surge and bubble about her, like rising water in a filthy tub, she saw at last what it was that the squatting spirit had been after.

"Why me?" she could only groan. "Why, in God's name, me? Was it such a crime to think that even their possessions were beautiful?"

The Double Gap

Memo from Albert Ellsworth to Philip Kyles, Oct. 10, 1969

YOU WILL BE SURPRISED, my dear Philip, to receive this missive
from your "alienated" grandfather. After our last altercation,
you may not have expected to hear from me at all. But we old
must be patient. We must be constantly exploring new methods
of communication. One of the things that is most difficult for us
is that we have to sit on our prejudices while you young crea-
tures are at liberty to blow yours to the sky. If I so much as
mutter the words "half-baked" or "irresponsible" or, worst of
all, "unpatriotic," I am shut up forever in the cubbyhole of the
seventy-seven-year-old Wall Street reactionary, the befuddled
yearner after "law and order." Prejudice in a young man is lovable hot headedness. In a dotard it is rot.

So I have dreamed up this form of communication as one that
may be conducive to calm and truth. I shall dictate my "apologia" to my machine and let my poor faithful Miss Downey, who
has suffered these forty years with my vagaries, type it up. You
may read it and come to my office and dictate your response. It
is my frail hope that in this fashion we may resolve some of our
differences. Believe me, dear boy, I do not mean to be arbitrary.
Your present decision not to work for Carter & Ellsworth after
your graduation from law school may be a perfectly sound one.
All I ask is that you reconsider it without emotion or prejudice,
or with as little of these obstructions as is possible in our troubled time. Hear my plea.

When you stalked out of my club the other night, after our rather tumultuous evening, you left me with many sad reflections. I do not want you to have any regrets about that. The excellent Haut-Brion had loosened our tongues, and we had both been sharp. I'm glad it happened. If you consider me a superannuated tool of the legal and financial establishments, a greedy old lawyer who has sacrificed his talent to the selfish interests of rich clients, I want to know it. And if you desire to practice law in a way that will benefit a larger segment of your fellow men, I want to know that, too. I must never assume that I cannot learn from my daughter's son. But so too must you not take it for granted that you cannot learn from your mother's father. What are the mere fifty-five years that separate us in the six thousand of recorded history?

I want you to try to see me as I am. I take back the word "apologia." I loathe apologies. What if my generation neglected Negroes? Whom will yours neglect? The future may condemn us both for not allowing euthanasia, as we condemn our English predecessors for hanging that thirteen-year-old girl who stole the silver spoon. If we can bring ourselves to understand just *one* generation other than our own, the past may be unlocked!

I also realize that your vision of me is shared by many in my own office. I see it in their cloudy glances: that of a dry, ascetic, neat old widower, living by the clock, obsessed with the minutiae of his law practice, knowledgeable about trees but lost in forests, a "character" famed for his memory and accuracy, but having the soul of a computer. What wonder that you should turn from such a picture to practice your new profession among the "disadvantaged," or fly to African nations on the wings of government grants and teach the Bill of Rights as missionaries once taught the gospels? What else can a grandfather expect, particularly a grandfather who has been so indiscreet as to have made you financially independent for life?

One thing you must first endeavor to understand — and if you can take this hurdle, the others should be relatively easy. I am an incurable romantic. I seethe with passion! Oh, I see you smiling. How laughable. How ridiculous. How pathetic, even. But it's still true. I do! And what is more, I don't believe that any of your generation, that anybody born after 1900, in fact, will ever know what true passion is. Born in 1892, I skimmed under the line. As you read my story, you must bear this in mind.

My father was a designer and decorator. He made lamps for Tiffany and stained-glass windows for churches. It was a minor talent, but it was accompanied by all the temperament of a major one. He felt that he had to travel in Middle Eastern nations in quest of color and atmosphere, and he not infrequently went off as guest lecturer on the yachts of rich friends. Naturally there was no idea of his large, rather grubby family accompanying him on his splendid missions, and Mother was left to struggle with seven children in the shabby old house on Flushing Bay. She never complained. She even accused herself of being in part responsible, by having given in so weakly to her selfish spouse, with the result that I, the eldest, on whom many of the neglected paternal duties naturally fell, grew up with an odd philosophic dichotomy. On the one hand, I glowed with pride and admiration before what I regarded as the fiery jewels of my father's windows in Manhattan churches, and on the other, I came to associate art and all beautiful things with a blamable casualness in the discharge of domestic duties. I did not presume to criticize my delightful parent — delightful, at least, on the rare occasions when he showed himself — but I may have effected a kind of psychological punishment of his image by denying to my dun-colored self even the contemplation of any such career. Somebody, presumably, had to pay the penalty for Father. What more could I do for my sainted mother than take that, too, upon my bowed shoulders?

I think I decided to go to law school because the law struck me as the opposite pole to art. The years that I spent working my way through Columbia have a drabness in my recollection, a sense of winter wind and nocturnal subways and Law Review notes pounded out in the gray early morning, that fits the chosen sobriety of my plumage, as did the gaudy colors of my father's artifacts blend with his waistcoats and ties.

I became editor in chief of the Law Review, which made it a simple matter (the first of my lifetime) to achieve a junior clerkship in the great office of Carter & Noles. There I worked for two years on a salary that was almost nominal before I was even introduced to Mr. Carter. I saw him, however, daily. Elihu Cowden Carter was to Carter & Noles what Louis XIV was to Versailles. The clerks and stenographers at least mentally genuflected when that stout, diminutive figure with the white curly hair and the flowing pince-nez rushed through the corridors, always late, always excited, shouting last-minute instructions to the secretary or lawyer behind him. The office buzzed with his sayings, his eccentricities, his wild, wonderful tempers, his court triumphs. But what Mr. Carter offered to me was nothing less than a way out of my dilemma of not being and yet yearning to be Father, a kind of miraculous compromise, a cake both kept and eaten. For he, unlike my wandering parent, was esteemed on the moral side as a husband, a father, a citizen, a philanthropist. And yet he was also a tyrant, a pagan god, a fascinating, dynamic genius who dared to wear huge ruby cuff links and twirl a gold-headed cane, a collector (it was rumored) of pornography and the author (in his youth) of two brilliant satirical novels. He pointed the way of salvation to Albert Ells-worth. One *could* be both artist and attorney. One could sing lyrics and pay one's bills.

My first contact with the great man, however, was not happy. I had been preparing the court papers in one of the many es-tates of which he was executor. His annual income in fiduciary commissions alone, it was whispered, exceeded a hundred thou-sand dollars. The older associate for whom I worked had to go to Albany for the day, and he told me to obtain Mr. Carter's signature. For a whole morning I hovered nervously outside the senior partner's office until the secretary found the proper minute to let me in. Mr. Carter, without a glance or a greeting, took the papers from me and, somewhat to my surprise, pro-ceeded to read them. He was not a "Where do I sign?" man.

I looked about. I might have been in a period room in a mu-seum rather than a downtown law office. Louis XV bergères took the place of the usual leather armchairs; a huge table of malachite surface and four curved gilded legs culminating in lions' heads with bared teeth served as a desk. On the walls were panels after Boucher; on the floor was an Aubusson. Only the window view over the smoky harbor betrayed the true locale.

"What's this?" the sharp voice demanded, and I turned from my reverie to take the document he stuck at me.

"It's an affidavit of debts and cash, sir."

"I can read, young man. I can read. What's it *for?*"

"The Surrogate's Court Act requires it, sir."

"Yes, but *why?*"

I had heard that he liked the unexpected, and I picked the wrong moment to be jocular. "It may be a vestige of the days when decedents' estates were handled in the ecclesiastical courts. Perhaps Henry VIII used it as a means of finding out how much cash the monasteries had."

Alas, Mr. Carter only glared. "Do you mean by this display of learning to imply that the affidavit has no current function?"

"None that I know of, sir."

"Then why the devil should I sign it?"

"Because the statute says you must."

"Must! Wasn't it the great Elizabeth, since we're so Tudor-minded this morning, who said, 'Little man, little man, the word "must" is never used to princes'? Well, I may not be a prince, but I don't like to be ordered about. What is the penalty if I refuse?"

"The penalty, sir?"

"Yes, the penalty, you numbskull!" he roared. "Do I pay a fine, and how much? Do I go to jail, and for how long?"

"I'll have to check the statute, sir."

"You mean you *haven't!*" He snatched the affidavit back from me and tore it in two. "Well, for your edification, Ellsworth, let me inform you there *is* no penalty. And never again come into this office and ask me to sign some meaningless piece of bureaucratic foolscap for the doing of which I am not paid and for the not doing of which I am not punished. If we must be fools, let it be either for greed or for fear. Good day, sir!"

I thought I would never see him again. He had a terrible reputation for judging clerks on a single test. But evidently I had not done as badly as I feared, for only three months later I was called in to confer with him about a matrimonial matter on which I had written an exhaustive memorandum of law.

It was the old case of the heiress who has eloped with the penniless young man and, five years later, repents of her bargain. She finds she is her father's daughter, after all, and quite as mean as her progenitor. The old man is willing to take her back and wants his grandchildren, but first all traces of the interloper must be obliterated. Counsel are summoned to preside over the touching reconciliation of Mr. and Miss Moneybags.

My sympathies were entirely with the son-in-law. There was nothing in the files to indicate that he had been mercenary; on the contrary, he seemed to be a nice if rather dull young man, who had a respectable job and loved his children. Yet now all the resources of a colossal fortune were aimed at taking them away from him. Nothing to me then or since has been more odious than the vindictiveness of the servants of wealth toward any humble person who gains an entry to the royal family.

I sat with Mr. Carter while he dictated a long, stiff letter to the young man's lawyer. Yet stiff as it was, I noticed that it considerably ameliorated the tone of what the client had wished him to write. When his secretary had gone to type it, he turned to me and asked my opinion.

"My candid opinion, sir?"

"That's what I pay you for," he growled. "So long as 'candid' is not a mere excuse for insolence."

"If I were you, then, sir, I should suggest a rather different approach. I should suggest to the client that in return for his son-in-law's consent to a divorce, he settle a million dollars on him, in trust. As to custody of the children, I'd split it fifty-fifty."

Mr. Carter's face was inscrutable. "And your reasons, young man, for this bizarre proposal?"

"It would cost the client nothing, for the trust would pass ultimately to his own grandchildren. It would save the son-in-law's pride and give him the means of living decently while his children were with him. It would avoid bitterness and resentment all around."

"And what about *me*, Mr. Ellsworth?"

"How do you mean, sir?"

"Where would I go for honey when you have plucked the fairest flower of my garden?"

"You mean the client would leave you? Oh, no, sir, no client would do that."

Mr. Carter gave a high squeal of laughter. "Dream on, my boy, dream on! It may interest you to know that I have already suggested a solution not too different from yours and that I have been told, in less than elegant terms, precisely what I could do with it! Yes, my dear Ellsworth, we are all slaves in this universe, only on slightly different levels. But you and I, I am glad to see, can share a few illusions together. Let us cherish them. In the long run, they may see us through!"

And from this point on I became Mr. Carter's principal clerk.

He was not a man who ever much cared for office hours. He carried his law practice in his head, under that rumpled sea of white locks, and he was as much at work in a dinner jacket, in his baroque dining room, as he was grandly orating and gesticulating before the Appellate Division. Often I would work all evening in his library until he came in at midnight, from the opera, whistling (very much off key) an aria and plunk down beside me to read over and revise a brief until the small hours. He had little depth of legal knowledge, in the scholastic sense, but he had a fantastic speed of comprehension, and he could translate my dull prose instantly into a sparkling narration in his own style. This latter may seem a bit florid to modern eyes, but it had a great effect on the courts of his day.

It was, of course, at the Fiftieth Street house that I met your grandmother. She was the only Carter daughter still unmarried, and she looked after her semi-invalid mother, who was as quiet and passive a peahen as one might have expected for such a mate. It fell upon Clarissa to manage the household and see that everything meshed with the comings and goings, or rather the rushings and dashings, of her eccentric papa. It was hard work, for however kind, however competent, she had not inherited his genius.

I fell in love with Clarissa at first sight. That is something else your generation doesn't believe in. You believe in bed at first sight but not love. To you, a man who was a virgin at thirty and loved only one woman all his life would be an incredible supposition. Yet just such a man was I.

I think what initially attracted me to Clarissa was her enchanting expression of mildly frenzied frustration. Her impulses of generosity reached out to everyone: to her parents, to the servants, to the hard-working clerks in the office, to the poor of her charities, to the world itself, but these impulses were continually being arrested by the exigencies of her father and mother, by her household duties, by her social obligations, by the general brutality of mankind, even by her own blessed, lovable inefficiency. Her large, worried brown eyes, her nervous gestures, her darting, at times almost clumsy movements, were occasionally irritating to her irascible sire, but when she entered the library, late at night, with a supper tray for the office slavey, she made all my toil worthwhile. I adored her from the day of our first meeting to the day of her death, and I think she loved me — a little better than she loved the rest of the world.

But the pace of love was slower in 1920, at least for young lawyers and the daughters of their bosses. The rattle of the jazz era hardly penetrated to the dark library at Fiftieth Street. It was to be a full two years before Clarissa and I spoke of love and two more before we married. Indeed, so great were my inhibitions about my social inferiority, and so intense was her concern with her domestic duties and charities, that we might never have got around to it at all but for the famous and (in other respects)

ill-fated trip that she and I made with her father to Central
America in 1921. It was just after I had been elected a junior
partner in the firm.

Mr. Carter's principal corporate client was the Great American Fruit Company which did much of its business in what we
used to call, in those less sensitive days, the "banana republics."
When Holland pulled out of Dutch Honduras, a bad situation
arose. The Dutch settlers, united with some of the rich Honduras families, seized the capital and purported to rule the country. A mercantile oligarchy, the tools of Argentinian capital,
they were overtly hostile to the Fruit Company. The popular
party, whom they described as "rebels," occupied the principal
seaport, Bazilla, and were supported by our client. Mr. Carter
and his party took up residence there in a big white multi-porti-
coed villa, from which he proceeded to direct the "revolution."

Those were thrilling days. Mr. Carter was at his greatest. He
became a kind of general in chief of the popular forces. Seated
on a veranda in a spotless white suit under a great sombrero,
sipping juleps, he received delegations and harangued them in
fluent Spanish on the necessity of unity and discipline. When
not so engaged, he and I drew up the new constitution (which is
still in effect), reorganized the army, arranged for elections and
drafted the correspondence to foreign powers, including the
United States. Of course, we had special communications with
the latter, and it was through our embassy in Panama that Mr.
Carter finally arranged the naval blockade which prevented the
"loyalists" from receiving help from Argentina and which
brought about their rapid bid for peace.

To me it was all a dazzling revelation of what the highest role
of a lawyer could be. Taken out of the library and set down at
the front, I watched my secret daydreams become actualities and
saw Mr. Carter take the shape to the world that he had always

taken to me. For the most niggardly clerk in his office would now be obliged to concede that behind all the bluff and bluster, behind the mannerisms and theatricality, there lurked a statesman with a heart and imagination big enough to play midwife to a newborn nation. Or to change my image, let me compare the constitution that I helped him to draft on a veranda overlooking the sparkling Caribbean to the golden cords that he wound around the bucking bronco of the Honduran state until it had been calmed into civilized submission. Small wonder that Mr. Carter's bust dominates the main square of Bazilla to this day.

Well, you know the tragic end of the story. You know how your great-grandfather met his John Wilkes Booth, the mad Dutch planter who shot him four times through the stomach as he was entering the Presidencia to attend the great ball that celebrated the adoption of the constitution. It was on the steamer returning to New York, two months later, after the national mourning and the funeral procession led by the president and cabinet of the new republic, that your stricken grandmother agreed to allow me to guide the destinies of her broken life.

In the years that followed, as I rose in the firm until I had taken his place, it was always my first policy to keep the spirit of Elihu Cowden Carter alive. I made his memory and his image the trademark of our organization. Each associate who came to work with us was given a copy, bound in morocco and illustrated with prints covered by onionskin, of my biography of our founder. The French furniture was moved from his office to our reception hall, as was his great portrait by Sargent, seated at the Empire table. Over the water coolers I placed bronze tablets with quotations from his public addresses. A glass-topped case stood in our library housing his decorations from foreign governments, and the bloody vest that was taken from his body in

Bazilla was hung in a frame in our principal conference room.

Oh, I know there are those who say I went too far. But if you don't overdo this kind of thing, you are bound to underdo it. The tendency to oblivion is a rushing torrent. Ideally, I should have stepped into Mr. Carter's shoes and provided the same dynamic leadership that he had. But I couldn't. I could only be my own, inferior kind of senior partner. I could only lead by reason, by watching, by patience, in my own drab way. The color and inspiration that we so desperately needed had to be invoked in the great spirit of our founder.

This, then, is the firm that you sneer at for being mercenary. Perhaps it is. But I wanted you, anyway, to see how *I* see it. For if I, as an idealist, have produced only what is sordid, you as an idealist may fare no better. What I suppose we must now do is try to analyze the nature of idealism. Maybe it will come to pieces in our hands. Let us take the chance. I exhort you, therefore, to utter candor: about me, about the family, about the past. Your witness, sir.

Philip Kyles to Albert Ellsworth

I accept your terms, Grandpa. I have always subscribed to the immortal sentiment of E. E. Cummings: "There is some shit I will not eat." So long as you merely pass it out, without requiring consumption, a declination ceases to be bad manners. You are warned! Read further at your peril!

I have always liked you, Grandpa, but my affection has been tempered with a good deal of resentment. As a child I yearned to have a special relationship with you. I suppose I wanted you to be a buffer against Mummie. But in every issue, in every crisis, you invariably took her side. I faced not one but two older generations, solidly united. It was poor Daddy's obvious role to come to my aid, but what can an alcoholic do? Oh, yes, I suppose, deep down, I blamed you for that, too. For Daddy's failure as a man. You overworked him, when he was in your office, to avoid any show of favoritism to a son-in-law. Then, when you discovered his drinking, you affirmed your probity by firing him. And finally, to salve your conscience, you completed his humiliation by supporting him. It was a pretty thorough job.

I find your story of Great-grandfather Carter absolutely fantastic. How could he have so deluded you? I can remember the exact time when I first began to suspect the stuffing in his idol-image. It was the summer of my seventeenth year. Until then I had never much cared for his relics: the pompous bad French furniture, the albums of photographs of him with his foolish hairdo and round pot, in the center of legal groups, the privately printed volumes of his windy letters and speeches, but I had held my peace. I had even assumed that there might have been a great man behind it all, that it might be the fate of great men to be survived by just such ineloquent memorabilia. And then came that spring when you suggested to Mummie that it would do me good to work as an office boy in Carter & Ellsworth. I had just been kicked out of Dunbar Academy for smoking pot (that was the difference between 1963 and 1969!), and it was generally felt that I needed a few more kicks.

Well, I am grateful for that summer. It made a man of me, though not at all in the sense you intended. It made me look about. It made me think. There *had* to be a reason for your fetish of Carter, for the grotesque fashion in which you had strewn garish reminders of him all over the three great floors of your law factory. Even the dullest of office boys found it funny. But why? What was the purpose of it?

At Yale I read up on Carter. I even did a term paper on him for my course in government and got an A. Needless to say, I never showed it to any of the family. My thesis, in brief, was that Carter was a brilliant ham actor who persuaded a credulous public to accept the hatchet man of a big, bullying corporation as a legal philosopher and statesman. In Dutch Honduras he used his client's gold to put a gang of political pirates in power. The job itself was simple. The hard part was to drape it in the glory of the Stars and Stripes. He succeeded in both.

At one point I almost came to like him. It occurred to me that he might be a jolly old buccaneer, cackling to himself at the naiveté of a sentimental world that insisted on sanctifying him. But later research compelled me to abandon this consoling theory. Nobody bought the legend of Elihu Carter more avidly than Carter himself. His art collection gave him away. Every one of his pictures, sculptures and furnishings was designed, like those of petty German royalties, to emphasize the grandeur of its owner. One would have thought that in all his many residences there had to be — by the laws of coincidence alone — one good thing. There wasn't.

It was not until the summer after my first year in law school, when I again worked for you, but this time as a clerk, that I finally discovered what you were up to. You gave the show away yourself, at one of our lunches at the Down Town Association. "A small law firm," you told me, "can be nothing more, if it chooses, than a group of lawyers practicing law. A big one, like Carter & Ellsworth, is lost without an *esprit de corps.*" So *that* was it. You deliberately set out to create the legend of Elihu Cowden Carter. You coolly manufactured a religion and a creed to hold your office together! What a magnificent old cynic you are, Grandpa! Why can't you admit it? Why do you have to daub life in strange colors even when you're all by yourself with a dictaphone? *That* is what my generation can never understand.

Take all this business about Grandma. I remember her distinctly. She was a very dear person, but her goodness was so widely scattered that it had lost some of its taste. It seemed to me that she was hopelessly vague, always inditing letters to the *Times* about the vivisection of dogs or the poisoning of pigeons, and gently haranguing her bored grandchildren about the poor and suffering. Surely, you must know that this kind of constant self-identification with pain springs from guilt. Grandma could no more love the people in the slums than she could love the members of her own family. She tried to cover the desert of a heart dried up by a psychic shame with the flowers of charity. When you say that she loved you a tiny bit more than she loved mankind, you show that you knew that. Oh, yes, you know everything that I know, Grandpa! You simply use a different vocabulary.

[*Typist's note:* I cannot help but enter a *caveat* here, Philip. You must *not* show this to your grandfather. Do you want to kill him? What makes you think you're entitled to say these things? I have known Mr. Ellsworth for forty years, and I utterly repudiate all your interpretations. Has it ever occurred to you, young man, that your sacred candor is nothing but your psychic impulse to revenge yourself on your elders and betters? Shame on you!]

Bravo, Miss Downey! You make the picture complete. If you hadn't existed, Grandpa would have invented you. The old guy is a great creative artist, a kind of capitalist Dickens. But what you don't appreciate is how tough he is. He can take all that I can dish out and more. So go back to your machine and remember what Harry Truman said: "If you can't stand the heat, get out of the kitchen!"

I have heard Mummie herself say, Grandpa, that you and Grandma had developed the perfect mechanism against the smallest imputation of selfishness. You lived for her and she for you, so you could both do exactly as you wished. What a marvelous solution of the ego! You let Grandma have all the money she wanted for her charities, and she let you give your life to Carter & Ellsworth, and together you grew old like two old folks in a valentine. Maybe my friends, who try to face their own selfishness without subterfuge, are wrong. Maybe you two had it licked. Whatever "it" is.

Except sex. I can't give you sex. I can see how it might be fun to build up the legend of Elihu Carter, even the legend of Carter & Ellsworth, but why is sex fun the way you played it? You're perfectly right that I find it difficult to conceive of a normal man who was still a virgin at thirty. I ceased to be one at seventeen, during that first summer in your office which you so rightly said would make a man of me. And ever since I've had more or less regular sexual relations. It's not promiscuity. I *need* the society of girls. Ruth and I have been going together for over a year now, and we may very well get married. But we don't see the need of talking about love all the time. We love each other, yes. But we know that very few people have the luck of loving "forever."

Perhaps that is why my generation goes in less for fraternities and secret societies than yours and Daddy's did. Perhaps it's why we prefer coeducation. Some of the emotions of sex in your day must have gone into those deep college friendships. But surely such sustained virginity as yours must have been rare even then. What did you do? Masturbate? Wasn't *that* promiscuous?

Let me end this tape with a more important question. I learned in sociology that the manners and fashions of any era are determined by a small, dedicated group of men and women.

Obviously, you are one of these. What I want to know is how you coped with the people of *your* generation who didn't go along. I know how you tried to cope with those of mine. How did you handle heresy in the ranks? How did you handle it in Carter & Ellsworth?

Let me rattle an old skeleton while I'm at it, one that Daddy used to drop hints about. Did one of your partners ever try to bribe a judge? Mummy always shut him up right away, and I tended to ignore it because Daddy was such a sorehead about Carter & Ellsworth. I knew he had been kicked out because of his drinking, though he always claimed that he took to drinking because he was kicked out. But in the past couple of years I have come to develop more sympathy with the poor guy's plight, caught as he is between Mummie's frantic social life (Granny's misty altruism in vicious reverse) and your austerity. *Was* there anything in that dark hint?

Albert Ellsworth to Philip Kyles

Let me say, straight off, Philip, that you're perfectly right about my being tough. I will not deny that reading the transcript of your tape was a painful experience, but it was one that I do not regret having solicited. I believe that our experiment may yet work. For you, too, dear boy, are tough. I was much amused at how you stood up to Miss Downey. Let me here put in an aside for her. She may be wondering why she is being put through this, why we do not play our tapes to ourselves. It is because I feel that the detachment of the typed word is indispensable to what we are doing, and I can only add, as a small recompense for her embarrassment, that she is the only person in the whole world whom I could entrust with such a task.

To turn, then, to sex, the topic A of your generation. Yes, I did masturbate (poor Miss Downey!). As you imply, a man must do something, and no doubt monks have so indulged themselves through the ages. But, strange as it may seem to you, and strange as it would have seemed to many of my contemporaries had I discussed my situation (which I never did), it did not seem strange to me. Much of my energy went into the fatiguing hours of my studies and law practice, and I was too afraid of venereal disease to go near a brothel.

Maybe there *was* more sex in my friendships and less in my marriage than I was aware of. We don't know where sex starts and where it stops. Maybe it permeates everything. I know that people who hold that theory tend to regard themselves, with a smug superiority, as down-to-earth realists. They see the sign of the phallus wherever they look. But if everything is sex, may not each of its manifestations be of equal importance? The sigh, the kiss, the wink, the shy compliment, the bold compliment, the daydream, the act of coition, the orgasm, the handshake — they are all facets of a revolving surface and perhaps glitter equally to the man from Mars. You undoubtedly speculate that your grandmother and I had an unsatisfactory bed life. You are wrong. And yet when I tell you that was the least important part of our marriage, I am sure you will snigger and consider that you were right in the first place. You're still wrong. Clarissa and I had something very beautiful together — something that I am afraid you and Ruth will not find until you have cast out Freud, or at least the Freud of the amateurs.

But enough of that. We might even quarrel about sex. It was my mistake to bring it up. My delusions, if such they are, about your grandmother can have no effect on your current decisions. The question on the table is whether or not you come to work for Carter & Ellsworth. Let us keep to that.

My greatest concern over the last thirty years has been the

increase in size of our office. We now number a hundred and twenty lawyers. You can't cope with the fantastic business regulations exacted by modern socialism with a much smaller staff. But how was I to preserve the individualist spirit and the moral standards of the old-time practitioner? How was I to avoid the "organization man's" point of view, so lamentably evident in the big companies, where the moral buck is passed from shoulder to shoulder until it is spilled?

I did what I could artificially. We had firm dinners, firm cocktail parties, "outings," departmental lunches. There was even an office mimeographed news sheet. I never lost an opportunity to dramatize for the younger men the history of the firm. Many mocked me, as you mock me, but it worked. I remember a journalist who came to interview me about a book that he wanted to write on the big New York law firms. He was frankly cynical about what he expected to find: nepotism, old school ties, inter-firm back scratching. I told him that none of the big firms could long survive those things, that character and brains were their indispensable stock in trade. I invited him to use a desk in our office and to open all files that were not privileged. After three months he wrote a piece that justified me!

All right. I know. I am beating around the bush. I am avoiding your question. Have we ever bribed a judge?

Not a United States judge. Thank God I can at least say that! But I have to confess that there were times when the Great American Fruit Company bribed courts in Dutch Honduras. Of course, I refused to have anything to do with it myself, but that's no excuse. I knew that it was going on. I was persuaded by the officers of the company not to ask certain questions. They claimed that judicial bribes were a kind of tax on foreign corporations, that one had to pay them, not to obtain an advantage over one's opponent, but simply to be placed on an equal footing with him. I hated it, but I knew that Mr. Carter himself had winked at the practice (which will come as small surprise to *you*), and I accepted it as a *sine qua non* to doing business in Central America. When in Rome . . .

But I am still stalling. Let's get at it. The incident to which your father referred occurred *in* the United States, in 1939, the last year that he clerked in my office. It had nothing, however, to do with my dropping him, and I do not know how he got wind of it. But then he was always snooping around in our files, looking for discreditable material. I'm sorry to say it, Philip, but your father has never been able to forgive himself for marrying your mother for her money. He has tried ever since to ease his conscience by reducing *me* to his level. Small wonder your mother goes in for jewelry and charity balls.

What happened was this. I had a partner, now deceased, Tom Ambrose, who was the kind of lawyer I dislike most in our profession: a one-client man. I may live for my clients, but I have never lived for one. Whenever I saw a clerk becoming so monopolized, I would correct the situation either by dividing his work with others or by arranging to have him leave us and go into the employ of the corporate client. But Ambrose defeated me. He made himself so essential to the Fruit Company that they asked that he be made the partner in charge of their business. I put it off as long as I could, but in the end I gave in, only because the company had been Mr. Carter's special pet.

I never ceased to regret it. Ambrose always made me feel that his first loyalty was to his client, never to the firm. He cared for our partnership only insofar as it was of service to the Fruit Company, and he would refuse even to discuss firm matters that did not affect his particular interest. I am afraid that I came to detest him. He was a short, stout, bullheaded man, who had a horrid habit of standing in my doorway, instead of walking into the room, and staring at me with his little pig eyes, puffing all the while at a cigar, before he put his question. The question, once put, invariably covered a sneer, a sneer at me, at my aspirations, at the firm, at everything in the world that was not Tom Ambrose or the Great American Fruit Company.

On one memorable morning, however, he did not pause in the doorway. He came straight into my office and closed the door behind him. He explained that he was representing Great American in a pending lawsuit in a federal district court in California, before a judge whose reputation in bar circles was beginning to acquire a faintly acrid smell. Only the night before, working alone in the company's confidential files, he had happened upon a memorandum revealing that this judge had just received an unsecured loan of a hundred thousand dollars from one of the executive vice presidents.

Oh, Philip! You will smile at my naiveté. You will say that all the big companies did this kind of thing. I wonder if it may not give you some pause to know that even so crude a man as Tom Ambrose was shaken to the core by his discovery. Why had the memorandum been written? Because bureaucratic habits are so rigid that wrongdoing officers must incriminate themselves as lemmings must leap in the sea. And why had Ambrose told *me*? Because, deep down, like all my partners, he believed that I could perform miracles. He believed that I could get him and his company and even the wicked judge off the hook, so that we could all be ethical and prosperous together once again in the best of all possible worlds!

Alas, there were limits to my miracle-working powers. I remember going to the window and standing with my back to Ambrose.

"Well, at least what we have to *do* is perfectly simple," I said. "We must go to the company and get them to rescind the deal."

"And get the money back from the judge? How the devil do they do that?"

I shrugged. "That's their problem. But I'm sure that His Honor, once that he has been apprised of the litigant's change in attitude, will cooperate to the fullest."

"How can you talk like that, Ellsworth? Suppose the judge coughs up the loan? What kind of justice is the Fruit Company going to get from him after *that?*"

"As just a justice as it was getting before."

"Make sense, man! You know Great American's never going to ask for that loan back."

"Very well."

"Very well, what?"

"Very well, we withdraw from the case."

"And prejudice our client? How will it look?"

"We don't have to say why we're withdrawing."

"Ellsworth for God's sake! You know the company would never forgive us. It would be the end of Carter & Ellsworth for them."

"But not the end of Carter & Ellsworth."

"No," Ambrose retorted bitterly. "Only the end of Tom Ambrose. I see your game. You've never liked me, and now you spy a chance to be rid of me, even at the cost of five percent of your gross. Well, we'll see what the executive committee has to say about that!"

The executive committee consisted of the five senior partners and included Tom Ambrose and myself. Its decisions on firm policy were final. That afternoon the committee met in my office for a tense two hour session, and I was overruled, three to two. The partners who joined Ambrose in making a majority took the simple position that it was not their duty as counsel to read and construe the private correspondence of an officer of a corporate client, which Ambrose had had no business to read in the first place. To do so, they maintained, and then to jump to criminal conclusions was nothing short of monstrous. How were they to know that the transaction might not have some perfectly innocent explanation? They preferred, in brief, to be know-nothings.

For twenty-four hours I debated resigning from the firm. In the end I decided that it was too great a part of my life. I simply could not bring myself to it. So Carter & Ellsworth proceeded to try and win a case before a judge whom I knew had been fixed. The following year the judge died of a stroke, and five years later Tom Ambrose followed him with cancer. Our little drama was to have no further consequences than the heartache of Albert Ellsworth. But that heartache was as bitter as Ambrose himself could have wished.

You see now, as you suspected all along, that there *have* been compromises. That was the greatest of which I have any knowledge. But give me credit at least for admitting the problem and my own failure. I do not know where you could go to work today and find better intentions than in this office. And now I hold my peace and let you be judge.

Philip Kyles to Albert Ellsworth

It may surprise you to learn, Grandpa, that I'm not particularly shocked by the Ambrose disclosure. It even seems to me that if you had walked out of the firm under those circumstances, you might have been taking yourself too seriously. But I think I am beginning to see at last what you mean by your "passion." You are really a survivor not of the nineteenth century, but of the age of chivalry. The *game* is what you care about, and what is the merit of winning a game unless you play by the rules? Your game — and I see that you play it passionately — is to be at once the greatest and the most ethical member of the whole wide bar. What satisfaction would there be to a man like you in winning a bridge tournament by the use of a finger code? You play a good game and a clean one, but to me it's still just a game.

From where I sit — and a lot of young people are sitting here with me — the gap seems to be narrowing between the big corporations and their lawyers and the Mafia and theirs. Now don't flip. I don't mean that you or your clients are crooks (that bribing officer in Great American Fruit excepted). What I mean is that the crooks are copying *you*. In a crowded planet people tend for their protection to form into big, selfish pyramids. The Mafia leaders copy the corporate hierarchy. They constitute a caricature — and a grim one — of the business world. I may be against the "establishment," but I wonder if I am much more against it than you are. The difference is that I want to bust it. You want to romanticize it. Neither of us can bear it as it is.

My particular friends at law school fail to see why a client's best interests should be the be-all and end-all of their professional lives. They fail to see why they should spend their existences as the tools of greed. Nor are they satisfied with the supposedly compensating game of ethical canons which has the function, at least in the minds of your generation, of raising the lawyer to a higher moral plane than that of his client. Do your dirty work, but do it ethically, and in heaven you'll be on a higher cloud than the punk who paid you. No, it won't wash.

We can't be satisfied with indirection. We want to benefit our fellow men directly, in the ghettos, the slums, the poor rural areas, the starving parts of the world. Those of us who have to earn our bread may go to work for firms like yours, but they won't buy the "mystique." Let me end where I began with E. E. Cummings' great quotation about what he will not eat.

Albert Ellsworth to Philip Kyles

I'm afraid you're like Tom Ambrose. You're a one-client man. Your client is the world. All the dangers of fascism are for me contained in this. Ponder — please ponder — my description of that man. What happened to him could happen to anybody. But good luck to you, anyway. I'm glad that I've made you independent so you won't be compelled, like your breadwinner friends, to go to work for a firm in whose "mystique" you cannot believe. I am convinced, sincerely convinced, that you will do big things. I am only disappointed that you will not be doing them with me. And I cannot help but wonder a bit, when you and your contemporaries have scraped all the gilt off the statue of life (gilt which I call passion and you call sentimentality), whether you will not be a bit disappointed at the dull gray skeleton that you find beneath. But that, of course, is a question for youth, not age. Farewell. When we meet again we will communicate (or fail to communicate) more normally. And good night, Miss Downey. I'm sure you're glad this is over.

The Collector

No MAN was more sought after as a speaker at club evenings or graduation ceremonies than Grenville Thorne. His presence on the dais ensured an audience that the occasion would be entertaining as well as edifying, as high in tone as it would be rich in humor. Thorne had the right to consider himself a rare page in the annals of mortal success, for he had achieved, in his fifty-six years, a renown for wit and erudition, for warmth of heart and public spirit, for gracious affability and old-world courtliness — all by doing the one thing in life that he most enjoyed: buying rare books and manuscripts.

He had imbibed a literary atmosphere from his earliest boyhood in the library of his grandfather, Richardson Thorne (a respected if now supplanted editor of Shakespeare) that had occupied the back of the old brownstone house on East Tenth Street. Books and associational items had been heaped everywhere, the valuable with the less so, folios and rare quartos stacked on the shelves with Victorian illustrated editions, fine old prints of the Virgin Queen and her favorites cluttered on the spare bits of wall space between sentimental lithographs, an ugly plaster reproduction of the funerary bust of the poet sitting under a perfect Hilliard miniature of an unknown youth. There had been no catalog; every record had been kept in the old man's mind. If young Thorne but put his finger on the back of a book, his grandfather, glancing up across the room, could tell at once which it was.

The house was Grenville Thorne's now and the library,

which he had vastly enhanced — far more than making up for what his rapacious mother had sold — but everything in it had been converted to the requirements of the nineteen sixties. Steel cabinets, fireproof, held the ordered rows of gleaming volumes; a card index file stood on the site of the Stratford bust; a vast blue safe, the holy of holies, massively filled one corner. Through the narrow corridors of the house, clogging them so one could hardly pass, were the glass cases for the books of lesser value, the sets, the "reading copies," the reference volumes, and in the parlor and even the bedrooms the tables were heaped with octavo tomes. Only the dining room was bare of literature, but it was dominated by the proprietor's portrait over the sideboard, smiling, pipe in hand, tweed jacketed, silver haired, eagle-eyed, the distinguished collector personified.

Thorne liked to believe that, if he had given his grandfather's hobby a contemporary suit, he had still retained its essence. He congratulated himself on having preserved from the past the only passion that could burn as brightly in the nineteen sixties as in the eighteen sixties. God and progress were dead, and love was mechanical; peace and salvation were pipe dreams, but whatever else he had missed, Grenville Thorne would be able to say, at the moment of his extinction, "Ah, but I owned the manuscript of 'Endymion'!" During the students' strike at Columbia, which as a trustee he had had to observe, he had felt only a faintly contemptuous pity for those shouting youths. "Collect, you fools, collect!" he had wanted to tell them. And he had smiled at the thought of what their stupefied reaction would have been.

His mind was particularly full of his grandfather on the winter afternoon when he sat alone in his library after his aunt's funeral service. Delia Thorne, a bedridden maiden lady of eighty-five, very pure, very fine, very lovely, had made her home for twenty years with her nephew, occupying her father's old bedroom where she had written her fragile poems, her *chinoiseries*, and received the daily visits of her loving relatives. Thorne stood now before the open safe and ran his fingers over the treasures that his grandfather had left to her and that were now to join their fellows in legal as well as actual entity.

"By God, Aunt Delia, you picked the best," he murmured. "Even with all I've bought, through all the years, the cream of the collection is still yours!" Moving his index finger over the backs of the cluster of volumes on the central shelf, he recited the names reverently, as if they were a part of the service just concluded: "The 1609 *Sonnets*, with the Aspley imprint, the 'Pied-Bull' *Lear*, the *Hamlet* third quarto, the *Palladis Tamia*, the *Venus and Adonis* with the arms of the Countess of Pembroke, the first issue of *Lucrece*, the four folios . . ."

He paused in his inventory, dizzy with the sense of what was now his, and pressed his lips against the box cover of the 1609 *Sonnets*. He would immortalize Aunt Delia for what she had done for him. He would write and print a monograph of her pale, uneventful life. It would be a beautiful slender volume, bound in blue morocco, with a frontispiece, protected by onionskin, of George de Forest Brush's idealized painting of her as a girl.

He heard his wife's step in the hall and drew back from the safe in a quick, automatic movement of guilt. It was not that he concealed his primary passion from Alma, but good manners required the formal observance of conventional emotional priorities. Alma, however, as always, knew just what he was doing.

"You've been looking at Aunt Delia's books? I was thinking of them myself during the service. What a beautiful thing it was, her refusing to sell them, way back, when your grandfather died, and everyone was so hard up! I know God is everywhere, but I wonder if just now, just for this moment, He isn't a tiny bit more intensely in this room."

Thorne nodded. Certainly, Aunt Delia had kept the torch lit in those terrible years when his own formidable mother had sold, one by one, the old man's unique assemblage of first quartos. He shuddered at the recollection of that roughly sweeping broom, which had spared humans no more than it spared books, which had sent him whisking out of Columbia into an uncle-in-law's textile factor business and dispelled forever his dream of becoming a professor. Yet he always had to concede that his mother's crude remedies had worked. Had he not learned his trade and earned the money that had replaced the old library with a greater one and supported Aunt Delia, impoverished but for her fiercely grasped treasure, to boot?

"I suppose Mother did the best she could — according to her lights," he said ruefully, trying to put away the memory of those quartos. "It's always a difficult task for sensible souls to find themselves responsible for impractical ones, like Aunt Delia and Grandpa."

"A very difficult task." Alma came over and slipped her arm under his. The courtesy of her tacit assumption that he was grief stricken at the death of an ancient bedridden aunt was exquisite. "But it's never been one, thank God, that I've had to shoulder. Your share of the Thorne mania has always been contained in the most beautiful little urn of common sense. No, not an urn. An urn is for ashes. A reliquary, a beautiful silver reliquary, all studded with jewels!"

"Usually semiprecious, I'm afraid. You're the one who's kept me rational. Without you, we'd have been in the poor house."

"Oh, Grenny, you old silly!"

Yet he had spoken the simple truth. Alma had been to him the wife men dream of. Even her least prepossessing aspect, her physical appearance, her large frame and broad shoulders, her round brown face and short bobbed hair, was redeemed by the radiant gaiety of her laughing blue eyes, eyes that were as spiritual as the rest of her seemed down to earth. Alma, though as much a New Yorker as himself by birth, had been raised in the depression years in Austria by parents who had found it more economical to live abroad, and had been converted early to Catholicism and to the Teutonic concept of the subservient wife and strong mother. In return for her husband's reluctant promise that they should have as many children as God should send — which turned out, happily for him, to be only two, Dick and Priscilla — she had thrown herself gladly into supporting his every ambition, his every whim. Alma had known how to pinch and scrape in the bad years of Thorne's business, how to cadge scholarships and borrow summer houses, but never had she suggested that he sell a book or manuscript, and once, in a particularly bleak winter — for textile factors were subject to sharp ups and downs — she had even managed to buy him for Christmas, out of her household savings, the 1619 quarto of *Henry V.*

"Dick wants to know if this is a good time to talk to you about Aunt Delia's will," she said now.

"Did Aunt Delia leave a will? She never spoke to me about it!" Thorne turned abruptly away from his wife as he said this. He did not like what his heart was suddenly doing.

Dick Thorne had just finished his first year as a law clerk in a downtown firm. He was a sober, hard working, rather literal young man who seemed more than necessarily resigned to a life of pulling other people's chestnuts out of the fire. Thorne was fond of him, but, as in all his family relationships, he found it wise to pretend to be fonder.

"I suppose there was no reason for her to mention it," Alma

replied. "Dick's the only lawyer in the family. I hope she left him something."

"Oh, I'm sure she did. He was always her favorite, you know."

He felt as if the air in the library had all at once congealed into a solid substance that was pressing hard against every square inch of his skin. He shook his shoulders to dispel the feeling, but it was not quickly dispelled. Moistening his lips, he paused before replying, to be very sure that his voice would sound natural.

"Is Dick here? Ask him to come in."

When Alma had gone, and Dick was standing before his desk, he examined the young man furtively. Dick had a craggy face that was more manly than handsome. He had his mother's health and strength, but his eyes lacked her radiance. They were brown and brooding and frequently sullen. Dick was as honorable as his mother, but, unlike her, he was aware of his honorableness.

"I understand you have your first estate to administer," Thorne began, in his most agreeable manner. "I am very proud that Aunt Delia should have confided in you."

"Well, it's a very simple estate, of course." Dick's tone was abrupt to the point of seeming faintly unpleasant. "It consists almost entirely of those books. The only complication will be how to pay the estate tax. Presumably, I'll have to sell some of them."

"Sell some of them!" Once again Thorne had to moisten his lips before speaking. "What do you mean, *you'll* have to?"

"I'm Aunt Delia's executor. Those books have great value. At least so you've always told me. There'll be an estate tax, and how else can I raise the money to pay it?"

"Isn't that up to the residuary legatee? Can't he put up the money?"

"Certainly. If he has it."

"And why do you assume I haven't?"

Dick's truculent manner now revealed itself as simple embarrassment. "Dad, I know this will come as a terrible shock, but I have to tell you. Aunt Delia left those books to me. I couldn't talk her out of it. I tried every argument, but I just plain couldn't. She kept saying over and over again that I was her father's only great-grandson and namesake. She said if she left them to you, they'd be taxed twice, which, of course, I couldn't deny. When I pointed out that it wasn't fair to Priscilla, she said you could make it up to her in *your* will. Finally, when she threatened to leave them to the Folger if I wouldn't take them, I had to give in. I figured you'd rather keep them in the family than lose them altogether."

Thorne was almost frightened by the pain in his chest. It was as if a lunatic were running about inside it, hitting wildly at his ribs, trying to get out. "Isn't there some rule against lawyers drawing wills for their own benefit?"

Dick closed his lips tightly. "You mean I should have sent her to another lawyer? I didn't think you'd have wanted me to go that far. Actually, I did have someone else in the firm prepare the will. But of course you're Aunt Delia's sole heir at law. If you wish to contest on the grounds of undue influence . . ."

"No, no, no!" Thorne was beginning to see what he was doing to his son, to his family. It was all a horrible madness, and the proof that it was madness was that he could not stop. As he saw himself suddenly through the young man's contemptuous eyes, he sickened with shame. "Try to see my viewpoint, Dick," he pleaded. "Those books are the cream of this library! You can't possibly imagine what they mean to me. Good God, I didn't know myself till this minute!"

"Dad, I *do* know." Dick's tone changed immediately with his father's. He sat down by him now, very kind and solicitous. "We all know how you care, Ma and Pris and I. Ever since I found that I couldn't make Aunt Delia change her mind, I've done a lot of thinking about what I'd do when the time came. Of course, the obvious thing would be to give you the books, but that would involve a big gift tax, which it seems absurd to pay. So what I decided was this. You keep the books for your lifetime, exactly as if they were legally your own — no questions asked. If you don't want to sell any of them, you can pay Aunt Delia's estate duties yourself. Then, on your death, if I survive you, I take them back, but only provided you leave Pris *your* library, to equal things up. Why doesn't that do the trick?"

For all his bitterness Thorne was able to see that the young man was behaving very well. That he was behaving, in fact, beautifully. That he was a son to be proud of, a true son of his mother. But the lunatic within him was remorseless, and nobody was to be spared.

"No, no, they're your books, and I want you to take them," he cried petulantly. "Take them away now, will you? Get them out of my sight. I don't want to have them under this roof another night. Take them to your apartment or your office, I don't care. I want to start right now getting used to living without them!"

He snatched the 1609 *Sonnets* from the shelf and threw it down on the desk before his astonished son. He had turned back to take down the first folio when the grating sound of Dick's sneer stopped him.

"It's only title you care about, isn't it, Dad? It's only owning. I can offer you the books to do as you like with, but that won't do, will it? Oh, no! They've got to be yours, all yours, legally yours. You're nothing but a miser, chinking his gold pieces together. Do you really expect anyone who's seen you at it, the way I have, to consider you a *literary* person?"

Thorne gaped at his son, but no words came to his aid.

"I'll tell you something more, Dad. I knew you'd scorn my offer. I only made it to prove the point. Oh, it was sincere enough. I'd have been only too happy to let you keep the books. I'd have been overjoyed to find you weren't the moral monster I've always suspected!"

Dick's eyes, so distant and scornful, might have been those of a judging angel. Thorne could only stammer out, "Monster?"

"You heard me. This is no time to mince words. If you'd only admitted from the beginning that all you cared about was your sacred library, I might have been able to come to some kind of terms with it. But oh, no! You had to be the great literary gentleman with the heart as big as a folio! You had to be adored and admired! And the worst part of it was the way you sold the whole rotten picture to Mummie and Pris. They've positively made love to being sacrificed! I suppose, to be absolutely fair, I should admit it wasn't all your fault. If women turn themselves into carpets, they must expect to be walked on. But you didn't just walk — you trampled! Mummie had to live in this old barn of a house and clean it herself, because *you* liked the library. She had to scrimp and cadge while you were spending thousands on quartos. And even after you'd made your money, she had to act as a companion and nurse to Aunt Delia because you wouldn't pay to put the old girl in a nursing home where she belonged. Not much! She had to be right here, under your nose, for fear somebody might get those books away from her! Well, I'm *glad* I've got them. And I'll tell you exactly what I'm going to do with them, now you've turned down my offer, which I shan't renew. I'm going to sell them, every last blessed one of them, and use the money to give Mummie and Pris some of the things you've denied them!"

"Sell them?" Thorne asked eagerly. "Will you sell them to me?"

"No!" Dick seemed actually to welcome this final evidence of his father's complete contemptibility. Any lingering doubts as to the justification of his patricidal outburst must have now been swept away. "You'd only gyp me. I'm going to sell them at public auction and at the highest price in the history of book collecting! If you want to bid for them, you're welcome!"

The worst jolt that his son had given Thorne was the revelation that somebody shared the horrid, half-stifled suspicion that had always made a vivid little hell out of odd corners of his bookish heaven, the suspicion that the passion which held him so tightly might, after all, be a vice. He had usually managed to make himself believe that as long as he alone entertained this idea, it did not have to be truth, or at least the whole truth. Why should not that other aspect of the collector, whose image he so constantly saw reflected in the eyes of a congratulating world, be also a part of verity? If everyone admired it, why might it not even be a moral passion? But now that Dick had come swinging into the temple with a scourge, it was difficult not to think of himself as a moneychanger.

The days that followed brought on a nervous collapse. Thorne would see nobody. He told his office that he was going south, and to lend verisimilitude to his story he ordered Alma and Priscilla to go to Florida without him. Alma's anguished solicitude had become unbearable to him. He was convinced that she had a secret sympathy for Dick. How could so adoring a mother not have? As for his son, he had ceased all communication with him after delivering Aunt Delia's books to his law firm, together with a grudging but duly executed consent, as sole heir, to the probate of her catastrophic will.

He spent the days alone now in his library or roaming the corridors of the empty house, examining his treasures, reliving the acquisition of each, considering, step by step, the long growth of what Dick had made him see as his moral malady. And the more intensely he looked into his own mental state, the more deeply he scrutinized whatever remained of his conscience, the more grimly was he convinced that Dick was right, that he *was* a monster, a moral leper. Indeed, after only a week, he began to wonder if he had not ceased altogether to be a human being and to doubt if the process were still reversible. Like Claudius in *Hamlet,* he could not pray for redemption while he was still in possession of the fruits of his crime, and he still loved his books as much as ever. One morning, after a night of little sleep, opening the safe before breakfast and staring at the empty shelf where Aunt Delia's books had been, he burst into hoarse sobs.

Yet there were clearer times, or so he deemed them. He began to recall symptoms of his malady in fellow collectors. He did not count as his fellows the millionaires who bought French impressionists for social prestige or the frivolous fashionables who collected because they had nothing better to do or even the generous souls who bought to give to museums or universities. No, the "real" collectors were those who had to grapple with the same soul searching that he did. Oh, he knew them! Even the ones who had seemed to bask in the same kind of reputation that he enjoyed, without so much as the tremor of a wrigglesome qualm, would betray themselves, on being shown a superior collection, by a green look in the eye, by a prehensile closing of the fingers as they handled an item. He could tell them, the real collectors, as one dope addict could tell another! And Dick had mercilessly divined that the essence of the craving was not for possession or lesser tenure or any mere opportunity to enjoy a treasure by sight or feeling. It was for nothing less than a fee simple absolute!

At last, one evening, he fell on his knees before the safe and prayed aloud: "I know you're only a golden calf, but who else can I appeal to? At least, you're a god, even if you're an evil one. If I destroy you, I destroy myself, and that may be the best thing to do. But if truth is what books are meant to stand for, you should not deny me that. We have both known all along, haven't we, that I'm a thief?"

He was able, after this, to take his seat almost peacefully in the armchair by the fire and go through the process of reliving an old crime, the only one he had ever committed, early in his collecting career. It had not been a dramatic crime, as in a problem play, to constitute the keystone of an otherwise blameless and splendid career. It had been a crime with no consequences and one from which he had derived no profit. But it perfectly illustrated the principle that Dick had divined.

A fellow collector had loaned him an early edition of Racine, bound in yellow morocco with the lozenge of Madame Sophie of France and inscribed to her by the Young Pretender. Shortly afterwards the lender had died, unexpectedly, and Thorne, who had been too hard up at the time even to contemplate bidding in the item at the executor's auction, had simply failed to return it. It had been a crime without the smallest risk. The collector had kept no inventory, and even if the volume had been traced, Thorne could have always claimed that it was a gift, or at least that he had thought it was. Indeed, might it not have been? His late friend had been a very generous man. Would he really have wanted that volume returned to his executor? Probably not.

Yet for two years afterwards the nagging knowledge that the book did not legally belong to him had destroyed all Thorne's pleasure in it, and one night, with a fierce little passion of relief, he had burnt it to nothing in the library grate.

Subsequently, in more prosperous years, he had assembled four whole shelves of volumes bearing the arms of the French royal family in memory of that incinerated piece. Rising from his armchair now, he pulled them out and arranged them on a table. He examined lovingly the splendid red of Madame Adelaide, the rich green of Madame Victoire, the bars sinister and dexter of the Duc and Duchesse du Maine, the castles of Madame de Pompadour, the lilies and dolphins of the Duchesse d'Angoulême, the bees of the Emperor. In the totality of his ownership they seemed to be singing to him, yet through their chorus he could make out the discord of Dick's indictment.

A still more horrid idea now occurred to his tormented mind. Did not the beautiful bindings suggest, in their very resplendency, a discrepancy between what was outside and what was in, the contents and the cover? How many of those dreary missals, of those histories of desert fathers, of those almanacs and forgotten five act tragedies, concealed under such glorious integument, had he read or did he ever intend to read? Was it not symptomatic of the progress of his vice that the young Grenville Thorne who had started his collection with a second edition of the *Lyrical Ballads,* a dear shabby torn volume in its original battered boards, should now be on the prowl for a manuscript of Carmen Sylva, bound in red velvet, with semiprecious stones, for the last Czarina? Was it not the ultimate proof of the viciousness of his passion that it should, through the years, have degraded his taste until he was dazzled by bindings and cases, by armorial stampings, by gilt edges and precious clasps? Ah, *that* was the difference between him and his sainted grandfather!

Was it conceivable that the Kohinoor itself could have turned the old man from the sonnets of Shakespeare to those of a Rumanian queen?

That night he came to a violent conclusion. If his vice had dehumanized him, the way to return to the world of men would be to sell his collection. By putting it on the auction block, he might redeem himself from the throttling grasp of his private fiend and become at last a husband and father. Until the early hours of the morning he roamed the house, touching the backs of his books, the tears streaming from his eyes. He recalled the description of the dying Cardinal Mazarin, tottering through the corridors of his palace, past the walls hung with the masterpieces of his vast collection, mumbling, "The way to leave all this? The way to leave all this?" If Thorne's was a noble decision, it was, alas, accompanied by no noble elation. The selling of the books would be only the draining of blood from a corpse. It would not be a resurrection; it would be an embalming. But maybe that was all that was left for him. Penance.

When he called his old friend, Tom Spofford, of the Leland Galleries, the next morning, to announce his dread resolve, he was startled to be interrupted before he had fairly begun.

"I was just about to call you, Grenny. What the hell is this all about?"

"What do you mean?"

"This business of your son selling the Delia Thorne books. Did you know they were in the gallery now? Did you approve it?"

All immediate idea of redemption vanished from Thorne's mind. "It's not up to me, Tom, to approve or disapprove," he explained. "Aunt Delia left her collection to Dick. He's his own boss. He knows what he's doing."

"Well, I figured he probably did. But with an old customer

like you, I thought I'd better call first. If you want to buy them in, the auction's set for the seventeenth. There should be quite a turnout."

"I imagine. I'll come and watch."

"Now what did you call me about?"

"Oh. Let's see. What was it? I must be losing my mind. Ah, yes. I wondered if you'd been able to find out anything about that Carmen Sylva book . . ."

Somehow Thorne got through the ten days to the seventeenth. Alma and Priscilla came back, and there was much desultory chatter about Florida. At Alma's timid suggestion, Dick was invited to a family meal, and no mention was made of Aunt Delia or her books. Thorne was aided in preserving the appearance of equanimity by the fact that he no longer knew what he was going to do or even why he was waiting for Dick's auction. All he could hope was that the sale might have some of the efficacy of a funeral. It would place a period on the first agony of grief. After that, it would be time enough to look about and see what he had to do. At the least, his attendance at the execution of Aunt Delia's books would prepare him for the sacrifice of his own.

At ten minutes to ten on the fatal day Thorne entered the familiar gray oblong room, already crowded with dealers. As he passed down the center aisle toward the stage with the maroon curtain backdrop to take his reserved seat by Tom Spofford in the first row, he heard the murmuring about him. "Isn't that Grenville Thorne?" "Do you suppose he's buying or selling?" Obviously the book world was agog with speculation as to the reasons for the sale. Thorne took his seat without nodding to anyone, simply touching Tom's shoulder as he might have greeted a friend in church.

The first item to be placed on the lectern was the least valuable, the *Pericles* quarto. Thorne remembered that Aunt Delia had asked her father to leave it to her because she had loved one line: "See where she comes appareled like the spring."

That had been like Aunt Delia. In more than eighty years at the altar of words she had not produced one such a line, and she had started knowing that she never would. The bidding began at a modest thousand, rose slowly to twenty-five hundred and stopped there. Thorne turned to glance around the room behind him. Everybody seemed to be watching him.

"Sold for twenty-five hundred! Come, gentlemen. This is the *Delia Thorne* collection. Are you all asleep this morning? Or is this the bargain day to end all bargain days?"

The *Venus and Adonis* was next, and to Thorne's consternation it was knocked down for only four thousand. He exchanged a glance with Tom in whose eyes he saw mirrored his own divination. The dealers were scared! Because the Thornes were selling, without any known financial crisis, the books were suspect! They had been on display, to be sure, but how did one *know,* unless one had examined every page and watermark? As Thorne heard the old roaring in his ears, he knew that he was no longer a free agent.

The "Pied-Bull" *Lear* was the third item offered, and Thorne entered the bidding at fifteen thousand. When it was knocked down to him at this figure, he could feel, even in his euphoric state, that the whole room behind him had come alive. There was a loud brouhaha of snorts, of exhalations, of whisperings. People poked shoulders, shifted seats. There would be no more bargains that day. Thorne thought he saw Tom signal by a wink to the auctioneer in the pulpit who raised his voice to a solemn cry like a muezzin's.

"Ladies and Gentlemen, we now offer the little volume you've all been waiting for: the Thomas Thorp 1609 edition of the sonnets of our 'ever living' poet. I will not insult the eminent bibliophiles present by describing it other than by saying that of thirteen known copies in the world it is the only one now available to collectors!"

Thorne's recollections of what followed were vague, but his hand was up at every bid, and he remembered the unprecedented burst of applause that followed the announcement of his successful purchase of his own son's property for a hundred and twenty-five thousand dollars. Thereafter the waters of his mania closed over him, and he bought in the balance of Aunt Delia's books for the highest prices, as Dick had predicted, that these items had ever brought. It was a heyday for dealers. They knew they were playing with a lunatic.

From his room in the psychiatric wing Thorne could watch the boats on the East River. He sat by the hour doing this, the 1609 *Sonnets* on his lap. Every now and then he read one. Alma tried to persuade him to let her take the little volume home to the safe and replace it with some less precious item.

"*I* can't get out," he retorted. "How do you think a burglar can get in? Don't worry. I sleep with it under my pillow. I would kill anyone who reached for it, and I think he'd know it. After all, look where I am."

"Oh, darling, it's only for a few weeks. A rest is all you need."

"A rest and a new soul."

Alma, since his collapse, had come down so violently on his side that even he could no longer doubt the completeness of her sympathy. She had excoriated Dick for his "heartless" course of action and had threatened the unhappy young man that she would never touch a penny of the proceeds of the fatal auction that he was holding "in trust" for her. She had discharged her two maids and was doing all the housework to help make up for the loss of Thorne's capital resulting from his rash bids. She had cleaned out the two top stories of the house and was planning to rent them as apartments. She had become, in short, a kind of fury of conjugal loyalty. But to Thorne, depleted, beaten, philosophic, in his chair by the window, it was all only further evidence of the ravage he had caused in her.

When Dick came to see him, tears of desperation in his eyes over his mother's attitude, and begged him to take the money back, Thorne simply shook his head.

"You were right, my boy," he said. "You were perfectly right."

"But Mother? She hates me now!"

"Oh, she'll come around. You'll see. She'll have to."

But Alma seemed incorrigible in her fanatic espousal of his cause. One day she came in with a package that was wrapped in the familiar green paper of his favorite bookseller. The sight of it alone quickened his heartbeat.

"What have you done?"

"Open it."

It was the *Pericles* quarto, one of the two items of Aunt Delia's collection that he had failed to get at the auction. Looking at it, he had the same sharp twist of pain in his stomach that he remembered feeling, long ago, in contemplating the little yellow stolen volume of Madame Sophie of France.

"Oh, Alma, you shouldn't have!"

"Darling, how could I let the poor thing be separated from the others? Think how lonely it must have been!"

That night, his lights off, watching the full moon over Queens, Thorne made his decision. He would go through with his original plan to sell his entire collection, except for Aunt Delia's books. He would dispose of the house as well. Together they should realize at least a million. He would give Priscilla out of this sum the equivalent of what her brother had made at the auction. Both children would then be independent. With the balance he would retire, travel, show Alma the world, make up to her for all her sacrifices. They would keep a small apartment in New York and a safe-deposit box for Aunt Delia's treasures. The latter would be to them the symbol of all the beauty behind the madness that had been cured.

Turning on his light he brought out the *Sonnets* from under his pillow and opened it.

Not marble nor the gilded monuments of princes
Shall outlive this powerful rhyme . . .

When he had read the sonnet over three times, he replaced the volume under his pillow and turned the light off. Perhaps it would not be asking too much of the future if, when his master plan had been executed, he allowed himself to keep an eye open for the chance of picking up at a bargain the *Venus and Adonis* that had gone for such a song at Dick's auction. After all, would it really be collecting again to try to recapture the one stray sheep from Aunt Delia's flock? Would it not be rather the pious act of a faithful nephew? Would his grandfather not have asked it of him? And with his fingers clutching the little book that Thomas Thorp had printed in 1609, he fell at last into that quiet sleep that is nourished by dreams of fantasy and illusion.

Second Chance

IT WAS DECIDED by all the Kilpatricks that I should represent my sister-in-law, Rebecca, in her divorce from Gilbert Van Ness. Gilbert insisted that he did not need a lawyer; he said he could represent himself. There were no legal complications. The two boys were almost of age, and Rebecca could have what money there was. He simply wanted "out." The Kilpatricks, furious as they were, agreed that it was better to keep things in the family. Everyone knew how tempers deteriorated when the lawyers took over. It killed any last chance of reconciliation, and what but reconciliation could poor Rebecca pray for?

Had the family aspect of the question not prevailed, I would have had an ethical problem. Gilbert was not only my wife's brother-in-law; he was one of my oldest friends. We had been together at Andover and Yale, and at Harvard as graduate students, he in business, I in law. We had courted the Kilpatrick twins in the same summer in Marigold, Long Island. Gilbert had been my youthful ideal of what a man should look like. At any point before my marriage to Belinda, I would gladly have swapped skins with him.

He is still very handsome. In his twenties he was almost too much so. His pale skin and delicate features, his thick curly red-blond hair, his laughing gray-green eyes, his tall slender figure made a distressing contrast to my dark, rough, rather huddled exterior. He dressed up to his appearance, too — in beautiful London suits and colored shirts. His family never seemed to have much money, but always enough for that. And his temper

was as cool and polished as his outward demeanor — except
when he was ruffled by a physical molestation. He could be dis-
gustingly violent if some joker messed his hair or dirtied his
clothes. Insults, on the other hand, made no dent on him, and
he would laugh off any criticism. He never seemed to take his
peers seriously after he had made his initial — and usually successful effort — to charm them. He mocked the world, but most
of all he mocked himself. He had no enemies and no intimates,
not even me. He existed, like a flower, to please all.

But that was twenty years ago. I have often thought that the
Kilpatricks, dear as they are, were not the garden to which that
flower should have been transplanted. They were all very well
for me and Belinda. We are both fairly tough, and Belinda had
the sense not to settle in Marigold. But Rebecca could not conceive of a happier place to live than right down the road from
her parents. She felt that the Kilpatrick atmosphere was the finest, the healthiest, the kindest, the coziest in the whole world.
And so in a way it was. But it was suffocating to Gilbert, not
because the Kilpatricks did not like him — they did, very much
— but because they lacked the discrimination to see that he was
made of finer material than they. It never crossed the mind of
big blond Rebecca ("Junoesque" is how we used to describe
her) that she had made a catch. And, to tell the truth, as the
years went by, and as Gilbert seemed more and more to wilt in
his chosen garden, it became less and less apparent that she had.

The best way to describe the Kilpatricks might be to say that
although not to any degree Bostonian in origin, they had many
of the characteristics associated with that city. They placed a
heavy emphasis on the virtues of family life and seemed to be
always proclaiming that what they might lack in style or polish
they made up for in heart. The big black shingle house with the
multitude of verandas that sprawled over the top of the little

hill overlooking the sailboat-clogged harbor of Marigold was the center of social life in that small commuting community. When I first used to visit there, there seemed to be a Kilpatrick child of appropriate age for every other child around the harbor. If I close my eyes to evoke those distant summers, I have an immediate sense of shrieks of laughter, of noisy parlor games, of loquacious mixed doubles, of closets ankle deep in tennis rackets and sneakers, of rather rank athletic clothing strewn about guest rooms, of a dearth of privacy.

It had its sunny side, but there were shadows, too. Why was Mr. Kilpatrick always reading the adventure novels of Stanley J. Weyman? Why did his wife have to sit in the cellar during thunderstorms? Why was it so important that they should always feel qualified to rate themselves "nice" (their favorite word), the nicest family that existed, perhaps the *only* really nice family in existence? Could it have been that they were diverting themselves against the panic of the idea that they were just as others? And could that idea of sameness have been the equivalent to them of annihilation? Was it *that* that kept them chattering?

Because Gilbert always tended to deprecate himself, he was singularly vulnerable to the Kilpatricks. He was well read, but he could not discuss books with those who never opened them. He was clever at parlor games, but his quiet voice was always drowned out. He was agile at sports, but he was far too scrupulous (unlike them!) about rules. He was astute in business, but he allowed himself to be drawn into the Kilpatrick textile firm where he was outvoted by his brothers-in-law whose heedless optimism made them ignore all warnings that the future was not for small family enterprises and spurn the merger that Gilbert suggested. He receded into passivity until he was so far in the background that it was difficult to remember he was there. He

faded to the point where one no longer quite knew what color
he had been.

When the textile business was finally and disastrously sold,
and all the Kilpatricks had to fend for themselves, which in one
way or another they succeeded in doing, Gilbert seemed the
only failure. At forty-five he was still handsome and red-haired,
but there was a gaunt look to him that made me think, when he
came to my office to discuss his future, of a Confederate officer
returning to his ruined plantation after Appomatox. As for myself, I had prospered vulgarly as a tax specialist, and Belinda and
I had six children. Indeed, in Glenhurst, the next station on the
Long Island Rail Road after Marigold, we probably corre-
sponded to the Kilpatricks.

To my relief but somewhat to my surprise, I found that Gilbert had no intention of remaining a failure. His recognition of
the bottom as bottom seemed to have aroused him at last from
his torpor, and he was very precise about what he wanted to do.
If he looked gaunt, it was evidently not because he had despaired. He asked me to write him a letter of introduction to
Victor Terhune, founder of Terhune Associates, the advertising
firm. He knew that I prepared Mr. Terhune's personal income
tax returns.

"Advertising?" I queried. "Isn't that a young man's business?"

"Of course, it is. But I've been studying it pretty closely for
five years now. I've made it a kind of hobby, ever since I saw the
handwriting on the wall in the woolen business. I think I'll get
on."

Never before had I heard him so confident! For a moment I
wondered if he was enjoying my astonishment, but his return
gaze was quite noncommittal. He was suddenly a stranger.

"But the textile business is so different," I protested.

"No business is *that* different. They all boil down to the same old question of selling yourself. You're thinking that to date I haven't shown much promise in that department, and obviously you're right. But there's no law that says I have to keep on being what I have been."

"What does Rebecca think of your plans?"

"I haven't told her."

"Don't you think you should?"

Gilbert took his gloves from my desk and rose. "Are you going to give me that letter, Joe, or aren't you?"

"Of course, I'm going to give it to you."

"Very well then. Make it a warm one. A *very* warm one if you don't want to find yourself having to help out with the college bills of two young Van Nesses."

I wrote the letter then and there, while he waited, feeling vaguely mortified at the coolness of his tone. Evidently, anyway, it worked. A week later he telephoned to inform me that he had been employed by Terhune. He thanked me, but only perfunctorily. That night, when I told Belinda, she hurled the bombshell at me that she had obviously been waiting all day to hurl.

"The bastard!" she cried. "He didn't happen to mention, did he, when he was asking for that reference, that he was planning to walk out on his wife the very first day he got the job?"

2

Belinda was much more violent about it than Rebecca. The latter was simply bewildered; she seemed to be looking about dumbly, like a stunned cow, to see where the iron mallet would fall next. As she had never seen why Gilbert Van Ness should not have been delighted and honored to become a member of the Kilpatrick clan, so now she could not conceive why he should want to leave it. But Belinda could. She entirely understood how her sister could bore a man to the point of taking such a step, and she could also see why her two nephews, bearded, radical students at N.Y.U. who spent much of their time in the East Village, would fail to hold him. These problems, however, only made Gilbert a bigger skunk.

"If you'd heard the way he talked to his own boys, and right in front of Rebecca!" she exclaimed to me. "He said they believed in nothing, so why should he? He asked them why there should be one standard for youth and another for middle age."

Belinda glared at me as if she were seeking for the smallest sign of apostasy on my part. I suppose Gilbert's defection had a peculiar terror to women her age. Who knew when the fire of such liberating ideas might not sweep the brush of their men's nostalgia for departed youth?

"I think Gilbert is perfectly outrageous," I agreed hastily. "But you must admit those boys are hard to take."

"And whose fault is *that?*" Belinda demanded. "Who was too soft with them? Who spoiled them rotten?"

Belinda was passionately curious to hear every word of the divorce conferences between Gilbert and me. Had she dared, she would probably have asked me to conceal her in my office closet. However bad Gilbert was, she was anxious to hear that he was worse. But had she found herself an eavesdropper, she would not have enjoyed the experience. For Gilbert, knowing that I would report back to the Kilpatricks, used our conferences, with a good humor that bordered on vindictiveness, to announce the credo which he must have put together, piece by piece, in the years of his self-imposed darkness.

I knew that he had consulted a psychoanalyst at the time of the collapse of the Kilpatrick Textile Company, and I asked him, a bit priggishly, if he held his doctor responsible for his conduct.

"Quite the contrary," he assured me. "He's all on your side. He says that he's only just succeeded in isolating the germ of my neurosis, and hasn't even started to cure it. Wait till he hears that he, too, has been abandoned. Oh, I promise you, he'll wail like a Frankenstein whose monster has just broken out of the laboratory!"

"You mean before the monster's complete?" I asked, surveying his red tie and yellow vest with renewed disgust. "What do you possibly suppose he left out?"

"I'm afraid he'd say a heart," Gilbert replied with a shrug. "Like most psychiatrists, he's a sentimental ass."

The disgust trickled out of me, as a kind of awe took its place. *Was* he a monster? Had my clumsy family-in-law really smothered his heart? "Maybe Doctor Kober's right," I muttered.

Gilbert shook his head; he was no longer smiling now. "He wants to play God. He wants to tinker with souls. He doesn't plan that I shall rise from his expensive couch until I can bow and say, 'Thank you, dear Doctor, I'm cured now, and I'm going back to my family in Marigold, the roundest little peg in the roundest little hole you ever saw.' But that's rubbish. All any psychiatrist can do is what Kober has done already. He can release, as Kober has released me. He can drain the mud out of the pool of a personality, so the patient can peer into its limpid depths and see what he is. And what he is, is basically what he always was."

"And what is that?" Staring, fascinated, into Gilbert's green-gray eyes, I felt as if I were looking into the very pool that he described.

"A son of a bitch! Isn't that what Belinda and her mother are calling me?"

"It is. But is that really what you call yourself?"

"Oh, I've given up nomenclature. I simply recognize the Gilbert Van Ness I have to live with. I admit I didn't like the draining process at first. I didn't like facing the fact that I'd never really loved Rebecca. That I'd never even much cared for the boys. I didn't like being confronted with the timid creature who had buried the childish guilt of his masturbating (or whatever it was he *had* done) under the odorous pile of the Kilpatricks' fatuities. But little by little, as my figure emerged under the clearing water, I began to see that certain traits, unused, had been perfectly preserved, like the flesh of a mammoth in a glacier. I saw the hardness, that fine, cold, clear hardness. It had a kind of royal beauty, like the stone images of early Aztecs. Not a *bad* roughness, mind you. It had nothing to do with spite or cruelty. Oh, nothing like that! It was simply the indispensable hardness that every man of stature must carry in his heart. Only I lacked the stature."

"Which is what you want now?"

"Why not, Joe?" Gilbert's gauntness seemed to recede as he smiled again, and I thought with a sudden pang of jealousy that he might have been thirty again. "What can I lose? I'm a failure already. One can always go back to that. What Kober helped me to see was that I was not necessarily born to be a failure. I might have been born to be one of those men whom everyone instantly recognizes as a person for whom things go well. You know the type. The type that gets taxis on rainy nights. That beckons to waiters, and the waiters come. That buys, and the stocks go up. Even in charities they're on the winning side. You find them on the boards of the great museums, the popular private schools. They 'swing.' They're 'with it.' They know by instinct how to avoid the dead end, the lost cause, the worthy bore. The Kennedy family is the type *par excellence!*"

"All right, be a Kennedy," I agreed. "Be president, if you like. My job isn't to persuade you to be a failure. Didn't I warn you from the beginning about the family textiles? Didn't I beg you to get the hell out of Marigold? Well, go ahead and be a great advertiser. I'm all for it. But let poor Rebecca share in the fun. Take her along!"

Gilbert shook his head very firmly at this. "My dear fellow, can't you see that would ruin everything? Rebecca is the very symbol of my degradation. It's absolutely vital that we separate. We're that notorious drowning couple who drag each other down. I've got to make my choice between sinking with Rebecca or staying on the surface. It's not such a hard one to make! I'm only really sorry about the boys, but they insist on taking their mother's side. I must say, it seems to be the first moral stand they've ever taken. I doubt if it's the last, however. They'll probably end up as stuffy as all the Kilpatricks. Must I go on with this, Joe? Surely, you see my point?"

The damnable part was that I did. I could entirely see that my poor sister-in-law was no companion for a man who was making so belated a start on Madison Avenue.

"There's such a thing as responsibility," I growled.

"Oh, Joe, for pity's sake, spare us both. Call me Gauguin, bound for the South Seas. Give me up. Let me get a Mexican divorce, and Rebecca can have everything I've got — less twenty-five thousand bucks to carry me for two years. You'll admit that's sporting. If I lose my gamble, I lose all. She can have the house, both cars, my interest in Dad's estate (it should come to a couple of hundred thousand) — even the few pictures I've bought. All she has to do is give me my clothes and change the front door key. Don't glower at me. As a lawyer you know it's a damn good offer!"

"The hell I do. Suppose you make a fortune?"

He laughed cheerfully. "What are my chances?"

"Not good, I admit."

"Well, there you are!"

"And yet I'm damned if I don't think you may pull it off. How about giving Rebecca a piece of your future? Just a small piece?"

Gilbert flung his hands up. "Never! Don't you see I must be free? If I carry Rebecca as a partner I'm bound to fail again." His voice rose in a curious new ecstasy of conviction. "Maybe, if I *do* hit the jackpot, I'll cut her in. I don't say I won't. But I shan't be bound to do anything. I *can't* be! There's my offer, Joe. She can take all and let me go. Otherwise, there'll be nothing for anyone. I'll go to the Bahamas and sit on my ass. I mean it! You know I mean it!"

I sighed. "I know. I'll draw up the papers. But I've never before taken a guy for all he's worth and still been so sure that *I* was the sucker!"

Gilbert jumped up and shook my hand. "Thanks! That's a real compliment coming from you. But then you and I have always been pals. We've always understood each other."

Looking at that bright mobile face that seemed to be growing younger by the minute, I sighed again. Never had *I* understood him less! Never, obviously, had I understood him at all.

3

The curious thing about Gilbert's immediate success in the advertising business was that it came as no surprise to the Kilpatricks. It was as if they secretly recognized that all along they had kept him down, or even as if they sullenly nursed some bitter superstition that any man who so brazenly subverted the moral code and kicked his basic responsibilities to the winds was bound to triumph in the big, hard world — at least in the big, hard world of Madison Avenue. Did I not detect in their attitude a feeling that if one dressed well and looked well, if one fussed about externals and went into the business of pushing deodorants, one might reasonably anticipate a commercial success corresponding to one's moral depravity? People like my family-in-law have never been satisfied since they gave up believing in hellfire. Where else was Gilbert Van Ness to get his comeuppance?

In the meanwhile they provided a good working purgatory for me. Each step in Gilbert's ascent was instantly converted into a form of robbery of Rebecca to which I had been accessory, if not in actual intent at least in criminal negligence. When Gilbert was credited with the American Fiat account, only a year after his employment at Terhune, the uproar was such that I had to walk out of a family dinner. After that Belinda took them to task and made them, through her father, formally apologize, but I knew that they still believed that I had let Gilbert off a percentage alimony because he was my pal. I would rather have had them believe that, anyway, than that his stronger personality had put it over my weaker one. Or that I had been dazzled — even envious — at the prospect of his liberty.

The first time that Belinda and I saw Gilbert after the divorce was at a dinner party given by the Terhunes in their triplex apartment on the East River. It was a very social affair, the kind that was apt to be written up in the *Daily News,* and all the "beautiful people" were there. We were asked only because the Terhunes made a point of asking us once a year. A tax lawyer in modern society, because he has to be admitted to secrets, has some of the status of a psychiatrist. He can be included in the larger parties.

Belinda and I knew nobody and felt like country cousins. We stood before dinner by a window and talked to each other. Mr. and Mrs. Terhune, like many people of fashion, had no breeding and never bothered to introduce their unimportant guests. Our tempers were not improved by seeing Gilbert, looking very young and almost flamboyantly handsome in a green velvet dinner jacket, chatting and laughing by the fireplace with the daughter of the house.

"If he marries her, I'll give up God!" Belinda hissed. "Do you know where Rebecca is tonight? At a reception for the opening of the Merchants' Exchange branch office at Seventy-third and Lex. They asked all their depositors."

"That sounds pretty stupid."

"It *is* stupid, you dope! The point is it's the only party she's been asked to all winter!"

I was surprised to find myself seated next to the heiress at dinner. Andrea Terhune was very beautiful, with delicate features and high piled, elaborately set, blond hair, but her manner was so artificial that she might have been playing a part. Despite her looks and fortune, she was still unmarried at twenty-seven. This, however, was not an unusual phenomenon in fashionable circles. A life devoted to haute couture and parties was sometimes deemed too sweet to be interrupted by domesticity. Andrea had all the chatter of her group and could no more talk to me than she could have to a Malay farmer.

"We were discussing Irene Bosworth," she began, when the conversational turn required her to pay me some attention. "Don't you think she's absolutely divine? I mean, literally."

"Do you mean she's God?"

"Well, one of His angels, anyway."

"I don't know her. Who is she?"

Andrea might have been able to take in the conception of a guest who was not acquainted with Irene Bosworth, but she had to reject altogether my ignorance of her identity.

"It's not only that she gives her life to the little people at the opera house. Oh, I don't mean just the bit part singers and the chorus. No! I mean the ushers and cleaning women — everybody. Yes! But in addition to all that — parties for them, outings to her place in Greenwich — yes! — she is going on her own (not her foundation at all) to do the new sets for the revival of *The Sicilian Vespers*. Yes! I mean, how much can one woman do for the city she lives in? How much?"

I realized now who she was talking about. "Mrs. Bosworth does what she can to minimize the cost," I observed churlishly. "She tried to get a charitable deduction for that big gala she threw for Callas. The Tax Court turned her down flat."

Andrea looked at me doubtfully. In her world one said only "lovely" things about "in" people. "I thought lawyers weren't meant to talk about their clients' cases."

"Mrs. Bosworth is no client of mine!" I retorted indignantly. "I read the case in the advance sheets. Would you like me to send it to you? She also tried to deduct the flowers she sent Mr. Bing when he was ill."

"I think you're horrid. But anyway I don't want to talk about Irene. I want to talk about Gilbert Van Ness. He tells me you're a great friend. That's why I wanted you next to me. Isn't he simply the most darling creature in the whole wide world? I mean really isn't he?"

"More than Mrs. Bosworth?"

"Oh, forget Irene."

"Forget a divinity?"

"When a greater one appears."

Really, she was too ridiculous. This kind of hyperbolic talk was bad enough in her parents where it was entirely hypocritical. The Terhunes, after all, had been Taubmans and had come up through the garment district. But it was much worse when it was sincere. That Andrea should believe her own fatuities was almost irritating enough to make one forget that she was the daughter of a client.

"I have always been able to look at Gilbert without blinking. Perhaps his halo needs shining."

She ignored this. "Dad says he's an absolute genius. Already, he's become his Number One man. I've never seen my father take to anyone in his office so quickly. And then Gilbert is such fun at parties. He's not always talking about how hard he works, like the other men. He despises drudgery. He says the art of living must be carried into one's daily work. He says he can think up a TV serial at a dinner party and choose his wines at the office. Isn't he fantastic?"

"Isn't he a bit long in the tooth for you?"

But she seemed utterly unperturbed by my rudeness. "Oh, nobody I know cares about age."

"What do you know about his marriage?"

"Isn't that ancient history? I gather she was a ghastly frump."

At this I *did* forget that she was a client's daughter. "The unfortunate woman to whom you allude happens to be my wife's sister. But that's not the point. Any more than her frumpishness or non-frumpishness is the point. The point is that the man who swore to love and cherish her left her, without a hint of warning, without even a stated complaint, after twenty years of married life. She woke up one morning, poor creature, to find herself both middle-aged and abandoned, with two disturbed sons, one of whom is now in a mental institution. You think the man who caused this mess is simply divine? I suggest he's simply a heel!"

"Why you're supposed to be his friend!" she exclaimed, horrified. "I never heard such disloyalty. We'll see what he thinks of your kind of affection. I'll tell him what you said this very evening!"

"Do!"

Andrea turned to her other partner and spoke to me no more that night. But she must have whispered her story to Gilbert while the ladies were leaving the dining room, for during the brandy hour he sauntered over to my table where I was smoking a cigar alone and settled into Andrea's chair.

"You lawyers!" he sneered. "You're so damn self-righteous! You can't face the fact that you've picked the wrong profession."

"Why have we picked the wrong profession?" I demanded, so surprised at his question that I forgot the issue between us.

"In a day when any numbskull can make money out of capital, you pick a trade where all your compensation is income. And you're a *tax* lawyer, too!"

"Some of us may care for something besides money."

"Yes, but not you, Joe. You just think you do. You kid yourself into believing that a tax lawyer is something more than a tricky accountant, that he's some kind of artist philosopher, but when you go out to dinner and see how well your clients live — by not paying the taxes that *you* pay — you're burned up. Oh, I could smell those cinders all the way across the dining room! You try to smother your jealousy by covering it up in sneers. Can't you guess what's wrong with those grapes?"

"Do you think I'm jealous of *you?*"

"Wildly. Why else would you fill poor Andrea's ear with all

that Victorian garbage about my being a cad? She thought you were crazy. Isn't it perfectly obvious that you envy my good fortune — in love *and* war?"

"Is she going to marry you?"

"Of course, she's going to marry me!"

"Poor kid. I can even feel sorry for her."

"Rave on, old pal. I see I must stand in your dim, dark legal mind for the personification of evil. But do you know what that evil really *is?* Do you know what my heresy really consists of?"

"Please instruct me, Bishop."

"In two words. Second chance. The idea that you can start again. Start again and win! Of course, you hate me. You hate me because I remind you in your indolence that you could do it, too. That it's *not* too late. You're shaken up by the wind of my liberation, and you snatch about for any old rope or rag to tie yourself down to the raft of old habits. You call these ropes moral principles. But you know they're only cowardice!"

Mr. Terhune joined us here, and the subject was changed. I contributed little to the discussion of advertising techniques that ensued, but I watched, hypnotized, the graceful manipulations of Gilbert's handling of his future father-in-law. Where in God's name had he learned it? How did he know how to put his own ideas on the old man's tongue and then brazenly flatter him for his perspicacity? Rumor had it that Terhune was slipping. Did the tycoon himself realize that his salvation might be to let a younger man of suave manners and easy charm (a rarity in his black forest) gracefully and almost painlessly convert him into a figurehead? The old wolf might prefer to be anesthetized to being torn to pieces by the pack. But had such plans been in the making on those long Sunday afternoons at Marigold during the hysteria of the mixed doubles by the iced tea tray?

When I told Belinda about Gilbert and Andrea in the taxi

going home, she became very grave. It was evident that she had come to share some of my awe.

"I guess we'd better give up hoping that Gilbert is going to stub his toe," she said. "I'm afraid the rest of his way is going to be up."

"Until he sits on the left hand of God the Father?"

"Or on the right hand of the other guy."

Belinda's concern lightened my own apprehension. "So now, like Andrea, you think he's divine?"

"I don't know what I think he is, but I guess it's not safe to get in his way. Stay clear, Joe!"

I went to bed that night reflecting that Gilbert had indeed become a formidable figure if Belinda was scared of him. But I did not go to sleep before I had repudiated his indictment of myself. I had been worried that there might have been something in what he had said, that I might, deep down, want to start over again and earn a bigger income and woo a younger wife. But the moment Belinda and I saw eye to eye on any subject, I was instantly aware of the unbreakable cord that held us. I wasn't kidding myself when I reasoned that I wouldn't really — in the long run — know what to do with an Andrea.

4

Belinda and I were not asked to the wedding, which came as little surprise, but some six months afterwards we were asked to dine with the newlyweds. I could see that Belinda, passionately curious, wanted to go, but that she could see no way to camouflage the enormity of such disloyalty to her sister. After a bit, I took mercy and came to her aid.

"I know it will be a disagreeable experience for you," I said, "but if you could possibly bring yourself to swallow it, I think

we ought to go for the sake of your nephews. After all, you and
I are their only link with Gilbert. It helps to keep those wires
open. Gilbert will undoubtedly have other children, and if we
don't watch out, he may disinherit Rebecca's."

Belinda was obviously grateful, but she was too much a
woman to admit it. She was even ungracious enough to make a
reference to the disastrous divorce settlement. "I guess you're
right, Joe. I guess we have to keep in with Gilbert. After all,
the boys have no legal claim on him now."

I uttered a silent prayer for patience and said nothing. Belinda was not the bully so many of her sex are. If you allowed
her to score one good blow, she would not insist on a second.
We got on perfectly so long as she was half a neck ahead. It was
not unreasonable.

The Van Ness house was disappointingly attractive. It was a
brownstone with a totally reconverted interior, so that the first
two floors formed one huge room with unexpected balconies
and beautiful ancient books above eye level, striking modern
pictures and venetian furniture, bright colors and lots of glass.
It was a perfect background for our relaxed, charming host and
his beautiful bride. I could see that Belinda was impressed, and
I wondered if Gilbert's charm might not in the end even work
on her.

We were eight at dinner, and the wines, constantly poured,
were so good that I almost forgave Gilbert his good fortune. I
found myself more interested in consumption than conversation, but this was perfectly acceptable, as Andrea kept breaking
up individual parleys in favor of a general one dominated by her
husband.

"Oh, you'll have to ask Gilbert that," she would say, or, "Gilbert has a marvelous story on that subject," or sometimes, a bit
breathlessly, "Oh, just a second, please. I want to hear what Gil-

bert is saying," or even, as a gentle admonition, "Gilbert's talking."

I looked at Gilbert to see how he reacted to this kind of lionizing, but he seemed perfectly unaware of it. If Andrea threw a direct question down the table, he would answer it at once, very politely, but he would not accept her proffered opportunity for a monologue. His modesty, his restraint, the courtesy with which he treated all his guests, were beyond even my power to criticize. I began to be afraid that he might have been right all along. Rebecca was a bore, stupidly self-absorbed, and the boys were hopeless. Could he be blamed for leaving the wreck and making what he had of himself? Now that I was satisfied that I was not more than superficially jealous of him, could I not be big enough to admit that Gilbert Van Ness was simply a successful man? Successful in no invidious sense of that dangerous word?

And then he did something. It was a very small thing, but it saved me. He handed a fork to his butler. He did not look at him, nor did the butler ask the reason. Gilbert did not interrupt his story, nor signify by the smallest gesture or frown why it was that he did not want that fork. Obviously, he had seen a speck on it. But what revealed the true Gilbert to me then was my immediate deduction of the enormous amount of domestic machinery that must have been hid beyond that simple gesture. He must have trained his servants like a drill sergeant if they knew instantly that a utensil so handed them was a reproof.

A small thing, but such are the things we judge by. The point was that Gilbert was not the free soul that he claimed to be. He felt that he had to conceal the elaboration that underlay his presentation of the casual. Gilbert had worked hard to attain the perfection of that house, that dinner party. Most of the particular charm at which he aimed was the seeming ease with

which it all was done. Any sense of the long rehearsals on a bare
stage would have ruined his effect.

Well, what was wrong with that? Couldn't a man take a little
trouble about a party? Wasn't it churlish of me, a guest, a bene-
ficiary, to sneer at the effort that had gone into my entertainment? No! For Gilbert was a fraud. He wanted his success to
seem to have dropped from the heavens upon his curly head. It
was his conceit to play the pampered child of the gods, a Gany-
mede beloved by Jove!

I now observed Andrea more closely. Surely, there was something more than love or admiration in her efforts to attract all
attention to her husband. Her eyes moved back and forth; her
hands fluttered; she even made, from time to time, a faint click-
ing noise as if she were grinding her teeth. She was nervous.
She was afraid! Gilbert had her as surely under control as if he
had a cord around her thin white neck which he could twitch
whenever he wanted her to do his bidding. She, like the butler,
was only another part of his machinery. She was a foil, a fall
guy. Worse, she was a stagehand in his burlesque. It was her
humiliating function, poor slavey, to stand in the wings and
catch, one by one, the flung garments of her strutting, stripping
spouse. And it was our function, as captive audience, to gawk
and gape at the revealed beauty of our naked host who, by the
very bareness of his ass, proclaimed his independence of all artificial aids!

Once again, after a dinner, Gilbert arranged to sit with me
alone for a brandy. On the excuse of showing me a new picture,
he took me off to his study.

"Tell me something, old fellow," he began. "I'm thinking of
coming to you for some legal advice. There's a piece in this
week's *New York Scene* about Terhune. Have you seen it?"

"Yes."

"What did you think of it?"

"Very complimentary."

Gilbert's eyebrows rose a bit. "Really?"

"Didn't you?"

"They used a highly offensive word about us. About the partners, I mean. Don't you recall it now?"

"No, what was it?"

"They referred to us as 'hucksters.' "

"They did?" I asked, staring.

"I'm surprised you should have missed it. Do you consider it actionable?"

I played for time. "You mean is it libelous?"

"Of course. If I called you a shyster, wouldn't you sue me?"

"Undoubtedly."

"Well, isn't it just as bad to use their term — I refrain from repeating it — to describe those of my profession? Of course, you realize, Joe, that the art of public relations is as high a discipline as any other?"

"Is that what you meant when you told me you were Gauguin, bound for the South Seas?"

Oh, I had him! The sudden sneer of his lower lip gave him away as surely as the slanty eyes of a villain in melodrama. He sat there exposed before me, a miserable, petty egomaniac, just another of the hundreds that swarmed on Madison Avenue! Oh, he could have his world now!

"What on earth are you talking about, Joe?"

"Simply that I can conceive of no word in the language more perfectly appropriate to describe you — personally, professionally, spiritually — than that word. A huckster you are, Gilbert, and a huckster you will die!"

Gilbert was in total control of himself again. The sneer had quickly vanished.

"Well, I see that I must seek more sympathetic counsel for *that* suit. And if you're any specimen of what I can expect to find in the jury box, I suppose I had better drop it altogether. Shall we join the ladies?"

When I told Belinda about it in the taxi, she did not applaud my candor. She did not think that the father of six children was entitled to the luxury of wantonly insulting the son-in-law of his biggest client. But she was not hard on me. The wonderful thing about Belinda was that when she saw that something was really important to me, she always went along. I did not have to tell her why it was so important. I did not have to say that I had lost a client and saved my soul. But that was what had happened. I had exorcised the demon of the second chance. I had saved my marriage, not from dissolution, but from the cloying idea that I wanted its dissolution. Or that I had wanted to be like Gilbert. Or that I had thought it might be unmanly *not* to be like Gilbert. Now he could go on handing spotted spoons to his butler for eternity. I simply did not care.

Suttee

AGNES LYNNE considered that, at sixty-seven, she was young to be widowed, but she was surprised to find how many of her contemporaries had preceded her to this condition. It was as if, while Percy had been alive, the widows had tried to camouflage their state of bereavement, rounding up a brother or nephew or cousin to accompany them to dinner at the Lynnes', or at least, if they had to come alone, making as much noise as two, but that now that Agnes was one of them, they could relax and admit the pleasures as well as the necessities of a purely female society, positively flaunting their assumption that she, like themselves, was henceforth dependent on the matinee, the bridge table, the book class, the garden tour. They beckoned to her, with a hint of grimness behind their friendliness, a note of subdued triumph in their very sympathy, like shades of the dead welcoming a soul newly arrived from our warm planet at the dreary realms of Pluto.

Agnes rebelled against what they so evidently deemed her doom. Having been childless, she could not join in their desolate, endless chatter about absent and indifferent children, and more absent and more indifferent grandchildren. She had a fierce little faith that, having been denied the early joys of motherhood, she was at least entitled to escape its later pangs. While her friends had been confined to the nursery, she had been more actively engaged in what she had dared to call "real life," and if this had provided a poorer show than the shining faces and curly hair of progeny, it ought, now that those faces had lost their glow and that hair its fresh abundance, to supply the compensation of an old age that refused to be relegated to the shelf of fruitless nostalgia and of rejected participation. Agnes was not yet prepared to admit that she was not still alive.

The "real life" in which she and Percy had been such close partners had been largely the life of his law firm, Lynne, Travers, Platt & O'Shea, on Court Street, one of the biggest in Brooklyn, rivaling all but the very biggest across the East River. The Lynnes had constantly entertained the partners and associates in their commodious, comfortable, old-fashioned apartment overlooking Prospect Park. Agnes had come to think of herself as a kind of office mother, giving quiet tips to the over-ambitious partners, helping the wives of the younger associates to find apartments and doctors and baby sitters, making herself available at teatime on weekends to lonely bachelor clerks. She had even fostered a romance between one of the loneliest of the latter and the almost old-maid daughter of a senior partner which had resulted in a surprisingly happy marriage.

But best of all had been the firm itself. Lynne, Travers had been a happy association of dedicated men. At least, so Agnes had seen it, or tried to see it. The partners had been gentlemen in the truest old sense of that now scorned word, united in their trust as well as in their affection. There had been no squabbles over dividing profits, no wrangling over precedence in the firm name, no squeezing out of old and failing members. The indigent client had received the same quality of service as the rich one, and both time and money had been liberally contributed to Legal Aid.

Oh, of course, it had not been all *that* perfect. Far from it! Agnes was not so fatuous as to suppose so, and if she had been, Percy, in the terrible misanthropic moods that had followed his rare drinking bouts, would have enlightened her. In a single one of these he used to be able to destroy the work of years. He would become sullen, bitter, vindictive. He would refuse to stay home, despite her begging, and would go to the office to taunt the clerks for their supposed laziness and stupidity. At times he had seemed to show a streak of near sadism. After the fit had passed, he had been disarmingly apologetic, and Agnes had usually managed to visit the bruised young men and to heal their wounds with the old saw about bark and bite, but for all his charm and for all her sympathy, these outbreaks had produced some permanent alienations.

Percy's last illness had been frightful, a culmination of all the most terrible of his depressions. The great, gaunt, fuliginous man had lain motionless on his hospital bed, his face turned sullenly away from visitors. But at the very end, just when she had thought that she could not bear it, just when it had seemed too hideously much that their whole life together should be smirched with this final gloom, he had turned and roughly seized her hand and pressed it until it hurt and then had hoarsely blessed her for forty-five years of patience and love. Oh, the difference that had made! She still ached in her heart at the thought of it, or rather at the thought of how long and hideously she would have ached without it. If their reach had exceeded their grasp, at least they had reached. And if he had found it difficult to love, at least he had tried.

And now she was left, stunned and groggy with the sense of all that was over. Not only was Percy over, and their life together over, but so was the firm itself, or at least the firm in any shape that she cared to recognize as such. It was not that she had been unprepared for change, even for annihilation. She had read "Ozymandias" and knew about those vast and trunkless legs of stone standing in the desert. But what she had not been prepared for was the speed with which the past could be wrapped up and put away. She had thought it might be decades, at least years. She had not dreamed that it might be a matter of months.

Yet so it was. Old Mr. Bry, who had been Percy's guide and mentor, had died at ninety; then Judge Satler, then Percy — all within thirteen months. In the same period Kings Long Island Trust Company, Percy's favorite client, had been merged with a Manhattan bank and lost to the latter's Wall Street counsel. And then the firm itself had joined up with a smaller firm and had acquired seven new partners, five of whom had never even met Percy. One miserable little year of death and mergers, and the whole character of a grand old law partnership was lost! Each time that Agnes, as executrix of her husband's will, went down to Court Street, there would like as not be a receptionist at the desk who did not even know her. "Mrs. Linn? L–i–n–n? Is that right?" It was worst when these girls were polite, solicitous. Agnes would have rather faced some blunt old dragon, waving her away with a snarl of "Scat, has-been!"

Determined to avoid both the altered firm and the beckoning widows, she found a temporary solace in a new friend, Ada Koepel. Ada, a tall, trim woman, with faded beauty, very gray, always in black, was also a widow and also the widow of a lawyer — Mr. Koepel had been a surrogate and a leader in Jewish philanthropies — but, like Agnes, she eschewed the company of bereaved females. They had met, not through what they had lost but through what they still had — their poodles — in Prospect Park, and they had slipped into the habit of meeting at the same bench, by the Botanic Gardens, at eleven. Ada Koepel lived alone — her two married daughters had moved to the West Coast — but she was devoid of the usual desperation. She seemed to accept the sun and the grass and the park as her natural companions. But Agnes soon discovered that the park Ada, so calm and seemingly gentle, had a lively counterpart in the

Ada of the Brooklyn Library, the Ada of the Philharmonic. If she was quiet in Prospect Park, it was because she needed the rest.

"You'll find that what gets you through is your intellect," Ada summed up one day, when she had completed what must have been a silent "diagnosis" of her new friend. Or had it been a testing period? "You must read with me, my dear. And don't tell me that it's a 'passive' occupation. Reading is only the converse to writing. Where would Shakespeare be without *us?*"

"You don't mean to compare a reader with a writer? A great writer? A writer like Shakespeare?"

"Why not? Appreciation completes the artistic process. Perfect appreciation is just as rare as perfect writing. I don't, mind you, say that mine is perfect. I'm not such an ass. But one can try."

Oh, yes, Ada, when she wanted, had the tone of a leader! She led Agnes now, to the library, to lectures, to museums, to concerts. To the latter such things had always been a fringe to life, an attractive fringe, to be sure, but nothing more. Now she tried to learn to respect the great reality that they were to Ada. But where she decidedly did not follow her new friend was in the latter's attitude toward the world of law in which both their husbands had been so importantly engaged. Ada cast an eye on this world which to Agnes was too cool, too balanced, too distinctly appraising. Ada's greatest principle in life, it sometimes seemed to Agnes, was to be "taken in" by nothing — but the sonnets of Shakespeare and the fugues of Bach.

Ada was not, for example, suitably impressed by the great "public spirit" of the old firm of Lynne, Travers, even when Agnes had broadly hinted how much of that spirit had been directly infused from the late Percy Lynne.

"Well, in the 'great old days,' as you call them," Ada wanted to know, "didn't your husband's firm discriminate against Jews?"

"Oh, I doubt that," Agnes answered, much embarrassed. "I just don't think Jewish boys cared to go into that kind of firm. At least in those days."

"What kind of firm?"

"Well . . . a non-Jewish firm."

"You mean it just used to happen that way? The Jews wanted to be with Jews and the Gentiles with Gentiles?"

Agnes, at this, was decidedly disappointed in her new friend. She had not believed that Ada would be so narrowly partisan. It was not, of course, that her tone was disagreeable. Ada's voice was as soft as ever. But the laughter behind it, if heard, would have been mocking. Agnes had sadly to conclude that Ada was never going to concede that Percy and his partners had lived on a higher moral plane than other lawyers. Certainly, she had to admit to herself, if Ada had heard any of the anti-Jewish stories that Percy had loved to tell, she would not. Ada would never have understood that a certain kind of jovial, conversational anti-Semitism had been a harmless trait in Percy and his friends. They had roasted Jews the way they had roasted Catholics — it had been a social habit, a men's convention, lacking in taste perhaps, but having nothing to do with any real animus, certainly having nothing to do with discriminations or persecutions. Had Percy not arranged the election of the first Jew to his fraternity at Yale?

"I don't think you understand the kind of firm Percy's was," Agnes told her friend with dignified regret. "He and his partners would never have held race or religion against their fellow men."

"Against their fellow clubmen," Ada corrected her. "I'm sorry, Agnes, but there are some things you have to be Jewish to understand. I am perfectly willing to concede that your husband and his partners were honest and industrious men, and in some ways high-minded. They trusted each other, but they kept 'each other' to a very small group. I know something about that, dear. Judge Koepel used to tell me."

Agnes was so indignant that she did not care if she was offensive. "Judge Koepel, I'm sure, knew everything."

"Ah, now you're cross, and there's no point talking when one is cross." Ada rose and called her poodle which she had let off the leash. She and Agnes had picked that bench because the policeman on the beat winked at this. "Let us change the subject. But just before we do so, let me assure you that I'm not being superior. Judge Koepel was no more public-spirited than anyone in Mr. Lynne's firm. Perhaps he was a tiny bit clearer on some of the issues, that's all."

Agnes might have succumbed to the widows after this altercation had not a third diversion unexpectedly offered itself. Upon her return from the park on the day of her difference with Ada, she found a letter from Decius Blount, now senior partner of Percy's firm, asking if he could call upon her the following afternoon. But much more important even than this pleasant prospect was the gracious paragraph that ended his letter:

I know that I must not lose touch with you. Now that I occupy the chief administrative position of the firm, I shall have a constant need of your advice and encouragement. You are the repository of all the old spirit and spark that made us great. Alas, we look about in vain for that today. If you would coach me — if you would simply talk to me, say, one day a week, or even a month, about yourself and Percy and all the wonderful things you planned together, I know that I should approach my task with a lighter heart and a bigger hope.

Agnes, standing by the window and looking out over darkening Prospect Park, put the letter to her heart and wept.

2

Decius Blount, who was a rather boyish fifty, with soft brown eyes and soft brown hair, the latter only very lightly touched with gray, would have been almost good-looking had he not been a bit too short, a bit too plump and a good deal too mannered. Agnes could never forget Percy's crude expression that he sat in a drawing room chair as if he had "a bug up his ass." Poor Decius tried desperately to make up for his self-consciousness by arraying his round, plump body in beautiful tweeds and by soldering up his natural furtiveness in a late-Victorian pomposity. But when he played with his watch chain, when he complimented Agnes on her tea, when he admired any of the rather indifferent trinkets that sparsely furnished the living room (Agnes and Percy had cared little for bibelots), he suggested a Cruikshank drawing of one of Dickens' parlor hypocrites.

Yet, as Agnes well knew, mannerisms could be very misleading, and they were never more so than in the case of Decius Blount. He was one of those brilliant, effeminate men who study, from childhood, how to adapt themselves to the world of their more masculine fellows and end by dominating it. In the Middle Ages he would have been a political prelate; in the Ottoman court a eunuch and vizier; in our own, he was a lawyer. So thorough had been his understanding of every partner and client of Percy's firm that on the latter's death his succession had been as unquestioned as it had been surprising. Percy had always told Agnes that Decius was a "frustrated pansy," but Agnes, as a woman, suspected that he was simply an inhibited male.

If Percy had regarded Decius, as a lawyer, with his rare admiration and, as a human being, with his much commoner contempt, Decius had returned good for good and good for bad. He had consistently worshiped Percy in every capacity, and if the latter's widow occasionally and uneasily suspected that, like most worshipers, Decius subconsciously preferred to have the founder of the cult dead and freed from the faults of clay, she nonetheless appreciated a zeal that did not seem to have notably survived in her husband's other erstwhile admirers. To hear Decius praise Percy was a greater pleasure than any matinee that the widows could offer.

"What Percy understood," he told her that afternoon, pacing from the fireplace to the window and back, "was that a law firm is something much more than its clients' problems. In a way, you might say, the latter exist *for* the firm, as cases exist to make up law. The practice of any profession is an art, and the joint practice of it by a group of dedicated men can be the greatest art of all. Ah, but they must be dedicated, that's the point! They must be dedicated to something higher than the client, something higher than mere monetary reward!"

And what was better even than all of this, what was almost enough, in fact, to make a life out of a widowhood, was the astonishing revelation of his absolute determination to see her regularly. His note had not been flattery, after all; it had not even been politeness. Decius Blount had simply made up his mind that he must draw inspiration from the distinguished dead through *her* medium. He wanted his "day" in her week; he insisted upon coming to her, directly from the office, at six o'clock every Wednesday. He would hold the firm under her regency, as she would hold her regency under the shade of Percy. The past would not be dead. It should direct the living!

The only thing that she worried about was that Decius might

ruin it all by too much solemnity. But even this fear proved unfounded.

"You know, Agnes," he told her, as early as their third Wednesday, "there is no reason that you should always be the one to entertain me. Suppose next Wednesday you come to my apartment? And not just for tea, but for dinner?"

Decius' apartment was unexpectedly charming, with a fine view of the harbor. It was on the top floor of an old brownstone mansion on Brooklyn Heights, and its walls were covered with his collection of baroque eighteenth-century stage designs. A grinning, white-coated Japanese houseboy served them steak and Burgundy, ice cream and champagne. Agnes became a little bit tipsy and listened with the greatest sympathy as Decius held forth on his lonely boyhod and his poor sad tubercular mother. Only with coffee did she suffer the dampening thought that this long dead parent must have been her own age. But when she mentioned this, Decius was unexpectedly explicit in his denial.

"Oh, Mummie was ages older than you, Agnes. You're only sixty-eight, and Mummie would have been ninety-three. She was forty-two, you see, when I was born. I really belong in your generation. You could be my older sister."

"Well, yes — I suppose."

"And what's more I *feel* we're the same generation. Don't you? Don't you think we talk as contemporaries?"

Agnes was going to pass this off with a shrug, but Decius was much too serious. His eyes were fixed on her, and for once he sat still, making none of his usual nervous gesticulations. Even in the gentle haze which the wine had created, she could sense his force.

"It's not only a question of age, Decius," she answered, with a rueful note. "A bachelor always has his life more or less ahead of him, while a widow has hers behind. So even if you were sixty-eight, and I — What are you? Fifty-one? — I'd still be the elder."

"Not all widows feel that way!"

"Indeed they don't. There are widows and widows. I'm the old-fashioned kind. The best of me was buried with Percy."

Decius rose at this, very solemnly, and, leaning down, kissed her hand. It was all very embarrassing, but it was still not quite as embarrassing as she had thought it was going to be.

"God bless you, Agnes. What is left of you is better than what any of the rest of us have. So long as we've got you, we'll get by."

Agnes could think of nothing to say, so she made a vague murmuring noise, and Decius resumed his seat. After a tense, stiff little pause he continued, but in a more relaxed tone than she would have thought, under the circumstances, possible.

"It's not just as a member of the firm that I need you, Agnes. It's much more personal than that. I need you to be my friend." Decius' face was actually serene, in the style of some very shy people when they manage at last to talk intimately. "I've had few friends in my life. Almost none, really. As a boy I was weak physically. I didn't get my strength till college. I was afraid of girls, and the other boys made fun of me. After Mother died I turned entirely into myself and my work. In the firm I admired some of the older partners, particularly Percy, but I was never intimate with any of them. Maybe they didn't want to be. Maybe I didn't know how. Anyway, I was always alone. But now that you're alone, too, I thought we might be friends. Real friends. You wouldn't be always expecting those other things of me, the way younger women do. Lord, you wouldn't believe what some of them will do to get a man! And I wouldn't be expecting anything of you but the chance to take you out to dinner and the theater. Why couldn't we have a wonderful, happy friendship? Oh, Agnes, please say yes! I need you so!"

"But, my poor boy," Agnes cried, taking both his outstretched hands in hers, "do you think it's such a favor for a lonely old widow to agree to be taken out to dinner by an attractive, successful man? By a leader of the bar? Why, Decius, you've got it all mixed up. I'd be honored and flattered to be your friend!"

After this their Wednesday evenings became more festive. Decius would take her to dine in Manhattan in restaurants like the Pavillon or Voisin's, and order fine dishes and great wines. Agnes had never been much interested in these, but Decius was a decided gourmet, and she was already learning to humor him. Their conversation, a bit to her surprise, even a bit to her disappointment, rarely struck again the intense personal note that he had sounded on the night of their dinner at his apartment. They talked now continually about the office, even more than she had done with Percy: which clerks should be promoted, which partners should be retired, which clients were more trouble than they were worth. Decius had soon brought her up to date with the events that had occurred since Percy's death. He made them come alive because he saw them as a drama. He seemed to see the firm, she gradually made out, as a kind of oriental court of which he was sultan, a wise young sultan of emancipated ideas, but surrounded by stealthy courtiers who, if not constantly watched, would converge upon him and knife him and fling his corpse in the Bosporus, giving over the empire to rapine and lawlessness. Agnes even began to see that it might be the function of Percy Lynne's widow to keep this obsession from getting out of control.

"Has it ever occurred to you that they may be afraid of *you?*" she asked him once.

His eyes narrowed. "They?"

"Everyone you fear. Anyone you fear. You can be quite formidable, my dear. I'm very glad that you're on my side."

The pale distant look in his brown eyes immediately softened. "Oh, you'll never have to worry about that," he said quickly.

Not all their evenings were so exclusive. From time to time Decius entertained other partners and their wives, and Agnes had the opportunity, in the case of those who had come into the firm after Percy's death, to catch up with the missing characters of the drama. Soon all the partners, taking their cue from Decius that Agnes' mourning did not exclude social life, invited her to their own parties. She found that on these occasions she and Decius were treated as a couple, and she began, in this rather curious sense, to occupy again the social position in the firm that she had lost with Percy's death. But she was not at all sure that she liked it.

In particular, she was embarrassed by Decius' public attitude toward her. She did not so much mind the excessive flattery of his demeanor to her: the little toasts at dinner parties after rapping his fork on his glass, the appeals down the table to her wisdom and judgment, the hushing of other people when she was talking, but she did mind his possessiveness. He always insisted on bringing her to a party and on taking her home, on putting on her coat and taking it off, on maneuvering her about as if she were an adored but petulantly exacting sovereign and he a wily and admiring premier, Victoria and Disraeli. But when she finally spoke to him about this, at one of their restaurants, she was startled to find that he was not in the least embarrassed. On the contrary, he seemed suddenly to spring into action, like a sailor long trained for combat, at the bell for battle stations.

"There's only one solution to this," he exclaimed in a high tense tone, imperially signaling to the waiter for two more cocktails. "We must marry. That's all there is to it. We must marry, and why not?"

"For God's sake, why?" she cried aghast.

"Listen to me, Agnes. I've thought it all out. Listen to me and be quiet." They were side by side on a bench seat, their backs to the wall, and he stared across the room into the huge mirror opposite as he talked. "I'm not intruding on your duties to Percy. I should not be so presumptuous. They are sacred to me. The marriage would be in name only, of course. Oh, I should venerate you like a vestal virgin! But such a union would at least enable me to give you my name and home and your proper position as senior partner's wife again. Oh, Agnes, let me take care of you! I think I might almost be able to make you happy again. Don't say anything tonight. Don't say anything for weeks. But think it over. Think it over carefully. I've deserved that much."

"But you dear crazy boy, how would you look, married to an old woman!"

"You're not an old woman."

"People would say so."

"Who cares what people say?"

"Oh, Decius, you're sweet!" Agnes closed her eyes and gasped at the sudden stroke of her headache. Then, just as suddenly, the pain passed, and her eyes were full of tears. "What would Percy say?"

"Do you know something? I think Percy would approve. I think somewhere he's watching us right now! I think he *wants* you to be looked after."

Again Agnes closed her eyes as she seemed to hear the whole dining room reverberate with her late husband's high screechy laugh. "I wonder," she murmured faintly.

"Look how I've upset you. I'm a brute! I promise not to mention the subject again tonight. And neither do you. You're to consider it, that's all. Just to contemplate it, that's all."

"But, Decius . . ."

"Not another word! Ah, good, here come our cocktails."

3

When Agnes, the next morning, was considering whose advice she might seek, she was not surprised to discover that the only name that survived all objections was Ada Koepel's. All of the people she knew best in the world were connected in one way or another with Lynne, Travers, and it was out of the question to consult any of them. Besides, Ada was freer than most of preconceived notions. She found her at ten o'clock at their old meeting place.

"Well?" Ada asked, with a cryptic smile, when Agnes had finished her story.

"*Well?* What do you mean, Ada, well? What should I *do?*"

"Of course, you must realize that any widow who advised you to turn him down would be instantly accused of rank envy. As a chance, it's a near miracle."

"Ah, but Ada, what do you and I have to do with vulgar attitudes? The question is: what is my duty?"

"Duty? Does the situation present one?"

"Of course it does! Would Percy want me to preserve his firm by marrying and guiding Decius? Or would he feel that I had simply made myself ridiculous?"

"Percy is dead," Ada said drily. "I think we had better consider what *you* want."

"But it's not what I want, or even what Percy wants, really. It's what's right!"

"I see." Ada's face was inscrutable. "Well, then, what Mr. Blount proposes seems to me entirely fitting. You have told me how he feels about his law firm. It's precisely the way you feel.

Indeed, from what you tell me, I don't see why you and the gentleman are not in total agreement about everything. I suggest that this marriage was made in heaven!"

"Except that it wouldn't be really a marriage," Agnes corrected her, a bit shocked by the levity of Ada's tone. "I hoped I had made that clear."

"You implied that it wouldn't be consummated," Ada said, with a crudeness that Agnes found in poor taste. "But it seems to me it's still a marriage. What else would you call it?"

"A partnership."

"Oh, Agnes, you and your partnerships! I'm afraid they're beyond me."

"But you must see, Ada, that Percy was my husband, for ever and ever, the way . . ." She knew that Judge Koepel's name had been Abraham, but she did not know by what diminutive Ada might have addressed him. "The way Judge Koepel was yours," she ended lamely.

"Then what are we discussing?"

"The form of a marriage. The form of a marriage to carry on the substance of all that Percy believed in."

Ada now really stared at her. "You're beyond everything, Agnes. You and all the good women like you. But have it your way, by all means. Marry Mr. Blount for Percy's sake and live happily ever after!"

"But do you really mean that?"

"I really mean it. I may find your motives bizarre, but I thoroughly applaud your actions. What would you like for a wedding present? Oh, I beg your pardon. It's not really a wedding, is it? What would you like for a partnership present?"

Agnes was not much satisfied with this, but she decided ultimately — after some days' consideration — that Ada, for all her sarcasm, did basically approve of the union. Ada obviously thought very little of her — that had been evident from the beginning. How much, after all, did she really think of Ada? The point of their friendship had been in the new lights that each could provide the other. And what more valuable light could Ada provide than the revelation that, silly as Agnes Lynne might be, she would be no sillier as Agnes Blount?

For a week she saw no one at all, not even Decius. She walked with her poodle in parts of Prospect Park where she would not be apt to encounter Ada and went over her albums at night. She reviewed the photographs of every trip that she had made with Percy and read all the clippings from newspapers and bar journals about his accomplishments and awards. Yet she could never bring herself to see the shade of her husband as taking any attitude but a ribald one about her contemplated step. She even at times had an uncomfortable glimpse of him sitting beside Ada on that park bench. Wasn't it possible that he and Ada would have hit it off? Wasn't it even possible that he might be speaking to her through Ada?

Never! She was standing before the marble statue of Mowgli in the Elephant House when the cold common sense of this negative answer rattled through her. *That* was what Ada had meant when she had said that Percy was dead! That the decision to remarry was hers, not his! The fact that Percy mocked her and had always done so, that Ada mocked her and would continue to do so had little to do with the separate and distinct question of the duty of Percy's widow. What *she* had to consider was how her marriage would strike the world. For even, if she decided, with both Ada and Percy against her, that it was her duty to Percy's firm to marry Decius and guide him as senior partner, she had still to contend with the fact that if the world laughed at her, the world might foil her plan. For how could she help anyone, let alone a law firm, if she were a figure of fun? Ah, but she would not be — *that* was what she finally took from Ada — if the world were *ignorant* of her motive! The world would forgive love, at any age, in any old fool; it would never forgive self-sacrifice. If she were to marry Decius and marry him, according to her plan, successfully, she would have to keep her mouth shut about why she was doing it.

When she had finally thought it all through, she left the zoo and went directly home. She telephoned Decius and asked him to take her out to dinner. When he inquired which of their restaurants she would prefer, she named the most expensive and knew that in doing so, she had informed him that her answer would be affirmative.

4

She told him with the first cocktail. She came straight out with it and hoped that she had succeeded in sounding gay. Decius turned pink. He insisted on kissing her hand and ordering champagne. She was almost afraid that he would leap to his feet and appeal to a roomful of strangers to drink their health.

"May we go to Venice on our honeymoon?" he asked excitedly. "I have always thought Venice the most romantic place in the world. Oh, Agnes, what a life we are going to have!"

He drank steadily through the evening, while Agnes took token sips to accompany him. Cocktails were followed by champagne and that by many brandies. She had never seen him in such a mood. His nervousness and excitement boiled over the brim of his normal discipline and seemed to inundate her with monologue. One subject triggered off another, but all were about Decius Blount and his long unhappy past and his long, now happy future. Nobody had understood him before Agnes,

not even his sacred mother, who now, it appeared, had been
rather an old bitch. He had never had a girl friend; he had
never, he managed to imply, had any relations whatever with
women. There had been two or three men, including Percy,
whom he had liked and admired, but none of them had really
cared for him. But now, with Agnes . . . well, people would
see what he had in him! His talk seemed to intoxicate him more
than the wine or brandy, but this intoxication did not in the
least affect his articulation or the lucidity of his thoughts. On
the contrary, he seemed to have been totally released from his
old formal and a bit formidable self. He seemed younger,
brighter, more ebullient. He was the least bit like — and the
thought struck her with something like dismay — a poet, a
Shelley, a bright-eyed idealist. He, Decius Blount! At fifty-one!

"Oh, my dearest, I feel I know everything tonight!" he exclaimed. "And that I can tell you everything, too. You're not
like other women because you don't expect things of me, if you
see what I mean. And for that very reason you're the one
woman in the world to whom I might be everything. Because
we've promised each other no love, it's precisely what may be in
store for us. Because to me you've been a priestess at the altar,
you may be the one woman I'm destined to possess!" At this
point Agnes' obvious disquietude briefly penetrated even his
mist. "But never mind that now, dearest. I see that the priestess
is alarmed. Which is, of course, the very thing to most excite the
moral acolyte. No need to think of that till Venice!"

He was good to his resolution, however drunk, and did not
revert to the subject, nor, needless to say, did Agnes. When she
finally induced him to take her home, he was still in the same
golden mood, and when she allowed him to kiss her good night
in the taxi, gently but definitely refusing to let him come up

with her, she was sure that he would go to a bar, perhaps to several. But he was better off alone, and certainly so was she. She knew what a night lay ahead of her.

After only an hour of anguished sobbing, however, she was able to dry the tears of mortification and take her seat at Percy's desk. There, looking over the moonlit park, she wrote what she hoped was a beautiful letter to Decius, breaking off their engagement and wishing him a happy and fruitful life with the younger woman "whom I feel confident that you will now find and whom I know that you richly deserve." After making a fair copy she went down herself to the lobby to mail it. At four in the morning she was able at last to sleep.

The next day in the park, as she told Ada the story, she felt that her conduct had been correct. It seemed to her that it had been both dignified and kind. Of course, it did not come to her as a surprise that Ada should take a less elevated view of the matter, but it certainly came as a shock, and finally as an outrage, that Ada should actually rail at her. She would not have believed that the woman could have been such a fishwife!

"When we first met," Ada exclaimed, in a tone that verged on the strident, "you complained about other widows because they were so removed from what you called 'life.' I thought that possibly we meant the same thing by the term, or at least something not too different. Indeed, I hoped it might prove the basis for a mutual sympathy. But now I see that I was very much misguided. For when life, poor wretched substance that it may be, dares at last to reveal itself to you — to Agnes Lynne — in any other form than a romantic illustration for a children's book, you beg off. Oh, Agnes, I have no patience with you! None! You and your kind are simply impossible. What in the name of Venus is your old body good for but to give some satisfaction to that poor frustrated man? Why are you always chattering about that law firm? *He's* the one who needs you. You ought to be proud!"

Agnes stared at the stranger beside her for a long moment and then slowly shook her head.

"I guess there are differences of opinion that are not argu-able," she said sadly. "Even if you should be right, it's much too late for me to learn. I think I must make do with myself as I am. For as long as may be necessary. Which I hope will not be long." She rose.

"Oh, Agnes, do sit down. I can't bear that high, injured look. Let's discuss this like two rational human beings!"

"How can we, when only one is present? Good day, Ada."

And as she moved away, she saw, ahead of her, unavoidable now, the widows looming.

The Sacrifice

CORNELIUS PLATT had had a horror of violence from his earliest years. It was not merely the violence that resulted in damage to flesh or windows, to bones or buildings, but the violence that tended in any way to shake up the natural order of things, whether its manifestation was casual, in riots, or serious, in revolutions, or simply in the shattering of the primeval silence with oaths and obscenities. Platt, a thoughtful youth and a philosophic adult, had from the beginning suspected that those who went about tearing off carpets and covers, pulling down curtains and throwing up sashes, in restless, insatiable quest for the "basic," might in the end only discover that they had made a mess of the living room. For how much was there to any chamber but the grace of its decoration? And how much, when all was badly said and badly done, was there to the human race when it had lost its manners?

But this horror of violence had always been accompanied by a very healthy respect for the perpetrators of violence, by a conviction, indeed, that such were the true rulers of the world, either boldly, with a display of brawn, or discreetly, with that same brawn concealed beneath traditional velvet. Platt's notorious father, the artist and playboy, from whose custody he had been early removed by his scandalized dead mother's family, had been a proof of where people's real, if not professed, sympathies lay. For all the senior Platt's wenching and extravagance, for all his passion for killing that had started with ducks, matured to rogue elephants and ended with Spanish rebels (and his own extinction), his name, even in the minds of his bitterest critics, still evoked the picture of a man. And so his son, through school and college, through early manhood and middle age, right into the evening of his sixties, in the black silk of his court robes, Mr. Justice Platt, heir of the dead adventurer of Barcelona, still looked out with a guarded caution on the world below his bench, a world that for all its lip service to his mistress of the balanced scales was stubbornly inclined to equate violence with vigor: in sport, in love, in politics, in art.

Oh, he had made his peace with the world! Few better. He had even snatched success from its massive jaws, under its mane and sleeping, grumbling head. He had made his reputation at the bar and was making another on the bench, reputations for wisdom, temperance and scholarship that fitted with his long, spare, lean build and what he liked to hear described as his "Roman" profile. More importantly, he had a still beautiful and still loving wife, famed for her work in civil rights, a strong, bright, splendid son who had given up his law practice to go into city government, and a nine-year-old grandson as beautiful as an English boy painted by Romney. It might indeed have seemed that, on the threshold of his seventh decade, Cornelius Platt, at least so far as he personally was concerned, had little more to fear from the dreaded violence of the outside world, that he had tiptoed successfully past the sleeping monster.

That it was never too late for life, however, to play dirty tricks, came as a small surprise to a pessimist like Platt. Even the dismay of his first discovery of the trick was accompanied by a faint, chilly admiration for the perfect irony of his situation. For what had happened was that the violence that he had so long eschewed had wreaked its revenge by taking up its roosting spot in the heart of Cornelius Platt! Oh, there was no mistaking it. No slightest possibility of error. He found in reading the

Times, in watching the news on television, in listening to his morning radio reporter while he shaved that a faint dull prick in the back of his neck would grow, with sickening rapidity, to a pain through his shoulders, down his back, from where it would clutch at his intestines and then spray upwards through his chest. It was rage, rage in *him,* the judge of judges!

It might have seemed, at first blush, the most natural, even the most banal of all experiences that could arrive at the spotless and polished doorstep of a respected sexagenarian: the indignant conviction that the bottom had been knocked out of society. Was it particularly unusual for a prominent member of the bar, a jurist "with good capon lined" to see doom in the strikes, the muggings, the robberies, the riots of modern urban life? What was his attitude but a typical letter to the *Times?* Yet Platt knew in his heart, from the very beginning of this new emotional stage, that there was a difference between his reaction and that of his complaining comtemporaries. Whereas his brethren of the bench and bar, his friends at the club, his golf and bridge cronies, would purse their lips and cluck and chatter, without particular animosity, with only stertorous disapproval, about the need of law and order, whereas the more reactionary might even postulate, as a kind of temporary necessity, the erection of some super police force, they had all essentially accepted the unrest of the age as they accepted the weather and the income tax. They did not, as *he* did, have gaudy dreams of a *Dies Irae.*

For what had slipped into the corners of his guarded heart, what had slunk by the sentries of his judicious toleration, to light up his interior with a fearful glow, was a passionate yearning to see the violators violated. It was a yearning with a force that could make him tremble and feel chills. It could even bring tears, in private, to eyes that stared in luminous shock and dismay at their own image in his shaving mirror. His mind seemed to be turning into a torture chamber of the Inquisition where modern offenders met a punishment unmitigated by modern humaneness. The muggers who infested the parks and streets, the union chiefs who denied heat or transit to a baffled populace, the ragged undergraduates who shouted obscenities at those who wished only to instruct them were hung by their thumbs, stretched on the rack, flogged and branded, before the throne of a robed and hooded priest who could have been only one person!

Sometimes, in the early morning, waking by Mary Ellen's calmly unconscious body and trembling at the memory of a dream of multiple horrors, he would try to console himself by supposing that many otherwise rational persons were subject to such fantasies and that so long as one never acted upon them, one was morally justified in dismissing them as hallucinations such as might have been brought on by drink or fever. But then he would have to face not one but a pair of reasons against his being entitled to any such relief, the same two reasons that formed the arches on which rested his very life. First, could he be sure, as a judge, that such fantasies might not affect his judgments? And, secondly, how in such a marriage as his could hatred live beside love?

He had a funny little hope, that lasted for the better part of a year, that he might create a drainage system by way of carefully controlled social conversations that would carry away some of the contamination within him in harmless little streams of anecdote ultimately eliminated by the chemical of human indifference. Thus at dinner parties he would contribute to the usual discussion of growing lawlessness, the perfect horror story, culled from his wide newspaper reading and high political connections. If the topic was crime, he would offer police details on the latest atrocity; if strikes, some jewel of union intransigence; if welfare, the most shocking new case of waste and extravagance. And in supplying these items he was scrupulous to avoid the least appearance of heat; he was always cool and clear, as if seeking only to get at the facts, never to take a position. He would raise an eyebrow in a manner more quizzical than critical; he would appear to invite the amusement of his audience, at most their tolerance of a state of affairs that was, after all, only part and parcel of the poor old human condition.

When Mary Ellen first spoke to him about this little habit, in a taxi returning from a dinner party given by the presiding justice, he recognized that a woman's strength may lie precisely in her contempt for subtlety.

"Why are you so down on welfare?" she asked. "Do you suggest we can do without it?"

"I suggest, my dear, that you have confounded criticism with condemnation. I don't suppose one must approve of waste."

"Don't play the judge with me, Neely. You and your 'brethren' can fool the world that you live in a kind of mental vacuum where any prejudice drops to the floor like a pin, but you don't fool your wives. The only people who tell the kind of story you told tonight — that one about mailing welfare checks to Miami — want to abolish welfare."

"I shall try to remember that."

"You *don't* want to abolish it, do you, darling?"

He knew that she was looking at him now, with her large worried eyes, but he dared not turn to her. Why should she leap to such a disparaging conclusion? Did it not show that, all along, she had secretly suspected him?

"Of course, I don't," he tried to assure her. "Perhaps I get too used, in my position, to the detached point of view."

"Because you're always judging? Do you call that detachment? You weigh us all and find us wanting. Don't do it, Neely. The terrible danger of sixty is for the heart to die, twenty years before the body!"

Platt, feeling the full intensity of her concern, stifled a near sob at the sudden bleakness of his own damnation.

"It will never be your danger, my darling!" he exclaimed fervently.

"How grossly you overrate me!" she answered, surprised. "I'm in your boat, Neely. That's how I know."

Platt did not for a minute believe that Mary Ellen's heart was in danger of dying. He did not even believe it of his own. There was nothing dead or even old in the dreadful passions that crackled in his chest. No, alas, the deadest, coldest grate would have been preferable to such a flame.

"Ah, if I could only be like you, dear," he murmured, "I'd be all right!"

Mary Ellen was one of those women whose beauty depends entirely on her skin and eyes. Her head, her limbs, her body were long and thin, her hair, a rather shabby blond, hung down straight and dank, so that her total effect, when she was tired or ill, was osseous, undernourished. But all this was more than redeemed, it was glorified by the glow in her nacreous flesh that made a shimmering background for large, lustrous, hopeful and ultimately rather threatening, yellow-brown eyes that seemed to give her interlocutor every last possible chance to be decent, to be good, even to be great, but which, at the same time, had a reservation, hanging there between observed and observer, that if he *didn't* . . . ! Platt had spent the thirty years of their marriage in distinct awareness of the crackle of the auto-da-fé that was ready to spring into an encompassing glare if the heretic should be finally impenitent. And what had been the murderous temptation of his lifetime but just to be impenitent? If only, at long last, to have the relief of the scorching fire after all the anticipation? The scorching fire that would match, that might cast out, his own?

Mary Ellen, in a word, was good, and her goodness had in it no hint of priggishness, no smallest aspect of fatuity. No, he could never lay that flattering unction to his soul that Mary Ellen's goodness was of the waxed doll's variety that justified his own badness as comfortingly, perhaps even lovingly mortal. Far from it. If there was any room for goodness in the world, a supposition increasingly to be doubted, then there had to be a place for Mary Ellen's goodness which was premised on the simple faith that one must help *everybody*. His last chance to scoff at her on the grounds that, loving the whole world, she might have rendered herself incapable of loving an individual, that she might have lost her humanity, her taste, her very character in a kind of misty saintliness, had expired on the day she had elected, with a total commitment that must have satisfied any but a fiend of jealousy, to love him.

It was Mary Ellen's warning that he had in mind when he dodged the responsibility of a "police brutality" case by persuading the presiding justice to reassign the writing of the decision to Judge O'Hara, a former district attorney. Platt joined the majority in quashing the conviction, not even availing himself of the opportunity, which would not have affected the outcome, of siding with Judge Dent, the court's right wing, in his lonely and embittered dissent. But immediately afterwards he was overcome with the darkest depression. For how could he continue to sit on the bench if his decision had been made in reaction to his own animosity? Perhaps, under the law, the conviction *should* have been sustained. His mind, at any rate, should have been clear of the least bias, for or against the policeman, for or against the accused. God knew, it had been far from that.

Yet if he resigned his position, Mary Ellen would have to know all. He had no excuse of age or health or even of fatigue. She was bound to flare, suspicious as she already was, that his problem was moral, and however she might appreciate, even applaud, his move, however high a tone she might take as to what her own soothing, curative role should be in his retirement, there would still be a horror to be smothered, a disgust to be concealed. He would have forfeited her respect, and Mary Ellen could never love where she did not respect. He would have fallen to the rank of one of her wrongdoers, one of her "lame ducks." He would feel the beneficence of her charity, not the sustaining life force of her wifely devotion. It would be far, far worse than her hate.

To lose not only the court but Mary Ellen's love was not to be thought of. What would be left of him but the remnant of a carapace stranded high on the bleak beach of pity? And then, too, did it not behoove him to effect a cure as a duty to society as well as to himself? Was such a man as he, in Macduff's phrase, fit to live, let alone to govern? For it was just the complication of his case that his mind and judgment remained at all times essentially clear of the contagion. Platt knew perfectly well that the police stick, the machine gun, the armed state were far more pernicious than the evils which they purported to correct. He had no illusions about the vicious circle of modern crime and modern punishment. And, even more importantly, he was perfectly convinced that the man who did not love his fellow men was already half dead. There was simply no way for civilized man to live amid the throng of his fellows: cheaters, hypocrites, lechers as they were, cowardly, inhumane, brutal as their behavior might be, without loving them. Oh, yes, if one could not love even the apathetic folk who slammed their windows to shut out the cry of the girl assaulted in the street below, the folk who would not be implicated even to the extent of picking up a telephone to call the police, one was, compared to enlightened souls, already in the shadow of the tomb. For what was poor shabby humanity but a mob of window slammers? And what was worse than such a mob but the man who hated it?

If the message of the church was love, then the church might be the place for him. He took to going on Sundays again, much to Mary Ellen's surprise, whose own goodness had never needed the support of faith, who even used to say that she liked the idea of personal extinction, but in the Church of the Holy Trinity Platt found the obstacle of his schoolboy associations too solidly in his path. The prayers were dull, the hymns were dull, the sermons were worst of all. The clean, antiseptic modernity of the church itself, with its bare limestone walls and nonpictorial stained glass, struck him as only coldly handsome. He could not seem to revive any relationship between a savior of mankind and a savior of himself. Perhaps he had trampled it out too completely. The mystic idea of a soul stripped of all its trappings: of flesh, of worldly rank, of ambition, of lust, of very appetite, struck him as not only poor but as somehow ridiculous, as a tricky substitute, in its denial of humanity, for Mary Ellen's "extinction." There was drama in the martyrs, but where was the drama in the Reverend Darlington holding up to the altar a silver plate stuffed with greenbacks and the discreeter envelopes of those who gave "more"? No, he had burnt his bridges to the Protestant God of his early years, and he felt that it was unseemly, at his age, to go courting another.

Without assistance from this world and without hope of a next, he began to wonder grimly how long he could continue before some terrible exposure, in his home or on the bench, should overwhelm him. The violence in the world about him and the violence that festered within him were bound, he feared, sooner or later to join forces, sweeping away the pale, interfering integument of Cornelius Platt's body. Yet just when he thought that merger most likely, just when he feared that his inner anger would detonate and blow his physical self to bits, he had the shock of hearing his own voice speak out sharply against his concealed emotions, taking the side of the angels against an angry, red neck taxi driver who sped him recklessly downtown while denouncing the city fathers as a "bunch of nigger lovers."

"How much longer is the little guy going to put up with it, that's what I want to know? It's all very well for people like yourself to be liberals, mister. You live in districts, like where I picked you up, that niggers and Puerto Ricans can't afford. But what about people like me? Where I live, we're afraid to send our kids to school! I tell you, mister, the day is coming when the people of this country are going to take the law into their own hands. And when that day comes, the Ku Klux Klan is going to look like a ladies' sewing circle!"

Platt felt a fierce dusky elation in the pit of his heart at the prospect of the collapse of all hope for Mary Ellen's little civic groups. What an answer to the muggings, to the rapings, to the pilferings, to see stark corpses swinging from streetlamps! But what he heard himself say was this: "Do you realize, my friend, that you are filled with hate? Right up to the brim? Do you realize it's coming out of your very pores? That's no way to live, you know. Not only will it kill your soul, it will kill your body. The adrenalin alone can do it. You've *got* to get rid of some of that hate. Take it from one who knows!"

The driver had stopped for a light, and he turned all the way around now, appalled, to stare at Platt.

"That's a hell of a thing to tell a man," he muttered. "What are you, anyway? Some kind of evangelist?"

"No. I'm just a poor hater like yourself. But I know what

it can do to the heart. Take it from me, my friend, I *know*."

"I don't hate no one," the driver grumbled and was silent. But when Platt paid his fare, the man spurned his tip.

After this he took the subway to his chambers. It was his theory — and one that few of his fellow New Yorkers would have disputed — that if one could love mankind in the rush hour, one could love it anywhere. It was underground, in the dreary stations, in the dusty cars, where every cubic inch of space seemed filled as instantly by clothed flesh as it might have been by rushing water, where men and women, dull eyed and self-absorbed, were crushed against each other without concupiscence, without hate, without charity, without love, with nothing but irritation, a terrible, soul-consuming irritation which wore down the heart and eroded the intestines, that humans were reduced, not to beasts — for do not elephants prop up the wounded, the lame? — but to mere cellular matter, responding with an automatism that only seemed sullen, to electric stimuli. And Platt, jostled or pulled, seated and smothered, looked into eyes a few inches from his own and wondered where Christ was.

It was after the rush hour, however, and after an unusually tense day of oral argument in a bitterly contested labor case, that Platt, much depleted, had his most unnerving experience. He was sitting in an uncrowded car, reading an opinion of the Court of Appeals in the *Law Journal,* when two Negro boys, hardly more than fifteen or sixteen years of age, came chasing each other down the aisle. As they passed Platt, the pursuer caught up with the pursued, seized him by the shoulders and sent him spinning so hard against Platt that he landed in the latter's lap, crushing his newspaper. Instantly the boy so thrown recovered himself and pushed his assailant into the lap of the woman opposite. Both boys were shrieking with violent laughter. It could have been dope; it could have been high spirits.

The car remained silent and still, tense and hating, as the boys pushed each other back and forth, screaming and laughing. They were not hostile or belligerent; they were, on the contrary, highly cheerful, except that in their total disregard of the other passengers, in their seeming oblivion to all but their scuffling selves, it was difficult not to read a demonstration of contempt. They might have been in a gymnasium, a park, a backyard. But they were not. Oh, no, they were not.

Platt felt an almost unbearable constriction in his chest, and he started, smothering, to cough. It was his first vivid realization of the sharp physical agony to which humiliation could subject a man. That he, a duly elected judge, in a car full of white men, should be so treated and so submit! No, no. It was too much, hideously too much. Suddenly, with a gasping, grating relief in his throat, he threw back his head and screamed, "How much will you all take from these nigger bastards? How much will you all take, for Christ's sake, before you string them up?"

Then his throat closed as if a huge hand had squeezed it, and as he struggled for breath, red lights, like rockets, seemed to come hissing in upon him. Finally, there was a hideous rending pain in his chest, and a sense of grayness everywhere, and he heard Mary Ellen's voice, very distinct, but low and rapid: "Can you hear me, Neely? You're perfectly all right. It wasn't a heart attack at all. It was just the heat of the subway after those pills you've been taking for your cold. Doctor Kilbourne says you're perfectly sound."

Platt opened his eyes and saw a white wall behind Mary Ellen's drawn countenance. He made out, too, the corner of a reproduction of a Van Gogh landscape.

"I'm in a hospital?" he murmured.

"You're at Saint Joseph's. You fainted in the subway. Fortunately Timmy Kohler, Judge O'Hara's law clerk, was in the same car. He called the police at the next station, and they got you here."

"Otherwise, you'd have ended up at Bellevue."

Platt, hearing this second voice, turned to see his son Bobby on the other side of the bed. The young man was all smiles, all sympathy, all love, but his father could only turn away from him with tears of shame.

"Was I hurt?" he asked. "Was I hit?"

"No, dear," Mary Ellen said soothingly. "It wasn't anything that happened to you. You just fainted, that's all. I know it's not like you, but . . ."

"But those boys? Did they *do* anything?"

"What boys?"

"He must mean the two boys that Timmy said were squabbling in the car," Bobby intervened. "Don't you remember, Ma? He said one of them brushed up against Dad. It may have been the surprise and shock that started this off."

Platt looked now from his son to his wife and wondered if he could read some faint suspicion in the latter's lowered eyes. But no, she was straightening his sheet with a brief, efficient gesture. She had served as a gray lady in that very hospital in World War II.

"And I didn't *say* anything? I didn't cry out?"

"No, darling, apparently you just slumped in your seat. You join the great multitude of those for whom the subway has proved too much. I know you turned down an official car on principle, but you're going to have to take it back now."

Platt closed his eyes in the bliss of his release. For if some private devil had made up the hideous farce of his outburst in that subway car, might not that same devil of hallucinations have created others? As he thought now of those two boys fighting, it seemed to him that his animosity was quite gone. Indeed, he seemed to have no attitude at all in their respect but a vague and soothing benevolence. He turned his head on the pillow, his eyes still closed. Surely this would have been the time to die. If there was a state of grace, he was in it now.

2

This episode was followed by a suspension of anxiety, and Platt began cautiously to wonder if his mental disease had not abated, if like some rare cancerous growths, despaired of by doctors, it had not suddenly and blessedly simply shriveled away. He no longer traveled by subway, as Mary Ellen absolutely prohibited it, and he found that he was working hard and well again. He even wrote two opinions on the police power of the state that were hailed by civil liberties groups. At dinner parties he was able now to censor his old habit of documenting disasters, and he had glimpses of an approaching old age when he might sit in the sun in a rose garden of human understanding, accepting and being accepted. Was it too much to hope? It was.

The blow that was now to fall seemed to have been heralded by his fantasies as the murders in Shakespeare are heralded by bloody images. His whole life was to take on the semblance of a poetic melodrama, too ghastly not to be real. And the victim was not himself — how easy that would have been! — but Bobbie's child, Alex, aged nine, the boy as beautiful as a painting by Romney, as gay and precocious as a lad in a tale by Henry James, the adored of his little family, the idol of Mary Ellen.

At noon on a winter morning Platt was summoned from the bench by his law clerk to meet the Chief Inspector of Police, green faced, in his chambers. Alex's body had been found in a men's toilet in Central Park after his nurse, alarmed at the time he had been away, had called a policeman. The child had not only been stabbed to death — he had been castrated. Whether the act of mayhem had been committed before or after death it was impossible to determine. The fiend or fiends had escaped without clue.

3

It seemed to Platt in later days that he had lacked the very time for the question of a personal reaction. The first thing had been to arrange that the mutilation of the child be kept from his parents and grandmother. The next had been to tell them without deranging their minds. Platt's horror at their horror left little room for the horror of what he had seen at the morgue. And then there were the newspapers and the frenzied hunt for the criminals who were never found. The only consolation, a small one, had been in knowing that he bore the knowledge of the mutilation alone.

What preoccupied him most in the gray days that followed was Mary Ellen's collapse. Bobbie and Bobbie's wife were nothing less than heroic, but Mary Ellen seemed to have crumpled into a formless heap. For days she sat in an armchair by the window in her bedroom, her eyes fixed dully on the wall of the building opposite. For weeks she refused to go out of the apartment. All her old activities were abandoned. She hated the universe now, except for Bobbie, and although she said nothing overtly hostile to Platt, he knew that somehow, for some arcane reason, she blamed him.

When the doctor suggested a cruise, Mary Ellen made no objection. She simply shrugged and permitted her packing to be done for her.

"I might as well be on the high seas," was all she said. "At least Bobbie will worry less about me."

But the big ship did nothing for her. Slumped in her deck chair, an unopened novel on her lap, the light wholly gone from her skin, she exuded the sullen acceptance of the postoperative patient who knows, without being told, that the surgeon couldn't "get it all out." She refused to meet anyone or even to smile at her fellow passengers.

"Pigs," she would simply mutter to herself. "Pigs."

Platt was haunted by the idea that the same hate which had eaten into his heart before the fainting fit in the subway might now be gnawing at hers. It was not, God knew, that he felt any enthusiasm for his cruise mates or for the big vessel that bore them over the Mediterranean, a huge, gaudy balloon painted with cartoonlike faces. Everything on board reminded him of death.

He saw it in the sagging shoulders and dropped jaws and brilliant shirts of the old men; he saw it in the stiff ankles and big buttocks and soft sweaters of their slowly moving wives. He saw it in the compulsive shopping in the bazaars, in the shrill sessions of bingo, in the ineluctable rubbers of bridge. He saw it in his own gaunt face, thrust at him by innumerable mirrors at close quarters, the face of another corpse on a boat load of eating, defecating zombies.

But there was still a compensation that obviously did not exist for Mary Ellen. There was still the compensation of the totality of disillusionment. For what did his fellow travelers represent but the very opposite of all the types who had used to outrage him? In the annihilation of the last vestige of his respect for man, he had annihilated the last vestige of his hate. A kind of peace had descended over him, a peace as flat and wide and inanimate as the Egyptian Sea around him. But might it not still turn into the peace of God?

One day, approaching Crete, without sight of land, a benign

brilliant day, he told Mary Ellen the whole story of his inner troubles. She hardly looked at him as he talked, but allowed her eyes, half-closed, to rest on the sharp line of the horizon over that dead water.

"Why do you tell me this?"

"Because I know you have always suspected that my detachment was a failure to care about people. It was the fear of caring too much — the wrong way. The fear of hating."

"And now you're free of it? Is that what you're saying? You find you don't hate as much as you thought you did?"

"I shouldn't say 'find.' I should say 'hope.' "

"And that's what poor Alex will have accomplished by dying? To have cast the hate out of his grandfather's heart?"

Platt, with rigidly tightened lips, followed her gaze to the horizon. He needed a minute to poke about in the bludgeoned house of his heart to see what had been broken. But for all the brutality of the onslaught, it seemed to be still intact.

"It will be one of his accomplishments, perhaps."

"Making his tragedy, I suppose, worthwhile?"

"It sounds very selfish, very egocentric of me, when you put it that way. No doubt you want to punish me for having anything left at all. It's perfectly natural."

She looked at him at last, and her yellow-brown eyes showed the first flicker that he had seen since the tragedy. But love was not the cause.

"What I can't bear is your seeing everything in terms of yourself!"

"How else can I see it? The condition of being human is the condition of being selfish. One is glad that Christ died for one."

"Oh, spare me that at least!"

Her face now, at their distance of not more than two feet, might have been a face in the subway, expressing not so much hate as the total rejection of love, rejection, anyway, of him and *his* love. Then her eyes clouded again as with the faintest of shrugs she turned back to the sea and into herself, pushing him off, in the manner that one animal pushes another off, unless it wants to eat it or copulate. To Mary Ellen the crowding bodies of other people had no function but to annoy.

He reached over to pat her hand and met, as he had expected, with no response. Then he rose to walk down the deck and to gaze over the stern rail at their tumbled wake. He had achieved an equanimity that, however precarious, might contain his clue to the future. There was not to be happiness in it, certainly, but neither might there have to be any great misery. The event which he had dreaded for thirty years had happened: Mary Ellen's love was gone; her light was out. She had become as merely mortal, as mechanically human, as the fancied individuals in the subway. That amorphous crowd of straphangers had grown, with Alex's death, to include everyone, even Mary Ellen. Like little particles of zinc they had merged with the larger trembling mass.

But this, the nightmare, had been only a nightmare. *He* had survived. For what he had discovered was that his love for Mary Ellen did not, after all, depend on her love for him. It existed of and by itself, and it might survive all her scoffing, all her cruelty, even all her hate. He would look after Mary Ellen, and this love, now proven so tough, so durable, so oddly independent, might expand indefinitely to take in the approaching coast of Crete and the whole of the big dirty world that he had left behind.

The
Mormon
Experience

The
Mormon
Experience

*A History
of the Latter-day Saints*

Leonard J. Arrington and Davis Bitton

Alfred A. Knopf   New York   1979

Copyright © 1979 by Leonard J. Arrington and Davis Bitton
All rights reserved under International and Pan-American Copyright Conventions.
Published in the United States by Alfred A. Knopf, Inc., New York, and
simultaneously in Canada by Random House of Canada Limited, Toronto.
Distributed by Random House, Inc., New York.

Library of Congress Cataloging in Publication Data

Arrington, Leonard J. (Date)
The Mormon experience, a history of the Latter-day Saints.

Includes index.
1. Church of Jesus Christ of Latter-day Saints—
History.   I. Bitton, Davis, joint author.
II. Title.
BX8611.A78   289.3′09   78-20561
ISBN 0-394-46566-0

Manufactured in the United States of America
Published March 30, 1979
Second Printing, July 1979

To our children

Contents

Preface

In the spring of 1967, while I was a visiting professor of history at the University of California, Los Angeles, I received a letter from Alfred A. Knopf in which he suggested the need for a reliable and scholarly one-volume history of the Mormons, and asked if I would consider writing one. I replied that I would be interested in doing so if I could obtain the permission of the Church of Jesus Christ of Latter-day Saints (the correct name of the church often popularly referred to as the Mormon church) to use its archives without restriction. Such permission was immediately granted by the First Presidency of the church, and in the summer of 1967 I began preliminary work on the volume. I received counsel from Professor Rodman W. Paul, a special friend of Mr. Knopf, who was in nearby Pasadena. Although I worked in the Latter-day Saint Church Archives each summer thereafter, my various duties at Utah State University, to which I returned as a professor of economics in the fall of 1967, prevented rapid progress on the book. In addition to my teaching responsibilities, other projects arose that were related to my work as an economic historian. Moreover, I discovered such a wealth of previously unused materials in the LDS Archives that I accumulated mountains of undigested notes requiring interpretative frames of reference. When I was named Church Historian of the Church of Jesus Christ of Latter-day Saints in January 1972, I was given the opportunity of helping to establish policies connected with the use and publication of historical materials, and of working with a sizable staff.

In the months that followed, church authorities organized the Historical Department of the Church into library, archival, curator, and historical research and writing divisions. I was given charge of the latter. Since this reorganization professional historians have been poring over the massive store of documents in the LDS Archives and preparing articles, papers, and books. Many of these have represented necessary steps in the writing of the present work. Seeing that my own administrative responsibilities were too great to permit me to complete this volume, I asked the Assistant Church Historian, Davis Bitton, to assist me in the task. A graduate of Princeton and former faculty member at the University of Texas and University of California at Santa Barbara, Dr. Bitton is also professor of history at the University of Utah.

The task of Dr. Bitton and myself has been lightened and speeded by the work of several research assistants. Richard F. Daines, Dean L. May, David Whittaker, Christine Rigby Arrington, Gordon I. Irving, Jill Mulvay Derr, Scott G. Kenney, and Richard L. Jensen have each assisted with one or more of these chapters, and we are grateful for their help. We have also benefited from the editorial work of Maureen Ursenbach Beecher, Sharon Lee Swenson, Eugene England, Rebecca F. Cornwall, and D. Michael Quinn. Our colleagues in historical activities, James B. Allen, Dean C. Jessee, and Ronald W. Walker, have rendered extensive help, as have many employees of the LDS Historical Department. Most of the typing was done by Christine Croft Waters and Nedra Yeates Pace. We are grateful for their competence and patience.

Rodman W. Paul has been kind enough to read the entire work in its penultimate draft and has given many suggestions. Jan B. Shipps has also generously read the first chapter and made helpful comments.

Several officials of the Church of Jesus Christ of Latter-day Saints made helpful suggestions, but they should not be held responsible for our interpretation, which is published entirely on our own personal responsibility.

One final note to the reader: Because the approach of this study is more topical than strictly chronological, the subject division of the three parts of the book is suggestive of general focus rather than precise delimitations.

Salt Lake City   LEONARD J. ARRINGTON
June 9, 1978

Introduction

When Colonel Thomas L. Kane, Philadelphia military officer and would-be philanthropist, visited the Mormon refugees in Iowa in 1846, he was touched to hear a Latter-day Saint woman singing the psalm "By the waters of Babylon we sat down and wept." During much of their history the Mormons were, figuratively speaking, by the waters of Babylon, trying to sing the Lord's song in a strange land. Theirs is the story of a religious minority, generally unpopular and often harassed—a group that some scholars think was the most persecuted religious community in early America. The intergroup friction between the Mormons and their neighbors tells something about American society and the limits of religious tolerance.

How the Mormons reacted to the almost constant opposition and changing environment facing them is essentially a study in survival. But survival at what cost? Mormons, while isolationist in some ways and resistant to modern trends in others, were not one of those sects determined to reject telephones, electricity, and zippers in order to preserve the old ways. From the beginning, Mormonism reached out to the world. Adjustments to changing circumstances were inevitable; this, of course, is the experience of all people. But the Mormons' struggle to preserve their uniqueness, coupled as it was with a missionary outthrust, makes a poignant study in proselyting effort and adjustment—a case study of the generational tension and international conciliation that have become part of the contemporary human condition.

Then, too, Mormonism provides a remarkable case study of the growth and development of a new religion—the only major religion with American roots. Now a worldwide movement of some four million people, its history has exhibited many of the problems and adjustments inherent in any religious movement. What would we not give to possess a history of the first century and a half of Christianity in the same detail that we can know the history of Mormonism from 1830 to the 1970s? There are differences as well as similarities, of course, but the student of comparative religions will find the Mormon experience instructive. Moreover, as sociologists and cultural geographers have pointed out, Mormonism is more than a religious movement; it is also a unique American subculture. A study of Mormonism is a justifiable aspect of the study of civilization and culture with roots in America and branches in most nations of the world.

Besides, the Mormons (they prefer to be known as Latter-day Saints) are interesting. They include such diverse personalities as Jack Dempsey, Laraine Day, J. Willard Marriott, Johnny Miller, the Osmonds, David M. Kennedy, and George Romney. Their welfare program; their missionary system, which maintains twenty-five thousand young men and women on proselyting assignments throughout the world; their temples, structures whose functions are unlike those of any other sacred buildings; and their microfilming enterprise of genealogical and historical records—such activities have attracted the interest of many observers of the contemporary scene.

There has been no single work that professors and students of American civilization and religion have been able to read and recommend as an introduction to the Mormons, as the one book a person might read who simply wanted to find out about the Mormon people. There are books by journalists, some of them sensationalist in tone, superficial introductions without historical depth; to us they seem to be the products of a few weeks' work, and they do not do justice to the complexity of the subject. A sociologist of the past generation wrote a book still worth reading—Nels Anderson, *Desert Saints: The Mormon Frontier in Utah* (Chicago, 1942)—but it makes little effort to deal with Mormons in the twentieth century, and even for the nineteenth century it suffers from weaknesses, such as its lack of information on doctrinal developments. A Roman Catholic sociologist of religion, Thomas F. O'Dea, produced *The Mormons* (Chicago, 1957), a one-volume study that contains valuable insights, but his references to the history of Mormonism were limited to available published accounts. His analysis of values and internal tensions is nevertheless a real contribution.

In 1976 the church-owned Deseret Book Company published James B. Allen and Glen M. Leonard's *The Story of the Latter-day Saints* (Salt Lake City, 1976). Although this well-written and comprehensive study can be recommended for many purposes, it was designed primarily for Mormons, and its narrative approach, with emphasis on institutional developments, may fail to highlight problems and comparisons that will be of primary interest to a reader approaching the subject for the first time. Marvin S. Hill and James B. Allen's *Mormonism and American Culture* (New York, 1972) contains about a dozen articles that will interest serious students, but it assumes at least some knowledge of the subject and makes no pretense of introducing Mormonism to those unversed in its history. And there are a few books that are frankly hatchet jobs—modern resurrections of the irresponsible anti-Mormon exposés that were common in the past century. All things considered, it seemed that the time was ripe for an analytical, interpretative, topical history designed for a broad readership.

Another reason a new book on the Mormons seems justified at this time is the considerable activity of scholars—archivists and historians—in the past generation, especially during the past five to ten years. Of course Mormons have always been a record-keeping people, but only recently has the "professionalization" of the LDS Church Archives been fully accomplished. This has meant a vigorous program of acquisitions and the turning up of new, valuable primary material. Equally important, the materials already in the archives have been organized and catalogued for ready access. In the meantime, important acquisitions were being made in the Mormon holdings at Brigham Young University, the University of Utah, Utah State University, the Utah State Historical Society, the Coe Collection at Yale, the Henry E. Huntington Library and Art Gallery, and elsewhere. From the point of view of primary source material, therefore, present-day scholars are in a position their predecessors would have envied.

During the same recent years the writing of books and articles on the Mormons has continued apace. When one of the present authors wrote *Great Basin Kingdom: An Economic History of the Latter-day Saints, 1830–1900* (Cambridge, Mass., 1958), it seemed that there was a wealth of monographic material to be considered. But never in Mormon history has there been such productive scholarship as during the period from that time to the present. In part the great expansion in studies about the Mormons has resulted from the increase in the number of trained historians with this field as their specialty. But organizationally, Mormon studies have been greatly stimulated by the historical work of the Mormon History Association (founded in 1965), the Institute of Mormon Studies of Brigham Young University (which began in 1966), and the Historical Department of the Church (created in 1972). As the footnotes and bibliographical listings indicate, we have tried to keep abreast of this scholarly activity.

A final word: Both authors of the present work are believing and practicing members of the Church of Jesus Christ of Latter-day Saints. As such, we hope we have been able to discern some features of Mormon history from the inside that would elude the outside visitor, however conscientious. At the same time we have not attempted to write a tract; we have sought to understand as scholars of any faith or no faith would seek to understand. Anthropologists studying primitive cultures, sociologists examining life on skid row, historians re-creating civilizations of the past—all have certain advantages of perspective that enable them to see things that even their subjects do not recognize. But anthropologists were neither the first nor the last to recognize the obverse of this coin: Some matters can never be understood adequately except from within. We have tried to take advantage of our empathy with our fellow Mormons, while preserving proper scholarly objectivity and availing ourselves of insights from a variety of disciplines. To the non-Mormon reader, who might believe us unduly favorable to the Mormon point of view, we can only say that we have tried to be fair and have called them as we have seen them. To the Mormon reader, who might be surprised at our frank recognition of problems within the faith, at our willingness to assign blame to Latter-day Saints, and at our sincere goodwill to the historical opponents of Mormonism, the answer is really the same.

There is one other aspect of our approach that deserves comment: Mormon writers have sometimes felt uneasy in acknowledging secular influences on developments in Mormon history. Yet it is readily apparent that church leaders have been, and still are, particularly sensitive to the movements and conditions of their times. In that awareness they have asked for and claimed heavenly inspiration for statements and programs. The problem is not a new one. The extent to which any specific doctrine or plan of action is drawn directly from the divine source of knowledge, is prompted by ideas and values in the surrounding environment, or is some mixture of the two is a question that believers have had to wrestle with from at least as long ago as the times of the biblical prophets. "Many religious believers have found it quite unnecessary to believe that the prophets operated in a vacuum by ignoring the surrounding culture," psychologist Gary L. Bunker has written. "On the other hand, to say that they simply took over existing notions and restated them seems a naive reductionism that fails to consider the nature of all creativity, the different ways in which inspiration can occur, and the importance of timing, of context, and of charisma." In this sense we see no necessary incompatibility between believing that LDS authorities benefit from divine inspiration and recognizing that they also have their eyes open to what is going on in the world generally.

Commenting on the faults of some early Christians, Edward Gibbon observed that the faith they professed was not necessarily impugned if one remembered "not only *by whom,* but likewise *to whom,* the Divine Revelation was given." The same point was made by Mormon historian Brigham H. Roberts early in this century. While the officers and members of the Restored church possess, and have possessed, the heavenly treasure of divine authority, he wrote, "they carried it in earthen vessels; and that earthliness, with their human limitations, was plainly manifested on many occasions and in various ways, both in personal conduct and in collective deportment."

Maps

by Nancy Sessions

Scenes of Early Mormonism, 1820-1846

Mormon Kingdom in the West, 1847-1900

Scenes of Early Mormonism
1820–1846

Sharon
Whitingham
Harmony
Palmyra
Lake Ontario
Susquehanna R.
Lake Erie
Kirtland 1831
Lake Huron
Lake Michigan

Major Mormon
Migrations

0 50 100
miles

Mississippi River
Nauvoo 1838–1845
1838–1845
Adam-ondi-Ahman
1831–1833
Far West 1836–1838
Liberty
1834–1836
Independence
Missouri River
St. Louis
1838–1845
English Saints
Mississippi Saints
1846–1848

1846–1852
Winter Quarters
Kanesville
Missouri River

Mormon Kingdom in the West
1847–1900

Alberta

Fort Lemhi

Rexburg
Idaho Falls
Snake River
Star Valley
Big Horn Basin

Logan
Fort Bridger
Ogden
Salt Lake City

Carson Valley

Elk Mountain
Manti
Colorado River

St. George
Bluff
San Luis Valley

Las Vegas

Little Colorado

San Bernardino

Gila River
Mesa

"Mormon Country"
Boundary of Proposed (1849) State of Deseret
Early Outposts
Settled Valleys
Outlying Colonies

Sonora
Chihuahua

Part One
The Early Church

When Joseph Smith organized the Church of Jesus Christ of Latter-day Saints in western New York on April 6, 1830, he launched a movement that by 1978 would spread to more than seventy nations. But its early growth was marked by turbulence and suffering. The first adherents, primarily from New England and the Middle Atlantic states, viewed Mormonism as "the Restored Gospel of Jesus Christ," and accepted Joseph Smith as God's prophet, authorized to organize a lay priesthood, gather "the honest in heart," and establish communities dedicated to Christian principles. Difficulties with neighbors—who disliked their claims of divine sanction and their strong sense of order and unity, even in matters of politics and economics—drove the Mormons, in succession, from western Missouri, northeastern Ohio, northern Missouri, and western Illinois. With their unity and sense of uniqueness forged in the fire of these persecutions, the Mormons migrated to the valley of the Great Salt Lake and there, in 1847, established a new Zion.

1

⸭ The Beginnings ⸭

The whole family were melted to tears, and believed all he said. Knowing that he was very young, that he had not enjoyed the advantages of a common education; and knowing too, his whole character and disposition, they were convinced that he was totally incapable of arising before his aged parents, his brothers and sisters, and so solemnly giving utterance to anything but the truth.

—William Smith,
brother of Joseph Smith(1883)

In the days of the Prophet Joseph, such moments were more precious to me than all the wealth of the world. No matter how great my poverty—if I had to borrow meal to feed my wife and children—I never let an opportunity pass of learning what the Prophet had to impart.

—Brigham Young (1868)

Mormonism began in a cauldron of religious excitement. The Pennsylvanians, eastern New Yorkers, and Yankees who left the rocky soil, rigid society, and lack of opportunity of the New England hill country in the 1790s to settle west of the Catskill and Adirondack mountains were mostly young, disillusioned with their previous economic and spiritual life, and ready to adapt to a new one. When in 1799 and 1800, the Second Great Awakening began to sweep the country, it struck a tinderbox in western New York.[1]

Following the revivals of 1800, religion entered a temporary decline in western New York, reawakened in 1807 and 1808, and then declined again during the political and military excitements of 1812. A new wave of revivalism began around 1815, subsided somewhat after 1820, and then peaked after 1824 in the enthusiasm aroused by the great evangelist Charles Finney. The religious aspect of the region took on additional excitement when innovative reformers were attracted to the area. Several communities of Shakers located in the region. Even farther from the mainstream was the small band that surrounded Jemima Wilkinson, "the Publick Universal Friend." The religious spectrum extended all the way from such radical fringe groups through liberal Unitarians and Universalists to conservative Congregationalists, Methodists, and Presbyterians. Not surprisingly, as the different groups participated in revivals, there was more than a little religious squabbling.

Into this maelstrom Joseph Smith, Sr.; his wife, Lucy Mack Smith; and their family of eight—Alvin, Hyrum, Joseph, Sophronia, Samuel, William, Catherine, and Don Carlos—moved in 1816. The paternal Smith line extended through five generations in Topsfield, Massachusetts, a typical Congregationalist town near Boston. The Topsfield Smiths were respected coopers, or barrel makers, who served in several civic positions. Asael, father of Joseph senior, left Topsfield to settle in Vermont. Religiously he was characterized as a Universalist, or believer in universal resurrection, and a seeker. His son Joseph had little to do with organized religion, but retained the liberal bent of his father.

The maternal Mack line was less socially and religiously settled than the Smiths. Lucy's father, Solomon Mack, fought bravely in the French and Indian and Revolutionary wars but never accumulated much of an economic stake. He, too, seems to have been something of a seeker. One son, Jason, called himself such and founded a short-lived communitarian colony in New York.[2]

Lucy and Joseph married in 1796, and for the next twenty years they attempted to prosper in New England. But a combination of poor judgment, bad luck, and adverse circumstances conspired to keep them continually on the move. In this rootlessness they were not unique, for frequent moves and poverty were often the fate of those who lost their initial stake but chose to remain in the settled regions of New England and New York.[3] Writing some fifty years later, Lucy revealed herself as a deeply spiritual person who saw the hand of God in many events of her life. "I said in my heart that there was not then upon earth the religion which I sought," she wrote, adding that her husband "contended for the ancient order as established by our Lord and Saviour Jesus Christ and his apostles."[4] She also recorded a number of "prophetic" dreams on the part of her husband. The whole question of the family's early religiosity, however, is colored by later controversial events; little contemporary evidence of their early lives is recorded. All that may be said with certainty of the Smith family as it moved once again in 1816, this time to western New York, is that its members were relatively unchurched yet spiritually inclined and the inheritors of a mild "seeker" tradition that may have been accentuated by the family's economic problems and social conditions on the New York frontier.

The distance of time and the distortions of both adulation and malice have obscured the beginnings of young Joseph Smith's "calling." As poor as other migrant families, the Smiths were an unremarkable addition to the small community of Palmyra, near Rochester. During their first two years in the area they ran a small shop in town, hired out as laborers to more prosperous citizens, and saved their money. By 1818 they were able to make the initial payment on one hundred acres of heavily wooded land, equidistant from Palmyra and Farmington (later Manchester).[5]

Joseph Smith, Jr.—the future prophet—was born in Sharon, Vermont, on December 23, 1805, and as a boy moved with his family to New York State. Any assessment of his youthful character is colored by conflicting evaluations of his later acts, for almost all documents extant concerning his early life were written after he had become a controversial figure. Lucy Smith remembered her son as a brave youth, solicitous of his mother and prone to deep thought.[6] Orsamus Turner, an editor and author of anti-Mormon tracts who knew him around 1819 and 1820, later wrote: "But Joseph had . . . some very laudable aspirations; the mother's intellect occasionally shone out . . . , especially when he used to help us solve some portentous questions of moral or political ethics, in our juvenile debating club."[7]

Smith was literate, but little more. His parents had both been occasional schoolteachers, so he probably received more education at home than did many a child growing up on the western frontier. But life in New York was a constant economic struggle for the Smiths, who worked hard to maintain themselves. For most of his youth Smith was occupied with land clearing, plowing, maple sugar gathering, house raising, and heavy manual labor. The harsh realities of the family's situation gave little opportunity for young Joseph to idle away his time in telling tall tales, as some subsequent accounts of his youth were to charge.

Joseph Smith's history began to depart from the usual pattern with his "First Vision," which occurred sometime between his fourteenth and sixteenth years and which he immediately reported to his family. Of course, the claim that God and Jesus Christ literally appeared and gave specific information to a human being in modern times was dramatic—and divisive. Such experiences, whether those of Saint Paul or Ignatius Loyola, do not lend themselves easily to dispassionate historical analysis. Faced with Joseph Smith's account of a subjective religious experience in a literal historical setting, writers of the past have either accepted it as fact or, more commonly, rejected it as falsehood or delusion. There has been no appropriate middle ground, as in the case of, say, Gandhi or Luther, where all parties could agree that an experience was valuable and an evidence of personal genius even if not a literal divine manifestation. The tools of secular scholarship are crude and inadequate instruments for measuring mystical theophanies, which for believers mean the excited discovery (as the Quaker mystic Rufus Jones expressed it) that "God is a living, revealing, communicating God—the Great I Am, not a great He Was."[8] What the historian can do is to analyze as fairly as possible Joseph Smith's own account of his experiences.

The 1838 account of the First Vision describes Joseph Smith's confusion as a boy of fourteen at the "war of words and tumult of opinions" accompanying the religious excitement in western New York. Powerfully impressed by the scriptural injunction in James, "If any of you lack wisdom, let him ask of God," young Smith went to the woods near his home to pray:

> I saw a pillar of light exactly over my head, above the brightness of the sun, which descended gradually until it fell upon me. . . . When the light rested upon me I saw two Personages, whose brightness and glory defy all description, standing above me in the air. One of them spake unto me, calling me by name and said, pointing to the other—*"This is My Beloved Son. Hear Him!"*[9]

To those who believed this really happened, powerful insights were immediately available: that God was, despite a glory "beyond all description," in fact a literal person such as biblical prophets claimed to see and speak with; that Jesus Christ was indeed resurrected and ascended to the Father; that the heavens were not closed, and God was able and willing to communicate with humans in the direct terms ancient Hebrews and Christians claimed.

Probably none of these interpretations of the vision occurred to young Smith, who was most impressed with its assurance that he was personally forgiven of his sins and the instruction that he was to join none of the existing churches. He was awed that God would choose to reveal himself to a backwoods boy, even though he knew the Bible well enough to find precedents there for God's selection of the weak and young and teachable over those already set in their ways. Much of his life Joseph Smith struggled openly with a sense of unworthiness and of possible failure. He was amazed that as an ingenuous boy he was treated badly when he related his vision to others.

> It caused me serious reflection then, and often has since, how very strange it was that an obscure boy, of a little over fourteen years of age, and one, too, who was doomed to the necessity of obtaining a scanty maintenance by his daily labor, should be thought a character of sufficient importance to attract the attention of the great ones of the most popular sects of the day, and in a manner to create in them a spirit of the most bitter persecution and reviling.
>
> However it was nevertheless a fact that I had beheld a vision. . . . I had actually seen a light, and in the midst of that light I saw two Personages, and they did in reality speak to me; and though I was hated and persecuted for saying that I had seen a vision, yet it was true; and while they were persecuting me, reviling me, and speaking all manner of evil falsely for so saying, I was led to say in my heart: Why persecute me for telling the truth?[10]

Some critics of Joseph Smith have made much of the fact that the officially accepted account of the vision was not recorded until 1838, claiming that it was a fabrication to provide a miraculous, revelatory foundation for

the struggling young church he had started. When, in the 1960s, earlier accounts of the vision were uncovered in the Mormon Church Archives, some
writers began to emphasize the discrepancies between them, arguing or implying that anyone who could not tell an experience the same way twice was
not to be relied upon. Another line of approach was developed in 1967 by the
Reverend Wesley P. Walters, who examined Palmyra church records and
failed to find evidence of a revival there in 1820.[11]

In the strict sense, historical research can never either confirm or disprove
alleged supernatural appearances. But it is quite within its proper limits in
raising questions about the surrounding environment and about the relationship of different texts. Milton Backman has shown that the "whole district of
country" (Joseph Smith's phrase) was indeed racked by religious excitement
during 1819 and 1820. Whitney Cross's earlier statement that the religious
enthusiasms subsequent to the War of 1812 died down "after 1820" adds cre-
dence to 1820 as the probable date of the first Vision.[12]

To assess the importance of discrepancies between different extant versions of the vision, it will be helpful to examine the earliest of these. This
version, recorded in the winter of 1831–32 in the handwriting of Smith himself, presents the simplest account of the event.[13] After sketching his early life,
Smith relates how, at about the age of twelve, his "mind became Seriously
imprest with regard to all the important concerns for the welfare of my immortal Soul."[14] Through his study of the Scriptures the boy became convinced of the general apostasy and darkness of the world and of his own
sinfulness. The vision itself grew out of his deep thoughts over the next several years.

> The Lord heard my cry in the wilderness. While in the attitude of calling
> upon the Lord in the 16th year of my age, a pillar of light above the bright-
> ness of the sun at noonday came down from above and rested upon me, and
> I was filled with the Spirit of God, and the Lord opened the heavens upon
> me, and I saw the Lord. He spoke unto me saying "Joseph my son, Thy sins
> are forgiven thee. Go thy way, walk in my Statutes, and keep my command-
> ments. Behold, I am the Lord of Glory; I was crucifyed for the world, that all
> those who believe on my name may have Eternal life. Behold, none doeth
> good, no not one. They have turned aside from the Gospel and keep not my
> commandments. They draw near to me with their lips while their hearts are
> far from me, and mine anger is kindling against the inhabitants of the earth
> to visit them according to their ungodliness and to bring to pass that which
> hath been spoken by the mouth of the prophets and apostles, behold and lo,
> I come quickly, as it was written of me, in the cloud clothed in glory of my
> Father and my soul is filled with love."[15]

Textual analysis shows several differences between this early version and
the later ones, but these are mainly matters of emphasis. The 1832 account

paints a picture of the boy's concern for his own soul and his sense of forgiveness as the Lord speaks to him. Later there is more specific indication of the background of sectarian controversy, the desire to know which church was true, and the divine instructions that Joseph Smith himself would later be an instrument in restoring the true church to earth. Yet the earlier version also had said that the inhabitants of the earth had "turned aside from the Gospel," and the Lord promised that his Second Coming would "come quickly." If the two personages of the Godhead did not clearly appear in the 1832 version, there is no mistaking the assertion that Jesus Christ did the speaking to Joseph and that the Spirit of God was also present.

If the later version was different, this was not a result of inventing an experience out of whole cloth, as an unscrupulous person might readily have done, but rather of reexamining an earlier experience and seeing it in a different light. As a teen-ager Smith had probably seen the experience primarily as a relief from anxiety about his sins and concerns about the jarring claims of the different sects. By 1838 Smith was head of a church, his prophetic status challenged both from without and from within. His shift of emphasis from the personal to the general was natural, as was his ability now to see the vision more clearly than before in terms of its ecclesiastical and theological implications. As Martin Luther was only gradually driven to recognize the implications of his theses of 1517 and 1518, Joseph Smith came only in time to recognize the larger implications of his initial revelatory experience.

Typical of the psychological phases following conversion, the ardor of Smith's First Vision experience faded somewhat over the next few years. In fact, his next recorded approach to the Lord was a plea for forgiveness for the petty weaknesses he had displayed in the interim. It seems safe to assert that until 1823 the Smiths and their neighbors had little sense of what was to come.

For Mormons the visit of an angel to Joseph Smith during the night of September 21, 1823, signaled the documentary foundation of Mormonism. A statue representing the angel now crowns the Salt Lake Temple. In one hand the figure holds a trumpet; in the other are clasped plates symbolic of the Book of Mormon, the ancient religious record whose existence Smith claimed was revealed to him in 1823.

The basic elements of Smith's account are easily told. Sometime after his First Vision he became concerned with his lack of spirituality.[16] He was guilty of what he called "a light, and too often, vain mind, . . . a foolish and trifling conversation." During the night of September 21, after praying for forgiveness and guidance, he was rewarded with the appearance of an angelic being who announced himself as Moroni (pronounced "more-own-I"), last prophet of a vanished race that anciently inhabited the Americas. Assuring

Smith that his sins were forgiven, Moroni went on to tell him of a collection of gold leaves or "plates" containing an abridged religious history engraved many centuries earlier by Moroni and his father, Mormon. "He said," Smith continued, "that I should go and get them. He also revealed unto me many things concerning the inhabitants of the earth which since have been revealed in commandments and revelations." The angel then left, but returned twice more during the night to reiterate the message.

The next day Smith was again visited by the angel, who commanded him to go to the site where the records were buried. He went to a hill, "convenient to the village of Manchester, . . . of considerable size, and the most elevated of any in the neighborhood." On the west slope he found a large rounded stone. Underneath he discovered a stone box containing the plates of gold and an instrument later used to aid in translation, which apparently consisted of two transparent stones attached like eyeglasses to a breastplate and which was identified by the angel as the biblical Urim and Thummim used by ancient seers.[17] Although he tried three times to remove the objects, he was unable to do so. The angel told him, "You have not kept the commandments of the Lord," and chastened him for having "sought the Plates to obtain riches."[18] The angel commanded him to appear at the hill once each year "until the time should come for obtaining the plates." He did so, receiving much instruction about his future mission. On the fifth such visit, September 22, 1827, he took possession of the plates. At the time he was twenty-one years of age.

Smith tried to keep the matter quiet, but did tell his immediate family of the angel and the plates. As his mother wrote:

> The ensuing evening, when the family were all together, Joseph made known to them all that he had communicated to his father in the field, and also of his finding the Record, as well as what passed between him and the angel while he was at the place where the plates were deposited.[19]

Mrs. Smith portrays her son Alvin's strong faith in Joseph. In mid-November 1823, Alvin became ill and was soon near death. Among his last words, as reported by his mother, were that Joseph must "do everything in his power to obtain the Record."[20]

In the intervening years, owing to the family's limited worldly circumstances, the Smith sons often hired out as laborers. One specific instance of such employment was Joseph Smith's work for Josiah Stoal (or Stowell) of Chenango County, New York, who engaged him to search for a silver mine in Susquehanna County, Pennsylvania. While working in this area, Smith met and later married Emma Hale. He claimed that he "prevailed with the old gentleman to cease digging," but the incident was later magnified when a series of money-digging activities was attributed to him.[21] Whether based on the single mine-digging project or on other similar activities, the charge that Smith was a "money digger" was used to discredit him in the eyes of the public.

Serving a similar purpose of discrediting Smith were assertions that his family was a collection of notorious undesirables. Virtually all allegations of the Smith family's bad character stem from affidavits collected around 1832 by D. P. Hurlbut (Hurlburt), an excommunicated Mormon who, at the request of an anti-Mormon committee, returned to the Palmyra region with the professed aim of gathering evidence to "completely divest Joseph Smith of all claims to the character of an honest man." The affidavits were published in E. D. Howe's 1834 exposé *Mormonism Unvailed.*[22]

The bulk of Hurlbut's seventy-two affidavits follow the tone and wording of two community statements from Palmyra and Manchester. Fifty-one Palmyra residents signed a statement that the Smiths were "destitute of moral character," given to "visionary projects," and "addicted to vicious habits." The remaining affidavits follow the same line and often, in fact, employ the precise phrasing of the Palmyra statement, which leads to the suspicion that Hurlbut's hand was in the preparation of many of them.[23]

The remaining affidavits may be divided into two classes. A number of local residents reported having observed Smith family members engaged in money digging or other superstitious or dishonest activities. Peter Ingersoll attests that Father Smith persuaded him to "douse" for a buried treasure, after which Joseph senior performed a strutting dance with a magical stone in his hat. William Stafford reports two occasions when the Smiths involved him in treasure-digging excursions. During one such nocturnal rite they tricked him out of a large black sheep. Willard Chase testified that young Smith found a "singularly appearing stone" while digging a well on the Chase property in 1822. Later, says Chase, Smith began to "publish abroad what wonders he could discover by looking in it." Such stories, buttressed by allegations of drunkenness and general bad character, comprise the bulk of the Hurlbut affidavits.

Taken alone, the Hurlbut affidavits are deficient. Not only do they contain a minimum of firsthand evidence, but on many points they are contradictory. The points on which they agree are worded so similarly that they smack of a plot to discredit the Smiths. On the other hand, it has not been possible to reject the affidavits totally. Smith's self-admitted employment by Josiah Stoal resulted in the youth's being brought to trial in 1826, charged with either vagrancy or disorderly conduct. Bills drawn up by the local judge and constable refer to Smith as a "glass looker" (one who, by peering through a glass stone, could see things not discernible by the natural eye). The bills class the offense as a misdemeanor and indicate that at least twelve witnesses were served with subpoenas. Summaries of the trial contain many contradictions but agree on the essential point that Smith was brought to court by Stoal's relatives to prevent the old man from squandering more money on the work of the youthful visionary. Several neighbors testified against Smith, but Stoal stood fast by his employee. Some accounts have Smith being acquitted by reason of Stoal's testimony; in others, he escaped or was convicted and moved out of town.[24]

Another negative evaluation of Smith is the affidavit of Isaac Hale, the father of Emma Hale, whom Smith married in 1827. Hale said that Smith had first made his acquaintance when he began boarding at the Hale household while working for a set of "money diggers." His chief job, according to his future father-in-law, was divining the location of treasure by peering at a stone placed in his hat. Hale denied the young man permission to marry his daughter on the grounds that Smith "was a stranger" and "followed a business" to which he objected. Later Smith returned, and he and Miss Hale, who was of legal age, were married while her father was away. Hale obviously mistrusted the young man and considered him a charlatan. At least this was his attitude in 1833–34, when he prepared the affidavit. His feelings were not always so strong, for earlier he had allowed his son-in-law to live with him during the period when the translation of the plates was begun.

Assertions that the entire Smith family was lazy, openly dishonest, and vicious seem malicious in view of the fact that between 1823 and 1827 the Smiths cleared large portions of their farm, hired out as day laborers to various neighbors, and somehow managed to support themselves. When a difficulty about the title of the farm arose in 1825, a Mr. Robinson obtained some sixty signatures attesting to the family's good character and industry. Throughout the period Mrs. Smith and several children retained membership in the Presbyterian Church.[25] Court records show that the Smiths were involved in several litigations, none of which seem to be the result of anything but severe poverty. Many Palmyra residents remembered the Smiths quite positively. One speaks of them as being the best family in the area in time of sickness. Others mention that young Joseph was a steady and diligent worker.[26]

The money-digging allegations require more thorough evaluation. Treasure hunts seem to have been a favorite avocation of many area residents. "There was considerable digging for money in our neighborhood by men, women and children," remembers one Palmyran. Many of those signing affidavits concerning Smith's money digging were devotees of the same activity. As employees in all manner of digging projects, the Smiths may have been unfairly thought to be directing some such operations. One 1833 statement reports that the author had known Smith for ten years and that "latterly" he was noted as a money digger. If this term refers to the period after Smith's

1827 announcement of the gold plates, it suggests how the money-digging story gained circulation.[27]

A combination of rumors concerning the First Vision, the visits from Moroni, and the use of a seer stone very probably attracted Josiah Stoal to the Smith farm in Palmyra. Smith may have encouraged the farmer to believe that he did possess a sort of second sight—not an illogical conviction in light of his background. Use of stones in divining was not uncommon for that time. One old-time resident recalled Joshua Stafford's peep stone, which "looked like white marble and had a hole through the center," and remembered that "Sally Chase, a Methodist, had one."[28] As late as 1841 Joseph Smith displayed a seer stone in Nauvoo, Illinois, although his attachment to such things had become qualified in two directions; he readily said every person was entitled to such a stone, and his own revelations and translations had long since ceased to require such physical aid.

Mormon historians may have been too ready to cast Smith in the mold of a modern, twentieth-century man sanitized from all superstitious or presently questionable activities; and critics may have been too ready to magnify into dire villainy activities probably as innocent and prevalent in the 1820s as astrology or health food faddism are among respectable people today.

Before 1827, knowledge of the golden plates was limited mainly to Smith's immediate family, although rumors may have been in the air. On September 22 of that year, Smith indicates that the angel finally allowed him to remove the plates and the Urim and Thummim from their resting place. His alleged possession of valuable artifacts must have aroused great interest in the region. Unable to find the seclusion he needed to begin translation, he and Emma decided to move to her parents' home near Harmony, Pennsylvania, but could not raise enough money to make the trip. At this point he asked his mother to approach Martin Harris, a prosperous local farmer who had learned of the plates and who had occasionally employed Smith. Harris donated fifty dollars and then followed the pair to Pennsylvania. Settled in his father-in-law's home, Smith commenced translating the plates with either his wife or Harris as scribe. He also made facsimiles of some of the characters before him.

Harris was interested in acquiring a scholarly opinion on the origin and meaning of the script. Prevailing upon Smith to allow him to submit the facsimiles to several antiquarians, Harris journeyed to New York and displayed the characters to Dr. Samuel Latham Mitchill, a scientist and classical scholar, and to Professor Charles Anthon of Columbia University, a noted student of ancient languages. According to Harris's account of his interview with Anthon, the professor was impressed by the facsimiles and gave Harris a certificate testifying that they were "true characters," and that "the translation of such of them as had been translated was also correct." Upon learning, however, of the supernatural origins of the golden book that they came from, according to Harris, the professor seized the certificate and destroyed it. Anthon's account of the interview differs considerably. Several years later he wrote that he remembered Harris's visit well but that stories that he had certified the translation were totally false. For Anthon the whole thing was either a scheme to defraud Harris or a hoax on the learned.[29]

In 1828 Anthon could have had no knowledge of Egyptian script, let alone "Reformed Egyptian," as Smith identified the language of the Book of Mormon.[30] Whether the scholar professed to understand the script out of academic bravado and then destroyed the certificate when he learned that he might be made a public laughingstock, or whether Harris's version does not accurately reflect the interview, is unclear. Whatever the sequence of events in New York, Harris returned to Pennsylvania convinced of the manuscript's authenticity. He arranged his affairs in Palmyra so that he could continue to serve as scribe in the translation. Later he would guarantee some three thousand dollars for the first publication of the book.

The work of translation proceeded haltingly through 1828. By June 14, Smith had dictated 116 pages of manuscript to Harris from behind a curtain erected to isolate Smith and the plates and Urim and Thummim from the scribe. Details of the actual process of translation are unclear.[31] The only statement by Smith himself, contained in a revelation dictated in 1829, indicates that the process of translation was not automatic, required considerable thought, and was ultimately governed by a feeling-state verification.[32]

After the completion of 116 pages, Harris obtained permission, after repeated requests, to take them to Palmyra to show to his wife, who was contemptuous of the whole affair. Harris made the trip to Palmyra, but somehow the manuscript disappeared.[33] The fate of the lost 116 pages has never been determined. Some have theorized that Lucy Harris destroyed them. Harris's first words upon returning are reported to have been: "I have lost my soul; I have lost my soul."[34] Smith responded to the loss with bitter remorse and retired to puzzle out a solution to his predicament. Whatever the nature of the translation process, Smith realized that he would be unable to duplicate precisely the 116 pages. If the lost portion was still extant, his enemies might alter it. To a people steeped in biblical literalism the existence of two divergent copies of the same inspired work would be unacceptable.

By July, Smith had received a revelation severely chastising him but promising that the work would go forth. At that time the Urim and Thummim were taken from him. Several days later he received a second revelation promising to restore his gift of translation. Rather than attempting to retranslate the lost portion, he was to render an alternative account of the same historical material that had been included among the plates.[35]

During the winter of 1828–29 Smith resumed the process of translation.

He made little progress, however, until Oliver Cowdery, a Palmyra school-teacher, arrived in Harmony along with Samuel Smith, Joseph's younger brother. As scribe, Cowdery immediately began recording the torrents of dictation that spilled forth from behind the makeshift curtain. Between April 7, 1829, and July of that same year Cowdery recorded the bulk of the 275,000-word work.[36]

The book that came from the plates is a chronicle of several peoples who lived in the Americas prior to the arrival of Columbus. It begins in 600 B.C. in the Holy Land, as a small band of Hebrews is inspired to escape Jerusalem just prior to the Babylonian invasion. Under divine guidance they travel by caravan to the Indian Ocean, construct a boat, and journey to a promised land on the west coast of the Americas. In the new land, conflict divides them into two groups, the Nephites and the Lamanites. The centuries before the birth of Christ are spent constructing elaborate cities and temples, warring, and conducting missionary expeditions. Following his crucifixion, Christ appears in the Americas and organizes his church, announcing that he will also appear to other separated branches of the House of Israel. For two hundred years following this visit the people unite to live in peace and harmony. When unrighteousness and disharmony reappear, the people again split into opposing groups. In approximately A.D. 421 one group destroys the other completely and, apparently mixed with other groups from Europe and Asia, becomes the ancestors of the Indians of North, Central, and South America. Moroni, the last prophet of the destroyed group, buries the records of his people in the "Hill Cumorah" where they are to remain preserved until brought forth as a needed witness to the divinity of Christ in "the latter days."[37]

The Book of Mormon (named for Moroni's father, an ancient American soldier-historian) was printed in 1829–30 by Egbert B. Grandin of Palmyra, Martin Harris's three thousand dollars providing for a first edition of five thousand copies. Included in the first and all subsequent publications was the testimony of Oliver Cowdery, Martin Harris, and David Whitmer (a Pennsylvania farmer who had befriended Smith) that they had seen the gold plates and knew by divine witness that the translation of them was correct. Eight other witnesses—members of the Whitmer and Smith families, and Hiram Page—also testified to having seen and handled the plates.[38] After displaying the plates to the witnesses, Smith gave them and the other artifacts back to Moroni.[39]

The reliability of these testimonies has naturally been questioned. All of the three original witnesses and several of the others later left the church. But despite differences with Smith, all of the witnesses remained confident of the ancient origin and divinely aided translation of the book. Before their deaths Harris and Cowdery both returned to membership in the Utah church and strongly reaffirmed their original witness.[40]

Smith's account of the origin of the Book of Mormon has, of course, never been acceptable to nonbelievers. But finding a creditable alternative explanation has been difficult. Soon after its publication several hypotheses for the "Gold Bible" were developed. The most popular theory, which survived well into the twentieth century, was that a manuscript romance written by Solomon Spaulding had fallen into the hands of Sidney Rigdon, who allegedly altered it and surreptitiously placed it in the hands of Smith, who then recited it to his scribes. But Rigdon did not meet Smith or become affiliated with the church until his baptism in November 1830. The Spaulding-Rigdon theory of the book's origin is based on a number of very superficial similarities between the two works, and modern textual analysis does not substantiate the theory.[41]

Fawn Brodie, Joseph Smith's eminent but unsympathetic biographer, has advanced the second principal countertheory of the book's origin. She pictures Smith as an uneducated but highly imaginative youth who conceived of writing the book as a means of impressing his wife and making a large profit from his reputation as a seer. Sometime during the process of "translation" he became convinced of his own powers of persuasion and decided to concentrate on the religious possibilities of the fabrication. To this school of thought the text of the Book of Mormon represents a rewording of Smith's private concerns and the larger issues swirling about western New York. Certainly the origin of the American Indian, anti-Masonism, anti-Catholicism, and questions of authority, predestination, and baptism loomed large in the minds of Smith's neighbors, and such concerns can be seen mirrored in the text of the Book of Mormon. Such parallels suggest to some scholars that the book originated in the fertile mind of a questioning youth in nineteenth-century western New York, not in ancient America.[42]

Mormons insist that Smith's limited education made it impossible for him to produce such a long and complex book by himself. The issues in the book are seen by defenders as universal, and likely to have aroused interest in ancient times as well as in modern America.[43] Some Mormons have pointed out a number of esoteric connections between their scripture and ancient Mediterranean cultures.[44] Since the Book of Mormon does not pretend to tell the history of all of the peoples of the entire Western Hemisphere, there is always the possibility that the particular peoples whose story is recounted in the Mormon scripture existed elsewhere than the places and times that have been thoroughly investigated by archaeologists. Meanwhile, as parallels continue to accumulate between the Old World and the New, it is natural to conclude that the material evidence is not all in.

Whatever the origin of the Book of Mormon, its translation raised doctrinal and procedural questions. As early as April 1829 Smith shared with Oliver Cowdery a divine admonition to "seek to bring forth and establish the cause of Zion." Beyond the preparation of the Book of Mormon, the exact nature of that cause was yet to be specified. In May of 1829, Smith wrote, he and Cowdery "on a certain day went into the woods to pray and inquire of the Lord respecting baptism for the remission of sins, that we found in the translation of the plates." While the two prayed, a being who identified himself as John the Baptist appeared to them and, laying his hands upon their heads, conferred upon them the "Priesthood of Aaron, which holds the keys of the ministering of angels, and of the Gospel of repentance, and of baptism by immersion for the remission of sins." At an unspecified date later that summer Peter, James, and John, the ancient apostles, similarly restored the Melchizedek, or high, priesthood, the authority by which Smith and his followers would establish a church.[45]

Immediately after their visit from John the Baptist, Smith and Cowdery baptized each other. Then Samuel Smith was baptized. Joseph Smith also baptized an older man named Joseph Knight from Colesville, New York, and several members of the Whitmer family of Fayette, New York. In June, Smith and Cowdery moved to the Whitmer residence, where they finished the translation of the book. That same month they baptized Hyrum Smith, David Whitmer, and Peter Whitmer. "From this time forth," Smith later wrote, "many became believers, and some were baptized, whilst we continued to instruct and persuade as many as applied for information."[46]

Throughout the remainder of 1829 Smith announced intermittent revelations regarding the future organization of the church. Late in the year he issued "A Revelation on Church Government," which would become the church constitution. The revelation identified Smith and Cowdery as the "first elders" and apostles of the church, established fundamental church doctrines and ordinances, and set down duties of a series of elders, priests, teachers, and deacons who were to be appointed later. On April 6, 1830, Joseph, Hyrum, and Samuel Smith, Oliver Cowdery, and Peter and David Whitmer met with others in the Peter Whitmer home in Fayette to organize officially the Church of Christ. By common consent the six accepted Cowdery and Smith as elders of the church and witnessed their ordination to that position. Afterward Smith served the sacrament (communion) and "confirmed" those present.[47] Mormonism as an organized movement—as a church—had come into existence.

At first, both the affection and the antagonism evoked by Mormonism centered around the personality of Joseph Smith. He was doubtless a complex person who reflected many of the tensions of his time. Few men have been viewed with such intense contradiction—as both a monstrous charlatan and a demidivinity.

"I've got the damn fools now," asserts the Smith of the Hurlbut affidavits. "Oh, may God grant that I may be directed in all my thoughts," wrote

Smith in his private diary. John C. Bennett, former mayor of Nauvoo, Illinois, and one-time close friend of Smith, embittered by his excommunication from the church, describes a prophet who proposed a side-show exhibit of falsified gold plates at "twenty-five cents a sight." But Smith's uncle John Smith remembered, "Joseph took the shoes from his feet and gave [them] to me." To many people Smith seemed an adulterous tyrant, a destroyer of home and family. To his own wife he wrote, "Emma, I received your letter which I read over and over again. It was a sweet morsel to me." While some shuddered at the thought of this fraud and fiend, others rejoiced at the memory of this friend. "I feel like shouting hallelujah, all the time, when I think that I ever knew Joseph Smith," said Brigham Young.[48]

This tall, robust, blue-eyed man could receive a revelation, wrestle a workman, outrun a mob, and develop plans for a model city virtually in the same day. He incited many to either despise or deify him. Inside him was a force that impelled him to prophethood and attracted devoted followers to him. As Albert Schweitzer notes in *The Quest for the Historical Jesus* (1906; Eng. tr. 1910), the best biographies have been written out of hate or disdain or contempt. The unsympathetic pictures of the Mormon prophet at least possess the stuff of life, portraying for our imagination a vibrant if rascally scapegrace. The saintly Joseph of Mormon biography, on the other hand, has often seemed to dwell above human passion and earthly circumstance. Both extremes miss the heart of the man, whose often contradictory acts and paradoxical rhetoric suggest that the stereotypes ignore his humanity.

A possible key to at least a partial understanding of Joseph Smith lies in recent studies that portray the will to prophesy as the reaction of a few brilliant, conflicted persons to the unbridgeable contradictions of life. Most individuals respond to inconsistencies and injustices by either enduring them or discovering conventional solutions. Others, of a different cast of mind, are called—or call themselves—to prophethood. In his thought-provoking study of Martin Luther, psychologist Erik Erikson comments on the connection between an inner life and a public calling:

> Millions of boys face these problems and solve them in some way or another—they live, as Captain Ahab says, with half their heart and with only one of their lungs, and the world is the worse for it. Now and again, however, an individual is called upon (called by *whom*, only the theologians claim to know, and by *what*, only bad psychologists) to lift his individual patienthood to the level of a universal one and to try to solve for all what he could not solve for himself alone.[49]

This kind of conflict can be seen in Moses—born Israelite but raised in the house of the pharaoh—who fled to the wilderness crying out against his people's degradation by the Egyptians whose culture had shaped him. He returned as a prophet to lead both himself and his people back to their identity as an independent nation. Martin Luther's conflict also arose early in life, son of a father alternately brutal and loving. The young Luther grew up with persistent ambivalences about authority, further strained by the conflict between his brilliance and his superstition, his spirituality and his coarseness, and his perception of the gap between preachment and practice in religion. In a different context Joseph Smith, too, can be viewed as finding his capacity for prophethood in a series of contradictions—of a somewhat different nature, however, from those of either Moses or Luther.

One looks in vain to find a deep-seated conflict between Smith and his father. Instead, some of the earliest objections to the young prophet were that he seemed to dominate his father. "A careless young man . . . very saucy and insolent to his father," declared Isaac Hale, Smith's father-in-law. Hale's testimony, however, was undoubtedly influenced by the treatment he felt he himself had received from his son-in-law.[50] The evidence, in any event, indicates that although Smith's family believed in his prophetic gifts, he deferred to his father in matters of family discipline until the latter's death in 1840.[51]

Some biographers have seen a key conflict precisely in Smith's relationship with Isaac Hale. But although it undoubtedly became bitter, the frustration it must have caused Smith came too late in life and was too easily avoided to have produced in him such spiritual turmoil as might have influenced his career as a religious leader.

In Smith's mind, the crucial inconsistency was not within his family but rather in the troubled relationship between his family and society at large. The Smiths conceived of themselves as an intelligent, patriotic, spiritual family which had suffered a series of misfortunes. One cannot read Lucy Mack Smith's history without becoming aware of her pride in her father's literary accomplishments, her belief that misfortune continually robbed the family of its rightful economic and social position, and her conviction that something important was bound to originate among her sons. She undoubtedly communicated this pride and expectation to her sons early in life. Outsiders, however, saw neither the glories of the past nor the possibilities of the future, but only the poverty of the present. One challenge for Joseph Smith was that of resolving the conflict between the family's self-image and its public image.

A second conflict that shaped young Smith was common in newly settled regions. The family moved several times within his memory. Nearly every one of the children was born in a different village. Joseph may well have connected this lack of roots with his family's lack of status. His desire for security thus helps to explain his lifelong effort to forge a powerful identity, infusing the biblical concept of prophet with new meaning, and to create for himself and others a system of cosmic sweep that would offer a sense of direction in a topsy-turvy world.

A third contradiction Smith faced was familiar to youths of that time. He experienced both the swirling emotionalism of revivalistic religion and a growing desire for rationalism and an empirical test for truth. A consequence of these two contradictory influences may have been a perception that his own inherited superstitions and folkways were out of joint with a nascent sense of practical rationality. Finally, he, like many others, felt a powerful need for deep religious experience and spiritual justification. For one reason or another, existing religions had proved incapable of filling his need.

Smith's efforts to bridge the gap between inner and outer realities often created new paradoxes, but they were significant enough to evoke either fervent love or hate from his contemporaries. He was, in the words used by Carl Van Doren to describe Benjamin Franklin, a "harmonious human multitude"—a complex mix of half a dozen different elements, each of which in a simpler man might have constituted an entire personality. This diversity may have helped to attract the wide variety of convert leaders that enabled the church to survive his death.

Admittedly the question of the origin and validity of Smith's claims is inherently controversial. Erik Erikson has reminded us of the difficulty of measuring extraordinary men by conventional yardsticks:

> In the case of great young men . . . rods which measure consistency, inner balance, or proficiency simply do not fit the relevant dimensions. On the contrary, a case could be made for the necessity for extraordinary conflicts, at times both felt and judged to be desperate. For if some youths did not feel estranged from the compromise patterns into which their societies have settled down, if some did not force themselves almost against their wills to insist, at the price of isolation, on finding an original way of meeting our existential problems, societies would lose an essential avenue to rejuvenation and to that rebellious expansion of human consciousness which alone can keep pace with technological and social change.[52]

Let us turn our attention to the movement that in April 1830 included only a few followers. For if Smith's own resolution of tensions has more than biographical interest, it lies in the fact that somehow he was able to forge answers that exerted an appeal for others.[53]

2

⟨ The Appeals of ⟩ Mormonism

Next morning I called at his house, where, for the first time, my eyes beheld the Book of Mormon—that book of books . . . which was the principal means, in the hands of God, of directing the entire course of my future life.

I opened it with eagerness, and read its title page. I then read the testimony of several witnesses in relation to the manner of its being found and translated. After this I commenced its contents by course. I read all day; eating was a burden, I had no desire for food; sleep was a burden when the night came, for I preferred reading to sleep.

As I read, the spirit of the Lord was upon me, and I knew and comprehended that the book was true, as plainly and manifestly as a man comprehends and knows that he exists. My joy was now full, as it were, and I rejoiced sufficiently to more than pay me for all the sorrows, sacrifices and toils of my life. I soon determined to see the young man who had been the instrument of its discovery and translation.

—Parley Parker Pratt (converted in 1830)

In listening to these modern prophets, I discovered, as I think, the great secret of their success in making converts. They speak to a common feeling; they minister to a universal want . . . . They speak a language of hope and promise to weak, weary hearts, tossed and troubled, who have wandered from sect to sect, seeking in vain for the primal manifestations of the divine power.

—John Greenleaf Whittier (1847)

Joseph Smith, like Martin Luther, was initially concerned primarily with the state of his own soul. Luther's "What shall I do to be saved?" became Smith's "Which church shall I join?" In both cases the implications of the question and the answer were more than personal; they were universal. If, as Smith believed, existing churches were inadequate, teaching as God's doctrines the commandments of men, people needed to be informed. If a new message was to come from heaven, people had to be prepared. Even before the spring of 1830, word was circulating of a new gospel that aroused ridicule and opposition from many but belief from a few. Mormonism was becoming a movement. As we have seen, the official recognition of its status as a church came with the formal organization on April 6, 1830, in Fayette, New York, of the Church of Christ, later referred to as the Church of the Latter-day Saints (emphasizing that this was Christ's Church in the last days), and in 1838, the Church of Jesus Christ of Latter-day Saints.

The banner of the restored gospel having been raised, the word was carried abroad. Several early revelations declared that the field was "white already to harvest."[1] Members of the Smith family rallied to the cause, as did a few friends and neighbors. One of the most significant early conversions occurred in late 1830 when four missionaries who had been sent to meet the Indians in Missouri stopped at Kirtland, in northeastern Ohio, and there recruited Sidney Rigdon—a prominent Campbellite preacher who had recently broken off from the main Disciples of Christ movement—together with part of his congregation. When Joseph Smith and other New York Mormons moved to Ohio in the spring of 1831, they joined about one hundred members of the church at Kirtland.[2] For about seven years Kirtland was to be a main center of Mormon activity. By the summer of 1835 there were fifteen hundred to two thousand Mormons in Kirtland and vicinity.

In the meantime a second center for the new church was established in Missouri, designated as Zion in the revelations of Joseph Smith. Feeling threatened by the influx of Saints, Missourians began the harassment or persecution that, as will be discussed in the next chapter, only confirmed the Mormons' conviction that they were the heirs of the early Christian saints. The sojourn of the Saints in Independence, Jackson County, Missouri, was short-lived, for they were forced to evacuate in 1833–34. Temporarily settling in northern Missouri counties, Mormons continued to flock into the area. The Missouri persecutions, which forced them out of the state by 1839, did not hamper the fervor of most Saints or their ability to attract others, and the movement now numbered several thousand.[3]

An observer of the scene in 1839, however, might have held out little hope for the continued success of Mormonism, for in addition to the natural ebbing of the fervor of conversion, successive blows had weakened it: financial reversals, internal dissension and apostasy, the abandonment of Kirtland, repeated persecutions in Missouri, expulsion from the state, and finally the incarceration of their leaders, including Joseph Smith, who languished in Missouri jails for six months. But the movement showed recuperative powers. Within a year Commerce, Illinois (rechristened Nauvoo), on the western border of Illinois, was its new center. Refugees and converts straggled in. Then, at the very moment when the impoverished survivors were trying to get back on their feet, when disease was rampant and most Mormon families were suffering severely, Smith sent the surviving apostles (seven of the original twelve) to England, to start preaching the new message in that foreign land. There Brigham Young, Heber C. Kimball, and their colleagues won quick successes. By 1841 there were several thousand Mormons in Great

Britain, many of them hoping to emigrate, four hundred of them crossing the Atlantic to Nauvoo in the first year of the apostolic mission.[4]

In the meantime proselyting continued in the United States, and Nauvoo soon became a city of approximately 11,000 inhabitants.[5] In addition, there were thousands of Saints in communities near Nauvoo and additional thousands in the United States and Great Britain who were unable to gather. Possibly as many as 35,000 persons joined the movement during its first fourteen years.[6]

After Smith's assassination by a hostile mob in 1844 the Mormons found themselves momentarily dazed. Brigham Young was president of the Quorum of the Twelve Apostles and had developed as an increasingly effective and accepted leader while welding the Quorum into a successful missionary force in England. Having responded to gradually increased responsibilities in Nauvoo, he moved to the fore in accordance with the covenants of the church, including the vote of a special conference in August 1844. Under his leadership proselyting continued, as did immigration to Nauvoo. Although there was growing opposition, eventually sufficient to force an evacuation of the city, the Saints continued to build houses and to complete the temple that had been started by Smith. With the abandonment of Nauvoo, in 1846, the exodus to the Great Basin repeated on a larger scale the pattern established earlier in Missouri and Illinois—a migration of the faithful, with, at the same time, continued recruitment in the United States and an expansion of the overseas missionary field. The word was carried into different parts of Europe, especially Scandinavia, and to far-off places like Hawaii and Australia.[7]

Sometime in the nineteenth century, births to Mormon families became the most important source of addition to the ranks, but conversions remained a significant percentage. A continued influx of converts meant for the church the "avoidance of sectarian stagnation," according to Thomas O'Dea, for the apostasies and losses through inactivity and indifference were counteracted by repeated transfusions of fresh blood.[8] If the loss in apostates and the disillusioned at Kirtland, for example, had not been outweighed by the conversions, Mormonism might very early have lapsed, as did most other nineteenth-century religious movements, into an insignificant sect.

Early-twentieth-century anti-Mormon diatribes, both in printed form and in the newer medium, motion pictures, showed handsome but licentious Mormon missionaries winning converts through the evil eye of hypnotism, then whisking them off bodily to their lairs in the American West. How else could so many have been won to such a sacrifice of the traditional values of Western civilization? To students of the Mormon phenomenon it is plain that the Mormon message had its appeals. To analyze these appeals is in a sense artificial, a removal from the world of actual experience to the efforts of scholarly dissection. An interview with a flesh-and-blood convert, who would be quite willing to give his "reasons" for joining the Latter-day Saints, might be more informative, or at least more in touch with the real world. But the explanation of such converts for their decision, in the past as at present, is in itself usually fairly simple. They joined the Mormons, they say, because they became convinced that Mormonism was "true." Some would admit to being influenced by missionaries as persons, or impressed by the sincerity and compassion of Mormons they had known. But such attractions were not likely to be sufficient to motivate such a psychically disruptive act as conversion.

Many Mormons, especially in the early years of the Restoration, were converted through reading the Book of Mormon. From the beginning, missionaries called attention to the following promise written by the ancient American compiler, Moroni, on the closing page:

> And when ye shall receive these things, I would exhort you that you would ask God, the Eternal Father, in the name of Christ, if these things are not true; and if ye shall ask with a sincere heart, with real intent, having faith in Christ, he will manifest the truth of it unto you, by the power of the Holy Ghost.

To judge from their statements, more than a few new members received what to them was a heavenly manifestation or personal assurance of the truth of the Book of Mormon, an assurance that then impelled them to accept the claims of the prophet and his successors. Personal "testimony" of Mormon converts—basically a claim that they "knew in their hearts" that the church was true—flowed from individual encounters with the Divine, but to those who did not share the experience they seemed inadequate and naive. It has been suggested that lower-class people in the eastern states and in Europe might have used Mormonism as the pretense for migrating and putting down stakes in a new location without necessarily having much regard for the religion. Brigham Young was one Mormon leader who acknowledged some truth in this view. "Many embrace the Gospel," he said in 1855, "actuated by no other motive than to have the privilege of being removed from their oppressed condition to where they will not suffer. They will embrace any doctrine under the heavens, if you will only take them from their present condition."[9] But all these explanations are not sufficient for a phenomenon so complex.

As previously indicated, when Mormonism appeared, the religious scene was already crowded and confused, a maelstrom of frenetic activity. Although the religious unity of Western Christendom had been broken at the time of the Reformation, the pattern in Europe was still, generally speaking, one of state churches. But the process of fragmentation continued through the seventeenth and eighteenth centuries and reached its *reductio ad absurdum* in America, where the lack of religious consensus was becoming ever more apparent. That all needs were not satisfied is clear enough from several manifestations of religious uneasiness, discontent, and searching at the end of the eighteenth and beginning of the nineteenth century.

For one thing, membership in the churches did not encompass anywhere near the entire population, and there was a noticeable weakening of institutional religion. Part of the dissatisfaction with established churches stemmed from the "enlightened" Christianity of the late eighteenth century, which, originating in Europe, crossed the Atlantic to appear in the writings of Ethan Allen, Thomas Paine, Thomas Jefferson, Benjamin Franklin, and others. A few extremists took the point of view of European deism, rejecting the Christian message per se while retaining a belief in God, in the immortality of the human soul, and in the necessity of living a good life. More typical were Christians who, inspired by the apologetic writings of John Locke and Bishop Joseph Butler, sought to retain the basic faith while stripping it of nonessentials, rejecting the creeds and abstruse theology of the Middle Ages, and grounding it whenever possible on rational arguments. Such an attitude looked for a statement of Christian theology that was logical and straightforward. These "enlightened" Christians tended to insist on man's free agency, to emphasize ethics as the chief end of religion, and to look forward optimistically to human progress. "In Christian terms," says Sydney Ahlstrom, "this would lead to a postmillennial eschatology; that is, the Kingdom of God would be realized in history, whereupon Christ or his Spirit would in some sense return."[10]

The "enlightened" Christians tended to be impatient with the traditional concept of the Trinity, the Nicene formulation that had been shared by Catholicism and magisterial Protestantism. "Three are one and one is three," said Jefferson, "and yet the one is not three, and the three are not one. . . . This constitutes the craft, the power and profit of the priests. Sweep away their gossamer fabric of factious religion, and they would catch no more flies."[11] Among Unitarians, who looked to Joseph Priestley as the founder of their movement in America, there appeared a willingness to see the Father and the Son as separate beings, although there continued to be differences among them as to precise details. Jefferson was among those who went so far as to deny the reality of "spiritual" (in the sense of nonmaterial) beings: "To say that the human soul, angels, God, are immaterial," he said, "is to say they are nothing, or there is no God, no angels, no soul. I cannot reason otherwise."[12]

One rationalist, Benjamin Franklin, remained outwardly observant of traditional Christianity, but found it impossible to worship what he regarded as the excessively narrow Christian God of his age. In 1728 he wrote:

> When I stretch my Imagination thro' and beyond our System of Planets, beyond the visible fix'd Stars themselves, into that Space that is every Way infinite, and conceive it fill'd with Suns like ours, each with a Chorus of Worlds forever moving round him, then this little Ball on which we move, seems, even in my narrow Imagination, to be almost Nothing, and my self less than nothing, and of no sort of Consequence. . . .

> I conceive then, that the Infinite has created many Beings or Gods, vastly superior to Man, who can better conceive his Perfections than we, and return him a more rational and glorious Praise. . . .

> Howbeit, I conceive that each of these is exceeding wise, and good, and very powerful; and that Each has made for himself, one glorious Sun, attended with a beautiful and admirable System of Planets.

> It is that particular wise and good God, who is the Author and Owner of our System, that I propose for the Object of my Praise and Adoration.[13]

Here was one American, at least, who was prepared to accept a plurality of worlds and even a plurality of gods while still advocating a kind of working monotheism, all within a framework of reverence and awe.

Through the "enlightened" thinkers at the end of the eighteenth century a new, critical attitude toward the Bible entered America. Its roots were not in "higher criticism," the critical study of the character, composition, editing, and collection of biblical texts—which did not make a major impact until the mid-nineteenth century—but in the literary analysis and internal criticism of Richard Simon and Pierre Bayle in the seventeenth century as continued and popularized by the philosophes in the eighteenth. European deists and their American counterparts—Thomas Paine, for example—ridiculed much of the Bible for its inconsistencies, its primitive science, the questionable morality of many Old Testament heroes, and the implausible miracles of the New Testament. Those unwilling to go so far as to reject the Bible used it with careful selectivity, emphasizing the moral message but ignoring the embarrassing details. Jefferson, for example, published a private version of the Scriptures that was limited to the moral and ethical message. The pitfalls of translation and the virtual impossibility of getting back to the original text of the Bible were recognized by educated people. At least some of the problems, it appeared, were due to scribal error in the process of copying and recopying over the centuries and to unintentional mistranslations.[14]

It was in an effort to counteract indifference and skepticism that revivalism entered the scene. Starting as part of the Second Great Awakening during the 1790s in New England, revivals continued decade after decade as a primary means for the conversion of the unchurched or the rededication of the indifferent. In the first generation of the nineteenth century, revivals swept across upstate New York so frequently that it came to be known as the "burned-over district." At times, as contemporary accounts make clear, the camp meetings got out of hand, with excesses of shouting, raptures, and swooning. "The cry went up against hierarchies, seminary professors, dry learning, 'hireling ministers,' unconverted congregations, and 'cold' formalism," in Ahlstrom's description. "Farmers became theologians, offbeat village youths became bishops, odd girls became prophets."[15] At their best the revivals succeeded in bringing about a personal experience that changed the lives of individuals. But even those who were willing to dismiss the excesses in order to benefit from the positive gains were often troubled by three disconcerting questions: First, the permanence of the revival fervor, that is, its long-range impact on a congregation, seemed debatable. Second, for many, the kind of conversion insisted upon—a subjective internal experience—was either unattainable or at least a questionable qualification for salvation. Third, the competitive spirit between denominations sometimes led to wars of words and mutual denunciations that raised doubts as to which of the various churches was right, or suggested that they might all be wrong together.

An alternative approach, of major importance to Mormon beginnings, was the "primitive gospel" movement, a reaction against the revivals being promoted by evangelical Protestantism and the sectarian conflicts of claim and counterclaim. The primitive gospelers were widely separated, yet there was among them a common set of assumptions. Each segment of the movement was led by a layman or a man with only limited training in the ministry. Often a critic of a trained and professional clergy, this man felt that religion must be made more personal, more independent of organized institutions. These leaders awaited an approaching better day which the apocalyptic books of the Old and New Testaments had promised. Rejecting the pessimistic predestinarian views of the Calvinist faith, they hoped for a mass conversion to Christianity that would prepare the way for the Second Advent of Christ. "Finally, each of these religious innovators felt deep anguish at the sectarian variety and conflict which bewildered American churchmen in these years."[16]

The primitive gospelers shared with other radicals, such as the Unitarian Joseph Priestley, the view "that the established churches were corrupt, having departed from the ancient, primitive Christian faith."[17] During its first phase two prominent leaders of this primitive-gospel movement were Abner Jones and Elias Smith (no relation to Joseph Smith). Elias Smith attacked the "hireling clergy" and, interpreting biblical prophecies, saw the American Revolution as a fulfillment of Daniel's prophecy. A millennial reign of Christ on earth was expected soon, and various events of the day were seen as "signs of the times." From its beginning, the Campbellite movement was strongly permeated with the primitive-gospel point of view. Starting in 1809 as the Christian Association of Washington, the Campbellites denounced the existing denominations. Alexander Campbell and his colleagues preached what they called the restored gospel. Instead of trying to bring about a subjective religious experience or conversion, they preached an objective "plan of salvation," which had the following points: faith, repentance, baptism for the remission of sins, receiving the gift of the Holy Spirit, and eternal life.[18] The movement enjoyed rapid growth in the Ohio Valley and elsewhere.

Finally, it should be noted that communitarian societies were enjoying some popularity. Not new to America in the strict sense, such societies took root in American soil and seemed to flourish. The most prominent of these were the communities established by the Shakers, a sect fundamentally biblical in orientation, millennialist in doctrine, and revivalistic in spirit.[19] The Shakers incorporated some highly unusual patterns of worship that bordered on later Pentecostalism, and they developed certain attitudes toward sex, marriage, and procreation that eventually doomed the movement to oblivion; they were open to heavenly manifestations and revelations through Ann Lee, their prophetess, and, after her death, through others.[20]

It would be misleading to see deists, Unitarians, Universalists, primitive-gospel advocates, Campbellites, and Shakers as constituting anything like a majority or even a substantial minority within American Christianity. The mainstream—representing perhaps 90 percent of church *members*—was still found in Episcopalian, Presbyterian, Congregationalist, Methodist, Baptist, and Roman Catholic congregations. But because of the large percentage of unchurched Americans (about 90 percent) and the simmering dissatisfaction within the established denominations, the fringe groups had an importance out of proportion to their numbers.

What did Mormonism have to offer in such a context? Its message as preached and accepted in the 1830s and 1840s was usually simple: God has spoken again, and Joseph Smith is his prophet. The heavens are not sealed but God is again revealing his will to men. God exists, a real being of material body. The Father and the Son are literal, separate beings. The true church of Jesus Christ is restored to earth with authority to act. The gifts of the spirit enjoyed by Christians at the time of the apostles are again available to the faithful. Salvation is to be attained by faith, repentance, baptism, and the laying on of hands for the gift of the Holy Ghost, steps to be followed, of course, by unbroken faithfulness to the end. In the Book of Mormon, in

Joseph Smith's revelations, in pamphlets and sermons, these were the claims advanced by Mormon missionaries:

1. Restoration of the true church. In a manner commending itself to the general restorationist position of the primitive gospelers, the Mormons claimed that the true church of Christ, which had been taken from the early church as a result of apostasy and corruption, was now again on the earth. The idea meant in part that the practices of the original Christianity were again on the earth—a lay ministry, baptism of believers by immersion, and the gifts of the spirit. But especially basic to the concept of Restoration was the priesthood. The priesthood, or authority to act in God's name, had been taken from the earth sometime in the early centuries of Christian history but was now restored to earth. The Mormon church, therefore, was not only like the original Christian church but had the same sacerdotal authority, without which any attempt to restore would result only in dead forms.

To many, this came as a recognizable variation of the primitive-gospel theme mentioned earlier: the assumed corruption and apostasy of Christianity, the need to return to pure biblical practices. The primitive-gospel frame of mind was prominent in the thinking of Joseph Smith's grandfathers, and his uncle, and his parents. His mother, Lucy Mack Smith, told of her efforts to obtain the "change of heart" advocated by evangelical Christianity:

> To accomplish this I spent much of my time in reading the Bible and praying; but, notwithstanding my great anxiety to experience a change of heart, another matter would always interpose in all my meditations: If I remain a member of no church all religious people will say I am of the world; and, if I join some one of the different denominations, all the rest will say I am in error. No church will admit that I am right, except the one with which I am associated. This makes them witnesses against each other; and how can I decide in such a case as this, seeing they are all unlike the church of Christ as it existed in former days![21]

Significantly, her conclusions were basically the same as those later reached by her son Joseph at the time of his First Vision. As for the father, Joseph senior, he "would not subscribe to any particular system of faith, but contended for the ancient order, as established by our Lord and Savior Jesus Christ, and his apostles."[22] The Smiths were, in contemporary terms, primitive gospelers.

Over and over again, the early converts to the Mormon faith turned out to have been of the same predisposition. Dissatisfied with revivalism and with the existing denominations, seekers of biblical Christianity, the converts recognized what they were looking for when they heard the Mormon message. Joel Hills Johnson, who later became a Mormon elder, told of his experience in about 1818: "I would often sit up almost all night to read religious tracts and papers by firelight [and] also read the Bible with much attention, and joy would spring up in my heart with a testimony that the time would come when I should come in possession of . . . the faith once delivered to the Saints."[23] Wilford Woodruff, a deeply religious young man, did not join any church before 1830 "for the reason that I could not find any denomination whose doctrines, faith and practice agreed with the Gospel of Jesus Christ, or the ordinances and gifts which the Apostles taught."[24] Oliver Huntington withdrew from the Presbyterian church in 1832, believing "they had a form of Godliness but denied the power thereof." He "searched the scriptures daily and found the faith once delivered to the Saints was not among men."[25] Other early Mormons whose positions were basically the same included Newel Knight, Edward Hunter, Amasa Lyman, Parley Pratt, John Taylor, Daniel Tyler, Willard Richards, Nathaniel Henry Felt, and Lorenzo Snow.[26]

Not all who joined the Mormons were primitive gospelers in the specific sense.[27] If many had remained aloof from church affiliation while awaiting the restoration of the ancient order of things, many others were members of the existing denominations. Analyzing the thirty-four men who were in the First Presidency and Quorum of the Twelve—the top echelon of Mormon leaders—between 1832 and 1849, one scholar has found that ten had been Methodist, one Baptist, five Disciples of Christ, two Presbyterian, three Congregationalist, one Shaker, eight unaffiliated (some of these were undoubtedly seekers), and four unknown, with several men having affiliated with more than one religious group before Mormonism.[28] What must be acknowledged is the possibility of belonging to a group such as the Methodists, even showing considerable fervor, while still remaining uneasy about certain questions. One example of more than passing interest was the Reverend Orson Spencer, a Baptist clergyman who had graduated from Union College in 1824 and Hamilton Literary and Theological College in 1829. A well-known preacher, Spencer was once invited to become minister of the church where the governor of Massachusetts worshipped. In trying to explain his conversion to Mormonism, Spencer wrote in 1842:

> The Spirit of God wrought mightily in me, commending the ancient gospel to my conscience. I contemplated it with peaceful serenity and joy in believing. Visions and dreams began to illuminate, occasionally, my slumbering moments; but when I allowed my selfish propensities to speak, I cursed "Mormonism" in my heart, and regretted being in possession of as much light and knowledge as had flowed into my mind from that source. When I preached or conversed according to my best convictions, peace reigned in my heart, and truth enlarged my understanding. . . .
>
> I counted the cost, to myself and family, of embracing such views, until I could read it like the child his alphabet, either upward or downward. The expense I viewed through unavoidable tears, both in public and private, by

night and by day; I said, however, the Lord He is God, I *can, I will* embrace the truth.[29]

It was the "ancient gospel" that attracted Spencer so irresistibly. "What could I do?" he asked. "Truth had taken possession of my mind—plain, simple Bible truth."

2. *Biblicism.* Mormons were believers in the Bible, but with a difference. The *Brookville* (Ind.) *Enquirer* noted that Orson Pratt made "no lame attempt" at presenting the plain meaning of the Bible.[30] Sidney Rigdon, preaching in Kirtland, presented what he called "plain scripture facts."[31] Whenever they could appeal their case to the Bible, said several Mormon elders, they were sure of victory in any contest. They confidently asked ministers of other faiths to meet them on "bible ground."[32]

In their use of the Bible, though persistently logical in presentation and appealing to "common sense," the Mormons were strikingly literalist, contemptuous of "spiritualizing" the prophecies. Not surprisingly, the Mormons cited most frequently those biblical passages that served their purposes. Topics buttressed by New Testament scriptures, for instance, included especially (1) the primitive church pattern; (2) the expectation of apostasy and later restoration; (3) millennialism; and (4) the uniformity of the gospel. Old Testament passages, too, were used with selectivity, emphasizing millennialism and gospel uniformity (that the patriarchs and prophets looked forward to Christ and his church) along with the special role of Israel in the divine strategy.[33] One could easily compile a Mormon Bible including only Mormon proof texts; the result would be, if not a pamphlet, at least a small book. Like the followers of other sects, the Mormons utilized "selective emphasis."[34]

There were more important qualifications of Mormon belief in the Bible. "We believe the Bible to be the word of God as far as it is translated correctly," wrote Joseph Smith in 1842.[35] *As far as it is translated correctly*—this dependent clause seems obvious enough. It showed at least partial awareness of the problems of transmission from the time of original writing to the present. The Book of Mormon explained more explicitly that "many plain and precious things" had been lost or removed from the Scriptures. Thus a huge loophole was identified: Passages that seemed to contradict the Mormon position could be explained as mistranslations. Starting as early as 1830 Joseph Smith began preparing a new version of the Bible, sometimes called a "translation" but actually the correction or expansion of certain passages in the King James Version.[36] Without consulting texts in the original languages (he did not then have the linguistic competence, even had such texts been available), Smith made changes on the basis of what he claimed was inspiration. Some examples:

KING JAMES VERSION	JOSEPH SMITH'S REVISION
Jer. 18:8 If that nation, against whom I have pronounced, turn from their evil I will repent of the evil that I thought to do unto them.	If that nation, against whom I have pronounced, turn from their evil, I will withhold the evil that I thought to do unto them.
Matt. 6:13 And lead us not into temptation, but deliver us from evil.	And suffer us not to be led into temptation, but deliver us from evil.
Matt. 7:1 Judge not, that ye be not judged.	Judge not unrighteously, that ye be not judged; but judge righteous judgment.

Many changes were innocuous, even commonsense in nature. Others were more elaborate, having important doctrinal implications. More than a few of the revelations Smith published during the 1830s were "triggered" by the systematic study of the Bible he was engaged in. Clearly he did not feel obligated to accept the Bible in its current authorized version as any kind of constraint on the unfolding doctrines of the church. Yet most, if not all, fundamental Mormon assertions could be supported by biblical scripture.

3. *The Book of Mormon.* Published in 1830, the Book of Mormon immediately set Smith's movement apart from other restorationist attempts. It was something tangible. It could be read and reacted to, in fact *had* to be accounted for in some specific way—not merely passed off as interesting or not, as ideas could be. Almost immediately upon its publication, as previously suggested, there were counterexplanations for the book: It had been secretly written by Sidney Rigdon, who was sometimes said to have used as his basis a romance written earlier by Solomon Spaulding. Later critics have rejected this theory as unproved and more willingly see Smith himself as author of the book.[37] In either case, of course, there is no inclination by non-Mormon scholars to accept the book's claim to be an ancient document written by prophets on the American continent between 600 B.C. and A.D. 421. The book is viewed by non-Mormons as a product of nineteenth-century America, whether actually written by Smith or simply taken over by him. Alexander Campbell's summary of the book has been widely quoted. It reproduced, he said,

> every error and almost every truth discussed in New York for the last ten years. [It] decides all the great controversies—infant baptism, ordination, the trinity, regeneration, repentance, justification, the fall of man, the atonement, transubstantiation, fasting, penance, church government, religious experience, the call of the ministry, the general resurrection, eternal

punishment, who may baptize, and even the question of free masonry, republican government, and the rights of man.[38]

Campbell's list is meant to suggest that the book substantially concerned itself with current issues. Granting this, the book could then be read, at least in part, as specifically designed to answer to the needs of its contemporary readers. Rev. Orson Spencer, who was familiar with anti-Mormon publications, tells of his own contrasting reaction:

> I arose from its perusal with a strong conviction on my mind, that its pages were graced with the pen of inspiration. I was surprised that so little fault could be found with a book of such magnitude, treating, as it did, of such diversified subjects, through a period of so many generations. It appeared to me that no enemy to truth or godliness would ever take the least interest in publishing the contents of such a book; such appeared to me its godly bearing, sound morality, and harmony with ancient scriptures, that the enemy of all righteousness might as well proclaim the dissolution of his own kingdom, as to spread the contents of such a volume among men; and from that time to this, every effort made by its enemies to demolish, has only shown how invincible a fortress defends it. . . . On this subject I only ask the friends of pure religion to read the Book of Mormon with the same unprejudiced, prayerful, and teachable spirit that they would recommend unbelievers in the ancient scriptures to read those sacred records.[39]

Spencer's observation suggests that for many converts, the Book of Mormon answered disquieting controversies.

Those who have not read the Book of Mormon, or have only sampled its contents, will find it difficult to understand why people of the 1830s and 1840s often found the work so exciting. It was not merely that answers to current problems were supplied by the book, although Campbell was correct in recognizing that the work did seem relevant to many issues of the day. Within the frame of reference of the time, the work had several features that a modern marketing expert could have turned into advertising "blurbs."

First, it was an interesting story. Lehi and his family were living at Jerusalem in the year 600 B.C. when they were called by God to lead a colony into the wilderness. A dangerous return to Jerusalem for forgotten records is followed by a harrowing struggle for survival in adjacent deserts. Finally they reach the sea and with divine guidance build a ship. Internal family squabbles have developed and continue. After an ocean voyage, the company finally reaches the New World, a promised land. Here the story of conflict between Lehi's sons and the eventual division of his descendants into two warring factions, the Nephites and the Lamanites, is recounted. After several centuries a time of culmination is reached with the comprehensively prophesied appearance of the resurrected Jesus Christ in the New World. Then, after a utopian period of righteousness and prosperity, human nature reasserts itself in further schisms and conflicts.

The work is incredibly complex. There are flashbacks and flashbacks within flashbacks, dramatic missionary journeys as well as terrible wars. Sermons and prophecies appear frequently, each of them containing important religious messages, and all unified by a concern to proclaim the divinity of Christ. Several prophetic dreams or visions provide a panoramic view of human history and its meaning, particularly of America and its European ("gentile") settlers as well as its native Indian ("Lamanite") occupants. To an age not yet surfeited with the novel or the mass media, an age that found the Bible itself interesting, the Book of Mormon could be read easily, if only for its compelling and fascinating narrative.

The book also clarified problematical passages in the Bible. It was not, in its own terms, a substitute for the Bible but rather a complement to it. In his appearance among the Nephites, Christ gives a modified version of his Sermon on the Mount, making clear that some of the exacting ethic of that statement was intended not for all Christians but for the immediate apostles with their special callings. He tells the Nephites that they are the ones he had in mind when, in Judea, he had said, "Other sheep I have which are not of this fold. Them also I must bring." The possibility of interpreting the sacrament of the Lord's Supper as transubstantiation was avoided by the inclusion of specific sacramental prayers. Throughout, the Book of Mormon contains this kind of information, never clashing with the biblical dicta, but frequently explaining and clarifying them.

While answering religious questions, the book does so with an occasional ambiguity that enhanced its appeal. On the question of the nature of God, certain passages blur the distinction between the Father and the Son, but others imply a distinction among the three divine persons. The nothingness of man—compared, that is, with God and man's own possibilities—is declared: "O how foolish, and how vain, and how evil, and devilish, and how quick to do iniquity, and how slow to do good, are the children of men. . . . O how great is the nothingness of the children of men; yea, even they are less than the dust of the earth."[40] But original sin is rejected, and a frequently reiterated theme is the free agency of man and the importance of his own works to his ultimate destiny. A profoundly optimistic—almost humanistic—view is taken of Adam, the Fall, and man's purpose: "Adam fell, that men might be; and men are, that they might have joy."[41] The work is not simply Arminian, as Thomas O'Dea maintains; a critic would find that it is both Arminian and Calvinist, containing elements that could appeal to both groups.[42] It has the complexity of the Bible, expressing itself as recounted human experience of the Divine rather than with the syllogistic unity of a work of theology or a tract.

Moreover, the Book of Mormon provided a sweeping historical context for the history of the New World, at once explaining the origin of the American Indian (a subject of current interest and speculation) and relating the New World to the divine plan for mankind.[43] America is declared "a land choice above all other lands," and its discovery by Columbus and even the winning of independence from Great Britain are shown, in prophecy, as fulfillment of God's will.[44] It seems doubtful that any reader would set out in a simpleminded way to find a work offering an enlarged historical context for America or that he would consider the Book of Mormon acceptable for this reason alone. But that it answered deep psychological needs of many of its readers seems clear, and the strong purposeful thrust of its narrative was to work in its favor.

Finally, the Book of Mormon could be viewed as a concrete piece of evidence, something that could be subjected to tests. From the first edition it was always printed with accompanying statements by witnesses who, as previously described, claimed to have seen and "hefted" the plates from which it was translated.[45] It could be scrutinized internally for contradictions. It could be compared with the Bible. It could be seen as the explanation of the ruins being discovered in Central America, the discoveries serving as further confirmation and proof.[46] And it could be read prayerfully in the expectation that God in his mercy would make known whether or not the work was what it claimed to be. In experimental terms, then, the book offered evidence at a time when Christian claims in general sometimes appeared fragile or indefinite.

4. *Modern revelation.* Along with the Bible and the Book of Mormon the new religion put forth various "revelations"—communications from God to his prophet. To understand why they would exert an appeal instead of simply appearing as transparent pretensions, it is necessary to read them. The revelations, as now published, fill up a medium-sized book. Removed from the circumstances in which they originally appeared, they are not always easy to understand.[47] Some points can be made, however, that will help to explain how they appeared to the early Mormon converts.

The revelations contained answers to members' current questions. God, who is the same yesterday, today, and tomorrow, would not reveal his will in the past without being willing to reveal it today—this was the premise. Is revelation to be received only by the prophet? No; others could enjoy the same gift. Should I expect the appearance of an angel in response to my prayer? No; you should study the matter out in your mind, prayerfully, and God will guide your thinking, causing a stupor of thought to come over you when considering possible "wrong" decisions, a "burning of the bosom" to attest to truths. May I receive a revelation for the whole church? No; such messages come to the designated prophet. Should I follow the recommendations of dietary crusaders? You should refrain from tobacco, alcohol, tea, and coffee and should eat grain, fresh fruits, and "little meat." How shall I prepare myself for service in the church? Study the best books, including the Scriptures, treasuring up words of life that can be used later in preaching. Can I read the Apocrypha as Scripture? You are free to read these works, for they contain much good, but as they also contain error, they should be used with caution.

Some of the revelations are constitutional documents setting forth the order and organization of the church. What are the offices in the church? What are the duties of the different priesthood offices? What church records should be kept when a member moves? Coming as revelations, they carried an authoritative force that might be lacking had they been the product of a committee.

Some of the revelations expand on theological questions. They explain to the believer that God is a being of body, parts, and passions, the Godhead consisting of three separate beings united in purpose. The postmortal existence of man is spelled out in greater detail than elsewhere: There are three kingdoms or degrees; all mankind (except a few sons of perdition) will be "saved" in one of these kingdoms; only the inhabitants of the highest, the Celestial, are in the presence of God; those who are faithful in all things can look forward to "exaltation" in the Celestial kingdom, qualifying them to become "gods" and "goddesses" and creators of worlds. The Mormon cosmology—"worlds without end have I created"—with a vast sweep extending from a preexistence to future divine possibilities, is thus set forth with the purpose, as one Mormon writer has said, not of humanizing God but of deifying man, not as he is but as he may become.[48] Universalists, who had rejected the notion of damnation and eternal hellfire for the majority of souls, could find such ideas extremely appealing. A Benjamin Franklin would not be put off by the expansive concept of a plurality of gods, and those who found the traditional description of heaven static and unexciting could respond favorably to the portrayal of future progress, a continued dynamic existence, the infinite potential of man, and the expanding universe. Baptism for the dead, mentioned only once in the New Testament (though fairly widespread in early Christianity), was introduced in one of the revelations. This restored practice was for Mormon believers a marvelous reassertion of Christ's emphasis on earthly baptism as essential to salvation for every person, together with a provision for those who had not had opportunity to make such a decision in mortal life to accept the truth in the future life if they wished and then have available to them a vicarious performance of the earthly ordinance done by others for them in this life. Thus there was regular opportunity for loving concern and service to be expressed from children to their ancestors, and at the same time a satisfying demonstration of the fairness and justice of God.

Although some of these "advanced" doctrines did not reach scattered members of the church at once, and there is evidence of reluctance on the part of some to go beyond the simple Mormonism they had accepted in the early 1830s, most believers saw them, not as a stumbling block, but as evidence that Joseph Smith was indeed a prophet of God. The power that had enabled the ancient prophets of the Bible to reveal God's will was again on the earth. The message was basically the same, but it was adapted to modern needs. The doctrines themselves were seen not as contradictory to the Bible or the Book of Mormon but as a magnificent amplification of them.

The revelations affecting the human condition were conditional prophecies. When fulfilled, these predictions were, for the faithful, powerful confirmation of Smith's prophetic role. When not fulfilled, there was an escape clause: Fulfillment had been conditioned upon repentance, or—as when Jackson County was not occupied as Zion but abandoned in the face of persecution—the Saints had been contentious or insufficiently faithful. In 1832 Smith prophesied in remarkable detail that a war between the states would break out in South Carolina. When it did not happen immediately, the believers simply bided their time and found Joseph Smith's status as a true prophet confirmed at the beginning of the Civil War in 1861.[49]

5. *Eschatology.* It would be a serious error to think of the appeals of Mormonism only in terms of its doctrines regarding God, man, and salvation. As important as they were, they were frequently overshadowed, especially during the 1830s, by millenarian and eschatological claims regarding the end of the world and the Second Coming of Christ. The hymns sung in the church during these years, to judge from those printed in periodicals before the first hymnal, usually proclaimed the imminence of the Parousia (Second Coming).[50] "Know assuredly," wrote Parley P. Pratt to Queen Victoria in 1841, "that the world in which we live is on the eve of a REVOLUTION, more powerful in its beginning—more rapid in its progress—more lasting in its influence—more important in its consequences—than any which man has yet witnessed upon the earth."[51] Although Smith himself was usually tentative and nonspecific regarding the exact timetable, some of his followers were emphatic that the conclusive scene would occur within a few years, within their own lifetimes at the outside.[52] All kinds of world events, especially calamities and wars, were "signs of the times," evidences confirming the forthcoming time when the earth would be renewed, receive paradisiacal glory, and Christ would reign personally upon the earth.[53]

Since adventism and millenarianism appealed to some Americans of the early nineteenth century, it is significant that Mormonism contained such an element. Nevertheless, as usual, there were differences. If premillenarians believed that the coming of Christ would precede the thousand-year reign of peace and postmillenarians thought his coming would conclude it, nineteenth-century Mormons have been described technically as premillenarians.[54] But of greater significance than the time of the miraculous events, for Mormons, was the place. And at that place—first Missouri, then Nauvoo, Illinois, finally Utah with promise of a future return to the Zion of Jackson County, Missouri—the Mormons were to establish the moral, social, and political conditions necessary before Christ's return could occur. There was something to do, here and now, an immediate challenge of kingdom-building that was still charged with eternal significance for the working out of God's purposes in history. As early as 1837, a Universalist visitor to Kirtland declared that the Saints had "too much worldly wisdom connected with their religion—too great a desire for the perishable riches of this world—holding out the idea that the kingdom of Christ is to be composed of 'real estate, herds, flocks, silver, gold,' etc., as well as of human beings."[55] But for the majority of early Mormons this was not a weakness but a strength, evidence that religion had application to the here-and-now rather than being concerned only with a "beatific vision" or "mansions above," and that it dealt with the whole man rather than dichotomizing the spirit and the flesh.

This brings us back to the question of economic motivation. Considering that many, perhaps most, Mormon converts throughout the nineteenth century were people of the lower classes, was not the promise of an inheritance in a new Zion (whatever the location) the most compelling feature of the Mormon message? This charge was especially prevalent after the exodus to the West and after the establishment of the Perpetual Emigration Fund, which offered (much like modern student-loan programs) an immediate payment of part or all of the emigration expenses with the expectation, which was to be only partially fulfilled, of a future reimbursement. In 1869 the Mormon apostle Lorenzo Snow implicitly acknowledged that the charge contained more than a little truth. After recalling Moses' preaching to the Israelites and his promise to take them out of bondage, Snow said:

> It is the same when a Sectarian minister goes to England. He knocks at a man's door and says: "I am a missionary from America." Well, the man on whom he calls is in distress. Says he: "I am sorry I cannot take you in; but I am in distress. It is mealtime but my family has nothing to eat. I am out of employment and have nothing to live upon. I wish I could relieve your wants, but I have nothing with which to assist you." Oh, says the minister, you must wait upon Providence, you must have a great deal of patience and long-suffering. I am come to preach to you the gospel, and you must pray and keep praying until you think you have got a pardon of your sins; but still remain where you are. No redemption!
> Well, now, that is different from the "Mormon" Elder's manner. He presents himself in something like this way: "I have come in the name of the Almighty, in obedience to a call from God, to deliver you from your present

circumstances. Repent of your sins and be baptised, and the Holy Ghost shall rest upon you, and you shall know that I have the authority to administer the ordinances of the Gospel by the power of the Almighty and the revelations of God. Gather out from this nation, for it is ripening in iniquity, there is no salvation here. Flee to a place of safety." And as the messenger who went to Sodom said to the family whom he found there, so says the Elder of Israel, telling them, as Moses did the children of Israel, "to go to the land that the Lord God has appointed for the gathering of His people."[56]

So the "gathering," involving a physical removal that symbolized and paralleled the spiritual removal, could hold out hopes of a better land in the West. The traditional forces that promoted immigration thus worked to stimulate the Mormon converts. But this cannot be seen as a simple factor: Moving to join the body of the Saints often entailed enormous hardship; the inevitable ridicule and persecution served as a kind of automatic screening device; and church leaders and missionaries tried to assure religious commitment on the part of those who gathered. If their efforts were not wholly successful, they were relatively so, and most converts to Mormonism must be considered, in the absence of clear evidence to the contrary, to have been sincere. Many lost property, money, and friends. If some did well for themselves in the new environment, they were people of an entrepreneurial spirit who, except for the rigid class distinctions of the time, might have succeeded in any community. If the economic consequences of conversion, whether positive or negative, were part of the picture, they should be seen within the context of Mormonism's answers to religious and psychological needs.

6. *Mythic potency.* In saying that the Latter-day religion gave satisfactory answers to many questions people asked about their relationship to society, to God, and to the universe, we are recognizing that Mormonism exerted what Mircea Eliade has called a "mythic potency." The lives of human beings, Eliade asserts, whether in archaic or modern societies, have been given meaning and importance by means of "myths"—what he also calls "true stories" or "sacred histories." In this sense the Christian gospel as restored by Joseph Smith provided a satisfying "true story" of sacred events. In fact, it was perhaps this characteristic that most clearly separated Mormonism from the many other restorationist groups, with which it shared many features and from which it drew many of its converts. A convert might have first been attracted to Mormonism's strong claim to be New Testament Christianity restored. But once in the church, he was soon involved, both intellectually and experientially, in what Smith often referred to as the "ancient order of things." For instance, when an economic system for the church was needed, Smith did not announce a carefully devised rational plan that appealed to contemporary experience, but issued a revelation that was essentially the story

of how things were done—what God's pattern was—in very ancient times, and the proclaimed system was in fact called the Order of Enoch. It may even be that this characteristic reaching back behind the modes of a rationalistic, individualistic political and social order that had gained ascendancy since the Enlightenment—to theocracy, communitarian living, temple rituals, and so forth—was a major cause for the perplexity and eventual fury that Mormonism aroused, but by responding to human yearnings with basic and lasting archetypes, the religion induced faith and understanding and commanded the loyalty of thousands who accepted it.[57]

7. *Religious authoritarianism.* In 1966 Mario S. De Pillis wrote "The Quest for Religious Authority and the Rise of Mormonism," in which he noted the widespread search in the nineteenth century for divinely authorized religion.[58] A Roman Catholic, De Pillis might be expected to understand this emphasis rather more than Protestant historians. He noted that the dismay over Christianity's divisions led to antisectarianism, the desire to establish not just another, alternative mode but the one true and divinely authorized Christian religion. Recognizing that others shared this concern, De Pillis noted "how much stronger the Mormon quest for authority was than that of the Campbellites, Shakers, and others who preached against sectarianism, how much more elaborate and theologically central was the Mormon concern for authoritative religion than, for example, Campbell's exaggerated reliance on the New Testament or the Shakers' faith in the postmillennial ministry of their foundress." For Mormons, De Pillis concludes: "Only the restored Priesthood could save a torn and divided Christianity."[59]

Joseph Smith's own spiritual pilgrimage was thus a paradigm of that of many who joined the movement. They shared a desire to know which church was right, a sense of repugnance at the "warring sects," impatience and rejection of the creeds and official orthodox theologies, and they found the answer in a restoration not only of propositional truths but, more important, of the sacerdotal authority that had been lost from the Christian church many centuries earlier. To the extent that "seekers" shared these concerns, Mormonism provided answers. Campbellite preachers who abandoned another restorationist movement for Mormonism—Sidney Rigdon, Lyman Wight, Parley P. Pratt, and others—were to some extent motivated by its superior claim to divine authority.[60] Likewise, the Irvingite congregation in England, already primitivist in its basic stance, would find in Mormonism the same idea of a return to the truths of primitive Christianity with the additional feature, indispensable to some minds, of a restored, divinely authorized priesthood.[61]

More concrete than the claim of "true authority" was the very real power that became increasingly available to Latter-day Saints through Mormonism's nearly universal male priesthood and the communitarian direction by that priesthood. The highest echelons of the Mormon ecclesia not only controlled the religious life but exercised direction over city building, education, politics, economics, and social activities. Those powers filtered down in varying degrees to the mass of the priesthood. At Nauvoo, Joseph Smith would unfold a system by which Mormon men and women might qualify to become members of a godlike nobility (in a preparatory, symbolic sense) on earth as a rehearsal for actual investiture hereafter. For the masses of Latter-day Saint converts, Mormonism supplied an opportunity for status, prestige, and power. The Nietzschean "will to power" is an aspect of religious conversion that virtually no proselyte would acknowledge, even if he were conscious of it. But Mormonism, like democracy, provided abundant access to power and influence for people who had not experienced enough of it. Access to power was a barely concealed motive for the conversion of John C. Bennett to Mormonism (as well as his later efforts as an ex-Mormon to assist the schismatics Sidney Rigdon and James J. Strang), and frustration in the exercise of that newly achieved power was a frequent cause of many ecclesiastical court trials during the first decades of Mormonism, in which men openly accused others of "diminishing my influence." The desire for power and prestige was undoubtedly one of the responsive chords that reverberated to the message of restorationist, authoritative, communitarian yet individualistic Mormonism.

But to see the claim to authority as the key to Mormon success is too narrow. If religious chaos was one part of the background, skepticism was the other. For those who tended toward a skeptical attitude Mormonism provided not tortured syllogisms but concrete evidence. The proofs the new faith brought in support of its claims fell into several categories. First, as we have seen, there were the Old and New Testament passages that enabled Mormon preachers to show that their religion had been foreseen. Acceptable or not, the Mormon use of the Bible was difficult to counteract. Second, there were gifts of the spirit, primarily healing and speaking in tongues. To those who experienced them and at least some who observed them, these were the New Testament "signs" promised to those who believed. Third, there was the Book of Mormon, a work that had somehow to be accounted for. Although the canons of proof were not clearly spelled out, it should be clear that within their frame of reference the Mormon claims appeared well supported.

Evidence was increasingly important in another stream of the Christian tradition: the reaction against revival preaching that removed faith "from the realm of introspection" and placed it "in the realm of evidence." Impatient with the emphasis on some kind of internal transformation that was hard to experience and impossible to prove, antirevivalists redefined faith as assent to propositions. Barton Stone and other "New Light" Presbyterians were preaching this notion, as, in the 1830s, was William Kinkade, who said, "Faith is a relying on evidence." Similarly, for Alexander Campbell there could be no faith without testimony. In this context a young scholar's recent summary of Mormonism is relevant:

> Mormonism demanded of its converts not only that they repent of their sins and reform their lives, but also that they make a number of unique belief commitments. Latter-day Saints were asked to affirm *that* Joseph Smith was a prophet of God, *that* the primitive gospel had been restored through him, *that* the Book of Mormon was a true record of ancient prophets on the American continent. The Book of Mormon itself was conceived as another piece of evidence "to the convincing of the Jew and Gentile that Jesus is the Christ, the Eternal God."[62]

There are difficulties for intellectuals with a conception of faith relying on testimony. How, asked J. B. Turner, were honest men to be protected from any knave who chose to "draw on a long face and come to you in the name of the Lord?"[63] But psychologically such a concept seemed fairly rational, and once certain assumptions had been accepted, the Mormon message had the support of confirming evidence in an age when such evidence was desperately sought by many Christians.[64]

One must avoid exaggerating the importance of all of this in the conversion experiences of the time. All agreed that the *sine qua non* was the manifestation of the Spirit, or the still small voice—some kind of inner confirmation by which one knew and knew that he knew. This sensation of conviction, usually referred to as the individual's "testimony," was maddening to outsiders, who found it hard to reason with or to combat. Orson Spencer concluded his defense of the Book of Mormon with an appeal to the reader to trust in his own prayerfully received witness: "On this subject [the Book of Mormon] I only ask the friends of pure religion to read the Book of Mormon with the same unprejudiced, prayerful, and teachable spirit that they would recommend unbelievers in the ancient scriptures to read those sacred records."[65] External evidence was not, therefore, the sole source of the decisions to convert. It was circumstantial, confirming, predisposing. And it was cumulative, multiplying its force with each additional factor. But conversion itself was individual, personal, spiritual.

Once in the fold, the convert found himself reinforced by a variety of influences. Immediately he became involved. The dramatic appeal of gathering required action that usually meant breaking with friends and relatives. Uprooting themselves and their families, the new Saints migrated to the gathering place of the moment and there attempted to put down roots. Once such decisions were made—and occasionally emotional scenes led to strong declarations—any reversal was extremely difficult. Involvement by physical removal was reinforced by the lay nature of the Mormon organization, which required most adults to take part in some kind of leadership or missionary role. Few sincere male converts failed to have the opportunity of preaching the restored gospel as missionaries. The movement was not designed to encourage lukewarm bystanders or occasional attenders; it required willingness to participate as teachers, branch leaders, missionaries, scribes. Activity created lines of connection that were difficult to sever. Finally, psychological bonds were reinforced by financial bonds, as the payment of tithing and other offerings in effect turned the faithful into stockholders.

Anti-Mormon writers of the past century did not portray all Saints as villains. Their explanation was that the mass of Mormons were sincere dupes victimized by a sinister group of leaders. While the evidence of sincerity on the part of Mormon authorities is overwhelming, it is undeniable that Mormon leaders did exert an immense influence over their followers. This direction was in the first instance personal. Joseph Smith was a man of enormous vitality and magnetism. Those who became his followers were drawn to him both as a person and as a prophet and held him in affection. What also needs to be recognized is that the second echelon of leaders included compelling preachers, deeply committed men who had excellent rapport with those they taught. Brigham Young, Heber C. Kimball, Orson Pratt, George A. Smith, Charles C. Rich, Franklin D. Richards, Erastus Snow, and others—these were men of real ability who possessed the spiritual fire needed to attract followers and the conviction necessary to buoy them up through adversity. In personal terms these traits could serve as a magnet in drawing converts into the fold.[66]

The authoritative nature of this leadership—the followers expected to "counsel" on such matters as place of residence, mission calls, occupation, and even whom to marry—gave the believers a sense of security. The responsibility was on shoulders other than their own; if they but followed faithfully, all would be right. Some reacted negatively, but the appeals of a "flight from freedom" should not be underestimated.[67]

The promises and hopes of material improvement, the charismatic leadership, and the involvement in a going concern are similar to the attractions that have drawn "true believers" to other movements.[68] Just as uprooted and confused people have rallied to various causes for largely psychological reasons, many Mormons were influenced less by the ideas than their own emotional and psychological needs. The spiritual alienation and lack of meaning in life characteristic of modern society were noted in the nineteenth century by Karl Marx, Sören Kierkegaard, and others. If Mormonism as it was preached to the confused and disinherited of America and Europe seemed to hold out hopes for a new tomorrow, the chance of putting down stakes in Zion, working out one's salvation, and an imminent coming of Christ; if it brought the cheerless and lonely into groups where they were called brother and sister and made to feel part of a family; if it provided a sense of direction and possibilities of progress to many who had fallen into despair—it should not be surprising that it attracted followers.

In Mormonism, then, the converts found security. And they found answers. What was the nature of God? What was the nature of man? What is the purpose of life? What reassurances can I look forward to in the future history of the world? What will be my status in the hereafter? What will be my relationship there to parents, wife, and children? Sydney Ahlstrom's observation about Emanuel Swedenborg is applicable with equal force to Joseph Smith:

> There are many clues to [his] amazing capacity to satisfy such varied yearnings, but first among them was his self-assured optimism and his sweeping comprehensiveness. He made the whole universe religiously intelligible, giving satisfaction to those who were surfeited with revivalism and narrow-mindedness.[69]

The unique feature of Mormonism's appeal was its combination of theological intelligibility and spiritual reassurance with a specific program offering material and emotional satisfaction in the present. When many motives coincide, the results are powerful.

3

┥Early Persecutions┝

But little more than two years ago, some two or three of these people made their appearance on the Upper Missouri and they now number some 1,200 souls in this country, and each successive autumn and spring pours forth its swarm among us, with a gradual falling off in the character of those who compose it; until it seems that those communities from which they come, were flooding us with the very dregs of their composition.
—Resolutions of old settlers at Independence, Missouri (July 20, 1833)

The Mormons must be treated as enemies, and must be exterminated or driven from the State if necessary, for the public peace.
—Lilburn W. Boggs, governor of Missouri (1838)

Hiram, Ohio, March 14, 1832: Joseph Smith, the twenty-six-year-old Mormon prophet, sleeps exhaustedly on a trundle bed beside a sick infant he has spent much of the night caring for. Awakened suddenly by the screams of his wife Emma, he is seized by a dozen men who burst into the room and carry him out the door. He kicks and struggles, but large hands encompass his neck and choke him into unconsciousness. His head swimming, he revives while they carry him and sees his friend and counselor, Sidney Rigdon, stretched out on the ground. Assuming that Rigdon is dead, Smith pleads, "You will have mercy and spare my life, I hope." Loud curses are the only response. Men mill about in confusion, shouting and swearing; some demand that he be killed outright. A brief council is held, and apparently the consensus is against immediate death. Instead they strip off his clothes except for his shirt collar. One man falls upon the naked Smith and scratches his body, shouting, "Goddamn you, that's how the Holy Ghost falls on folks!" A vial is pushed into his mouth, but he breaks it with his teeth and spits it out. A bucket of steaming tar arrives, and his body is covered. Someone tries to force the tar paddle into his mouth. Suddenly the mob scatters, leaving him tarred and bruised on the ground. He struggles to rise but falls back. He jerks the tar away from his lips so that he can breathe more easily. After a moment's rest, pulling himself to his feet, he notices two lights in the distance. He staggers toward one of them, which turns out to be the house of a recent convert, John Johnson. As the young prophet reaches the door, naked and besmirched with tar, his (Smith's) anxious wife sees him and assumes he is covered with blood. He asks for a blanket, wraps it around himself, and goes inside.[1]

Independence, Missouri, July 20, 1833: A noisy mob of more than 300 men gather outside the residence of Mormon Bishop Edward Partridge. When he comes outside to inquire what they want, he is informed with much angry shouting that the Mormon store and printing establishment he directs must be closed. When he refuses to comply, he is seized and dragged to the public square near the courthouse. There the mob strips him of his outer clothing, daubs him with tar, and covers him with feathers. The mob gives Charles Allen, another Mormon, the same treatment. Meanwhile the house of W. W. Phelps, which contains the printing press, is reduced to rubble; scores of other Mormons, including women and children, are driven from their homes with yells and threats. Furniture from Phelps's house is scattered about his garden. As darkness falls, the Mormons straggle back from their hiding places in cornfields and thickets. Family members scrape the tar from Bishop Partridge.[2]

Haun's Mill, a small settlement near Far West, Missouri, October 30, 1838: In a state of anxiety because of growing general persecution and roving hostile "militia" bands, but feeling secure for the moment because of a recent treaty made with nearby militia, about thirty Mormon families, some recently arrived from the East, are camped in wagons and tents near homes and a mill belonging to some other Mormons. In the late afternoon the militia, about 240 strong in military formation, suddenly rides into the settlement and begins firing without warning. Despite no initial resistance and shouts of surrender, they continue firing, eventually killing seventeen and wounding twelve, some of whom die later. The main slaughter occurs when a number of Mormon men take refuge in an old blacksmith shop that has such large crevices in the walls that volley after volley fired through them turn it into a deathtrap. An old man, lying wounded, is shot through the heart and his body hacked at and mangled with a corn knife. A boy of nine, found hiding under the bellows of the blacksmith shop, is shot through the head with the comment, "Nits will make lice." When all who have not been able to flee have apparently been killed, the militia men loot the houses and tents, in some cases stripping the dead, and drive off with the horses and wagons.

Morley's Settlement, near Nauvoo, Illinois, September 10, 1845: Filled with fear inspired by recent events, the Mormons in this small settlement are disturbed to notice groups of men on horseback gathering nearby. Several of their haystacks and outbuildings soon burst into flames. This violence to property is only an overture to the actions of the next day. Despite a driving rain, the

e Mormon men, women, and children into the surrounding bushes.
nine houses, virtually the entire settlement, are burned to the
After huddling together for warmth during the night, the drenched
and pitiful group of Mormons make their way to Nauvoo.[3]

Why did the Mormons arouse such active hostility? It was present in
New York, Ohio, Missouri, Illinois, and Iowa. It followed them to Utah.
Manifestations of what most Mormons perceived as persecution moved west
with the church, including the "invasion" by the U.S. Army in the Utah
War of 1857–58, the legislative-judicial-executive campaign against Mormon
polygamy (mainly in the 1870s and the 1880s), and acts of hostility—including lynching—against individual Mormon missionaries, even in the twentieth century. Other minority religions—Shakers, Disciples, and Public
Friends—never attracted the persecution that followed the Mormons from
county to county, and from state to state. Persecution was not behavior that
most Americans praised; it was rather something from which they had hoped
to escape by coming to the New World. Religious tolerance was incorporated into the Bill of Rights and, by the early years of the nineteenth century, had been further strengthened by its inclusion in various state
constitutions. Yet the Mormons attracted animosity everywhere they went.
What was it about them that inflamed their enemies? What was it, indeed,
that turned friends into enemies?

To begin with, there was the repugnance felt for a religion that challenged many accepted values. Except for the small minority who greeted
Mormonism as the answer to unmet spiritual needs, most felt that its beliefs
were superstitious, disgusting, repellent. What was apparently most galling
was a mixture in Mormonism of what seemed to outsiders as a primitivistic
reversion to "unenlightened," even "un-American," beliefs. Mormon claims
to have witnessed divine revelations were ridiculed. Since this kind of denunciation began early in Joseph Smith's career, even before the church was organized, it formed a kind of substratum of animosity. In 1827 Smith said,
"rumor with her thousand tongues was all the time employed in circulating
falsehoods about my father's family, and about myself. . . . The persecution,
however, became so intolerable that I was under the necessity of leaving
Manchester" and moving to Pennsylvania.[4] The general attitude in New
York, to judge from the few contemporary accounts, was one of disdain for
claims to revelation in the modern age.

In Kirtland, Ohio, in 1830, the Mormons made an impressive conversion
in Sidney Rigdon and much of his Campbellite congregation. But the popular attitude toward the new religion, as expressed in the press, was one of
continuing contempt. The newspapers scoffed at the claims to modern revelation: The *Painesville* (Ohio) *Telegraph* referred to Mormonism as a "strange

delusion and imposition." Ohioans derided the Mormon belief in the imminent Second Coming, and their spiritual manifestations were subjected to incessant ridicule. Latter-day Saints were seen as wild-eyed zealots.[5]

In Jackson County, Missouri, in 1833, the Mormon immigrants were regarded as "deluded fanatics, or weak and designing knaves." "They openly blasphemed the Most High God," anti-Mormon spokesmen said in a manifesto, "and cast contempt on His holy religion, by pretending to receive revelations direct from heaven, by pretending to speak unknown tongues, by direct inspiration, and by divers pretenses derogatory to God and religion, and to the utter subversion of human reason."[6] Another document, known as the "Propositions of the Mob," derided the Mormon claims: "Of their pretended revelations from heaven . . . and the contemptible gibberish with which they habitually profane the Sabbath, and which they dignify with the appellation of unknown tongues, we have nothing to say; vengeance belongs to God alone."[7] In 1837 Samuel Owens, one of the most energetic leaders of the mob activity, portrayed the Mormons as a "fanatic tribe" guilty of "disgusting folly." Their religion, he said, was a "delusion," the Book of Mormon "a ridiculous farrago of nonsense."[8]

The same ridicule of the Mormon religion continued in Illinois from 1839 to 1846, especially after the resumption of violent opposition in 1843. The main source of this vitriol was the pen of Thomas Sharp, editor of the Warsaw (Ill.) *Signal.*[9]

Linked very closely with the disparagement of the Mormon religion was the description of the Saints themselves as low-class, degraded types. They were, in a word, undesirables. Nancy Towle, as early as 1831, described Joseph Smith as "good-natured" but "low bred."[10] The Hurlbut affidavits collected in Palmyra viewed the Smith family in similar terms.[11] In Missouri the Mormons were described as "the very dregs of that society from thich they came, lazy, idle, and vicious."[12] The mob's "Propositions" were even more emphatic: "Elevated, as they mostly are, but little above the condition of our blacks, either in regard to property or education; they have become a subject of much anxiety.[13] In 1837, Samuel Owens reached a rhetorical apex. The Mormons, he said, were a "tribe of locusts, that still threatens to scorch and wither the herbage of a fair and goodly portion of Missouri by the swarm of emigrants from their pestilent hive in Ohio and in New York." They were, he continued, a "mass of human corruption."[14]

Revulsion at the Mormons' religious claims and practices and what their detractors perceived as their despicable, degraded social status was not, of course, the whole story. This basic prejudice, which at the outset provided virtually the only basis for their mistreatment in New York State, continued throughout their migrations but was reinforced by other, more immediate reasons for alarm. It is understandable, perhaps, that the Mormons viewed some of the later explanations of opposition as excuses for the religious persecution that, as they knew, had started early in their history.

Not in New York or Ohio, but in Missouri and to some extent in Illinois and Iowa, the Mormons were accused of agitating among Indians.[15] The Mormons did regard the Indians as a people destined to rise again and assume their rightful heritage in the promised land their ancestors had come to in 600 B.C. The first mission to Missouri specifically included preaching to the Indians. But such activity appeared dangerous to Missourians, who remembered battles on the frontier. In 1832 their newspapers carried vivid accounts of the Black Hawk War raging just to the north in Illinois. In the northern Missouri counties, volunteers eagerly enlisted to assist in subduing the rebel Indians. Strongly opposed to the federal government's policy of concentrating Indians on their frontier, the Missouri representative in Congress pleaded for protection by government troops. And it was in 1832, only a few months after the arrival of the first Mormon settlers, that Jackson County organized three volunteer military companies, "ready at a minute's warning to march into the field in defense of their country." The Mormons, on the other hand, viewed the gathering of the Indians as "gratifying" and "marvelous," and the government as an unconscious ally in the work of the Lord. Although there is no evidence of Mormon efforts to encourage violence, their efforts to proselyte among the Indians were "a serious subject of alarm." The Rev. Isaac McCoy, after mentioning the popular suspicions, added his own opinion: "I could not resist the belief that they had sought aid from the Indians though I have not ascertained that legal evidence of the fact could be obtained."[16] It was on the basis of these fears and rumors, with statements by some Mormons undoubtedly providing plausibility, that the "mob" demands usually charged the Mormons with tampering with the Indians.[17] Later, in Illinois, there were at least some efforts to preach Mormonism to neighboring Indians, and the fears of a Mormon-Indian coalition occurred again in Iowa and during the Utah War in the 1850s.[18]

In Missouri the Mormons were also accused of tampering with Negro slaves.[19] In 1833, an editorial in the Mormon newspaper *The Evening and the Morning Star*, of Independence, Missouri, seemed, at least to sensitive Southerners, to offer asylum for "free people of color." Although a clarifying statement immediately denied any such intent (in any case the total number of Mormon Negroes must have been less than a dozen), the fear was implanted. As one of the anti-Mormon statements explained: "With the corrupting influence of these [the free blacks] on our slaves, and the stench, both physical and moral, that their introduction would set afloat in our social atmosphere, and the vexation that would attend the civil rule of these fanatics, it would require neither a visit from the destroying angel, nor the judgments of an offended God, to render our situation here insupportable."[20] Samuel Owens denounced their "impertinent and mischievous interference" with the slaves.[21] The calmer statement of the Clay County anti-Mormons in 1836 seems closer to the truth: "They [the Mormons] are eastern men, whose manners, habits, customs, and even dialect, are essentially different from our own. They are non-slaveholders, and opposed to slavery, which in this peculiar period, when abolitionism has reared its deformed and haggard visage in our land, is well calculated to excite deep and abiding prejudice in any community where slavery is tolerated and protected."[22]

These charges of Mormon agitation among Negroes seem unfounded, but the important thing is that such rumors were being circulated and believed.[23] Such talk, like allegations of Mormon involvement with the Indians, touched a tender nerve. It raised the specter of violence and suggested that strong measures were needed to protect "the cause of public morals."

If reports of tampering with slaves and Indians were based primarily on rumor, the same could not be said of other Mormon activities which were regarded as more than a little menacing to the old settlers in Ohio, Missouri, Illinois, and Iowa. These can be conveniently summarized as economic, political, and religious threats. Individuals regarded as degraded and superstitious can be simply discriminated against, as American history abundantly demonstrates, but when they appear to constitute a group, more decisive action may seem necessary. It is important to recognize, in other words, that the Mormons were not only despised but also feared.

In Jackson County, Missouri, some of the most prominent spokesmen against the Mormons were the merchants of Independence. It might be expected that such men would regard the Mormons as a boon, an additional pool of hundreds of customers. But the fact was that the Mormons traded almost entirely through the store of Sidney Gilbert, a church member.[24] In effect, they had pooled their meager resources and were functioning as a cooperative community. From the outside the Mormons, however destitute individually, must have looked like a fairly powerful economic bloc, with resources far exceeding those of any one individual. Such an economic unity would be seen as operating in restraint of trade. It would also be an influence on the land market.[25] Prices would be artificially elevated for choice pieces of property. The Mormons, after all, had indicated their firm intent to buy up the region. The land market thus was thrown into an unnatural upward spiral, much to the disgust of prospective purchasers, who had to compete with the Mormons. This perception of the Mormons as an economic threat—with respect to their control over their own trade and their effect on the land market—was repeated with variations in Ohio, Missouri, and Illinois. The Mormon economic role was complicated by land speculation and by ventures into banking; the failure of the Kirtland bank, despite the general suspension of banks in 1837, was a major cause of resentment.[26] On another level neighboring towns were alarmed by the influx of Mormons into these different gathering places. Warsaw, Illinois, for example, had seen itself as a natural river port for the carrying trade but suddenly found Nauvoo, twelve miles upriver, outstripping it. Painesville, Ohio, and perhaps Saint Joseph, Missouri, may earlier have experienced some of the same resentment against Mormons in Kirtland and Independence, respectively.

Mormon economic separateness had its obverse (and perhaps a partial cause) in the refusal of some Gentiles (non-Mormons) to do business with the Saints. This refusal became particularly painful during the panic of 1837. "It seemed that our enemies were determined to drive us away if they could possibly, by starving us out," wrote Caroline Barnes Crosby. Wilford Woodruff wrote that the Gentiles "would be glad to starve the Saints to death."[27]

The tendency of anti-Mormons to brand the Saints as the "dregs of society" also had its economic aspect. In 1834, for example, an anti-Mormon group meeting in Kirtland complained of the "impoverished" Mormons who threatened to become "an insupportable weight of pauperism."[28] In short, many people who had no interest in their theology saw the Mormons, in one way or another, as an economic threat.

Non-Mormons also viewed the Mormons as a political problem. The Saints almost always voted as a bloc, which created strong apprehension in opposing camps. When they made the difference in the results of an election, it was easy to use them as a scapegoat: "If it had not been for the Mormons, we would have won." Even the party that benefited from the Mormon vote had reason to beware of Greeks bearing gifts, for Mormon votes meant, or could mean, Mormon control. Moreover, there was the tendency, especially in Illinois and to a lesser extent in Iowa, for Mormons to use their political weight by attempting to arrange for support from the different candidates. It was natural for them to do so; for them to vote for known enemies or to fail to take advantage of the highly American institution of the ballot box to improve their situation would have shown a lack of good sense. Still, resentment was intensified.

During the Ohio period the Mormons were strongly Jacksonian in their party allegiance. In the 1836 presidential election, although Martin Van Buren lost Geauga County, Ohio, and the entire state as well, Mormon Kirtland voted overwhelmingly for him. The Mormons "began to make their boasts that in a short time they would control all the county offices and elect a member of Congress for their own ranks," wrote non-Mormon newspaperman E. D. Howe in recalling the Kirtland period.[29]

In Jackson County, Missouri, as early as 1833 the Propositions of the Mob stated:

When we reflect on the extensive field in which the sect is operating, . . . it required no gift of prophecy to tell that the day is not far distant when the civil government of the county will be in their hands; when the sheriff, the justices, and the county judges will be Mormons, or persons wishing to court their favor from motives of interest or ambition.[30]

Resettling in the northern Missouri counties of Daviess, Carroll, and Caldwell, the Mormons ran into similar problems. In Daviess County, where the Whigs and Democrats were about evenly divided, strong opposition to Mormon political influence led to the formation of anti-Mormon groups, resolutions to prevent the Mormons from voting, and finally an election day riot at Gallatin on August 6, 1838, that set off a conflagration of persecution culminating in an "extermination order" by Governor Boggs and the expulsion of the Mormons from the state.[31]

In Illinois, politics were a constant point of friction.[32] As early as 1839, the Mormon apostle Lyman Wight published letters in the Quincy (Ill.) *Whig* blaming the Missouri Democrats (and indirectly national Democrats) for the persecutions. Wight's statement was repudiated, and soon the Mormon leaders began working for Illinois Democrats. During the 1840 election several candidates visited Nauvoo in their quest for votes. Disgusted with President Van Buren because he refused aid in their attempts to receive remuneration for the lands they had been forced to abandon in Missouri, the Mormons voted for the Whigs nationally, but for state and local candidates they split their votes, leaning toward the Democrats. Whig newspapers denounced "the awful wickedness of the party that would consent to receive the support of such miscreants."[33] Joseph Smith, apparently influenced by such Whig denunciations, exhorted his followers to unite with the Democratic party. In 1841 an Anti-Mormon party, composed of Whigs and anti-Mormon Democrats, was formed.[34]

In 1842 Smith tried to modify the church's political stance. "We care not a fig for a Whig or Democrat," he said. "They are both alike to us; but we shall go for our friends, our tried friends and the cause of human liberty, which is the cause of God."[35] This was interpreted as an open invitation for candidates to court the Mormon vote. Some of the confusion implicit in this situation became explicit in 1843 when Smith, in order to obtain the services of Cyrus Walker as a defense attorney, agreed to vote for him for the legislature. He did so personally. But shortly before the election Hyrum Smith announced, undoubtedly with Joseph's approval, that he had received a revelation that Walker's Democratic opponent, J. P. Hoge, should receive the Saints' votes. Hoge received 629 votes in Nauvoo; Walker, the Whig, 71. It was from this time, Thomas Ford later wrote, that "the Whigs generally, and a part of the democrats, determined upon driving the Mormons out of the State."[36]

It was such bloc voting more than anything else that aroused opposition in Illinois. In 1841 William Harris asked if Mormonism were not "inimical to the institution of our country" and provided his own answer: "Let the ballot box, at every election where they have voted answer, and it will be found that they have voted almost to a man, with Smith."[37] To this charge Joseph Smith gave the following answer:

> With regard to elections, some say all the Latter-day Saints vote together, and vote as I say. But I never tell any man how to vote or whom to vote for. But I will show you how we have been situated by bringing a comparison. Should there be a Methodist society here and two candidates running for office, one says, "If you will vote for me and put me in governor, I will exterminate the Methodists, take away their charters," etc. The other candidate says, "If I am governor, I will give all an equal privilege." Which would the Methodists vote for? Of course they would vote EN MASSE for the candidate that would give them their rights.
>
> Thus it has been with us. Joseph Duncan said if the people would elect him he would exterminate the Mormons and take away their charters. As to Mr. Ford, a spirit in his speeches was manifest—instead of any such threats—to give every man his rights; hence, the members of the Church universally voted for Mr. Ford and he was elected governor.[38]

This explanation, however, although probably accurate, did little to mollify those who did not receive the Mormon vote.

For those who saw the Mormons as an unholy, corrupting influence in politics, the events of 1844 provided additional evidence. Early that year the Kingdom of God—a cadre to coordinate gathering and to prepare for the expected millennial reign—was officially organized under the direction of a discreetly formed Council of Fifty.[39] Although not well or widely known, the increased ambitions of the Prophet were the subject of various rumors. What was widely known was the decision of Joseph Smith to run as a candidate for the U.S. presidency. Possibly intended as a means of avoiding the tangled maze of appeals to the national parties, or even as mainly a proselyting device, this decision nevertheless signaled continued Mormon involvement in politics. Those who already hated Smith became almost maniacal in their determination to put him out of the way.

It is worth noting that even during their temporary stay in Iowa in 1846 after Smith's death, the Mormons could not resist using the ballot box to protect their interests. Once again the result was inevitable: animosity from those who suffered from the Mormon votes. Later, when political differences led not only to opposition from outside but also to dissension within Mormon ranks, Brigham Young wrote from Utah to the leaders at Kanesville, Iowa:

> Now we do not care about your political differences, but wish to say confidentially to you, keep them up, outwardly for that may be good policy. But

let it be distinctly understood between you and him [Orson Hyde and Almon Babbitt] as good brethren, that you are seeking to accomplish the same grand object namely admission [of Utah territory] into the Union as a free, and Independent State. Do not permit (trivial) matters to influence you in the least; and never! no never!! again drag Priesthood into a Political gentile warfare.[40]

Despite the evident frustration here, it is clear that there was still a basic assumption of Mormon political unity, an assumption that would not be finally abandoned until the early 1890s, when church members, in the interests of gaining Utah statehood, were allowed and even encouraged to divide their votes between the national parties.[41]

In addition to their economic and political influences, the Mormons posed a religious threat. It would seem, on the face of it, that a religion held in such contempt would not be a serious contender against more established denominations. But to examine this problem in a contemporary frame of reference it is important to realize that in the 1830s the older denominations were not firmly entrenched in Ohio, Missouri, or Illinois. In Missouri, especially, these denominations were barely able to maintain a few congregations and preachers. For the pioneer ministers of Christianity on the frontier, consolidation and conversions were an uphill battle.[42] Suddenly a new religion appeared, full of enthusiasm, growing in numbers, confident, and well organized. It was difficult for orthodox Protestants to assume an attitude of superior indifference or Christian tolerance toward the Mormons, whose missionaries continually called their neighbors to repentance. And individuals and families were responding to the call and converting. It is no accident that those often in the forefront of the persecution were ministers of other religions, who viewed the Mormons as actually or potentially taking converts from their small flocks. "Who were the leaders and foremost in the ranks of the Savior's persecutors?" asked Brigham Young in 1871. "The Scribes and the Pharisees. Who were foremost in the ranks in persecuting Joseph Smith, even when he had the pledge of the governor of the State of Illinois that he should be preserved, and when not one scratch or law could be found against him? Who led the blackened crew who said that, if the law could not reach him, powder and ball should? The priests; they have always led the van, and always will."[43] Besides resenting the "sheep stealing" that threatened to reduce their own congregations, the clergy undoubtedly saw themselves as defenders of true Christianity against false prophets and heterodoxy.

That the Mormons were seen as a threat—economically, politically, and religiously—was in a large measure a result of their corporate, organized nature. Individually they might be despised, but scarcely feared. As a group, however, they had to be reckoned with. One is reminded of the difference between individual workers attempting to negotiate contracts with employers and powerful labor unions engaged in collective bargaining. Or of the difference between individual Indians pressing a claim and organized tribal councils, who have the "clout" to exert influence on political leaders and to buy substantial properties. Similarly, organized corporate Mormonism was regarded as representing a threat to the established ways.

In addition, there were accusations that the Mormons were guilty of theft, counterfeiting, and even murder. It is impossible to substantiate any such charges in New York or Ohio, although the failure of the Kirtland bank, in 1837, caused some holders of its notes to feel they had been taken advantage of. In Missouri it seems clear that some Mormons were guilty of responses that led to criminal behavior.[44] With or without the support of church officials—the evidence is not conclusive—Sampson Avard in 1838 organized a vengeance-taking society called the Daughters of Zion, or Danites. Unquestionably this secret group, in its final stage, went beyond the bounds of legality and propriety in defending the Saints and retaliating against those who had committed crimes against them. When, after months, Avard and some of his associates were arrested, their testimony that at least one high church official (perhaps Sidney Rigdon) had approved of their activities created a legend of "Mormon Destroying Angels" that is still alive in the literature of the "Wild West."[45]

In Illinois, too, there were frequent charges of theft and counterfeiting. Samuel W. Taylor has posited the theory that a few criminals joined the Mormon church in order to benefit from the protection of the Nauvoo city charter, which guaranteed a great degree of independence and which was interpreted broadly by church leaders. Almost certainly there were cases of theft, counterfeiting, and harassment of visitors by individual Mormons.[46] But were there two or three such instances or several hundred? Although reliable evidence is hard to come by, the following statement of Illinois Governor Thomas Ford in 1845 is relevant:

> Justice, however, requires me here to say, that I have investigated the charge of promiscuous stealing, and find it greatly exaggerated. I could not ascertain that there were a greater proportion of thieves in that community than any other of the same number of inhabitants; and perhaps if the city of Nauvoo were compared with St. Louis, or any other Western city, the proportion would not be so great. I think it very possible, however, that the Mormons sometimes erred in protecting members of their community from prosecution and punishment, who were accused of offenses, under the belief that the accusation against them, was a persecution of their enemies on account of their religion.[47]

Nonetheless, to whatever extent such crimes as theft were committed by Mormons, even with near-civil-war conditions as the context, their enemies would have cause for hating them. The victims of the crimes could not be expected to make fine distinctions and recognize the element of self-protection in Mormon behavior. An innocent bystander, once his cattle had been driven off, readily became a Mormon hater. (This whole question is complicated by the willingness of the mob element to charge the Latter-day Saints with crimes they themselves had committed, and perhaps similar behavior could be found on both sides.) The fact remains that criminal activity on the part of some Mormons or pretended Mormons did take place, and it reinforced prejudices and created opposition where it had not existed before.

Finally, there were specific circumstances that did, in given locations, turn suspicion into resentment. In Ohio, there was the failure of the Kirtland bank. In Illinois, a case in point was the establishment of a Masonic lodge at Nauvoo in late 1841. Immediately the widespread anti-Masonic sentiment was transferred to the Mormons; and ironically, the Mormon Masons, because of their rapid growth, became equally unpopular among their fellow Masons. "Within five months," Kenneth Godfrey has pointed out, "the Nauvoo Lodge initiated 256 candidates and raised 243 more, which was six times as many initiations and elevations as all of the other lodges in the state combined."[48] Some Masons were further angered by Smith's purported use of the Masonic ceremony in Mormon temple ordinances. (While recognizing that there were similarities as well as differences, the Mormons insisted that their own ceremonies were divinely revealed.) An additional element contributing to the Mormons' problems in Illinois—as if more were required— were the rumors of plural marriage that began to circulate in Nauvoo.

Clearly there were ample reasons for the unpopularity of the Mormons.[49] The appeal the new faith had for some does not negate the fact that the common reaction to it, almost everywhere, was distaste and antipathy. Early critics were right in one way: A group that succeeds in turning friends and the far more numerous "neutrals" into enemies, as the Mormons did in one place after another, must have exhibited some repellent characteristics, at the very least.

But unpopularity is one thing, persecution another. Why did the Mormons' enemies not content themselves with verbal condemnation? A pluralistic society does not, after all, require that all factions join in a love feast. One answer, of course, is that the resentment had become too intense to be channeled or sublimated. The "anti's" experienced enormous frustration, for none of the normal, legal procedures seemed able to cope with the Mormon threat. Pent-up frustration eventually reached a bursting point; the slightest provocation could then trigger a violent outbreak.

The persecutors were usually referred to by the Saints, and sometimes by others, as a "mob." The term has connotations of a faceless monster, of a milling, seething crowd without organization, without direction. It was a term of opprobrium, but in a curious sense may also have been a convenient term of defense, for it seemed to imply a kind of irresistible and irrational will of the people welling up to manifest itself. Recent studies of crowds in widely varied historical contexts have thrown into doubt these notions of mass behavior.[50] In ways not always discernible at the time, riots and popular disturbances have a structure and a shape. To understand the Mormon persecutions, therefore, it is necessary to consider the kinds of punishment inflicted, the occasions for violence, the makeup and leadership of the crowds, and the efforts at rationalization and legitimization.

Those who made up the mobs, who did the actual burning, beating, driving, and even killing, who responded with enthusiasm to the call to join in a "wolf hunt," obviously included some rough types. Violent persecution was expedited by a pool of ruffians either unemployed or temporarily idle between harvest and planting. Perhaps every community in the nineteenth century had such an element in its population. It was not a time of universal compulsory education, and it seems likely that the adolescent element, at least, was quite ready to kick up its heels when offered the opportunity. Besides, frontier regions such as Missouri and Illinois included in their population an inordinate number of illiterate, hard-drinking, hard-swearing, lawless men.[51] In Illinois, Governor Ford attended circuit courts in Hancock County between 1830 and 1834. "To my certain knowledge," he wrote, "the early settlers, with some honorable exceptions, were, in popular language, hard cases."[52]

If "hard cases" or seasonally unemployed youths made up a large portion of the mob, it is not surprising that they were capable of drunken brawls. The first attempt to form a plan for expelling the Mormons in Jackson County broke up in a "Missouri row,"[53] and there was some wanton destruction. Most of the persecutors' actions, however, fell into the following categories: raising the red flag; "disturbing" the Mormons; uttering horrid yells and blasphemous epithets; threatening to shoot cattle, whip Mormons who resisted, demolish houses, or kill Mormons who sought redress; stoning, brickbatting, or breaking into houses; throwing furniture out of doors; breaking windows; stealing or destroying property; overturning or burning haystacks; unroofing houses; burning, razing, or otherwise destroying houses and mills; whipping and beating or tarring and feathering men; turning people out of their homes; "driving" groups of Mormons to new locations.[54]

If these actions are examined dispassionately, it becomes apparent that noise and threats, however horrendous they were to the Mormons who experienced them, were more common than actual violence. Hoots and catcalls, stones thrown against houses, and general disturbance of the peace added to the intolerability of the situation, but were a far cry from unrestrained massacres. Usually the targets were selective: the houses of the leading men, printing establishments, or stores. When outlying settlements were hit, it was with a view to forcing the Mormons to pull back and reverse their outward expansion. Women and children were usually allowed to flee for their lives. Men were humiliated by beatings and tar-and-featherings but not—except at Haun's Mill—indiscriminately slaughtered. The fatalities, with few exceptions, occurred when Mormon defensive units were functioning as troops in the field.

This is not to minimize the suffering. Even threats and broken windows create an atmosphere of insecurity and fear. Nor should the destruction of property and expulsion from homes be dismissed lightly. Setting fire to barns, fields, and haystacks meant destroying the food needed for survival during winter months, and unroofing or burning houses left many Mormons without habitations, at least temporarily. Colonel Thomas L. Kane, who visited the Mormons while they crossed Iowa to Winter Quarters, Nebraska, was convinced that much of the sickness and death they experienced was due to exposure and suffering caused earlier by the mobs. Even a dozen whippings were too numerous. A single murder was too many; and there must have been one or two score in Missouri alone, not counting the deaths from exposure of the aged and infirm driven from their homes. J. B. Turner, no sympathizer with the Mormons, wrote the following in 1842:

> Who began the quarrel? Was it the Mormons? Is it not notorious, on the contrary, that they were hunted, like wild beasts, from county to county, before they made any desperate resistance? Did they ever, as a body, refuse obedience to the laws, when called upon to do so, until driven to desperation by repeated threats and assaults on the part of the mob? Did the state ever make one decent effort to defend them, as fellow-citizens, in their rights, or to redress their wrongs? Let the conduct of its governors, attorneys, and the fate of their final petitions answer. Have any who plundered and openly massacred the Mormons ever been brought to the punishment due to their crimes? Let the boasting murderers of begging and helpless infancy answer. Has the state ever remunerated even those known to be innocent, for the loss of either their property or their arms? Did either the pulpit or the press through the state raise a note of remonstrance or alarm? Let the clergymen who abetted, and the editors who encouraged the mob, answer. We know that there were many noble exceptions; but, alas, that they were so few! We hate the Mormon imposture; it is from beginning to end utterly detestable, both in its principles and its effects. Mormonism is a monstrous evil; and the only place where it ever did or ever could shine, this side the world of despair, is by the side of the Missouri mob."

Yet despite other examples of despicable behavior by the Illinois mobs, and however harrowing and oppressive the persecutions in their cumulative effect, the Mormons were not slaughtered indiscriminately.[56] There was some degree of control and rationality in the choice of means to achieve agreed-upon objectives. If the mob was a monster, it was a monster with a head. To appreciate this point it becomes necessary to examine mob membership—not the rank and file, the riffraff, or the farmers and laborers who made up its mass but those who stood at the head, those who called the shots.

A clue to the nature of the anti-Mormon leadership in Jackson County is contained in the following sentence from the Mormon appeal to Missouri Governor Daniel Dunklin in 1833: "Knowing . . . that every officer, civil and military, with a very few exceptions, has pledged his life and honor to force us from the county, dead or alive, . . . we appeal to the Governor for aid."[57] The mob leaders were, in most instances, men of substance and position. Heading the movement to eliminate the Mormons from Jackson County were S. D. Lucas, colonel and county judge; Samuel C. Owens, county clerk; Russell Hicks, deputy clerk; John Smith, justice of the peace; Samuel Weston, justice of the peace; William Brown, constable; Thomas Pitcher, deputy constable. "Besides these," says B. H. Roberts, "there were Indian agents, postmasters, doctors, lawyers and merchants."[58] Standing by and allegedly giving "secret assistance" was Lieutenant Governor (and later Governor) Lilburn W. Boggs, a native of Jackson County who carried local grudges to a state level. When hostilities resumed in the northern Missouri counties in 1838, the anti-Mormons were led and encouraged by people like Judge Adam Black of Millport and Judge Austin A. King. In Ray County the sheriff served trumped-up writs on the Mormon leaders. When these leaders did not respond to the writs, since they lived outside of their jurisdiction, Governor Boggs gave orders to General David R. Atchison to raise a force of four hundred men to be held in readiness to deal with "Indian disturbances on our immediate frontier" and "civil disturbances in Caldwell, Daviess and Carroll" counties. In Illinois, too, there were prominent citizens among the persecutors, ranging from Warsaw editor Thomas Sharp to prominent citizens and community leaders in other towns.[59] Even before the calling up of militia companies gave "official" sanction to the persecution, the prominence of civil authorities in the "complaints" legitimized the anti-Mormon movement in the eyes of the common people.

This legitimization of the violence was greatly increased when the armed men who meted out the punishment were not "mobs" but a kind of official or quasi-official militia. In Missouri, it was of great psychological encouragement when Governor Boggs called up the militia companies. Many of the most heinous acts were the work of these troops. The Mormons accurately judged them as guilty of mob behavior, but it was of no small importance, especially after Boggs had issued his "extermination order," that the troops acted under the aegis of the state.[60] In Illinois, the same device did not at first seem a possibility, so the determined anti-Mormons formed private contingents of troops. Recognizing that they had no legal sanction for such units, they justified them by the expected arguments: The problem was too pressing to be dealt with by the usual procedures of law, and they were acting in defense of the safety of the community. Later, Governor Ford called up units of the state militia in an effort to preserve the peace. It was one of these units—the Carthage Greys—that would storm the jail and murder Joseph and Hyrum Smith.[61]

It is important to understand that various actions against the Mormons usually took place within a verbal atmosphere that was anything but calm and dispassionate. Among the incitements were statements, delivered as speeches and published in newspapers, of ex-Mormons who chose not to leave the church quietly but continually stirred up opposition. In Ohio there were Simonds Ryder, Ezra Booth, and Philastus Hurlbut, who wrote and lectured against their former brethren and, in the case of Ryder, participated actively in leading mob violence.[62] In Missouri, George M. Hinkle and others became turncoats and encouraged the state militia in their efforts to capture the Mormon leaders.[63] In Illinois, as Smith well knew, his most bitter opponent was his former right-hand man, John C. Bennett, who wrote and lectured throughout the state, returned to Missouri to charge Smith with complicity in the attempted execution of Governor Lilburn Boggs, and enraged fellow Masons with details of Smith's "transformations" of Masonry. In the end it was another who had been a close counselor to Smith, William Law, who with his friends published the *Expositor,* which precipitated the series of events that culminated in the lynching of the Smiths.[64]

The verbal atmosphere conducive to persecution was further electrified by books, pamphlets, and newspaper articles. An examination of the persecutions that followed the publication of certain books strengthens the impression that they must have been a significant part of the provocation. Some of the books that exacerbated hostilities are

Eber D. Howe, *Mormonism Unvailed, or a Faithful Account of that Singular Imposition and Delusion* (1834)

John Corrill, *Brief History of the Church of Christ of Latter Day Saints* (*Commonly Called Mormons*) (1839)

William Swartzell, *Mormonism Exposed* (1840)

William Harris, *Mormonism Portrayed; Its Errors and Absurdities* (1841)

E. G. Lee, *The Mormons; or, Knavery Exposed* (1841)

John C. Bennett, *The History of the Saints; or, An Exposé of Joe Smith and Mormonism* (1842)

J. B. Turner, *Mormonism in All Ages; or The Rise, Progress, and Causes of Mormonism; with the Biography of Its Author and Founder, Joseph Smith, Junior* (1842)

Joseph H. Jackson, *A Narrative of the Experiences of Joseph H. Jackson in Nauvoo, Exposing the Depths of Mormon Villainy* (1844)

Even more inflammatory were newspaper articles damning the Mormons and demanding their expulsion or extermination. John Hay, a Warsaw resident who was later secretary to President Abraham Lincoln, recalled, "The newspapers of the county grew hysterical with exclamation points and 'display type.' "[65] Hay quoted one example from the Warsaw (Ill.) *Signal:* "War and extermination is inevitable! CITIZENS ARISE, ONE AND ALL!!! Can you *stand* by, and suffer such INFERNAL DEVILS! to ROB men of their property and RIGHTS, without avenging them? We have no time for comment: every man will make his own. LET IT BE MADE WITH POWDER AND BALL!!!"[66]

Additional, oral provocation emerged in speeches and sermons. These are practically impossible to document, but undoubtedly the writers of published sentiments such as those just noted spoke out strongly at anti-Mormon rallies. During elections, when speeches were given in the small towns of Illinois, some candidates may have indulged in anti-Mormonism because it would attract votes. Ministers were in the forefront of much of the agitation, and without question statements from these leaders of the community conscience—indeed, their very presence in the mobs—helped to legitimize the persecutions.

The clearest examples of such verbal justification were the manifestos and ultimatums, expressed in "mass" meetings and in writing to prove the "will of the community." Popular sentiment was aroused not to justify rebellion against a tyrannical establishment but to rationalize suppression or rejection of an unpopular minority. The ultimatums helped to legitimize harsh measures by making them appear as last resorts after patient warnings. The Mormons were warned of the consequences of their continued ingathering; if they then persisted, their enemies argued, they brought the attacks upon their own heads.

Leadership by "people of quality," use of public officials and militia units where possible, verbal rationalization of extralegal strategies—these are among the conditions for "guilt-free aggression." Also helping to explain the notable lack of guilt or remorse among the persecutors was the persistent effort to "dehumanize" the victims.[67] To describe the Mormons as the "dregs of society" was a step in this direction, and the general contempt for their social status served the same purpose. An additional stimulus began in the Nauvoo period, when the influx of mostly lower-class converts from England easily aroused nativist prejudice. The new Mormons were portrayed as the "offscourings of Europe." (This image of illiterate Europeans making up the mass of Mormon immigrants continued throughout the rest of the nineteenth century, and made it easy for opponents to regard Mormons as un-

American.) Another effort to lower the Mormons' image on the social scale were the attempts to identify them with Negroes and Indians, the two groups repeatedly seen in the American tradition of violence as deserving forcible repression.

The dehumanization of the Japanese into "Japs," of Koreans and Vietnamese into "gooks," is familiar to us in the twentieth century. With the Mormons the process began when they were called "Mormonites," a term of opprobrium. By implication if not explicitly, they were denounced as dupes, foreigners, Negro-lovers, Indian-lovers, trash, and vermin. Various images tended to degrade the Mormons into animals: swarms, hives, locusts, geese, and droves. (It was a small step later in the century to entitle a book on the Mormons *Uncle Sam's Abscess,* for a cancerous growth was properly removed by surgery.)[68] Conceptually the Mormons were removed, if not from the human race, at least from "our kind of people." They were the *other,* the evil principle, appropriately resisted by violent measures that one would never think of using against normal neighbors and fellow citizens.

Persecution of the Mormons in a land of religious toleration seemed outrageous to the victims and to many observers. But recent studies compiled in *The History of Violence in America* suggest that the response of the anti-Mormons was consistent with vigilante strategies widely adopted for dealing with similar problems at the time.[69] Vigilante movements arose mainly on the frontier as conservative attempts to preserve "the values of a property holder's society." The leaders were community stalwarts, the "frontier elite," who had a stake in the community, entrepreneurs whose personal finances could be easily upset. The vigilantes usually subscribed to a written constitution, articles of grievance, or a manifesto, often citing the inadequacy of law enforcement and the unreliability of the judicial system as justification for extralegal measures. They frequently attracted "a fringe of sadists and naturally violent types," who used the movement as an excuse for "giving free rein to their unsavory passions." When the vigilantes encountered strong opposition, the result was "an anarchic and socially destructive vigilante war."

These conditions are certainly descriptive of the Mormons' troubles. If there is a feature unique to the persecutions of the Saints, it may be the fact that the real conflict was not so much between the community and fringe criminals (although this happened at times) as between two different, mutually irreconcilable communities. But although in conflict, the Mormons and their enemies were living in the same world. They worked from similar assumptions, spoke the same language, and commonly resorted to like patterns of behavior. If the persecutors dehumanized the Mormons, the Mormon tendency to see their enemies as ripe for divine judgment made them also offensive. If the persecutors published manifestos and propositions, the

Mormons utilized the printed word with equal vigor; accounts of atrocities, with supporting affidavits, filled the newspapers, and petitions to governors, Congress, and the President set forth the offended innocence of the Mormons and the malice of their enemies. If anti-Mormon firebrands were intemperate in their denunciation of the Mormon scum and their demands for using "powder and ball," Mormon preachers were on occasion equally abusive and loud in their claims of their right to use force in their own defense. If the persecutors formed militia companies, the Mormons tried to organize their own volunteer forces in Missouri and succeeded in constituting the Nauvoo Legion under the "sponsorship" of the Illinois state government. If the persecutors utilized mobs and vigilantes when official military units did not suffice, the Mormons put together an unofficial army, Zion's Camp, in 1834; a secret, unsanctioned paramilitary force, the Danites, in 1838; and an organization of teen-age intimidators, the Nauvoo Whittling and Whistling Brigade, in 1844. If the persecutors cited the inadequacy of existing judicial machinery as a reason for extreme measures, the Mormons found their own justification.

Perhaps the most obvious exception to this picture is the simple desire for plunder on the part of some of the persecutors—either outright looting or forcing extremely cheap sale or abandonment of homes, land, and belongings. This was particularly true in Nauvoo in 1845–46, where some mob action intentionally aimed at, and succeeded in, preventing the sale of property left behind in the hands of a few trustees—including the temple and other church property, which some parties were considering buying for one million dollars.

Unlike the *ex parte* treatments of past generations, recent scholarship dealing with the Mormon persecution has been reluctant to view it in simple terms.[70] There is agreement that the Mormons did suffer from persecution, that they brought at least some of it on themselves, that the anti-Mormons overreacted and resorted to a violence that deserved condemnation. Was it really religious persecution? The Mormons had no doubt about the proper term for the treatment to which they were subjected, and many neutral observers concurred. It is important to recognize, however, that among the Mormons "religion" encompassed much more than it did for their contemporaries.[71] The Mormon religion included not only theology and a standard of morality but also an eschatology, an economic philosophy, and a goal of community-building that inevitably meant political and economic tension with their neighbors. Contemporary observers who urged the Mormons to break up and scatter, living as people of other faiths did, were in their own terms correct: This was one way of avoiding persecution.[72] Latter-day Saint spiritual assumptions and practical community goals were, in important ways, inconsistent with American pluralism; therefore, in the final analysis, given Mormon determination to gather together rather than live scattered in small numbers among others, there were only three "solutions" to the Mormon problem: (1) protection by the government—a false expectation, as the Mormon efforts to obtain redress revealed; (2) extermination, an "ultimate solution" that almost no one really advocated except to force consideration of the third alternative; and (3) expulsion or voluntary departure of the Mormons into previously unoccupied lands where they could live in isolation. On a small scale the last alternative was attempted in Missouri and in Illinois. But only with the massive exodus to the nearly absolute isolation of the Mountain West was it successful for long. Perhaps, after all, it was an unavoidable conflict in that the only way to avoid it would have been for one or the other of the parties to have become different from what they were. (One is reminded of the Protestant-Catholic violence in Ireland or the Christian-Moslem conflict in Lebanon, for which no easy solutions have yet been found.) Fortunately for the Mormons there was the "escape hatch" of the frontier, and their numbers were still sufficiently small for a mass exodus to be feasible.

Not that the opposition stopped with the migration of the Mormons to the Great Basin. In the West, however, the situation changed in two respects: Polygamy was openly acknowledged and practiced and became the major grievance, at least to judge from its prominence in the national press; and the Mormons in the West were not a minority seeking to intrude themselves. At least in Utah, they were the majority; they were the "old settlers." But the idea that polygamy was the main reason for opposition did not ring true to Mormons, who remembered New York and Ohio and Missouri and Illinois and Iowa. For them it was all part of the persecution that, whatever excuses might be offered, would always be the lot of the Saints of God.

The Mormons could also regard persecution as "a blessing in disguise," a perception that helped them in dealing with the psychological trauma. After fleeing to refuge in the Salt Lake Valley, when the possibility of survival was still sometimes in doubt, Brigham Young was able to say to the Saints gathered to celebrate the fifth anniversary of their arrival:

> If the Saints are persecuted, it is for their good; if they are driven, it is for their good; . . . I have nothing to fear in all the persecutions or hardships I may pass through in connection with this people, but the one thing, and that is, to stray from the religion I have embraced, and be forsaken of my God. If you or I should see that day, we shall see at once that the world will love its own; and affliction, persecutions, death, fire, and the sword, will cease to follow us.[73]

This sense of persecution as both fate and test of the chosen people had developed early in the church—and with ample incentive. "Christ and his Apostles were never known to persecute," wrote Mormon Bishop Edward

Partridge to his parents in 1834, "but bore all things which that wicked generation was pleased to put upon them. From this we learn that those who have the Spirit of Christ never persecute, but are always persecuted, as we may learn both from sacred and profane history." He spoke from experience, having been among the first to be tarred and feathered and threatened with death in Jackson County. "I can assure you it is not a trifling thing to give up all for Christ's sake, to be willing to even lay down our lives in His cause," Partridge wrote—and then added, in a marvelous understatement, "I know more about these things than I did when I saw you last."[74]

4

{ Triumph and Tragedy } In "The City of Joseph"

I love you all. I am your best friend, and if persons miss their mark, it is their own fault. . . . You never knew my heart; no man knows my history; I cannot tell it. I shall never undertake it. If I had not experienced what I have, I should not have believed it myself. I never did harm any man since I have been born into the world. My voice is always for peace, I cannot lie down until my work is finished, I never think any evil nor do anything to the harm of my fellow man. When I am called at the trump of the archangel and weighed in the balance, you will all know me then.

—Joseph Smith (1844, two months before his death)

The most perfect union, peace and good feeling has invariably prevailed in our midst, and still continues. It seems like a foretaste of celestial enjoyment and Millennial glory. . . . There are many good buildings erecting in different parts of the city, there is not much sickness in the place, and there never was a more prosperous time in general, among the Saints, since the work commenced. Nauvoo or more properly, the "City of Joseph," looks like a paradise. . . . Many strangers are pouring in to view the Temple and the city. They express their astonishment and surprise to see the rapid progress of the Temple and the beauty and grandeur of Mormon looks.

—Brigham Young (1845, two months before agreeing to abandon the city)

The feelings that led to persecution in New York, Ohio, Missouri, Illinois, and Iowa were not limited to those states. Fear that monolithic Mormonism might insidiously engulf broad areas of the nation was widespread, as this 1843 comment from the New York *Sun* shows:

Should the inherent corruption of Mormonism fail to develop . . . sufficiently to convince its followers of their error, where will the thing end? A great military despotism is growing up in the fertile West, increasing faster, in proportion, than the existing population, spreading its influence around, and marshalling multitudes under its banner, causing serious alarm to every patriot.[1]

The reality of the Mormon situation differed greatly from this popular image. Between 1840 and 1845 the movement was subject to a complex process of both adhesion and dispersion—opposing tendencies centripetal or centrifugal, promoting either union or fragmentation.

Much Mormon history has emphasized the centripetal aspect of the faith, the drawing-in power of the religion. Early in the church's history the concept of a Zion, a gathering place for God's people, gained a place in the Mormon mind. Like the Hebrews of the Old Testament, the Saints were to be gathered out of the world and established as a cohesive economic, social, and political entity insulated from divisive outside influences. Mormon unity was further enhanced by the basic claim of direct, continuous revelation, the emphasis on new scriptures, the merging of the spiritual and temporal in the Kingdom of God on earth, and the repeated efforts to construct a temple at the heart of Zion. The persecutions also did much to draw the Mormons together. Most important was the unifying dynamism of the charismatic authority centered in the person of Joseph Smith.

But the same principles that united the church also contained seeds that threatened disunion. The concept of a gathering brought many of the Saints together but left unclear the status of those unable or unwilling to move bodily to Zion; and the emphasis on modern revelation and new scriptures created the possibility that individual members might seek or claim instructions for the entire church. Together these two concepts precipitated a condition of dissent: At each stage some Mormons were left behind, disagreeing with the latest revelatory changes. Especially in the 1840s, because of poor communications and the secrecy necessitated by persecution, the central body of the church had received new doctrines different in some ways from those still taught at the fringes of Mormon influence. Finally, from the beginning the tendency to merge spiritual and temporal values grated on many members, and the persecution that forced abandonment of temples and other laboriously developed properties struck some at a vulnerable time, when the initial fervor of conversion had begun to fade.

The murder of Joseph Smith in 1844 removed one of the most powerful binding forces. It brought the whole issue of unity versus fragmentation to a head, as the choice of a successor had to be made. But that issue itself antedated the immediate crisis. The problem of prophetic power had been broached soon after the formal organization of the church in April of 1830. In September of that year Smith recorded a revelation informing Oliver Cowdery, Smith's scribe and one of the three witnesses to the Book of Mormon, that "no one shall be appointed to receive commandments and revelations in this church excepting my servant Joseph Smith, Jun., . . . And thou shalt not command him who is at thy head, and at the head of the church."[2]

This revelation did not satisfy everyone. Breaking away in 1831 to found the Pure Church of Christ, Wycam Clark hoped to convert the whole world by preaching "pure" Mormonism. The sect disintegrated after a few months.[3]

A little later, a man named Hawley condemned Smith in Kirtland for allowing women to wear caps and men to sport pads on their coat sleeves, and for
excommunicating another professed prophet, John Noah. Brigham Young
later recalled his own vigorous reaction to Hawley's claims:

> I put my pants and shoes on, took my cowhide, went out and, laying hold of
> him, jerked him around and assured him that if he did not stop his noise and
> let the people enjoy sleep without interruption, I would cowhide him on the
> spot, for we had the Lord's Prophet right here and we did not want the
> Devil's prophet yelling around the streets.[4]

Between 1831 and 1838 several other splinter groups formed. An independent Church lasted for two or three months, while Warren Parrish's Church
of Christ persisted in Kirtland into the 1840s.

Dissent was not left behind in Kirtland and Jackson County. Even before
he arrived in Missouri in early 1838, Joseph Smith sent a communication alluding to "transgression" by Oliver Cowdery and to other officials who
"come not to build up, but to destroy and scatter abroad." Cowdery was soon
excommunicated from the church on charges of neglect of duty, financial
chicanery, and opposition to the Prophet. One day later, David Whitmer, a
witness to the Book of Mormon, was likewise read out of the church. William E. McLellin, Lyman E. Johnson, and others were excommunicated on
various charges. When Smith's counselor, Sidney Rigdon, delivered a sermon
describing dissenters as salt that having lost its savor was to be trodden under
foot, eighty-four churchmen signed a paper ordering the dissenters out of the
county within three days, at the risk of suffering "a more fatal calamity." In
this atmosphere the celebrated Danite avengers, a secret paramilitary group
sworn to defend Mormonism, arose under the direction of Sampson Avard.
Ironically, Avard himself soon became one of the bitterest enemies of the
church and was later excommunicated.[5]

As the Missouri settlements were fragmented by persecution and dissension, defections were a constant source of irritation. Many members, including several leaders, left because of disillusionment or dissatisfaction. Without
a constant influx of enthusiastic new converts from the East and Canada and
after 1840 from England, the church might have disappeared or dwindled to a
position of insignificance. As it was, from the converts and from a core of
members and leaders still loyal to the Prophet a new gathering would arise
"phoenix-like," in Robert Flanders's apt phrase, "from the camp of the
refugees."[6]

With Joseph and Hyrum Smith, Sidney Rigdon, and several other prominent Mormon leaders imprisoned in Liberty, Missouri, in 1838 and early
1839, the task of directing the retreat from Missouri and choosing a new

gathering place rested upon the Quorum of the Twelve Apostles, which had been organized in 1835. It fell to Brigham Young, senior apostle, to direct the movement of several thousand Saints from Missouri to the area of Quincy, Illinois, where local residents opened their homes to them. Young had learned a lesson from the disorderly flight of the Saints from Kirtland, Ohio, and from Jackson County, Missouri. Before leaving Missouri, he had members and leaders sign a pledge acknowledging themselves "firmly bound to the extent of all our available property, to be disposed of by a committee who shall be appointed for the purpose of providing means for the removal from this state of the poor and destitute who shall be considered worthy."[7] He and others made many trips back and forth to redeem this pledge and to shepherd a relatively orderly exodus that, unknown to anyone at the time, would serve as training for the larger, more difficult exodus of 1846–47.

Joseph Smith and his party escaped from Missouri in April 1839. Soon the Saints began to build "Nauvoo the beautiful," some fifty-three miles north of Quincy on a peninsula jutting into the Mississippi River from the Illinois side. Equally as important as brick and timber in building the city were the energy and dedication of new converts. Many came from Europe as the first fruits of a missionary effort that can be seen, if not as divinely directed, at least as an extremely courageous gamble. For at the very time the severely wounded church, dispersed in swamps on the banks of the Mississippi, would seem to have needed them at home for mere survival, Smith had sent his proven inner core of leadership strength on a mission to England.

From their organization in 1835 the apostles had been called to proselyte in the East. In 1837 two apostles, Orson Hyde and Heber C. Kimball, opened a mission in England, where they baptized more than 1,300 people. When the full body of apostles (led by Young) arrived there early in 1840, they found a fulfillment of Smith's prophecy to them—a field of converts "white already to harvest."[8] The depression of 1837, social oppression, Chartist schemes, disillusionment with the Church of England, and various religious agitations had prepared the way. Mormon preachers could promise not only salvation and truth but also the tangible reality of a prosperous Zion in the New Eden of America, a city where the common man could find employment, inexpensive land, dignity, and peace. In one year (April 1840 to April 1841) the Twelve Apostles baptized about 4,500 people and dispatched over 800 members to America, thus launching a major emigration effort that lasted almost fifty years. Between 1837 and 1846 Mormon missionaries in England baptized almost 18,000 English citizens. Of these, 4,733 emigrated to Nauvoo and its environs in the early 1840s.[9]

Nauvoo was situated at the heart of an agricultural hinterland that funneled produce and commerce into the center. Under Smith's leadership, members donated labor and capital to the erection of an impressive temple, a large hotel, sawmills, a flour mill, a tool factory, a foundry, and a chinaware factory. With a liberal charter from the Illinois legislature, the city enjoyed wide powers of self-rule. A militia was recruited, trained, and staffed with Mormon officers. Joseph Smith was given the rank of lieutenant general by the state's governor. An embryonic university, an agricultural and manufacturing society, and a large community field where the landless could farm were only a few of the attractions the city offered. Nauvoo prospered as no previous Mormon undertaking had. By 1844 the population had grown to about ten thousand, making it, next to Chicago, the largest city in Illinois.[10]

Despite signs of outward growth and prosperity, however, Nauvoo always rested on a precarious economic foundation. In time the growth of industry might have solved this problem. Human relations were something else, for in the founding of Nauvoo were planted seeds that would lead to its destruction at the hands of outsiders. The mere existence of a Mormon city-state on the Mississippi invited opposition. Less apparent were the flaws that would weaken Mormon solidarity from within.

Paradoxically, continuing revelation, considered by many converts as one of the appeals of Mormonism, contributed to the divisions of Nauvoo because of the development during this period of certain unusual doctrines, including plurality of gods, ceremonial temple rites, baptism for the dead, and, especially, plural marriage.[11] The allegation that Mormon leaders were practicing polygamy was the most sensational aspect of the exposés of John C. Bennett, the brilliant but mercurial former mayor of Nauvoo. Smith publicly denied all such charges and in turn accused Bennett of immoral behavior. As we shall see, there is evidence that by 1841 some form of plurality (though not the licentious form of "polygamy" Bennett accused them of) was practiced among a tightly closed circle of high church officials. During 1842 and 1843 rumors to that effect were widely circulated. From the first, polygamy was an explosive issue. A scandal to non-Mormon neighbors, it also caused a number of defections within the Mormon camp even before the death of Joseph Smith. Afterwards it became a barrier to reconciliation between Mormon factions, a prime cause of hostility between the church and the federal government, and the practice by which Latter-day Saints were most readily identified, and ridiculed, in the media.[12]

About the same time came the revelation of new rites for the Nauvoo temple. Even before the temple was finished, selected leaders underwent ceremonies of washing, anointing, and sealing in eternal marriage. (Sealing, in Mormon terminology, means "uniting for eternity husbands, wives, and children in the sacred bonds of the family.") In some instances men were sealed (or married) to more than one wife. By the fall of 1843 the subject of plurality was on every tongue in the city. Charlotte Haven wrote a letter to her family alluding to "wonderful revelations not yet made public"and discussing the case of Elder George Adams, who had returned from England with a second wife. "I am told that his first wife is reconciled to this at first unwelcome guest in her home," wrote Haven, "for her husband and some others have reasoned with her that plurality of wives is taught in the Bible, that Abraham, Jacob, Solomon, David and indeed all the old prophets and good men, had several wives, and if it is all right for them, it is all right for the Latter Day Saints."[13]

Perhaps partly to counter the tendencies toward disunity but, more important, to implement his vision of the temporal kingdom of God on earth, Smith established the Council of Fifty in March of 1844. The council brought together "a select circle of the prophet's most trusted friends, including the twelve [apostles] but not all the constituted authorities of the Church."[14] Powerful church and civic officials and prominent businessmen met together in the council to plan and regulate the temporal affairs of the Kingdom. For most of the Nauvoo period the existence of the council was semisecret. After Smith's death, particularly when the Nauvoo charter was repealed, the council emerged as a powerful unifying force for many Saints, but also as an apparent example of group temporal ambition repugnant to some Mormons and to many non-Mormons.

This paradoxical combination of forces that was simultaneously both strengthening and weakening is characteristic of much that occurred in Nauvoo. Indeed, the city itself was an apt symbol of the complex character and fate of Joseph Smith. In only five years it had risen from an impassable, malaria-ridden swamp to become one of the largest and loveliest—and yet strangest—cities in America. It impressed visitors with its civil order, but along its waterfront thieves and counterfeiters continued to operate; its heights were crowned with an imposing white limestone temple, which Mormons revered as the House of the Lord and used for the most sacred ceremonies but which their enemies imagined as the scene of barbarous rites, even sexual orgies. At the height of Nauvoo's elegance and industry, only seven years from its founding, its citizens were driven out and most of their properties seized. The temple was desecrated and within a few years destroyed by fire and tornado. But the city's inhabitants, institutions, records, and spirit were moved essentially intact across fifteen hundred miles of plain and desert to make an almost instant new City of Zion for the Mormons in the Salt Lake Valley.

Even Nauvoo's beginnings were paradoxical. The land was bought from Isaac Galland at what appeared to be very favorable terms for the dispossessed and penniless Saints. Galland seemed an altruistic benefactor, but turned out to be a promoter who had sold lands he didn't own and a swindler who made off with the funds of the church. Nonetheless, Nauvoo remained a great opportunity, and Mormon energy and cooperative efficiency soon made the best of it, despite a period of intense suffering and many deaths from disease. The enterprise was given indispensable assistance by an influx of converts who possessed some money and skill and much devotion. Leaving nearly intolerable conditions in the mines and mills of the English midlands, these immigrants came with the expectation, possibly encouraged by the missionaries who converted them, of finding a paradise—at least of opportunity—in the American Zion with its strange name. Naturally, some found the reality disappointing, but almost all adopted the attitude expressed by Edwin Bottomly in a letter back to his father: "There is plenty of Fruit and fish and fowl but they are the same in this country as in any other, *no catch no eat.*"[15]

The large majority responded eagerly to Smith's vision of a literal Zion. Brigham Young, who knew firsthand the challenge of organizing the European immigrants, described Smith's achievement this way in 1843: "No other man, at this age of the world, has power to assemble such a great people from all the nations of the earth, with all their varied dispositions and so assimilate and cement them together that they become subject to rule and order. This the Prophet Joseph is doing. He has already gathered a great people who willingly subject themselves to his counsel, because they know it is righteous."[16]

As the city mushroomed, it attracted attention to itself and its prophet-designer. A young man who began serving as Smith's clerk in 1840 wrote:

> The Prophet had a great many callers or visitors, and he received them in his office, where I was clerking—persons of almost all professions—Doctors, lawyers, Priests and people seemed anxious to get a good look at what was then considered something very wonderful; a man who should dare to call himself a prophet, announce himself as a seer and ambassador of the Lord . . . he was always equal to the occasion, and perfectly master of the situation, . . . I could clearly see that Joseph was the captain, no matter whose company he was in.[17]

The most distinguished visitors to Nauvoo were Charles Francis Adams, son of former president John Quincy Adams, and Josiah Quincy, soon to become mayor of Boston. Quincy later stated that Smith remained an enigma to him, but suggested that he might well turn out to be the nineteenth-century figure with the most powerful influence on the destinies of his countrymen:

> Born in the lowest ranks of poverty, without book-learning and with the homeliest of all human names, he had made himself at the age of thirty-nine a power upon earth. Of the multitudinous family of Smith . . . none had so won human hearts and shaped human lives as this Joseph. His influence, whether for good or for evil, is potent today, and the end is not yet.[18]

Many visitors had their prejudices removed, or at least radically altered, by seeing Nauvoo. One wrote in May 1844:

> Before visiting the place, my mind was very much prejudiced against the Mormons . . . and I presume, if I had never taken occasion to inform myself of their religion and views, my mind would have remained in the same condition. There is not a city within my knowledge that can boast of a more enterprising and industrious people than Nauvoo. Her citizens are enlightened, and possess many advantages in the arts and sciences of the day, which other cities of longer standing cannot boast; in a word Nauvoo bids fair to soon outrival any city in the West.[19]

Some, however, responded quite differently. On April 6, 1841, Smith, who enjoyed ceremony and celebrations, conducted a day of exuberant spectacle in his young city, with many non-Mormon guests from surrounding towns. The fourteen companies of the Legion drilled and paraded, with Smith commanding in his splendid lieutenant general's uniform. At noon the eleventh anniversary of the church and the laying of the cornerstone of an ambitious temple were feted with hymns, prayers, and oration, followed by a magnificent turkey dinner. Such displays were in part an innocent diversion for Smith, a manifestation of his boyish love of play-acting, games, and entertainment. But a few observers saw something ominous in the martial display. Thomas C. Sharp, young editor of the Warsaw (Ill.) *Signal,* fifteen miles downriver, who shared the dinner and the stand with Smith at the cornerstone laying, returned home to open a determined campaign against the Mormon presence in Illinois. His motives are made a little clearer by the information that a real estate development he had invested in failed because Mormon immigrants lost interest in it.[20]

John C. Bennett, whose feelings were not as simple or as direct as Sharp's, was also present, as a newly ordained assistant to Smith in the church presidency. Strikingly handsome and patently ambitious, he had quickly moved into the inner circles of power in the city and in the church. It was probably out of sincere sympathy that he had written Smith in the summer of 1840 to urge draining of the marshes that plagued the settlers, and he provided a supply of the drug quinine as a cure for the "swamp fever." These remedies were effective. Bennett was soon baptized, and moved to Nauvoo. In January 1841, Smith announced a revelation giving the Lord's approval of Bennett, but one so interlaced with "if" clauses as to seem, on hindsight, to be premonitory: "His reward shall not fail if he receive counsel. . . . I have seen his works . . . which I accept if he continue. . . ."[21]

After he was made Smith's counselor, Bennett gradually assumed many of the duties of the ailing Sidney Rigdon. And in the meantime, he used his influence at the state capital to obtain approval for the Nauvoo city charter and a charter for a university and the city militia. After being elected mayor, he moved with remarkable speed toward making Nauvoo a major commercial city by planning a wing dam in the Mississippi and a canal to a reservoir two miles inland to provide a harbor for steamboats and waterpower for industry. Before long he was appointed chancellor of the embryonic university, president of the Nauvoo Agricultural and Manufacturing Association, and second-in-command to Smith in the Nauvoo Legion, which he organized, outfitted, and trained.

Bennett's fall was nearly as meteoric. In the summer of 1841, Hyrum Smith discovered that the self-styled bachelor had an estranged wife and children in Ohio. When confronted with this information, Bennett confessed, made a dramatic show of contrition, and remained in fellowship. But he apparently learned something of the doctrine of polygamy then being taught by Smith to a few intimate friends. Bennett began to use his position and his reputation to seduce women, under the guise of practicing the new marriage form—the women had probably heard enough rumors to make his pretensions somewhat credible. When Smith gathered testimony from a number of women and confronted Bennett in May 1842, the latter made another dramatic show of repentance, swearing that he had not been acting under Smith's teachings. After his excommunication in June, however, he immediately published a series of letters in a Springfield newspaper claiming to have been coerced into writing the confession. He accused the Prophet of being a lascivious, power-mad charlatan. The letters caused a sensation throughout the state. They were picked up by other newspapers and even published as a book, *The History of the Saints, or, An Exposé of Joe Smith and Mormonism* (Boston, 1842). Bennett's determined, articulate opposition, in print and in speeches throughout the country, gave apparent substance to Sharp's vitriolic attacks in the Warsaw (Ill.) *Signal* and thus helped bring about the downfall of Nauvoo and its Prophet.

Actually, the apparent flaw that allowed Smith to misjudge Bennett is more complex than first appears—a universalism that was a major source of Mormonism's early success.

Smith was not interested in a narrow religion. As time permitted, he read and attended lectures, studied languages, and spoke and wrote on a wide range of topics—from how to cultivate peace with animals to the origin of the American Indians, from the pre-mortal development of man's intelligence to the nature of godhood. Curious and searching, he reached out to books, to other faiths, and to all people he met for new ideas. He sent the Quorum of the Twelve and other missionaries to the Indians, to Canada, Europe, Russia, the East Indies, the Pacific Islands—even one to dedicate Jerusalem for the regathering of the Jews. The restored gospel, he said, was "for everyone."

As a result of this broad appeal Smith attracted a remarkably wide range of able people. He placed many in positions where their diverse talents could be used—the tough frontiersman Porter Rockwell, who became his bodyguard; the brilliant Baptist minister Orson Spencer, who was a powerful early writer and missionary; and the ingenious mathematician and astronomer Orson Pratt, who became an apostle and indefatigable missionary. It is an important key to his character that Smith won the admiration and devotion of a variety of talented, strong-willed people.

But such diversity exacted a price. It led him to appoint men to positions of trust who later became weak or disloyal. And as he continued to add revelations and practices in Mormonism, he ran the risk of losing those who preferred the original ways. One group of followers tended to reject the doctrinal developments at Nauvoo, especially the temple ordinances, plural marriage, and belief in the eternality and potential godhood of man.[22]

For those Utah Mormon followers who affirmed the Nauvoo experience, one of the most impressive attestations is the funeral sermon Smith gave for his friend, King Follett, in April 1844, just two months before his own death. The sermon makes specific certain ideas about the relationship of God and man that were only hinted at in previous revelations.

> If the veil were rent today and you were to see the great God who holds this world in its orbit and upholds all things by his power, you would see him in the image and very form of a man; for Adam was created in the very fashion and image of God. He received instruction from and walked, talked and conversed with him as one man talks and communes with another. . . .

> The mind of man is as immortal as God himself. . . . I take my ring from my finger and liken it unto the mind of man, the immortal spirit, because it has no beginning. Suppose I cut it in two; as the Lord lives, because it has a beginning, it would have an end. . . . If that were so, the doctrine of annihilation would be true. But if I am right, I might with boldness proclaim from the house tops that God never did have power to create the spirit of man at all. God himself could not create himself. Intelligence exists upon a self-existent principle. . . . Moreover, all the spirits that God ever sent into the world are susceptible to enlargement. . . .

> God found himself in the midst of spirits and glory, and because he was greater, he saw proper to institute laws whereby the rest could have the privilege of advancing like himself—that they might have one glory upon another and all the knowledge, power, and glory necessary to save the world of spirits. I know that when I tell you these words of eternal life that are given to me, you taste them, and I know you believe them . . . you are bound to receive them as sweet and to rejoice more and more.[23]

The sermon is the main statement of the faith that God and man are fundamentally related, the same kind of race of beings, though quite different in degree of development, both having existed forever.

To believers such ideas provided a challenging vision of their relationship to God and their own eternal potential. But to those outside of Nauvoo who heard rumors of the strange new doctrines they seemed the worst kind of blasphemy.

Smith generally followed the structure of the Puritan sermon tradition but opened it up, rather in the style of some revivalist preachers. Spontaneously he erected lasting symbols of his concepts: "I take my ring from my finger and liken it unto the mind of man. . . ." He appealed to the spirit of each hearer: "When I tell you these words of eternal life that are given to me, you taste them, and I know you believe them." Aware that some of his enemies were in the crowd, he also spoke directly to them: "When a man begins to be an enemy, he hunts me; he seeks to kill me; he thirsts for my blood; he never ceases. He has the same spirit of those who crucified the Lord of Life— the same spirit that sins against the Holy Ghost."[24] Surely this antagonized them further. In closing he appealed for understanding: "I love you all. I am your best friend. . . . You never know my heart; no man knows my history; I cannot tell it." To a believer this means: Even you who are close to me cannot know the complexity of a normally flawed and limited human spirit driven by divine imperatives and given divine instruction and aid.

Much has been made of Smith's charismatic hold on others. Emmeline B. Wells, a remarkable leader of Mormon women, later in life reported her first sight of Joseph Smith in these terms:

> His majestic bearing, so entirely different from anyone I had ever seen (and I had seen many superior men) was more than a surprise. It was as if I beheld a vision; I seemed to be lifted off my feet, to be as it were walking in the air, and paying no heed whatever to those around me. . . . When he took my hand, I was simply electrified. . . . The one thought that filled my soul was, I have seen the Prophet of God, he has taken me by the hand, and this testimony has never left me in all the "perils by the way." It is as vivid today as ever it was. For many years I felt it too sacred an experience even to mention.[25]

Some have suspected that Smith was attractive only to women, but he affected men the same way. His wife Emma's amusing comment makes this clear: "I never wanted him to go into the garden to work for if he did it would not be fifteen minutes before there would be . . . half a dozen men round him and they would tramp the ground down faster than he could hoe it up."[26] Anson Call remembered: "He was one of the grandest samples of

manhood that I ever saw walk or ride at the head of a legion of men. In listening to him as he has addressed the Saints his words have so affected me
that I would rise upon my feet in the agitation that would take hold of my
mind."[27]

After visiting Nauvoo, Josiah Quincy compared Joseph Smith with Elisha
R. Potter of the U.S. Congress: "Of all men I have met, these two seemed
best endowed with the kingly faculty which directs, as by intrinsic right, the
feeble or confused souls who are looking for guidance."[28] Smith himself explained that moral force in rather different terms:

> Sectarian priests cry out concerning me, and ask, "Why is it this babbler
> gains so many followers, and retains them?" I answer, It is because I possess
> the principle of love. All I can offer the world is a good heart and a good
> hand. The Saints can testify whether I am willing to lay down my life for my
> brethren.[29]

Whatever the exact nature of the magnetism, its effect on his followers was
unmistakable. Brigham Young, who of all his adherents perhaps most unre-
servedly gave his loyalty to Smith, later said with uncharacteristic abandon, "I
feel like shouting hallelujah, all the time, when I think that I ever knew Joseph Smith."[30]

Of course while the Mormons saw their prophet in these enthusiastic
terms, and while some visitors recognized his magnetism, others viewed him
as a fanatic, a would-be dictator, a leader profiting from deception. "One of
the grossest and most infamous impostors that ever appeared upon the face of
the earth," John C. Bennett called him.

Which was the real Joseph Smith? There can be no simple answer to this
question. From the beginning of the movement anti-Mormon literature established a caricature that he never lived down. If his friends and family also
had a one-sided view, it was at least based on close experience. At the very
least, therefore, some attractive personal characteristics should be recognized
as part of the three-dimensional person that Joseph Smith was in real life.
Otherwise the powerful loyalty of people from diverse backgrounds is
inexplicable.

Even more revealing than the testimony of others were Smith's words and
actions at the times of his greatest extremities. His letters while imprisoned
for six months in Missouri in 1838–39 were especially important. The hardships he endured while incarcerated in the dark, narrow confines of Liberty
Jail tempered his personality and refined his spiritual qualities. "No tongue
can tell what inexpressible joy it gives a man to see the face of one who has
been a friend, after having been enclosed in the walls of a prison for five
months," he wrote. "It seems to me my heart will always be more tender after
this."[31] Parley P. Pratt, a fellow prisoner, told of the filthy conditions, bad

food, and dehumanizing treatment they received, including the taunting of guards who boasted of their deeds of pillage, rape, and murder performed in driving out the Mormons.[32] Yet after nearly six months of such treatment, Smith was able, with his fellow prisoners, to record a tender, magnanimous revelation that has become a classical source for Mormon thinking about the relationship between love and power:

> The rights of the priesthood are inseparably connected with the powers of heaven, and the powers of heaven cannot be controlled or handled only upon the principles of righteousness. . . . No power or influence can or ought to be maintained by virtue of the priesthood, only by persuasion, by long-suffering, by gentleness and meekness, and by love unfeigned; by kindness and pure knowledge, which shall greatly enlarge the soul without hypocrisy, and without guile—reproving betimes with sharpness, when moved upon by the Holy Ghost; and then showing forth afterwards an increase of love toward him whom thou hast reproved, lest he esteem thee to be his enemy; that he may know that thy faithfulness is stronger than the cords of death.[33]

Smith was not like those crusaders who become so involved in their public life that they have little left for those closest to them. For his deepest satisfactions he drew back to his family.[34] His letters to Emma from Liberty Jail confirmed this unusual bond:

> O God, grant that I may have the privilege of seeing once more my lovely family in the enjoyment of the sweets of liberty . . . to press them to my bosom and kiss their lovely cheeks would fill my heart with unspeakable gratitude. . . . Tell little Joseph he must be a good boy. Father loves him with a perfect love; he is the eldest—must not hurt those that are smaller than he, but care for them. . . . Julia is a lovely girl . . . tell her Father wants her to remember that I am a true and faithful friend to you and the children forever. My heart is entwined around you forever and ever.[35]

> Affectionate wife . . . I was sorry to learn that Fredrick was sick but I trust he is well again and that you are all well. I want you to try to gain time and write to me a long letter and tell me all you can and even if old Major is alive yet and what those little prattlers say that cling around you[r] neck.[36]

In 1844, during the last few days of his life, the same tender regard appeared in the hastily scrawled notes of reassurance to Emma.

In the spring of 1844, following a barrage of accusations by John C. Bennett, a small group of Mormon dissidents founded a counterorganization and began publishing the Nauvoo (Ill.) *Expositor.*[37] They got out only one issue, on June 7, which contained inflammatory allegations about the sex lives of

Mormon leaders and members. Smith, who was mayor, his brother Hyrum, vice-mayor, and the city council, citing Blackstone on a community's right to abate as a nuisance anything that disturbs the peace, declared the newspaper libelous and a public nuisance endangering civil order, and directed the city marshal to destroy that issue and the press. Some had argued for merely fining the libelers or simply burning the papers, but Smith said he would "rather die tomorrow and have the thing smashed, than live and have it go on, for it was exciting the spirit of mobocracy . . . and bringing death and destruction upon us."[38] The council, which included at least one non-Mormon, concurred.

Nothing could have provided better ammunition for the anti-Mormons in Illinois, who had already organized into vigilante groups dedicated to the destruction of Mormonism. Although suppression of inflammatory periodicals was not without precedent and abatement of a nuisance was within the powers of the city council, leaders of the anti-Mormon party were quick to raise the issue of freedom of the press.[39] Ironically, considering that they were protesting against violation of civil rights by the Mormons, the anti-Mormons took no care to retaliate through moderate or lawful measures. Thomas Sharp, editor of the Warsaw (Ill.) Signal, proclaimed, "We hold ourselves at all times in readyness to co-operate with our fellow citizens . . . to exterminate, utterly exterminate, the wicked and abominable Mormon leaders."[40] Encouraged by such statements, the small cabal of Mormon dissenters went to the county seat at Carthage, about fifteen miles east of Nauvoo, and filed charges of inciting a riot against Smith and the other Mormon leaders. A constable was sent to arrest them.

Knowing the danger of going to Carthage, Joseph and Hyrum Smith asked to be tried anywhere else. When that was refused, they obtained a writ of habeas corpus from a city court and were tried and acquitted before a non-Mormon judge in Nauvoo. When the constable returned to Carthage without Smith, the fury among the "old settlers" exploded. In the vigilante tradition men took up arms in parts of Illinois, Missouri, and Iowa, some starting for Carthage. Messengers were sent to Gov. Thomas Ford demanding that he bring in the state militia and end Smith's defiance of the law.

In response Smith declared martial law, mobilized the Nauvoo Legion, and wrote the traveling apostles and other leaders to return home. Arriving in Carthage on June 21, Ford reviewed the evidence. He then declared the destruction of the Expositor illegal and demanded that the Smiths submit to the original charges levied by Judge Thomas Morrison in Carthage. If they refused, Ford warned, Nauvoo would probably be destroyed and many Mormons would be killed because the assembled militia might well "disregard the authority of their officers."[41]

The circle was narrowing. Smith recognized full well his limited options.

In a letter written late at night on June 22 he expressed willingness to be tried again on the original writ, even though that constituted double jeopardy. He had acted in the *Expositor* matter on legal advice, but if he had erred, it was a civil matter that the courts could determine and he would pay all costs. But he could not go to Carthage:

> We dare not come. Writs, we are assured, are issued against us in various parts of the country. For what? To drag us from place to place, from court to court, across the creeks and prairies, till some bloodthirsty villain could find his opportunity to shoot us. We dare not come, though your Excellency promises protection. Yet, at the same time you have expressed fears that you could not control the mob, in which case we are left to the mercy of the merciless. . . . Sir, you must not blame us, for "a burnt child dreads the fire. . . ." We dare not do it.[42]

Desperate, Smith even considered going to Washington to lay the case directly before President John Tyler, whom he had written a few days before, claiming the constitutional right of federal assistance because forces from both Missouri and Illinois were joining in an "insurrection." Later he read the governor's letter over again to a group gathered at his home. Sitting slumped, head in his hands, he murmured, "There is no mercy—no mercy here." Abraham Hodge reports that as they discussed Hyrum's comment that they were dead men if they fell into the mob's hands, "All at once Joseph's countenance brightened up and he said, 'The way is open. It is clear to my mind what to do. All they want is Hyrum and myself. . . . We will cross the river tonight, and go away to the West!' " The last entry in Joseph's personal journal, probably written late that night by a clerk, reads:

> I told Stephen Markham that if I and Hyrum were ever taken again we should be massacred, or I was not a prophet of God. I want Hyrum to live to avenge my blood, but he is determined not to leave me.[43]

Smith bade farewell to his family, leaving instructions for them to be taken to Cincinnati. At midnight Porter Rockwell rowed him and Hyrum and Apostle Willard Richards across the Mississippi. Rockwell returned at daybreak for horses. That morning a posse arrived in Nauvoo to arrest the brothers and left empty-handed, having threatened to occupy the city until the Smiths were taken. In the afternoon Emma sent Rockwell and Reynolds Cahoon to entreat Smith to return; they found the Smiths packing flour and provisions. The messengers presented Emma's letter, told of the posse's threats on the city, and the governor's reassurances of safety if they submitted. Finally they accused Joseph of cowardice. According to Willard Richards, who was keeping Smith's journal, Smith replied, "If my life is of no value to my friends it is of none to myself."[44] After consulting briefly with Rockwell and Hyrum, he agreed they would all return. From that moment Smith had a strong premonition of his death, although he never stopped hoping that it might be avoided. On the way to Nauvoo he spoke of his desire to preach one last time to the Saints, but instead spent the evening with his family. The next morning as he was passing through the city a friend heard him declare, "I am going as a lamb to the slaughter."[45]

On the road to Carthage the entourage met a detachment sent to collect state arms held by the Nauvoo Legion. Smith returned to assist them. Arriving finally in Carthage at midnight, he was met by loud threats to kill him from a tumultuous crowd. Only the governor's assurance that the Smiths would be displayed to them on the morrow calmed the clamor. The next day, when the various troops of militia were lined up for review, the Smiths were shown to them by Governor Ford. The local militia, known as the Carthage Greys, were hard to control and almost mutinied. The Smiths first asked to be returned to their hotel for safety, but later gave themselves up to the constable on the original charge of riot. Instead, however, of being taken to Judge Morrison, the issuer of the original writ, as Ford had before insisted was essential to proper legal process, they were arraigned before Justice of the Peace Robert Smith, an outspoken anti-Mormon who was also captain of the Carthage Greys. He set a high bail, but it was met by friends of the Smiths. They would have gone free, but in the evening they were arrested on a writ for treason on the grounds of having declared martial law in Nauvoo. Without any hearing, the justice ordered the prisoners committed without bail until June 29, on the claim that a material witness, Francis Higbee, could not appear until then. Justice Smith had his Carthage Greys carry out the order by incarcerating the Smiths and eight of their friends in the unbarred debtors' room on the second floor of the small, two-story jail on the edge of town. Despite the clear illegalities of this procedure, Governor Ford refused to interfere with what he called "a civil officer in the discharge of his duty."

Joseph had written Emma a reassuring note: "When the truth comes out we have nothing to fear. We all feel calm and composed."[46] But his deeper fears were revealed in a note sent at the same time to Porter Rockwell ordering him to stay in Nauvoo and not to allow himself to be taken prisoner by anyone. An ominous undercurrent of foreboding continued in Carthage all the next day. Leading anti-Mormons such as Dr. Charles Foster were heard to say, "The law is too short for these men, but they must not be suffered to go at large; if the law will not reach them, powder and ball must." Robert Smith ordered the prisoners before him again. At first, the jailer refused to give them up but was intimidated by a detachment of the Carthage Greys sent by Justice Smith in his capacity as their captain. According to Willard Richards, Joseph expected to be massacred by the mob in the streets as they were taken to the courthouse. He walked boldly through the Carthage Greys and in a gesture of defiance "politely locked arms with the worst mobocrat he could see, and Hyrum locked arms with Joseph, . . . escorted by a guard."[47]

On the morning of the following day, June 27, Governor Ford broke his promise not to leave Carthage without taking the prisoners along. He chose as his escort the only group of militia that had shown any neutrality and left the most obvious conspirators, the Carthage Greys, guarding the jail. Again Smith tried to reassure Emma, writing her, "There is no danger of any extermination order. Should there be a mutiny among the troops (which we do not anticipate, excitement is abating) a part will remain loyal and stand for the defense of the state and our rights." But in a hasty postscript his fears show through: "Dear Emma, I am very much resigned to my lot, knowing I am justified, and have done the best that could be done. Give my love to the children and all my friends."[48]

That morning Dan Jones, a diminutive Welsh convert acting as a messenger for the Smiths, heard several threats on the brothers' lives. Jones pleaded with Governor Ford to protect them, but Ford answered, "You are unnecessarily alarmed. The people are not that cruel." He disbanded the thirteen-hundred-man militia and set out for Nauvoo. The militia from Warsaw had already started for Nauvoo. When they received the governor's orders to disband with no provision for the officers to march them home, Thomas Sharp called for volunteers to go back to Carthage. Some of the men daubed their faces with mud and set out. In the meantime, a six-shooter had been smuggled in to Joseph by a visitor who was certain an attack on the jail was imminent. By afternoon all of the Smiths' friends had been forced to leave except the apostles Willard Richards and John Taylor. As the day grew hotter, the prisoners took off their coats and sat silent and depressed. Taylor, who had a rich voice, was asked by Joseph to sing a newly popular inspirational song, "A Poor Wayfaring Man of Grief."

At about four o'clock a boy watching from the courthouse cupola saw men assembling on the prairie outside town and warned the captain in charge of the company of Carthage Greys left on guard. The captain told him to remain on watch and report further developments. But when the boy saw men approaching the jail at about five o'clock, he could not find the captain. Quickly surrounding the jail, the men were fired upon by the guards, who were apparently part of the conspiracy and used blanks. One group of attackers then stormed up the stairs. Within three minutes Hyrum and Joseph were shot to death and Taylor severely wounded. Hyrum was killed immediately, but Joseph fired three times down the stairs wounding three men. As he leaped from a window, he was hit fatally front and back. The attackers inside the jail rushed back down the stairs. By the time they returned, Richards had dragged the wounded Taylor into a separate room where they were not noticed. When someone shouted, "The Mormons are coming," the attackers fled. Captain Smith and the main company of guards arrived after the action was over. They, too, quickly dispersed.

Sure that the Mormons would retaliate, the people of Carthage evacuated their town by nightfall. After hearing the news, Governor Ford returned briefly and then went south. But the Mormons were entirely subdued by the shattering loss of their leaders. Samuel Smith, who had been chased by part of a group in mud-daubed faces as he galloped toward Carthage and who died within a month from the ordeal, carried his brothers' bodies by wagon back to Nauvoo. Thousands of grieving people filed by their coffins. After a show of burying them publicly, the bodies were hidden and guarded in fear of desecration.

Brigham Young and the absent apostles did not learn of the assassinations until July 16 and were not able to return to Nauvoo until August 6. They found the Saints still bewildered. Young wrote his daughter on August 11:

> It has been a time of mourning. The day that Joseph and Hyrum were brought in from Carthage to Nauvoo it was Judged by menny boath in and out of the church that there was more then five barels of tears shead. I cannot bare to think enny thing about it.[49]

Within six months Young, as the new leader of the church, had begun to call Nauvoo "the City of Joseph." In little more than a year raids by anti-Mormons started up again. In two years the Mormons had been driven out, and the city lay deserted.

5

⟨ Dispersion and the Exodus ⟩ under Brigham Young

I have seen some sorrowful days since I left you and some happy ones. But I can tell you it is a sorrowful time here [Nauvoo] at present. Those that stood up for Joseph before his death are getting divided among themselves.

—Sarah Scott (1844)

We'll find the place which God for us prepared,
Far away in the West;
Where none shall come to hurt, or make afraid:
There the Saints will be blessed.

—William Clayton (1846)

The martyrdom of Smith plunged the church into a state of sadness and confusion. In addition to his religious role, Joseph had been the political, economic, and social mainstay of Nauvoo. The first impulse of the Saints in and around Nauvoo was to find a leader who could fill all of the dead Prophet's roles. But the means of orderly succession had not yet been clearly established.[1]

As head of the Quorum of the Twelve Apostles, Brigham Young had shepherded the church through the exodus from Missouri. He had led the Twelve on their eighteen-month mission to England. Their success in that country—attended by healings, mass conversion, and innovations in proselyting and emigration—had welded them into a forceful, unified apostolic body. Impressed, Smith gave them additional duties and began to rely on Young's close association and counsel. Thus the Quorum, led by Young, assumed increasing importance. In Nauvoo its members were soon collaborating closely with Smith in both economic and ecclesiastical action. They further proved their mettle by a series of missions. The last of these, in 1844, was an assignment to travel throughout the East campaigning for Smith's candidacy for the American presidency—an effort apparently designed to disseminate Mormon political and religious views. It was while serving on this mission that Young learned of the assassination of Joseph and Hyrum Smith.

When Young arrived in Nauvoo from New England on August 6, he found that Sidney Rigdon had preceded him. Rigdon had been a counselor in the presidency of the church. Young met with the rest of the apostles at the home where John Taylor was recuperating and planned with them how to deal with this challenge for leadership of the church. On the following afternoon a general meeting of church members was held. Rigdon asserted that no one could take Smith's place but that he, as Joseph's counselor, would serve as the church's "guardian." Young answered with his own conviction that the Twelve held "all the keys and powers" for church leadership.

A dramatic general meeting was held the following day. Rigdon addressed the assembly at length but apparently gained little support. Then Young arose and dramatically reinforced his own and the Twelve's claim to preeminence.

> Attention all! . . . For the first time in my life, for the first time in your lives, for the first time in the Kingdom of God in the nineteenth century, without a Prophet at our head, do I step forth to act in my calling in connection with the Quorum of the Twelve, as Apostles of Jesus Christ unto this generation—Apostles whom God has called by revelation through the Prophet Joseph, who are ordained and anointed to bear off the keys of the kingdom of God in all the world.[2]

After Young's speech and those of others supporting the Twelve, the Nauvoo congregation voted overwhelmingly to sustain him and the apostles as leaders of the church.[3]

An earlier revelation had stated that the Twelve formed a quorum "equal in authority and power" to the First Presidency. The First Presidency having been dissolved by the death of Joseph and Hyrum Smith, only Rigdon was left to argue that he should take the reins of power. In pragmatic terms there was no viable alternative to direction by the tried and proven Twelve under the leadership of Brigham Young. Remembering another early revelation to the effect that church leaders were not ordained until after a vote of the church, most Latter-day Saints were satisfied after the August 8 meeting that Young was the choice of both God and the people. "Brother Joseph," concluded Young, "has laid the foundation for a great work and we will build upon it. There is an almighty foundation laid, and we can build a kingdom such as there never was in this world."[4]

Many who were present at the August 8 meeting later remembered seeing in Brigham Young that day a new appearance and hearing from him a new voice—one that was very familiar, that of Joseph Smith. For them the "Mantle of Joseph" was given directly, miraculously, to Young. George Laub later recorded in his journal that that day Young's "voice was the voice of Br. Joseph and his face appeared as Joseph's face."[5] Apostle Wilford Woodruff later remembered, "When Brigham Young arose and commenced speaking . . . if I had not seen him with my own eyes, there is no one that could have convinced me that it was not Joseph Smith."[6]

Certainly most of the people wanted a legitimate successor, one similar to Smith, to fill the spiritual and emotional void caused by the death of their beloved Prophet. However social psychologists might explain the change of Young's voice and appearance at the August 8 meeting, he was in fact a Joseph Smith to those who accepted him—in some ways he became more. The next day, after the vote of confidence indicating the "common consent" of those assembled, he met with church leaders and proceeded with remarkable assurance to tighten up church organization. Such had not been necessary earlier, he explained, because of Smith's personal magnetic leadership: "I remarked that Joseph's presence had measurably superseded the necessity of carrying out a perfect organization of the several quorums."[7]

A few selected entries from Young's holograph diary give the best indication of how his activities and sense of assurance developed over the next few months:

Sunday, August 18, 1844. I preached to the Saints in the morning. I had good liberty and by the help of the Lord I was enabled to satisfy the Brethren and unite them together so they will finish the Temple.

Friday, September 20. Went to the temple, called on Sister Evans, sealed her up to her husband; Horace, her oldest son, stood as proxy. Laid hands on Sister Hurley; the Lord is with me.

Sunday, September 22. I preached to the congregation of the Saints, had a good time. Told the Saints some new things.

Friday, January 24 {1845}. Brothers H. C. Kimball and N. K. Whitney was at my house; we washed and annointed and prayed. Had a good time. I inquired of the Lord whether we should stay here and finish the Temple. The answer was we should.[8]

They did finish the temple. In fact, Young motivated the Nauvoo Mormons to do as much in the next eighteen months as had been accomplished in the previous three years. Here perhaps can be seen a quality in Young that distinguished him from Smith—not mere practicality, because Smith had that too, but a willingness, even a compulsion, to organize and *do,* to take Smith's plans and visions, even roughshod, and drive people to get things completed. Young moved directly ahead. He had his own style. These leadership qualities would come to fruition on the trek west and in the Great Basin. After the church's early surge of expansion and growth under Joseph Smith, Young led the church through a phase of consolidation, organizational strengthening, doctrinal clarification, and coming to grips with practical problems.

Brigham Young's early development was in many ways similar to Joseph Smith's, but it also contained the seeds of their differences. Like the Smiths, Young's family emigrated from New England to frontier New York in Brigham's boyhood. As he said much later, he was "brought up from [his] youth amid those flaming, fiery revivals so customary with the Methodists."[9] He neither rejected nor fully accepted the strict, Methodist piety of his parents. Although he was interested in finding religious truth, he remained apart from the organized religion of his parents and friends. He did not find his answer in a vision. Young said that his prayer as a boy was "Lord, preserve me until I am old enough to have sound judgment, and a discreet mind ripened upon a good solid foundation of common sense."[10]

Brigham's mother died in his fourteenth year. He was apprenticed out and soon became a skilled carpenter, painter, and glazier. Meanwhile he continued to seek religious satisfaction: "I used to go to meetings—was well acquainted with the Episcopalians, Presbyterians, New Lights, Baptists, Freewill Baptists and Reformed Methodists—lived from my youth where I was acquainted with Quakers as well as the other denominations."[11] On the one hand, his concern for common sense was deeply offended by the revivalists: "Men were rolling and hollering and bawling and thumping, but [they] had no effect on me. I wanted to know the truth that I might not be fooled."[12] On the other hand, his yearning for spiritual nourishment was not met by established churches with their doctrinal contentions and arid moralizing. His reaction to hearing the famous Methodist preacher Lorenzo Dow was restrained: "He could tell the people they should not work on the Sabbath day; they should not lie, swear, steal, commit adultery, etc. but when he came to teaching the things of God he was as dark as midnight."[13] Young accepted traditional moral teachings, but his yearning for answers did not stop at that point.

Spirit and emotion but not to excess, common sense and good judgment but something more—such was the combination that haunted Young through his long quest for a religious "home." After his marriage in 1823 to Miriam Works, who had tuberculosis and slowly declined until her death in 1832, he tried mainly to be a moral, hardworking, and tender husband and father. But he also joined with various groups of independent "seekers" in the several towns in western New York where he pursued his carpentry and painting. When he moved in 1829 to Mendon, New York, where others of his family were also established, he joined with such a group, led by his brother Phineas, who described it thus: "We opened a house for preaching, and commenced teaching the people according to the light we had; a reformation commenced, and we soon had a good society organized."[14] From such groups, as we have seen, came many of the early converts to Mormonism.

Young's conversion began with the Book of Mormon, a copy of which he saw, fresh off the press, in the spring of 1830. But he was not baptized until 1832. He said later, "I examined the matter studiously for two years before I made up my mind to receive that book. . . . I wished time sufficient to prove all things for myself."[15] On another occasion he added, "I sought to become acquainted with the people who professed to believe that book. . . . I watched to see whether good common sense was manifest."[16] Not that he rejected all spiritual gifts or manifestations. At a small branch of the church in Pennsylvania he first heard speaking in tongues—the glossolalia that had been mentioned in the New Testament. He also heard a missionary without eloquence or talent for public speaking say: "I know by the power of the Holy Ghost, that the Book of Mormon is true, that Joseph Smith is a prophet of the Lord." "My own judgment, natural endowments, and education," said Brigham, "bowed to this simple, but mighty testimony."[17] Though he had earlier been repelled by the excesses of evangelical groups, Young found in Mormonism a counterpoise of rationality—"good common sense"—and a practical orientation that made the experience quite different.

The lay-priesthood dimension of Mormonism was especially satisfying to Brigham Young. He started keeping a diary the day after his baptism, which he described as follows: "Before my clothes were dry on my back Brother [Eleazer] Miller laid his hands on me and ordained me an Elder, at which I marvelled."[18] He later remembered the elation that came from being called and authorized to *do* something. Soon he embarked on a series of proselyting missions throughout New York and up into Canada.

Anxious to meet Joseph Smith in person, Brigham and his brother Joseph found the Prophet chopping wood. After hours of intense conversation Young spoke in tongues their first evening together.[19] But from what we can learn of Young's development in the church before he even met Smith, and of their subsequent relationship, it is probable that Young found in Smith the fullest human embodiment of the values he had already discovered for himself in Mormonism.

Young responded to Smith's call for the few hundred members of the infant church to gather at Kirtland in 1833. That winter he was especially diligent in learning from the Prophet and the other leaders in conversation and meetings. He volunteered for the Zion's Camp march to the aid of the church in Missouri that next spring. His faithful performance led to his being called, along with his closest friend, Heber C. Kimball, into the first Quorum of Apostles in 1835. Young later recalled that when two such relatively rough and untutored laborers were chosen, "some of the knowing ones marvelled . . . their looks expressed, What a pity."[20] Indeed, it seems that Kimball and Young were more eagerly employed in finishing the Kirtland Temple for the 1836 dedication than in participating in the School of the Prophets, where Smith studied doctrine and languages with other church leaders. But as Smith later pointed out, among that original Quorum of the Twelve only Kimball and Young did not ever "lift their heel against me."[21]

Young's loyalty to Smith had an emotional quality. Such fealty was crucial in Kirtland, where Smith's failed bank led to internal dissension. Young's fierce defense of Smith led to threats being made against himself, and he had to flee Kirtland for his safety, even before Smith himself was forced to leave in January 1838.

Over the next few years Young demonstrated not only tenacious loyalty but also the courage and competence to succeed in increasingly difficult assignments. He shepherded the migration from Missouri to Illinois; in mortal danger he returned with the Twelve from Illinois to Far West, Missouri, in order to fulfill to the letter Smith's revelation requiring them to take leave from the Saints at the temple site on April 26, 1839, for their mission to England; he led the apostles in England with a degree of success perhaps even beyond Smith's dreams. As a result of the confidence he developed during the mission, he went on more completely to establish the role of the Twelve when they returned. In 1844, as we have seen, most Mormons accepted Brigham Young as Smith's obvious successor.

During the year and a half after the martyrdom, Young marshaled the support of the badly shaken church. He told the beleaguered Nauvoo Saints, "I have traveled these many years, in the midst of poverty and tribulation, and that, too, with blood in my shoes, month after month, to sustain and preach this Gospel and build up this Kingdom."[22] At times his forthrightness was costly. Although in some ways he admired Orson and Parley Pratt and Orson Spencer, he tended to be suspicious of smoothly articulate but "impractical" intellectuals. He was particularly distrustful of Sidney Rigdon. On September 1, 1844, a few days before being excommunicated for refusing to follow the Twelve, Rigdon addressed a meeting. Young wrote in his diary: "His discourse was complicated and somewhat scattered. He said he had all things shone [shown] to him from this time . . . but he did not tell what the saints should do to save themselves."[23] Young knew what the Saints needed to do to save themselves.

The members of the church had to come to grips with three questions: Who would assume Smith's prophetic mantle? What would be their attitude toward the new doctrines that had appeared in Nauvoo preceding Smith's death? And what should be the temporal role of the church? On the whole, the Nauvoo Saints under Young's leadership supported continuation of his predecessor's policies. Less comfortable with these policies and Young's leadership were a few Latter-day Saints who were geographically removed from Nauvoo and its "mysteries."[24]

Predictably, the first dissenting body to organize after Young's assumption of leadership was headed by Sidney Rigdon. Upon his return to Pittsburgh, Rigdon called together a small group of followers and began publication of the *Latter-day Saints' Messenger and Advocate.* By the spring of 1845 the Church of Christ had voted Rigdon its president, denounced polygamy, and claimed that Joseph Smith had been a fallen prophet. By 1847 this small organization had virtually disintegrated, although Rigdon continued for another thirty years trying to rally support.[25]

The most important of the splinter groups that formed immediately after Smith's death was led by James J. Strang, "prophet and king" of a group at Voree, Wisconsin. Brilliant but unstable, Strang had been baptized in Nauvoo in February 1844 by Joseph Smith himself, then sent to survey the Burlington area of Wisconsin as a possible new gathering place for the Saints in that part of the country. In May he wrote to Smith praising the Racine and Walworth county regions and asking for permission to establish a stake (a kind of diocese of several congregations) there. After learning of Smith's death, Strang claimed to have received a letter from the Prophet naming himself as prophet and president of the church and designating Voree as the new gathering place for the entire church. Strang showed the letter to a conference of elders in Florence, Michigan. Some were persuaded, others were not. The presiding elder excommunicated him. By the time word of the incident reached Nauvoo, the Twelve were firmly established as controllers of the church's interests. On August 26, 1844, they confirmed the excommuniation.

Undeterred, Strang and his counselors proselyted throughout the Midwest and publicized a purported revelation in which Strang was ordained by an angel to be Smith's successor. During 1845 Strang and his followers gathered a small colony of believers at Voree. Eventually he won over two former apostles, William E. McLellin and John E. Page, who had lost their standing in the Nauvoo-based church, plus William Smith, brother to Joseph, as well as William E. Marks, who had previously followed Rigdon, and other, less prominent members. Later that spring John C. Bennett joined Strang's movement.

The diverse group of former church leaders who gathered with Strang at Voree were not destined to harmonize. Dissension and excommunications forced Strang in 1847 to relocate his colony on Beaver Island in northern Lake Michigan. By 1849 most of the Voree Saints had gathered there, and in 1850, in an elaborate ceremony, Strang was crowned King of the Kingdom.

But tragedy quickly ensued. On June 16, 1856, Strang was assassinated by alienated followers, and the next month his twenty-six hundred adherents were driven from Beaver Island. As late as 1977 there were three congregations and scattered families of Strangites totaling about four hundred members.[26]

Strang's relevance to the Mormon dispersion arises from the fact that he succeeded in attracting a number of disgruntled former Mormon leaders. He secured his influence by patterning himself after Smith's career. Strang's professed angelic ordination, his claimed discovery of a buried record, his introduction of polygamy and a temporal kingdom, even his final martyrdom, seemed a replay of previous events. It was not surprising that some Mormons were attracted to a leader whose very eccentricities reminded them of their first prophet.

Prior to the exodus from Nauvoo, Strang and Rigdon offered the only organized alternatives to Brigham Young and the apostolic regime. With the disintegration of Rigdon's church and the Voree group, a number of scattered dissenters, all baptized Mormons, including some who had suspended judgment since Smith's death, remained aloof from any of the possible successors to Smith's seat. As the westward-looking Saints conducted the great migration and built a mountain-desert empire, these undefined collections of believers began to coalesce around certain centers. Each represented a different concept of Mormonism's nature.

The first trend was toward the founding of short-lived "personality cults," centered around striking, often bizarre, leaders. For instance, George J. Adams, a noted Boston actor, followed Strang for a short while but broke with "King James" when the Voree prophet would not extend the privilege of polygamy to his counselor (Adams). In 1861 Adams organized a tiny sect called the Church of the Messiah. When he attempted to move the cell to Palestine in 1865, he provided humorous grist for Mark Twain's *Innocents Abroad* (1869). Charles B. Thompson also left Nauvoo to join with Strang. One year later he was called to "lift up his voice" as "Baneemy, patriarch of Zion." Thompson-Baneemy acquired a retinue of fifty or sixty families, including that of William E. Marks, who had been Nauvoo stake president. In 1853 Thompson founded the Community of Preparation in southern Iowa. When the community broke up, Thompson moved to Saint Louis and continued publishing a newspaper there until 1888. In a similar manner James Brewster; Apostle Lyman Wight, who led a group to Texas; Alpheus Cutler; Francis Gladden Bishop, the oft-excommunicated Nauvoo member; and William E. McLellin, along with Martin Harris and David Whitmer, all established tiny religious edifices on the shakiest of foundations.[27] A somewhat larger group than any of these, the Bickertonites, grew out of Sidney Rigdon's Pittsburgh apostasy.[28] None of the ten or so such splinter groups was numerically consequential.

It was a later Reorganization movement that became a genuine rival to mainstream Mormonism. The milieu that spawned this Reorganization was most notable in the beginning for its diversity. Many Saints outside Nauvoo, as well as residents not privy to the doctrinal innovations of the period, had been surprised by the rumors that reached them after the death of Joseph Smith concerning secret temple rites, the plurality of gods, and especially plurality of wives. Such practices and beliefs immediately became linked, for them, with Brigham Young. Other Mormons, finding the rigors of travel and Young's strong hand on the march west unbearable, filtered back from Iowa or beyond to seek out old homes and comfortable ways. They sought shelter from the conflicts that had convulsed the preceding years of Mormon history.

The Reorganization began in Wisconsin among a small band of families that had outgrown the flamboyant pretenders of the immediate post-Nauvoo period. Among these unquiet spirits was Jason W. Briggs. Baptized in Potosi, Wisconsin, in 1841, Briggs and the branch he led renounced Brigham Young as a successor to Joseph Smith and at first joined with James Strang. Briggs soon found that "some of the doctrines of Strang did not suit me." Accordingly, his branch moved, practically as a unit, into the party of William Smith, brother of the Prophet, who claimed leadership in the movement by right of blood relationship. But the peripatetic Briggs again became disaffected, perhaps by rumors that William Smith, like Young and Strang, favored polygamy.

His nostalgia for pristine purity drove Briggs to prayer in November 1851. "The elders whom I have ordained by the hand of my servant Joseph," the word of the Lord seemed to say, should fulfill their duty of preaching the restored gospel. In due time the Lord would call upon the seed of Joseph Smith and "bring one forth and he will be mighty and strong, and he shall preside over the high priesthood of my church; and then shall the quorums assemble, and the pure in heart shall gather, and Zion shall be reinhabited."[29]

During the next several weeks Briggs and his friends revealed this "word of the Lord" to several nearby branches. Briggs had become convinced that Joseph Smith III, the Prophet's oldest living son, a nineteen-year-old boy, who remained in Nauvoo with his mother, was the promised "mighty and strong" heir to the presidency of the church.[30] Over the next year and a half several other groups of Mormons seeking an alternative to Young's leadership joined the "Young Joseph" movement.[31] The first conference of the Reorganizers convened on June 12, 1852. Those who assembled published a pamphlet entitled "A Word of Consolation to the Scattered Saints" and began a missionary effort. By April 1853 the movement was growing appreciably, but young Smith had still not stepped forward to take his place.

Soon another revelation came, this time to H. H. Deam. It called for a provisional president, seven apostles, and several other officers for the incipient movement. When read and accepted by the small flock of waiting Saints, it provoked several spiritual manifestations. Zenos H. Gurley (a former Strangite) and Deam were named senior apostles but declined the presidency, so the office went to Jason Briggs.

In the years immediately following, the Reorganized branches waited in vain for their new leader to take his place. Nevertheless, the movement gained momentum. Priesthood quorums were developed, a pamphlet was published, and some congregations that had chosen not to migrate with Young joined the cause. Still young Smith did not appear.

By 1860 he was at last ready to assume leadership. Four years earlier he had rejected the plan, but now, in Amboy, Illinois, he told the church:

> I came here not of myself, but by the influence of the Spirit. For some time I have received manifestations pointing to the position which I am about to assume. I wish to say that I have come in obedience to a power not my own, and shall be dictated by the power that sent me.[32]

The twenty-eight-year-old man who accepted the call to head the Reorganized Church of Jesus Christ of Latter Day Saints probably played as great a role in forming its identity as did the teachings of his father. Joseph Smith III had grown up in Nauvoo with his mother, Emma, who trained her son in the Christian graces but taught him little about Mormonism. He was, as Alma Blair has characterized him, "open minded, slow to form opinions, logical with a sense of humor, able to see various sides to a question, but capable of coming to his own conclusions and holding to them." Charles Derry, who left the Utah church to join the Reorganized group, was impressed by his first meeting with Smith but added, "his appearance was more like that of a farmer than a church president."[33]

Smith was faced with a difficult challenge. To prosper, the Reorganization had to forge for itself an identity based on something more than feelings of anti-Brighamism and antipolygamy. Its response was a conservative one. Eventually, Reorganized officials rejected virtually the entire Nauvoo experience. Its branch of Mormonism was redefined within the safer limits of Smith's earlier years. Polygamy, plurality of gods, baptism for the dead, temple ordinances, the literal gathering of the Saints, the establishment of an earthly kingdom—these and other subsequent additions by the founding Prophet to Mormon theology were progressively expunged from the faith. Thus the Reorganization came to occupy a stance between standard Protestantism and Utah Mormonism. It retained a belief in a reopened canon, but its doctrinal position edged closer to a socially conscious, conservative sort of Protestantism.[34]

Difficulties with identity, however, have continued among Reorganized Saints. When the church in the West abandoned polygamy and emphasized the spiritual rather than the temporal Kingdom of God, the distance between sectarian America and western Mormonism appeared to diminish. The result has been to leave the Reorganization without a clearly defined role. It is no longer sufficient, Robert Flanders has pointed out, for members of the Reorganized movement to say, "We are not Mormons" or "We don't believe in polygamy." To maintain their identity a new footing is currently being explored. Flanders sees a possibility that increasing decentralization, pluralism, and "demythologization" will lead to "a new identity based on both early Mormon and modern ecumenical Christian principles."[35]

Whatever their present situation, Reorganized Mormons were successful in the nineteenth century in welding together several remnants of dissident Mormonism, including some dissenters from the western church itself. Nourished by a small influx of converts from foreign and domestic missions, by the 1970s the Reorganization could claim some 220,000 church members, concentrated mainly in the Midwest.[36] Headquarters are in Independence, Missouri. Relations between this group and the larger church, with its headquarters in Salt Lake City, are polite but not warm. Both accept Joseph Smith as a Prophet, but they draw different conclusions about the meaning of the Restoration.

For the majority of Saints, the death of their Prophet did not require such a searching reexamination of faith. They believed that the mantle of leadership and continuity had fallen upon the Twelve Apostles, led by Brigham Young. Thus the largest group of Mormons united under Young's leadership and, under the duress of continuing persecutions, reached westward for the long-sought dream of a Kingdom of God on earth.

But temporarily, for a year or two, they clung to Nauvoo. The murders of Joseph and Hyrum Smith had brought a short respite from the pressure of mob violence. During a period of relative peace, stretching through September 1845, Young and the Twelve Apostles moved ahead with a number of important tasks. First, they decreed that the vital missionary work in the eastern states and England should continue. "It is necessary," said Brigham Young in a general conference convened in October 1844, "that the Saints should also be instructed relative to . . . spreading the principles of truth from sea to sea, and from land to land until it shall have been preached to all nations."[37] Young sent Parley P. Pratt to the East to reassert apostolic control over missions there. There Pratt found William Smith, George Adams, and

Samuel Brannan leading rival factions of eastern members. He managed to impose some order and retain most of that vital missionary field for the Nauvoo Saints. Wilford Woodruff, the Welshman Dan Jones, and several other missionaries continued the work of the Twelve in the British Isles, which had long been the special preserve of the apostles. Contending "toe to toe and inch for inch for every bit of ground," in Jones's words, the Nauvoo missionaries converted more than six thousand Britishers in three years. Jones himself was responsible for thirty-six hundred baptisms in three and one-half years in Wales.[38]

The second goal of the apostolic regime was to complete the Nauvoo Temple and share with as many members as possible the sacred rites performed only in that edifice. "You cannot obtain these things until that house is built," affirmed Young. More than two hundred laborers worked at cutting stone and wood for the temple. The Relief Society, a Nauvoo women's organization, had donated two thousand dollars to the project; Joseph Toronto, an Italian sailor, added twenty-five hundred dollars to the fund. By October 5, 1845, the ground floor of the temple was ready for use. Even before that date the upper sealing rooms were packed with faithful Saints who participated in sacred ceremonies under the direction of Young and other apostles. In the winter of 1845–46 they gave as much attention to the temple as to the preparations for the trek they knew was ahead of them.

A third objective of the Nauvoo leadership was to consolidate and strengthen the internal structure of the church. Young increased the number of the Seventies, a priesthood group under the Twelve, and charged them with conducting a vast missionary effort throughout the world. Missionary districts were established in each of the country's congressional precincts. By such efforts Young assured a steady influx of converts, minimized the possibility of further division in outlying branches, and institutionalized the loyalty the Saints had previously felt toward Joseph Smith.

Persecution began again in the fall of 1844, when Mormon homes in Illinois were subjected to "wolf hunts"—freewheeling raids. The mobs disbanded under pressure from a state militia unit, but the latter soon let it be known that it could not be counted upon to protect Nauvoo. In January 1845 the Nauvoo charter, which had granted such extraordinary powers as the right to have a militia, was repealed by the Illinois legislature. That spring, harassment of the leaders with legal writs recommenced. In September, after barn-burning and crop-burning attacks on surrounding settlements, harassed Mormons flocked into the city for protection. While they might have been able to defend their outlying settlements if they had earnestly tried, the hostility of those in control of the state and neighboring towns assured that such success would be short-lived, or at least very costly in lives. Young at first responded with tough language ("at the first sign of aggression . . . give them the cold lead") and sent out a posse led by a sympathetic non-Mormon sheriff. But as soon as he saw bloodshed occurring, he began to negotiate.

By the end of September 1845 it was clear to the Saints that they would have to leave Nauvoo. In the years before his death Smith had discussed a number of colonizing projects in the West. He had looked to the Republic of Texas as a possible haven for the Saints. The Voree settlement in Wisconsin was part of the same expansive impulse. Early in 1844 he had planned an expedition to explore "Oregon and California" (terms then including practically the entire unexplored region of the present far western United States).[39] Even earlier, some associates later remembered, he had prophesied in August 1842 "that the Saints would continue to suffer much affliction, and would be driven to the Rocky Mountains. . . . Some would live to go and assist in making settlements and building cities, and see the Saints become a mighty people in the midst of the Rocky Mountains."[40]

Determined to find a haven well away from the increasingly populated Midwest, Brigham Young discussed the problem with his advisers in the fall of 1845, read John C. Fremont's *Report of the Exploring Expedition to the Rocky Mountains* (1845), and decided to send a party of fifteen hundred men to the Great Basin in the Rocky Mountains the next year. Almost immediately Nauvoo became a vast outfitting and blacksmith shop. Thousands of Latter-day Saint families struggled to sell their farms and homes and gather one good wagon, three yoke of oxen, two cows, two beef cattle, three sheep, one thousand pounds of flour, twenty pounds of sugar, one rifle and ammunition, a tent and tent poles, from ten to twenty pounds of seed, and some farming tools. Such an outfit was necessary, in Apostle Parley P. Pratt's calculations, to transport a family of five to the new gathering place.[41] The departure was set for the spring of 1846, as soon as water was flowing and there was sufficient grass for the animals.

Rising persecution, and indictments charging Young and the apostles with counterfeiting and other crimes, accelerated the departure. Young also heard rumors that there would be federal military intervention to prevent their movement on the ground that the Saints were intent on setting up an independent commonwealth. On February 2, 1846, despite the continuing winter cold, Young and the Twelve decided it was time to leave. They were delayed several days by members who, anxious to experience the temple ceremonies, lined up from early in the morning until late at night, the apostles serving as officiators in the ordinances. Finally, on February 15, Young joined the growing camp in Lee County, Iowa, across the Mississippi. Intending that a small group led by the Twelve would move ahead to find a settling place and plant crops, he had advised the main body of Saints not to leave until they were well prepared. But a steady stream of Nauvoo Mormons left the city throughout the winter and spring, the flow of refugees swelling and ebbing with fluctuations in the pressure applied by non-Mormons. Despite the token prices paid for the Saints' property and the unready condition of many of the families, the evacuation of Nauvoo was virtually complete by September. Some Mormons later trickled back into the city, but in the fall of 1846 Nauvoo the Beautiful, the "City of Joseph," stood almost empty.[42]

The exodus to the Far West, stretching as it did over several years and thousands of miles, is not easy to portray. It was not the movement of a single horde but rather a chain of sometimes loosely linked companies inching toward a destination at first ill defined. At one end of the chain, converts and refugees were continually beginning migration. At the other, almost immediately after the arrival in the Salt Lake Valley, they were dispersing into planned colonies throughout the Great Basin, that vast intermontane region whose waters drain toward the Great Salt Lake. The trek west added migration to the processes of conversion, gathering, and persecution in the Mormon panoply of formative experiences. It was a refiner's fire from which emerged tougher Saints.[43]

Young and the other leaders compared the Mormon movement to the exodus from Egypt under Moses, calling the leading party the Camp of Israel. Biblical rhetoric was used to heighten the Saints' sense of leaving a place of persecution for a Promised Land and of being miraculously blessed and guided. Their safe crossing of the Mississippi on the ice, the flocks of quail that descended to feed the most ill-prepared group to be expelled when they were starving on the west bank, and the last-minute assistance from the federal government (in exchange for the Mormon Battalion volunteers) that tided them over the necessary eight-month delay in Winter Quarters, Nebraska—such experiences could not help but remind the Saints of Moses and the Children of Israel.

This biblical identification was given particular point in the leaders' emphasis that they, like the Children of Israel, were being continually tested in order to prepare a fit generation for that Promised Land. When his brother apostle at Winter Quarters warned that the advance company could not make the journey with the one hundred pounds of provisions available per person, Young replied that he "did not want any to go who had not faith to start with that amount."[44] Moreover, they must learn to share: "Brother Perkins wanted to know something about our going west; I [Brigham Young] told him that those who went must expect to go on the apostles' doctrines and no man say aught that he has is his own, but all things are the Lord's; and we His stewards."[45]

The earliest refugees crossed the Mississippi on rafts and flatboats in February 1846. Later the river froze, the ice permitting many families to walk their teams directly across to Iowa. On the other side of the river the refugees streamed into the Sugar Creek camp, some nine miles inland from the Mississippi. They camped there in the most primitive conditions, awaiting spring weather. Nine babies were born the first few days at Sugar Creek. As early as February 25, one group set out in ten-degree weather for the Des Moines River. On March 1, with refugees still streaming into the Sugar Creek camp, other wagons prepared to leave. Brigham Young departed from the camp late in the afternoon, traveled five miles, and camped with a party of more than a thousand.

The progress of the Camp of Israel across Iowa was less than steady. Many of the Saints were penniless: "We have sold our place for a trifle to a Baptist Minister," wrote Martha Haven. "All we got was a cow and two pairs of steers, worth sixty dollars in trade."[46] As a result, most of the parties were continually on the lookout for employment in the many small Iowa towns through which they passed. The Mormons stopped over to earn what they could by building jails, courthouses, fences, and furniture, and by sending their band to play at funerals and wakes as far away as Saint Louis. Since many had crossed the Mississippi on foot, carrying their possessions in a handcart or box, they salvaged scraps of lumber and iron to piece together into wagons.[47]

By June 22 five hundred wagons had reached the Missouri River above its union with the Platte. There, at Council Bluffs, Young established a temporary terminus for the migration. Behind him, twenty-five hundred wagons and perhaps as many as twelve thousand Saints were scattered across 120 miles of sparsely inhabited prairie. Despite the confusion that developed, organization was quickly reasserted. Prominent Nauvoo leaders such as Gen. Charles C. Rich, Apostle John Taylor, Bishop George Miller, Charles Shumway, and Brigham Young himself had each taken charge of companies of four to five hundred wagons. Within each camp a pyramidal organization grouped families into tens, fifties, and hundreds, provided leaders for each unit, and distributed specialized guards and pioneers evenly among the groups of fifty. When the leaders of the entire camp met in March at Shoal Creek, 100 miles out of Nauvoo, they reconstituted this organization (which had been scrambled in the rush out of Nauvoo) and approved regulations that would keep the Saints from bidding against each other for scarce supplies of grain and other foodstuffs in the surrounding country. Thus, early on, the special circumstances of the Mormons' overland migration enjoined a centralized organization quite unlike that of most travelers of the period.[48]

During the fall and winter of 1846 several advance companies pushed past Council Bluffs. They spent the winter there on the Missouri, Platte, and Niobrara rivers. Young's group later backtracked three miles and established

Winter Quarters, now part of Omaha, Nebraska. Mount Pisgah, Garden Grove, and Council Point, Iowa—these were the main way stations established to raise food for those following.

Life was difficult in the winter of 1846–47. Some two hundred people died at Winter Quarters alone—perhaps one in thirty. Petty quarrels frequently disrupted life in the camps. James Hemmick challenged Wilbur J. Earl to a duel and was expelled from the camp. Counterfeit money was circulated by a few in the community, leading to incidents with Indians as well as trouble in the camps. Although each succeeding party of pioneers planted or cultivated plots of public land to provision those following them, this food supply was sometimes insufficient. Many families survived on the charity of their neighbors.

Weather, varying degrees of unpreparedness, and human cussedness combined in such a way that it took four months to cross Iowa's three hundred miles. For comparison, it took the pioneer company only three months to cover the remaining one thousand miles to the Salt Lake Valley in 1847. Of course, that later company was designed for speed and provisioned and organized in the way Young had intended the first trail-blazing group across Iowa should be. But in 1846, despite the energy with which he threw himself against all obstacles, Young's plans repeatedly broke against human and physical reality. The epic journey he led the next year to the mountains was a dramatic achievement. It was in Iowa in 1846 that Young learned to be the Moses his people needed.

One example of Young's ability to land on his feet was his handling of the noted Mormon Battalion experience. Back in January, Young had instructed the church's leading authority in the East, Jesse C. Little, to "take every honorable advantage of the times you can" to get assistance from the national government for the destitute church in its migration west.[49] He apparently hoped to obtain a contract to build a series of forts to protect the developing Oregon Trail. In May, Little met young Thomas Kane, a member of a prominent Pennsylvania family who had been reading sympathetically about the Mormons. Using Kane's connections in Washington, Little was able to obtain a series of interviews with President James K. Polk, who was naturally preoccupied with the recent declaration of war on Mexico. One suggestion was that the assistance take the form of enlistment of one thousand Mormon soldiers to march to California under General Stephen Watts Kearny and another one thousand to go by sea. By June 5 Polk had consulted with his cabinet and gave approval, but only for five hundred soldiers by land, apparently because of the opposition of Sen. Thomas H. Benton of Missouri, who impugned Mormon loyalty and persuaded the president that Mormons should constitute no more than one-third of Kearny's forces. Young was convinced by private informants that Benton was looking for a pretext to raise a military force in Missouri with which to pursue and disperse the whole body of Saints. This perception was recalled in an early speech in the Salt Lake Valley in 1847 when Young "damned President Polk for his tyranny in drafting out 500 men to form a Battalion, in order that the women and children might perish on the Prairies. [And] in case he refused their enlisting, Missouri was ready with 3,000 men, to have swept the Saints out of existence."[50] Two days later, in an emotional welcoming-home ceremony for Battalion members just arrived from California, Young stated that, because of Benton's dangerous intentions, "the Battalion saved the people by going into the army."[51]

Although the fear of being pursued by Missourians may have been exaggerated, Young was probably right that there was some kind of dirty work afoot. An intriguing letter from Thomas Kane on July 11, 1850, mentions the existence of some persons "besides the President who were willing to see you driven by force out upon the wilderness." The letter does not give further details, but Kane promised to write them up for the church to have from his executors when he died.[52] (Such a document may exist among those still closed to researchers at Kane, Pennsylvania.) If Kane did learn of such a plot, it was only on his return to Washington in the fall of 1846, because he traveled out to Council Bluffs in June to assure the Mormons that Polk's overture was in good faith. Whether Young suspected anything at the time is not clear. At any rate, he could see that the Battalion provided opportunities that might indeed save the Saints. After moving from camp to camp, speaking before campfires and from wagon tongues, he accomplished the impossible by persuading five hundred Mormon boys and men to leave their families and enlist.

Young argued that sufficient men would remain to conduct the exodus and that the Battalion wages would be an indispensable source of "hard cash" income. Moreover, cooperation would guarantee government permission to camp on Indian lands and use grass and timber. In their extremity it was no small consideration that five hundred men would be transported to California at government expense, thereby assuring Mormon prominence in the new territory expected to be established there.

The Mormon Battalion left Council Bluffs on July 20 to march to Fort Leavenworth, Kansas. Outfitted there, they began what probably was the longest march of infantry to that date in American history. A year later they arrived on the Pacific Coast, where they disbanded after earning some seventy thousand dollars in wages and allowances.

During the winter, Young further strengthened the lines of internal organization and communication necessary to administer a church spread out over several thousand miles. He established an internal mail service to communicate between the camps. When word reached the Missouri of the miserable condition of the last Saints to leave Nauvoo, he sent a relief team to bring the stragglers to join the main body.[53] To complete the lines of communication, he dispatched several apostles to England to oversee the missionary and emigration apparatus in that country.

On January 14, 1847, Young announced "The Word and Will of the Lord" to the Camps of Israel. The revelation reaffirmed the pyramidal organization of the previous summer and required the captains of each company to decide "how many can go next spring; then choose out a sufficient number of able-bodied and expert men, to take teams, seeds, and farming utensils, to go as pioneers to prepare for putting in spring crops." This document further required each company to care for its share of families of Battalion members, widows, and indigents and provided for extensive planting and building by those staying behind.[54]

Early in April, Young and a party of "able-bodied and expert men" left Winter Quarters to scout the trail and establish a preliminary settlement in the Salt Lake Valley, which church leaders had already selected as the destination.[55] As they commenced, some 143 men, 3 women, and 2 children, traveling in seventy-three wagons, comprised the company. The party traveled on the north side of the Platte River instead of the south side, which was the route for most groups heading west. As Wilford Woodruff later remembered, "We thought it best to keep on the north side of the river and brave the difficulties of burning prairies to make a road that should stand as a permanent route for the Saints independent of the then emigrant road, and let the river separate the emigrating companies that they need not quarrel for wood, grass, or water." [56]

The first destination of the pioneer party was Fort Laramie, 543 miles up the Platte River from Winter Quarters. They arrived there on June 1, 1847. That leg of the journey was not extremely difficult, for there were few streams to be crossed, the terrain was flat, and the teams were in good condition. The pioneers did have a few mild encounters with Indians and often had difficulty finding forage for their draft animals.

At Fort Laramie the pioneers were pleased to encounter a group of Mississippi Latter-day Saints who had wintered in Pueblo, Colorado, with the Mormon Battalion and then headed north to join the main group. From that point the company traveled west along the North Platte to Devil's Gate, up the Sweetwater and over the South Pass, then diagonally south and west to Fort Bridger on the Green River. Along the way they met mountain men Jim Bridger, Moses Harris, and Miles Goodyear, who gave varying views of the Saints' prospects in different parts of the Great Salt Lake area. They took the rather new Sublette Cutoff down Echo and Weber canyons and then the trail made just the year before by the Donner-Reed company up East Canyon and through the mountains. Although aided by some of the clearing that had

been done by the Donner-Reed party, the Mormon company made sl
progress through the tortuous canyons. Young lagged to the rear owing
an attack of Rocky Mountain (tick) fever that nearly killed him. Orson Pratt
and Erastus Snow, advance scouts, entered the Salt Lake Valley on July 21.
Three days later Wilford Woodruff's carriage, in which Brigham Young lay,
climbed the last incline before the valley. Young raised himself from the carriage floor and surveyed the new gathering place of the Saints. "The spirit of
light," he later wrote in his journal, "rested on us and hovered over the valley, and I felt that there the Saints would find protection and safety." [57]
Erastus Snow recalled him as saying: "This is the place whereon we will plant
our feet and where the Lord's people will dwell." [58]

The pioneer company immediately began planting crops, laying out a
stockade, and preparing for the arrival of the larger parties, which were en
route to the valley. Characteristically, they dedicated the land to the Lord,
prayed for rain, and built a dam for irrigation in case the rain failed to come.
After setting the process of settlement in motion, Young and a large party of
men left to return to the Missouri River Valley for the winter. As his band
retraced the route of the migration, it passed each of ten companies heading
west. Approximately seventeen hundred Saints traveled in these ten companies; these pioneers of 1847 formed the nucleus of the Mormon domain in
the West.

Historians have called the Mormon migration the best-organized movement of people in American history. Unlike other contemporary journeys to
the Far West, it was religiously motivated. The Mormons went without the
guides and professional outfitters employed by most westering emigrants. A
poverty-stricken band of people, in many cases unable to outfit themselves
properly, the Saints were not frontiersmen; they were artisans, farmers, businessmen, and clerks. The organization and cohesion of the Mormons was in
marked contrast to "the process of disruption [that] prevailed so generally"
in overland trail movements. [59] Unique to the Mormons were the planting and
building for the benefit of those to come later, sending back from Salt Lake
City relief and supply parties to aid others on the last and toughest part of the
route, and establishing a Perpetual Emigrating Fund to finance the poverty-
stricken so that they could make the journey and pay later. The entire community of Nauvoo, a whole culture, was transported to a completely uninhabited location. Other frontier communities either grew slowly, adding a
few families at a time until local government and trade became possible, or
materialized overnight in the boom-bust syndrome of the mining exploitation of the West. In contrast, Salt Lake Valley was, within three months of
its settlement, home to nearly two thousand people and was well organized
for trade and government.

Many of the characteristics of orderliness and obedience had previously been exhibited by the Saints, but the journey west reinforced them. Discipline, cooperation, and organization were essential; priesthood and camp leaders had authority to instruct members where and when to build fires, when to get up, when to stop, where to camp. One camp historian wrote that Brigham Young had instructed a company "not to abuse cattle but take care of them—not to yell & bawl or make any noise nor to be up at nights— but attend prayers & go to bed by 9—& put out the fires. It is best to tie up the cattle outside—horses inside—hogs & dogs to be tied up or shot—the sheep to be taken care of &c." [60] In large measure the people recognized Young's authority as necessary, and the exigencies of the trip and his successful leadership further strengthened his influence.

In addition, a certain resiliency, a feeling of having undergone the worst, grew in the Saints. "Mother, these western moves are hard on cattle," wrote Martha Haven, acknowledging that the move was also hard "on the people." Toughness led to pride. Martha Haven's letter concludes: "Truly, we have no abiding City. The ensign is to be reared upon the mountains and *all* Nations to flow unto it. We are not going to a remote corner of the earth to hide ourselves far from it." [61] And early in the migration William Clayton penned the anthem of a generation of Utah Mormons:

> Come, come ye Saints, no toil nor labor fear;
> But with joy wend your way.
> Though hard to you this journey may appear,
> Grace shall be as your day.
> 'Tis better far for us to strive,
> Our useless cares from us to drive;
> Do this, and joy your hearts will swell—
> All is well! All is well!
>
> Why should we mourn or think our lot is hard?
> 'Tis not so; all is right.
> Why should we think to earn a great reward,
> If we now shun the fight?
> Gird up your loins, fresh courage take;
> Our God will never us forsake;
> And soon we'll have this tale to tell—
> All is well! All is well!
>
> We'll find the place which God for us prepared,
> Far away in the West,
> Where none shall come to hurt or make afraid
> There the Saints will be blessed.
> We'll make the air with music ring,

Shout praises to our God and King;
Above the rest these words we'll tell—
All is well! All is well!

And should we die before our journey's through,
Happy day! All is well!
We then are free from toil and sorrow too;
With the just we shall dwell!
But if our lives are spared again
To see the Saints their rest obtain,
O how we'll make this chorus swell—
All is well! All is well! [62]

Having traveled back to Winter Quarters, Young reiterated his leadership by calling a general conference in December to sustain him as president of the church, with Heber C. Kimball and Willard Richards as counselors. Then, during the winter of 1847–48, Young and his fellow leaders organized five emigrating companies that would transport twenty-five hundred more Saints to their new home during the following summer.

For those in the Salt Lake Valley, the chief task was to survive the winter and then prepare for the flood of new immigrants expected the next summer. In addition to the pioneer companies, the Mississippi Saints and a number of ex-Battalion members swelled the settlement's population. In Young's absence during the first winter in the valley, government was in the hands of a stake presidency composed of John Smith (uncle to Joseph Smith), Charles C. Rich, and John Young. Under this leadership the Saints were organized into teams to construct a stockade lined with individual cabins; to plow, plant, and irrigate as much land as possible; to lay out a city; to bring in timber from nearby canyons; and to explore and hunt through the whole area.

On July 25 and 28, 1847, Young had preached sermons that, like John Winthrop's sermon aboard the *Arbella,* established the guidelines for the new community:

Those that do not like our looks and customs are at liberty to go where they please. But if they remain with us they must obey the laws sanctioned by us. There must be no work done on the Sabbath. As soon as we select a place of permanent location we shall take the compass and chain and lay out a city, and every man shall have his inheritance therein. We shall also lay out ground for cultivation, and every man shall have his inheritance and cultivate it as he pleases. Only he must be industrious. We do not intend to buy any land or sell any. . . .

We propose that the streets will be 88 feet wide, sidewalks 20 feet, the lots to contain 1 1/4 acre, eight lots in a block, the houses invariably set in the center of the lot, 20 feet back from the street, with no shops or other buildings on the corners of the streets. . . . [63]

From the beginning, Young sought to eliminate the divisive influences that had speeded the destruction of Nauvoo. Speculation, private ownership of natural resources, trade with Gentiles, and in fact almost all contact with the outside world were abjured. This Zion was to stand alone. That, at least, was the hope, the ideal.

By winter the pioneers had enclosed three blocks within a crude adobe wall, circled the city with eleven miles of fence and ditch, and prepared more than 5,000 acres for spring planting. Some 872 acres were sown in the fall with winter wheat. Captain James Brown of the Mormon Battalion was dispatched to California to collect Battalion pay and to purchase cattle and wheat and other seed. Roads, bridges, sawmills, and flour mills appeared as the council allocated public labor and directed private individuals in the task of preparing the valley for habitation.

Although the seventeen hundred Saints in the valley did not falter in their concerted efforts, a food shortage developed early in the winter. Too many poorly provisioned families had followed the pioneer company into the valley. The crops planted on July 24 had barely sprouted before untended animals grazed them to the ground. Indians and wolves decimated the livestock herds. The 1847 harvest consisted of a meager quantity of marble-sized potatoes. By winter the high council was asking for donations "in behalf of the destitute" and had inaugurated a voluntary rationing system. By spring the hungry farmers were reduced to eating crows, wolf meat, tree bark, thistle tops, sego lily bulbs, and hawks. Priddy Meek's dilemma was typical: "I would dig until I grew weak and faint and sit down and eat a root, and then begin again. I continued this until the roots began to fail." [64]

Just when the prospect of an abundant spring harvest in 1848 lifted pioneer spirits, hordes of crickets—"wingless, dumpy, black, swollen-headed, with bulging eyes in cases like goggles, mounted upon legs of steel wire, . . . a cross of the spider on the buffalo"—swarmed over the sprouting grain.[65] Neither fire nor water nor broomsticks could halt the invasion. At the height of the plague Charles C. Rich cautioned the pioneers not to dismantle their wagons "for we might need them." He may have been contemplating a move to California. At this point flocks of sea gulls from the Great Salt Lake appeared over the fields and began devouring the crickets. Many witnesses saw the intervention as providential; a remnant of the harvest was preserved, encouraging the Saints to remain in the valley. A Salt Lake City monument now commemorates the timely intervention of the birds.[66]

In 1848 the arrival of twenty-four hundred immigrants more than doubled the new colony's population. Some of them were put up in the "old fort" erected by the pioneer company of 1847, others were located in log cabins, tents, and wagons in blocks laid out around the projected site of the temple. The Mississippi Saints were located in Cottonwood, an irrigable farming region ten miles southeast of Salt Lake City. Under Brigham Young's direction the Council of Fifty replaced the high council as the de facto governing body of the colony. Under the council's close supervision food was rationed through another winter, more stringently than during the previous one. Cooperation was enjoined; speculation and private monopoly were denounced. "Natural feelings would say let them and their cattle go to Hell," exclaimed Young when some refused to join their cattle with the community herd, "but duty says if they will not take care of their cattle, we must do it for them." Of the surplus of those reluctant to share, Young said, "We will just take it and distribute among the Poors, and those that have and will not divide willingly may be thankful that their heads are not found wallowing in the Snow." [67] If the Saints' natural inclinations did not lead them to cooperation, the exigencies of their environment did.

During the winter Young established a court system, formed a provisional government for "the State of Deseret," distributed city lots and five- and ten-acre farming plots to nine hundred applicants, appointed trustees for natural resources, started several public works projects, coined several thousand gold pieces from dust brought by Battalion members returning from the California gold fields, and instituted a tax for public improvements.

Despite their industrious labors and careful planning, the Saints faced a gloomy future in the winter of 1848–49. In their two years in the valley the settlers had yet to reap a decent harvest. As reports of the gold strike in California trickled in, even the most loyal Saints began to wonder at their leaders' wisdom in choosing the inhospitable Great Basin for settlement. A few departed for the gold fields; others returned to the East. Brigham Young and the bulk of the church stood fast, but when Heber C. Kimball rose before them that spring to prophesy that the Saints would soon be able to buy eastern goods cheaper on their own streets than they could in the East, even the most faithful shook their heads. "I don't believe a word of it," declared stolid Apostle Charles C. Rich. [68] But within weeks thousands of forty-niners began to pass through the Salt Lake Valley on their way to the gold fields of California, leaving a wake of abandoned or cheaply traded goods and wagons. A fluke of fortune—or, as the Mormons interpreted it, a special blessing of Heaven—at once fulfilled a prophecy and combined with a good harvest and Mormon self-help to guarantee survival and make the continuing colony viable. Over the next half-century the settlement would grow to a network of nearly five hundred communities housing tens of thousands of Latter-day Saints. [69]

Part Two

The Kingdom in the West

⬦━━━⬦

Beginning in Nauvoo, Illinois, in February 1846, the Mormons carried out one of the great migrations of history. Over a period of forty years some one hundred thousand converts were organized and assisted across the ocean, inland by railroad or riverboat, across the Great Plains to the Salt Lake Valley, and thence to one of the five hundred Mormon communities in Utah, Arizona, Idaho, Nevada, Colorado, Wyoming, California, Alberta (Canada), and Sonora and Chihuahua (Mexico). In establishing their home in the West, the Mormons developed a subculture that added to the variegated patchwork quilt of America's heritage.

Under constant pressure to conform with dominant national patterns, the Mormons were in sporadic conflict with the American government for half a century. That conflict brought about creative adjustments. By the end of the century Mormon institutions were undergoing profound changes, but the basic religious programs were as vigorous as they were during the administration of Brigham Young.

6

{The Challenge of Building the Kingdom}

This [the Salt Lake Valley and Great Basin] is a good place to make Saints, and it is a good place for Saints to live; it is the place that the Lord has appointed, and we shall stay here, until He tells us to go somewhere else.

—Brigham Young (1856)

At the end of 1863 he writes, "I raised this year a good crop of corn, some wheat, and some oats." The sentence carries no overtone of the labor so strange to a mechanic. Jonathan [Samuel Dye] would have had trouble forcing this harvest from the earth anywhere, even in Illinois bottomland, where the soil is forty feet deep and is watered by generous summer rains. But at Easton [Uinta, Weber County, Utah] there were no rains and the thin soil was poisoned by alkali. The sagebrush was the index. Where sage grew, there other stuffs would grow also, after heartbreaking labor had cleared it away. Jonathan hacked at that hellish growth. Spines and slivers that no gloves can turn fill one's hands, the stench under the desert sun is dreadful, and the roots, which have probed deep and wide for moisture, must be chopped and grubbed and dragged out inch by inch. Then, before anything will sprout in the drugged earth, water must be brought. Through a dozen years of Jonathan's journal we observe the settlers of Easton combining to bring water to their fields. On the bench lands above their valleys, where gulches and canyons come down from the Wasatch, they made canals, which they led along the hills. From the canals smaller ditches flowed down to each man's fields, and from these ditches he must dig veins and capillaries for himself. Where the water ran, cultivation was possible; where it didn't, the sagebrush of the desert showed unbroken. Such cooperation forbade quarrels; one would as soon quarrel about the bloodstream. A man was allotted certain hours of water. When they came, at midnight or dawn or noon, he raised the gates into his own ditches and with spade and shovel and an engineering sense coaxed the water to his planting.

—Bernard DeVoto (1933)

Shortly after entering the Salt Lake Valley in the summer of 1847 the Mormon pioneers dammed a small creek to form a pool, and most of the company participated in a ritual rebaptism. "We had, as it were, entered a new world," Erastus Snow explained, "and wished to renew our covenants and commence a newness of life."[1] The symbolic act placed the group within a tradition extending to the earliest discoveries of America. In the sixteenth century the European mind sensed the significance of a vast, hitherto unknown and unexplored continent—a new world. A virgin land promised new beginnings: the opportunity of escaping difficulties of the past and of consciously shaping with deliberate design a better future. During the succeeding three centuries Europeans and Americans never quite gave up the hope that "if there were new lands and new inventions, there could be new societies molded by man's accumulated knowledge."[2]

To the Mormon pioneers of 1847 the eastern United States assumed the role Europe had traditionally occupied in the greater American consciousness, while the unsettled Great Basin offered the promise of a new world. Rebaptism, as Erastus Snow observed, underscored a desire by the Mormons to quit "Babylon"—to put behind them the misunderstanding, dissension, persecution, and temptation of contemporary American society and to build a new and better civilization in the Zion of their mountain stronghold. They were soon to find, as their New England ancestors had discovered, that a "newness of life" is more readily imagined than effected and that the past clings tenaciously to men, even in a new land.

The process of new settlement, of course, was central to the early American experience, repeated by groups from the sixteenth century to the nineteenth, from Newfoundland to Patagonia. For the Mormons, as for earlier colonists, establishing a viable new settlement required that, after traveling to a new homesite, people be domiciled, fed, and clothed while saving any surplus to increase the efficiency of future production and finance necessary outside purchases. It required the establishment of a trading system, including transportation. Institutions for facilitating both internal and external exchange had to be developed. A pool of folkways and traditions could set rules for everyday social life. Also necessary for enlisting community resources in collective enterprises were more formal institutions of government. The Mormons brought with them as part of their cultural baggage some institutions and values, but these now had to be adapted and implanted in the new western setting. It was, or seemed to be, a chance for a fresh start.

The site of the future Mormon domain had clear limitations as a center of new settlement, but to the Saints it possessed some distinct advantages as well. That some explorers doubted the soil and climate of the area would permit the growing of crops, that it was one thousand miles from any major population center, and that it was filled with several groups of Native Americans may have intimidated some, but to the Mormons these realities meant a land that was not attractive to anyone else—one that offered scope for development without interference from envious "old settlers" or ambitious speculators. The bulk of the population would settle within the Great Basin, the region bordered by the Rocky Mountains on the east, the Colorado River on the south, the Sierra Nevada on the west, and the watershed of the Columbia River on the north. The boundaries of Mormon settlement included about 210,000 square miles, encompassing almost the whole of present-day Nevada, the western half of Utah, the southwestern corner of Wyoming, the southeastern part of Idaho, a large area in southeastern Oregon, much of southern California, and a strip along the eastern border of northern California. Several minor settlements would spill over into the Colorado River drainage in the south and west, especially along the Virgin River, and into the Snake River drainage in the north. A crescent of high mountains, the Wasatch Range, rose abruptly from the valleys to rim the northeastern and eastern edges of the region, but toward the south and the west the landscape stretched out into flat desert broken by occasional minor mountain ranges. The settlers tended to huddle against the western flank of the high mountains curving along the northeastern rim of the Basin.

Arable land lay for the most part in narrow strips flanking streams running through the valleys. The quantity of land level enough to cultivate or close enough to water to irrigate was a small proportion of the total area.[3] In addition, much of the potential farm acreage was highly alkaline or saline, necessitating the development, through trial and error, of special farming techniques. There were rich, deep soils in the northern valleys, but in the south the soil was thin and fine—a slight integument above a broken sandstone terrain.

In an area where annual precipitation averaged only ten to twelve inches per year, it was critical that water resources be made adequate for agricultural and domestic needs.[4] In this respect the Mormons were especially fortunate because most valleys in the Great Basin and contiguous areas were crossed by several small streams originating high in the nearby mountains. The gradual melting of winter snowpacks sustained a flow of water throughout most of the summer. The supply was nevertheless limited and unquestionably restricted the long-term agricultural potential of the region.

Of the three major lakes, Bear Lake was northernmost, a high (6,000 feet above sea level) mountain lake surrounded by conifer forests. Utah Lake lay along the western edge of the rich Utah Valley, a freshwater body with a shallow, marshy shoreline. Forty miles north of Utah Lake was the Great Salt Lake, the most dominant geographical feature of the region, stretching eighty miles from north to south and thirty-five miles from east to west. Like Utah Lake, it had a nearly flat, marshy shoreline that changed dramatically as water levels in the lake fluctuated. Long an object of interest and curiosity, the "vast inland sea" imparted an air of the mysterious and exotic to the region. The connotation of lifelessness and sterility it carried had tainted the reputation of the whole Great Basin as a site for settlement and helped keep it uninhabited by white pioneers before 1847, despite early references to the promise of several valleys within it.

There was virtually no timber in the valleys, although an occasional clump of cottonwood and box elder grew along the streams. Nearby canyons and mountains, however, provided supplies of softwoods, primarily pine and fir, adequate for initial development. Church leaders early recognized that timber, as well as water, had to be carefully husbanded to ensure a supply for future needs.[5]

The region was rich in mineral resources. Copper, iron, lead, silver, and gold ores were to be found in substantial amounts, and there were large deposits of coal. Though the earliest settlers were keenly interested in the mineral deposits, the costly exploitation of these valuable resources was left, for the most part, to later, non-Mormon developers.[6]

There was considerable variation in growing season and precipitation. On any given day there could easily be a twenty-point spread in temperature between habitable northern mountain valleys and the southern "Dixie" region. In some localities frosts could occur as late as June and as early as September; other areas rarely experienced frost at all. Annual precipitation ranged from five inches a year in the southeastern deserts to nearly seventeen in Cache Valley.[7] The well-watered areas tended to have exceptionally short growing seasons, and areas with longer growing seasons tended to have less water and less fertile soils, thus further limiting the modest agricultural potential of Mormon settlement sites.

Several groups of Native Americans were resident in the Great Basin when the Mormons arrived. The Salt Lake Valley was a fortuitous location for the white settlers, serving at the time as a no-man's-land between the Utes, who ranged to the southeast near Utah Lake, and the Western Shoshoni, who peopled the land west and southwest of Great Salt Lake (there is some evidence that Jim Bridger gave Young this information). Southern Paiute groups lived in the extreme southwestern portion of the present state of Utah, and other tribes, the Walapai, Havasupai, and Navaho, controlled regions across the Colorado, directly south of the Paiute domain.[8]

Though settling initially in a buffer zone between competing tribal groups, the Mormons soon began to expand, encroaching primarily upon the territory of the Utes, who occupied most of central Utah. Some Western Shoshoni were displaced in the north, and some Southern Paiutes in the south, but the density of Mormon settlement in Ute territory and the desirability of Ute lands made the impact there especially heavy,[9] prompting armed resistance in 1850, 1853-54, and 1866-67.[10]

The distance of the Great Basin from main population centers was to be of great significance to the Mormons. Their new home was over a thousand miles from the western fringes of American settlement along the Missouri.[11] Inhabited parts of Oregon and California lay almost as far beyond. The journey to Salt Lake City from the nearest populated areas took over twice as much time as that from Boston to London in the mid-nineteenth century; the expenses undoubtedly were much greater.[12] The Mormons had, in effect, leaped beyond the line of American frontier settlement, moving to a region that others would not approach in significant numbers for three decades.

The remoteness of the site was initially seen as an advantage by the Mormons, who felt, as a favorite hymn phrased it, that in the valleys of the Rocky Mountains they had at last found a land where "none shall come to hurt or make afraid."[13] To a people with understandably ambivalent attitudes toward the United States, the Great Basin seemed curiously attractive: its very waters did not mingle with those from the outside. But the "blessed isolation" was costly. Although the Great Basin offered the Mormons an opportunity to control their own destiny, a large proportion of the time and energies of church members, especially during the first two decades after settlement, was spent in transporting goods and new settlers and in building transportation links between scattered communities separated by the mountains and deserts of the newly found refuge.

Reports of the lush, well-watered abundance of California had been brought by Sam Brannan, a promoter who in 1846 had taken a shipload of Mormons from New York around Cape Horn and established a settlement near present-day San Francisco. Some members recently discharged from the Mormon Battalion also arrived in the Salt Lake Valley and enthusiastically recommended a move to the coast. Brigham Young was unpersuaded. Despite the paucity of arable land, rainfall, and timber, and the potential threat of native inhabitants, the Great Basin was the place God had chosen and preserved as a refuge for his people; its disadvantages would guarantee the isolation that would make it a safe place to gather. "We are gathered here not to scatter around and go off to the mines," the First Presidency announced, "but to build up the Kingdom of God."[14] In Young's language, it "is a good place to make Saints, and it is a good place for Saints to live; it is the place that the Lord has appointed, and we shall stay here until He tells us to go somewhere else."[15] Like the Adam of Mormon theology, Young chose a world of struggle and growth over an easy but static Eden. Under his leadership the overwhelming majority of Saints, perhaps with some grumbling and dissent, turned away from dreams of golden California in order to dig ditches, grub out sagebrush, and erect adobe homes in the Great Basin. The major challenges to the Mormons in settling Utah were the necessary accommodation to the Native Americans, adapting to the conditions created by the dryness of the region, and overcoming the problems associated with the isolation of the Great Basin.

During the first few weeks the community functioned under the same organization by which they traveled to the West; that is, with a president of the entire company (Brigham Young), and with captains over tens, over fifties, and over hundreds. One party of ten was assigned to explore the surrounding countryside, another to dig ditches, another to fence off prospective fields from wandering livestock, still another to get timber from the canyon, and so on. Prior to leaving for the States, Brigham Young organized a stake presidency and high council to serve as the civic and ecclesiastical government. The Salt Lake organization was one "stake in the tent of Zion." Its presidency consisted of three individuals appointed by Brigham Young to serve as a president and two counselors. The high council was a group of twelve men, also appointed by Young, who were convened by the stake president to discuss policy, arbitrate disputes, and take over the leadership of various community religious and civic projects. Upon Brigham Young's return with additional settlers in the fall of 1848 the community was organized into nineteen territorial wards, or congregations, of seventy to one hundred families each. In charge of each ward was an appointed bishop responsible for seeing that the ward built and operated a school; built fences, roads, and canals; and conducted Sunday worship services. If there were poor people, he must provide for their needs; if new immigrants arrived, he must find a place for them to live and work. He adjudicated disputes between members, collected tithes and offerings, and supervised the planting of common fields and the management of collective herds of cattle. All such officers, who served without pay as a part of their religious responsibility, were presented to the congregations for their approval or "sustaining vote."

Also important was the militia, which grouped the male population into officers, companies, and ranks. Originally developed in response to persecutions in Missouri and Illinois, it retained the name of the Nauvoo Legion. Officers in the Legion were often officers in the priesthood groups as well, an example of the naturally interlocking religious and secular domains that disturbed non-Mormons who drifted into the region.

In 1849 the Mormons organized a provisional State of Deseret (a Book of Mormon term meaning "honeybee"), complete with a governor, lieutenant governor, and various government officials. Constitution and officers were approved by an election, but Congress, torn by disputes between slave and nonslave states, accepted Utah (named by congressional committeemen for the Ute Indians) into the Union only as a territory. For the next forty years the territory would be administered by federally appointed officials. Although Young himself was named as the first territorial governor, and some other governors were fair-minded administrators, the appointed officials were usually unsympathetic to the Mormons and their strange ways.

The challenges of new settlement in the harsh environment of the Great Basin were greatly compounded by the large numbers involved. During the summer of 1846 in the Mormon camps on the road from Nauvoo there were about fifteen thousand persons, three thousand wagons, thirty thousand head of cattle, and substantial numbers of sheep, horses, and mules.

After reaching their destination, the first priority was testing the agricultural potential. "We had a desire to try the soil to know that it could produce," Wilford Woodruff recalled many years later.

> Of course all this company—nearly the whole of us were born and raised in the New England States, . . . had no experience in irrigation. We pitched our camp, put some teams onto our plows . . . and undertook to plow the earth, but we found neither wood nor iron were strong enough to make furrows here in this hard soil. It was like adamant. Of course we had to turn water on it. . . . We went and turned out the City Creek. We turned it over our ground. Come to put our teams on it, of course they sank down to their belleys in the mud. We had to wait until this land dried enough to hold our teams up. We then plowed our land.[16]

Thus during the summer of 1847 the pioneers built a diversion dam across City Creek, which flowed through the center of their camp, and by this means were able to plow and plant a potato patch and a wheat field. When they discovered that grain sown in the early spring of 1848 would not mature without water supplied during the summer, they dammed Big Cottonwood Creek toward the north of the valley and dug a canal along the east side of the ten square miles of land known as the Big Field. From this mainline canal ditches were dug to each ward and then distributed by gravity flow to the various home lots and farming acreages. Each bishop was appointed to be watermaster for his ward to assure ample channels and equitable division of the water. Originally, the fields were flooded with water once or twice a week; later, rows of seeds were planted and individual "corrugates" were dug to carry tiny streams of water to each row.

The water came from streams that drained the mountains rimming the Salt Lake Valley. Diverted from these streams by means of dams and canals, it supplied homes, gardens, orchards, livestock, and farms. As the number of families under a canal multiplied, longer highline canals were constructed along the sides of the mountains to carry water to as much land as possible.

Many early ditches were dug without surveying instruments. A wooden triangle with a plumb supported from the apex was commonly employed for determining the run of a new canal. Makeshift levels were fashioned from wooden pipes and bottles filled with water. One bishop laid out a canal by filling a broad milk pan with water and sighting along the surface. Construction equipment consisted of little more than teams and plows, although an improvised device called a go-devil was sometimes used in larger projects. The go-devil consisted of heavy planks or logs bolted together in the shape of an

A. Pulled by a pair of draft animals, it dug deeply into the soil with its pointed end, throwing dirt up and out at the sides. A farmer would often be assigned a certain section of a canal to dig and maintain proportionate to his share of lands to be irrigated by the proposed project. He used his own simple agricultural implements to complete his section after the initial trench had been routed through by a collectively owned go-devil.[17] The whole project was to bring water to the land with a minimum of capital investment. No attempts were made until the 1870s to build large reservoirs for water storage. Learning the fine arts of field irrigation—how much water to carry to crops and how often to water—required years of trial and error.[18]

The new gathering place and headquarters city of the Mormons was named Great Salt Lake City, Great Basin, North America. Starting from the Temple Block, which was to be in the center, the settlers laid out 135 ten-acre blocks, each divided into eight home lots of one and one-fourth acres each. The streets were all 135 feet (8 rods) wide and followed the cardinal points of the compass. Each street was named for its direction and distance from the projected temple site. Fifth East Street was the fifth street east of the temple, running north and south. Second South Street was the second street south of the temple, running east and west. Besides the graphlike rationality and completeness of address thus achieved, the central importance of the religious base of the community was underscored with all locations designated by their relationship to the temple. Because of the shortage of timber, houses were characteristically constructed of sun-dried clay adobes, like those that Mormon Battalion members had seen in the Southwest. Each home was set back from the sidewalks twenty feet, with the sidewalks another twenty feet from the street.[19]

One block of the city survey was reserved as the site of a fort or stockade of log cabins that would serve as temporary housing. By September 1847, two months after the first Mormons entered the valley, twenty-nine log houses had been built in the fort and an adobe wall erected along three sides. More cabins were completed during the fall and winter. Since not all of the seventeen-hundred-odd settlers who wintered there could have been housed in the cabins, many lived on in their solid, canvas-covered wagon boxes, lifted from the running gears and set upon the ground, with lean-tos built alongside for extra room. Over the next two decades many families, arriving late in the fall, spent the initial winter in the wagon that had taken them across the plains.

The first religious services and civic meetings—the two were generally combined—were held in the "bowery," a forest of tall posts set into the ground to support a roof of brush, boughs, and dirt. Reconstructed on a larger scale in 1849 to accommodate three thousand people, the bowery was the community hearth and central meeting place until 1851, when it was replaced by a plain large adobe building called the Tabernacle. This building was superseded in 1867 by the elliptical structure now standing on Temple Square, also known as the Tabernacle, which still functions as the seat of semiannual general church conferences and of other major social and cultural events in Salt Lake City.[20]

The sacred center of the Mormon kingdom was to be the great temple. Begun in the 1850s, the building was an adaptation of features common in New England church architecture. Although the angles, detailing, and decorative carving were significantly altered, the main part of the structure was almost a replica of the temple built in Nauvoo under Joseph Smith's direction. Six towers topped with spires, three at each end, represented the orders of the Mormon priesthood. Each of the six pyramidal spires was flanked at its four corners by a descending set of three small pinnacles. A massive project requiring forty years to complete, the Salt Lake Temple absorbed a good portion of whatever resources could be spared from the fulfillment of vital physical human needs. This imposing "Chartres of the Desert," as Aldous Huxley once half-mockingly called it, though extravagant in its overall impression, nonetheless bespeaks the devotion of its builders and the sacred uses for which it was intended.[21] Here, as in Nauvoo, Mormons received their spiritual endowments, married "for time and eternity," and performed the same ceremonies on behalf of dead ancestors. In Mormon symbolism, the temple was the place where man met God—where the temporal met the spiritual, where the mortal met the immortal.

As the temple neared completion during the last half of the nineteenth century, the massive upthrust of the carved granite towers echoed the surrounding peaks and stood out as a powerful symbol to the immigrating and visiting Saints as they came into the valley and to those who lived in sight of it. Seen in its historical and religious context, the building possessed a strength unusual in American church architecture. It took daring and skill to conceive and begin such a structure early in the stage of settlement.[22]

From the beginning, Mormon leaders saw the Salt Lake Valley as only the point of initial settlement in the Great Basin. Once a bridgehead had been established there, colonization of every habitable part of the region would commence. During the first winter in the valley (1847–48) they decided to spend nearly two thousand dollars of Mormon Battalion pay to buy out the one white settler in the region, trapper Miles Goodyear, who claimed ownership of large portions of the Weber Valley, the present site of Ogden, Utah.[23] Several thousand Saints were still in camps along the Missouri River, awaiting an opportunity to come to the valley. A constantly growing stream of European converts was also eager to gather with the Saints in the Great Basin. Realizing that the Salt Lake Valley would not be able to contain everyone, Brigham Young and his associates planned a far-flung commonwealth of Mormon settlements.

The initial pattern of geographic expansion in Mormon colonization was the successive filling of contiguous irrigable valleys lying mostly in a north-south line along the western edge of the Wasatch Mountains. In September of 1847 settlement began edging north of Salt Lake City to the present site of the city of Bountiful. In the next year settlers moved onto lands farther north in Weber Valley. Southern settlement began in 1849, when colonists encroached upon Ute lands in Utah Valley and Sanpete Valley.

Three more distant colonies were founded as supply stations for trading caravans, immigrants traveling to the Great Basin, and those leaving the area on proselyting missions. Inspired by a proposal to "establish a chain of forts from Great Salt Lake City to the Pacific Ocean,"[24] Mormons founded a colony at San Bernardino, California, in 1851, but in 1857 most of them were recalled because of the Utah War. An 1855 settlement at Las Vegas was also situated along this southern route to the Los Angeles–Pacific Coast area. It is sometimes said that this place, too, was abandoned because of the Utah War, but the Las Vegas colonists were released from their mission in February 1857, before news of the approach of the Utah Expedition had been received, and all returned in September of that year.

Lying on the route to the Sacramento Valley and San Francisco Bay, Carson Valley, Nevada, became the site of Mormon colonization in 1851. The initiative here was taken by Saints acting independently of the central leadership of the church. By 1856 Young was persuaded to call an official colonizing mission to the area, but disputes with resident non-Mormons limited development, and the colony was abandoned in 1857.

The overland route to the Missouri River in Iowa was of great importance to Mormon trade and travel. The point where that trail met the Green River, in southwestern Wyoming, was especially significant because it marked a major intersection as the route divided into trails heading toward the Northwest, Utah, and California. Jim Bridger's fort dominated the site from 1843 until he abandoned it in late 1853. The next spring a colonizing mission was sent from Salt Lake City to occupy it. Opposed by a group of trappers who had taken up residence in the fort, the colonists moved twelve miles to the south to found Fort Supply. Church leaders purchased Fort Bridger in 1855, but by that time the Green River missionaries had decided to make a permanent colony of Fort Supply. Both settlements were burned in 1857 by the Mormons themselves, as part of the "scorched earth" policy they followed in response to the U.S. Army's movement against Utah.

Two, perhaps three, of the outlying colonies were founded primarily as bases for missionary work among the Indians. Fort Lemhi was established on the Salmon River in central Idaho in 1855 and abandoned because of Indian hostility in 1858. The Elk Mountain colony, close to the site of present-day Moab, in eastern Utah, was also founded in 1855 along the seldom used Old Spanish Trail. The obvious purpose of the group was to convert the local Indians to Mormonism. After several conversions the colonists became resentful of the freedom with which the new communicants helped themselves to the sparse supply of vegetables. The missionary-settlers began storing the food in the fort, an act that apparently angered the Indians and precipitated an attack on the fort during which three missionaries were killed. The effort was abandoned three months after it had begun.[25]

Colonies were established in every practical direction: to the north, in the 1850s in present-day Davis County, in Weber Valley, in Box Elder Valley, and in Cache Valley; in the 1860s in Bear Lake Valley and northern Cache Valley in Utah-Idaho. Brigham Young also favored expanding colonization toward the south. His dream of self-sufficiency meant the successful production of sugar, cotton, and other semitropical staples, and it was thought that severe frosts would limit agricultural production as settlements moved north. Interrupted momentarily by Indian uprisings in the late 1860s, the colonies reached their southernmost point north of the Colorado River by 1870. After a brief hiatus when several southern Nevada colonies collapsed, settlement began again in 1876 along the Little Colorado River in Arizona, preparing the way for colonization in the Salt River Valley, the Gila River Valley, and finally along the San Pedro River, only forty miles above the Mexican border. The later movement into Mexico to escape antipolygamist raids in the 1880s was only a slight extension of the southern point of Mormon colonization.[26]

Not until the 1880s, after Brigham Young's death, was there substantial colonization of the Snake River Valley, in southeastern Idaho, and the Star Valley, in western Wyoming. These later Mormon settlements tended to be less closely directed by central church leaders. Now settling in already partially occupied areas, the Mormons could not always follow earlier patterns of village-building and land apportionment.

Increasing pressures on the available land led to a second set of outlying colonies in the 1880s and 1890s. The San Luis Valley of southern Colorado was settled in the late 1870s and early 1880s by Mormon converts from the southern states. The several colonies founded there formed an enclave nearly three hundred miles from the closest centers of Latter-day Saint population.[27] At about the same time, the famous San Juan Mission to southeastern Utah was launched, an effort requiring an incredible feat of lowering wagons through a precipitous ravine very appropriately called Hole-in-the-Rock. The heroic effort was a monument not only to the faith and tenacity of the pioneers but also to the desperate need, by the end of the 1870s, for more lands to colonize.[28]

Antipolygamy raids in the 1880s led to settlements in southwestern Al-

Canada, far beyond the northern outposts of established Mormon domain. Another leap north took place in the late 1890s, when church leaders sponsored settlement in the Big Horn Basin, in northern Wyoming. This was the last important colonization in the traditional Mormon pattern—colonists supervised by church-appointed leaders settling in square-surveyed villages flanked by farmlands watered with cooperative canals—in effect weaving once more the fabric of religious, social, and economic practices that had become characteristic of rural Mormon life.[29] In the twentieth century Mormons would tend to follow the same pattern of migration as was occurring on the national level, that is, from farm to city. The presence of growing numbers of non-Mormons in what was originally Mormon country made it impossible to perpetuate the "traditional" form of colonization. In rural as in urban areas the religious and social cohesiveness that village life had once reinforced was now provided by the ecclesiastical ward.

For a half-century or more, starting when in 1831 Joseph Smith urged a move to the site of the New Jerusalem in Jackson County, Missouri, the Mormon colonization process presented a strong contrast to the rugged individualism of most American pioneering. In the Mormon pattern, a preliminary exploration was made under church sponsorship. A company was chosen and equipped to pioneer the settlement. These settlers were fortified by strong sermons reminding them that their mission was a necessary part of building the Kingdom of God and that strict religiosity and cooperation should attend their labors. The group, organized in a quasi-military fashion, first erected a fort where they spent several months. New colonists left in the fall or winter, so that they might build rudimentary shelters, construct irrigation works, and prepare land before time for planting spring crops. The pioneering company normally was heavily dominated by men; many wives and children remained behind until houses were built and security assured.

By the time colonization from the Salt Lake Valley base began, the process had become almost routine. Community institutions were patterned after those of Salt Lake City, which in turn followed those of Winter Quarters, Nebraska; Nauvoo, Illinois; and Far West and Jackson County, Missouri. One such colony was that headed by George A. Smith (an apostle and cousin of the founding prophet), who left Salt Lake City on December 7, 1850, with the Iron County Mission of 167 persons. The company reached Parowan, in southern Utah, the unsettled site of their future home, on January 10. On January 15 county officials were nominated; two days later formal elections were held under the supervision of three "judges of election" and a clerk. Sixteen officials were elected, including a representative to the territorial legislature, county judges, a sheriff, an assessor and tax collector, a road supervisor, a "weigher and sealer," a recorder, and four constables. On January 28 crews began hewing logs for a meetinghouse. Smith sent three letters to Washington, D.C.: one requesting a post office for the new town of Parowan, another asking the Smithsonian Institution for a barometer and other meteorological instruments, and a third informing the Mormon representative in Washington of his other two letters.

By the end of the month the essential community development allowed a moment of individual enterprise. "I called the camp together this morning," Smith wrote in his diary, "and told them that there was no call for public work today and that every man was at liberty." This news evoked "a regular stampede for the kanyon [sic], every man taking his axe and leaving his gun." It was the first time the men had had time to build homes for their own families. The next few months saw a school organized, canals and roads built, houses raised, a gristmill put into operation, and a site for an ironworks scouted. On July 4 the celebration of Independence Day was respectably calm and placid. "All was silent, not a gun fired, nor a drunken man seen in the streets," Smith wrote. This casual reference to peaceful Parowan attested to a remarkable colonizing accomplishment, for when the year began, this had been a solitary stretch of salt grass and sagebrush, disturbed only by occasional travelers between California and the Salt Lake Valley or nomadic Indians. Now, in a village surrounded by fields heavy with ripening wheat, there was concern that local rowdies might disturb the placid little city in its celebration of the national holiday.[30]

Within the decade the experience would be repeated at least one hundred times in other localities. By the end of the century more than five hundred communities in the American West would bear the distinctive stamp of Mormon colonization. A century later many villagers in southern Utah continue to surprise tourists with their determination to maintain homes in a forbidding land. The brick houses are plain, even severe, in design. Green lawns, gardens, and fields fade quickly to sun-baked desert where irrigation ends. The Mormon leaders of the nineteenth century had designated this area as a refuge and domicile for their people. Recognizing that it was no lush paradise, the Saints planted their roots deep.

Supplying clothing and manufactured goods for both domestic and industrial uses presented enormous difficulties. The nation's textile mills were still in New England, and shipping bolts of machine-made fabric to the region was prohibitively expensive. Homespun woolen goods were the main source of clothing during the early years of settlement. Tanning leather was a complex and difficult process that local facilities never mastered to the satisfaction of Mormon consumers. The cost of importing such goods and the outward flow of cash for them made it clear that local industries should be established. Yet an industrial plant could be built only by withholding investment capital from the often critical current consumption needs. Nevertheless, Brigham Young, determined that the Saints should have factories as well as dairies, devoted much energy to assuring industrial self-sufficiency for his people. "We do not intend to have any trade or commerce with the gentile world," he told the pioneer company almost immediately upon their arrival in the valley, "for so long as we buy of them we are in a degree dependent upon them. The Kingdom of God cannot rise independent of the gentile nations until we produce, manufacture, and make every article of use, convenience, or necessity among our own people. . . . I am determined to cut every thread of this kind and live free and independent, untrammeled by any of their detestable customs and practices."[31]

Suffused with a desire to promote economic independence, the church became involved in nearly every important industrial development during the first two decades of settlement. In addition it urged the establishment in local communities of such light industries as gristmills, sawmills, woodworking shops, hat factories, soap factories, tanneries, broom factories—anything that might promote self-sufficiency.

It was the stake high council, serving as a provisional government in the Salt Lake Valley during the winter of 1847–48 and the ensuing year, that led the first efforts toward industrialization. In 1849 Brigham Young, after spending nearly two years organizing the immigration, assumed a more active role in governing the infant empire. That spring the Mormon leader sat down with his advisors to plan the economic development of the Great Basin.[32] Most American-born Mormons were lifelong farmers possessing few industrial skills. Foreign converts, on the other hand, tended to be craftsmen and mechanics, reflecting in the variety of their skills the higher stage of industrialization Europe had achieved. One contemporary listing of the skills of emigrants leaving Liverpool for the Salt Lake Valley ran alphabetically from accountant to yeoman, and included 10 boilermakers, 46 engineers, 2 ironmongers, 226 miners, 8 printers, 22 spinners, 9 weavers, and representatives of other specialized trades.[33] Quick to recognize the importance of this expertise to his dream of building an independent commonwealth, Young instructed church agents and missionaries in Great Britain to seek out skilled workers, especially iron manufacturers, metal workers, textile manufacturers, and potters. Such persons were to be encouraged to "emigrate immediately . . . in preference to anyone else."[34] Each of the major industrial enterprises attempted by the church during the first decade drew upon European converts for technical expertise.

In addition to foundries, machine shops, and nail mills set up under the department of public works in the 1850s, the church became involved in attempts to launch five major industrial enterprises: a pottery works, a paper mill, a beet sugar factory, a textile establishment, and an iron smelter. Converts from Staffordshire, England, were asked to establish the Deseret Pottery in 1851, but its production was apparently never sufficient to have an important effect on supplies of dishes in the region.[35] The paper mill was a more successful operation. Beginning with a simple machine designed by an English convert, it was frequently updated with new machinery from the East and functioned efficiently to mitigate the natural paper shortage in Utah until 1883.[36]

The ill-fated attempt to launch the beet sugar industry in the early 1850s was a typically frustrating episode in the economic development of the region. Repeated efforts to import necessary machinery and to cultivate sugar beets failed to produce any palatable product.[37] Success came only when church leaders found an alternative in several varieties of cane that could be raised in southern Utah. For several years the molasses of sorghum cane became the staple sweetener of Mormon cuisine. Only after 1890 did the sugar beet become a significant source for local factories.[38]

The textile industry similarly began with bold plans and ended, in the short run, with modest results. After a woolen mill faltered because of lack of wool, its facilities were dismantled and sent to southern Utah, where cotton was being produced in sufficient quantity to make effective use of the machinery.[39]

The early attempts to develop an iron industry also ran aground, but not due to lack of organization or skill.[40] Part of the reason for establishing the colony of Parowan was for the production of iron. Former coal miners and iron workers were chosen to help found the new settlement. After the initial colonizing period a group of "iron missionaries" was called to move twenty miles south and build a small blast furnace. By the next September the furnace was ignited and "a small quantity of iron run out, which caused the hearts of all to rejoice."[41] In the meantime church officials had canvassed European congregations to raise funds and find the skilled workers needed to launch a substantial iron industry. In late April 1852, even before the first iron had been produced at the new town of Cedar City, the Deseret Iron Company was organized in London with a capitalization of nearly five million dollars. Leaders of the company, Erastus Snow and Franklin D. Richards, purchased machinery in Europe and arrived in Salt Lake City just in time to witness the presentation of the first Utah iron to Brigham Young.[42]

A rich vein of coal was located and a new furnace built. But Indian problems and a disastrous flood halted further work in 1853. In 1854 there was some iron produced, but the workers were primarily engaged in building a new blast furnace and six coke ovens. These improvements seemed to assure success. Nearly eleven tons of iron were manufactured in April 1855, and production continued into November. A bell was cast from the iron, the only known surviving casting from the ironworks.[43] Subsidized by both the church and the territorial government, the operation continued to expand. Troubles developed in 1856, however, when Cedar City coal did not produce an ideal coke, leading to consideration of an alternate site close to better coal deposits in Sanpete County. The accidental burning out of a blast pipe, followed by a drought that cut off necessary water, caused long delays. Devastation of their crops by grasshoppers forced workers to devote most of their time to production of foodstuffs, further postponing production.[44]

The 1857 season was also a near total loss. Continuing flood danger led to rebuilding on higher ground. This task was barely completed when the approach of federal troops led to the mobilization of all able-bodied men. The Utah War occupied the attentions of the group for nearly a year. Other problems plagued the operation when production was resumed in 1858, and in October of that year the experiment was given up.[45] Not until the capital and expertise of giant companies came to the region in the twentieth century were Utah's iron and coal deposits significantly developed. By 1965 Utah was the fourth largest producer of iron ore in the United States, a belated tribute to the imagination of pioneers of the 1850s.[46]

Whether in fighting grasshoppers, constructing iron furnaces and gristmills, or erecting telegraph poles, the Mormons functioned cooperatively. On the very day Salt Lake City was tied to a national telegraphic system, Brigham Young called church officials to his office to propose a north–south line connecting Utah settlements to the Salt Lake Valley. Scarcities of wire and other supplies caused by the Civil War delayed the project until 1866. Work began in earnest that spring, and one year later five hundred miles of line were in operation. Built almost entirely by volunteer laborers supervised by local church officials, the system was eventually extended to almost every Mormon settlement from Idaho to Arizona. Operators were supported by voluntary donations collected by the bishops. Charges for personal social messages were minimal, and church business of all kinds was free. Service to non-Mormon mining communities helped pay operating costs, and deficits were made up by the tithing office until the system was sold to eastern interests in 1900.[47]

Equally impressive were the efforts to construct a railroad network. Mormon settlers had gained experience in railroad building through contracts awarded them by the Union Pacific and Central Pacific railroads in the mid-1860s. As the transcontinental line neared completion, church leaders met to plan the Utah Central Railroad, which would tie Salt Lake City into the national system at Ogden, thirty-seven miles north of the Mormon capital. Mormon wards and settlements along the proposed route were asked to do the grading for portions of the line within their boundaries. Local ward bishops (parish ministers) organized the efforts, promoting friendly competition between neighboring communities. The symbolic importance of this first link in the internal Mormon railroad network was underscored in the dedication ceremonies on July 10, 1870. The last spike of native iron was made especially for the occasion by the department of public works. Both it and the steel mallet Young used in the ceremony were engraved with the words "Holiness to the Lord." Addressing the fifteen thousand Saints at the dedication, he emphasized the theme of self-sufficiency. "Since the day that we first trod the soil of these valleys, have we received any assistance from our neighbors?" he asked rhetorically.

> No, we have not. We have built our homes, our cities, have made our farms, have dug our canals and water ditches, have subdued this barren country, have fed the stranger, have clothed the naked, have immigrated the poor from foreign lands, have placed them in a condition to make all comfortable. . . . We have fed the Indians to the amount of thousands of dollars yearly, have clothed them in part, and have sustained several Indian wars, and now we have built thirty-seven miles of railroad.[48]

The Utah Central Railroad, built almost wholly by volunteer labor and without outside financing, stood as the ultimate symbol of the determined independence of the Mormons. In 1871 the line was extended northward, connecting settlements in northern Utah and southeastern Idaho, but it remained economically unprofitable until the Union Pacific assumed management in 1877.[49]

Church leaders also started construction of another railroad line southward. As the line moved into Utah Valley and then further south, spurs were built eastward to the granite quarries and mining camps of Little Cottonwood Canyon and westward to Bingham, the center of Utah copper mining activities. This track gradually became entwined in the intrigues of national railroad magnates and was completely out of Mormon hands by 1879. Some Utah citizens were so disillusioned that Provo newspapers advised members to travel to general conference in Salt Lake City by wagon rather than line the pockets of railroad magnate Jay Gould.[50]

Frequently Mormons launched cooperative projects that businesses with greater capital and the favors of national politicians were later to expand and exploit. Constructing railroads by volunteer labor worked well in Mormon-settled areas, but successful completion depended on a ready supply of iron rails and rolling stock from the outside. This seemed to be the point at which involvement with national railroad interests became necessary. The Mormons sought to expand the home-sponsored roads beyond the more heavily settled areas of Utah Valley in the south and Cache Valley in the north, but they lacked the voluntary labor that had facilitated their progress to those points. Inevitably the railroads passed out of Mormon hands and became links in a national system.

Not only did the Mormons cooperatively build fences, canals, roads, public buildings, telegraph lines, and railroads, many of them also functioned for a period in cooperative communities. In the 1860s each village or settlement was asked to establish, under the managership of its bishop, a cooperative store that handled all commodities sold at retail. "Profits" of the store were used to establish supporting industries—livestock herds, woolen mills, tanneries, and boot and shoe shops. As this movement progressed, manufacturing and merchandising interests in each community were welded into a single large locally owned cooperative called a United Order.[31] The emphasis was on "home" (that is, village) industry, unity, and brotherly love. In establishing several dozens of these United Order communities in the 1870s, Brigham Young envisioned a society in which the people would make and raise all they needed to eat, drink, or wear and still realize a surplus for sale to outsiders. There must be greater self-sufficiency; people must overcome selfishness and prepare for the millennial reign of Christ.

There came to be a variety of types of United Orders. In some villages residents ate in a common dining hall, wore clothes from the same bolts of cloth, labored under the direction of an elected board of management, and shared equitably in the community product. In others, farms, shops, and factories were run by the central cooperative, but families divided the proceeds according to their labor and ate separately. In still others, the community operated several cooperative enterprises on which dividends were paid to the investors, but some economic activity continued private in nature. Some of these idealistic communities lasted for many years, while others were discontinued after functioning for only a few months or years.

Success in such ventures is often measured both by endurance and by the degree of equalitarianism achieved. If these were the sole criteria, the cooperative communities did not approach the success of Hutterite or Shaker communes, for Mormon experiments were short-lived, and "free agency" and economic inequalities persisted among the Saints.[32] But if it were possible to measure the value of property thus "consecrated" and the number of manhours devoted to the Mormon experiment, the totals would be impressive. There were, in addition, personal rewards. Many of those who lived in the United Order, especially in the more rigorous communities such as Orderville, Utah, saw their experience as a time of near-perfection in Christian living, a spiritual success if not an economic one. The ideal remains a part of twentieth-century Mormon awareness.

7

{Immigration and Diversity}

A church without a gathering is not the church for me;
The Savior would not own it, wherever it might be.
   But I've a church that's called out,
   From false traditions, fears and doubts,
A gathering dispensation—O, that's the church for me.
                              —Mormon song (1845)

In the milieu of the founding of Mormonism the idea that the "elect" or converted should gather together was hardly surprising. The Book of Mormon narrated a dozen or more gatherings of people who traveled across oceans or deserts to escape the wicked. Only months after the formal organization of the church Joseph Smith made public a revelation calling the scattered New England and New York Saints to join together:

> And ye are called to bring to pass the gathering of mine elect; for mine elect hear my voice and harden not their hearts.

> Wherefore the decree hath gone forth from the Father that they shall be gathered in unto one place upon the face of this land, to prepare their hearts and be prepared in all things against the day when tribulation and desolation are sent forth upon the wicked.[1]

Mormons thus tended to see themselves as modern Children of Israel, chosen to raise a holy city to the Lord. As Saints of the latter-days, looking forward to the Second Coming of Jesus Christ, they had to unite and purify themselves.

Besides such religious beliefs there were practical reasons for gathering the Saints together. Persecution had begun almost simultaneously with the birth of the new religion. Scattered believers saw themselves as easy victims of torment; grouped together, they could more easily protect themselves. Then, too, the "world" (Mormons used this word in the New Testament sense) was seen as dominated by corrupt institutions, values, and practices. In such a setting the vacillating Saint was likely to fall away rapidly. New converts and the more stalwart believers longed to come together for mutual support and to establish institutions and practices appropriate for Zion.

The call to gather to Zion was at once a religious principle, a test of faith, and a lure. Most obviously, the doctrine that each convert join the main body of the church was presented as a heavenly commandment:

> Yea, verily I say unto you again, the time has come when the voice of the Lord is unto you: Go ye out of Babylon; gather ye out from among the nations, from the four winds, from one end of heaven to the other. . . . Let them, therefore, who are among the Gentiles flee unto Zion.[2]

Such phrases reached deeply into Mormon eschatology. For many faithful Latter-day Saints, the world was balanced precariously on the brink of destruction. Each new flood, earthquake, or war was noted by Mormon newspapers, often with an editorial opinion that such events heralded the day when the wicked would "be burned like stubble" and only the pure-in-heart of Zion would remain. In the terminology of the new religion, the faithful became the descendants of Israel through Ephraim, non-Mormons became Gentiles, the nations of the world became Babylon, and the home of the church "in the tops of the mountains" as prophesied by Isaiah became Zion. In the words of a song often sung by the soon-to-be-gathered Saints: "O Babylon, O Babylon, we bid thee farewell; we go to the mountains of Ephraim to dwell."[3]

Religious commandment merged with economic enticement to stimulate the gathering of Mormons. The Book of Mormon itself spoke of America as "a land choice above all others."[4] The Bible prophesied of the wonders and glories of the city of Zion. Not that conversion and gathering meant immediate economic rewards. For many, conversion to Mormonism meant the loss of whatever economic and social privileges they possessed before joining the church. Schools, employers, and friends often closed their doors to new Mormons, forcing even those who had not originally intended to emigrate to travel to the Mormon homeland. To provide encouragement, Mormon leaders were not reticent to extol the economic advantages of emigration. In 1852 the *Millennial Star,* published in England, commented:

> For the Saints to get themselves to the Valley, is a good thing. Few of them can be worse off there than they are here. Many of them here have not the necessaries, to say nothing of the comforts, of life. There, all would have the

necessaries, and most would obtain many of the comforts. As a whole, the Saints of Utah are far better fed and clothed than their brethren and sisters in this country. Then how unwise it is for anyone to delay gathering till he gain sufficient means here to make himself what he thinks comfortable on the journey to, and after he arrives at, the Mountains.[5]

Such sentiments fell on eager ears among the working classes of Europe. The Mormon migrations from Europe began in 1840 during a time of poverty and unrest in Britain.[6] And throughout the century the combination of destitution at home and the "mirage in the West" (Durand Echevarria's phrase) that released the great flood of emigration to the New World provided powerful reinforcement to the Mormon gathering.

Certainly most Mormon converts felt they had undergone a spiritual change. But without the lure of a home in America would there have been fewer of them? One must remember that in many ways Mormonism was the least attractive of the several available means of emigration to a new country. Demanding of the emigrant strict obedience and continuing economic sacrifice, it offered in return a home in one of the least inviting regions of the hemisphere. Clearly the Mormon religion itself, if not the sole factor behind emigration, was the key to the process.

Mormon missionaries in England early demonstrated their ability not only to convert Britishers to the church but also to persuade the new converts to emigrate to the United States. During the first decade of the British Mission, 1837–1846, there were 17,849 English baptisms.[7] Of these, more than 4,700 converts journeyed to the United States to gather with the Saints in Nauvoo. At first the British converts received little official aid in the process of emigrating. Mission officers in Liverpool helped emigrating converts to reserve room aboard oceangoing vessels, but the Saints themselves were expected to pay all costs. Missionary elders returning to the States after several years abroad generally accompanied the groups and served as temporary leaders and guides. Emigrating Britons generally embarked at Liverpool, traveled for several months in cramped steerage, then debarked at New Orleans, where they caught a Mississippi River boat upriver to Saint Louis and then on to Nauvoo. Other converts reached Illinois overland from New York, Boston, or other Atlantic Coast seaports.

In the mid-1840s some church officials began to assist emigrants. Reuben Hedlock, American president of the British Mission, created a scheme whereby British Saints would send English goods to the Mormon headquarters in America. When they emigrated, they would in return receive livestock and land in the gathering place. The motives behind this Joint Stock Company, as the plan came to be called, were mixed. Undoubtedly a goal of some of the men involved was profit. "There is abundant room for enterprise," wrote David Kimball, "and surely we have as much right to dip our bread in the dish, to gather up the wealth of nations, as any one else."[8] The plan soon broadened to include plans for a trade circuit including the California coast, Latin America, and Britain.

In 1846 the apostles Orson Hyde and John Taylor arrived from America and immediately quashed the scheme. Apparently feeling that the joint-stock form of organization would be more of a distraction than a boon, they issued a proclamation denouncing it:

> That holy zeal for the conversion and salvation of souls, which ought to burn in the bosom of every man that has been honoured by the priesthood . . . has been quenched and smothered by the damps of a misguided ambition. . . . the Spirit of God never sent forth men to preach Joint Stockism.[9]

The next attempt to lend official support to the migration arose after the expulsion from Nauvoo. Faced with the problem of large numbers of impoverished Saints remaining in Iowa while the main body of the church moved on to Utah, Brigham Young was anxious to prevent the lingerers from falling into apostasy or joining a rival faction. His solution was for Utah members to donate money and goods to help others to make the journey west; those assisted were expected to repay the church when they established themselves in the Great Basin. In 1849 when the windfalls of the gold rush brought a new prosperity to the Salt Lake Valley, the Mormon leaders decided to expand the plan to include needy British Saints who desired to emigrate.

The resulting official plan for aiding immigrants was ratified by a general conference of the church in Salt Lake City in 1849. A committee in Utah was appointed to gather funds. The money was then entrusted to Edward Hunter, who would travel to the eastern states, purchase cattle for the emigrating companies, and then return with the companies to Utah. When the immigrants arrived in the Salt Lake Valley, Hunter would sell the cattle to finance the next season's emigration. One year later the Utah legislature incorporated the Perpetual Emigrating Company, commonly known as the Perpetual Emigration Fund, or PEF. The preamble to the company charter compared the dreary lot of the oppressed in Europe, whose labor was "insufficient to procure even the most common necessaries of life," with life on the "genial soil" of Utah, where "labour and industry meet their due reward."[10] The advantages were not all to the immigrants. As the preamble continued:

> Labor, industry, and economy is wealth, and all kind of mechanics and laborers are requisite for building up and attending the benefits of civilized so-

ciety, subduing the soil, and otherwise developing the resources of a new country.[11]

The church leaders clearly felt that the immigration process should play a part in building the kingdom. Potential emigrants were divided into three classes. The first were those unable to pay any part of their way from Europe. The fund covered all expenses of their trip, but they were expected to reimburse such expenses after they reached Utah, either by working on church projects beyond the 10-percent labor tithing expected of all Mormons or by donating their surplus produce or cash to the church. A second class of PEF-assisted emigrants, known as ten-pound companies, was composed of those able to donate some part of their expenses. As expenses rose, the ten-pound plan became thirteen- and then fifteen-pound plans. A third group were the cash companies, those able to pay all costs of the journey but who utilized church-chartered ships and organizational facilities.

In 1853, 2,312 persons emigrated to the Great Basin with assistance from the fund. Four hundred were in the "poor companies," 1,000 were in the ten-pound class, and the final 955 paid their own expenses. Between 1852 and 1855 the PEF helped approximately 10,000 Latter-day Saints come to Zion. By 1870 the fund had assisted more than 38,000 from the British Isles and 13,000 from Scandinavia and the European continent.

The financial arrangements of the PEF were complicated by the general poverty of the Mormon converts. As soon as potential European emigrants were baptized, they were encouraged to begin saving for the trip by making regular deposits in either the Emigration Deposit Fund, the Individual Emigration Account, or the Penny Emigration Fund, all maintained by mission personnel. The fund received additional monies from contributions by wealthy members, tithing payments by European Saints, and commissions earned by Mormon shipping agents who sold space aboard Mormon-chartered ships. The bulk of the PEF finances, however, came from donations by church members already established in the Great Basin. Between the formation of the fund in 1849 and its dissolution near the end of the century Great Basin Mormons gave approximately eight million dollars. Nearly all contributions were made in kind: livestock, grain, produce, hay, or other goods. Such donations were collected in bishops' storehouses and later arduously converted into the cash needed to charter ships, buy equipment, and pay for provisions. The territorial legislature sought to aid the fund by directing that all unclaimed strays and other incidental sources of territorial income be directed to the PEF. Each year church leaders determined how many emigrants could be handled. If donations fell below the required amount, general tithing funds were transferred to make up the difference.

After arranging sufficient financing for the voyage, a potential emigrant gave his name to the PEF shipping agent in Liverpool. When the agent had enough applications to fill a ship, he chartered a vessel and notified passengers of the time of embarkation, price of passage, amount of baggage allowed, and other particulars of the voyage.

Local church organizations were responsible for organizing their potential emigrants and shepherding them to Liverpool, the chief port of the European Mormon emigration. For British Saints this meant little more than a short train or ferry ride, but Scandinavian, German, French, and Italian converts, who made up a significant portion of the emigration by the mid-1850s, often found the first leg of the journey difficult. The Scandinavian Saints usually united to charter their own ship to Liverpool.

At Liverpool the emigrants boarded waiting vessels. If the ships were late in arriving or had been commandeered for naval service, the travelers were lodged at the expense of either the PEF or the delinquent shipowner. Aboard ship, the agent appointed a president and two counselors (usually missionaries returning to America) to preside over the company. After receiving the sustaining vote of the group, the "presidency" divided the company into wards or branches, usually along the lines of the travelers' home districts. Each ward or branch was then provided with presiding officers and assigned a separate portion of the ship. Single men and women were usually assigned to opposite ends of the ship; on at least one occasion they were separated by the family section.

Once underway, the emigrants were expected to rise at an early hour, clean their quarters, assemble for prayer, and then eat breakfast. Choirs, language classes, dances, and theatricals occupied much of the time while onboard ship. Contemporary observers were impressed by the prevailing order, cleanliness, and decency aboard Mormon ships. Charles Dickens, novelist-chronicler of Victorian life, described the Mormon emigrants in a chapter of *The Uncommercial Traveler:*

> They had not been a couple of hours on board when they established their own police, made their own regulations, and set their own watches at all the hatchways. Before nine o'clock the ship was as orderly and quiet as a man-of-war . . . there was no disorder, hurry, or difficulty. . . . I afterwards learned that a Despatch was sent home by the captain, before he struck out into the wide Atlantic, highly extolling the behavior of these Emigrants and the perfect order and propriety of all their social arrangements.[12]

A select committee of the House of Commons studied the emigrant shipping in 1854 and concluded that "no ships under the provisions of the 'Passengers Act' could be depended upon for comfort and security in the same degree as those under the Mormon agent's care."[13]

Converts often arrived on the American frontier with only a short time to prepare for the trek to Utah. At the outfitting point they were provided by the emigration agent with their "outfit," consisting usually of one wagon, two yoke of oxen, two cows, and a tent, worth a total of $250 to $500 in the 1850s. To economize, emigrants were expected to purchase cotton fabric for the wagon covers in England and stitch it during the voyage. Ten immigrants were assigned to each wagon and provided with one thousand pounds of flour, sugar, bacon, rice, beans, dried fruits, and other supplies sufficient to last the trip. Provisioning several thousand emigrants a year was no simple task. Horace S. Eldredge, head agent during 1853–54, wrote that in 1853 he purchased four hundred wagons, two thousand oxen, supplies for four thousand persons for three months and a large quantity of merchandise and machinery needed by the church in Utah. The wagons and cattle alone cost $120,000.

After 1854 the main debarkation port of the immigration was shifted from New Orleans to New York to avoid the cholera epidemics that were sweeping through the southern riverport. Later immigrants traveled by the expanding railway network to the jumping-off point in the west.

The route from Kanesville (Council Bluffs), Iowa, to Salt Lake City was well established. For a few cents travelers could purchase one of several small guidebooks giving exact distances, camping conditions, precautions, and directions for the entire trip. Nevertheless, the trip was arduous for European members, who were unaccustomed to the rigors of frontier travel. Urban converts had little faculty for handling teams, camping, repairing wagons, or hunting. Experienced Mormon guides, often missionaries crossing the continent for the third or fourth time, escorted most companies. Brigham Young also asked the Utah settlers to send out relief trains to meet the incoming parties somewhere in Wyoming with fresh food and strong teams. In 1852 the immigrating companies were welcomed at the midpoint of their journey by two hundred wagons carrying fifty-thousand pounds of flour and vegetables. "I care not what you believe about the resurrection," the practical Young said, inducing his followers to volunteer for the relief trains, "if I can only get religion enough in the people to accomplish that [sending relief trains], it will satisfy me for the present."[14] In 1853 Fort Bridger and Fort Supply, in western Wyoming, were secured in order to service the immigrants better.

By 1856 the expense of outfitting several thousand immigrants each year was becoming too great for the church. To supplement the wagons, leaders decided to furnish immigrants with small two-wheeled carts, close in size to those used by apple peddlers in eastern cities, which could be pulled by hand from the Missouri to the Salt Lake Valley. The vehicle required no time-consuming harnessing and no concern for maintenance of livestock. Each cart would carry the provisions and a few personal effects for four or five people.

Heavier possessions and food supplies would be transported in wagons accompanying the train, one for each twenty handcarts.

The idea seemed so practical and promising that nineteen hundred people signed up for the handcart immigration in 1856, traveling by rail from the ports of Boston and New York to Iowa City, Iowa, where the handcarts were waiting. Organizing into companies of one hundred carts, the immigrants spread out along the twelve-hundred-mile trail from Iowa City to Salt Lake City, the first company arriving at its destination in September. Two later companies arrived in good spirits and without mishap. The final two companies were delayed, however, while waiting for handcarts to be built. They left Iowa City on July 15 and 28 under the leadership of James G. Willie and Edward Martin. Although seasoned travelers advised them not to travel beyond Winter Quarters, Nebraska, that late in the season, their eagerness to reach the valley overruled their judgment. Both groups were overtaken by early winter storms in Wyoming. Rescue teams sent out from Salt Lake City did not arrive in time to prevent many deaths from exposure to the severe weather, and of the 1,076 immigrants in these two companies over 200 died.[15]

Brigham Young was conducting a religious service in Salt Lake City when he learned that rescue missions were bringing the last company into the valley. He turned to the audience, announced that there would be no afternoon meeting, and then asked the women present "to go home and prepare to give those who have just arrived a mouthful of something to eat, and to wash them and nurse them. . . . Prayer is good, but when baked potatoes and milk are needed, prayer will not supply their place."[16] One of the arriving party told of their reception after the grueling journey as they entered the city with frozen feet and near starvation, despite the assistance from the rescue parties that had met them earlier:

> We arrived in Salt Lake City nine o'clock at night the 11th of December 1856. Three out of four that were living were frozen. My mother was dead in the wagon.
>
> Bishop Hardy had us taken to a home in his ward and the brethren and sisters brought us plenty of food. We had to be careful and not eat too much as it might kill us we were so hungry.
>
> Early next morning Bro. Brigham Young and a doctor came. The doctor's name was Williams. When Bro. Young came in he shook hands with us all. When he saw our condition—our feet frozen and our mother dead—tears rolled down his cheeks.[17]

The tragedy of the Willie and Martin companies was a setback from which handcart migration never fully recovered. With PEF funds at an all-time low, the European Saints had the choice of handcarts or delay until teams and wagons could be afforded. Most chose to delay, and immigration dropped to 480 converts in 1857. That year church leaders developed a bold design for a chain of way stations stretching from the Missouri to the Great Basin that would make handcart migration much safer and facilitate transportation to and from the Missouri. But the Utah War destroyed this plan, halting all immigration in 1858. In the prosperous years of 1859 and 1860 only three companies chose to travel by handcart, and no handcart companies were organized after that. All told, approximately three thousand persons had carried their possessions in handcarts across the twelve-hundred-mile route during a period when fifty-two hundred came by team and wagon.[18]

The plan devised as a substitute for the handcarts called for each Utah settlement to donate teams, wagons, and drivers to form a church train that left for the East as soon as spring weather permitted. Initially the train traveled to the Missouri, but later it merely had to meet the westward-moving railhead. At the eastern terminus of their route, church wagons were loaded with machinery, merchandise, and immigrant baggage. Wagons then made the return trip to Utah before mountain passes were blocked by snow. Between 1860 and 1869 most immigrants arrived in Utah walking beside one of the church trains. After 1869 completion of the transcontinental railroad revolutionized immigration.

Whether they arrived by wagon, handcart, or railroad, the immigrants were greeted warmly in Utah. Many were eagerly awaited by relatives who had come to Zion and sent back money for their families. Those who arrived without prior arrangements could still look forward to excellent treatment from their "brothers and sisters in the gospel." Here, for example, is a *Deseret News* reporter's comment on the arrival of one company in 1864:

> The Bishops and their assistants have had a stirring time since Captain Hyde's train got in, enormous quantities of meat, pies, bread, potatoes, and other consumables having been "taken up" through the wards and "put down" with considerable gusto by the arrivals on emigration square.[19]

The already established Saints were under instructions to take the new arrivals into their homes, care for them, and provide employment until they could begin to farm or practice their own occupations.

The sense of gathering was confirmed by the food and festivities that welcomed immigrants on Emigration Square. Soon afterward they dispersed to the colonies scattered throughout the Great Basin. The dispersal began with a "placement meeting" attended by all local bishops. Each was asked how many families could be absorbed into his ward for the winter and what special skills were desirable. The British traveler and editor William Hepworth Dixon told of a placement meeting in which one bishop said he could "take five brick-layers, another two carpenters, a third a tinman, a fourth seven or eight farm-servants, and so on through the whole bench." In a few minutes, Dixon observed, "two hundred of these poor emigrants had been placed in the way of earning their daily bread."[20]

The first spring after their arrival the immigrants often traveled to more distant settlements. Some joined relatives, others sought one of the small communities colonized by Mormons from their own country. Many stayed in Salt Lake City to use their skills as artisans on the large public works programs always underway in the city. Still others applied for an "inheritance" of land and began farming. Very few became dependent upon the church, or burdens on those already established. Young often reiterated his view of church responsibility:

> True charity to a poor family or person consists of placing them in a situation in which they can support themselves. In this country there is no person possessing an ordinary degree of health and strength, but can earn a support for himself and his family. But many of our brethren have been raised at some particular trade or employment in the old country, and have not the tact and ingenuity to turn their hand to anything, which forms a strong feature in American character. It therefore becomes our duty to teach them how to live.[21]

On the whole, immigrants responded well to the encouragement and guidance of the Mormon leaders. Although there were exceptions, most became as well adjusted to the territory as the earlier pioneers.

Between 1846 and 1887 European emigration to Utah totaled over 85,-000. Through 1855 the 21,911 emigrants included 19,535 Britons, 2,000 Scandinavians, and a few French, Italians, and Germans. In the late period the non-British nationalities made up a larger portion of the total.[22] The number of Scandinavians eventually reached over 30,000 before the end of the nineteenth century. Not all of those who came were assisted by the Perpetual Emigrating Fund; many paid their own expenses. But by 1880 those who had received help owed $1,604,000 to the fund. Half of these debts were canceled by John Taylor, president of the church, to celebrate its jubilee year of 1880.

The Mormon emigration of the nineteenth century resembled the great efflux of dissatisfied Europeans to the New World, but it differed in important respects. It followed an internal dynamic, ebbing and flowing more with changes in the church's situation and the missionary effort than with the economic and political cycles that determined the rate of most emigration.[23] It was marked by a degree of order rarely seen in secular migrations. Finally, the attitude of the early Mormon settlers toward the immigrants was remarkable. Although some signs of nativist resistance to newcomers appeared from time to time, the Saints by and large showed a great willingness to extend a welcome. Most of them had experienced the gathering impulse themselves and could empathize with their fellow believers. And of course they were repeatedly reminded of their religious obligation to love and help their "brothers and sisters in the gospel." If the reality fell short of the ideal, it seems fair to say that the usual harsh lines between different nationalities and between old and new arrivals were softened by Mormon values and programs.

The sight of each new company of immigrants marching through Salt Lake City was designed to stir the soul of every faithful Mormon: brass bands playing, flags waving, and children singing hymns. Zion was growing, and soon she would be delivered from her enemies.

Among non-Mormons, however, the arrival of fresh converts was more of a cause for consternation than rejoicing. The prospect of shiploads of foreigners being channeled yearly to Mormon Utah was enough to arouse intense opposition to Mormon immigration in the national press and political circles. As early as 1865 Samuel Bowles, editor of the Springfield, (Mass.) *Republican,* described the Mormon immigrants as "simple, ignorant people beyond any class known in American society, and so easy victims to the shrewd and sharp and fanatical Yankee leaders in the Mormon church." Gentiles in Utah were not slow to add their voices to the Eastern cry against the immigration. The anti-Mormon *Handbook on Mormonism* classified Mormons as "low, base-born . . . hereditary bondsmen . . . serf blood." Others described the converts as a barely human crop harvested from the slums and fields of Europe.[24] Mormon spokesmen like Apostle George Q. Cannon (himself a British immigrant) responded to the charges, but could do little to alter the public image of Mormon immigrants.

Despite the general verbal opposition to the Mormon immigration, little concrete action was taken to stem it until the 1870s. In 1876 the United States Supreme Court ruled that immigration policy was a matter strictly confined to the federal government. In 1879 Secretary of State William Evarts became uneasy about Utah's "accessions from Europe . . . drawn mainly from the ignorant classes, who are easily influenced by the double appeal to their passions and their poverty." Evarts soon sent a formal note to several European governments requesting aid in stopping the Mormon stream at its sources, but he received little response to his move. The Danish government dismissed it as manifestly absurd that they seek to interfere with law-abiding citizens on grounds that such converts were "potential lawbreakers" and polygamists.[25] Even the London *Examiner* opposed the secretary's move:

> We repeat, therefore, that it is not in the power of the United States, with regard for the law, the Constitution, and the rights of man, to prevent the Mormons entering the country merely because they are suspected of polyga-

mous views. In England there are several thousand Mormons, and in Scandinavia quite as many. They hold their meetings publicly, and try to make proselytes. Yet though their views may be abhorrent to everyone of common sense and decency—yet, so long as they do not transgress the law of the land, there is not injustice enough in England to punish them simply because some of their faith may have 10 wives in another part of the world.

In reporting the above, *The New York Times* stated that many considered the Evarts proposal "a canard" and were unable to believe that "anything so absurd could be seriously fathered by the American Government."[26]

But national concern over immigration in general grew throughout the next five years. More and more Americans felt that the nation was becoming a dumping ground for foreign undesirables. Although not dealing directly with the Mormon question, a congressional act of 1882 established a selection system that excluded certain elements from the country. The first list weeded out lunatics, foreign convicts, idiots, and persons likely to become wards of the government. It also levied a fifty-cent tax on all immigrants to finance the necessary administrative apparatus. The act had little effect on Mormon migration, although in one case a group of Swiss converts were delayed as "paupers" because of the church's policy that immigrants not carry cash on the voyage. In 1885 and 1887, at the urging of organized labor, Congress passed two laws designed to prevent immigration financed by contracts pledging immigrants to repay their expenses after arrival. Although the act might have been interpreted as a challenge to the Perpetual Emigration Fund system, it was never used for that purpose, probably because after 1869 the PEF functioned only as a facilitator.[27]

In 1887 the Tucker Amendment to the Edmunds Act struck at Mormon immigration. A direct effort to destroy the temporal power of the Mormon church, the amendment provided "that the Perpetual Emigrating Company be dissolved, its charter annulled, and its resources escheated and expended by the Secretary of the Interior for the use of the district public schools of Utah." Further, the territorial legislature was prohibited from supporting any plan for the "bringing of persons into the said territory for any purpose whatsoever." The church's attorneys asserted that the Perpetual Emigrating Company

has never held or owned at any time since its incorporation any real estate whatsoever;

That the contributions to its funds have been by it expended, as they have been contributed, and that at no time has any fund remained on hand for any length of time;

That it did not, on the 19th day of February, 1887, nor on the 3rd of March, 1887, hold any real or personal property whatsoever, save and except certain promissory notes, which had been heretofore given it by emigrants in payment of advances by the said corporation to them to assist them in their emigration, and which said notes are for the most part barred by the statute of limitations, uncollectable, of no value and wholly worthless.[28]

When the federally appointed receiver actually took control of the fund, he found the church attorney's statement generally accurate. Nevertheless, the Edmunds-Tucker Act destroyed the financial and organizational machinery that had assisted the immigration process.

The second law aimed directly at Mormon immigration was passed in 1891—curious timing because by then church leaders had already formalized their intention and advice to abstain from plural marriage. The exclusion list of 1882 was now expanded to include "persons convicted of other infamous crimes or misdemeanors involving moral turpitude, polygamists, aliens assisted by others by payment for passage and contract laborers under the 1885 statute."[29] Perhaps Congress feared that the Mormons would revive polygamy when they had gathered sufficient converts to Utah, or possibly the 1891 law was merely a delayed response to the vigorous anti-Mormon campaign of the previous decade.

Actually, the shift in American attitudes toward immigration had little effect on Mormon policies, for the Saints themselves had undergone a change of heart and circumstance. The relative importance of immigration had peaked during the 1860s, when the foreign-born population of Utah comprised 35 percent of the territory's total population. After 1870 that percentage declined; in 1880 it was 30 percent, ten years later only 25 percent. By the turn of the century it was below 20 percent and still dropping.

There were many causes for the decline in Mormon immigration. The ratio of conversions had declined since the earliest missionary period of the church. The conflict between the church and the nation often diverted energy from missionary effort and finally brought an effective halt to conversion and immigration. The first clash occurred during the Utah War of 1857–58, when all foreign missionaries were called home to defend Zion. The peak immigration years of the Civil War period marked a time when the nation was preoccupied with its own difficulties, so that the Mormons were able to pursue their ideal of the Kingdom. In the 1880s friction between Utah and the nation reached new heights. With the passage of the Edmunds Act (1882) and the Edmunds-Tucker Act (1887), the church became involved in a battle for survival. Defense, not growth, was emphasized during these years. To these causes must be added the factors that generally influenced immigration. Although the Mormon immigration did not precisely follow general trends, the drop in newcomers to Utah mirrored a comparable decline in national figures.[30]

In addition, the constant flow of new Saints from Europe had weakened the European missions. Enthusiastic converts, most capable of building a dynamic local organization, consistently went to the United States, leaving behind the sick, the poor, and the lukewarm. In 1880 out of a total church membership of 160,000 only 11,000 remained in Europe. American missionaries could not always fill the void.

The first suggestion of a change in official church policy on immigration may be seen in a *New York Times* article in 1890 which quoted George Q. Cannon, member of the church's First Presidency, as saying, "Our converts are made abroad by missionaries just like those of any other Church, but instead of inducing them to come to this country, we really urge our missionaries to dissuade them in any way they can. It is not to our advantage to have any come who are not thoroughly grounded in the faith."[31] At first the new policy was not unequivocally announced or enforced. Gradually the principle of gathering was de-emphasized, but in 1891 the *Millennial Star* was still informing the British Saints that "those who receive the gospel among the nations are to be assembled in the land of Zion, which is in the western hemisphere. . . . "[32]

The ambiguous situation continued through most of the 1890s. Cannon's conference speech of October 1898 clearly counseled the Saints not to emigrate immediately:

> There is one course that has been taken which I think will be attended with good effects, that is counseling the Saints in the various lands where they embrace the Gospel to remain quiet for a while; to not be anxious to break up their homes to gather to Zion. This counsel is being given by the Elders now in various lands.[33]

But Cannon's advice did not eliminate the gathering. He merely wished the Saints to prepare themselves before gathering. By 1907 the temporary injunction had developed into a policy that foreign members stay in the country of their conversion and build up the church there. The church began buying or building permanent mission headquarters and chapels in countries with stable local congregations. A 1911 message of the First Presidency urged members not to emigrate. In 1913 and 1915 sites for temples were dedicated in Alberta, Canada, and Laie, Hawaii. As time went on, statements instructing converts to remain in their native lands became even more definite. Although a few converts continued to emigrate to Utah each year, the heyday of gathering was over. Zion was moving to the scattered members rather than the scattered members to Zion.

The consequences of the gathering were diverse and often subtle. At times the survival of the church may have depended on the success of the gathering. During each early crisis, missionaries went out to recruit converts to Zion. While dissension and difficulties grew in Kirtland, Joseph Smith sent the first missionaries to England. As the Saints struggled to establish a new home in Illinois after their expulsion from Missouri, Smith again called the apostles to proselyte in England. The influx of British Saints into Nauvoo immeasurably strengthened that city and formed a large group loyal to the apostles who had originally converted and guided them. Subsequent to Smith's death, the apostles once more took steps to maintain the connection between the British Isles and the Zion they hoped to establish in the West. After the settlement of the Great Basin, successive waves of immigrants helped bring in the numbers necessary to colonize remote regions, stabilize the industrial base, and provide technical skills for specific undertakings.

The gathering infused Mormonism with the cultures of several different ethnic or national groups. Today a visitor to Cache Valley, eighty-five miles north of Salt Lake City, finds a remarkable complex of different cultures still in existence. Wellsville, the first town in the valley, was founded by Peter Maughan, one of the early English converts to the church. Hyrum, three miles to the east, was a Scandinavian town from its beginning, and names such as Liljenquist, Olsen, and Carlson still predominate. Five miles north sauerkraut is traditionally produced by the largely German residents of Providence. In Logan, the largest town in the valley, the oldest bank, which was founded by a Yankee who once presided over a Mormon colony in Mexico, later became part of a financial empire built by the sons of a Scottish immigrant. The Logan hospital was founded by the sons of another Scottish convert. One of the city's jewelry stores is managed by the descendants of Waldensian converts from the Italian Alps. In Smithfield and Newton one can sample the valley's famous Swiss cheese. A tour through Utah's other towns or valleys yields similar results. A half-century of missionary work and gathering made the Mormon church as notable for its diversity of national background as for its religious solidarity.

In 1870 British-born immigrants made up nearly one-quarter of Utah's total population. The significance of this total is minimized by the ease with which these immigrants blended into the American environment. The majority of the British converts had urban and industrial backgrounds. In Utah they tended to locate in the principal cities, where they could find work in the trades, business, or small industries. Salt Lake, Weber, Utah, and Davis counties were the most densely populated areas of the territory, and each received a large share of the British immigrants. Unimpeded by the language or cultural difficulties that slowed others, Britons were easily absorbed into local populations and soon moved into leadership positions. John Taylor, born in England and converted in Canada, succeeded Brigham Young as president of the church. Other Britons served as stake and temple presidents, general church authorities, and mission presidents.

Scandinavian immigrants were next to the British in number. When Mormon missionaries first approached the poor farmers and tradesmen of Denmark, Sweden, and Norway with "the restored gospel" and glowing pictures of Zion, their listeners must have felt a sharp contrast to their own meager incomes and low-ceilinged homes. Between 1850 and 1880 more than thirty thousand became convinced that their spiritual and temporal state would improve through their joining the Mormons.

As they traveled to Utah, some visualized their future activities idyllically:

> We plow, we sow and irrigate,
> To raise the golden grain;
> And diligently labor
> To independence gain;
> Some haul the wood from canyons wild,
> Some tend the flocks and herds,
> And all our moments are beguiled
> By industry's rewards.
> My Valley Home, my Mountain Home,
> The dear and peaceful Valley.[34]

Once in Zion, the Scandinavians encountered unforeseen difficulties. More than the English settlers, they faced economic problems in their first years in the territory. Arriving later than the English, the bulk of the Scandinavians were forced to go farther afield to find land and water. The first newcomers colonized the Sanpete Valley. Later immigrants followed to Sanpete or went north to Box Elder and Cache counties. Many skilled workers could remain in Salt Lake City, where clerical, sales, and administrative jobs were usually filled by American or English natives. As the Scandinavian immigration continued, although at a diminished rate, church leaders were forced to find new areas for colonization. In the second wave of Mormon settlement, during the last quarter of the century, Scandinavian members helped establish colonies from Arizona to Canada and shared the trials and disappointments of such expeditions as the Hole-in-the-Rock mission in the far southeastern corner of Utah. In 1878 Bishop Hans Jensen Hals of Manti explained the decision to colonize the San Luis Valley in southern Colorado: "Utah is becoming too crowded for us. . . . Because our poor brethren and sisters who come to these tightly populated towns in Utah have no chance to get land to cultivate for themselves, the Lord has led our brethren the apostles to take this step for Zion's outspreading."[35]

The Scandinavian immigrants eventually solved their economic dilemma. The Cache and Sanpete valleys, both containing large Scandinavian populations, became the granaries of the territory. Other immigrants found different economic niches. Lars Jensen built a ferry on the Green River in 1885. Anders Borgeson erected a molasses mill in Santaquin, Utah. Many Danish and Swedish immigrants developed dairy farming near the state's heavily populated areas. Other Scandinavians resumed their former trades of carpentry and stonemasonry as the growing territory allowed such specialization.

Language and cultural differences provoked a number of squabbles between the Scandinavians and Anglo-Saxons, as well as among the Scandinavians themselves.[36] Both the Danes and the Swedes soon had newspapers in their own languages, and at times allegations of church preference given to other groups appeared in their pages. Mormon leaders took a firm hand with such breaches of brotherliness. Early in the twentieth century the First Presidency issued a long epistle clarifying the church's position against ethnic separatism or preference and strongly condemning any who sought to divide church members along ethnic lines.[37] Like the English Saints, the Scandinavians eventually found a satisfying place in the Mormon culture and blended their unique characteristics with it. Ultimately they, too, had their representatives among church leaders: Christian D. Fjeldsted (Danish) became a general authority in 1884. Anthon H. Lund (Danish) was made an apostle in 1889, and John A. Widtsoe (Norwegian) assumed that office in 1921.

The persistent themes of Mormon emigration, adaptation, and assimilation are well illustrated by the British and Scandinavians. In addition, a number of smaller groups—French, Belgians, Dutch, even a few Armenians and Polynesians—added diversity to the Mormon commonwealth in the West. Although German-speaking immigrants were fewer—between three and four thousand lived in Utah in 1890—they made signal contributions. Karl G. Maeser, an experienced teacher from Germany, was one of the founding fathers of higher education in Mormon country.[38]

If the Mormon gathering did not bring people from every country, this was not due to narrow goals, for church leaders repeatedly insisted that the restored gospel was for all the world—"every nation, kindred, tongue and people." But numbers of missionaries have been limited, and the effort has been concentrated where the receptivity was encouraging. More important, many countries have simply prohibited proselyting by the Mormons. Few if any Mormons gathered from Spain, Portugal, Italy, Greece, the Balkans, or Eastern Europe. And for practical purposes there were none from Asia, Africa, or Central and South America. The recent successes in countries like Japan, the Philippines, Mexico, and Brazil have occurred in the post–gathering era, when the thrust has been to build up Mormon congregations abroad.

For those Mormons who did gather, it was a bittersweet experience. As William Mulder has observed:

> The Mormon immigrant, like every immigrant, crossed more than an ocean and a continent—his traveling was, in John Ciardi's phrase, ". . . across the

sprung longitudes of the mind/ And the blood's latitudes." From earliest
voyager to latest refugee the personal record of that experience holds an un-
failing fascination, whether set down in William Bradford's "plain stile;
with singular regard unto the simple trueth in all things," or in the broken
tongue of the lowly Scandinavian Mormon.[39]

Whatever the experience of individual families, it is clear that without the
gathering, without the infusion of new blood, without the buildup of Zion
as both symbol of achievement and nerve center, Mormonism might have
lost its sense of destiny. The arrival of converts from other lands year after
year, from 1840 to the end of the century, and then at a diminishing pace in
the twentieth century, served as a reminder of the worldwide scope of Mormonism's message and a reassurance of its validity and appeal. Having drawn
strength from the gathering, in terms of population, and a constantly renewed enthusiasm, Mormonism was later in a position to accelerate its missionary program to a much higher level of intensity and to establish viable
congregations and leadership programs in other parts of the world.

8

{Mormons and Native Americans}

The Lamanites [Indians] must rise in majesty and power.

—Spencer W. Kimball (1947)

I challenge you that between now and when you come back next fall to general conference that you love each other as children of God and not as different races and cultures.

—George P. Lee, first Native American to become a Mormon general authority (1976)

Accommodation to the Native Americans in the Great Basin was more difficult than the assimilation of British and Scandinavian immigrants. When Joseph Smith published the Book of Mormon in 1830, he had offered special reasons for concern over the welfare of American Indians. The Book of Mormon, as mentioned earlier, purported to be a history and religious record of three groups of Middle Easterners who traveled to the Western Hemisphere over a fifteen-hundred-year period and who played an important role in the establishment of an ancient American civilization. It was regarded as evidence that American Indians, like some of their Hebrew ancestors, were part of God's chosen people, and that they had flourished in North and South America under his protecting care. According to the Book of Mormon, they had once practiced an advanced form of Christianity, having been taught its principles by Jesus Christ after his Crucifixion; but through their "abominations and loss of belief," these early settlers had eventually become "wild," "full of mischief," "loathsome," and "full of idleness."[1] The Latter-day Saints had the responsibility, according to this theology, of introducing this "covenant people" to the Book of Mormon and teaching them the ways of their ancestors, who once followed Jesus. Eventually, these Lamanites, as the Book of Mormon called them, were destined to become revitalized, and the Latter-day Saints were expected to lead in this process by carrying them "in their arms and upon their shoulders" to help them "blossom as a rose."[2]

At first glance the Mormons' perception of the Native Americans seemed combine two ideas that make strange bedfellows: (1) the idea of the "noble savage," recognizing a certain moral superiority in the past and future of the Indians if not always in their present; and (2) the idea of the "white man's burden," the obligation to help civilize and elevate the native race. Actually the Latter-day Saint view was richer and more complex than these secular traditions, for it combined under a religious canopy the duty to convert and civilize with a respect for the past accomplishments and the religious record of the Indians and with an attitude of awe toward a chosen people of destiny whose prophesied role in the divine economy was equal if not superior in some ways to that of white Mormons.

Imbued with the concept that they had the responsibility of helping the Indians, early Mormons sent representatives to various tribes. In October 1830 Joseph Smith sent Oliver Cowdery, Parley P. Pratt, Peter Whitmer, and Ziba Peterson, all residents of western New York, to preach to the Native Americans on the western frontier. They met with the Catteraugus nation in western New York, the Wyandots in western Ohio, and the Shawnees and Delawares in eastern Kansas.[3] Although the Indians listened respectfully, federal agents soon ordered the missionaries out of Indian country as "disturbers of the peace." Similar opposition frustrated other efforts to establish contact with the Indians before the Mormon hegira to the Great Basin in 1846.

One of the factors causing the Mormon expulsion from Missouri in 1833 and 1839 was the fear on the part of other settlers that the Mormons might give the Indians a false sense of power and importance. The Mormons were accused of "keeping up a constant communication with the Indian tribes of our frontier, with declaring, even from the pulpit, that the Indians are a part of God's chosen people, and are destined, by heaven, to inherit this land, in common with themselves."[4]

Even after the Mormons settled at Nauvoo, Illinois, Indian agents continued to be suspicious of the Saints. On one occasion several Potawatomi chiefs visited Joseph Smith to discuss their grievances.[5] Following a lengthy "powwow," the agent Henry King, who interpreted for the Prophet, reported to Iowa's governor John Chambers that "It seems evident, from all that I can learn . . . that a grand conspiracy is about to be entered into between the *Mormons and the Indians* to destroy all white settlements on the Frontier."[6]

When expelled from Illinois in 1846, the Mormons fully expected that in their new setting they would be able to render service on behalf of the Indian. Their leaders issued this challenge:

> The sons and daughters of Zion will soon be required to devote a portion of their time in instructing the children of the forest. For they must be educated, and instructed in all the arts of civil life, as well as in the gospel. They

must be clothed, fed, and instructed in the principles and practice of virtue, modesty, temperance, cleanliness, industry, mechanical arts, manners, customs, dress, music, and all other things which are calculated in their nature to refine, purify, exalt and glorify them, as the sons and daughters of the royal house of Israel. . . . The despised and degraded son of the forest, who has wandered in dejection and sorrow, and suffered reproach, shall then . . . stand forth in manly dignity. . . . His heart shall expand with knowledge . . . and his mind shall comprehend the vast creations of his God and His eternal purpose of redemption, glory, and exaltation.[7]

Upon reaching the Great Basin, the Mormons had the unique opportunity to apply this philosophy in their association with several thousand Indians in the new Mormon territory.[8] Generally speaking, there were four culture types of Indians in residence. In the Wasatch Mountain and Uinta Basin areas to the east the Shoshoni and Ute nations practiced a modified Great Plains culture based partly on the buffalo. In the south lived the Hopis, with a settled agricultural economy of corn, beans, squash, and small game, and the nomadic Navahos and Apaches, with their herds of sheep and goats and their skills in silverwork and the making of rugs. In the desert areas to the west the Gosiutes and Paiutes eked out a precarious existence from roots, berries, insects, and an occasional rabbit or antelope.

In establishing their settlements near these native peoples Mormon leaders tried to follow a conciliatory policy.[9] Although they did not pay the Indians for their land after the manner of William Penn, they met in council with the chiefs of local tribes and secured their consent to settle. The Mormons promised to give the Indians whatever livestock and produce they could spare, on the occasion of their periodic visits, and the Indians agreed not to molest the settlers or their livestock. In June 1849, for example, Brigham Young met with Chief Wakara (Walker) and twelve Ute Indians to discuss the prospects of settlement. In describing this incident, Brigham Young's scribe recorded: "When Walker had filled his pipe, he offered the Lord the first smoke pointing the pipe and stepping towards the sun. Walker then smoked it and passed it round the ring by the right hand to H. C. Kimball, who smoked. It was then passed by the left (hand to) . . . the rest of the company, ending with the Indians."[10] The resulting agreement permitted the Mormons to settle the Sanpete Valley of central Utah.

Although relationships were usually harmonious, conflicts inevitably arose over land, water, and the treatment of individuals on both sides. From the time of settlement of the Great Basin in 1847 until the removal of the Indians to reservations in eastern Utah and elsewhere beginning in the late 1860s, Mormon policy may be summarized in terms of two opposing principles. On the one hand, the Mormons kept in mind that the Indians, however threatening and however pitiable, were their brothers and that they deserved understanding and help. On the other hand, Mormon survival and development of the Great Basin required tactics designed to assure the physical protection and economic expansion of the white settlers. Young summarized the policy in his address before the Utah legislature in 1854: "I have uniformly pursued a friendly course of policy towards them [the Indians], feeling convinced that independent of the question of exercising humanity towards so degraded and ignorant a race of people, it was manifestly more economical and less expensive, to feed and clothe, than to fight them."[11]

Above all, he opposed the customary frontier theory that "the only good Indian was a dead Indian," and the resulting practice of indiscriminately killing Indians.

> I wish to impress [all] with the necessity of treating the Indians with kindness, and to refrain from harboring the revengeful, vindictive feeling that many indulge in. I am convinced that as long as we harbor in us such feelings towards them, so long they will be our enemies, and the Lord will suffer them to afflict us. . . . Why should men have a disposition to kill a destitute, naked Indian, who may steal a shirt or a horse and think it no harm, when they never think of meting out a like retribution to a white man who steals, although he has been taught better from infancy? . . . We exhort you to feed and clothe them so far as it lies in your power. Never turn them away hungry from your door, teach them the arts of husbandry, bear with them in all patience and long suffering, and never consider their lives as equivalent for petty stealing.[12]

Having suffered from the vengeful behavior of Indians who had been fired upon by isolated groups of overlanders passing through the region on their way to California, the Mormons found it necessary to distinguish themselves from other Americans. This, along with the Mormon belief that the Indians would experience a time of renewal, led to the charge, often made by federal Indian agents, that the Mormons were plotting with the Indians against the United States and its citizens. Most authorities agree that Mormon missionaries did not deliberately stir up the Indians. Yet the contrast between the benevolent policies of the "Mormonee" and the careless actions of some passing "Mericats" had an inevitable effect. The indifferent attitude of the federal government did not warm the hearts of the Indians, and when they learned that the Mormons, too, were refugees whose rights had not been protected by Washington and who were pursued by a federal army (the Utah Expedition) or by federal judges, it was natural to perceive them as fellow sufferers if not blood brothers. Illustrative is the story, probably apocryphal, of a Mormon testimony meeting (a meeting at which any person in the congregation may stand and speak) in which an Indian chief arose, drew himself up to his full height, assumed a very dignified manner, and delivered the following short sermon: "Mormon weino [*bueno,* or good]. Mormon tick-a-boo [friend]. Make-em water-ditch. Plant-em grain. Feed-em Indians. Mormon tick-a-boo. White man, son-of-a-bitch!"[13]

In carrying out their benevolent yet self-protective policies, the Mormons followed four practices:

First, Mormon communities were usually settled in a fortlike arrangement, with a wall around each village, so that the temptations of "sneak" attacks would be materially reduced. At least this was the official advice; sometimes accomplishing it took a long time and meant an increase of danger for a while. The territorial militia, the Nauvoo Legion, composed of all the male members of the community over eighteen years of age, conducted regular drills and exercises, and militiamen were subject to instant mobilization in case of an attack on their own or a nearby village. A group of young minutemen were on call to track down marauding groups who had stolen livestock.[14]

Second, Mormon leaders eliminated a potential source of trouble by appointing a number of persons who had an understanding of Indian language and culture to conduct all the trading for the Mormon community. This kept individual Indians from circulating in the villages, eliminated competitive bargaining among Indians and Latter-day Saints, and ensured that relationships with Indians were carried out by those best acquainted with them.

Third, a community storehouse, or tithing house, was maintained by each village to which Latter-day Saint members brought one-tenth of their production of calves and colts, grain and flour, butter and eggs, potatoes and carrots, and other commodities. Stores of these could be drawn upon in presenting gifts to visiting groups of Indians. The records of each of the tithing houses contain an "Indian Account" that details each item disbursed, the names of the Indians receiving it, the date, and the value. The 1864 Indian Account of the Cache Valley (Utah) Tithing House shows disbursements during the spring and summer of that year of more than a ton of flour, four beeves, and thirty bushels of vegetables.[15] To give another example, a band of about one thousand Shoshoni Indians camped near the Mormon settlement of Huntsville, in Ogden Valley, Utah, during the summer of 1866. The local bishop, Francis A. Hammond, invited them to the public square to receive their "presents." After they had sung and danced and performed a sham fight, they received the community's gift consisting of four beeves, nine sheep, several sacks of flour, and something like seventy bushels of potatoes, carrots, beets, and turnips.[16]

Fourth, as an extension of the tithing-house arrangement, the women of many wards and settlements were organized into what was called an Indian Relief Society, which met once a week to make articles of clothing and bedding for Native American women and children. Records in the Church Archives show that the women of one of the Salt Lake wards, or congregations, over a four-month period turned over to the tithing house for distribution to Indians twenty-six undergarments, twenty-nine dresses, twenty-four baby dresses, and three quilts. In agricultural settlements they arranged with their husbands for Indian women to glean after the harvest in Mormon grain fields.[17]

One problem encountered by the Mormons in relation to the Indians was the rather extensive slave trade in the Great Basin. Various groups of Mexicans and Ute Indians circulated through the territory buying or stealing children of the weaker tribes for sale to Mexicans. Reputedly, each child would bring from one hundred to two hundred dollars and was condemned to a lifetime of slavery in a Mexican village. The whole business was repulsive to the Mormons, but there was no easy solution, inasmuch as stopping the trade would suspend an important source of Indian revenue.[18] The nature of the dilemma was illustrated during the winter of 1848–49 when a band referred to in contemporary literature as Cumumbah or Weber Utes came into the Salt Lake Valley desiring to trade. They had previously taken two girls about four and five years old as prisoners and wanted to sell them. When the Mormons declined, the enraged chief took one of the girls by the heels and dashed her brains out on the hard ground, "after which he threw the body towards us, telling us we had no hearts, or we would have bought it and saved its life."[19] Charles Decker, a young scout and brother-in-law of Brigham Young, moved quickly to prevent the same thing from happening to the other girl, and purchased her with his rifle and pony. He then took her to the home of Lorenzo Dow Young, a brother of Brigham, to be washed and clothed. John R. Young, son of Lorenzo, wrote:

> She was the saddest-looking piece of humanity I have ever seen. They had shingled her head with butcher knives and fire brands. All the fleshy parts of her body, legs, and arms had been hacked with knives, then fire brands had been stuck into the wounds. She was gaunt with hunger, and smeared from head to foot with blood and ashes. After being washed and clothed, she was given to President [Brigham] Young and became as one of his family. They named her Sally.[20]

After this experience Brigham Young encouraged his followers to adopt Indian children offered for sale. His advice to the little settlement of Parowan just six months after the founding of that community is characteristic:

> He advised them to buy up the Lamanite [i.e., Indian] children, as fast as they could, and educate them and teach them the Gospel, ... He remarked that the Lord could not have devised a better plan, than to have put the

Saints where they were, in order to accomplish the redemption of the Lamanites.[21]

In urging the legislature to pass an Indian slave act that would decree the stopping of the trade, Brigham Young "drew a fine distinction between actual slavery to the Mexicans and purchase by the Mormons," insisting that in the latter case the Indians were being purchased into freedom instead of slavery.[22] The Mormons could "help the process of civilizing the natives," he thought, by taking them into the family, training them to do home work and farming, and teaching them religion.[23] At least fifty or sixty Indian children were raised in Latter-day Saint homes. Some of them married Mormon whites and became the progenitors of important Utah families; others lived lonely lives, feeling at home neither in white Mormon society nor in their own tribal society; still others fell victim to such white man's diseases as measles and smallpox.[24]

Another problem with which the Mormons came to grips was the occasional testing of their determination by hostile raiding parties. In 1849 Timpanogos Utes from Utah Valley, south of Great Salt Lake, raided the range in Tooele Valley, west of Salt Lake City. Forty Mormon militiamen rode off in pursuit, surrounding the band, and killed several of the Indians at a location known thereafter as Battle Creek (now Pleasant Grove). Daniel H. Wells, commander of the troops responsible for routing the Indians from the Utah Lake area, recorded to relatives in the East his sympathetic response to the military duty just completed:

> After two days hard fighting among those brushy ravines the Indians took to the mountains where rocks and narrow passes furnished them ample natural defenses. Long and weary was the pursuit, but they were overtaken in their mountain home. Being routed far and near, they fled like the mountain roe. The Indians were cleared from the valleys, the slain have gone to their place to rest.
>
> The mountain dell, alone, can narrate the sufferings of those poor wretches who, wounded and naked, fled for their lives over mountain heights of snow where snowshoes alone could keep them from being buried alive. The campaign is now brought to a close.[25]

A more important test occurred in 1853, when Chief Wakara (Walker), the powerful Ute leader who had welcomed the Mormons into the region (and had even been baptized and ordained a Mormon elder), found himself unable to control young hotbloods thirsting for retaliation against the white invaders.[26] When the raids began, Brigham Young counseled the abandonment of some of the more isolated settlements and sent out various peace overtures to Wakara to ensure at least his neutrality. During the ensuing Walker War, the Mormons were counseled not to kill but to be patient and firm. Protected by walls and vigilant guards, the Mormons lost no women or children and only twelve men. None of the latter died in military action; two met death in performance of community guard duty, and the remaining ten were killed because they failed to observe the precautions announced by military authorities. Approximately four hundred head of livestock were lost.[27]

Brigham Young's letter to Wakara in July 1853, in the midst of the hostilities, held forth a carrot of reward and also appealed to the chief's sense of right:

G.S.L. City, July 25, 1853

Captain Walker:

I send you some tobacco for you to smoke in the mountains when you get lonesome. You are a fool for fighting your best friends, for we are the best friends, and the only friends that you have in the world. Everybody else would kill you if they could get a chance. If you get hungry send some friendly Indian down to the settlements and we will give you some beef-cattle and flour. If you are afraid of the tobacco which I send you, you can let some of your prisoners [Mormons] try it first and then you will know that it is good. When you get good natured again I would like to see you. Don't you think you should be ashamed? You know that I have always been your best friend.

Brigham Young[28]

Apparently the diplomacy paid off, for Wakara was able to gather the various old chiefs together for a council at Nephi.[29] When the cavalcade arrived on the road opposite Wakara's camp, Governor Young sent a delegation to inform the chief that he had arrived and would be ready to give him audience. Wakara sent back word that if Young wanted to see him, he would have to come to the Indian camp. "If the mountain will not come to Mohammed, Mohammed will go to the mountain," said Young, and gave orders for the troop to proceed to Wakara's camp.

After the ceremony of shaking hands the chiefs began to speak, one by one. "I am for war," said the first. "Mericats and Mormonee no friends to Utahs [Utes]," said the second, and so on. When most had spoken, some for peace and some for war, Young asked Wakara to speak, but he shook his head, "No. I got no heart to speak. No can talk today." Young then handed him a pipe. Wakara took it, gave one or two puffs, and told the governor to smoke, which he did and passed it around to all the party.

Young commenced by telling the chiefs that he wanted to be friends with all the Indians, loved them like a father, and would always give them plenty of clothes and good food. He then presented them with gifts he had brought along for the occasion: sixteen head of cattle, blankets and clothing, trinkets, and arms and ammunition.[30]

Wakara then spoke:

> Wakara has heard all the talk of the good Mormon chief. Wakara no like to go to war.... Wakara no want to fight more. Wakara talk with Great Spirit; Great Spirit say "Make peace." Wakara love Mormon chief; he is a good man.... If Indian kill white man again, Wakara make Indian howl.

The calumet of peace was again handed around, and all the party took a smoke. The council was then dissolved.[31]

Shortly after this settlement, the Mormon church inaugurated a three-phase program aimed at preventing hostilities from flaring up again. Refinements were made in the distribution of goods to visiting and nearby tribes. These included improvements in tithing-house arrangements and in the work of Indian Relief Societies.

The Mormons also established Indian farms designed to teach native peoples the art of agriculture and assist them in their production operations. Mormon supervisors, called Indian farmers, were assigned to work with the natives in raising crops and improving their livestock.[32]

Finally, outpost missions were established, each of which was manned by thirty to forty men, who were "called" to preach the Mormon vision of Christianity and demonstrate desirable agricultural practices to potentially hostile tribes on the fringe of Mormon country. Mormon missionary agriculturists lived among the Indians, spoke their language, and occasionally intermarried.[33] The instructions given by Brigham Young to these missionaries were exemplified by the following:

> Beloved Brethren. We wish you to devote your time and energies to the great duty of instructing the Lamanites [Indians] in the knowledge of the Gospel.... You will need to be wise servants and harmless as doves, preserving an unblemished integrity towards them in all your words and actions.... Teach them by precept and example, to labor and cultivate the earth.... Teach them to respect each others rights; to cease the shedding of blood; and to promote peace. Teach them to know the value of their time, and how to appropriate it in such a manner as to make themselves self-sustaining and independent.... Be not discouraged if the work progresses slowly, but remember that if you spend a whole life and by so doing serve one soul of the seed of Abraham, your joy will be very great; and how much greater indeed will be your joy if your ministry should result in the salvation of many souls.[34]

Illustrative of the attitudes, concerns, and problems in the Indian missions is the legendary Jacob Hamblin. An Ohio convert to Mormonism,

Hamblin was living in Tooele, Utah, thirty-five miles west of Salt Lake City, in 1853. This little community had often experienced raids on its cattle and horses by Gosiute and Shoshoni tribesmen. After one raid, Hamblin was appointed leader of a posse to find the livestock and punish the Indian thieves. Traveling at night, the posse located the camp, surrounded it, and started the attack. Hamblin told the sequence as follows:

> The chief among them sprang to his feet, and stepping towards me, said, "I never hurt you, and I do not want to. If you shoot, I will; if you do not, I will not." I was not familiar with their language, but I knew what he said. Such an influence came over me that I would not have killed one of them for all the cattle in Tooele Valley. The running of the women and the crying of the children aroused my sympathies, and I felt inspired to do my best to prevent the company from shooting any of them. Some shots were fired, but no one was injured, except that the legs and feet of some of the Indians were bruised by jumping among the rocks.[35]

Hamblin induced the chief and three of his men to accompany him to Tooele, giving his assurance that they would be returned without injury. They agreed to go. When he arrived in the village, however, Hamblin's military and ecclesiastical superior refused to go along with the promise of safety and "decided to have them shot."

"I told them," Hamblin later recalled, "I did not care to live after I had seen the Indians whose safety I had guaranteed, murdered, and as it made little difference with me, if there were any shot I should be first. At the same time I placed myself in front of the Indians. This ended the matter, and they were set at liberty."[36]

As a dedicated disciple, Hamblin began to have second thoughts about his defiance of his bishop, and prayed earnestly to know if he had done the right thing. During this period of reconsideration he was called out once more to lead a posse, go after the Indians, "to shoot all we found, and bring no more into the settlement." Again they traveled at night, again they intercepted the band. An Indian surprised him, and Hamblin leveled his rifle at him, but it misfired. The Indian sent an arrow at Hamblin, but it struck his gun. A second arrow passed through his hat; the third barely missed his head; the fourth went through his coat and vest but did not touch his body. The Indian ran by other members of the posse, but their guns also misfired. No one was able to discharge his gun within range of an Indian. Hamblin saw his escape from bullets and arrows as an answer to his prayer:

> It appeared evident to me that a special providence had been over us, in this and the two previous expeditions, to prevent us from shedding the blood of the Indians. The Holy Spirit forcibly impressed me that it was not my call-

ing to shed the blood of the scattered remnant of Israel, but to be a messenger of peace to them. It was also made manifest to me that if I would not thirst for their blood, I should never fall by their hands. . . . When I saw the women and children fleeing for their lives, barefooted over the rocks and through the snow, leaving a trail of blood, I fully made up my mind, that if I had anything more to do with the Indians, it would be in a different way. . . . I thanked the Lord, as I often felt to do, for the revelations of His Spirit.[37]

Perhaps word of this inward call to Hamblin to be a messenger of peace to the Indians was relayed to Brigham Young. At any rate, the next year the president called him to the Southern Indian Mission, where he settled at Santa Clara, Utah, and devoted the remainder of his life to helping the Indians. Like some other Mormon missionaries, Hamblin retained a core of common prejudice. "I have wished many times," he once said, "that my lot was cast among a more cleanly people; where there could be found something desirable, something cheering to a person accustomed to a civilized life." Yet he could empathize with the Indians, listen to their point of view patiently, and respond with honesty and candor. He did not laugh at them or scold them.[38] Tutsegavit, the chief of the primitive Paiutes with whom he worked, fully admitted the difficulty of getting his tribe to change. "We only Paiutes," he said. "We cannot be good. Some day, maybe, our children will be good. Now we only Paiutes."[39]

Near the end of his life Hamblin did get a chance to work among what he called "the nobler branches of the race"—the Navahos and Hopis who lived south of the Colorado River. He moved to Kanab, Utah, to be closer to the Navahos. Juanita Brooks gives a delightful account of an occasion when the Navahos came to Kanab to trade. They stopped, as was their custom, on a knoll just outside of town, built a smoke, and with a blanket signaled that they were there. This time Hamblin sent his son, Jacob junior, with a pony to exchange for blankets.

> The boy, eager to make a good bargain, kept demanding more and more, and the Indian gave what he asked without much protest. When he [the boy] arrived home, pleased with himself as a good trader, his father looked at the blankets, and without comment counted out one pile.
> "You take these back," he told the boy. "You charged too much for the pony; this is all he is worth."
> At the camp the Indian was evidently expecting him.
> "I know you come back," the native said. "Jacob your father? He my father, too."[40]

In 1876 Brigham Young denominated Jacob Hamblin Apostle to the Lamanites. He died in 1886, still among his Indian people.

The principal problem of these farms and missions was the hostility of federal Indian agents, who regarded the Mormon efforts as "tampering" with "their" Indians.[41] Conflicts between the Mormons and the federal government over other issues, such as plural marriage and political sovereignty, increased the hostility and suspicion. The willingness of the Mormons to make separate treaties and to assume responsibility only for their own actions was regarded as a dangerous precedent. Nor could federal agents countenance the impression given many Indians that the Big Chief was in Salt Lake City rather than in Washington, D.C. Related to the opposition of the Indian agents was the enmity of the mountain men, who saw Mormon diplomacy as a serious threat to their own profitable trapping and trading operations. These men often used both federal agents and Indians to limit the influence and activities of the Mormons. Many Indians, on the other hand, regarded the Mormons as natural kinsmen, for both Saints and Indians sought to manage certain property interests collectively, practiced cooperative herding, and shared with the poor.[42]

The year 1865 was a watershed in Mormon-Indian relations because of the treaty signed that year by which Utah chieftains conveyed to the United States title to the land in the settled areas of the territory. In return the tribes were allotted land in the Uintah country of eastern Utah for a reservation. By this time, there were perhaps sixty thousand people in Utah Territory, and unquestionably the Mormons were pressing hard on Indian hunting and fishing grounds. The treaty settlement, in which the Mormons were active participants, was a necessity for both Indians and Saints. The actual removal of most of the Indians from Mormon neighborhoods roughly coincided with the 1869 adoption of President Ulysses S. Grant's "Quaker" policy of making the Indians wards of the nation.[43]

The Saints faced the most serious Indian uprising in 1865, when a minority of Indian militants rejected the reservation solution and began guerrilla warfare. A young Indian outlaw by the name of Black Hawk, with a hard core of perhaps thirty leaders and two or three hundred warriors, conducted a four-year campaign against the Mormons that resulted in the death of seventy white men, the loss of two thousand head of horses and cattle, and the abandonment of twenty-five settlements.[44] Despite requests by Mormon officials and Indian agents, the federal army units in Utah refused to intervene or to provide protection for the white settlers; the entire responsibility for defense was placed on the Nauvoo Legion.[45] Four years after the war began, the Saints of Fillmore, Utah, were assembled for their regular Sunday services when Black Hawk and his militants walked in. Surprisingly contrite, Black Hawk said they had come to prove to the whites "that their hearts were good, and that they desired a lasting peace." The following September Black Hawk became ill and died. He was buried in special religious ceremonies near Spring Lake where he was born. In a funeral sermon Brigham Young said, "He was the most formidable foe . . . that the Saints have had to encounter for many years."[46]

Another minority of Indians rejected reservation life. Instead of taking the militant stance of Black Hawk's men, they simply left the reservations, wandered from place to place, and eked out a meager existence. One band of Shoshoni, who frequently passed through southern Idaho, northern Utah, and eastern Nevada, was of this type. Worried by the possibility of conflict, the Mormon missionary and Indian interpreter George Washington Hill traveled into southern Idaho, met this band of Indians, and baptized many of them during the spring of 1873. Eventually these Mormon Indians settled on a site some thirty-five miles north of Brigham City, Utah, named Washakie after a famed Shoshoni chief. By 1889 the Washakie Indians had surveyed some seven thousand acres of land, cleared much of it for farming, dug a canal system, and built a sawmill, chapel, schoolhouse, mission home, and houses for most native families. In addition, the Washakie Ward was organized, with Isaac E. D. Zundel as bishop. Within three years he had established the Sunday School, Mutual Improvement Association for the youth, an Indian Relief Society among the women, the Primary Association for the children, and priesthood quorums similar to those normally found in white Mormon wards. James J. Chandler, a man of considerable teaching experience, was asked in 1885, "to labor as school teacher." After obtaining some books and apparatus, he began school with ten whites and ten Indians. The Washakie Indian Farm served as a model for collecting other nonreservation Indians onto farming sites located in Sanpete Valley, Deep Creek, and Grass Valley.[47]

For the vast majority of Indians who stayed on reservations, the Mormons introduced various programs. The mission to the three hundred Indians on the Catawba Reservation in York County, South Carolina, deserves special mention because it was outside the accustomed sphere of Mormon interest. Within a year or two after Mormon missionaries visited the reservation in 1883, virtually the entire nation was baptized and a branch of the church was established. This was the only instance in which an eastern tribe moved from paganism to Christianity in the Mormon path. But not without opposition. One evening after dark, an anti-Mormon crowd of whites gathered at the reservation, shot one of the missionaries and stripped the other of his clothes and whipped him. Not succeeding in forcing whiskey down his throat, the mob poured a bottle over his face and warned him not to come back to the reservation.[48] The missionaries left, but the Catawbas maintained a separate (ethnic) Mormon ward for seventy years.

This episode suggests the strong feeling against the Mormons in most parts of the nation.[49] There was a widely believed allegation that Mormon elders had participated in the ghost dance ceremonies, which, after misunderstanding and overreaction by Indian agents and the U.S. Army, eventually triggered the infamous massacre at Wounded Knee, South Dakota. After investigating the Messiah craze that preceded the massacre by a few weeks, General Nelson A. Miles reported that Indians on the Utah, Montana, and Cheyenne reservations believed the Messiah would restore them to their former glory, bringing back the buffalo and driving the whites from the land. When asked who he thought "responsible for this imposition upon the Indians," General Miles replied,

> It is my belief that the Mormons are the prime movers in it. This is not a hard statement to believe, for there are 200,000 Mormons and they themselves claim to believe in prophets and spiritual manifestations, and they even now claim to hold intercourse with the spirit of Joe Smith. Besides, they have had missionaries at work among the Indians for many years and have made many converts.[50]

In addition to Miles's indictment, the authoritative study of the ghost dance printed in the 1890s stated that the Paiute prophet Wovoka, who started the movement, had learned his religious doctrines from the Mormons and, in order to prepare his red brothers to meet the Messiah, had woven them together with Indian legends.[51]

The Latter-day Saints, already facing enough problems because of their unpopularity, had no stomach for additional conflict over this issue. In a time of readjustment and accommodation they quietly dropped their Indian programs on the reservations. It began to seem that their vision of redeeming the Indians was spent, and that their attitudes toward Indians were not unlike those of many other westerners.[52]

Nevertheless, the prophecies of a glorious future for the Indians remained in Mormon scripture. Some few examples of continued patient hoping by Native American Mormons and by whites living in close proximity to them can be cited. It appeared to be a question of priorities. Energies had to be expended elsewhere until the time was ripe for a renewal of the determined missionary thrust among the "Lamanites." That moment arrived late in 1942 when Mary Jumbo, a Navaho residing in Shiprock, New Mexico, pleaded with President Heber J. Grant to send missionaries to her people. The First Presidency authorized George Albert Smith, an apostle and special friend of Native Americans, to organize the Southwest Indian Mission, with headquarters in Gallup, New Mexico.[53] It was the first formal Mormon Indian mission in five decades. Later, the Northern Indian Mission, with headquarters in

Rapid City, South Dakota, was also organized. The dire need of the Indians, particularly during the harsh winter of 1948–49, led to the inauguration of a greatly expanded program in the 1950s.

The program has four phases. The first is a kind of Mormon Peace Corps, which preceded that of John F. Kennedy's administration. Several thousand young Latter-day Saint men and women have engaged in a voluntary ministry among Native Americans. These "missions," typically lasting two years, have involved not only proselyting but labor, assisting Indians with their farming, cooperative enterprises, small businesses, and recreational and educational programs.[34] For example, the president of the Northern Indian Mission to the Sioux, Arapaho, Shoshoni, Omaha, Winnebago, Chippewa, and Northern Cheyenne tribes in the 1960s was Harvey Dahl, who had operated a cattle ranch at Deeth, Nevada, and who oversaw the ten agricultural and cattle projects of the Indians of the region. "The Indians need economic help as much as spiritual help," he asserted. "Our aim is to build men to be good ranchers and farmers, heads of their homes, and good church leaders." These Indians own forty-five thousand acres of good land in South Dakota, and Dahl and his missionaries, some of them Indians, taught managerial farming. Experienced agricultural supervisors were appointed as resource persons to suggest ways of improving the operations of these and other tribal groups or nations.[35]

A second phase of the current policy is the Indian Seminary Program, in which more than twenty-five thousand Indian boys and girls attend classes in religion and participate in various kinds of organized activities, including two thousand from the Alberta-Saskatchewan area. These seminaries are located adjacent to federal and public schools from the Mohawk community at Hogansburg, New York, in the East, to federal schools at Riverside, California, and Salem, Oregon, in the West. A cadre of some two hundred men— many of them Indians themselves—are employed full-time as seminary teachers.

The third phase is a special program of Brigham Young University in which more than five hundred Native American students representing seventy-one tribes from twenty-seven states have been enrolled annually, many of them on special scholarships. The university also sponsors the Institute of American Indian Studies, which encourages research, makes available university resources for the study of Indian history and culture, and offers practical assistance in solving current Indian problems.

Finally, there is the voluntary Indian Placement Program. Over a twenty-five-year period approximately sixty thousand young Mormon Indians were temporarily placed during the school year in homes of white Mormon families, who paid the full expense of their upkeep. Nearly every classroom in most Mormon communities since the 1950s has contained a number of Indian students living in the homes of local families. At the end of each school year the children are returned to their natural homes to share experiences with their family and friends and to maintain ties with their tribe. One aim of the program was for students to go back to the same foster home each fall until graduation from high school, thus making the natural parents and foster parents partners in providing the student the best opportunities available in both Native American and white cultures.[56] Despite problems and objections, more than 80 percent of the young Native Americans graduated from high school. Critics have viewed the placement program as a wrenching of young Indians from their own families and cultural surroundings. Other denominations have been wary of the proselyting work of Mormon missionaries among the Indians. But to Mormon host families the presence of these young people, and the occasional visits of their parents and relatives, have resulted in the sloughing off of prejudices and the development of love, friendship, and concern. In the 1970s, with the improvement of educational facilities among the Indian nations themselves, the placement plan began to be phased out. Mormon efforts to help Indians were rechanneled into a larger stream, as educational, medical, and agricultural programs were introduced among Indian peoples in Central and South America.

A significant milestone in the Mormon mission to the "Lamanites" was reached in the appointment in 1975 of George Patrick Lee as a member of the church's First Quorum of Seventy. A full-blooded Navaho, Lee was thirty-two at the time of his appointment. In the 1950s he was one of the first participants in the church's Indian Placement Program and later went on to receive a bachelor's degree from Brigham Young University, a master's from Utah State University, and a doctorate from Brigham Young University. Prior to his appointment he served as president of the College of Ganado, a two-year community college on the Navaho reservation in Arizona, the first Indian to hold that position.

9

{ The Kingdom and the Nation }

I tell you Mormonism is one great surge of licentiousness; it is the seraglio of the Republic, it is the concentrated corruption of this land, it is the brothel of the nation, it is hell enthroned. This miserable corpse of Mormonism has been rotting in the sun, and rotting and rotting for forty years, and the United States Government has not had the courage to bury it.

—the Reverend T. De Witt Talmage (1880)

Many persons suppose that there is some provision in the United States Constitution touching this subject. This is an error. The constitution leaves all matters relating to marriages to be regulated by the people of the various states; and hence it is that so many diversified marriage and divorce codes exist throughout the country. Congress claims the power to regulate these matters in the territories. We do not admit that this right belongs to the general government, but claim that in matters of local concern the territorial legislative assemblies are manifestly the proper parties to act.

—John Taylor (1884)

Throughout America there was admiration, often grudging, for the persever-ance the Mormons brought to the task of conquering the Great Basin. Many of the positive qualities and ideals Americans had prided themselves on—toughness, determination, ambition, hard work, expansionist vision—were exemplified by this group. Yet just as there had been persecution of the Mor-mons in the different localities they had tried to settle, now the question was raised to a higher level, and there were higher stakes. Was there room in the United States for a sect like the Mormons? What were the limits of American tolerance?

Besides the psychological and religious elements mentioned earlier and the vigilante tradition that found many communities drawing lines and re-jecting unacceptable behavior or cultural types, the core of the problem lay in the Mormon concept of a divinely authorized earthly religious kingdom, in which secular and religious concerns were fused under the central authority of the priesthood, as represented by the prophet-president of the church. Certain economic practices appeared to clash with American free enterprise and competition. Mormon bloc voting conflicted with the political pluralism of many parts of the nation. Finally, the public announcement of Mormon plural marriage in 1852 affronted the most basic social institution, the monogamous family. Could such institutions be absorbed? Or would they be rejected as incompatible with the larger organism?

By embarking for the remote and unsettled Great Basin, the Mormons were hoping for tolerance under conditions of geographic separation. While several splinter groups chose to surrender the principle of corporate action rather than leave their homes in the already established United States, the exodus to the Great Basin demonstrated that the majority of Smith's followers sought release from harassment and did not wish to surrender their institutions. Nevertheless, despite their physical removal they maintained ties that inevitably brought them into renewed conflict with the United States.

The Mormons never seriously contemplated secession from the United States. Both Parley P. Pratt and Brigham Young expressed the goal of the migration as "a foundation for a territorial or state government under the Constitution of the United States, where we shall be the first settlers and a vast majority of the people."[1] The majority of pioneers had been born in the United States, and the others had willingly come as immigrants. They could not easily cast off their bias in favor of American institutions. Loyalties aside, the Mormon colonies in the West depended on the nation for capital, for consumer goods, and for protection.

Established in the Great Basin, church leaders soon undertook to formalize their governmental structure and cement their ties to the nation. Until 1849 government in the valley remained in the hands of the Salt Lake Stake Presidency and High Council, a Mormon ecclesiastical body. But in 1848 the Council of Fifty, a secretive general leadership quorum that included the apostles, began deliberating on the nature of civil government to be established in the valley. Their planning resulted in the establishment of a provisional secular government called the State of Deseret. Named for a Book of Mormon word meaning "honeybee," Deseret began with a constitutional convention assembled on March 5, 1849. Three days later a proposed constitution typical of state constitutions of the day was presented to the body. The assembled priesthood leaders wasted little time in its adoption. Although the document fixed an election date in early May, ballots were actually cast on March 12, in accordance with a previous council decision, scarcely allowing time for normal political processes. A religiously orthodox slate of officers, including Brigham Young as governor and Heber C. Kimball, his counselor in the First Presidency, as chief justice, was unanimously approved.[2]

The establishment of the State of Deseret exemplified a problem that pervaded nineteenth-century Mormon political life. While the leaders were perfectly willing to conform outwardly to typical American political practices, the inner character and authority of Mormon government derived from religious sources. Saints could always argue that such government expressed the will of the governed, but non-Mormons forced to work within such a system could scarcely be pleased by a structure that fulfilled the letter but not the spirit of "the law."

Although the proposed State of Deseret was satisfactory to the Mormons, getting it recognized by the national government was not so easy. John Bernhisel was dispatched in 1849 to Washington to seek admission into the Union. Later, Almon W. Babbitt joined Bernhisel and non-Mormon Colonel Thomas L. Kane, a resolute supporter of Mormon interests, in lobbying for statehood. A Kentucky congressman responded to the application by reading a lengthy statement by William Smith, the embittered brother of Joseph Smith, accusing the "Brighamite" Saints of polygamy, murder, and oaths of vengeance against the United States. Two other factors further weakened the Mormon position. The question of slavery in the western territories paralyzed congressional action on admitting them as states. Finally, the Mormon proposal appeared geographically exorbitant to congressmen, who were not anxious to place a vast region of two hundred thousand square miles (which included a portion of California's southern boundary in the statehood petition) under the control of a religious hierarchy reconstituted as a civil government.

Instead of statehood, the Mormon colonies, with boundaries reduced from the original proposal, were given territorial status under the name of Utah. This was part of the Compromise of 1850. Bernhisel expressed the feelings of many Mormons when he spoke of the "risk of having a set of whippersnappers or brokendown politicians to tyrannize over us . . . for I have every reason to apprehend that we should be brought into collision with the Central Government."[3] Under the territorial system the local settlers would be unable to elect their own officials except at the lower levels. The specter of rule by hostile officials aroused concern among the Mormons.

These fears subsided temporarily when word reached Utah that President Millard Fillmore had selected as governor Brigham Young, who held both the religious and secular reins of the "Kingdom." The other appointed officials were evenly divided between Mormons and Gentiles (non-Mormons). Even before the arrival of the federal appointees Young moved quickly to convert the State of Deseret into the territorial government authorized by Washington, to declare an earlier census to be official, and, based on its information, to establish districts and a date for election of representatives to the territorial legislature. As Superintendent of Indian Affairs, he also divided the territory into several districts, anticipating concurrence by the Washington-appointed officials.

When Secretary of State Broughton Harris, Chief Justice Lemuel H.

Brandebury, Associate Justice Perry E. Brocchus, and two Indian agents (all non-Mormons) arrived during the summer of 1851, instead of a governmental vacuum they found an efficient system that made their own appointments appear superfluous. Harris soon became embroiled in disputes with Young over the governor's hasty actions in such matters as the census, and steadfastly refused to release any of the twenty-five thousand dollars he had been authorized to disburse in the territory. Even had Young waited patiently for the eastern officials and scrupulously followed the letter of each regulation, the end results would certainly have been the same. To the Mormons, Harris was little more than an officious young bureaucrat.

Judge Brocchus's falling-out with the Saints was even more precipitous. Only weeks after his arrival he was invited to address a general conference of the church. He praised Mormon industry and order but went on to impugn the loyalty of the Saints and the virtue of Mormon women. Young managed to quell the angry congregation but denounced Brocchus as a worthless political hack. Brocchus, Brandebury, and Harris ultimately fled the territory and denounced the Mormons in the East. Attempting to counteract this bad press, Mormon representatives in the East managed to publicize their view: that the runaways had abandoned their offices without just cause. Although much was made in the national press of supposed Mormon sedition, President Fillmore closed the incident by appointing another group of officers, this time of higher caliber.

Between 1852 and 1857 little was done to alter the balance of power in Utah. As federal appointees followed each other to serve for brief intervals in the territory, the Mormons tended to the business of economic development, missionary proselyting, immigration, and the settling of new colonies. Relations between Mormons and "Gentile" officials varied from the cordial to the acrimonious, depending on circumstances and personalities. In the presidential election year of 1856 the national Republican platform expressed the sentiment of many easterners and midwesterners when it declared opposition to the "twin relics of barbarism"—slavery and polygamy.

In 1857 Utah territory was invaded by a hostile force of American soldiery. The events and influences that led to this confrontation are difficult to establish. The conflict was triggered in 1855 when David H. Burr, a non-Mormon appointed to be surveyor general of the territory, found his work impeded by Saints understandably anxious about any official survey of lands that they possessed only by right of occupation, not by any explicit declaration or approval of Congress. Burr and his assistants left the territory and reinforced the reports of Mormon skullduggery already prevalent in Washington. Garland Hurt, an energetic Indian agent, added his disturbing opinion that the Mormons were teaching the Indians to distinguish between the

"Mormonee" and other Americans. Not willing to accept the explanation that Mormons had to adopt some means of letting the Indians know that *they* shouldn't be held responsible for the brutality practiced by other Americans, Hurt alleged that the Mormons were planning to employ Native Americans in a war of vengeance against all non-Mormon settlers and travelers.

Troubles with surveyors and Indian agents were overshadowed by continuing strife between Mormons and federally appointed judges. After 1855 the Utah judiciary was headed by three non-Mormons: W. W. Drummond, George P. Stiles, and John F. Kinney. While on the surface Kinney was friendly to the Mormons, he represented them to Washington as being seditious and unruly. Stiles and Drummond did not bother to temper their distaste; the latter, especially, came to personify for the Mormons all the injustices of the territorial system.

The Mormons found Drummond to be a "loathesome specimen of humanity." Norman Furniss, a recent historian, wrote that he was "as unsavory as any man appointed to office."[4] Drummond's flagrant association with a prostitute offended the moral sense of the Saints. Perhaps most threatening was his attack on the probate courts, with Mormon bishops as probate judges, which had ruled on both civil and criminal cases. At the time he accused Mormons of destroying court records, an accusation later proved false. Offensive as his personal character might have been, Drummond played an important role in sparking the national reaction to Utah.

By the spring of 1857 the disgruntled officeholders were assembled in Washington clamoring for the newly inaugurated president, James Buchanan, to do something about the state of affairs in Utah. Although he had not considered the Mormon issue important enough to mention in his inaugural address, Buchanan was sensitive to public opinion. Between April and the early part of May he decided to replace Brigham Young as governor. By the end of the month he had chosen an even more drastic course of action. What had led him to these two momentous decisions? We do not know exactly, but there are several clues.

The Mormons had picked an awkward time to establish their semi-independent kingdom in the West. The issues of slavery and states' rights were already dividing the nation. Northerners wanted to make an example of Mormon rebelliousness, while some Southerners hoped an anti-Mormon campaign might relieve the pressure on them. One Southern leader wrote to Buchanan urging a vigorous Utah policy that would "supersede the Negro-Mania with the almost universal excitement of an Anti-Mormon Crusade."[5] The thousands of European Saints flocking to Utah made it difficult to ignore the "Mormon problem," and in fact aroused some early anti-immigrant nativism.

But such considerations lay in the background as predisposing conditions.

On the front of the stage Drummond, Hurt, and others somehow persuaded Buchanan that the Mormons were in a state of rebellion. They contended that through threats, boycotts, and murder the Mormon leaders hoped to drive all non-Mormons from the territory. A stream of newspaper articles, pamphlets, novels, and public speeches enumerated supposed Mormon treacheries and called for reprisals as extreme as a holy war of extermination. When Apostle Parley P. Pratt was murdered in Arkansas in May 1857, many newspapers greeted his death with undisguised glee.

Buchanan and his cabinet officers found themselves in a climate of public opinion that seemed to support any move to protect the rights of non-Mormons, suppress Mormon home rule, and eradicate polygamy. The President became convinced that a vigorous anti-Mormon action could only be to his credit. By May 1857 he had decided upon a show of military force as the best and quickest solution. But he seriously underestimated the degree to which it would be opposed by the Mormons. In the ensuing two years he found that his solution was anything but quick, and even the political popularity of a Utah campaign was to prove disappointing.

Indecision, incompetence, and competition for lucrative contracts surrounded the preparations of the Utah Expedition. The first body of soldiers did not leave Fort Leavenworth until mid-July. Others did not straggle out until September. Within weeks they were plagued by foul weather and the indecision of their officers. William S. Harney, originally chosen to command the army, was replaced by Colonel Albert Sidney Johnston. During the winter Johnston engaged in a running dispute with the newly appointed governor of Utah, Alfred Cumming of Georgia and Missouri, who accompanied the troops West. The Colonel seemed to be intent on a military victory over the Mormons, whereas Cumming was primarily concerned with acceptance of himself as governor.

Although Mormon leaders had suspected something was afoot, they first heard of the impending invasion on July 24, 1857, the tenth anniversary of their entrance into the valley. Four dust-covered horsemen galloped into a festive assembly and announced that a large force of American soldiers was on its way to install a non-Mormon governor and prevent any further "rebellion." Buchanan's action conjured up memories of Missouri and Illinois—of mobs aided and abetted by the military. The President had even neglected to send an official communication to Brigham Young, who, in his own mind still the official governor, chose to regard the approaching troops as a hostile army invading Utah Territory.

Determined to greet the invaders with force if necessary, the Mormons hoped to avoid bloodshed with "scorched earth" and harassment policies that would leave the invaders with a precarious line of supply. Young called out the territorial militia and asked each community to donate men, firearms, and provisions to the defense. By the fall of 1857 eleven hundred men were fortifying the mountain passes east of Great Salt Lake. Other parties were dispatched to burn Fort Bridger and Fort Supply, Mormon-owned outposts at the eastern entrance to the territory. By November 1857 a troop of eighteen hundred federal soldiers and camp followers were huddling around the charred ruins of Fort Bridger, desperately trying to avoid starvation until spring, when they could resume their campaign. Mormon raiders managed to burn three wagon trains sent to supply the expedition, destroying three months' provisions and bringing federal troops to the brink of starvation. Young added insult to injury by offering to provide the embattled U.S. troops with salt, flour, and cattle.

It was miraculous that the Utah Expedition did not end in a bloodbath. Unleashing military force is always easier than restraining it, and for the Mormons to attempt harassment of the invaders and destruction of supply trains while avoiding the taking of life and open battles was, on the face of it, a delicate combination that would not seem to have much chance of success. Yet there were practically no casualties except from frostbite and exposure.

The one exception was the Fancher train, a company of overland immigrants from Arkansas and Missouri that passed through Utah in August 1857 just when Mormon tempers and fears were at a fever pitch. In a remote, grassy valley in the south of Utah this company was virtually annihilated by a combined force of Mormon militia and Indians. This Mountain Meadows Massacre, in hindsight, was so obviously out of line with Brigham Young's instructions to avoid bloodshed, so inexplicable in terms of the military situation, and so counterproductive in terms of public opinion that it has intrigued historians ever since. At the time the episode was presented as a horrifying example of the depths of infamy to which Mormons were willing to descend. It becomes historically understandable if not pardonable when viewed as the result of a combination of Mormon hysteria during the early stages of the Utah War, the rumors that this company was a reconnoitering party in advance of the main federal army, and the misbehavior of some members of the Fancher train, mainly a few hangers-on known as Missouri wildcats, who forcibly expropriated supplies and made profane, provocative boasts that they had participated in the Haun's Mill Massacre and other mob actions against the Saints. Add to this the volatile, agitated state of the Indian tribes, who had determined to attack the train because its members had poisoned some of their wells, and the convergence of factors became such as to allow an explosion of passion that under most circumstances simply could not have occurred. Efforts were made by the Mormon leaders in southern Utah to find out what Brigham Young wanted them to do, but without benefit of telegraph his instructions to leave the Fanchers alone arrived just hours too late to prevent the carnage. Some 120 persons were killed by Mormon militiamen and Indians working together. When the incident was reported to Brigham Young, he was at first told that it was an Indian massacre. Only gradually did the bitter truth of Mormon participation and deception emerge. Some local church officials were released from their positions, others were excommunicated, and twenty years later the government convicted John D. Lee, a Mormon Indian farmer, for his part in the crime. He was executed by a firing squad at the site of the massacre.[6]

Young's initial anger at the Utah Expedition was tempered as he realized the futility of open warfare against the U.S. Army. He cautioned raiders to do all they could to delay the force but not to heighten the troops' belligerence toward the Mormons, but the official position emanating from Washington had already begun to change. Through Colonel Thomas L. Kane, Young had initiated peace feelers. While Kane was sailing to California to mediate between Governor Cumming, Young, and Colonel Johnston, Buchanan dispatched a presidential peace commission overland, an action motivated mainly by congressional unrest over the vast amount of money and manpower being used to provision and reinforce the Utah Expedition. Both Young and Buchanan, therefore, now sought a peaceful settlement.

While negotiations were still in process, Young decided on a dramatic gesture. This was a decision to "move South," to abandon the entire northern sweep of the territory to the army, leaving men behind with instructions to set fire to any settlement the soldiers made moves to occupy. Hosea Stout recorded the decision in his diary:

> *Thursday 18 March 1858:* Attended a general Council at the Historians office of the first Presidency, Twelve, and officers of the Legion. The object of which was to take into consideration the enemies, whether to attack them before they came near us or wait until they come near, or whether it is yet best to fight only in unavoidable defense or in case a large force is sent against us this spring whether to fight or burn our houses and destroy every thing in and around us and flee to the mountains and deserts.[7]

Adopting the "Sebastopol plan," which had served a similar purpose during the Crimean War, Young was attempting to muster some national sympathy while demonstrating that the Mormons were not willing to submit to a blatant military occupation of their homes. Throughout the spring the Mormons streamed south to temporary encampments near Provo and farther south.

Meanwhile, Governor Cumming made a trip to the Salt Lake Valley, assured himself there was no rebellion, and returned to Camp Scott, the bivouac at Fort Bridger. In April, agreement was reached that the expedition would be allowed to march through Salt Lake City and establish a position some forty miles distant from which it could ensure the rights of the presidential appointees without seeming to "occupy Mormon territory." In June, after announcing that Buchanan had granted the Mormons "free and full pardon," the new territorial officers and an escort of more than fifty-five hundred soldiers, teamsters, and suppliers marched through the abandoned streets of Salt Lake City. To the south, some thirty thousand Mormon faithful waited, fearful that their homes might be either occupied or destroyed. Nothing of the kind occurred. The Utah Expedition marched beyond the city and across the Jordan River to Cedar Valley, some forty miles south of Salt Lake City. There they established Camp Floyd, named in honor of the Secretary of War who had supported their mission.

The peaceable march of the army through Salt Lake City, the unopposed installation of Cumming as governor, and the subsequent return of the Mormons to their abandoned farms and homes ended a confrontation that had been heralded as apocalyptic but had always had something of the incongruity of comic opera. The President of the United States had dispatched the largest peacetime army in the nation's history to oversee the installation of half a dozen officials in a minor territory. He had done so without thorough investigation of charges made by a few disgruntled or economically interested individuals. He had neglected to notify the Mormons or to inquire after their viewpoint until nearly a year after the expedition was sent. The Mormons, in turn, had once more been uprooted from their homes, interrupted in their development of the territory, and labeled a rebellious people.

The aftermath of the war diminished its unpleasantness for the Mormons. Between 1858 and 1860, while finding that the soldiers interfered little with Mormon life, they reaped sizable economic rewards from the occupying army. The impoverished pioneers who had sadly watched the Utah Expedition march through the heart of the territory returned time after time to Camp Floyd to trade milk, butter, eggs, fish, and wheat for cash, clothing, iron utensils, and tea—items scarce in the isolated Utah economy.

Politically, too, the Mormons found their compromise less crushing than expected. The gentile officials soon split into two factions. One, led by Governor Cumming, followed a policy of tolerance. The other, headed by Justices Delany R. Eckles, John Cradlebaugh, and Charles E. Sinclair, failed to see any change in the state of affairs. Eckles wrote to Lewis Cass: "Brigham Young is de facto governor of Utah, whatever Governor Cumming may be de jure. His reign is one of terror . . . to me the future is dark and gloomy."[8]

The Cumming faction attempted to keep the army out of Utah affairs and avoid antagonizing the Mormons about their religious practices as long as the Saints remained outwardly loyal. Conversely, the judges were not reluctant to call in the army as a special posse to bring Mormons to trial and enforce their writs. Eckles concentrated on prosecuting polygamists, while Sinclair attacked the probate courts. Their zeal was stifled when they received official notice that "The Governor alone has power to issue a requisition for the movement of troops" and that they should "confine themselves strictly within their own official sphere."[9]

One case the judges did feel to be within their official sphere was the Mountain Meadows Massacre. Soon after Cradlebaugh's assignment to the southern judicial district of the territory he conducted an investigation and succeeded in implicating a number of important southern Utah settlers. Failing to get indictments from a grand jury and losing his military posse, he was forced to abandon the case. He was soon thereafter transferred to the Carson Valley, Nevada, court. Nevertheless, reports, not always evenhanded, of the Mountain Meadows Massacre reappeared from time to time to rekindle the national unpopularity of the Mormons.

The deepening national crisis over slavery rapidly drew national attention away from the distant Utah territory. In 1861 the forces at Camp Floyd were withdrawn, and the provisions, supplies, and facilities they left behind were disposed of advantageously for the Mormons. For a time Utah was left largely to its own devices. This was a relief to the Saints, who had expected an increased drive against their peculiarities as a result of the 1860 election victory of the Republicans, whose party platform repeated the 1856 pledge to eradicate polygamy. Yet the Saints found that Lincoln had little interest in conducting more than one crusade at a time. The President's droll parable as related to Mormon diplomat T. B. H. Stenhouse characterized his feelings well:

> Stenhouse, when I was a boy on the farm in Illinois there was a great deal of timber on the farm which we had to clear away. Occasionally we would come to a log which had fallen down. It was too hard to split, too wet to burn, and too heavy to move, so we plowed around it. You go back and tell Brigham Young that if he will let me alone I will let him alone.[10]

Despite Lincoln's tolerant attitude, circumstances would make Utah's stance during the Civil War vital to the Union. Early in the war it became necessary to shift the transcontinental stage lines northward, out of the reach of Confederate troops. The new route passed directly through Salt Lake City and the Utah Territory. Even more important, a key segment of the transcontinental telegraph, completed in 1861 with the help of the Mormons, ran through Utah. If the Union were to maintain the loyalty of California and other important western areas, it was essential that Utah remain firmly in the North's control.

Mormon attitudes toward the war were a curious mixture of loyalty, aloofness, and vindication. Looking back to an 1832 revelation in which Joseph Smith spoke of "the wars that will shortly come to pass, beginning at the rebellion of South Carolina,"[11] Saints found a certain amount of satisfaction in the troubles that had befallen their tormentors. "But let me tell you," spoke Heber C. Kimball, "the yoke is off our neck and it is on theirs, and the bow key is in. The day is not far distant when you will see us free as the air we breathe. President Young is our leader and has been ever since the death of Joseph the Prophet. He can govern this people with his hands in his pockets, and they are not governed one whit by the men that are sent here."[12] The troubles of the nation seemed heaven-sent to relieve the Saints of the burden of outside control.

Not that Mormons saw themselves as disloyal to the country. But some of their sermons suggest that deeper currents were at work: "We shall never secede from the Constitution of the United States. We shall not stop on the way of progress, but we shall make preparations for future events. The South will secede from the North and the North shall secede from us."[13] Loyalty qualified in such a way was consistent with the belief that the Constitution was divinely inspired but that the government had often been corrupt and misguided. "Utah in her rocky fortress," said Brigham Young, "is biding her time to step in and rescue the constitution and aid all lovers of freedom . . . irrespective of creed or party."[14] Understandably some observers read such statements as evidence of impending secession.

Early in 1862 federal officials in Utah notified the War Department that military protection of the overland route was urgently needed. Although they recommended that the non-Mormon superintendent of Indian affairs be authorized to raise a contingent, Brigham Young soon succeeded in transferring the assignment to the Nauvoo Legion. Lincoln bypassed the territorial governor and wired the church president authorizing him to "raise, arm and equip a company of calvalry for ninety days service, to protect the property of the telegraph and overland mail companies."[15] Under the leadership of Lot Smith, a hero of the Utah War, the Saints performed the service well. Hoping to be rewarded for their loyalty by obtaining recognition as a state, Mormon leaders established the State of Deseret as an invisible government behind the territorial apparatus. Similar to governments-in-exile that have been maintained in anticipation of later recognition, the ghost government, fully staffed with Mormon priesthood leaders, continued to meet annually on a ceremonial basis until 1870.[16]

Unfortunately for Mormon hopes, the national government's response was not affirmative. Early in 1861 Congress had pared Utah of all territory west of the thirty-ninth meridian. Probably triggered by the discovery of silver in the Carson Valley area of Nevada, the action was a reminder that the retained the right to govern the region. In 1862 Utah's petition for statehood was denied. While the short-lived debate over statehood was going on, Representative Justin R. Morrill of Vermont introduced legislation banning polygamy in the territories and divesting the church of all assets in excess of fifty thousand dollars. The bill became law but was not enforced for more than a decade.

Stephen S. Harding, who became Utah's governor in 1862, announced a policy of neutrality concerning the Mormon question. But within months he was reporting to Washington that the Saints' loyalty was questionable. He reported that he had heard no expressions of sympathy for the government of the United States, "now struggling for its very existence."[17] In July 1862 Colonel Patrick Edward Connor of Stockton, California, was ordered to raise a body of California and Nevada volunteers and move them to Utah, ostensibly to relieve the Nauvoo Legion of the responsibility for protecting the telegraph. Connor stationed his troops east of the city on a height (now part of the campus of the University of Utah) from which they could control the Mormon population. Connor's correspondence indicates that he felt his duty of assuring Mormon loyalty was at least as important as preventing Indian raids along the overland mail and telegraph route.

The presence of troops polarized sentiments in the territory. The small non-Mormon population in Utah at the time consisted mainly of a few merchants, some immigrants staying over in Utah instead of traveling on to California or Oregon, and the federal officials sent to govern the territory. This group was heartened by the arrival of Connor's forces. While Governor Harding accelerated his campaign in the East to expose Mormon wrongdoing, the federal judges in Utah made several unsuccessful attempts to prosecute Mormon polygamists and to investigate the Mountain Meadows affair. The soldiers themselves established the *Union Vedette*, the first daily newspaper in the territory, and filled its pages with attacks upon the Mormons and their leaders.

The Mormon majority—nine-tenths or more of the population—reacted to the new situation by proclaiming a policy of nonintercourse with the soldiers and Gentiles. The minimal trade with the army camp was channeled through a church committee, at officially set prices. Connor in turn demanded that all Mormons who traded at Camp Douglas first pronounce an oath of allegiance to the United States. Seeing this as an unwarranted insult to their patriotism, most Mormons declined to take the oath.

Tensions mounted. A mass meeting of the Saints declared Harding and the associate justices "hostile to the interests of the people of Utah" and dispatched a petition to Washington demanding that Lincoln remove the offending officials.[18] The Gentiles responded with equally vitriolic denunciations. Scaffolds were erected outside Brigham Young's home, and Mormon militiamen took up positions inside to repulse a rumored attempt to arrest him. Brigham Young defused the situation by surrendering himself on a charge of polygamy, but the case was soon dropped. For the Gentiles the arrest was a simple attempt to enforce the law. The Mormons, on the other hand, saw themselves as victims of persecution and violence. They well remembered what had happened the last time they allowed a prophet to place himself in gentile hands.

A compromise was finally reached. Connor was allowed to maintain a small provost guard within the city for the protection of the non-Mormons who felt themselves to be threatened. But he was warned by his commanding officers to refrain from any confrontation: "Under the circumstances, it is the course of true patriotism for you not to embark on any hostilities. It is infinitely better that you should avoid contact with them. . . . This will undoubtedly tax your forbearance and prudence to the utmost, but the General trusts it will not do so in vain."[19]

The Civil War period ended in Utah as enigmatically as it had begun. When Lincoln's second inaugural address reached Utah, both Mormons and Gentiles celebrated the occasion. At a memorial service for the President after his assassination, sorrowers were comforted by the oratory of both the Mormon apostle Amasa Lyman and the Reverend Norman McLeod, a Protestant stalwart.

Despite invasion, occupation, and legislation, the Mormons had managed to preserve the essentials of their kingdom. Polygamy was untouched. They still looked to Young for leadership in political, economic, and social as well as religious matters. In the actual government of the territory federal officeholders remained frustrated and largely impotent.

The Civil War era marked the appearance of forces that would soon challenge the unity and self-sufficiency of the Mormon kingdom. So long as the Saints did not obstruct overland travel, outsiders found little reason to interfere with the territory's internal workings. A massive gentile immigration would have shifted the political balance within the territory, but for several years outsiders saw little in the Great Basin to attract them. During the 1860s, however, these economic-geographic conditions began to shift.

Colonel Connor, an entrepreneur to the core, devoted most of his time to searching for valuable minerals in the mountains surrounding Salt Lake City. On September 17, 1863, Connor, several of his officers, and an independent-minded Mormon bishop filed claim to strikes in what later became known as Bingham Canyon, southwest of the Salt Lake Valley. Connor could scarcely conceal his glee over the challenge mining would present to the Mormon leaders:

> The results so far have exceeded my most sanguine expectations. Already reliable reports reach me of rich gold, silver and copper mines. . . . If I be not

mistaken in these anticipations, I have no reason to doubt that the Mormon
question will at an early date be finally settled by peaceable means.

Mormon leaders had always opposed deserting agriculture to mine for precious metals. Rich strikes would unavoidably attract a flood of gentile miners.
This was exactly what Connor hoped would occur: "My policy in this territory has been to invite hither a large Gentile and loyal population, sufficient
by peaceful means and through the ballot box to overwhelm the Mormons
by mere force of numbers."[20] Although a small influx of miners did follow in
the wake of Connor's discoveries, no profitable mining ventures were actually
undertaken until a revolution in transportation facilitated shipment of ore to
the East.

But a much more fundamental change was approaching the territory. On
May 10, 1869, the driving of the golden spike joining the Union Pacific and
Central Pacific railroads at Promontory Summit near Ogden punctuated the
close of one era and the beginning of another. Incomprehensibly to the Gentiles, the Mormons were ardent supporters of the railroad. The pioneer company of 1847 had dreamed of a transcontinental railroad following the route
they established. The territorial legislature passed a memorial in 1852 pressing
for a railroad to the Pacific. When the Union Pacific Railroad Company was
incorporated in 1862, Brigham Young in behalf of the church subscribed to
five thousand dollars' worth of stock. Gentiles, however, saw the railroad as a
final solution to the problems created by Mormon isolation and independence. Apostle George Q. Cannon advised his listeners of such threats in
1868: "We are told—openly and without disguise, that when the railroad is
completed there will be such a flood of so called 'civilization' brought in here
that every vestige of us, our church and institutions, shall be completely obliterated."[21] Brigham Young's evaluation of the situation was succinct and to
the point: Mormonism "must indeed be a ——— poor religion, if it cannot
stand one railroad."[22]

Mormon leaders took several steps to prepare for the railroad. To promote
social and economic unity Young revived the School of the Prophets, a study
group of leading men earlier established by Joseph Smith, and redirected it to
the problem of reshaping the Latter-day Saint economy to survive and take
advantage of the circumstances evolving in the territory. The School of the
Prophets made specific plans to counter what were anticipated as the railroad's most pernicious effects. In order to minimize the influx of Gentiles
into the territory, Young, as trustee-in-trust of the church, took up a contract
to do ninety miles of the grading work through the heart of the territory.
This action prevented the intrusion of large groups of non-Mormon laborers
and railroad boomtowns.

On a second front, there was action to counter the growing importance of gentile merchants in the territory. Local Saints were encouraged to establish industries ranging from knitting mills to bucket factories; they advocated abstinence from coffee, tea, and tobacco—three perpetual drains on Mormon currency; and they established local cooperative general stores. The partial boycott of gentile merchants had some effect. Walker Brothers, local merchants who had left the church, found that their receipts dropped from sixty thousand to five thousand dollars per month. The Walkers and others made an offer to the Mormon leaders, promising to leave the territory if they could dispose of their holdings at even fifty cents on the dollar. Church leaders refused the bid, possibly hoping that the Gentiles would soon depart on their own. The Walkers stayed, diversified into mining, and relied on the trade of nearby mining towns, but others did leave. The School of the Prophets also spearheaded drives to build local, Mormon-owned railroads, consolidate Mormon land titles, and finance immigration via the transcontinental railroad.

The railroad marked the territory's entry into the mainstream of American economic life. Mormon leaders had created an agriculture-based economy that they hoped might become self-sufficient. When the first shipment of silver ore left Utah by wagon, moving toward the approaching railhead, it became clear that mining would loom large in the territory's economy. The Walker brothers were soon shipping thousands of tons of ore out of the territory each year and reaping enormous profits. Others scrambled to get a share.

While the mines and the railroad created a larger population of non-Mormons in the territory, this community still probably amounted to less than 10 percent of the total population. But the results of the boom were significant. The rise of a stable group of Gentiles who did not depend on the Mormons for their survival created an anti-Mormon lobby that, unlike the official "carpetbaggers," could claim to speak in the interest of Utah. And although the non-Mormon community would never rival the Mormons at the polls, they could use judicial methods to challenge the validity of elections that placed Mormons in office.

The new challenges to Mormon supremacy began as early as 1866, when Sen. Benjamin Wade of Ohio introduced a bill that would have eliminated Mormon control over the territory's militia and probate courts, prohibited marriage ceremonies by Mormon religious officials, subjected the church to taxation, and allowed trials for polygamy without a jury. The bill did not pass, but it marked the beginning of a new legislative campaign. Gentile Utahans nominated William McGroarty to oppose William Hooper in the election for territorial representative to Congress in 1867. Although McGroarty received only 105 votes (a good measure of the size of the gentile community), he challenged the election in Congress on the grounds that Hooper represented a population hostile to the United States, condoned poıygámy, and had taken a secret oath transferring his allegiance from the United States to the Mormon church. Although McGroarty's claims were denied, they symbolized the direction the conflict would take.

Actually, the most serious threat to the Mormons in the 1860s came from divisions within their own ranks. In 1869 William S. Godbe and a number of disaffected Mormon businessmen and intellectuals, including Amasa Lyman, T. B. H. Stenhouse, and Edward Tullidge, urged the church to adapt to the new era by participating in mining and trading. Godbe and his friends were disillusioned with several aspects of Mormonism, especially the "interference" with what they regarded as private concerns. They dabbled in spiritualism and criticized the frank materialism and authoritarian leadership style of Brigham Young.[23] When Godbe and his associates were expelled from the church, they established the New Movement, often known as Godbeites. As a religion the movement soon floundered, but its periodical, *Utah Magazine,* continued and later, as the Salt Lake City *Daily Tribune,* became the most effective organ of the territory's Gentiles.

The anti-Mormon sentiment that through the 1860s had resulted in occasional legislation or clashes between Mormons and their enemies broadened in the next decade into a veritable crusade on several fronts. While seizing every opportunity to challenge Mormon political control in the territory, Utah Gentiles kept up a steady barrage of criticism. In 1870 a group of prominent non-Mormons known as the Gentile Ring formed the Liberal party of Utah. For a few years the Liberals held control of Tooele County, southwest of Salt Lake City, where mining and railroad interests produced a small gentile majority. Despite its energetic efforts and frequent appeals to Mormons to discard their "oppressive leaders," the Liberal party was successful only in the sense that it influenced public opinion against the Mormons and provided a coterie of advisors to national and territorial politicians.

While local non-Mormons were incapable of changing conditions in the territory from within, Washington legislators were confident that by strong supervision of territorial affairs they could eradicate "the Mormon problem." The congressional crusade took the form of a series of bills aimed at reducing the power of the church and removing any legal smokescreens behind which the Mormons might carry on their objectionable practices. Following the defeat of Wade's bill in 1866, Sen. Aaron Cragin of New Hampshire proposed a nearly identical bill in 1867 and 1869. When Congress failed to approve the Cragin proposal, he withdrew it in favor of legislation sponsored by Rep. Shelby Cullom of Illinois. Cullom's bill concentrated on eliminating polygamy by placing such cases in the hands of the federal courts and juries. Mormon wives were to be deprived of immunity as witnesses against their husbands, the president was authorized to use the military to enforce the law, and the property of anyone imprisoned under the act or leaving the territory to evade prosecution would be confiscated and distributed among cooperating church members. The Cullom bill was defeated, as was the Ashley Bill, which proposed dismembering Utah by division and redistribution among Nevada, Wyoming, and Colorado.

The first legislation passed by Congress during this period was proposed by Representative Potter Poland of Vermont. Strengthening the 1862 law which had limited the amount of property the church could hold and made polygamy illegal in the territories, the 1874 Poland Act extended federal judicial control over all criminal, civil, and chancery cases and placed the offices of territorial attorney general and marshal under federal direction. Strengthened by the new legislation, federal appointees in the territory launched new attacks on Mormon leaders and institutions. The statement of Chief Justice James B. McKean illustrates the determination to let nothing stand in the way:

> ... the mission which God has called upon me to perform in Utah, is as much above the duties of other courts and judges as the heavens are above the earth, and whenever or wherever I may find the Local or Federal laws obstructing or interfering therewith, by God's blessing I shall trample them under my feet.[24]

This attitude was encouraged by the public outcry against Mormonism. Evangelical zeal had already saved the Mississippi Valley from "the clutches of Popery" and fomented the demand that the slavery question be "arbitrated by the appeal to arms." Now, according to Catholic historian Robert Joseph Dwyer, evangelical Protestants found polygamic theocracy in Utah a perfect target.[25]

Protestant incursions into the Salt Lake Valley had begun with the activities of the Rev. Norman McLeod, who had aroused eastern interest in "Christianizing" the Utah pagans. In 1870 Episcopalian bishop Daniel S. Tuttle supervised construction of a cathedral in Salt Lake City. Tuttle's missionaries concentrated on establishing schools in the chief cities of the territory, hoping to attract young Mormons away from the often backward Latter-day Saint schools and thus develop a generation of liberal Utahans. Tuttle was careful not to attack the Mormons, and even praised their industry and order. When the Mormon newspaper expressed its gratification for the bishop's temperate, friendly approach, the *Tribune* was quick to respond: "Our Malicious *Grandmother* [the *Deseret News*], seeing that this Christian minister had laid himself open to censure, hastened to slime him over with her blighting pestilential praise."[26]

Episcopalians and Catholics tended to avoid open conflict with the Mormon majority, while the evangelistic churches courted it. In 1870 John P. Newman, leading Methodist minister in Washington, D.C., and chaplain of the U.S. Senate, traveled to Salt Lake City bearing a challenge to Brigham Young to meet in a public debate on the burning question "Does the Bible Sanction Polygamy?" Neither a Bible scholar nor a debater, Young deferred to Apostle Orson Pratt, who contended against Reverend Newman for three days in the Tabernacle. While inconclusive, the famous Newman-Pratt debate illustrated two principal features of the Protestant anti-Mormon crusade. First, would-be reformers seized on polygamy as the most visible symbol of Mormon peculiarity. Although actual differences between Utah and the nation went far deeper than the unique marital arrangements of a minority of the Saints, antipolygamy became the rallying point of the crusade. The debate also exemplified the inconclusiveness of the verbal disputes that raged during the crusade: Mormons would remain convinced of the legality and superiority of their system, while Gentiles could not comprehend how the Latter-day Saints could resist the overwhelming show of public disapproval. On both sides, rhetoric was aimed at affirming the convictions of the committed rather than clarifying a middle ground of possible compromise.[27]

The Presbyterian and Methodist churches began in Utah with small congregations centered in Salt Lake City and in the gentile stronghold of Corinne, in northern Utah. Soon zealous evangelists were establishing schools and churches throughout the territory. In 1876 there were approximately 14,000 non-Mormons in the territory out of a total population of 150,000. Far more influential than the physical presence of local Protestants was the flow of letters from Utah to the East praising the industry and progress of the Protestant cause, adding a new charge or an illustration of a past accusation to the weight of anti-Mormon literature, and appealing for teachers, funds, and more active public support. Protestant ministers not only wrote letters and sent memorials or petitions to Congress but they often returned to their home states to further arouse feeling against the Mormons, as this 1884 account in the Salt Lake City *Tribune* shows:

> Dr. Iliff has returned from an extended visit to sixteen Eastern Methodist conferences, where he met with such pleasing success and made so favorable an impression the six bishops with many ministers and laymen, have requested him to take another eastern trip to explain more in detail the condition of affairs and prospects in Utah.... The Doctor found a remarkable interest in Utah's religious condition.... They were all eager to see the Asiatic Church crushed, wiped off the face of the earth.[28]

The energetic activities of the "Utah missionaries" had their most telling effect in arousing moralistic zeal in thousands of American women, whose idealistic fervor had earlier fostered abolitionism and now adopted a new cause. Harriet Beecher Stowe wrote an appeal to the women of America:

> Let every happy wife and mother who reads these lines give her sympathy, prayers and efforts to free her sisters from this degrading bondage. Let all the women of the country stand united for them. There is a power in combined enlightened sentiment, before which every form of injustice and cruelty must finally go down.[29]

The trouble was that "combined enlightened sentiment" flourished in one of the most morally contradictory periods of history. In England Prime Minister William Gladstone might patiently strive to reform each prostitute who accosted him as he strolled the back alleys of London, while at the same time he frequented the salon of a noted courtesan. In America rigidly moralistic men and women decried the sins of Mormondom in much the same way that their English counterparts gravely attended illustrated lectures on the fertility rites and sexual habits of primitive cultures while regarding the glimpse of even an ankle as high impropriety. Journalists painted an ugly picture of polygamous license and theocratic dictatorship holding sway by terror and ignorance. For most Americans the moral correctness of a crusade against "the Mormon monster" soon became axiomatic.

Antipolygamy groups, growing naturally out of the abolitionist societies of the 1850s, promised to attack the aberration on its home grounds. Gentile women in Utah cooperated by forming their own antipolygamy societies. In 1880 the Utah group began publication of the *Anti-Polygamy Standard,* which provided a forum for three years. Such literary efforts culminated in a series of heartrending fictional treatments of the horrors of polygamic autocracy. *The Fate of Madame la Tour, A Tale of Great Salt Lake,* by Mrs. A. G. Paddock, sold more than one hundred thousand copies.[30]

With each new tale of horror the women's crusade gained momentum. Despite the assertions of many Mormon plural wives that they were content with their situation, crusaders continued their resolutions, letters, and exposés. An ironic dilemma confronted them, however, on the question of suffrage. Women in Utah Territory had been enfranchised under an act of the Mormon-controlled legislature in 1870. Although many exercised their right to vote, it is clear that no significant ballot box rebellion developed after the privilege of voting was extended to the supposedly misused chattels of Mormon men. Since suffrage in Utah contributed to the strength of the Mormon establishment, eastern antipolygamist women found it advisable to oppose the Mormon feminists. Latter-day Saint women were eventually disfranchised by Congress under the Edmunds-Tucker Act of 1887.

*   *   *

By the end of the 1870s the crusade was in full cry. The long series of proposed bills and the passage of the Poland Act did not augur well for the Saints. Accusations by Utah clergymen and other Gentiles received great attention in the eastern press, while the counterarguments of Mormon advocates were largely ignored. More importantly, from the Mormon standpoint, Brigham Young was dead. The great colonizer died in 1877 of complications from a ruptured appendix. Leadership then reverted to the Quorum of the Twelve, presided over by John Taylor, senior apostle. Although Taylor was a man of ability and courage, the loss of the central figure of more than thirty years of Mormon history weakened the Saints in the face of the anti-Mormon offensive.

As early as 1879 it became clear that the final confrontation between church and state would occur not in the newspapers nor in the pulpit but in Congress and the courts. In 1875 George Reynolds, secretary to Brigham Young and a polygamist, had gone to court to test the constitutionality of the 1862 antibigamy legislation, which had hitherto remained unenforced. The first trial resulted in acquittal on technical grounds but the second trial was appealed to the U.S. Supreme Court, which ruled that the antibigamy law was constitutional and also confirmed Reynolds's guilty verdict and his sentence to a fine and two years' imprisonment. The Mormon legal defense had been that polygamy was a religious belief and was therefore protected by the Bill of Rights. The Supreme Court, while recognizing that the Bill of Rights extended freedom of religious belief to citizens, enumerated certain limitations to the privilege: "Laws are made for the government of actions and while they cannot interfere with mere religious beliefs and opinions, they may with practices."[31]

For some time the Mormons continued to resist federal authority. Local courts were still controlled by the Mormons; the right to pick juries was also firmly in Mormon hands because of the U.S. Supreme Court decision of 1872 in the *Englebrecht* case. Thus antipolygamy prosecutions were infrequent and generally resulted in acquittal. When John H. Miles was convicted of polygamous relations, the Supreme Court overruled the decision in 1881 on grounds that Miles's wife had unlawfully been required to testify against him.

Congress discovered the futility of trying to force compliance with unpopular laws when the local judiciary was controlled by those who opposed the law. In 1882 Senator George F. Edmunds, a Republican from Vermont, introduced an amendment to the Anti-Bigamy Act of 1862. Edmunds's proposal was aimed at disqualifying George Q. Cannon as the territorial delegate to Congress. It declared polygamy a felony, defined unlawful cohabitation and provided a misdemeanor penalty for it, disfranchised polygamists, nullified their eligibility for office and jury duty, and placed territorial elections under the control of a presidential commission instructed to issue certificates of election only to qualified (that is, nonpolygamous) candidates.

The battle over passage of the Edmunds Act was bitter. Many non-Mormons, especially Democrats and other westerners, opposed the bill on the grounds that it was an unwarranted encroachment on the constitutional rights of the Mormons. Mormons themselves mustered every voice they could against the bill. John Taylor, the new church president, expressed the church's official position and renewed the issue of constitutionality:

> We have no fault to find with our government, we deem it the best in the world, but we have reason to deplore its maladministration. . . . We shall abide all constitutional law, as we always have done; but while we are God-fearing and law-abiding and respect all honorable men and officers, we are no craven serfs, and have not learned to lick the feet of oppressors, nor to bow in base submission to unreasoning clamor. We will contend inch by inch, legally and constitutionally, for our rights as American citizens and plant ourselves firmly on the sacred guarantees of the constitution.[32]

Despite opposition, the Edmunds Act was signed into law by President Chester Arthur on March 22, 1882. The final grounds of the confrontation were fixed.

Bolstered by the new legislation and the supervisory power of the newly created Utah Commission, federal judges in Utah launched the first sustained offensive against polygamists. Deputies of the U.S. marshal pursued accused "cohabs" (persons suspected of "cohabitation") from haystack to haystack across the territory. Once captured, a suspected polygamist was dispatched to trial by a gentile judge, with jurors selected for their disbelief in plurality. Rudger Clawson, the first prominent Mormon convicted under the new law, was indicted on charges of both polygamy and unlawful cohabitation, convicted by a jury composed of twelve Gentiles, and sentenced to three and one-half years in the Utah Territorial Penitentiary. The U.S. Supreme Court upheld the decision.

Viewing with alarm the convictions obtained under the new act, the church leadership decided that new steps were necessary to circumvent the legislation. When Salt Lake Stake President Angus M. Cannon was arrested in 1885, John Taylor, George Q. Cannon, and other prominent churchmen decided to go on "the underground"—drop from public sight—and begin a migrant life of hiding a few days at a time in a succession of Mormon houses and barns. Life on the underground was a wearying cycle of travel, hardship, and close escapes. John M. Whitaker, a son-in-law of President Taylor, described the life of the time:

> The president and his associates had to move from place to place very frequently. At this particular time President Taylor was stopping out at Cot-

tonwood [immediately south of Salt Lake City]. Breakfast was just prepared under the trees in a grove near the home of his brother. They had just arose from morning prayer when President Taylor arose and said, "Charlie [the coachman] hitch up the horses as quickly as possible; I feel that the deputies will be here." Within twenty minutes here comes a number of deputy marshalls. Someone had informed the deputies of the whereabout of the President, but the Lord had inspired him to move in time.[33]

While one body of church leaders stayed near Salt Lake City in a succession of hideouts, another group sought more permanent asylum in Mexico, Canada, and Hawaii. Day-to-day direction of church affairs was left to a small number of nonpolygamists, who communicated by letter and nocturnal visits with high officials in the underground. A fourth body of Mormons made their residence in the territorial penitentiary, where they peacefully served terms ranging from six months to several years. They were generally treated humanely, although there were complaints about mail privileges, food, bedding, and especially the requirement that the bearded patriarchs be clean-shaven. Since the great majority of Mormons were not involved in polygamous marriage, they moved about freely and often served as intermediaries and protectors for underground polygamists.

President Taylor died while underground on July 25, 1887, in Kaysville, near Salt Lake City. His body was returned to the city, where Mormons lauded him as a "double martyr"—not only had he shed his blood in the Carthage jail where Joseph and Hyrum Smith were murdered but he had "been killed by the cruelty of those officials who have, in this Territory, misrepresented the Government of the United States." To Gentiles he was simply "a worn out old man."[34] Following Taylor's death, Wilford Woodruff assumed the leadership of the church from another series of hideaways.

The first step toward compromise was taken when Frank J. Cannon, representing the Mormon leaders, successfully lobbied to have the moderate New York judge Elliott F. Sanford appointed as chief justice of the Utah territorial courts. Sanford significantly reduced the sentences given convicted polygamists and thus persuaded a number of previously unrepentant "cohabs" to surrender. On September 17, 1888, George Q. Cannon, a symbol of Mormon resistance, surrendered voluntarily and was sentenced to only 175 days in prison. Sanford's policy was one of moderation. And he was candid in explaining what the Mormons must do:

> We care nothing for your polygamy. It's a good war-cry and serves our purpose by enlisting sympathy for our cause; but it's a mere bagatelle compared with other issues in the irrepressible conflict between our parties. What we most object to is your unity; your political and commercial solidarity; the obedience you render to your spiritual leaders in temporal affairs. We want

you to throw off the yoke of the Priesthood, to do as we do, and be Americans in deed as well as name.[35]

When it became evident that the Mormons would submit to the harassment of the 1882 law rather than surrender their cherished practices, Congress passed the Edmunds-Tucker Act in 1887.

The new act maintained the individual penalties of the previous statute but also provided for the legal dismemberment of the church itself. The Corporation of the Church of Jesus Christ of Latter-day Saints was dissolved.[36] Any church property in excess of fifty thousand dollars was to be applied to financing district (non-Mormon) schools in the territory. Such measures seemed extreme, but on May 19, 1890, by a five-to-four decision, the U.S. Supreme Court declared the seizure and redistribution of the church's holding to be legal:

> Then looking at the case as the finding of the facts presents it, we have before us—Congress had before it—a contumacious organization, wielding by its resources an immense power in the Territory of Utah, and employing those resources and that power in constantly attempting to oppose, thwart and subvert the legislation of Congress and the will of the government of the United States. Under these circumstances we have no doubt of the power of Congress to do as it did.[37]

Earlier, in February, the Court had upheld the constitutionality of disfranchising all Mormons, even those that were not polygamists. During the summer of 1890 bills were drafted in both houses of Congress that would have accomplished that purpose in all territories under federal jurisdiction.

As Mormon leaders met throughout the summer of 1890 to discuss the effects of these rulings, it became clear that the church had few options left. There was earnest prayer—and a response that many felt was from God. On the night of September 25, 1890, President Wilford Woodruff wrote in his journal, "I have arrived at a point in the history of my life as the president of the Church . . . where I am under the necessity of acting for the temporal salvation of the church." That day he issued a statement to the Saints which became known as the Manifesto:

> Inasmuch as laws have been enacted by Congress forbidding plural marriages, which laws have been pronounced constitutional by the court of last resort, I hereby declare my intention to submit to those laws, and to use my influence with the members of the Church over which I preside to have them do likewise.[38]

"It is not wisdom for us," said President Woodruff, "to go forth and carry out this principle [plural marriage] against the laws of the nation and receive the consequences. . . . I have done my duty, and the nation . . . must be held responsible."[39] On October 6 the general conference of the church "unanimously sustained" the act of their president as "authoritative and binding."

The antipolygamy stance of Woodruff did not, of course, satisfy everyone. A few Mormons continued to enter into plural marriages without the sanction of church authority. Some local and national political leaders found Woodruff's statement incomplete. They would have preferred a renunciation of the principle of plurality, not just a resolution to abide by the law. Others noted that the statement said nothing to suggest a discontinuance of what they regarded as pervasive church control in the political and economic spheres. But most Americans were glad to accept Woodruff's official declaration as adequate evidence of Mormon accommodation. Between 1894 and 1896 the church's property was returned by joint resolution of Congress, minus losses incurred during eight years of receivership. In return, Mormon leaders never attempted to reassert pervasive control over the territorial economy. The People's party, the Mormon political instrument in territorial elections, was dissolved. Mormon voters were advised to join either the Republican or the Democratic party. The process of "Americanization" was formalized in 1894, when Congress passed the enabling act permitting Utah to form a state government.

From time to time old bitterness would revive. Charges of church influence in politics appeared regularly well into the new century. In 1898 Mormon B. H. Roberts was denied a seat in the U.S. House of Representatives on the ground that he was a practicing polygamist. In 1903 Reed Smoot's election to the Senate was contested because he was an officer (apostle) in the Mormon church—a church that, according to the charge, conspired to control the state's political life. Smoot, unlike Roberts, was seated and became one of the most powerful Senate leaders of the first third of the twentieth century.

The political activities of prominent churchmen such as Smoot and the importance of businessmen such as David Eccles (a pioneer Western industrialist) illustrated the new individualistic trends within Mormonism. A half-century and more of heated confrontation with the U.S. government had taught Latter-day Saints the practical limits of religious life in America. By the end of World War I, if not before, the Mormons were more American than most Americans. Patriotism, respect for the law, love of the Constitution, and obedience to political authority reigned as principles of the faith.

10

{ Marriage and }
{ Family Patterns }

H.G.—With regard, then, to the grave question on which your doctrines and practices are avowedly at war with those of the Christian world—that of a plurality of wives—is the system of your Church acceptable to the majority of its women?

B.Y.—They could not be more averse to it than I was when it was first revealed to us as the Divine will. I think they generally accept it, as I do, as the will of God.

—Horace Greeley interview with Brigham Young (1859)

No other success can compensate for failure in the home. The poorest shack in which love prevails over a united family is of greater value to God and future humanity than any other riches.

—David O. McKay (1964)

For most non-Mormons in the nineteenth century (and many in the twentieth) the predominant and peculiar feature of Mormonism was plural marriage, or polygamy. This rallying point for the anti-Mormon crusades of the 1870s and 1880s established a persisting stereotype. But the great majority of Mormons have had no direct experience with polygamy. Considering that the church is approximately 150 years old, that polygamy was in effect for about one-third of that time, and that at the maximum less than one-fifth of the church population lived in polygamous families while the principle was in effect, then less than one-fifteenth of all Mormons have been so involved. But even that figure fails to consider the geometric growth of the church. Just as most of the scientists who have ever lived are alive at the present moment, more than half of those who have been Mormons were baptized since 1950. Thus the percentage of all Mormons from the beginning to the present who were parents or children in plural households is something less than 1 percent. These are rough figures, but they help make a point: To understand the Mormon family it is important to look for characteristics and values that did not depend on polygamy. Indeed, even for that small percentage of Mormons who were directly involved in polygamy, the heart of this understanding of marriage lay not in plurality of wives but in the much broader principle of "eternal marriage."

* * *

From at least as early as 1842 Mormons have believed that a man and woman could be married, or "sealed" together, for eternity in sacred temples or (in the early days of the church) other specially consecrated places. If they are true to the exacting covenants of fidelity to each other and obedience to God that are part of the ceremony, Mormons believe they can not only enjoy a never-ending union but, through the special creative powers made possible by that union, can realize most fully their own true natures. This will ultimately enable them to become like God himself—if they meet the tests of life successfully. This belief has implications for the nature of God, the nature of man, and the path of salvation. On a more mundane level it has had a strong effect on patterns of courtship, expectations in marriage, views on divorce, and ideas about the roles of men and women.

It is possible for Mormons to take quite literally the announcement in Genesis that both male and female were created "in the image of God." The New Testament statements that God is the father of human spirits is explained in Mormon theology as follows: All men and women, in an existence long before they came to this earth, were actually born of Heavenly Parents; that is, for each person an eternally existing "intelligence" was given a spirit body so that it could begin to learn and exercise choice and thus progress. As spirit children they were taught and assisted by those Parents—God the Father and their Heavenly Mother—in preparation for coming here to mortality for further advancement. Because the Divine Parents impart something of their own nature to their children, human beings can think of themselves as "gods in embryo," as being able to continue on the path those Parents started them on—until eventually, if they remain faithful, they become like them, just as mortal children become like their mortal parents. Being parents in mortality is an opportunity to share in God's divine, creative work. The marriage relationship is thus seen as a necessary step (for those who make the appropriate covenants) toward the ultimate form of personal salvation—the highest purpose of existence itself—which is godhood.

The apparent exclusiveness of this doctrine (that only the few who are worthy and are sealed or married for eternity in Mormon temples can attain the highest degree of the "celestial kingdom") is offset by another fundamental doctrine. Mormons believe there is no final judgment immediately after death but that life goes on in another sphere. The eternal spirit, separated from the mortal body, returns to a spirit world and continues the process of learning and making choices while awaiting the resurrection of all God's children. In that spirit existence all who did not have the necessary opportunities for progress and fulfillment while on earth will have a fair chance.

This central perspective helps explain why the church holds to a strict standard of chastity, condemning without exception premarital and extramarital intercourse and all forms of extramarital eroticism. Yet those very proscriptions stem from recognition of the positive place sexuality plays in human happiness, self-fulfillment, and progress toward godhood.[1] Sexual characteristics are seen as ongoing parts of each individual's nature that make possible the fullest realization of his or her true self, both in mortality and beyond.

This understanding of the eternal meaning of the sex roles has produced characteristic patterns of courtship and marriage. Mormon youth are taught to take very seriously their selection of a mate, seeing it as a religious responsibility that will determine not only their earthly happiness but their eternal welfare. Sometimes this idealism produces problems. The inner conflict and guilt that sometimes accompany the strong emphasis on sexual purity occasionally carries over into marriage as sexual incompatibility or as naive shirking of the need for honest confrontation of real problems. And the strong emphasis on marriage sometimes takes a toll on those who for various reasons remain single, for the difficulty of finding an accepted place in a family-oriented culture may cause a loss of self-esteem. In recent years the church has paid increasing attention to the single minority—the unmarried, divorced, or widowed. But it continues to advocate successful marriage partnership and stable, mutually fulfilling family experience as the best builders of both individual and social strength.

Like other Americans and western Europeans, nineteenth-century Mormons believed in "romantic love." If there was any important difference in Mormon romantic love, it was in its religious context. At least the devout were anxious to find partners who were equally committed to the restored gospel. Sometime after the enunciation of the doctrine that human beings had existed as spirits prior to their birth, it became fairly common to think that one's special "one and only" had been known in the preexistence, when a covenant or promise had been made. A novel by Nephi Anderson, *Added Upon* (1898), and a more recent musical, *Saturday's Warrior* (1975), have popularized the idea; it has become a Mormon version of the standard literary device of bringing family members back together after amnesia or a lapse of time. Patriarchal blessings ("official" individual blessings under the hands of spiritual older men ordained to be patriarchs) promised many young Mormons that, if faithful, they would find and marry the "choice spirit" they had known in the preexistence. The idea received some discouragement from church leaders, who considered it too fatalistic, and the church never has held that all marriages were of this type. In popular lore the idea, when it cropped up, served mainly to give religious overtones to the common conception of a "one and only."[2]

The position of the wife and mother in the Mormon home was considered fundamental. The highest role for women was serving as helpmeet for husband and mother for the children God would "send" to them. There her importance as shaper of the future generation was inestimable. In December 1893 the *Young Woman's Journal* contained a pseudonymous article entitled "The Wife I Want," which set forth a catalogue of virtues including the following:

> She should be religious, yet not sanctimonious.
> She should be honest, truthful and candid, yet not consider it hypocrisy to refrain from telling people all that she may think or hear about them that is disagreeable.
> She should be kind and attentive to all people, but reserve her sweetest smiles and kindest acts for me. . . .
> She should love children, and never consider them "nuisances" or "wish them dead," and yet not be so indulgent as to allow them to grow up in idleness, disobedience or sin.
> She should make her home so pleasant that angels will delight to make it their abode, and that the family may consider it the one place on earth where a foretaste of heaven is obtained; yet she should not make herself a slave to the home, but move around in the world and improve mankind by her noble life. . . .
> She should find some time each day for intellectual culture, even though this may make early rising necessary, and to her physical health she should give due attention. . . .
> I should be the ONE man on the earth whom she is constantly studying and trying to please, and for whom she is willing to forsake kindred, home, country and everything except God and what pertains to celestial glory.[3]

The article provoked some lively commentary from female readers: "The husband I would not have," wrote one young lady, "is the man who wrote 'The Wife I Want'!" But generally the letters and editorial comments recognized the validity of the original ideal. Mormon women were not confined to household duties, but there is no doubt of their basic and continuing commitment to the traditional virtues of wife and mother.

The role of the male as husband and father was also basic. Strong statements from church presidents ranging from the negative ("No success can compensate for failure in the home") to the positive ("The most important work you will ever do will be within the walls of your own home") epitomize the extensive efforts recently made to "liberate" men. There has been intense training and exhortation to free the Mormon male from his modern American stereotype as a prisoner of circumstance who works long hours at the office in order to buy material things for his family, spending his leisure time as a macho sports addict or a swinger chasing other women. Such an emotionally starved life is not consistent with Mormon ideals. Mormon men are urged to take equal responsibility for the spirit of the home, for the teaching and emotional nurturing of the children, and for the quality of the husband and wife relationship. They are specifically encouraged to organize family activities such as the Family Home Evening each week, to be directly engaged in the religious, moral, and emotional training of their children, and to constantly "court" their wives.

Although success in marriage is difficult to measure, the majority of participating Mormons expressed satisfaction concerning their families and married life. Some 48 percent of U.S. Mormons go to the temple to begin "eternal marriages." (The others may be married by a Mormon bishop, another clergyman, or a justice of the peace because one of the spouses is not a church member, because one or both of the spouses cannot pass the rigorous examination for "worthiness," because it is not financially possible for them to travel to a temple, or simply because they prefer a nontemple marriage; many of these later are "sealed" in the temple.) There are 3.01 divorces per thousand of the U.S. Mormon population, compared with a national average of 4.8 divorces per thousand. Obviously the Mormon practice falls short of the ideal. Since Mormon divorce rates, too, are rising and the percentage of temple marriages has been declining, it may be conjectured that the difference is only one of time lag. Those who marry in the temple not surprisingly enjoy better success, for they have gone through a preliminary screening that assures a common religious commitment at the very least. For whatever reasons, it is impossible to deny that the concept of eternal marriage has added "importance, dignity, and glory to the idea of marriage."[4]

One consequence of the increased emphasis on family as an earthly focus of stability and a foreshadowing of eternal progress together was the formation of family organizations. Reunions were held as early as the Young and Richards gathering in Nauvoo in 1845. The process continued in the Great Basin, where the extended family was given great importance. If a person belonged to one of the leading families, relations were everywhere. Consider the situation of an imaginary family as follows: Three brothers join the church, and all take plural wives; each plural wife has four children; one of the boys enters polygamy, and one of the daughters becomes a plural wife, the others marrying "monogamously." The situation becomes too entangled to diagram, but it is obvious that in the third generation there would be half-siblings, cousins galore, and affinities by marriage with many other families. In terms of psychological security—"a friend in every port"—and actual "looking out for" each other, the system offered a great deal. D. Michael Quinn has demonstrated that influential families promoted a kind of dynasticism in the hierarchy of the church.[5] Actually the "looking out for" took other forms as well and was not limited to prominent families like the Cannons and the

Snows. To this day family reunions and organizations are a strong tradition in Mormon culture, and it is common to find a highly developed awareness of uncles, aunts, cousins, and the larger kinship group.

Closely related to eternal marriage was parenthood, which was regarded as both an obligation and a blessing. "Blessed is the man whose quiver is full of them"—this biblical appreciation of children was common among the Saints. Living in the agricultural or frontier environment where sons and daughters meant additional manpower for planting, harvesting, and the endless household chores, Mormons had practical reasons for placing a high valuation on children. Besides, as suggested earlier, their religion provided a frame of reference for the Mormons' procreative enthusiasm. Spirits destined for birth on this earth were thought to be waiting eagerly. They would all be born sooner or later, but how much better for them to be born of believing parents, Latter-day Saints who understood God's plan. It would be deliberately selfish to have no children or an unseemly few.

The belief was occasionally expressed that in the preexistence children had already picked the parents who would usher them into earthly life, by mutual consent of course. Since eventual eternal exaltation included a multitude of progeny, it was natural for some to develop what one writer has called a "quantum theory of salvation"—the more, the holier.[6] Strictly speaking, this unofficial theology at its best was never quite so crude, but it did allow room for an expansive view of family, stretching back into the preexistence and forward into eternity.

Mere physical propagation of offspring was not of course the end of parental responsibility. Although the concept of original sin had been rejected by the Book of Mormon and there was a certain idealization of little children, there was no doubt about the parental responsibility to care for, train, and indoctrinate their children. The age of baptism for children whose parents were church members was set at eight, and a revelation in 1831 announced that if Mormon parents did not teach their children the principles of faith and repentance, the sins they might commit were "upon the heads of the parents." A later verse added, "And they shall also teach their children to pray, and to walk uprightly before the Lord."[7] The obligation to teach children properly was a frequently reiterated theme in church conferences, sacrament meetings, and newspapers and periodicals.[8]

To deal with their obligation, Mormon parents often held regular family meetings. In the family of Daniel Wood during the 1860s, Charles E. Pearson, an adopted son, kept the minutes of such conclaves and wrote several homey poems and songs for use in them. The following was sung to the tune of "Marching to Georgia":

Come all my young companions, let's go to Brother Wood's,
For he's going to have a meeting to teach us what is good,
And we'll be sure to hear what'll make us all rejoice.
And be learned to make our lives useful.

Chorus
Hurrah, Hurrah, come let us all be going.
Hurrah, Hurrah, for meeting time is coming.
And we will always go when we can get the chance.
God bless Brother Wood forever.

Since the Wood family meetings included other young people from the neighborhood, they were actually an early form of youth association.[9]

Although the ways the Mormons chose to reprimand and punish their children were probably close to the standard American practices of the time, there were some expressions of forbearance in Mormon literature. In 1864 Brigham Young reminded parents that application of the rod was frequently counterproductive. Children reared under such harsh punishment "become so stupified and lost to every high-toned feeling and sentiment, that though you bray them in a mortar among wheat with a pestle, yet will not their foolishness depart from them." He continued:

Kind looks, kind actions, kind words, and a lovely, holy deportment towards them, will bind our children to us with bands that cannot easily be broken; while abuse and unkindness will drive them from us, and break assunder every holy tie that should bind them to us and to the everlasting covenant in which we are all embraced.

Denouncing "tyrant parents" who were "more like taskmasters than natural protectors," Young uttered this gentle admonition: "Let parents treat their children as they themselves would wish to be treated, and set an example before them that is worthy of you as Saints of God."[10]

There was great affection for children in Mormon families. One of the most moving passages in the Book of Mormon account of Jesus Christ's post-Resurrection visit to the Western Hemisphere tells of the people bringing their children to him:

and he took their little children, one by one, and blessed them, and prayed unto the Father for them.... And he spake unto the multitude, and said unto them: Behold your little ones. And as they looked to behold they cast their eyes towards heaven, and they saw the heavens open, and they saw angels descending out of heaven as it were in the midst of fire; and they came down and encircled those little ones about, and they were encircled about the fire; and the angels did minister unto them.[11]

This veneration of the innocence of children, echoing the New Testament blessing of children, influenced Mormon family life. Obtaining a firsthand impression of affectionate family relationships from the past is not easy, since they were rarely committed to writing. However, there are examples in the letters of the first two church presidents. This is Joseph Smith writing to his wife Emma on April 4, 1839, after he had been incarcerated in Liberty Jail for five months:

> I think of you and the children continually. If I could tell you my tale, I think you would say it was altogether enough for once, to gratify the malice of hell that I have suffered. I want to see little Frederick, Joseph, Julia, and Alexander, Joana, and old major [their dog]. And as to yourself if you want to know how much I want to see you, examine your feelings, how much you want to see me, and judge for yourself. I would gladly walk from here to you barefoot, and bareheaded, and half naked, to see you and think it great pleasure, and never count it toil. . . . I want you should not let those little fellows forget me. Tell them Father loves them with a perfect love, and he is doing all he can to get away from the mob to come to them. Do teach them all you can, that they may have good minds. Be tender and kind to them, don't be fractious to them, but listen to their wants. Tell them father says they must be good children, and mind their mother.

Here is Brigham Young writing to his wife, Mary Ann, on June 12, 1844, en route to the East on his last mission for Smith, just before the Prophet was killed:

> My beloved wife, while I am waiting for a boat to go to Buffalo, I improve a few moments in writing to you. . . . This is a pleasant evening on the Lake but I feel lonesome; O that I had you with me this summer, I think I should be happy. Well, I am now because I am in my calling and doing my duty, but [the] older I grow the more I desire to stay at home instead of traveling. . . . How I want to see you and the children. Kiss them for me and kiss Luny twice or more. Tell her it is for me. Give my love to all the family. . . . I do feel to Bless you in the name of the Lord.

And the parental love of a church member is conveyed in the following letter written by Albert Carrington in 1869 when he was a missionary in England, to his nine-year-old son:

> My very Dear, Good little Son Calvin. Your very good little letter of Jan. 14 came safely to me, and I was ever so much pleased to learn that your health was so good, that you are such a good boy, and grow so finely, and to see that you improve so fast in your writing. I am glad that your good Ma, has made you some knickerbokers and that you are to have your photograph to

take [and] send to me. I hope it will come safely, for I very much want to see it. Please ask your Ma to give you some good, sweet kisses for me, for you are quite right when you tell Ma that Pa would like to see you, for I would ever so well be pleased to see you, hug you, kiss you, romp with you, and hear you sing and play on your drum and the organ; and as soon as your Pa is through in England, he will go straight home and see you and Tenny and Ma and the rest of you. Now, my dear little son, that our Father in Heaven will ever preserve you in health and from error and evil and harm, and make you among the mightiest of his servants in working righteousness upon the earth is all the time the prayer of your affectionate father, Albert Carrington.[12]

As always, of course, there was a gap between the ideal and the reality: some Mormon children were neglected or overworked. Some were a disappointment to their parents.[13] But the high valuation placed on children and the recognition of their lofty eternal potential are clear.

The Mormon understanding of the family had its unique characteristics: the idea of eternal marriage, the concept of children entering earthly life after a premortal existence, certain scriptural passages and sermons about the obligations of parents, and the expectation of a continued family relationship in the hereafter. But these were ideas, assumptions about life and its meaning, that could either underlie activities and decisions in a significant way or be conveniently ignored. On a more practical level Mormon family life often included experiences not easily disregarded—actual life as opposed to beliefs. For one thing, there was the original conversion to Mormonism, which often meant the schism of families. In the sense that it was virtually impossible to bring all of one's extended family into the new faith, some kind of religious separation was inevitable. The tears and heartache that followed such division, especially when it occurred in the immediate family, are incalculable. In 1832 Orson Hyde traveled through New York State preaching to friends and family. One of his diary entries reads:

> Called on sister Laura and her husband Mr. North. They disbelieved. We took our things and left them, and tears from all eyes freely ran, and we shook the dust of our feet against them, but it was like piercing my heart; and all I can say is "The will of the Lord be done."[14]

The obverse of such heartrending experiences was the unity and solidarity among family members who together embraced the new religion.

Another divisive experience in many Mormon families was the absence of the father on missions. Around the turn of the century the missionary program was reorganized so that the bulk of the responsibility was carried by young, single men, but for the first fifty years or more of the church's existence it was not uncommon to call husbands and fathers to spend two, three, or as many as six years preaching the gospel outside of Utah. No more than a few hundred families experienced such paternal absences to any significant degree, but for those who did it must have seriously affected the family. And the possibility of such a call constantly hovered in the background. Another practical difference in Mormon families was the frequency and extent of moves made in response to their religious belief. Many Saints endured the hardships of being driven by persecutors or of responding to church calls to move to new settlements. The result, of course, was deprivation, a sense of loss, and often actual suffering, mitigated only by religious commitment.

Except for such ideological and practical differences, the Mormon family was essentially Victorian. And the Victorian family was itself heir of the Puritan "spiritualization of the household" described by Christopher Hill in *Society and Puritanism in Pre-Revolutionary England* (1964). Emphasis on the family unit and on the importance of religious teaching in the home was thus scarcely unique or new to Mormonism. The "cult of true womanhood"—the standard nineteenth-century American assumption that woman's essential role was to be pious, pure, submissive, and domestic—was understood in a different theological context by the Mormons.[15] It belonged to a larger set of tacit assumptions about the nature of family life and the ideal goals that included marriage for romantic love, idealization of the wife and mother, warmth and affection in the family circle, games and conversation around the hearth, helpful participation of the children in family chores, and visits to relatives "over the river and through the woods." This was the nineteenth-century family, not necessarily in actual experience but in the ideal, the family that comes across in, say, the poetry of James Whitcomb Riley. And the Mormons spoke the same language. The ideological and practical differences were few, and some of them even had parallels in the common Christian tradition. To a surprising degree this ideal of Mormon family life continues to be accepted today, but new problems and pressures have meant some readjustment and evoked defensive mechanisms.

Although monogamy has been the most common marriage form among Mormons, polygamy was considered the ideal from the mid-1840s to 1890 (and even beyond, for a few fundamentalists). Understandably the practice—known variously as polygamy, polygyny, plural marriage, celestial marriage, patriarchal marriage, plurality, or the principle—aroused much curiosity. It appealed not only to the prurient interest but also elicited a reforming zeal and sometimes even a sincere desire to understand Mormonism. In recent years those interested in alternative life-styles and marital arrangements have looked at the Mormon experiences with more sympathetic interest.

Considering the origins of plural marriage in the lifetime of Joseph

Smith, one can more readily understand the *how* than the *why*.[16] The motivation behind the introduction of a practice shocking to Gentiles and Mormons alike can scarcely have been as trivial as the usual anti-Mormon explanation suggests—Smith's personal lust. The standard Mormon explanation is simply that God chose to introduce the practice, as he had in ancient Israel, and he therefore made his will known to his spokesman on earth. However that may be, it is clear that the Prophet typically went to the Lord with problems and then received answers. A naturalistic approach would pay a good deal of attention to the kinds of problems that entered the Prophet's mind in the first place. Among these might well have been the practical difficulty of providing for all the unmarried females who were attracted to the new religion. (For some reason, perhaps the same that explains church attendance in all denominations, a slightly higher number of females than males accepted Mormonism.) Theologically there was the concept of "restoration of all things," meaning that the biblical mores could again be regarded as normative. Since Smith's revelations and writings show a great attraction for the Old Testament patriarchs as culture heroes, it was quite natural to ask how these great men of God justified a practice that seemed so abhorrent. In Book of Mormon passages dealing with the question there was strong disapproval of most Old Testament polygamy—apparently that motivated by lust or mere custom—but at least one passage suggests a possibility of exceptions:

> Wherefore, my brethren, hear me, and hearken to the word of the Lord: For there shall not be any man among you have save it be one wife: and concubines shall he have none: For I, the Lord God, delighteth in the chastity of women. And whoredoms are an abomination before me. . . . For if I will, saith the Lord of Hosts, raise up seed unto me, I will command my people; *otherwise,* they shall hearken unto these things.[17]

Here is one of those single words destined to have great importance, for it recognized the possibility of polygamy under certain conditions with divine approval.

Could it have been the prophesied and hoped-for conversion of the Indians that prompted the Prophet to consider the new marriage system? A recently discovered document is a copy of a purported revelation of 1831 that instructed seven missionaries in Missouri as follows: "For it is my will, that in time, ye should take unto you wives of the Lamanites and Nephites that their posterity may become white, delightsome and just, for even now their females are more virtuous than the gentiles." A note of W. W. Phelps explains more fully:

> About three years after this was given, I asked brother Joseph, privately, how "we," that were mentioned in the revelation could take wives of the "na-

tives" as we were all married men? He replied instantly "In the same manner that Abraham took Hagar and Keturah; and Jacob took Rachel, Bilhah and Zilpah; by revelation—the saints of the Lord are always directed by revelation."[18]

Obviously possibilities were being considered in the early 1830s, but the new system was not then formally established or widely discussed.

In 1842 a strange pamphlet entitled *The Peacemaker* was published in Nauvoo by Udney Hay Jacob.[19] Behind the pamphlet's intricate reasoning and unorthodox biblical exegesis was an underlying concern about social disorder and a breakdown of traditional family relationships. Divorce and the lack of uniform standards from state to state were denounced; they were, in the author's mind, a manifestation of alienation between men and women. What was needed, according to Jacob, was male leadership if the family and the social order were to function properly. The work expressed a strong aversion to promiscuity: The married man who took a maid must marry her and support her as a wife. No room here for dalliances leading to pregnancies for single girls who would be abandoned and disregarded. The intention and significance of the pamphlet are unclear, but it does suggest a desire by the author for a more stable, male-led family.

It is significant, too, that during the Nauvoo period Mormon doctrine and practice were broadened to include the concepts of a graded salvation, future possible godhood for the righteous, and unbreakable relationships with an extended family by means of vicarious ordinance work for the dead.[20] The phrase that summed up the "sealing" of parents to both children and ancestors was the verse in Malachi promising a return of Elijah, who would "turn the heart of the fathers to the children, and the heart of the children to their fathers."[21] Although none of these concepts required polygamy, they indicated a boldness and expansiveness that could accommodate an enlarged family pattern associated with the Old Testament patriarchs. In short, there were practical, sociological, and theological predisposing tendencies within the new movement that required only a word from God, a revelation, to initiate the practice of plural marriage.

When did the crucial authorizing revelation occur? Closely related is the question of when and to what extent was plural marriage practiced during the lifetime of Joseph Smith. There is no precise answer. One point of view, that of the Reorganized Church of Jesus Christ of Latter Day Saints, is that the system was introduced not by Smith but by Brigham Young. Since for various reasons Smith officially denied approval of polygamy, those disturbed by the principle could easily construct a case absolving the Prophet of responsibility. But this convenient argument was decisively refuted by, among others, Charles A. Shook, in *The True Origin of Mormon Polygamy* (1914).[22]

The most careful students of the subject seem agreed that Smith (*a*) had mentioned polygamy to associates as early as the Kirtland period of the mid-1830s; (*b*) had himself formed several plural relationships before 1843, when a revelation was announced; (*c*) had contracted some plural marriages that were platonic "eternity only" relationships; (*d*) may have sired in polygamy several children whose identities were obscured by their being raised under other surnames (but there is no hard evidence of any children except to his wife Emma); (*e*) had difficulty persuading Emma, his first wife, that the practice was approved by God. Although sexual attractiveness was probably an element of Smith's charisma, it is far from likely that his personal sex drive was the motivation. If he had been unprincipled, motivated solely by a desire for sexual gratification, there were tried and proven ways of satisfying such desires in American society without the burden of providing for additional families. Whatever the ultimate explanation of the reinstitution of polygamy, if Smith's religious sincerity is conceded, then he would naturally see the whole idea in religious terms, as, among other things, a restoration of the Old Testament practice.

Starting sometime in the early 1840s, Smith introduced a few chosen associates to the practice. Then, in 1842, John C. Bennett, who had for two years been a prominent adviser to Smith but whose character was, to say the least, unstable, left the church and published an exposé portraying the Mormon marriage system as an elaborate excuse for licentiousness. All during this time the Mormon leaders were publicly denying the practice. Whatever the ethics of these denials—which were rationalized by saying that the kind of polygamy the questioners had in mind was not the system being practiced—they were a practical requirement for gradual introduction to the church of such a difficult doctrine, necessary in fact for survival. Never during Smith's lifetime was the system publicly acknowledged, and in fact it was officially denied by Utah Mormons until 1852.

The response of the men who were introduced into polygamy between 1841 and 1846 was anything but enthusiastic. The same was true of the women who were offered the chance of becoming plural wives. Apart from the fact that the new system collided with moral assumptions they had grown up with, there were practical difficulties that made polygamy less attractive. For the men to support additional wives was seldom easy. And for women to be married on this basis without being legally acknowledged as wives can hardly have been reassuring. It was not the kind of scheme that aroused cheers and applause.

Yet such was their dedication to Mormonism and its prophet that several score were early persuaded that polygamy was a religious obligation. This belief did not come easily. Brigham Young declared that when he initially heard of the revelation on plural marriage, "it was the first time in my life that I desired the grave."[23] Orson Pratt, later a vociferous defender of polygamy, came close to abandoning the faith after his first encounter with the new marriage system.[24] Others were equally distraught. Disbelief was followed by a reluctant willingness to consider the possibility and finally by acceptance of the reality. Some received their personal conviction in dreams or revelations. An intolerable tension was established in the minds of Mormon leaders who were told about polygamy. On the one hand, they believed Smith was a prophet of God and they had committed their lives, their fortunes, and their sacred honor to the cause of the restored gospel. On the other hand, polygamy flew in the face of their traditional sense of morality. Something had to give in order for them to regain psychic equilibrium. Accepting a spiritual confirmation of the new revelation after intense personal soul-searching was the way most Mormon leaders were able to retain the consistency of their commitment.

Not all women approached with offers of plural relationships were discreet. From some of them came accusations that were magnified by rumor. Those women who accepted the system were faced with the same challenge their leaders had confronted: something had to give, and most often their faith in the gospel proved stronger than their inherited prejudice. Several of these women later described what happened. One of the frankest accounts was written by Lucy Walker, an orphan girl of sixteen who joined Smith's household in 1842. She said the following year Smith explained to her that God had commanded him to take her as a plural wife. At first she was astonished and insulted. He asked if she believed he was a prophet of God. After she answered affirmatively, he said that the principle of plural marriage had been restored by God and would "prove an everlasting blessing to my father's house, and form a chain that could never be broken, worlds without end." She was told to pray and that she would receive a personal testimony of the truth of what he said. She was angry, feeling that she was being asked "to place myself upon the altar a living sacrifice—perhaps to brook the world in disgrace and incur the displeasure and contempt of my youthful companions." She would rather die, unless she knew that God approved. After a long night of earnest prayer she felt as though her room were lighted "by a heavenly influence." "Supreme happiness took possession of me," she said, "and I received a powerful and irresistible testimony of the truth of plural marriage." On May 1, 1843, she was "sealed" to Joseph Smith "for time and all eternity" by Elder William Clayton.[25]

The number of women so sealed to Joseph Smith is not known. One biographer listed forty-eight, but many of these were undoubtedly wives in name only, officially "sealed" to him for the future life but not living with him conjugally in the present.[26] As for the others, abundant discussion has failed to establish whether or not Smith actually cohabited with them, and the lack of evidence of children from these relationships has not clarified the question. Several women later did testify that they were wives in the full sense of the word. Emily D. P. Partridge said she "roomed" with him,[27] and Melissa Lott Willes testified that she was his wife "in very deed."[28]

From a clandestine arrangement, limited to the Prophet and two or three dozen leading men and the wives who were party to the practice, Mormon polygamy slowly expanded after the Prophet's death in 1844, especially during ceremonies in the newly completed Nauvoo Temple at the end of 1845 and beginning of 1846. After the Mormons arrived in the Great Basin, plural marriages continued to be performed. Finally, in 1852, the practice was openly acknowledged at a general church conference, at which Apostle Orson Pratt gave a lengthy defense of polygamy.

How many Mormons practiced polygamy? This question does not have a simple answer and cannot be determined with the precision demographers prefer. But to reckon whether half of the Mormons or a third or a tenth were in the plural relationship, approximate figures suffice. When dealing with percentages it is important to know whether we are speaking of married men, wives, or total family members. Based on the best information now available, we estimate that no more than 5 percent of married Mormon men had more than one wife; and since the great majority of these had only two wives, it seems reasonable to suppose that about 12 percent of Mormon married women were involved in the principle. The birth rate among plural wives being somewhat lower than among monogamist wives, certainly no higher than 10 percent of Mormon children were born into polygamist families. These are general figures for the period from about 1850 to 1890. More precise calculations, which will show fluctuations year by year and variations from place to place, must await the completion of demographic research now in progress.[29]

Although the national press portrayed plural marriage as a monstrous dehumanization of women, Mormons, including many leading women, spoke out in its defense. For them it was a practical, honorable means of providing marriage and motherhood for thousands of deserving women who would otherwise be condemned to a life of spinsterhood;[30] it was an alternative to a variety of social evils; and it was commanded by God as a means of raising up a righteous generation. That its primary justification—and the primary motivation of its practitioners—was religious obligation, no one who has examined the diaries and letters of the time can deny. Even the Supreme Court in the crucial *Reynolds* decision did not deny that plural marriage was part of the Mormon religion but maintained that society had a right to forbid what were regarded as antisocial practices even if they were part of a religion.[31]

Usually a man did not merely decide to take an additional wife; he was asked to do so by church authorities after being selected on the basis of religious and economic qualifications. Then, in theory at least, the first wife was to give her permission before her husband named anyone else, and generally this sensible procedure was followed. Sometimes the first wife flatly refused. One Mormon raised the question with his spouse, who minced no words in replying, "All right Jody—you get another wife and I'll get another husband!"[32] No one knows how many of the 95 percent of Mormon husbands who remained monogamists had asked for permission and were refused, or how many sought permission while hoping they would be turned down, or how many did not bother to ask.

What seems even less clear is why some Mormon women responded affirmatively to such a question. The supernatural explanation they often emphasized indicated that an original reluctance was followed by prayer and then a dream or some other manifestation that brought peace of mind and a willingness to accept the difficult but divinely ordained principle. Lucy Hannah Flake asked for time to think and pray. After a few days she invited her husband to go outside with her after the evening meal. It was twilight. She looked at him and asked, "Will, who is the young lady we are going to marry?"[33] Some women, especially those raised in polygamous families that were relatively harmonious, needed no special sign. They were already persuaded of the religious basis of the system, having seen it in their parental families; they were not surprised or insulted when they were asked to be plural wives or, if they were first wives, when they were requested to allow the husband to take other women. Indeed, a few women were so full of zeal that the initiative came from them, for they insisted that the husband fulfill his responsibility.

But there were other considerations not readily apparent within our modern frame of reference. Once the religious nature of the plural marriage relationship had been established so that the new system did not seem immoral, it offered several immediate practical advantages. Wives who were barren could see that children were produced in the family and could share in their care, thus fulfilling the maternal instinct. Loneliness, a constant problem on the frontier when the husband was frequently absent on church assignments and working in the fields or canyons, could be alleviated with an adult female companion. True, she would be a plural wife, but for many hours of the day she would be working alongside or nearby the first wife. When sisters were married simultaneously, or when the first wife asked her husband to take her unmarried sister as plural wife, the arrangement seemed to be a way of perpetuating an existing congenial relationship. And there were older women beyond the usual marriageable age, scarcely able to arouse the lust of Mormon men, for whom plural marriage meant a respectable means of family and support. "Was this worse than the alternatives of leaving them to live alone

Founding prophet of the Mormons,
Joseph Smith, Jr. (1805–1844).

The jail in Carthage, Illinois, where Joseph Smith was murdered
by a lynch mob in 1844.

Brigham Young (1801–1877),
second prophet of the Mormons and
governor of Utah, 1852–1858.

inting of Mormons crossing the frozen Mississippi River
as they leave Nauvoo, Illinois, in February 1846.

Eliza R. Snow (1804–1877),
"Zion's poetess," president of
the Relief Society and a leader
of Mormon women's movements.

John Taylor (1808–1887) succeeded Brigham
Young as president of the Latter-day Saints
in 1877.

Painting of the organization of the Relief Society in Nauvoo,
Illinois, in 1842. Joseph Smith is on the left,
Emma Smith conducting.

Emmeline B. Wells (1828–1921), outspoken
editor of the *Woman's Exponent* and president of the
Relief Society, 1910–1921.

Susa Young Gates (1856–1933), daughter of
Brigham Young, founder of the *Young Women's
Journal,* editor of the *Improvement Era* and
the *Relief Society Magazine,* author, active
suffragist, and delegate to the International
Council of Women.

Wilford Woodruff (1807–1898), indefatigable diarist, ardent missionary,
and president of the church,
1887–1898, who issued the 1890 Manifesto that officially ended polygamy.

Mormon volunteer laborers helping construct an extension of the transcontinental railroad from Ogden to Salt Lake City in 1870.

Painting of a Mormon handcart company crossing the Great Plains in 1856.

An artist's depiction of a general conference in the Mormon Tabernacle
in Salt Lake City, 1870.

Sketch of Salt Lake City in the 1850s.
The wide streets were characteristic of all Mormon towns and villages.

Salt Lake Theatre, constructed in 1862.

The central tithing office and church store
in Salt Lake City in the 1850s.

Official residences and offices of Brigham Young in Salt Lake City, built in the 1850s. *Left to right:* the Lion House, the President's Office, the Beehive House. The rock wall was put up around the property in 1856.

Farmington, Utah, a typical Mormon village, as seen from the Wasatch Mountains in 1896.

Chapel in Pine Valley in southern Utah, built in 1868.
The architect was Ebenezer Bryce, an Australian
convert and shipbuilder.

This chapel in Preston, Idaho, is a "standard" LDS chapel of the 1970s.

Tabernacle in Brigham City, Utah, originally constructed in the 1870s.

Engraving of a painting of a Mormon missionary preaching in a cottage in Jutland in 1856. Scandinavia was a fruitful source of Mormon converts.

Missionaries presenting the Mormon message to a family in Bolivia.

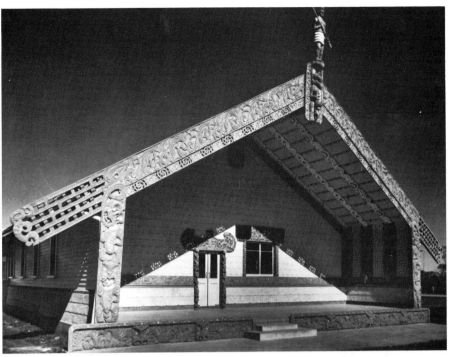

The "carved house" that served for many years as a chapel for the predominantly Maori Nuhaka Branch at Hawkes Bay, New Zealand.

Mormon elders in Polynesia confirming an eight-year-old girl after her baptism.

The original tabernacle built in
Salt Lake City in 1851.

Temple Square in Salt Lake City, showing the temple constructed from 1853 to 1893, and (behind to the left) the tabernacle without nails in the 1860s. On the left is the Bureau of Information, constructed in the early years of this century.

Spencer W. Kimball (1895–   ), president
of the church from 1973 to the present.

Belle Smith Spafford
(1895–   ), president of
the Women's Relief Society,
1945–1974, and president of
the National Council of
Women, 1968–1970.

Barbara Smith (1926–   ),
general president of the
Relief Society from 1974
to the present.

David O. McKay,
(1873–1970), member of
the Quorum of Twelve Apostles
from 1906 until his death
and member of the First
Presidency from 1934 to 1970.

as wards of the church or state?" argued the rhetoric of the system's proponents. Within their new families, when it worked out well, they had chores to contribute to the operation of the household, children to call them aunt or grandma, food to eat, a place to sleep—in short, a hearth and home. Finally, from the point of view of the first wife, plural wives were seen as additional help in the home. In Virgin, Utah, a man was reminded by his stake president of his duty to enter polygamy. He was reluctant to do so but asked his wife, who had borne him seven children. She consented, provided he married "a sensible helpmeet and not a silly little girl."[34] Two wives could share household duties, taking turns, leaving one free for other assignments, even work outside the home. It increased the flexibility and broadened alternatives, at least when it functioned at its best and when there was affection and good humor between wives.

The Mormons presented a united front against the attacks on their marriage practices. During the 1870s and 1880s, with the national legislative-judicial campaign increasing in intensity, women met in indignation meetings, where they gave speeches and signed petitions. Some of these are eloquent statements, but there were concessions that the principle was a "trial," although God certainly expected his people to be "tried." The following by Artimesia Beman Snow is typical:

> Sisters, I am a sincere believer in plural marriage. In 1844 my husband first asked my consent to take to himself other wives. I freely gave it, believing such an order of marriage to be a pure and holy principle, revealed from the heavens to our beloved Prophet, Seer, and Revelator. Knowing it to be a principle practiced anciently by those, who now sit at the right hand of our Father in Heaven, and knowing also my husband to be a virtuous man, and entering into that order out of pure motives in obedience to the will and commandments of Heaven, I say I freely gave my consent. I have lived in the order of Celestial marriage thirty-five years. I have no wish—I have no desire—to have it changed or abolished. . . .
>
> I have not been without my trials in the practice of this principle, but I have had peace and comfort, and I have had sorrow. I expected to be tried. . . . I entered into it with that expectation. I had my prejudices to subdue, my selfishness to overcome, and many things to contend with.
>
> The Lord has said, He would have a tried people, that they should come up through great tribulation, that they might be prepared to endure His presence and glory. If I had no trials, I should not expect to be numbered with the People of God, and therefore not be made a partaker of His blessings and glory.
>
> I have reared a large family in the marriage system. I have been the mother of eleven children. My husband has been the father of thirty-five, twenty-six now living, all equally honorable in as much as they pursue an

upright, righteous course through life. Out of that number there are sixteen sons. Not one of them has ever committed any crime that has brought a stain upon their character or a dishonor upon the heads of their parents. Not one of them is given to tippling or drunkenness, not one smokes or chews tobacco, and as fast as they arrive at mature age, earn their living by the sweat of the brow, or by the labor of their own hands. Why should they not be honorable? Their father is an honorable man. He is honored with that priesthood that emanates from the Gods.[35]

The admission that polygamy introduced trials is a clue that it often led to heartache and suffering. The initial discussion between husband and wife presented opportunities for misunderstandings and tears. If there was agreement that another wife would enter the family, deciding just who it would be presented other grounds for bickering. Once the new wife was in the home, the wisdom of a Solomon was required to prevent jealousy from developing. Who would do what chores? Who would accompany the husband to church meetings? To the theater? How much time would he spend with each? Possibilities of friction led those who could afford it to build separate houses, and when polygamists were prosecuted, it became prudent to maintain households in different settlements. Spending alternate nights or alternate weeks with each family was a common method of attempting to be fair to both wives, but even here there were practical obstacles. Whether admitted or not, the fact that only the first wife had married status in the eyes of the federal law gave her an advantage over the others. And although in theory all wives (as well as all children) were equal, jealousies between different families could easily make the plural families feel like second-class citizens.[36]

One could find many specific examples of unhappiness. Olive Andelin Potter's husband simply did not have the money to support her as a plural wife. The result was grinding poverty and resentment at the system that allowed her to be mistreated.[37] Juliaetta Bateman Jensen's sister, a plural wife, evidently led a tragic existence.[38] One of the most fully documented accounts is by Annie Clark, a highly intelligent, sensitive young woman who became the plural wife of J. M. Tanner, a leading Mormon educator.[39] Married during the late 1880s, she suffered at first from the secrecy and ignominy of living plurality secretly, giving birth to her children at the home of her parents or other relatives, still using her maiden name. It was a dangerous time for plural marriages to be widely known: men and some women were serving time in the penitentiary for polygamy, and the trials leading to these convictions could be heartrending experiences as wives were called to testify against their husbands. The psychological and legal pressures led, in some instances, to abandonment of wives, who, having sacrificed much, suddenly found themselves without even the tenuous security of status as a plural wife.

Although polygamy produced some sorrow and unhappiness, he alternative was not a perfect system guaranteeing a life of bliss. As one Mormon woman wrote in 1882, trying to answer the questions of a Mrs. Scott:

> Each man who marries two or more wives manages his family affairs according to the best of his judgment and the dispositions of those with whom he is associated, just as men do that have but one wife. Some men think they can manage the wife or wives and some allow them to manage themselves. Some families are very agreeable and study each other's welfare and happiness, while others, I am sorry to say, are not quite so harmonious in their relation with each other. As far as my observation extends that is generally the case when there is but one wife. That does not by any means condemn marriage, which we believe to be a sacred and holy institution.[40]

In the 1960s and 1970s, when it is possible seriously to ask whether monogamy has failed and when various forms of group marriage are being tried in communes, the statement that polygamy worked about as well as monogamy, depending on the persons involved, rings true.

But in the 1850s, 1860s, 1870s, and 1880s the Mormons were "voting with their feet" by declining to enter the polygamous relationship in overwhelming numbers. In the 1880s they voted overwhelmingly in favor of a proposed state constitution that would prohibit polygamy. In 1890, when their president, Wilford Woodruff, presented the Manifesto indicating a willingness to obey the law of the land, they "sustained" him by a virtually unanimous vote. And in 1895, when the present Utah state constitution was drafted, it included an antipolygamy plank that promised the practice would not be revived in the future. Even if some of these actions were calculated with loopholes in mind—obeying the law of the land would still leave room for plural marriages on the high seas, in Mexico, or in Canada—it seems evident that the great majority of Mormons had had enough. It is a tribute to their conscientious tenacity that for several decades they persisted in insisting on their constitutional right to practice their religion. When the *Reynolds* decision appeared to strike down that defense by insisting that certain practices could not come under the cloak of religious freedom, they did not immediately submit. God was all-powerful; certainly he would not expect his people to abandon a practice he had commanded. Hence the period of the "underground" and the simultaneous efforts, through national lobbyists, to obtain some kind of concession. This was the era when Mormon men served prison terms as "prisoners for conscience' sake." Finally, after increasingly heavy-handed federal pressure that excluded Mormon voters from the polls and confiscated church property, the Manifesto was presented to the church members by President Woodruff as a divine revelation countermanding the revealed instructions that had inaugurated polygamy fifty years before.

In retrospect, it is clear that polygamy caused an incredible amount of publicity for Mormonism. George Q. Cannon observed in 1879 that "Mormonism has become famous, because of the practicing, by a portion of the people, of this doctrine, until the whole earth resounds with the talk of 'the Polygamy of the Mormons,' as though the Mormons were half the people of the United States. In fact, if they numbered twenty-five millions instead of two hundred thousand, they could not have received more attention."[41] Mormons could regard the publicity as a means by which God kept his people in the view of the world; not for them the obscurity of most small denominations. Closely related to publicity was persecution—the Mormons' own word to describe the hostility and opposition culminating in the Edmunds-Tucker Act that confiscated their property. Such persecution was not pleasant, but social psychologists have recognized that there is nothing so effective as outside pressure to create a sense of group identity and cohesiveness.

In emphasizing how small was the percentage of Mormons who were directly involved in polygamy it is important to recall that all the central church leaders were polygamists. From the president down through the apostles and the Presiding Bishopric during the period, no general authority was a monogamist; the same was true of most bishops and stake presidents, as well as, for all practical purposes, their counselors. The privilege of polygamy was granted to the pure in heart and hence was a clear sign of worthiness for promotion in the Mormon hierarchy. Although no one ever explicitly said so in the nineteenth century, it appears to have been an effective device for gauging and assuring loyalty. As those who entered polygamy learned at the very beginning, it brought such a difficult clash with general moral assumptions that accepting it was a declaration of irrevocable commitment to the Prophet and his movement. It did the same with a man's first wife, with the plural wife, with the parents of the plural wife, and with their children. Self-image and self-respect were inextricably part of these plural relationships. The system was surely not contrived with anything quite this simple in mind, but in practice it served as a powerful reinforcement to existing loyalty.

Another way of conceptualizing this aspect of polygamy is to recall the potential disintegration of the church in the early 1840s. Leading apostles had been defecting since 1838, and in Nauvoo John C. Bennett was playing the turncoat and William and Wilson Law and Elias Higbee were threatening to lead a schism. Meanwhile, persecution from the outside was intensifying. With the death of Joseph Smith centrifugal forces could have broken the movement into different groups. What was needed was to enlarge the core of strong, faithful families, tying them to each other and to the church. A means of accomplishing this was a new system of adoption by which one could become recognized as the son or daughter of a prominent leader, with reciprocal loyalty and obligations.[42] More consequential was polygamy. Through it the Smiths, Youngs, Kimballs, Richardses, Woodruffs, Snows, and others became related to dozens of other families. The ceremonies of eternal marriage were known as "sealings," an apt word to describe the cementing that resulted. Although Mormons have not pretended to be able to discern perfectly God's motives, it has been suggested that this was his way of holding things together during a difficult period. Later, when times were more normal, the special arrangement was withdrawn.

The minority of Mormons that practiced plural marriage was bound by the same injunctions that directed monogamous families: Marriage was a blessing and a duty; children were to be welcomed in quantity (although no one expected unrestrained propagation); they were to be raised gently but firmly by parents who were obligated to teach them religious truths and train them for adult responsibilities; and the family unit was to be at once a school of experience, a haven of affection, and a foreshadowing of and preparation for eternal blessedness. To a large degree this was the standard ideology of family in the nineteenth century, but the Mormons saw it in their own religious framework. For them, the family has always been the basic unit for progress and joy in this life and in the life hereafter.

11

{ The Nineteenth }
{ Century Ward }

It is the Bishop's duty to attend to temporal matters. To see that the people are not idle. To give them counsel in temporal matters, and to acquaint themselves with every principle temporal or spiritual, that is revealed this side of the veil for the good of the people and their own exaltation.

—Brigham Young (1854)

Although Mormons from the beginning maintained a hierarchical structure of church government, the everyday life of the church was in the local ward, settlement, or congregation. Students of Mormonism have largely given primary attention to the activities of the central organization and to the upper echelons of leadership. This is understandable; most histories of nations have similarly focused on the central government. But what happened at church headquarters was not always an accurate indication of what was going on in the local congregations. No societal picture is complete without attention to small groups and their relationship to the central organization. For generations, certainly since the settlement in the Great Basin, it is in the activity of their local ward or congregation that Mormons have found their greatest sense of group identity.

Initially the church had no need for a complex structure. But as original members won converts among friends and relatives—more than a hundred in the year following the founding—decisions had to be made about who would supervise the budding congregations in New York State and Ohio and how these bodies should relate to the central church. There was to be no official clergy set apart from the larger class of lay members. Instead, all worthy male members were ordained to a lay priesthood, of which there were two levels: the lesser, or Aaronic, priesthood, which administered ordinances of the preparatory gospel, including the basic rites such as baptism and the sacrament of bread and wine; and a higher, or Melchizedek, priesthood, which held "the keys of all the spiritual blessings of the church" and supervised generally the new Kingdom of God. Offices in the Aaronic priesthood were deacon, teacher, and priest; those in the Melchizedek priesthood were elder, seventy, and high priest. None of these was a paid office; every member was a volunteer "laborer in the Lord's vineyard."

The most common office of the higher order of priesthood was that of elder. As local congregations sprang up—at first referred to as churches and then later as branches of the church—they were directed by a local or presiding elder. Frequently growing up around an initial convert family, the branches met in the homes of members such as Isaac Morley of Kirtland, Ohio, at whose home Sidney Rigdon was converted while attending a Sunday preaching meeting.[1] There were also prayer meetings during the week. Members were instructed to meet together often to pray, teach one another the doctrine, and partake of the sacrament in memory of Christ.[2] Since all of the men, unless disqualified by unfaithfulness, were ordained to the priesthood, the burden of preaching was widely shared. From the beginning there was congregational singing, an activity promoted through the publication in 1835 of the first of the Mormon hymnals.

These separate branches were not left without direction from the top. Periodically, in theory four times a year, officers and members from various branches were invited to attend regional conferences to report local conditions and receive instructions.[3] When missionaries traveled through a county on a tour to strengthen the churches, congregations within a radius of fifty or even a hundred miles would gather for a three-day conference, lodging in the homes of local members. Contact with church headquarters also came through newspapers, beginning in 1831 with *The Evening and the Morning Star,* the first in a long series of Mormon periodicals.[4]

As mentioned earlier, in the larger centers of church population Mormonism combined temporal with spiritual religion, as members shared their substance as well as beliefs. This linking of the earthly with the heavenly was typified by the office of bishop. Joseph Smith remained head of the higher priesthood, but in 1831 he named Edward Partridge as bishop of the church and leader of the lesser priesthood. Later Newel K. Whitney was also ordained a bishop to direct the care of the poor and supervise the Mormon communities in Ohio, leaving Partridge the responsibility in Missouri.[5]

The bishop's principal duty was to look after the poor. When the church moved to Illinois in 1839, the number of indigent members entering Nauvoo and nearby villages was so great that a single bishop could not attend to all their needs. Since the city had been divided into municipal wards as part of the civil government, it was decided to establish a parallel ecclesiastical unit, retaining the name *ward* and appointing a bishop over each.

This bishop was not elected by the people of his congregation. He was appointed by higher church authorities, a reflection of the tight central control and hierarchical nature of the church. At the same time, before making these "callings," the officials compared qualifications of potential bishops, tried by private interview or otherwise to ascertain opinion within the congregation, and prayed for the divine guidance that enabled the faithful to see their leaders as "called of God." When the bishop was formally named in a ward meeting, the higher authority asked the congregation to manifest by uplifted hand willingness to accept their new leader and support or sustain him in his calling. This process, still continued in the church, is not an election; it is closer to the acclamation that ended a coronation ceremony and served primarily to symbolize acceptance by the people.[6]

This system of geographically defined wards managed by bishops continues to be the pattern of church government at the local level. Originally limited to providing for the poor, the ward functions soon expanded. Church meetings held in "the grove" below the half-built Nauvoo Temple were attended by the entire community, but in winter, since no building was large enough for all the members, meetings in homes or small public halls were attended by neighbors of the organizers, thus becoming semiofficial ward gatherings. As the principal line officers of the church, bishops conducted ward meetings, collected tithes and contributions, gave counsel to ward members, relayed policy decisions, solicited volunteers for proselyting missions, and, in Brigham Young's expression, "notified everyone of his duties."[7] Each bishop appointed two "counselors" to help him and assigned lesser priesthood officers to visit the homes of members and learn who was in need of financial help and spiritual encouragement.[8]

Although the forced departure of the main body of the church from Illinois disrupted the congregational patterns, companies organized under a captain (often a bishop) were the standard administrative units during the trek west. At settlements like Winter Quarters and Council Bluffs, wards were organized in 1846, and once the Saints had arrived in the Great Basin the following year, wards quickly became the church's primary building blocks.

In pioneer Utah the ward was more than the basic ecclesiastical unit—it was the most important political unit and, except for the family, the most important social unit as well. As the central and largest concentration of population, Salt Lake City was divided into many wards. The same organizational unit was used for colonizing the various outlying settlements. Soon after its founding, a colony or village was designated a ward and a bishop appointed, often the man who had been commissioned by Brigham Young to lead the colonizing. It was in the process of community building that the bishop earned his substantial place in the Mormon organizational structure. Not only did he continue to care for the poor and watch over the spiritual well-being of members, but he now directed the difficult task of subduing the land and providing for its settlers.

Each ward was shaped to some extent by the character and personality of its bishop. The ward was the unit of welfare; the unit from which younger men (and later women) were called on missions to proselyte in "foreign" fields of labor; the unit where babies were christened or "blessed," younger men (and older men as well) ordained to the priesthood, funerals held, dances, musical festivals, and bazaars sponsored, young people taught, and group consciousness established.

In 1861 Presiding Bishop Edward Hunter said it was easier to be the bishop of a city ward than a country ward.[9] In the city a bishop had the support of other bishops, the city council, most of the general authorities of the church, and the protection of numbers. A bishop in a lonely settlement on the Bear River or in the southwest desert had to be more self-reliant. Having only irregular contact with Salt Lake City, he was, besides statesman and theologian, "pastor, constable, judge, arbitrator, foreman, and mayor."[10]

In most respects the city bishop and his country counterpart shared the same problems and duties. They were to take the lead "in every domestic improvement"; establish and supervise schools; assist the farmers; supervise the cultivation of public property and the repair of ward fences; assign to new arrivals their farm and town lots; see personally to the distribution of irrigation water and the maintenance and construction of ditches; keep cattle out of the fields, imposing sanctions on uncooperative owners; assign men to work on community road crews; and direct construction of schools, meetinghouses, and other public buildings. The pioneer bishop's concerns were overwhelmingly temporal. For the Sunday sermon he or a designated person might speak one week "upon the Ditch to convey Water to the 18th Ward" and the next week on why the Lord's people were subject to persecution. Whatever the theme, it was regarded as an aspect of "the restored gospel."[11] Occupationally the bishops during the nineteenth century were with few exceptions farmers and businessmen, practical-minded, effective motivators of men and women.[12]

In some respects Mormon wards were adaptations of the New England town form of government. When major decisions were to be made, priesthood holders (and sometimes their wives) were summoned to the meetinghouse. This decision-making process was sometimes formalized as a regular council meeting between the bishop and the three or four dozen "block teachers" who maintained personal contact with ward members. Called from the various priesthood quorums, the teachers were assigned, in pairs, to visit the homes of each ward family living on a particular block. Home visits were supposed to be made monthly, except during the busy summer season, to carry requests and instructions from the bishop, to gather contributions, and to see to the spiritual and temporal welfare of each family.[13] In essence, block teachers served as lesser bishops to their districts of as many as ten to twenty families. They were urged by the bishop to "stir the people up to diligence" and to settle disputes or chastise a wayward member so that the bishop would not have to deal with all such minor problems himself.

Although a bishop shared his duties widely with the priesthood quorums and other ward members, he remained the dominant figure in his ward principally because of his role as financier. The Mormon practice—since the late 1830s—of paying a tenth of one's income to the church became a system of voluntary taxation. In 1857 more than half of the heads of families in Salt Lake City's Thirteenth Ward paid a full 10 percent, and another third paid part tithing, with a total of 60 percent of the possible tithes being paid.[14] Most wards did not have such a good record. The payment of tithes varied from community to community and from year to year, depending on such variables as popularity of the bishop, the zeal of ward members, the presence or absence of the various alternative schemes for organizing economic life, and, most important, the general economic situation. At the end of the century the collection of tithing had lagged, but it was reestablished as the main source of financial support for church programs.[15] Besides tithing, there were special contributions to the Relief Society, missionary fund, telegraph office, building funds, Perpetual Emigration Fund, and fast offerings for the poor. And in the absence of civil government, or in some cases in his function as a city administrator, the bishop also collected road and school taxes. Most donations were made in kind—building supplies, livestock, produce, or labor.

On the first Thursday afternoon of every month (until 1896) farms and shops were closed and members came to "fast meeting," bringing the equivalent of several meals in foodstuffs for the poor. Fast meetings were well attended, not only because it was collection time for offerings but because it was the meeting where every member who wished could "bear testimony" before the congregation, as "led by the spirit of God."[16] After one meeting in 1856, when donations were delivered to the bishop's storehouse across the street from the chapel, Bishop Lorenzo D. Young of Salt Lake City's Eighteenth Ward received:

> LD Young 12 eggs and 8 lbs meal, G Toronto ½ lb coffee and 1 lb pork, Bro Thomas 4 lbs Flour, R Crookston 5 lbs Flour, Geo. Wallers 1½ lb pork, ¼ lb butter, D H Wells 12 lbs flour, Fanny Taggart 5½ lb meal, Prest B. Young 13 lb Flour, 6 lb Beef, 2 Pork.

At the same time the bishop distributed to the poor: "JB Lewis 4 eggs, Aunt Fanny 4 eggs, E C Brand 8 lbs Meal and 4 lbs Flour and 1 lb Pork, 1¼ beef, Bro Lyon ¾ lb Pork and 4¾ Beef, Adelia Young 13 lb Flour, Sister Christensen 6 lbs Flour, Bro Lyon 6 Flour, Sis Core 4 eggs, 5½ Meal, 1 lb Pork, ½ lb Coffee, Sis Crookston 5 lb Flour, ¾ Pork."[17] Since this was during a hard winter following a lean harvest, distributions may have been greater than normal.

The church inevitably dominated public and private economic life. The influence of church leaders in 1852 is suggested by Presiding Bishop Edward Hunter's saying that the authorities would "keep up the price of wheat to encourage the farmers."[18] When the railroad threatened to create an imbalance of cash flow between Mormons and Gentiles that would perpetuate Mormon economic dependence, Brigham Young encouraged each ward to form a manufacturing and mercantile cooperative which would keep Mormon money among Mormons. Instead of patronizing non-Mormon shops, members were asked to rely on the ward cooperative to buy their supplies. Never totally successful in sealing off Mormons from economic contact with their neighbors, the cooperative program had a spotty record. Eventually it gave way to free-enterprise capitalism, leaving as a vestige some church ownership of business. Nevertheless, for a period of several years bishops were involved in such mundane activities as supervising the ward cooperative store.

Establishment of territorial government in 1851 had little effect on the bishop's status. The distinction between church and civil government was hard to discern when, as sometimes occurred, a town's offices were located in the basement of the church. In most settlements the bishop served as court agent in the supervision of irrigation. As such, he could personally monitor streams and grant irrigation rights or, more commonly, appoint watermasters. Even after 1876, when supervisors were elected by the water users, water business was frequently a topic of discussion in priesthood sessions. When there were disputes, the bishop or ward teachers served as mediators.[19]

Another example of the lack of distinction between civil and religious jurisdiction was the operation of the schools. In most communities a small building served as church, community hall, and school. At first bishops were solely responsible for overseeing the schools. Soon school trustees were elected at meetings of ward priesthood holders. The trustees saw to the hiring of a "competent, sensible" teacher early in the season and the provision of books and fuel to heat the building. A "school tax" was assessed by the ward school committee. Collecting the tax was not always easy, as this early newspaper notice shows:

> Great SLC, Utah, July 18, 1850. Look here. All persons owning lots in the Tenth ward, who have not paid their school tax, are hereby notified that if the same is not paid forthwith, their lots will be returned to the office. Signed, Esaias Edwards, bldg committee.[20]

Until the federal government granted private title to lands, the bishop controlled the allocation of property, a power he used as final collection agent.

In 1851 the territorial legislature ruled that each town must have a public school supported by taxation. By the next year county courts were supervising construction of school buildings. But in difficult times, when cash short-age and poor crops left 40 percent of the tax levies unpaid, much of the school fund came from ward donations and tuition fees. The bishop was al-ways the last recourse in collections.[21] And in many small communities school was held in the ward meetinghouse—or church meetings were held in the ward schoolhouse.

The bishop was the uncontested if benevolent master of the community. When asked by the presiding bishop how he saw his duties, Bishop Edwin D. Woolley summed it up as follows:

> A bishop should act as a father to the people, who should be obedient to him as children to their parent. And the bishop should not require of the people what they are unable to do, so that his reasonable requests may be respected and attended to.[22]

It was a high ideal of service and one that was often realized. Surviving records indicate that early bishops were remarkably successful as fathers to their people.

The stake, a unit of several wards with its own presidency and council, had been inaugurated during the 1830s and later became an administrative unit of considerable importance. But for several decades stake organization was rather feeble. Although there was a functioning stake organization in Salt Lake City, many parts of the church had none, and where stakes existed, their functions were mainly two: holding meetings or conferences, quarterly in theory, that brought together the members from several wards; and trying some disciplinary cases in the stake high councils. Most direction from the top jumped over any stake level and proceeded directly between ward bishops and general church authorities, especially the presiding bishop. And in Salt Lake City at least, the bishops met regularly to discuss common problems and receive instructions.

The "Reformation" of the 1850s provides an interesting study of the in-teraction between a ward and the higher church authorities.[23] From the day the pioneers entered the valley, they had backsliders among their members. Once settled in, a certain number of immigrants preferred to be left alone. The images of the toilsome journey across the plains and the demanding task of building new homes and cultivating the desert have often given the ro-mantic impression of complete devotion to the Mormon cause, but such fi-delity naturally was not unanimous. In 1856 and 1857, under the guidance of Brigham Young's counselor Jedediah M. Grant, a major effort was made to "wake up the saints." Grant appointed reformation missionaries, who visited outlying wards, holding meetings reminiscent of Protestant revivals, with fiery sermons designed to make the listeners vividly aware of their personal sins. Such conferences were popularly attended, for the general authorities and their select corps of missionary-reformers were generally better preachers than the home bishop.

But the grit of the reformation work fell to the bishops. And too often "grit" was meant literally. At the presiding bishop's meeting of September 13, 1856, Jedediah Grant asked the bishops to stand who prayed alone and with their families and who "washed themselves at least once a week." When most remained seated, he threatened to send marshals out to wash them. The bishops must be the first ones to repent, he shouted, then their counselors, and then the block teachers, who were, after their own reformation, to go from house to house seeing that the people and their homes were clean and tidy as a prerequisite for the spiritual orderliness that would be effected by the reformation missionaries. "In this way the whole wards will be fired up, and prepared for the missionaries, and we shall see such a waking up throughout the Territory, that the Lord will pour his blessings upon us in a wonderful manner."[24]

Some bishops were not enthusiastic about the superficial manifestations of the Reformation—rebaptism, visions, and speaking in tongues—or the directions from Grant to continue "until it had become a boiling heat." One bishop said, "as to the reformation, when he saw good fences, clean streets, debts paid, tithing receipts &c he should then think the work of reformation was really progressing."[25] Like ministers who must stay on the scene looking after the souls of their parishioners long after the revivalist has come and gone, the bishops were interested in religious improvement that would be steady and permanent. But if a few bishops had reservations and expressed them mildly, they nevertheless carried out the instructions in their own way. Among the people, as one observer put it, there continued to be "a mixture of evil with a vast amount of good."[26]

The tight little Mormon island during the pioneer period of Brigham Young's lifetime was modified in important ways during the last quarter of the nineteenth and the opening years of the twentieth centuries. For one thing, the stake began to come into its own as an intermediate administrative unit. If the ward was equivalent to a parish, the stake—so named after the biblical analogy of a large tent held in place by stakes on all sides—was equivalent to a diocese, encompassing several congregations. Starting with a major administrative reform in the final year of Young's life, the church was divided systematically into stakes, and the process was accelerated at the turn of the century.[27]

Even with the streamlining of church administration through the stake organization, however, the ward remained (and remains) primary in many respects. Other changes occurring in the generation from 1877 to about 1910 both contracted and expanded its role. The contraction occurred quite naturally as activities once supervised by the bishop—schools, taxes, irrigation, business enterprises, judging civil disputes—were taken over by the state and local governments or by private enterprise. The expansion of the ward's role was accompanied by the rise of auxiliary organizations and of reorganized priesthood programs, which had the cumulative effect of multiplying points of contact—and time spent—between the individual member and his ward.

As early as 1849 some wards experimented with Sunday Schools for children. Like those in nineteenth-century England, they gave practical and moral training as well as classes on church history and theology. In 1867 the General Sunday School Union was founded to coordinate the work in the wards. In 1877 Brigham Young directed the bishops to include the sacrament (communion) in the Sunday School exercises, since few children attended the afternoon sacrament meeting with their parents. About the same time, Aurelia S. Rogers, who observed that boys in her rural ward were too much influenced by frontier conditions and by "worldly" values, recommended that a weekday meeting for children be established, resulting, in 1878, in the Primary Association. For older youths a system of religious classes was appended in 1890 to the public schools, which leaders felt were not providing sufficient religious training. One or more times a week Mormon students met with a church teacher after school.[28]

The Retrenchment Associations, founded by Brigham Young as a defensive measure to keep girls from following the ways of the world, was renamed the Young Ladies' Mutual Improvement Association in 1875, and the same year the Young Men's MIA was founded. A Young Men's and Young Women's Association was established in each ward, and an MIA General Board was appointed to supervise and improve these ward programs. Courses of study included history, literature, debate, and elocution, and Mormon youth could participate in ward dramas, concerts, dances, and picnics. Foreshadowing the development of a fairly broad athletic program, a gymnasium was built in Salt Lake City. In 1911, soon after the establishment of the Boy Scouts of America, the church incorporated scouting into its young men's organization. It experimented with the new Campfire Girls program but soon replaced it with a girls' activity program developed by its own general board.

The youth auxiliaries served educational, recreational, and religious purposes. In Granite Stake, Salt Lake City, "Mutual Missionaries," including sixty women, campaigned among inactive members and nonmembers, doing "much good among careless girls."[29] Without the Mutual Improvement Association, said President Heber J. Grant, "we would have large numbers of our young men joining the various secret societies for cheap insurance and sociability."[30] The auxiliaries helped to satisfy the Mormon urge for self-improvement in all aspects of life. In particular, they provided an expanded role for women, for as the auxiliaries developed and the need for teachers increased, women supplied much of the need.

The women's organization, the Relief Society, broadened its emphasis from charities, home manufacture, and abstaining from "the ways of the world" to include studies in theology, literature, applied social work, and home economics. It was common for a Relief Society hall to stand across the road from the ward chapel. Built by Relief Society members and their husbands, the halls were designed and paid for by the women in many ways. Some societies raised funds through donations of "Sunday eggs," reporting that "the hens seemed to lay better on Sunday than on any other day." One group of women loaded three thousand tons of sugar beets at thirty-four cents a ton to finance their building. More traditional methods of fund-raising were ward dinners, bake sales, bazaars, quilting, variety shows, and wheat cultivation. There were also cooperative stores, investment in real estate, and woolen manufacturing.[31] One churchwide Relief Society program was the raising and storage of wheat instigated by Emmeline B. Wells in 1876 at the request of Brigham Young. The *Relief Society Magazine* in 1917 reported:

> One of the best looking wheat fields in Millard county is that of the Leamington Relief Society, a branch of 37 members. After a fruitless effort to secure a portion of farm land upon which to produce wheat, these energetic women secured a lease on the town baseball field, where they now have a fine stand of wheat. It is estimated that the yield will be 40 bushels per acre. The grain will be cut by a self-binder and gathered by the women themselves for threshing.[32]

While the Sunday School Union, the Primary Association, the Mutual Improvement Association, and the Relief Society were vigorous new activities, each holding weekly meetings on the ward level, the priesthood activity of boys and men remained what it had been. After Brigham Young's directive to ordain boys as deacons at age twelve, the Aaronic priesthood gradually became a young men's calling. The deacons' quorums had "no set lessons, sometimes a talk, often musical numbers and readings, and admonitions from leaders."[33] The deacons were assigned to gather fast offerings and make distributions for the bishop, but although "the boys said they would gather," more often than not a pair of deacons would report having done no gathering for the month. The lessons, selected by boys, were lectures and readings from the Scriptures and from such books as *Ben Hur, Tom Sawyer, The Jungle Book,* and *Pigs Is Pigs.*[34] One secretary wrote, "A story was read. It got tiresome. Was moved and seconded that it be stopped."[35]

In 1908 President Joseph F. Smith assigned a committee to review the situation and make recommendations. The result was that methods of strengthening quorums were adopted from the successful auxiliaries. Priesthood meetings, which had been held irregularly and primarily for business reasons, were now turned into weekly instructional sessions with lesson manuals.[36]

The meetings were divided into classes for each of the six offices in the two priesthoods. Bishops began special efforts to win indifferent boys back into activity. One bishop took a boy with him every time he made some of his annual house visits; older boys were assigned specifically to be ward teachers to the widowed, aged, and poor; boys were appointed to tend church lawns; others helped older ward teachers in church visits, Red Cross work, War Saving and Thrift campaigns, and fuel surveys. Boy Scouts and the lesser priesthood members were made ushers in stake conferences instead of the older men.[37]

A graphic demonstration of the expanding number of organized activities in the ward was provided by the evolution in design of ward buildings.[38] The pioneer meetinghouse had been a simple rectangular building with a single large room on the ground level that could be converted from chapel to recreation hall as the occasion required. In the basement might be a small assembly hall, classrooms, food storage area, municipal offices, perhaps even a jail. After the turn of the century the increased responsibility of auxiliaries necessitated rooms for special purposes. The small basement assembly hall, which could no longer contain youth activities, was brought upstairs and appended to the main building. More classrooms were added to accommodate the expanding Sunday School program. In 1911 Boy Scout rooms were encouraged. After 1921 the church discontinued building separate Relief Society halls; instead, a special room, furnished and used by the women, was included in every chapel. By the beginning of World War I the ward meetinghouse had developed the functions and form it has kept to the present, with some modification, and it is now characterized by a variety of suborganizations designed to uplift and instruct members and by numerous social and religious meetings.

Like small towns, the wards had elements of similarity. In any Mormon ward one would encounter the same meetings, the same kinds of activity, the same shibboleths marking believers off from the outside world. The expression *ward family* early came into use as a designation of this group of perhaps 150 or 200 families with which one would inevitably become well acquainted. Visiting different wards when traveling or moving to another ward has seldom caused much of a shock to Mormons, who often remark that the "church is the same anywhere in the world." Common programs and common experiences did much to mold a common identity. If Thomas O'Dea and Rodman Paul are correct in their view that Mormons have become a "near-nation," or, as Dean L. May has maintained, a kind of ethnic group, it must be partly because of the manner in which wards contributed to a common culture, social institutions, traditions, and of course religion—adding up to a sense of group identity.[39]

And yet there are perceptible differences between wards, and some ethnic diversity. There were some predominantly Scandinavian wards, and others that were "old American." The several Swiss congregations were located in Bear Lake Valley in northern Utah and southern Idaho, with its alpine atmosphere, where they specialized in making cheese and butter, and in Santa Clara in southern Utah, where most of the church's sacramental wine was produced (in 1896 the church shifted definitely to water). The Sanpete Valley in central Utah contained a number of predominantly Scandinavian wards, some of whose members established dairies and creameries. In Skull Valley there was a Hawaiian ward—Iosepa, for "Joseph"—which for a few years served as a gathering point for converts from Hawaii. There were Welsh wards, which sponsored periodic *eisteddfods* and boasted the best choirs in the church. Because of different language mixes some wards even developed distinctive dialects and pronunciations.[40]

Every nineteenth-century ward had its own stories and legends, heroes and heroines—and members who were eccentric, or "different." One bishop exercised his prerogative and chose as one of his counselors a nonmember of the church. A new beet sugar factory had been built in the village, and most adult members of the ward worked there, so the bishop picked the factory superintendent as a counselor to ensure a harmony of interests between the ward and the management of the factory. Another bishop selected as his counselor a cowboy who was too bashful even to pray. In a southern Utah ward a bishop's counselor thought the village had become so dull that he decided to inject a little life into it by a practical joke. So he secretly made some huge boots. After a rain he would tramp around in the boots at night. People wondered about the giant, and some began to fear. Although the perpetrator soon owned up to the hoax, ward members talked for years of their temporary terror.[41] In another ward a young man with a well-developed sense of humor managed the ward store. After preparing a special ink that could be read only after heat was applied, he wrote scriptural messages on a certain brown hen's eggs. Soon the ward gathered to see what the hen had to say about the latest gossip in town. When the young man's father, an apostle, returned from Salt Lake City and observed the situation, he called a special priesthood meeting. To the assembled men he explained that he had just visited Brigham Young and had verified that God was still speaking to his prophet. The Lord, said the apostle, had not yet resorted to the hind end of a hen to convey messages to his people.[42]

Nor were all meetings of the ward cut-and-dried. When a stake president gave a brief sermon on shortening prayers, the bishop, on being called to close the meeting with prayer, said simply, "O Lord, make something of us if you can."[43] In a Danish ward that was in dire need of rain in late summer a certain brother was called upon to pray. Remembering the experience of early

June, when the prayed-for rain had come down in such a torrent that it destroyed their fields, the brother decided to be specific:

> Heavenly Fadder, ve air drying up down here. Ve need rain and ve need it qvick. What's the use of rain vit nothing left to rain on? Now if it wouldn't be too much trouble, ve don't vant vone of those big tonder and lightning storms, like the von ve got in Yune, which ruined the oats by the east hay-field. Whut ve vould appreciate very much is von of those nice long quiet rains, without any hails, that soaks everyting up nice. Amen.[44]

In one ward the young men found the impulse to swear irresistible. The bishop "bore down on them" and appointed one of the young men to be in charge of the group that was most guilty, a group working on the construction of a railroad grade:

> We soon commenced work, but found we had a hard job. The ground still frozen and full of solid roots and holes. This caused the boys to indulge in more or less swearing. We had a well organized camp having prayers every evening and blessing at every meal. After a week or so, I proposed to the boys that we make it a rule that when one of them swore during the day, he should do the praying at night. They all agreed to it unanimously. So I commenced listing them in my book and calling on them in turns. This soon put a stop to all profaning, and all were glad of it.[45]

Most wards maintained musical and dramatic associations, and many of these went well beyond the occasional production of a play or pageant to enhance a Twenty-fourth of July celebration. Cedar City Ward, for example, founded in November 1851, was putting on theatrical performances as early as the fall of 1852—a play with the sinister title *Priestcraft in Danger*.[46] Within two years the Cedar Dramatic Association was formed, supporting a repertorylike theatrical schedule that offered a new production every other week for a two-night run during theater season. The program usually began with a play expressing extravagant emotions and high sentiment. Musical numbers were normally offered between acts, and the evening was brought to an end with the performance of a short farce, "to dry the tears that rained down our faces at the tragedies of the drama," as one participant recalled. The plays were normally sentimental or farcical situation comedies wholly unknown to theater audiences today. They bore such titles as *David and Goliath*, *Forty Nights in a Bar Room*, *Farmer's Daughter*, *Miller and His Men*, *Slasher and Crasher*, and *Box and Cox*. Occasionally a work of Shakespeare was presented, but this was rare. Something of the scale of theatrical activity in that particular ward is suggested in the fact that the dramatic association in 1854 consisted of sixty-one members, with regular stage managers, prompters, call-boys, six musicians, and a clerk. At the time the ward could not have had more than two hundred persons. In the 1860s the association was producing such classics as *The Rose of Ettrick Vale* and *Grimshaw, Bagshaw, and Bradshaw*. During the winter of 1880, according to surviving records, the society produced a play each week for thirteen weeks. Season tickets, valued at three dollars, were usually paid in produce.

Theater was not the sole cultural interest of the members of this ward. Choirs for the singing of both religious and secular music were maintained from the earliest period. In 1866 fund-raising activities were underway for the purchase of instruments for a brass band and for a cabinet organ.

Several fiddlers were usually available for the dances, which capped every celebration and were the most important amusement in all early Mormon wards. The dances were presided over by a "floor manager" whose duties were to admit only people of good standing and to see that all the men who danced paid their tickets, tickets that could be paid for with beets, carrots, beans, or other produce, or with an order for ditchwork or barbering—anything the musicians could use. Popular dances included the quadrille, Virginia reel, and the minuet. Round dances, such as the waltz, the polka, and the schottische, which became popular with young people in the 1870s and 1880s, were at first forbidden, then limited to one or two such dances per evening, and finally allowed as long as propriety of dress and demeanor was observed.[47]

From the beginning and throughout the pioneer period and the period of proliferating programs in the generation following Brigham Young's death the ward was the center of Mormon worship, religious learning, humanitarian service, recreation, and friendships and associations. Since it was staffed by lay members of the congregation—even the bishop was a member of the congregation who temporarily became leader—the ward provided numerous kinds of activity and responsibility to every willing member. Speaking, teaching, acting, playing a musical instrument—such opportunities were sometimes accepted reluctantly but contributed to growth and enlarged self-confidence. Organizing and staffing auxiliaries, meeting with counselors as a kind of board of directors, and making administrative decisions were experiences available to almost any Mormon from the teen-age years through adulthood. The ward was far more than a place for listening to a sermon each Sunday. For the Latter-day Saints it was an arena for growth, a network of personal relationships, and a focal point of identity. It was a little commonwealth.[48]

12

{ Mormon Sisterhood: } Charting the Changes

Daughter, use all your gifts to build up righteousness in the earth. Never use them to acquire name or fame. Never rob your home, nor your children. If you were to become the greatest woman in this world, and your name should be known in every land and clime, and you would fail in your duty as wife and mother, you would wake up on the morning of the first resurrection and find you had failed in everything; but anything you can do after you have satisfied the claims of husband and family will redound to your own honor and to the glory of God.
—Brigham Young, as told to his daughter Susa Young Gates (ca. 1870)

I am glad there is a little spirit among our sisters, and that they dare say their souls are their own.

—John Taylor (1871)

"Thou art an elect lady, whom I have called," reads *Doctrine and Covenants,* section 25—"the word of the Lord directed to Emma Smith," through her husband Joseph Smith in July 1830. Here, in an extensive revelation addressed to a woman, Emma was admonished to be a comfort to her husband "in his afflictions with consoling words, in the spirit of meekness." She in turn was promised his support and his special blessing conferring upon her the Holy Ghost and appointing her to "expound scriptures, and to exhort the church." She was directed to give her time to writing and to learning and to making a selection of sacred hymns for the church. For short periods she served as a scribe for her husband, and her compilation of hymns was published in 1835. However, like most women of the time, she spent most of her energy as homemaker and mother, not an easy assignment in view of repeated moves and her husband's frequent absences. A support and helpmate to him during the seventeen years of their marriage, she showed no desire to exercise a leadership role in the ecclesiastical hierarchy. Not that Mormon women were ignored or kept at home. From the beginning they attended church meetings and exercised spiritual gifts along with men, voted in general church assemblies, and contributed time and means to such projects as the Kirtland Temple.

*   *   *

In 1842, twelve years after the organization of the church, Joseph Smith "ordained" Emma to preside over the new Female Relief Society of Nauvoo, Illinois, the official organization of women within the church, still extant today. The women had previously discussed among themselves forming a ladies' society to assist with the building of the Nauvoo Temple. When they presented a constitution and bylaws for the proposed society, Joseph Smith complimented them on their efforts but explained that within God's church they should be organized "under the priesthood after a pattern of the priesthood."[1]

The twenty women gathered in the upper story of Smith's Nauvoo store on March 17, 1842, elected a president, two counselors, a secretary and treasurer, and selected their own name (instead of adopting that suggested by the three men present, Joseph Smith among them). The Prophet told them that their presidency would preside over the society just as the First Presidency presided over the church. He further explained that they were to administer to the wants of the poor, to assist in strengthening the virtues of the community, and to "provoke the brethren to good works." He affirmed that "the Church was never perfectly organized until the women were thus organized." At the society's sixth weekly meeting, held at the end of April, he "turned the key" to them and promised that "this society shall rejoice and knowledge and intelligence shall flow down from this time."[2]

Mormon women traditionally trace their collective advancement to this turning of the key, for the Relief Society organization did substantially expand their opportunities for expression. Five months after their first meeting they petitioned the governor of Illinois for protection from illegal suits pending against Joseph Smith. Like the literary, benevolent, and antislavery societies of other American women, the Relief Society taught Mormon women how to organize and address public meetings. Weekly they met to conduct their business according to the rules of parliamentary procedure. Their recorded minutes indicate that the women contributed flax, wool, yarn, and old clothes and then worked together in sewing clothing for the poor and the temple workers. Details such as the following give some sense of the eagerness of the women to contribute:

> Mrs. Durfee said if the heads of the society wished, she is willing to go abroad with a wagon to collect wool, etc. for the purpose of forwarding the work.
>
> Sister Stanley proposed giving every tenth pound of flax, also one quart milk per day.
>
> Counselor Whitney spoke of a young man from England, who has been ill for a year now at her house.... Sister Jones said she is willing to take the

sick man to her house if it is thought wisdom—that her house is not so still as desirable for a sick person.

"It is natural for females to have feelings of charity," Smith had told the women. "You are now placed in a situation in which you can act according to those sympathies which God has planted in your bosoms."[3]

Within two years Relief Society membership expanded from twenty to more than thirteen hundred. Women not only learned to manage secular affairs ("Joseph Smith counseled the sisters to do business," one member recalled years afterward), but they also grasped a new spiritual understanding. "The propriety of females administering to the sick by the laying on of hands," was discussed by Joseph Smith, who "said it was according to revelation." He promised the women that if they were faithful, the angels could not "be restrained from being your associates," and assured them that "females can come into the presence of God."[4]

Concurrent with the development of this organization for women, Smith quietly introduced the practice of plural marriage on a limited basis. The new doctrine and practice met with diverse reactions from women in the church. Some, who heard only whisperings, were appalled. In September 1842 a group of Mormon men and women published in the Sangamo (Ill.) *Journal* their wish "publicly to withdraw" from the church and "no longer claim allegiance thereto" because they had "been most scandalously imposed upon in matters and things of a Divine character."[5] Other women, directly approached by one or another of a handful of priesthood leaders, resisted. "Early in the year 1842, Joseph Smith taught me the principle of marriage for eternity, and the doctrine of plural marriage," recollected Relief Society stalwart Sarah M. Kimball in the 1880s. "He said that in teaching this he realized that he jeopardized his life; but God had revealed it to him many years before as a privilege with blessings, now God had revealed it again and instructed him to teach it with commandment. . . . I asked him to teach it to some one else."[6]

Others embraced the principle and kept the silence. Eliza R. Snow said that when she was married to Joseph Smith she "did not know if ever [I] would be owned as a wife." Her own personal struggle in accepting the principle was recorded in her 1885 reminiscence:

> In Nauvoo I first understood that the practice of plurality was to be introduced into the church. The subject was very repugnant to my feelings— so directly was it in opposition to my educated prepossessions, that it seemed as though all the prejudices of my ancestors for generations past congregated around me. But when I reflected that I was living in the Dispensation of the fulness of times, embracing all other Dispensations, surely Plural Marriage must necessarily be included, and I consoled myself with the idea that it was far in the distance, and beyond the period of my mortal existence. It was not

long however, after I received the first intimation, before the announcement reached me that the "set time" had come—that God had commanded His servants to establish his order by taking additional wives. I knew that God, who had kept silence for centuries, was speaking. I had covenanted in the waters of baptism to live by every word He should communicate, and my heart was firmly set to do His bidding. As I increased in knowledge concerning the principle and design of Plural Marriage, I grew in love with it, and to-day esteem it a precious, sacred principle—necessary in the elevation and salvation of the human family.[7]

Among those most distressed about the practice of polygamy was Emma Smith, who allegedly burned the revelation on plural marriage first recorded by Smith's scribe, William Clayton. She is reported to have declared shortly before her death in 1879 that "there was no revelation on either polygamy or spiritual wives" and that her husband "had no other wife or wives than myself, in any sense, either spiritual or otherwise."[8] There is good evidence, however, that Emma Smith was not only aware of the new doctrine but made use of her position as president of the Relief Society to undermine its acceptance. "She tried to influence my wife and to make her believe that the revelation was not correct," recalled John Taylor. Perhaps because of such opposition Relief Society minutes end abruptly in March 1844, and after the death of Joseph Smith, Brigham Young and his associates "thought it best to defer [i.e., suspend]" the operations of the Relief Society organization.[9] It was not revived for nine years, although many of its functions were informally continued by small sewing circles and study groups.

While Emma Smith and others remained in Nauvoo (in 1847 she married Lewis Bidamon and lived in Nauvoo until her death in 1879), the main body of the Latter-day Saints began a mass exodus westward, encountering the deprivations and hardships typical of frontier migrations, the women alongside the men. "Two months today since I left my house," midwife Patty Sessions recorded in March 1846, "I have been in the cold in the snow and rain without a tent. . . . My health is poor, my mind weighed down, but my trust is in God."[10] Mormon women drove teams and walked alongside wagons, or jostled their way in wagonbox beds, sometimes ill, sometimes heavy with child. They gave birth to sons and daughters in wagons, tents, and lean-tos and buried infants and children in shallow wayside graves. Mary Ann Weston Maughan was grateful to have a dry-goods box to use as a coffin for her three-year-old son, Peter, killed when he fell beneath rolling wagon wheels. "It even was a mournfull satisfaction to us," she wrote, "for we had seen our brothers and sisters bury their dear ones without a coffin to lay them in. . . . A few days after, we heard that his grave had not been touched, but another little one made beside it."[11]

Women turned their wagons into homes insofar as that was possible. The large, cumbersome wagon in which Bathsheba Smith rode to Utah she fitted out with a carpeted floor, a comfortable bedstead and four chairs, and a head-high osnaburg wagon cover lined with blue drilling, the monotony of which was broken by a workable door and window, a looking glass, a candlestick, and a pincushion.[12]

Many found reminders of their previous home along the way. Jean Rio Baker had sailed from England to cross the American plains and join the Saints in Utah. "We have had a very pleasant week," she noted in April 1851. "Lovely weather and I have been reminded of the days we used to spend in Epping Forest, lang syne." Cooking up a catfish brought to her mind "halibut suppers in Bowlane," and the song of a whippoorwill, she thought, resembled that of a nightingale.[13]

For over twenty years, from 1846 to the coming of the railroad to Utah in 1869, crossing the plains was an experience common to Mormon women. Converts from the eastern states along with thousands who had emigrated from the British Isles and Scandinavia sang around their campfires in anticipation of "the place which God for us prepared, far away in the West." A promised land perhaps, but not a very promising one to women who arrived there weary from the long trek. "Teams, men and women completely worn down. I have scarcely life enough to rejoice that I am so near my journey's end. Everything seems lifeless and tasteless. I can anticipate no rest or pleasure, all appears dark and wild," wrote Angelina Farley in 1850 upon her arrival in the valley of the Great Salt Lake.[14] "I do not think our enemies need envy us this locality or ever come here to disturb us," noted Eliza Partridge Lyman as she settled with seven others in a log room in the "Promised Valley."[15]

There was, as Angelina Farley anticipated, no rest for women in Utah in the late 1840s and early 1850s. Women worked side by side with men in building homes of sun-dried adobe, digging irrigation ditches, planting and harvesting crops, and fighting grasshoppers and crickets. "In the early days of Utah, the struggle for bare sustenance was so severe that there was little time or opportunity for anything else," reminisced Lucinda Lee Dalton years later.[16] As men and women struggled together, sex roles often merged. But in doctrine the Victorian concept of "true womanhood" held sway: Woman's duty was to be "subservient and dependent," the women reminded each other, as they set about building houses, managing herds, establishing schools, creating communities, seemingly unaware of the irony.

"I do not know of any religion except doing as I am told," affirmed First Presidency member Heber C. Kimball in 1857.[17] Submission and obedience were prevalent themes during the early development of the church. It was to be a kingdom of order, and that demanded organization—a system of leaders and followers. All church members were to follow the directions of the First Presidency and the Twelve Apostles. Ward members were to abide by the counsels of their bishops. And wives and children were to submit to their priesthood-bearing husbands and fathers. "Women are made to be led, and counselled, and directed," declared Kimball. "Let our wives be the weaker vessels, and the men be men, and show the women by their superior ability that God gives husbands wisdom and ability to lead their wives into his presence," Brigham Young advised.[18]

The positioning of priesthood bearers "in the front rank," as one apostle termed it, could pose dilemmas for some Latter-day Saint women. Martha Spence Heywood, mother, schoolteacher, and occasional "scribbler," mulled over in her journal part of a sermon she had heard Brigham Young deliver in April 1856. "I prayed my Heavenly Father that I may receive it in honesty," she wrote, "especially the principle that a woman be she ever so smart, she cannot know more than her husband if he magnifies his Priesthood. That God never in any, any age of the world endowed woman with knowledge above the man." She must have misunderstood, for Brigham Young was far too perceptive to have said something like this, and on several occasions spoke just the opposite. What he did counsel was stewardship and submission—but not inferiority, intellectual or spiritual. Martha, who recognized the strength of her mind, met with a biweekly assembly of men and women known as the Polysophical Society, where she presented her own literary selections as part of a program of poetry, essays, and music—"a magnificent moral, intellectual and spiritual picnic," one member of the group called it.[19]

In what, then, did woman's subservience consist? Martha Heywood might have observed that there were circumstances under which women assumed roles similar to rather than subordinate to those of men—in taming the land, in gathering for cultural and intellectual exchange, in disciplining children—but not in the government of the church. Order required leaders and followers within a hierarchical system extending down to individual family units, where husbands were expected to govern. "The head of every man is Christ; and the head of the woman is the man," Mormons echoed Paul's ancient epistle to the Corinthians. Drawing from the long-accepted Christian tradition that woman was naturally under subjection to man because Eve, the archetypal woman, had been "first in transgression," church leaders taught that woman's obedience to priesthood leadership, particularly to her own husband (provided he was righteous), would redeem her from the "curse of Eve."[20]

But although these ideas were variations on Christian themes, most non-Mormons saw the practice of polygamy as degrading to Mormon women. Horace Greeley reported after visiting with Brigham Young in Utah in 1859:

> I have not observed a sign in the streets, an advertisement in the journals, of this Mormon metropolis, whereby a woman proposed to do anything what-

ever. No Mormon has ever cited to me his wife's or any woman's opinion on any subject; no Mormon woman has been introduced or has spoken to me: and, though I have been asked to visit Mormons in their houses, no one has spoken of his wife (or wives) desiring to see me, or his desiring me to make her (or their) acquaintance, or voluntarily indicated the existence of such a being or beings. I will not attempt to report our talk on this subject, because . . . it assumed somewhat the character of a disputation, and I could hardly give it impartially; but one remark made by President Young I think I can give accurately, and it may serve as a sample of all that was offered on that side. It was in these words, I think exactly: "If I did not consider myself competent to transact a certain business without taking my wife's or any woman's counsel with regard to it, I think I ought to let that business alone." The spirit with regard to Woman, of the entire Mormon, as of all other polygamic systems, is fairly displayed in this avowal. Let any such system become established and prevalent, and woman will soon be confined to the harem, and her appearance in the street with unveiled face will be accounted immodest.[21]

Had Greeley returned to Utah ten years later, he would have found not the veiled female faces he had predicted, but rather a platform of articulate women speaking from the pulpit of Salt Lake City's Tabernacle—women defending their right to "holy, honorable wedlock," the practice of plural marriage. "Were we the stupid, degraded, heartbroken beings that we have been represented, silence might better become us; but as women of God, . . . we not only speak because we have the right, but justice and humanity demand that we should."[22] So proclaimed sixty-five-year-old Eliza R. Snow, intellectual and spiritual leader of Mormon women. She and five thousand Latter-day Saint women were gathered in the Tabernacle in January 1870 to oppose antipolygamy legislation then pending in Congress, and this Great Indignation Meeting, as it was called, sparked similar assemblies among Mormon women in towns and settlements throughout Utah.

In 1867 Latter-day Saint women began the process of establishing Relief Societies in every ward. After the dissolution in 1844, they had organized in a few wards early in the 1850s, but their activities had been cut short by the Utah War in 1858 and were not resumed until Brigham Young made the call late in 1867. In the Salt Lake City Fifteenth Ward women set about discharging their responsibility to the poor, the sick, and the sorrowful. That accomplished, they found they had accumulated a surplus of donated funds, which they determined to put "to usury [i.e., to use]." They purchased a lot and sold shares toward the construction of a building, a two-story Relief Society hall where sisters could gather for meetings and display and sell their homemade goods on commission. Ward Relief Society president Sarah M.

Kimball made an occasion of the laying of the cornerstone for the hall, the first of its kind in the church. She spoke to assembled ward members, expressing "thanks to the Almighty God that the wheels of progress have been permitted to run until they have brought us to a more extended field of useful labor for female minds and hands," and predicting that the Fifteenth Ward Society Hall would be "a stepping stone to similar enterprises on a grander scale."[23]

In March 1888 Latter-day Saint Emily S. Richards stood before assembled delegates at the First International Council of Women in Washington, D.C., and reported the activities of twenty-two thousand members of four hundred Relief Societies in and out of Utah:

> They own many of the halls in which they meet, and such property is valued at $95,000. They have laid up wheat in granaries to the amount of 32,000 bushels, for seed or relief in case of scarcity. They assist in caring for the distressed, help to wait upon the sick and prepare the deceased for burial. They have a bi-weekly paper called the *Woman's Exponent,* with a woman editor, women writers, women business agents and women compositors.... The Deseret Hospital, with a lady M.D. as Principal, and skilled nurses and attendants, is under their direction. They have fostered the silk industry, producing the raw material and manufacturing it into various articles. Some of their Relief Societies have stores for the sale of merchandise, particularly home manufactures, as they encourage industry as well as intellectual culture. The entire organization is a live, active and growing institution, and its benefits are felt in every place where it extends, all its tendencies being to make women useful, progressive, independent and happy.[24]

During these twenty years (1868–1888) Mormon women experienced an impressive individual and collective blossoming, due in large part to the reorganization of the Relief Society. But the revival of that organization in itself manifested a shift in emphasis. Obedience may have been the prevalent theme in the 1850s, but by the end of the following decade a new theme had clearly emerged: cooperation. Gentile influence, growing in the Great Basin with the development of mining and the coming of the transcontinental railroad, threatened to undermine the economic stability of the Kingdom. The call went out to all hands, male and female. "It is the duty of every man and of every woman to do all that is possible to promote the kingdom of God on the earth," Brigham Young admonished.[25]

Young could sense how much was possible among Latter-day Saint women. "We have sisters here who, if they had the privilege of studying, would make just as good mathematicians or accountants as any man," he affirmed:

We believe that women are useful, not only to sweep houses, wash dishes, make beds, and raise babies, but that they should stand behind the counter, study law or physic [medicine], or become good book-keepers and be able to do the business in any counting house, and all this to enlarge their sphere of usefulness for the benefit of society at large. In following these things they but answer the design of their creation.[26]

Consequently, when the University of Deseret reopened in 1869, there were enrolled 223 pupils, 103 of whom were women. The same year, as Elizabeth Kane traveled through Utah, she noted young women serving as telegraph operators. Young named both women and men as trustees of his namesake colleges in Provo and Logan in 1875–76. Two women were admitted to the Utah bar in 1872, and the first of several Latter-day Saint women graduated from the Women's Medical College at Philadelphia in 1877. Moreover, after the Utah legislature passed a law in 1870 allowing incorporation of businesses by counties, women often served as directors and officers of business corporations (including mining companies).

Women likewise were given new collective responsibilities and opportunities. In 1869 Young commissioned Relief Society leaders to organize younger Latter-day Saint women into local Retrenchment Associations, where style-hungry daughters could pool their resolve to dress in Utah-manufactured garments rather than imported ones. The focus soon turned from retrenchment to "mutual improvement," complete with manuscript newspapers and courses of study. In 1878 women decided they needed to reach youth at an even younger age and proposed to church leaders that women establish Primary Associations for the education of children. Within a year there were over one hundred such associations scattered throughout the territory, organized and directed by women.

Probably the most impressive collective contribution of Mormon women was that of the Relief Societies themselves, which, community by community, made their impact on economic and social life. A report of the Sanpete Stake Relief Society for May 19, 1879, proclaimed that over a two- to three-year period the Sanpete women had:

Gathered 21,507 dozen Sunday eggs to use for charitable and philanthropic purposes.
Made 504 quilts.
Made five rugs and 3,633 yards of rag carpet.
Gathered 11,093 bushels of wheat.
Collected 111 books for their library.
Acquired four acres of land.
Manufactured 1,084 yards of cloth.
Donated $5,310 to temples.

Helped 399 families of missionaries, and sent off $2,925 to missionaries in the field.

Made 52,550 visits to the sick.

Clothed and prepared for burial 299 corpses.

Built seven Relief Society halls.

Held two bazaars or fairs.

Built one co-op store, acquired shares in three stores and two mills and one thresher.

Made 11,199 pounds of cheese.

Donated $5,965 to the emigration fund.

Spent $2,159 for surprise parties for the poor.

Women involved in these economic responsibilities considered themselves to be "doing just as much [for the building of the Kingdom] as an elder who went forth to preach the Gospel."[27]

New political frontiers opened to women during the same period. Utah females were enfranchised in 1870 and soon began to take part in local party caucuses. They were not allowed to hold public office, although they were sometimes nominated. Ida Cook was elected school superintendent for Cache County in 1877 but, according to one of her contemporaries, "owing to existing laws against women holding office was not allowed to act."[28] Although women frequently petitioned against such political disabilities, the most avid campaign for female rights among Mormons took place after Utah women were disfranchised in 1887 under the Edmunds-Tucker Act. Then Latter-day Saint women joined forces with national suffrage leaders in pressing for national and local suffrage legislation. The Utah Woman Suffrage Association was organized in 1889, and local Relief Society units began to sponsor suffrage meetings all over the territory, singing songs of woman's rights to their Mormon hymns, such as the following to the tune of "Hope of Israel":

> Freedom's daughter, rouse from slumber;
> See, the curtains are withdrawn,
> Which so long thy mind hath shrouded,
> Lo! thy day begins to dawn.
> Woman, 'rise! thy penance o'er,
> Sit thou in the dust no more;
> Seize the scepter, hold the van,
> Equal with thy brother, man.[29]

In 1895, after a series of debates over the issue of suffrage, Utah women were again enfranchised in the newly adopted state constitution. Before the turn of the century several women were elected to the state legislature, where they introduced bills providing for, among other things, a state board of health and a state institute of fine arts.

One of these legislators, the first woman state senator in the United States, Dr. Martha Hughes Cannon, was a physician and plural wife of the president of Salt Lake Stake. In an interview following her election (in which she defeated her husband and others who also sought the office) she observed that a plural wife was not a slave. "If her husband has four wives," she explained, "she has three weeks of freedom every month."[30] Likewise Mary Isabella Horne, a stake Relief Society president, said that since her husband's plural marriage, she felt better and could "do herself individually things she never could have attempted before; and work out her individual character as separate from her husband."[31]

From the 1850s, when plural marriage was publicly acknowledged as church doctrine and practice, to 1890, when it was discontinued, Mormon women spoke and wrote in its defense, holding mass meetings and sending several petitions to Congress demanding that their families not be destroyed by antipolygamy legislation. But the frequency with which church leaders advised women not to complain about their marital struggles is an indication that some at least felt sorely tried. Said one woman at a Relief Society gathering in 1870, "I have taken pleasure in practicing this pure principle [of plural marriage] although I have been tried in it. Yet ever since the birth of our first child by the second wife, I have never felt to dissolve ties thus formed."[32]

Some were not so ambivalent. Fanny Stenhouse's 1874 exposé, *"Tell It All": The Story of a Life Experience in Mormonism*, explains how her contempt for the system of plural marriage led to her deserting the Mormon cause.[33] Other plural wives divorced their husbands (divorces were easily granted to women, not nearly so easily to men) or deserted them. Some silently suffered what they felt to be injustice and passed on to their sons and daughters hostility for the system or the church itself. But for the most part Mormon women saw the anxieties and frustrations of polygamy as no greater than the tensions of the monogamous marriages some of them had known in their younger days.

President Wilford Woodruff's 1890 Manifesto counseled Saints to refrain from contracting plural marriages. Though full implementation of the edict took several years, it heralded an era of conformity for Mormon women and men. As Utah celebrated statehood in 1896, a new generation of Mormon women began to come into their own. They had experienced some of the persecutions of their foremothers when federal deputies attempted to enforce antipolygamy legislation in the 1880s, but theirs was certainly not a history of privation. Since these young women were less isolated from the gentile world, they were able to take advantage of the educational opportunities it offered them.

In 1892 Alice Louise Reynolds left the family of her polygamous father for courses in English at the University of Michigan at Ann Arbor. After returning two years later to Provo, Utah, to teach the first classes in Chaucer and Shakespeare offered at the Brigham Young Academy (now Brigham Young University), she continued graduate studies at the University of Chicago, and thereafter alternated her college teaching in Provo with summer graduate studies outside of Utah.

In 1897 Emma Lucy Gates left Salt Lake City at age seventeen to study music in Europe. Chaperoned by her grandmother, Lucy Bigelow Young, a wife of Brigham Young, she studied in France and Germany and made her formal debut with the Royal Opera of Berlin. She toured the continent and sang leading roles in the German State Opera until World War I broke out. Returning to Utah, she gave concerts, established her own opera company, and made recordings.

Mary Teasdel, daughter of a well-to-do Utah merchant, studied painting in Paris in 1899 with Jules Simon and James Abbott McNeill Whistler. Before she left France in 1902, she exhibited works at the International French Exposition and afterward returned to Utah to teach art and work with the Utah Art Institute. Her paintings have been on display at such art centers as the National Gallery in Washington, D.C.

After the turn of the century Mormon women began attending national social welfare institutes and international women's peace conferences. Amy Brown Lyman attended classes at the University of Chicago while her husband was studying there during the summer of 1902. She enrolled in a course in sociology—a new academic field at that time. Excited by the subject, she invested her time in the Chicago area in volunteer work at Jane Addams's Hull House.

This increased awareness of the larger world affected many women through the courses of study adopted by the Relief Society and the Young Ladies' Mutual Improvement Associations (formerly Retrenchment Associations). In 1914 the society moved away from locally planned lessons toward the adoption of a churchwide uniform course of study consisting of one lesson each month in each of four areas: theology, social sciences, literature, and homemaking. Early social science courses dealt with health, sanitation, and social welfare. Literature courses covered English and American poetry, novels, and plays—not only established classics but the works of contemporary writers as well.

Younger women studied the Bible, ethics, and literature, and received some marital and vocational guidance. Lessons from 1905 indicate that Mormon girls were reading Corneille, Descartes, Goethe, Locke, and Swift, and at the same time considering such topics as "The Girl Who Earns the Money." One lesson in the *Young Woman's Journal* for April 1905 explained that Mormon girls could "enter any avenue of artistic or business life without question," listing such fields as medicine, music, and astronomy, and they could involve themselves in church activities as well: "A girl in our Church may and does go upon missions to preach the Gospel; she can pray, preach and prophesy under the restrictions of wisdom and propriety." All of this, proposed the *Journal,* "with only the limitations of her true womanhood as a restraint."[34] What that meant is seen in the emphasis of subsequent materials: home and family responsibilities would be taught as the primary focus of a woman's activities.

Motherhood was one of several aspects of the Latter-day Saint woman's life, but it was to be given top priority. The Relief Society had begun motherhood training classes in 1902, emphasizing prenatal and infant care and childrearing. Such classes have continued in various forms to the present. "Mormon women," observed Susa Young Gates in 1926, "generally choose home life as their major occupation, making public activities incidental,"[35] though Susa herself was a prolific writer, musician, genealogist, teacher, home economist, suffragist, traveler, and church worker in addition to being the mother of thirteen children. Relief Societies and YLMIAs both tried to educate women for meaningful marital and family relations. A course of study for older girls in 1928 focused on the "everlasting covenant"—marriage and family life. Lessons dealt with the marriage contract, mutual obligations and expectations of husbands and wives, the rights of children, and childless parents. A lesson on the destiny of unmarried women within the church emphasized that the first duty of the unmarried was "to take their active place in society." Ultimately, the lesson explained, they would marry and raise up posterity in the postmortal existence if not in this life.

There was some effort to place this strong emphasis on home responsibilities within a broader context. Louise Y. Robison, a counselor in the general presidency of the Relief Society, in 1921 observed at a conference of Mormon women:

> Many of our beautiful girls marry and think they are faithful when they give their all in the home with their little people. They are so anxious to be good mothers, so anxious to be good wives, that they feel that they have not time for anything outside. They feel that life is long and after the children are grown and after they get through with their busy work, they will take up some outside work. It is too bad that the young mothers do not know that it is during the time when they are rearing these children that they need the broadening things of outside work and of the Spirit of the Lord that is obtained in mingling together.

Robison encouraged women to attend Relief Society meetings, where the weekly courses might broaden their horizons. "The Relief Society people are accomplishing such wonderful things," she concluded, "and if we stay home we are being left far behind."[36]

Although their silk raising and cooperatives and halls fell further into the past as the twentieth century moved forward, Mormon women recommitted themselves to the community virtues Joseph Smith had admonished them to strengthen in Nauvoo. The Relief Society, for example, used the wheat they had stored in local granaries to provide relief to victims of the San Francisco earthquake in 1906 and to relieve famine in China in 1907. During World War I, Relief Society women involved themselves in food production, in the sale of Liberty bonds, in sewing, knitting, bandage making, and home nursing courses for the Red Cross, and in administering aid to church members abroad. They also sold two hundred thousand bushels of wheat to the U.S. government to use for Allied relief.

A further indication of the outward reach was the establishment, in 1919, of the Relief Society Social Service Department in Salt Lake City. Amy Brown Lyman, general secretary of the Relief Society, whose training in the Chicago area had given her a strong background in social work, was named as director. The center worked with needy transients and served as an employment bureau for women and girls. In 1920 the center sponsored a six-week institute in family welfare work for sixty-three women representing stake Relief Societies throughout the church. Later, additional institutes were held in various localities, where over four thousand Relief Society women received social-work instruction. Since Relief Societies still collected and disbursed funds for the poor (they paid out nearly seventy thousand dollars for charitable purposes in 1935), learning how to work effectively with needy families was important.

Influenced by the 1921 Sheppard-Towner Act providing for federal-state maternal and child health care, the Relief Society invested interest on proceeds from the wheat sale in stake-sponsored programs for child and maternity care. Health care clinics for preschoolers were established; corrective dental work, eyeglasses, tonsillectomies, and other required surgery, medicine, and baby layettes were provided for mothers and children unable to pay. Some stakes equipped and managed maternity homes.

In 1911 women directing the Primary Association, the church's weekday organization for children, raised funds to provide for needy children patients at the Latter-day Saints Hospital in Salt Lake City. In 1923 the Primary established its own convalescent home for children, where afflicted youngsters could receive treatment free of charge, physicians donating their services and Primary "Birthday Penny Funds" maintaining operation of the home. Five thousand patients later, in 1952, this home was outgrown, and the Primary Children's Hospital was built in Salt Lake City with a governing board composed of Latter-day Saint women. In the 1920s local Primaries concerned themselves with private care of dependent orphans and neglected children, preadolescent recreation, and day nurseries. For their part, female leaders of the Young Ladies' Mutual Improvement Association took on leisure-time education, citizenship training, and vocational guidance for girls. All three of the church auxiliaries headed by women—the Relief Society, the Young Ladies' Mutual Improvement Association, and the Primary Association—raised and disbursed their own funds and could finance such projects on the general level as well as on ward and stake levels.[37]

"Mormon women are steadily and lovingly rearing their sons and daughters with American ideals in American homes," wrote Susa Young Gates in 1926.[38] Nineteenth-century Mormons had emphasized their differences with the gentile world, but as the century turned, Mormon women held mass meetings to speak not for polygamy but for peace. Their Relief Societies advocated not home-owned commission stores but consumer responsibility. Dramatic spiritual gifts such as speaking in tongues and anointing and blessing the sick, widely exercised by Latter-day Saint women through the nineteenth century, became less a part of the experience of Mormon women as the healing ordinance evolved into a strictly priestly function. Relief Societies maintained one monthly lesson in theology, during which women shared spiritual sentiments, but for the most part, gatherings of Mormon women resembled the social and educational exchanges of other American women. "You have more or less taken on the attributes that are attached in the world to cultural clubs," a member of the First Presidency told the Relief Society in 1936.[39]

Years of economic depression in the 1930s followed by World War II united Mormon women in the widespread production and collection of bedding, clothing, and food for American and European Saints. During the war LDS women's auxiliaries used their funds to purchase war bonds, and some local Relief Societies acted as Red Cross units or provided hospital supplies. Many Latter-day Saint women joined the labor force, but when their husbands returned home from the war, most of them resumed homemaking. Normalcy, for Americans at least, demanded breadwinning men and homemaking women, and Mormon customs were very much in the American pattern.

"Women's first concern must ever be the home," confirmed one Latter-day Saint woman, associate editor of the church's official magazine in 1947.[40] Through the 1950s and 1960s the traditional home theme received renewed emphasis among Latter-day Saints, an emphasis usually directed at women. Across the nation thousands of mothers began to reenter the labor market. American teen-agers, freed by postwar prosperity from family financial responsibilities, enjoyed their own cars and pursued their social life apart from their families, contributing to nationwide concern over juvenile delinquency. The American family was being threatened.

Church interest in working with state agencies had diminished in 1936 with the establishment of the Church Welfare Plan. Faced with new social problems, church leaders insisted that prevention was more effective than cure and that the best antidote to social problems was a strong home. Consequently, though the Relief Society continued to operate licensed social service agencies in several states, widespread involvement of Latter-day Saint women in social work became a thing of the past. Monthly lessons which had earlier focused on social work and psychology now dealt with social relations within the Latter-day Saint family. Literature lessons were abandoned for courses such as "Teaching the Gospel in the Home." As always, motherhood was lauded as woman's "prime and most important calling." Apostle Spencer W. Kimball (later church president) asked Latter-day Saint women in 1958:

> What would be the condition in our communities of youths if the modern mothers, with their freedom from household drudgery, wealth of facilities, increased time, and greater training, were to concentrate upon the training of their children; if they were to come home from the factory and the office and the schoolroom in those years when children are in the home; if they were to reduce their social obligations, their entertainment, and selfish diversions; if they were to dedicate the major part of their time and energies and powers to the creation of a small heaven in their home, total co-operation with their husbands, and a limitless devotion, teaching, training, leading, developing their children; investing their lives in their families, using the Church, the gospel to the fullest extent in that training?[41]

The implication for Mormon mothers with working husbands was obvious. Alternatives for other women—childless, unmarried, divorced, or widowed—were not addressed at that time.

Renewed emphasis on the woman in the home was not only a restatement of a dominant American theme. Church population more than tripled between 1940 and 1970, and much of the growth was in foreign nations. Following the war, Relief Societies, Mutual Improvement Associations, and Primaries scheduled conferences and conventions outside the United States, where home, wifehood, and motherhood were common denominators, and all three auxiliaries found that to the extent that lessons and programs were family centered, they had worldwide applicability.

Generally the church as a whole was moving in a similar direction. Throughout the 1960s church leaders were involved in "correlating" church programs—that is, in bringing the work of six or seven church auxiliaries under the direction of the general authorities—so that a unified program rather than several different programs would go out to expanding wards and stakes around the world. This correlated program structured priesthood and auxiliary lessons and activities to meet the needs of individual families. Under pressure from federal and state tax regulations, and with tighter administration through the church's hierarchical priesthood organization, all church auxiliaries turned over their general, stake, and ward funds to the First Presidency, stake presidents, or ward bishops, as the case might be. This effort at centralization at all levels served to streamline the production and distribution of materials and the carrying out of programs worldwide.

As a by-product, seen by some as an unfortunate result of the centralizing and consolidating process, priesthood correlation served to divest women of some administrative responsibility. The Relief Society had held control of its own funds; it had been required to raise its own operating money and had had control over its own disbursements. Now these responsibilities were incorporated under general ward, stake, and central budgets. The *Relief Society Magazine*, along with the organs of the Sunday School Union, the Primary Association, and the Mutual Improvement Association, were consolidated into three age-group magazines with more general appeal. Relief Society social service agencies were subsumed under a general church department, and the administration of the Primary Children's Hospital was taken over by a health services corporation.

Most Latter-day Saint women did not find that these changes reduced their ward responsibilities. They still taught the gospel to children, youth, and adults in programs that required several hours per week, and they were called upon by local bishops to perform charitable services at a moment's notice. Since church programs were family-centered, women as wives and mothers retained high status within the church community. One church leader suggested that men and women were being afforded separate but equal opportunities within the Kingdom: priesthood and motherhood.[42]

Such ideals would have seemed unobjectionable, even admirable, a generation earlier. But as the American woman's movement gained momentum in the early 1970s, the commitment to priesthood and motherhood seemed a dissonant counterpoint. Church leaders saw publicized demands for women's rights and freedom as yet another attack on the family. "We hear so much about emancipation, independence, sexual liberation, birth control, abortion, and other insidious propaganda belittling the role of motherhood, all of which is Satan's way of destroying woman, *the home, and the family—the basic unit of society,*" warned First Presidency member N. Eldon Tanner in 1973.[43] Feminists, on the other hand, criticized Mormon ideology as forcing women into menial, self-denying roles and robbing them of decision-making power. Belle S. Spafford, general Relief Society president who served as president of the National Council of Women from 1968 to 1970, found herself confronted with such questions as: "How does a woman of your experience feel having to be subservient to men in your own Church?" and "Why can't you do something to elevate the women of the Mormon Church from their positions as second-class citizens?"[44] Spafford affirmed the "position of dignity, respect, and trust" afforded to Mormon women in a response somewhat reminiscent of the indignation meetings of her nineteenth-century counterparts: Latter-day Saint sisters were women filling high and responsible positions in the church and the community.

This defensive posture made difficult for many Latter-day Saints a thorough appraisal of issues raised by modern feminists. During 1971 and 1972 a proliferation of literature regarding women by church members and leaders for the most part defended the status quo. But not without exception. A group of Latter-day Saint women in the Boston area pleaded for acceptance of a wider variety of Mormon models. "The standard for Mormon womanhood," one woman commented, "is the supportive wife, the loving mother of many, the excellent cook, the imaginative homemaker and the diligent church worker, a woman whose life is circumscribed by these roles." She continued:

> This model has been so clearly presented to us in sermon and story that we feel strong responsibility to cleave to that ideal and guilt when we depart. And so our group, largely made up of supportive wives and loving mothers who are also excellent homemakers and Church workers, has discussed the genesis of that model, how much of it is scriptural and how much traditional, and whether other models have met with acceptance in Church history.[45]

This group's search for alternative models in the Mormon past and present resulted in the publication of a new unofficial quarterly, *Exponent II*, "poised on the dual platforms of Mormonism and feminism [with] two aims: to strengthen The Church of Jesus Christ of Latter-day Saints, and to encourage and develop the talents of Mormon women."[46]

Other Mormon women began to sponsor classes and lectures dealing with the roles of Latter-day Saint women in church and society. Brigham Young University opened its 1975–76 academic year with a major address to students entitled "Feminism at BYU," in which Mormon feminist Elouise Bell questioned whether or not women at BYU were experiencing "educations in some senses quite inferior" to those men were receiving. The school's first women's conference was held some months later.[47]

Responding to such discussion, Barbara Smith, who succeeded Belle Spafford as general Relief Society president in 1974, made conciliatory efforts toward uniting Mormon sisterhood threatened by polarization over women's issues. Denouncing the proposed Equal Rights Amendment as "inflexible and vague," she advocated court and state legislative action to correct legal inequalities. Designating family as the top priority for both men and women,

Smith underscored woman's identity—be she unmarried, married, divorced, or widowed—as a daughter of God and responsible for her own choices and reasserted that self-fulfillment and community and social improvement are continuing concerns of Latter-day Saint women.[48]

A personal relationship with God is seen as fundamental for the individual Mormon, but unlike traditional Catholicism, which has seen the celibacy of holy orders as the highest state of human existence, Mormonism has maintained that marriage is necessary for fulfillment in this life and in eternity. To those who from this premise might draw unwarranted conclusions about female dependence on males for salvation, Eliza R. Snow explained in 1881, "We understand that instead of depending entirely on our husbands for salvation and position, we have to work them out ourselves."[49] John A. Widtsoe, writing in 1943, repeated that "the Lord loves His daughters as completely as His sons, and promised blessings are the same for both." They are individuals, he continued, "persons with the right of free agency, with the power of individual decision, with individual opportunity for everlasting joy—for whom all the ordinances of the Gospel are available alike, and whose actions throughout the eternities, with the loving aid of the Father, will determine individual achievement."[50]

Exhortations to Mormon women to be home-centered, pious, chaste, and submissive (all elements of the Victorian role expectation) seem less sexist when it is remembered that similar behavior standards have been set for Mormon males. Perhaps departing from the Victorian prototype in this respect, church leaders have denied the notion that a man is free to sow his wild oats or that a woman is incapable of assuming responsibility in her own right. Intense focus on the home as the singular sphere of women, tending to imply that it is not likewise man's sphere and his most important obligation, has had to be countered consciously in recent years, along with the equally unacceptable implication that unmarried, childless, or divorced women make a lesser contribution than married mothers.

But church leaders have made no concessions to the rising numbers of income-earning women. It is in the home, according to Nathan Eldon Tanner, that "a woman will find greater satisfaction and joy and make a greater contribution by being a wise and worthy mother raising good children than she could make in any other vocation."[51] There is tension between the real and the ideal, for many Mormon mothers—more than one-third in 1977—found it necessary (or desirable) to work outside the home. Perhaps in recognition of these facts of life, Camilla Kimball, wife of church president Spencer W. Kimball, urged Mormon women to pursue education and learn skills. "I would hope that every girl and woman here has the desire and ambition to qualify in two vocations—that of homemaking, and that of preparing to earn a living outside the home, if and when the occasion requires."[52] Obviously many women are following this advice and taking up occupations. The rhetoric emphasizing the importance of the home should not hide the fact that Mormon women, like women everywhere, are expanding their role far beyond what it was a generation ago.

Thus, while the church has, by preserving traditional roles, done everything in its power to resist the erosion of family life, the response of Mormon women to official expectations has not been unanimous. For example, church leaders' strong stand against the Equal Rights Amendment has not stopped individual Mormon women from campaigning in its favor. Esther Peterson, Utah-born consumer advisor to the Jimmy Carter administration, attacked the pointedly pro-family stance of the largely Mormon Utah delegation to the International Women's Year Convention in Houston, Texas, in November 1977. "We're all pro-family," she said, with reference to the largely feminist audience at the national conference. "The basic unit of our society is the family, and we want to strengthen the family." But reinterpreting the issues against which the Mormon women were speaking, she went on: "It's pro-family to have good day care. It's pro-family to have a good education so you can hold your family together with the substance it really needs." She reaffirmed her support of the Equal Rights Amendment, thus dissociating herself from her coreligionists on this issue. "That's difficult for me to do," she added: "These are my people."[53] For the most part, however, Mormon feminists have been a quiet minority, and the majority of Mormon women appear to be content with the traditional models as long as they are somewhat elastic.

Except for the hierarchy of the general authorities, women often work within the church on an equal basis with men. "In the Church and Kingdom of God the interests of men and women are the same," said Eliza R. Snow in 1875. Woman "bears joint responsibility with men in establishing the Kingdom of God," affirmed Widtsoe, adding that "the work will fail unless both do their duty."[54] And though Latter-day Saint women are not ordained to share the priesthood, they have come to hold substantial positions of leadership on all but the highest executive level of church government, including board positions with many corporations owned or partially owned by the church.

There has been among Mormon women little evidence of a demand for greater equality; certainly there are no great pressures from Latter-day Saints for priesthood for women, despite similar demands in other contemporary faiths. Feminists on the more radical edge of the movement express dismay at what they see as complacency on the part of Mormon women. The observable gap between the ideals of the most vehement feminists and most Mormon women might be seen as evidence of a cultural lag, the Latter-day Saints still being entangled in the mores of their past and its basically rural values. In this sense Mormons share many values with conservative Americans of the Midwest and the South. At the same time the self-perception of most Mormon women includes two other important elements. Aware that there has always been a discrepancy between their own ideals and the "ways of the world," they tend to see their defense of the nobility of the wife-mother role as part of an overall stance of maintaining standards against the erosion of the modern age. And their own past is complex enough and populated with enough strong, achieving female personalities that they are able to continue pushing on the boundaries, trying different options, and resisting an excessively narrow conception of their role.

Part Three
The Modern Church

The twenty years following the Woodruff Manifesto brought critical choices to Mormon leaders. Throughout the 1890s important social, political, and economic adjustments were made to save the church. After decades of determined resistance some of the distinctive characteristics of nineteenth-century Mormonism were finally suspended. Plural marriage, economic separatism, and a church-sponsored political party were surrendered or modified for an accommodation with the plenary powers of Congress over the territories. As a result, church leaders were able to return from exile and come out of hiding, polygamous husbands and fathers released from prison were reunited with their families, escheated church property was returned, and civil rights and self-government were restored. Then, in 1896, statehood was finally granted to Utah.

The church was saved, but what of the Kingdom? Latter-day Saints had viewed Mormonism as not just another sect, not just another church, but as a new Israel, the people called to establish the Kingdom of God that would usher in the millennial reign of Christ. The social, economic, and political concessions of the 1890s therefore contained important implications for the religious identity of the Saints. That in its adjustment to the pressures for conformity Mormonism retained a distinctive character helps to explain its remarkable growth in the twentieth century.

13

{ Church and Kingdom: Creative Adjustment and Reinvigoration }

How the people have grown and increased! It is like a field of lucerne after it has been cut. Take the harrow and go over the field, tear it to pieces, and you get a better crop. The harrow has been upon this people, and they have thrived under it, because God is at their head.

—Brigham Young, Jr. (1901)

The enforcement of the Edmunds-Tucker Act and its vindication by the U.S. Supreme Court in 1890 forced the church to discontinue the performance of plural marriages. At the same time, following understandings implicit in the arrangements by which Utah was granted statehood, the church abandoned its traditional promotion of cooperative or group economic enterprises, sold most of its business properties, disbanded the People's party, and in general adopted a "line" consistent with the dominant policies of the nation. Protestant elites reckoned that they had finally forced the Mormons to conform to a generally accepted image of "Christian practice." But the Mormons sought to preserve as many of their traditional goals as national sentiment would permit. While the church yielded on the key issues of polygamy, economic separatism, and political theocracy, the imagination and intelligence of its response perhaps deserve the term *creative adjustment* rather than such customary terms as *accommodation* or *surrender*.

Responsibility for preserving the church as an institution and the Kingdom as a vision belonged primarily to the men sustained by Latter-day Saints as "prophets, seers, and revelators," especially the one designated prophet and president of the church. Three men presided over the transition from nineteenth- to twentieth-century Mormonism: Wilford Woodruff, Lorenzo Snow, and Joseph F. Smith. Woodruff had been an eyewitness to many of the significant events in Mormon history: Zion's Camp, Nauvoo, the mission of the Twelve to Great Britain, the exodus from Illinois and the pioneering of the Great Basin, the Utah War, United Order, the antipolygamy raid, dedication of the Salt Lake Temple, and statehood for Utah. The seven-thousand-page handwritten Woodruff journal is a magnificent primary source, covering sixty-four years of Mormon history. Woodruff became president of the church in 1889. From his conversion in 1834 to his death in 1898, he traveled 175,000 miles to proclaim the Restoration, baptized 2,000 converts, and recorded numerous spiritual manifestations.

Lorenzo Snow had participated in the events of Missouri, Illinois, and territorial Utah. His church assignments had included missions to Italy, Switzerland, India, Palestine, and Hawaii. Sentenced to eighteen months in prison on three counts of plural marriage in 1885, he served nearly a year before being freed by a Supreme Court decision striking down such "segregating rulings." In 1898, at the age of eighty-four, he became president of the church. With his death in 1901 the Saints lost the last prophet who as an adult had known Joseph Smith personally.

Joseph F. Smith provided for twentieth-century Mormons the link with their religion's origins. The son of Hyrum Smith, Joseph F. at age five lost his father and Uncle Joseph at Carthage and at fourteen saw his mother succumb to the rigors of persecution and pioneer life. At age fifteen he was called on a four-year mission to Hawaii. Upon his return he enlisted in the militia opposing federal troops in the Utah War of 1857. Ordained an apostle, he served several missions to Europe, Hawaii, and the eastern states. He was elected to several terms in the territorial legislature and to the Salt Lake City Council. As a counselor in the church's First Presidency, Smith served presidents Taylor, Woodruff, and Snow. Husband to six wives and father of forty-three children, he was subjected to frequent harassment by federal officials during the antipolygamy raid of the 1880s.

In 1894, four years after the Manifesto, which officially ended the contracting of church-sanctioned plural marriages, Congress passed an enabling act that put Utah on its way to statehood. President Grover Cleveland granted amnesty to Mormon polygamists, and the following year Utah's constitutional convention added teeth to the Woodruff Manifesto by including a constitutional provision that "polygamous or plural marriages are forever prohibited." The constitution was ratified, and Utah became a state on January 4, 1896.

The great majority of Latter-day Saints accepted the suspension of plural marriage. Throughout the half-century of its practice there had always been Mormons who were less than enthusiastic about it. For the others, those who had practiced and defended it, it was necessary to remember that Mormonism had been founded on the principle of continuing revelation and that the ultimate earthly authority on religious matters resided in the living prophet. They remembered the words of an earlier revelation, when the Saints were prevented from fulfilling the divine command by the action of others: "It behooveth me to require that work no more . . . but to accept of their offerings."[1] If revelation from God could authorize the practice of plural marriage, revelation from the same source could discontinue it. This was the rationale that allowed the cessation of a system staunchly defended for nearly forty years.

But the polygamy issue continued to disrupt the tranquility of the Latter-day Saints for several more years. The problem existed on two levels. First, there were the plural relationships entered into prior to the 1890 Manifesto. Many of these were terminated; the plural wives received some kind of subsistence or none at all, depending on the persons involved, but cohabitation was carefully ended. Others married before 1890 chose to continue living as husband and wife, seeing such companionship as a moral and spiritual obligation even though it clashed with the law. Recognizing that such plural relationships from the past would produce fewer and fewer children as the participants advanced in age and that, deprived of new recruits to polygamy, the system would gradually disappear on its own, most political leaders and judges of the new state, Mormon and Gentile alike, saw it as humane to refrain from vigorous prosecution of the pre-1890 polygamists. On another level, however, was a small minority of Mormons who refused to accept the demise of a principle they had supported resolutely through years of criticism and prosecution. These few, thinking that the Manifesto must have been issued as a temporary political expedient, looked for loopholes such as the possibility of being married on the high seas or in other countries without violating the "law of the land" in the United States. During the period from 1890 to 1904 perhaps a few score new plural marriages were entered into by these diehards.

That Mormon polygamy was in a sense lingering on in these two ways was easily overlooked. But on occasion national attention was focused on the Mormons, and into the early years of the twentieth century pressure was brought to bear that continued their sense of being hounded and persecuted. Most of this publicity and pressure resulted from the election of Mormon officials to high political office. When B. H. Roberts, a member of the First Council of Seventy and a known polygamist, was sent to Congress in 1898, the Salt Lake Ministerial Association (the local Protestant organization) and its sister organizations across the country mobilized a responsive American public. In the year between election and the beginning of Roberts's term, a petition purportedly containing seven million signatures arrived in the nation's capital imploring Congress to refuse to seat him. Public opinion would not tolerate a Congressman who had more than one wife, and Roberts was denied his seat by an overwhelming vote in the House of Representatives.[2]

Four years later, Reed Smoot, a monogamist, was elected to the Senate. Protesting clergy and businessmen demanded that he be refused admittance to the Senate because he was an apostle in the church. Mormons, they charged, violated the separation of church and state by granting to their religious leaders absolute authority in all matters, spiritual and temporal. They further alleged that the Mormons continued secretly to advocate the practice of plural marriage while publicly claiming its end. Although the attempt was frustrated and Smoot was seated, petitions continued to be received, and the Senate finally voted to appoint an investigating committee.

When the Senate Committee on Privileges and Elections began hearings in January 1904, it became clear that the committee's work would be an investigation of the church rather than of Senator Smoot. President Joseph F. Smith and several other high-ranking officers were called to testify. Of four subpoenaed apostles accused of taking new plural wives, two were in poor health and died before they were able to travel; two, John W. Taylor and Matthias F. Cowley, refused to appear. Smith was placed in a difficult position. A father of five families, he had suffered vilification, economic hardship, and voluntary exile for plural marriage. He understood those who considered it a duty to perpetuate the principle. On the other hand, the church could not survive another battle over polygamy. To the committee he acknowledged living with his plural wives, a technical violation of the law, but denied personal involvement in or knowledge of any new plural marriages authorized by church authorities.[3]

Returning to Utah, Smith decided to reaffirm church policy and allay public suspicions. To the church's general conference in April 1904 he presented a manifesto declaring that new plural marriages were forbidden and parties entering such marriages would be excommunicated. The congregation voted to accept and sustain the statement. A year later the two apostles who had refused to cooperate with the Senate investigations submitted their resignations, claiming that the Woodruff Manifesto should have been applied only within the United States. One of them was later disfellowshipped and the other excommunicated. In 1907, three years after the investigation began, the Senate voted, by a narrow margin, to permit Smoot to retain his seat. He served a long and distinguished career in that body.

Since the Woodruff Manifesto small splinter groups have broken away from the main body of the church in order to practice plural marriage. Although these groups maintain that church leaders erred in abandoning the practice, many still acknowledge the validity and necessity of solemnizing the marriage in Latter-day Saint temples and try to stay within the fold while secretly practicing plural marriage. This has led to vigorous efforts on the part of church leaders to uncover and excommunicate them and their sympathizers. In this respect Latter-day Saints have been thoroughly converted to the more traditional standards and ideals of monogamy.

During the same transitional period following 1890, recognizing what was necessary for statehood, the Saints went about the process of political adjustment. In 1891 their People's party was disbanded, and the Saints were encouraged to align themselves with the national parties. Fearing their good intentions would be misunderstood if Mormons migrated en masse to the Democratic party, which had shown the most sympathy for the Saints during the last half of the nineteenth century, church leaders encouraged some to take up the Republican banner. Mormon folklore describes some bishops standing before their congregations and assigning the right half of the chapel to one party and the left to the other. Apostle Moses Thatcher, Elder B. H. Roberts, and Charles W. Penrose of the Salt Lake Stake Presidency campaigned openly in behalf of the Democrats. Apostles John Henry Smith and Francis M. Lyman supported the Republicans. It was also widely known that President Wilford Woodruff's counselors, George Q. Cannon and Joseph F. Smith, were Republicans.

In the 1892 congressional race for territorial delegate, Democrat Joseph L. Rawlins defeated Frank J. Cannon, son of George Q. Cannon. In the following election the Republicans took control, turning Rawlins out and sending Cannon to Washington. Rumors circulated that the Republican party had offered to stop the movement for an antipolygamy amendment to the national Constitution if the church would swing Utah into the Republican column.[4] The church was also charged with conspiring to deliver the Mormon vote to the Republicans in return for which eastern politicians would use their good offices to influence certain large trusts to help bail the church out of its financial difficulties. Although George Q. Cannon denied the charges, it was becoming apparent that the Republican party, with its big-business connections and increasing support for Utah's statehood, was becoming the party most amenable to Mormon interests.[5]

The Republicans swept the 1895 contest, electing every state and national candidate in the territory. Democratic church officials Moses Thatcher and B. H. Roberts were defeated, at least in part, by a statement of Joseph F. Smith that they had violated church policy in accepting their party's nomination without consulting their ecclesiastical superiors. Following the election the church's general authorities signed a "political rule," as it was called, or "political manifesto," which required its leaders to obtain permission before accepting any appointment that might interfere with their religious duties.[6]

In spite of the gradual identification with Republican philosophy, Utah voted overwhelmingly (82 percent) for William Jennings Bryan, in preference to Republican William McKinley, and also elected a Democratic legislature in 1896 and 1898. But in 1899 Democratic gains were reversed when the legislature could not agree on a choice for the U.S. Senate, leaving the state with only one senator.

Following that fiasco, Republican Thomas L. Kearns, a Roman Catholic, was elected senator with the rumored backing of Mormon church president Lorenzo Snow. Three years later, however, he failed to gain the support or endorsement of Snow's successor, Joseph F. Smith. Realizing he could not win his party's nomination, Kearns withdrew to help organize the anti-Mormon American party of Utah. But before leaving Washington he surprised Congress and the church with a scathing attack on "the Mormon monarchy" from the Senate floor. During the Smoot hearings Kearns charged the church with monopolizing business, taking the economic surplus of its members for an immense secret treasury, controlling politics in Utah, extending its dominion into other states, and secretly promoting polygamy.[7]

Returning to Utah, Kearns appointed former U.S. Senator Frank J. Cannon editor of the Salt Lake City *Daily Tribune*, which Kearns had acquired in 1901. Once an intimate of the First Presidency and a church agent in Washington, D.C., working for statehood, Frank Cannon had become disaffected from the church with the passing of his father, George Q. Cannon, in 1901. As editor of the *Tribune*, he launched a bitter five-year campaign against the church and Joseph F. Smith.[8] Earlier, Smith had refused to support Kearns's reelection bid partly because he wanted Reed Smoot to have the seat. In 1901 Smoot had withdrawn from the race in Kearns's favor, but now church leaders felt it important, and possible, to have their interests represented in the Senate. Theodore Roosevelt made it known he hoped no apostle would be nominated and strongly advised against it, but he provided moderate support at the Smoot hearings.[9] Smoot was reelected four times. During his thirty years in the Senate he became a prominent advocate of the high tariff (the Hawley-Smoot tariff bears his name), a supporter of some aspects of the progressive movement, and a respected kingmaker within the Republican party.[10] For many years he was chairman of the Senate Finance Committee.

Through the 1890s and early 1900s the church's growing identification with business and the eventual seating of Smoot, coupled with the Democratic debacle of 1899 and the "blistering" anti-Mormon plank of the 1904 national Democratic platform, helped convert many Saints to the Republican party. But the presumed solidarity of Mormon and Republican interests has often been exaggerated. The Anti-Mormon party, for example, won control of municipal government in Salt Lake City from 1905 to 1911 largely because of the large number of Democratic Mormons who spurned their party's banner. In 1914 Smoot retained his Senate seat by a slim three-thousand-vote margin over the popular Democratic Mormon James H. Moyle. And in 1916 the Utah vote went for Woodrow Wilson, even though the president of the church had publicly endorsed Taft in 1912 and presumably favored Hughes in 1916.[11]

Religion was declining as the decisive political issue. For example, despite renewed emphasis on the Word of Wisdom, which prohibited Latter-day Saints from using tobacco or alcohol, Mormons divided on the Prohibition question in the early 1900s. In 1908 Apostle Heber J. Grant, a Democrat, and Presiding Bishop Charles Nibley actively campaigned for prohibition legislation in Utah.[12] Grant told a Salt Lake Stake conference that no man who dealt with liquor could be in good standing in the church. But the wholesale division of a department store in which the church had an interest was one of the largest liquor dealers in the state, and a drugstore owned at least partly by Reed Smoot carried some intoxicating beverages. Reluctant to raise the specter of church influence and fearing the loss of non-Mormon votes, Smoot urged the local-option approach rather than statewide prohibition.

Smoot's effective political machine was successful in defeating Prohibition for Utah in 1908, but by 1916 the fact that forty-three other states had gone "dry" convinced Utah's Republicans that Prohibition was popular enough nationally that they could afford to endorse it. They were unable to convince Utahans that the tiger had changed his stripes, however, and lost the statehouse to Democrat Simon Bamberger, a known dry and the first non-Mormon governor since statehood.[13]

Utah politics had been thoroughly Americanized. To be sure, politicians continued to court the Mormon vote—just as New York politicians courted the Irish Catholic vote or the Jewish vote—but religion had become only one issue among many. The political tendency of Mormon voters has fluctuated, the result of several factors, economic, political, and social rather than the supposed dictation of religious leaders. Infrequently there have been allegations of efforts by Mormon leaders to influence elections, probably stimulated by occasional endorsements of candidates by individual general authorities and the fact that on the local level stake presidents and bishops have themselves been candidates. But any impression of a Mormon cabal attempting to manipulate every election or establish church control over elected officials is belied by the presence of Mormon leaders in both parties, by elections in which the vote went against the assumed church position, and by careful statements of the First Presidency explaining that members were to vote for honest candidates of either party.[14] With rare exceptions Utah's vote in presidential election years has gone with the national majority. And two Mormon presidential candidates of recent times, Republican George Romney and Democrat Morris Udall, were well known for their independent positions.

The financial condition of the church throughout the 1890s was desperate. Contributions had dwindled to a trickle due to hard times and fear that donations would end up with the federal government. When escheated church properties were finally returned after statehood, their value had been substantially reduced by mismanagement and the sale of several revenue-producing properties. The prolonged depression of the 1890s cut income from church-supported industry, while calls for welfare expenditures increased.

Completion of the four-million-dollar Salt Lake Temple also helped to deplete the church's resources. The seriousness of the situation at the end of 1896 was described in a journal entry by Wilford Woodruff: "The presidency of the church are so overwhelmed in financial matters it seems as though we shall never live to get through with it unless the Lord opens the way in a marvelous manner. It looks as though we shall never pay our debts."[15]

The way was "marvelously" opened in 1899 when Lorenzo Snow reemphasized the principle of tithing as a binding obligation of church membership. Tithing, he said, had been given as a lesser law when the Saints proved they could not live the higher Law of Consecration. Because of their love of money, he went on, the Saints in Missouri had failed to live the Law of Consecration and Order of Stewardships, and "the Lord could not sustain them against their enemies."[16] They were driven from the land of their inheritance, which would have to await redemption by a more righteous generation. The various efforts to implement the United Order in Utah had also been unsuccessful. In the meantime, Snow said, tithing was the system instituted to provide for the church's economic needs. In virtually every stake and general conference tithing was now advocated as the standard of righteousness. In 1901 Joseph F. Smith declared, "You may call it a prophecy if you will. Those who are and continue to be enrolled in the book of the law of the Lord—on the tithing records of the church—will continue to prosper, their substance will increase, and they will have added unto them in greater abundance everything that they need; while those whose names are not recorded in the book of the law of the Lord will begin to diminish in that which they possess, until they will feel sorely the chastening hand of God."[17]

By 1911 tithing receipts annually totaled up to $1.25 million—considerably less than the $15-million to $20-million figure reported in the national press but a yearly revenue equal to the entire church debt of 1898.[18] In addition, President Snow decided in 1898 to issue two $500,000 church bonds to help relieve the financial pressure. Aware of an earlier failure to sell church bonds in the East, he disposed of them locally. The $1 million in bonds was redeemed by 1906.

Finally, Snow called for the liquidation of several church-owned businesses. By selling them to private citizens the church freed itself from the burden of low-yield industry. Disposed of were the Deseret Telegraph, Utah Light and Railway Company (later Utah Power & Light), the Saltair recreational properties on the Great Salt Lake, and several mining and milling interests. The amalgamation of some church businesses with national corporations resulted in prominent Latter-day Saints being appointed to the boards of directors of several large trusts. Other church businesses, such as Zion's Cooperative Mercantile Institution (ZCMI), Zion's Savings Bank & Trust Company, and the Utah Sugar Company (later U & I Sugar), were partially retained, their stock sold on the open market, with the church maintaining a controlling interest. As the economic climate improved, the church began or participated in the organization of new ventures, such as the Beneficial Life Insurance Company and Hotel Utah. Profit-oriented business management combined with the new emphasis on tithing to produce a strong recovery. By 1904 the church had overcome the 1898 deficit of $1.25 million and had a net worth of $3.2 million.[19]

Most Latter-day Saints rejoiced at the improved economy and the increasing stability of church finance. But some concern was expressed that adoption of "worldly" business practices would result in the sacrifice of public welfare and religious principles for business profit. Nineteenth-century Mormon home industry was intended to be a cooperative enterprise operated for the direct and equal benefit of all. Now the church enterprises jostled with others, each competing for its own interests. Presiding Bishop Charles W. Nibley explained the position of twentieth-century Mormon business to a congressional committee investigating the sugar industry: The purpose of church-controlled industry, he reported, was to get the highest price it could for its product. The higher the profit, the greater the expansion, the more jobs and the higher the salaries.[20] The general welfare was best promoted through free private enterprise competing in a free and open market.

The survival of the Church of Jesus Christ of Latter-day Saints had thus required certain anguishing accommodations to American culture: Plural marriage was abandoned; the People's party was replaced by mainstream partisan politics; and group economics, no longer feasible with the separation of church and state, disappeared as competitive individualism was embraced. In each adjustment a certain amount of transvaluation was inevitable; but each seemed necessary for survival. The church was, in effect, reoriented to incorporate the standards of social, political, and economic behavior imposed by American society, while at the same time it attempted to retain as much of the "Kingdom" outlook as possible.

For many Americans the first serious test of Mormon "patriotism" occurred with the outbreak of the Spanish-American War. Although a few Mormons, most notably Brigham Young, Jr., spoke out against the war, most Latter-day Saints, like other Americans, gave it their enthusiastic support. With official encouragement from church leaders, several hundred young Mormons enlisted. There were cheers and waving of flags as the young men marched through the streets of Salt Lake City before boarding the train that would take them to their destination. These troops acquitted themselves well in Cuba and later in the Philippines. Although it may not have been precisely the war they would have preferred, Mormons responded with general enthusiasm to an opportunity to demonstrate their national loyalty.

World War I presented another such opportunity. At first, like other Americans, the Mormons and their leaders were content to adopt a hands-off attitude. Although William Howard Taft received most of Utah's votes in 1912, Wilson, who "kept us out of war," was victor in 1916. With the entrance of the United States into the war in 1917, church leaders showed no disposition to do other than follow the mainstream of national sentiment. They encouraged Mormon boys to enlist, and more than twenty-four thousand did so. Pacifism, which had its followers in Utah in the nineteenth century, was not popular among Mormons. The Saints had become Americans "lock, stock, and barrel." Not until after midcentury would the expansion of the church into Third World countries require a broader interpretation of this patriotism.

Nevertheless, on close analysis it is apparent that in the years following statehood the church fell deliberately short of complete congruity with the larger national culture. Mormonism was not destined to become one denomination among many in its own self-definition; that clearly would have been a betrayal of its own *raison d'être*. In politics, where accommodation was most complete, there continued to be the hovering specter of religious influence that set Utah apart from most states, even though in general there was restraint by church leaders, who only rarely unleashed their latent power of "advising" their members. In economic life, the powerful surge of competitive capitalism was always diluted to some extent by the undeniable egalitarian and cooperative ideal still explicitly set forth in Latter-day Saint scriptures. With the depression of the 1930s, church leaders drew from earlier wellsprings to inaugurate a welfare program that was seen as a step back in the direction of the Law of Consecration. Even in marriage, although the church's commitment to monogamy was quite clear, at least after 1904, it would be a mistake to think of the twentieth-century Mormon family as middle-of-the-road American. Resisting the trends represented by the revolutions in manners and morals after World War I and World War II, the Latter-day Saints continued to advocate relatively large families, family togetherness, and traditional roles for most men and women. If this seems much like the family ideal of Catholics and rural Protestants, it must be remembered that the eternal-marriage concept gave a unique flavor to the Mormon home. In short, accommodation was less than total, but in outward respects the remaining differences from the national norm were less noticeable than the similarities. In the minds of most persons, Mormonism ceased to be a monster breathing fire and threatening American institutions.[21] It became safe. The way was clear for it to pursue other goals.

Even after abandoning some controversial practices, the church continued to influence most facets of its members' lives. In no field was this more significant than in education. As the barriers between them and the greater world came down and the defense fortress mentality began to fade, young Mormons eagerly aspired to high school and college education. And in doing so they had the encouragement of church leadership. "If we are to be a powerful people in the near future," wrote the First Presidency in an official statement, "wielding potent influence for good among the people of the earth, we must prepare ourselves for those responsibilities."[22] For many, particularly of the third generation, it brought about Mormonism's first confrontation with serious, persistent intellectual challenges.

The approach to education in the late 1880s and 1890s included the sponsorship of religion classes for children in public elementary and intermediate schools, the establishment of the academies and colleges providing basic secondary education, and the institution of a central planning board for Young Men's and Young Ladies' Mutual Improvement Associations. The success of these programs made it possible for the church to retain the loyalty of most of its young and well-educated members; they, in turn, upon reaching maturity, developed and directed programs that were effective in helping the church to serve its youth.

The key development that caused the church to launch these programs was the necessity of converting the tithe-supported ward schools, which, like Catholic parochial schools, were religious in their orientation, into tax-supported public schools with a strictly secular focus. The Edmunds-Tucker Act required that the Utah school laws, which had been designed to sanction and support the ward school system, be suspended, that the territorial schools be placed under the control of the territorial supreme court and a court-appointed (non-Mormon) commissioner, and that the financial resources of the Corporation of the Church and the Perpetual Emigration Fund be disposed of by the secretary of the interior for the use and benefit of the public schools.[23] These federal requirements, as well as other considerations, led the Utah legislature to establish a tax-financed territorial system and to require compulsory attendance of all children through age fourteen. To help counteract the "tendencies that grow out of a Godless education," the First Presidency instituted the religion-class movement, as a part of which Mormon teachers, on a volunteer basis, taught "the Restored Christian Gospel" once a week to all pupils who would come.[24] Before the religion classes were discontinued in 1929, because the church had confidence that its seminaries would take care of the same need, an average of about thirty thousand children in the first decade of the century and sixty thousand in the second, in grades one through nine, annually enrolled for this weekday instruction.[25]

At the same time, seeing that the public school system was not prepared to open high schools—which would mean instruction beyond age fourteen—the First Presidency appropriated tithing funds to establish thirty-five stake academies, covering every "valley" or network of Mormon communities in the Mountain West.[26] The academies and other Latter-day Saint schools were supervised by a church superintendent of schools (later called church commissioner of education), a church board of education, and stake boards of education. The academies were modeled after the Brigham Young Academy in Provo, Utah, and the Brigham Young College in Logan, Utah. Sixteen academies were opened in 1888, and another nineteen by 1909. By 1905, in the infancy of the American high school movement, about 60 percent of Utah's high school students and a substantial proportion of Latter-day Saint teen-agers in Arizona, Idaho, Wyoming, and Nevada were enrolled in Latter-day Saint academies.

By 1920 state-supported high schools had proliferated to such an extent that the church adopted a policy of transferring its academies to local districts for use as public high schools. A few academies were upgraded to junior college status, and they had the primary responsibility of training teachers for public schools. In 1903, after the Salt Lake Academy (later Latter-day Saints University) was relinquished in favor of the University of Utah, the Provo academy was designated Brigham Young University, the church university.

As the number of public high schools increased, the church extended religion classes to include high schools as well. The first such program was initiated in 1912 at Granite High School in Salt Lake City, where the principal and district officials granted permission to conduct daily classes on a released-time basis in a neighboring church-owned building, called a seminary. One unit of credit was given for courses in Bible literature and history, and there were noncredit denominational classes as well. This may well have been the first released-time program of religious instruction in the nation.[27]

In 1926 the church withdrew from higher education, except for Brigham Young University, Ricks College (a two-year college in Rexburg, Idaho), and the Latter-day Saint Business College in Salt Lake City. It launched a program of religious studies on the college level, similar to the religion classes and seminaries at the elementary and secondary levels. The first of these institutes of religion, as they were called, was established adjacent to the University of Idaho campus at Moscow, Idaho. Non-Mormon faculty members sympathetic with the program's objectives helped secure elective credit at the university for nonsectarian courses taught at the institute.[28] By 1977 seminaries adjacent to high schools enrolled more than two hundred thousand students annually in classes in the Old Testament, the New Testament, the Book of Mormon, church history, and Christian history and doctrine. Religion thus continued to be a part of the daily routine for these seminary students, who could elect to meet for religious instruction each day before school or on a released-time basis.

Soon institutes of religion were established at many other colleges as well—at the Utah State Agricultural College (now Utah State University) in

1928, the University of Idaho, Southern Branch (now Idaho State University) in 1929, and the University of Utah in 1934. Thus, by 1935 Latter-day Saint students at the major universities in Mormon country were offered college-level courses in religion, as well as an extensive social program. By 1977 some seventy-five thousand students were attending classes in five hundred institutes throughout the United States and overseas.

Church leaders also undertook to supervise the recreation and cultural development of young people. There were admonitions to dress modestly, marry within the church, and avoid the temptation to postpone the responsibilities of marriage and children. Young people were urged to remain aloof from Sunday sports, pool halls, card games, and non-Latter-day Saint dance halls. To provide alternative activities to "satisfy their righteous ambitions and develop their talents,"[29] the programs of the Young Men's and Young Ladies' Mutual Improvement Associations were strengthened. "No outside organization is necessary," said Pres. Joseph F. Smith in 1902. "There is no call for individuals to organize clubs, or special gatherings in social, educational, or national capacity, in order to express wishes or desires for reforms that can always be expressed in the organizations that already exist in the Church."[30] Under this paternalistic regimen each of the ward MIAs sponsored musical and dramatic entertainment, athletic tournaments, picnics, weekly dances, and weekly classwork in "practical religion." Summer conferences were held in recreation resorts owned by stake MIAs or by the church. There were committees on amusements and entertainments on the general, stake, and ward levels to direct this program.[31] In 1911 churchwide competitions were initiated in athletics, drama, and music with stake and regional winners traveling to Salt Lake City for the finals. Activities that might have lured young Latter-day Saints from church participation were thus legitimized by church supervision and sponsorship.

Under the sponsorship of these auxiliary associations were new magazines that facilitated communication with a generation benefiting from enlarged educational opportunities: for young men, *The Improvement Era* (1897–1929), for young women, *The Young Woman's Journal* (1889–1929), and after 1929 an enlarged *Improvement Era* serving both organizations for the next forty years. These magazines carried not only organizational instructions but also articles on philosophy, politics, history, and literature. They are a major source of information for those seeking to understand Mormonism during the first half of the twentieth century or longer.

In practice the church did not find it necessary to prohibit all organized activity outside its own control. Service clubs, community projects, fund raising, politics, and a large number of private clubs and study groups continued to attract the energies of Latter-day Saints. But there can be no mistaking the tendency of Mormonism to penetrate the life of its members, to develop organizations and programs as the need arose, and to adapt these pragmatically under the pressure of changing circumstances.

The Mormon response was not isolationist in the sense of trying to prevent all contact with the "outside world." Possibly as many as a hundred Latter-day Saint men and women, some subsidized by the church, attended universities in the Midwest and the East in the decade after 1890, matriculating at Michigan, Chicago, Columbia, Cornell, Johns Hopkins, and Harvard. Most returned to Utah to teach in the church educational system or at the University of Utah or Utah State University, or to practice law or medicine. Among those who went east to study for advanced degrees were James E. Talmage, who studied science at Lehigh and Johns Hopkins, became the first president of the Latter-day Saint College, wrote the first text used in Latter-day Saint university instruction, *The Articles of Faith* (1899), and became an apostle; Richard R. Lyman, who studied engineering at the University of Michigan, obtained a Ph.D. at Cornell, became an apostle, and was employed as consulting engineer on the Sanitary District of Chicago, the Grand Coulee Dam, the Columbia Basin Project, and the Metropolitan Water District of Southern California; John A. Widtsoe, who graduated from Harvard with highest honors in biochemistry, completed a Ph.D. at the University of Göttingen in Germany, acted as president of Utah State Agricultural College and the University of Utah, and was ordained an apostle; James H. Moyle, who took a law degree at the University of Michigan and later was the first Mormon to hold high office in the national government, serving as assistant secretary of the treasury in the cabinet of Woodrow Wilson; and Amy Brown Lyman, who studied at the University of Chicago, did volunteer work with Jane Addams at Hull House, and later became general president of the Relief Society.

Likewise, several students were set apart by church authorities in the 1890s as "art missionaries" to study painting at the Académie Julian in Paris. Despite its adverse financial condition, the church supported these students with the understanding that they would return to paint murals for temples. These artists became the teachers of most of Utah's art students for the first half of the twentieth century.

As with the fine arts, church architecture after the Manifesto reflected the desire of Latter-day Saints to put isolationism behind them and participate in the artistic currents of the time. Church structures exhibited an eclecticism that included gothic and classical styles along with baroque, neoclassic, Romanesque, and even Muscovite and Byzantine elements. In 1910 Frank Lloyd Wright's prairie style began to be felt in Mormon architecture as well.

The influence of higher education on Mormon theology and culture, primarily as mediated by Mormons who studied at various universities, would not be felt without some "growing pains." The anguish and excitement of the search for truth and excellence may be illustrated in the experiences of two men, one a general authority who often served as a missionary, the other a professional student who served as a teacher in several of the institutions of higher learning in Utah.

Of all the advocates of quality education among the Mormons, none was more enthusiastic than Brigham H. Roberts (1857–1933).[32] A poor emigrant from England, Roberts walked across the plains to Utah at the age of nine. He had little opportunity for formal education, but he became a voracious reader, devouring books of history, science, philosophy, and religion. Possibly no other Mormon leader before or since has mastered such a range of scholarly works or published more prodigiously.[33] Roberts's faith in the divine origins and destiny of Mormonism was unquestioned, but he frequently took a broader view of its place in the heavenly scheme of things than did some of his colleagues. In 1902 he told the Saints that "while the Church of Jesus Christ of Latter-day Saints is given a prominent part in this great drama of the last days, it is not the only force nor the only means that the Lord has employed to bring to pass those things of which His prophets in ancient times have testified." Roberts saw the hand of God in the scientific and artistic advances of civilization as well. Mormonism, he said, is "one of the great world-movements for the accomplishment of the mighty purposes of God. It is connected with all the other great world movements that are bringing to pass the revolutions now going on in the earth." Through science "physical conditions are being brought into existence that will coordinate with those spiritual and moral conditions which 'Mormonism' will yet establish and will bring to pass, the realization of the world's hope for that reign of peace and righteousness called the millennium." Roberts was anxious for Latter-day Saints to take full advantage of educational opportunities in order to advance the cause of God.[34]

His magnum opus, "The Truth, the Way, and the Life," perhaps the most significant product of a Mormon mind in the first half of the twentieth century, was never published. Roberts's intention in this three-volume work was monumentally ambitious: "a search for THE TRUTH, as it relates to the Universe and to man; a consideration of THE WAY as it relates to the attainment of those ends which may be learned as to the purpose of man's earth-existence; and the contemplation of THE LIFE—that will result from the knowledge of the Truth and the Way." The title was chosen, as Truman G. Madsen has observed, "because through a lifetime of reflection he saw that the great system of 'truth' that 'gives unity to all history and proper relationship to all existing; that fills life with a real meaning, and makes existence desirable,' centers in and is embodied in Jesus the Christ."[35]

Roberts's theology was bold and audacious, for it "combined elements of traditional fundamentalism with the modern liberal doctrine of man and the optimism of the nineteenth century, and it required a bold, rebellious, and spacious mind to grasp its full implication." He "not only shaped the outlines of a systematic theology but developed, as well, the perspectives which placed the Church as an institution within the framework of history and provided the Mormon people with the instrument of rationalizing and defending their beliefs and practices."[36] This and Roberts's other numerous writings introduced Mormons to some of the most advanced thinkers of the age as no other church authority or educator could. In 1906 he characterized the activity of Mormon intellectuals in his and subsequent generations:

> [Mormonism] calls for thoughtful disciples who will not be content with merely repeating some of its truths, but will develop its truths; and enlarge it by that development. Not half . . . of that which Joseph Smith revealed to the Church has yet been unfolded, either to the Church or to the world. . . . The Prophet planted by teaching the germ-truths of the great dispensation of the fullness of times. The watering and the weeding is going on, and God is giving the increase, and will give it more abundantly in the future as more intelligent discipleship shall obtain.[37]

The spirit of intellectual liberality fostered by Roberts in his position as member of the First Council of Seventy was furthered by several Mormon educators of the early twentieth century, notably William H. Chamberlin (1871–1929).[38] While Roberts was outspoken, obstinate, and always ready to interject himself into the fray, Chamberlin was quiet and unassuming, and published very little. His influence was in the classroom, where he taught a large share of the men and women who later became professors, department heads, and deans in universities attended by Latter-day Saint students during the half-century after 1900. After his graduation from the University of Utah, Chamberlin served a three-year proselyting mission in Tahiti, studied ancient languages and biblical higher criticism at the University of Chicago, completed a Master of Arts from the University of Chicago, and learned philosophy under Josiah Royce at Harvard. He taught in public schools (1889–1891); science and mathematics at the Latter-day Saint College (1891–1897); geology and mathematics, then theology at Brigham Young College (1900–1901, 1903–1904); philosophy and ancient languages at Brigham Young University (1909–1916); philosophy at the University of Utah (1917–1920) and the Utah State Agricultural College (1920–1921).

When Chamberlin went to Brigham Young University in 1909, he joined his brother Ralph, and Henry and Joseph Peterson on the faculty. Ralph had completed his Ph.D. in biology at Cornell in 1905, the year the Peterson brothers graduated from the University of Chicago. Henry Peterson went on to earn a Master's degree in psychology from Harvard (1906), and Joseph to earn a Ph.D. in literature from Chicago (1907). Brigham Young University had recently been confirmed as the church university, and the four new faculty members had high hopes of helping to lift the quality of education at the school to the level of a major university. The four worked energetically—and successfully—to stimulate interest in intellectual pursuits. They spoke to church groups and student audiences on higher criticism and evolution, and both subjects became popular topics for debate and discussion on campus. Although other Latter-day Saints before the Chamberlins and Petersons had advocated evolution as God's means of creation, none had attracted so much attention.[39] Ralph Chamberlin spoke at a memorial service commemorating the births of Darwin and Lincoln, and described Darwin as one of the greatest scientific minds of the age. In the school paper he published "The Early Hebrew Conception of the Universe," and "Early Hebrew Legends," drawing upon higher criticism to point out the "constant evolution" of Hebraic thought and "the progressive unfolding of the divine Will" revealed in the Bible.

William Chamberlin published a monograph entitled "The Theory of Evolution as an Aid to Faith in God and Belief in the Resurrection," in which the philosophy of "personal idealism" played an important role. Stressing divine immanence in the processes of nature, Chamberlin found in the theory of evolution evidence for faith in the resurrection. He also spoke of the allegorical and mythical elements in Old Testament writings, which when properly understood as literary and didactic elements effectively disarmed petty critics of the Bible who objected to stories such as that of Jonah and the whale. In addition to accepting evolution and higher criticism, Joseph Peterson's theory of cognition apparently contradicted what some understood to be the Mormon concept of free will.

Although the modernist ideas of the Chamberlins and the Petersons seem to have met with the enthusiastic approval of faculty and student body alike, Superintendent of Church Education Horace H. Cummings reported that more than a dozen stake presidents had complained of heresies being taught at Brigham Young University by the new faculty members. Opposed to both higher criticism and theories of evolution, Cummings was motivated more by a concern for what he regarded as the spiritual welfare of the students than by scientific implications. After a brief investigation he reported that the teachers were "applying the evolutionary theory and the other philosophical hypotheses to principles of the gospel and to the teachings of the Church in such a way as to disturb, if not destroy, the faith of the pupils."[40] The Petersons and Ralph Chamberlin were named as chief offenders. The church board of education informed the three that they would have to alter their teachings or face dismissal.

A storm of controversy was raised in the Salt Lake City and Provo press.

This was intensified by the publication of a petition reportedly signed by 90 percent of the student body protesting the board's action. Nevertheless, the decision remained, and the Petersons and Ralph Chamberlin left the university for teaching careers outside the church educational system. William Chamberlin remained five more years, prepared his lectures with care, and continued to teach among his people.[41]

Mormonism had had its first brush with modernism. The trauma could have been worse; there were no books banned, no excommunications or schisms.[42] No official church position was taken with regard to evolution or higher criticism. In a church magazine, the *Juvenile Instructor*, President Joseph F. Smith wrote that the decision had only been not to discuss evolution in church schools. He described it as "a question of propriety [without] undertaking to say how much of evolution is true and how much false."[43]

By deciding not to decide the evolution question, Smith averted a head-on confrontation between those newly educated Saints who found in it support for Mormon doctrine and those of a more traditional persuasion who perceived in the theory the seeds of apostasy. By removing such controversial issues from the classroom, officials hoped to avert a doctrinal crisis, for the popularity of the professors' innovative interpretations had threatened to undermine the authority of the apostles and prophets as sole adjudicators of church doctrine.[44]

It should be noted that the erring professors were not excommunicated. There had always been, and would continue to be, room within the fold for a certain range of opinion. Historically, excommunication for apostasy has been mainly limited to those who wish to disassociate themselves from the church or to the rare case of an unbeliever who speaks out publicly against the church.[45] In the action against the professors, the prerogatives of the church's priesthood leaders were affirmed, but not without adverse repercussions. BYU gained an anti-intellectual reputation that persisted for several years. To many Saints the academic world became suspect; professions in the life sciences, religious studies, and philosophy were especially distrusted.[46]

As time went on, an expanding percentage of Mormons sought and obtained higher degrees. The challenge of such an experience to religious faith would continue down to the present, but the basic institutional response— organizations, programs, and publications to help religious knowledge develop simultaneously with secular knowledge—had been established during the first quarter of the century.

Years before, Joseph F. Smith had warned of the dangers inherent in an education that exaggerated the importance of book learning. In 1903 he admonished the Saints not to "allow our sons to grow up with the idea that there is nothing honorable in labor, except it be in the profession of law, or in some other light, practically unproductive . . . employment. . . . We need manual training schools instead of so much book-learning and the stuffing of fairy tales and fables, which are contained in many of our school books of today."[47] From this point of view higher education was good—up to a point. Smith concluded with a quotation from the Book of Mormon: "To be learned is good, if they hearken unto the counsels of God."[48]

There is a standard interpretation of the time between 1890 and 1918 that sees them as years of accommodation. Indeed, the church did give in to and align itself with national custom in its marriage system, its political and economic practices, and some of its educational patterns. According to this interpretation, the social, political, economic, and educational Kingdom was relinquished in order that the church could survive as an ecclesiastical institution with its own unique theology and religious practices.

Without question there is truth in such an interpretation; it explains much about how Mormons got where they are today and why they differ in important respects from their predecessors of the past century. Nevertheless, there are important qualifications that must be examined if the whole adjustment is to be properly understood. These qualifications explain not only how Mormonism now differs from its positions in the nineteenth century but, equally important, how and why Mormons are still different in important ways from the American mainstream. The church survived, but its survival was not simply a sliding-on once the concessions had been made. The adjustment required continued adaptation, formulation of new programs, flexibility, and pragmatism. Moreover, adjustment did not mean a total melting into the national patterns. It is still a distinctive church, not liberal Protestant, not fundamentalist Protestant, not Catholic.

In short, the accommodation thesis is partially correct, but inadequate as an overall interpretation of the status of Mormonism in the twentieth century. By 1910 educational, social, and cultural programs sponsored by the church were serving as a hedge against secular influences and reinforcing the sense of community among the believers. Though shorn of its overt political and economic power and clothed in twentieth-century garb, the restored church established by Joseph Smith survived—and flourished.

14

{ The Temporal }
Foundation

It has always been a cardinal teaching with the Latter-day Saints that a religion which has not the power to save people temporally and make them prosperous and happy here, cannot be depended upon to save them spiritually, to exalt them in the life to come.

—Joseph F. Smith (1905)

In recent years it has been common for national publications, in referring to the Mormon church, to use the adjective *wealthy* or *well-to-do*.[1] Part of this is explained by the centralized character of the church; its income and expenditures are handled by a central treasury rather than by each separate congregation as in many churches. Moreover, the church requests the payment of a full tithe—10 percent of a member's income—and the majority of its adherents are faithful in making such contributions. The Mormon work ethic has helped many individual Saints to do well financially, and thus they have earned substantial incomes on which to pay their tithes. Finally, the continued increase in church membership, particularly internal growth, has added to the accumulation of its financial resources.

This was not always true. The tempestuous early experiences of Mormonism made it impossible for members to accumulate substantial property and necessitated heavy church expenditures for nonproductive purposes. The expulsions from Missouri in the 1830s forced the Saints to leave behind all or nearly all of their property. Because of the haste of their departure, little was realized from sales of their property in Nauvoo. The difficulty of supporting several thousand new immigrants each year and the problems of making a living in the arid West militated against an early social surplus in the Great Basin. The antipolygamy raids of the 1880s and the depression of the 1890s added to the financial drain on the church and its members. Although the diary of Wilford Woodruff fully reflects his anxiety during the years he was president (1889–1898), he firmly believed that the church should not discontinue its program of economic development. Bonds were floated in 1898 to secure the funds to pay promissory notes as they came due. In the years that followed the restoration of prosperity, the increased payment of tithes and the sale of many of the church's business interests produced an improvement in its financial position. Although the church does not give a detailed accounting of its annual revenues and expenditures, there have been occasional summaries, and its financial position has continued to improve.[2] The 1959 summary, covering the year 1958, was as follows (on December 31, 1958, the membership of the church was 1,555,799):

Expenditures of the Church in 1958

For missions and missionary work	$13,034,893
This does not include approximately $5,000,000 paid by members and friends for support of the 5,485 full-time missionaries; nor does it include the value of the time given by missionaries.	
For ward and stake buildings and activities	28,313,005
Approximately half of this sum was raised in the local wards and stakes and half came out of general church funds. There were at the time 273 stakes and 2,205 wards.	
For construction and operation of temples	2,756,550
There were twelve operating temples in 1958.	
For church schools	15,508,502
These included church appropriations for Brigham Young University, Ricks College, LDS Business College, Church College at Laie, Hawaii, institutes of religion and seminaries, and schools in Mexico. Enrollment in the church school system in 1958 included 22,822 college students and 48,203 high school and elementary students.	
For welfare	6,881,667
Some 87,419 persons were assisted from bishops' storehouses in 1958, 16,640 were placed in remunerative employment, and 231,443 man-days of work were donated to the Welfare Plan. These figures do not include the value of the donated labor. About four-fifths of this sum came from fast offerings and other special cash donations.	
For buildings and grounds of central church buildings	1,242,913
For the LDS Genealogical Society	1,748,831
In 1958 genealogical records were microfilmed in nine countries; these were equivalent to 142,575 printed volumes of approximately 300 pages per volume.	
For expenses of the auxiliary General Boards (Sunday School, Young Men's and Young Women's MIA, Relief Society, and Primary, including Primary Children's Hospital)	664,625
All of this expenditure came from funds of the auxiliaries.	
For general administrative expenses of the church	2,264,940
For all other purposes	378,380
Grand total of expenditures in 1958	$72,794,306

Source: Conference Report, April 1959, pp. 91-93.[3]

The largest single expenditure in the general church budget, understandably, is that for church buildings, most of them chapels and facilities for religious education and recreation for members in all the stakes and missions of the church.[4] These structures become the temporal as well as spiritual focal point of the faithful. Family life, as indicated earlier, divides itself between the home and the church house, and has done so since the early settlements, when the first community project, even before the irrigation canal, would be a rude bowery where religious services could be held. That would be followed by the construction of a church-schoolhouse, usually a one-room building serving community educational, social, and religious purposes. Some few of those first Utah meetinghouses are still standing, rock structures mostly, with pitched roof, gable end to the street. Most, such as the one at Grantsville, some thirty miles west of Salt Lake City, have since found use as relic halls for the Daughters of Utah Pioneers or as town museums, private homes, or social halls.

Across the street and to the east of the little first churchhouse at Grantsville stands the second edifice raised by the Mormons there to accommodate the growing membership in the area—again typical of others of its time. Solidly built of adobe bricks in 1866, it was still in use in 1978, classrooms having been added on as church programs required. Those buildings of the 1860s resembled the earlier ones in that they were basically rectangular, gabled, and entered from the street. Some, such as the carefully preserved Parowan, Utah, church, were two-storied, separating divine worship from secular functions. Each floor had its own front entrance, the two stairways providing a characteristic appearance which identified the buildings.

Mormons invested more than just their tithing labor and their Sunday eggs in their buildings, and received from them more than mere protection from the elements during once-a-week services. As small communities found continuity and group cohesiveness through their building projects, larger regions found strength and a sense of support in the building of larger edifices—tabernacles as they were called—whose seating capacity might reach two thousand. There the people could gather for special meetings, stake conferences and the like, and be instructed by leaders from church headquarters. The tabernacle at Bountiful, twenty miles north of Salt Lake City, for example, took some eleven years to build, and in the interim served as a storage bin for community grain during the threat of invasion in 1857. When the Saints returned to their homes in 1858 after the move south, it took some prodding from Brigham Young to get the building finished; but once it was dedicated, with great celebration and pride, it became the center of the community temporally—the business district grew up around it—and spiritually. More than a century later, townspeople, Mormons and non-Mormons alike, fought official attempts at replacing the old building and won a program of restoration and preservation. The tabernacle at Logan, serving residents in Utah's Cache Valley, grew likewise slowly; so slowly, in fact, that at one stage Brigham Young, noting the growth of the valley's population since the building had been started, had the members tear out the old footings and expand the foundation. The structure, first used in 1877, is still the central gathering place in Logan.[5]

Construction of church buildings fostered economic growth in Mormon communities. To facilitate the building of the Logan temple, an even larger edifice than the tabernacle, six industries were established: a sawmill, a wood camp, a lime kiln, a stone quarry in Green Canyon, and another in Hyde Park Canyon for the wall quartzite, and a third quarry for the sandstone for water tables, caps, and ledges. The network of temple industries provided materials not only for the temple, but for the construction of homes, barns, and shops—many of the temple builders receiving their pay in such materials.[6]

To the twentieth-century church, in the Mountain West as in the mission areas farther afield, chapel building has represented the most frequent occasion for personal sacrifice on the part of members. The requirement that a local unit contribute from 30 to 50 percent of the cost of its building—the central church coffers providing the rest—works in many cases the kind of hardship perceived by church leaders as beneficial. One bishop commented that he "would hate most of all to be bishop in a ward which has no building project."[7] The benefits in terms of member cohesiveness, of increased growth, of justifiable pride are registered in the account by a mission president from Switzerland of how a little branch of thirty-six members in the village of Ebnat overcame governmental stumbling blocks and community prejudice to put up their building, and more obliquely in the comment of a member from Sweden who, on first visiting a Mormon meeting, was appalled at its location on a street "so repulsive and old."[8] "Building missionaries," young men called not as proselyters but as bricklayers, carpenters, or whatever, to work on the building, assisted in the project, and from the mission leader's point of view, "we gained good friends in that valley area as a result of that project."[9]

The early tithed labor, usually the largest portion of the building budget, has in the twentieth century given way to donations in cash. But in the meantime there is a history of community fundraisers, many of them reflecting the characteristics of the region as well as the ingenuity of the Saints. In West Virginia in 1905, two missionaries assigned to help build a chapel mowed, raked, and stacked hay for neighbors; they threshed wheat, and shucked corn, gathered chestnuts, and helped make cane sugar. One had a camera, so took family portraits on request. They sawed logs and hauled them to a sawmill, and in all won support of members and outsiders for the project.[10] More typical are the joint projects sponsored by whole wards: bazaars, banquets, booths at state and county fairs; invited speakers, performers, dramatic productions; sales of a variety of commodities, from children's books to home-made chocolates; auctions of help services—a member would mow your lawn four times for the highest bid, another volunteered ten hours of baby-sitting, still another a batch of homemade bread. The extracurricular benefits from such cooperative ventures were perceived by one contemporary church leader as doing more "to stimulate duties of the priesthood and growth of members than anything that could ever happen" in his stake.[11]

Enthusiasm for the present-day church building program is not universally shared.[12] Today's standardized meetinghouses, very similar in style, repeat themselves not only throughout the United States, where they blend most readily with the surrounding architecture, but in other areas of the world, where they stand out as uniquely American-Mormon. Voices pleading for greater individuality, for local initiative in design and materials, have been drowned out by the sounds of the construction of chapels from "cookie cutter" plans. One observer sees in the look-alike appearance of Mormon churches a positive response to the increased mobility of twentieth-century Saints. "Coming upon a Mormon meetinghouse in a strange town is like finding your favorite food franchise when you are traveling," he remarks. "Once you've located the church and Colonel Sanders it's as if you never left home."[13]

The similarity of programs for all units of the church makes very reasonable the standardization of building plans. Most facilities contain a chapel or worship space seating about three hundred people; recreational facilities for social, sport, and cultural activities; offices for ward and stake officers; a Relief Society room for the women's auxiliary; a Junior Sunday School or Primary room for the children; and classrooms for groups of all ages. Such a structure, usually housing two wards, cost upwards of $800,000 in 1977. In the 1970s one such building was dedicated somewhere in the world on the average every day.

The most elaborate, and, to the Mormons, significant church buildings are the temples. The most recognized shape in Mormondom is the outline of the six-towered Salt Lake Temple, a granite structure of mixed architectural style which took from 1853 to 1893 to build. The greatest skill and most generous funding which the church afforded was put into that and subsequent temples, each representing its period and, in some way, the feelings and concerns of the members at that time. There are the bastion-type early temples at Saint George, Logan, and Manti—seen by an 1880s observer as seeming to be "constructed for defense rather than for worship";[14] the early twentieth-century temples in prairie style, with motifs reminiscent of Central American Indian architecture, in Cardston, Alberta, Mesa, Arizona, and Laie, Hawaii; the mid-century romantic feeling of the central-spired temples at Idaho Falls,

Idaho, and Los Angeles and Oakland, California; and the modest simplicity of the first temples abroad—rectangular buildings with a front spire at London, England, Berne, Switzerland, and Hamilton, New Zealand. The 1970s saw construction of two temples rounded in appearance in Provo and Ogden, Utah, and then a recognition of the strength of symbolism of the six towers from the Salt Lake temple repeated in a modern setting in the Washington, D.C., temple.

That most controversial structure, costing $16 million, signified to the East Coast Mormons what temples mean to members wherever they are constructed: that the church in their region has arrived. No longer must the faithful make the long trek to larger Latter-day Saint populated regions of the Mountain West or California; Zion, they perceive, has extended its borders to include them.[15] In 1978 temples were being constructed in Mexico City, Mexico; São Paulo, Brazil; Tokyo, Japan; Seattle, Washington; Mapusaga, American Samoa; and West Jordan, Utah, in the Salt Lake Valley.

While the bulk of the expenditure from general church coffers goes to house the Saints generally, there are other structures and properties in Salt Lake City of no small value. The business of running an organization of four million members more than fills a twenty-eight-story office building, the descendant of the little one-room office across the plaza. In the one block, across Main Street from Temple Square, can be seen in a glance an evolution in church administration, as represented by three adjacent buildings: the Beehive House and its attached presidential office, constructed in 1854; the stately columned five-story Administration Building, built of Utah granite in 1917, containing offices of the First Presidency and other general authorities of the church; and the towering new General Church Office Building in the background, which houses the administrative departments of the church. Fittingly, the latter building was designed by George Cannon Young, A.I.A., a grandson of Brigham Young. The four-story east wing is the home of the Historical Department of the church, including the Church Library-Archives; the four-story west wing contains the Genealogical Department, with its enormous accumulation of books and microfilm holdings. Nearby is the Relief Society Building, completed in 1952, which houses offices and committee rooms, a women's library, and various exhibits and displays.

Beginning in 1902, with the construction of the Bureau of Information, the church sought to develop Temple Square in Salt Lake City as a visitors' center. By 1930 about 300,000 tourists were calling on the bureau every year. Volunteers served without salary to guide the visitors through the facilities at Temple Square and tell "the Mormon story." The bureau maintained a museum with relics pertaining to Mormon and Utah history. In 1970 an additional visitors center was located in Temple Square, and in 1978 the "old" Bureau of Information was replaced by a new one. Approximately 2.5 million persons now pass through Temple Square annually. The church also maintains a number of historic sites and buildings. The most important of these are at Nauvoo, Illinois, where, under the supervision of the nonprofit corporation Nauvoo Restoration, Inc., an attempt is made to perpetuate in history the work of the Mormon pioneers along the Upper Mississippi before their expulsion in 1846.

One of the most unusual structures built in recent years is the mammoth subterranean archival storage facility in Little Cottonwood Canyon, about twenty miles southeast of Salt Lake City. A huge vault bored through the sheer granite rock, this impregnable repository, with more than an acre and a half of storage area, is designed to last for centuries. It contains church records and the microfilm negatives of a vast accumulation of genealogical records—more than two billion pages of records.

On a seventeen-acre site in southwest Salt Lake City is the Distribution Center, which with its branches provides supplies and materials for the six thousand wards and branches throughout the world. There are church-owned mission offices in approximately two hundred locations, and "mission homes," where the mission president and his family live. The church also owns a thirty-six-story building in New York City that contains apartments, religious facilities, and administrative offices.

Most of these properties—the equivalent of chapels, parsonages, and church administrative buildings owned by other churches—are non-income producing and, as ecclesiastic properties, are nontaxable. They are held in the name of the Corporation of the President of the Church, a corporation organized in 1921. Like other churches, universities, charitable institutions, and fraternal organizations, the Mormon church receives donations of improved and unimproved land, bonds, and common stocks. These are administered by a solely owned subsidiary of the Corporation of the President, Deseret Trust Company, created in 1972. In addition there are some other assets—income-earning, nonecclesiastical, and hence taxable—that in 1967 were transferred to Deseret Management Corporation.

Consistent with its strong missionary impulse, the church began with the publication of a book, the Book of Mormon, and has almost uninterruptedly maintained a strong publication program. Its first magazine was the *Evening and the Morning Star*, published in Jackson County, Missouri, during 1832–33, which contained scriptures, hymns, and news of note. The *Latter-day Saints' Messenger and Advocate* was issued in Kirtland, Ohio, from 1834 to 1837, followed by the *Elders Journal*, 1837–38. In Nauvoo, Illinois, the church published *Times and Seasons* from 1839 to 1846. Meanwhile a British publication, *Latter-day Saints' Millennial Star*, was issued in Liverpool beginning in 1840 and continued without interruption until 1970.

After removal to the Great Basin the church initiated in 1850 the *Deseret News*, first newspaper west of the Mississippi. A weekly supplement, the *Church News*, is distributed each Saturday evening and is also mailed to subscribers in many parts of the world.

Auxiliary organizations have published materials in periodical form, beginning in 1866 with a magazine for the Sunday schools called the *Juvenile Instructor*, changed in 1930 to the *Instructor*. A group of Young Men's Mutual Improvement Association officers commenced publication of the *Contributor* in 1879, and it continued to 1896. Susa Young Gates began publishing the *Young Woman's Journal* in 1889, and it continued to 1929. Meanwhile the Young Men's MIA started publication of the *Improvement Era* in 1897, and it continued until 1929, when the *Young Woman's Journal* was merged with it under the same name, *Improvement Era*, which then represented both the young men's and young women's associations. The Primary Association inaugurated the *Children's Friend* in 1902. Women of the church, as noted in Chapter 12, initiated the *Woman's Exponent* in 1872. By the time it was replaced by the *Relief Society Magazine* in 1915, it had long since become the quasi-official organ of that organization.

In 1971 the church made a decision to drop all existing magazines and publish only four: one for the children, the *Friend* (a replacement for the *Children's Friend*); another for young people, the *New Era* (a replacement for the youth section of the *Improvement Era*); the third for adults, the *Ensign*, a replacement for the adult section of the *Improvement Era*; and the fourth an international magazine (with a different name for each language) for persons of all ages in seventeen different languages. These official publications stopped running advertisements in their pages. Since subscription prices are comparable to other magazines of similar quality that contain advertising, the periodicals are liberally subsidized.

The Deseret News Printing and Publishing Company, wholly owned by the Corporation of the President, publishes Salt Lake City's afternoon newspaper, the *Deseret News*, with a circulation of around one hundred thousand, and operates a commercial printing plant. For many years the *Deseret News* operated a paper mill in the Salt Lake Valley and later acquired an interest in a paper mill in Oregon. The latter was eventually transferred to the Times-Mirror Corporation of Los Angeles in return for a block of stock in that company, which publishes the *Los Angeles Times* and other newspapers. As the costs of paper and printing continued to mount after World War II, the *Deseret News* entered into a struggle for circulation and advertising with its two competitors in Salt Lake City, the morning *Tribune* and the evening *Telegram*. In 1952 the church purchased the *Telegram*, giving the *News* a clear field in the afternoon. Two years later an arrangement for trimming expenses and cooperation was worked out between the *News* and the *Tribune* in which the Newspaper Agency Corporation, owned by both, was formed to handle the printing, advertising, and circulating for both papers.[16]

Closely related to the *Deseret News* is a church publishing and retail outlet, the Deseret Book Company, which came into existence in 1866 when George Q. Cannon began publication of the *Juvenile Instructor* and established, at the same time, George Q. Cannon & Sons Company to publish and sell books, pamphlets, and instructional materials that would be helpful in the Sunday school program. With the death of Cannon in 1901, the church purchased the establishment and operated it under the name Deseret News Bookstore. In 1909 the Deseret Sunday School Union of the church decided, once again, to institute its own bookstore at an adjacent location. Deseret Book Company was formed in 1919 with the merger of the Deseret News and Sunday School bookstores.[17] Operating eight stores in Latter-day Saint centers in Utah and southern California, and with marketing outlets in many parts of the world, Deseret Book, a wholly owned subsidiary of Deseret Management, is one of the largest bookstores in the West. The company publishes about thirty books a year, and its annual sales of sixteen million dollars in 1977 included a wide variety of volumes and genealogical supplies. Until the establishment of the Church Distribution Center in the 1960s, Deseret Book was the principal agency for the publication and distribution of church literature and materials sold to church members and organizations. Closely related to Deseret Book is Deseret Press, with 1977 sales of twelve million dollars, which prints more than fifteen million copies of magazines, paperback books, and hardback books a year. A similar publishing and distributing house is Deseret Enterprises Ltd., located in a London suburb, which publishes and handles church books and supplies for Great Britain, South Africa, Australia, and New Zealand.

As the expansion of media to create a "global village" of instant communication has changed the ways information is conveyed, church leaders have taken advantage of the new technology. In 1922, after experimental transmission demonstrated a listening radius from Salt Lake City of a thousand miles, the *Deseret News* established a radio station, later to be known as KSL, which broadcasted the general conferences of the church, instituted a regular Sunday evening program of music and sermon, and in 1925 began the Tabernacle Choir broadcasts, which since 1929 have been a weekly network feature of CBS and is the longest-running program in broadcast history. The church transferred ownership of KSL to the Radio Service Corporation in 1929 and in recent years to Bonneville International.

Through a subsidiary corporation, Bonneville International, the church owns thirteen commercial radio and television stations. These include KSL-AM and KSL-TV in Salt Lake City; WRFM in New York; KBIG and KBRT-AM in Los Angeles; KIRO-AM and KIRO-TV and KSEA-FM in

Seattle; WCLR in Chicago; KMBZ-AM and KMBR-FM in Kansas City; KAFM in Dallas; and KOIT-FM in San Francisco. In addition to the holdings of Bonneville International, the church owns three noncommercial educational stations. KBYU-TV and KBYU-FM are operated by Brigham Young University, and KRIC-FM by Ricks College.[18] A subsidiary of Bonneville International, BEI Productions Inc., with headquarters in Los Angeles, evaluates, creates, and produces commercial entertainment films, television specials or packages, and other productions. Another subsidiary, Bonneville Productions, produces commercials and public service announcements.

The Public Communications Department, which is involved in Mormon broadcasting activities, is an international network, with 1,200 stake and mission public communications directors and coordinators. Charged with spotlighting the church—its people, programs, and beliefs—before the eyes of the world via the news media, motion pictures, and television and radio programming, the department designs and produces displays for the thirty or more Latter-day Saint visitors' centers, supports the production of church pageants and dramas, and sponsors a variety of television family programs.

Whether the church's system of communications—book publishing, periodicals, radio, television—is vast and powerful or moderate and reasonable depends on one's point of view and the basis of comparison. In a sense the controlled printed matter is minuscule compared with the overall quantity of publications in the world each year. Broadcast outlets are gauged to serve the interest of a broad, heterogeneous listening audience. The church has made vigorous efforts to expand its use of the media in order to communicate effectively with its own members and, where possible, to add important positive stimuli for a sound, stable society.

After World War II the church established what came to be known as the Latter-day Saint Church Hospital System.[19] By the 1960s there were seventeen such hospitals in Utah, Idaho, and Wyoming, fourteen of which were owned by the church. By 1974 the hospitals had a capacity of more than sixteen hundred beds, and some four hundred medical students regularly underwent training in them.

The emphasis after World War II was on expansion and improved service and efficiency, and gradually a cooperative hospital system was evolved. Each hospital was separately incorporated and was managed by local church and civic leaders. The chairman of the board in each instance was a member of the Presiding Bishopric of the church, with trained hospital administrators employed to manage them. Clarence E. Wonnacott, executive director of the entire system in the 1960s and early 1970s, worked with the Presiding Bishopric in planning, setting standards, coordinating personnel, and generally keeping all church hospitals moving forward. The church matched the funds of local congregations in financing the original structures, but each hospital was expected to be self-sufficient as far as operating costs were concerned. The church absorbed the cost of expansion but made some use of federal grants under the Hill-Burton Act.

In the fall of 1974 the First Presidency announced that the church was divesting itself of the hospitals it had been operating for so many years. The money could more wisely be spent, it was declared, on the health needs of members around the world rather than in a few intermountain states. The hospitals were turned over to a nonchurch, nonprofit corporation, Intermountain Health Care, Inc. At the same time health services in Third World areas, or where there was great need, were expanded, as additional health service missionaries were called to augment the 120 already serving on Indian reservations in the United States and among members in twenty foreign countries.

The Welfare Services program of the church is a natural outgrowth of the Mormon past. The economies of Utah and bordering states were hard hit during the Great Depression. Income dropped to less than half that of the 1920s. Agriculture- and mining-related industries were forced to reduce their working forces drastically, and many went bankrupt. Government services, such as education and public works construction, faced reduced revenues from the agriculture, mining, and related sectors, which paid the bulk of the region's taxes. Private production fell off precipitously; bank runs and failures were common. The rate of unemployment by 1932 exceeded the 25 percent of the work force unemployed nationally.

The responsibility for alleviating the suffering and hopelessness produced by the depression fell first upon local and state governments and charitable institutions. Mormon church units assisted with relief programs as early as 1931. Members were asked to report vacant lots that might hold gardens to their bishops, who would then distribute the land among needy families. Boy Scout troops and Relief Societies collected clothing and food supplies and took them to central receiving storehouses of local government and church authorities. The church also assisted needy people with fast offerings and tithing funds. But the situation became steadily worse through 1933.[20]

Late in the term of Herbert Hoover the first federal relief aid came to the region. During Franklin Roosevelt's presidency a succession of depression agencies provided relief and employment—the Civilian Conservation Corps, Federal Emergency Relief Administration, Civil Works Administration, and other agencies set up by the states with federal aid. Nevertheless, Mormons were not wholly satisfied with the government programs. Not only were these programs sometimes inadequate and late in coming, but Mormons felt a religious obligation to care for their own, reduce dependence on outside aid, and see that those capable of working had remunerative employment.

In 1933 the First Presidency ordered a survey of the economic status of church members and cautioned the Relief Society to expect "a considerable burden." Exhorting local officials to use existing ward and stake organizations to provide relief, leaders warned members against becoming dependent on "the dole"—any money given without requirement that the recipient work.[21]

Especially successful in providing relief assistance was the Pioneer Stake of Salt Lake City, more than half of whose men were unemployed in 1932. The stake presidency found employment for members through contacts with the industries and businesses. When that source was exhausted, the stake received permission to keep its tithing revenues rather than send them in to central church offices. A farm was managed by the stake, which also arranged to exchange stake labor for food grown on local farms. The stake purchased warehouses and a canning factory, shipping produce not needed by stake residents to markets where cash was available. Using cash and canned goods, the stake welfare project then expanded to include the purchase and renovation of unsalable clothing produced at the Logan Knitting Mills in northern Utah. By 1935 the Pioneer Stake project was almost self-sustaining and had become a pattern for the Church Welfare Plan initiated that same year.[22]

Ambivalence about the precise purpose of the Mormon effort existed from the beginning. Some saw it as a supplement to government projects. Need for such an activity became especially critical in 1935, when the Roosevelt administration announced its intention of ending direct federal relief and shifting it to state and local governments. The emphasis of the federal government, Roosevelt said, was hereafter to be given to work relief. The direct dole, he declared, was contributing to "spiritual and moral disintegration."[23] Agreeing with this philosophy, J. Reuben Clark, Jr., member of the church's First Presidency and an international lawyer and diplomat, added that "no man is politically free who depends upon the state for his sustenance."[24] At the same time the Mormon leadership was aware that the Utah and Idaho state governments were in no condition to bear additional burdens. Viewing the imminent change, the *Deseret News* commented, "Where preparation is being made to meet this problem there will be but little difficulty. But where no preparation has been made, suffering, difficulties, and bloodshed are not remote possibilities."[25] "Get off relief just as soon as you can," admonished Apostle Melvin J. Ballard. "If you don't you will be thrown off and it will be a sorry day when that time comes."[26]

The need of church members for a work relief program was real. A September 1935 survey indicated that 88,460 members, representing 17.9 percent of the total membership, were receiving some sort of relief—about 16.3 percent were dependent on public sources, while 1.6 percent obtained church assistance. Some 13,455, or 15 percent of those receiving relief, were unemployed, while the others were working on government-sponsored programs. The report also stated that between 11,500 and 16,500 members "did not need such assistance."[27]

In the April 1936 general conference a new Church Security Program, as it was then officially called, was approved. The program was designed to assist church members who were idle by providing employment in church-operated enterprises. The resulting products would assist them and other poverty-stricken church members. A chain of storehouses was to be built from which bishops or authorized members could make withdrawals to fill the needs of the poor. Three already existing groups—ward bishoprics, male priesthood quorums, and the female Relief Societies—were directed to determine need, establish enterprises, manage them, and distribute products to the poor. The rank and file of church membership would donate both labor and goods. A proportion of tithes and all the fast offerings collected in each area would be apportioned to the program. The size of the individual's family and the availability of other resources, rather than the strict value of labor, would determine the compensation returned for work under the system. "One gives what one has and gets what one needs," was the official description of the plan.[28] President Heber J. Grant summed up the multiplicity of goals of the program as follows:

> Our primary purpose in organizing the Church Security Plan was to set up a system under which the curse of idleness would be done away with, the evils of a dole abolished, and independence, industry, thrift and self-respect be once more established amongst our people. The aim of the Church is to help the people to help themselves. Work is to be re-enthroned as the ruling principle of the lives of our Church membership.[29]

Any church member who had accepted, or would otherwise be forced to accept, direct relief was to be aided by the Church Security Program. The aged who were not covered by Old Age and Survivor's Insurance, enacted in 1935, and who had no other means of support, would contribute funds and labor to the church's welfare system in their productive years and draw it out after retirement or when they became incapacitated. The church also instigated resettlement in order to make better use of productive land. Aid was given in obtaining implements and seed. Another feature was vocational education for unskilled workers.[30] Because the plan supplemented federal programs in a region where federal agencies were not as effective as in more heavily populated areas, Franklin Roosevelt gave his personal commendation of the Mormon Church Security Program and promised "full cooperation" on the part of the federal government. The president told church officials that he hoped Mormon efforts might inspire other groups to do something of a similar nature.[31]

The plan (the name was changed to Church Welfare Plan to avoid confusion with the national Social Security Act) brought the church back into some of the temporal roles it had abandoned at the turn of the century. It represented a fusion of modern "American" business practices with the distinctive Mormon heritage of cooperation and shared burdens.

An experience growing out of national antipathies illustrates the activities and spirit of Church Welfare. At the end of World War II the president of the Netherlands Mission, Cornelius Zappey, found the Dutch Latter-day Saints bitter—about war tragedies, about the German Nazis, about the Dutch who had collaborated. American relief, including many tons of Church Welfare goods, was helping alleviate postwar hunger, but Zappey felt the need for a "Love One Another" campaign and so initiated a project under which Dutch branches of the church would obtain government seed potatoes and plant them in backyards, on medians between highways, and on vacant lots. During the summer of 1947 Dutch Mormons spent hundreds of hours weeding, watering, and guarding the new plants. The potatoes were destined originally for the destitute Saints in Holland, but as harvest approached, Zappey decided to test the success of his "love" campaign by asking the Dutch Saints to contribute them instead to the Germans, even though many of the Dutch were still on food rations. The Dutch members accepted the change, and when they learned that government regulations forbade the export of food, they initiated a fast and prayer. Soon a coincidental meeting with American food officials opened the necessary government doors, and permission was granted for export of some of these potatoes. One November midnight ten rented trucks rolled into Germany carrying seventy tons of precious potatoes. They were distributed, at the rate of about one hundred pounds per family, to Latter-day Saint members in Hamburg, Celle, Berlin, and elsewhere.

The next spring, in 1948, Berlin Latter-day Saints planted two tons of the Dutch potatoes and harvested some sixteen tons. That year the Dutch, repeating their project, sent an additional ninety tons of potatoes to Germany. Dutch donations also purchased eighty barrels of newly harvested herring, which were sent with the potatoes to provide oils badly needed in the German diet. In a similar manner Swedish members aided the Finns, the Swiss the Austrians, and the Belgians the Germans. The magnitude of the Dutch potato project, especially in light of the Nazi starvation policy in Holland three years earlier, made this one of the finest chapters in the history of Church Welfare.[32]

The Church Welfare Plan continues functioning as the charitable arm of the church. In an effort to "spiritualize the temporal," it calls upon church members to share their time and money by voluntarily contributing the price of two meals monthly, by hauling hay, by sewing, and by canning fruit or vegetables. It helps the handicapped, widows, the aged and infirm, and those who are passing through temporary crises of illness, unemployment, or financial overextension. It also organizes the church's efforts to assist members and nonmembers at times of natural disaster or other crises.

After World War II the Church Welfare Plan expanded, under the name of the Cooperative Security Corporation (a nonprofit Utah corporation), into several major investments. (Since 1935 these had been held in the name of the Corporation of the Presiding Bishop.) The Deseret Mills and Elevators of Kaysville, Utah, was acquired in 1944 to mill flour, cereal, and feed for livestock on welfare projects. These elevators, remodeled in the 1970s into a modern feed mill, have a capacity of several hundred thousand bushels of grain. The Deseret Coal Mine of Emery County, Utah, acquired in 1947, and since divested under a special purchase agreement, produced up to 150,000 tons of coal per year to supply chapels, church institutions, and welfare recipients in Utah and Idaho. The Deseret Transportation System operates a fleet of seventeen tractors, twenty-four trailer trucks, and two service garages in Utah. On Welfare Square in Salt Lake City are a number of enterprises including a meat market, grocery store, clothing department, cannery, modern milk-processing plant, and an elevator that holds two hundred freight boxcars of grain to serve the needy. The nonprofit Deseret Industries organization, a branch of Welfare, operates thirteen processing plants in Utah, Idaho, California, and elsewhere that process or recondition, repair, sell, and distribute clothing, shoes, furniture, toys, and other commodities. There is also in Salt Lake City a Deseret Industries Rag Rug Factory, and facilities for making mattresses and box springs. These are not commercially oriented enterprises; they are designed to funnel goods to the needy, provide gainful employment for some 1,400 handicapped persons, and salvage many consumer goods that would otherwise be wasted.

In addition to these general welfare projects, approximately 650 separate enterprises are owned and operated by various wards and stakes throughout the United States and Canada. (Since 1974 welfare farms and factories have also been launched in Australia, England, Korea, and islands in the Pacific.) They include peanut farms and peanut butter factories in Texas, cotton farms and grapefruit orchards and canneries in Arizona, orange groves and canneries in southern California, apple orchards in Washington, pineapple and sugar plantations in Hawaii, dairies and a cheese plant in northern Utah, salmon canneries in Portland, Oregon, a gelatin factory in Kansas City, Missouri, a soap factory in Salt Lake City, and cattle ranches in Wyoming. There are some thirty-two fruit and vegetable canneries, and approximately six hundred separate farming projects producing a wide variety of crops: sugar beets, hay, beans, peas, soybeans, and dairy, poultry, sheep, and hog farms. The total value of all welfare properties has never been published, but probably would aggregate in the tens of millions. Welfare projects produce 90 percent of all welfare needs, including such items as soap, shoe polish, bowl cleaner, clothing, blankets, dairy products, and canned fruit and vegetables. These are distributed to those in need through some seventy-eight bishops' storehouses located at Latter-day Saint centers throughout the nation. In this way, some 110,000 persons are assisted with approximately ten million dollars in cash and welfare products each year. Total church welfare expenditures in 1977 were forty million dollars.[33]

Other aspects of the welfare program include the operation of employment centers, vocational training and career preparation, training in home financial management, family home improvement, and a food storage program in which each family is encouraged to store a one-year supply of foodstuffs and water in order to be prepared for natural or human disaster. Each family and individual is encouraged to strive to become self-reliant through family preparedness.

A contemporary example of welfare in action is its role in providing emergency assistance to approximately forty thousand persons, over 90 percent of them Latter-day Saints, who were affected by the collapse of the Teton Dam in Idaho's Upper Snake River Valley on June 5, 1976. This break released some 250,000 acre-feet of water trapped in a reservoir seventeen miles long. In the course of an eighty-five-mile rampage, a torrent of water spread out up to eleven miles in some places and engulfed a number of communities and farms. Although only six people were drowned, the flood wreaked havoc on all kinds of buildings and machinery, killed fifteen thousand head of livestock, and damaged or destroyed approximately 250 business structures, 3,500 farm buildings, and about 4,000 homes. The total property loss has been estimated at about two billion dollars.

Fortunately, Ricks College, on a hill in the center of the disaster area, was vacant of students for the summer. The college provided emergency living and sleeping facilities for several thousand families, served up to thirty thousand meals per day in its cafeteria, in addition to sack lunches for many thousands more. The college administration also operated a baby-care center.

Less than three hours after reports from the flood area reached Salt Lake City, trucks were dispatched from Welfare Square to supplement supplies of commodities already available in nearby bishops' storehouses. The church organizational structure was employed in subsequent weeks to account for missing persons, provide temporary food and housing for the more than 15,000 homeless, and, after the waters receded, to clean and repair hundreds of damaged homes. During the summer of 1976 crews of Latter-day Saint volunteers from areas in other parts of Idaho and from Utah, Wyoming, Montana, and California were bussed or flown in regularly to assist in the massive reconstruction effort. For several weeks an average of 2,000 volunteers rode daily from Cache Valley, Utah-Idaho (two hundred miles away); Star Valley, Wyoming; Davis and Salt Lake counties in Utah; and elsewhere to help in the cleaning and rebuilding process. Church leaders from the flooded areas, requesting electricians, were supplied with more than 400 trained men in one week, including 263 of them from the Kaysville, Utah, Stake, three hundred miles away. Federal officials were delighted with the manner in which the Mormons organized and saw to the completion of the rehabilitation of the communities affected by the disaster. More than one million man-hours of labor were contributed by those outside the flood area in the two months after the dam broke.[34]

At a time when natural disasters are normally followed by heavy federal assistance, the Mormons were responding in ways that demonstrated their complex inheritance. They did not reject government help. It is inaccurate to praise them for "taking care of their own," if that phrase is meant to imply total self-sufficiency. Both during the Great Depression and the Teton Dam catastrophe most Mormons looked upon themselves as taxpayers entitled to the benefits of relief assistance that were available to others. Yet there was a difference. The Mormons drew also from a tradition of self-help, sturdy self-reliance, and a desire to do as much as lay within their power to meet their own needs. And the tradition of sharing and cooperation that stretched all the way back to the beginnings of Mormonism could still manifest itself in group projects and charitable work.

For long years the church has operated ranches in several states and in addition furnished capital and encouragement for the construction of canals and irrigation projects. Since World War II, however, the church has acquired a number of ranchlands on which it has pioneered in the adoption of new practices. Under the Deseret name the church now operates two large ranches in southern Alberta; a large ranching complex in Florida; a ten thousand-acre hay and grain farm near Pecos, Texas; a five thousand-acre farm producing walnuts and almonds near Sacramento, California; and an eleven thousand-acre general agricultural ranch at Elberta, Utah.

The largest of these ventures is in Florida. In 1950 the church acquired for ranching and development purposes approximately 220,000 acres of swampland not far from Cape Canaveral (and Disney World). Situated in one of the least productive and least populated areas of Florida, this vast holding offered a challenge. Drainage ditches were constructed to handle the excess water of the rainy season, and irrigation canals were dug to carry water to the land in the dry season. Timber was cleared, roads were built, and hundreds of artesian wells were installed. Running over thirty thousand head of young cattle on land once described as worthless for the cattle business, these twentieth-century pioneers converted a Florida wasteland into a center of cattle feeding, as though making deserts—or swamps—"blossom as the rose" were part of the inherited makeup of the Mormons. Additional ranches and properties were subsequently acquired by the church, and the program of development continues. In 1977 some one hundred thousand head of Aberdeen Angus and Hereford cattle were being raised on 360,000 acres of church land in Florida.[35]

The expansionary and development activities of the wholly owned subsidiary of Deseret Management Corporation, Zion's Securities Corporation, began in 1922. This commercial real estate arm of the church pays property and corporation taxes on its net income. Worth $2.5 million at the time of its incorporation, it has grown steadily as its profits and gains have been reinvested. Until recently this was primarily an agency for the acquisition and management of real estate and the collection of rent. As an administrator said, "Once, Brigham Young had assigned 40 acres in the center of the city [Salt Lake City] to be held by the Church. Somehow, the 40 acres was whittled down to 10 acres. Now, Zion is trying to recover that 40 acres."[36]

The activities of Zion's Securities since World War II have been ambitious. Holding nearly all the real estate on the four sides facing Temple Square and Administration Square, and many other blocks and lots in Salt Lake City and County (an estimated sixty-five acres of land), it has cooperated with owners of neighboring parcels in developing modern business and shopping areas in downtown Salt Lake City. In the past few years Zion's Securities has built the twenty-story Beneficial Life Office tower, the eight-story J. C. Penney Building, the eighteen-story Kennecott Building, a modern Prudential Federal Savings Branch, a four-hundred-car parking terrace for the Temple Square Hotel, a two-hundred-car underground garage for Hotel Utah, the Hotel Utah Motor Lodge, the ZCMI Center or Mall, a one-thousand-car parking terrace on Regent Street, and a nine-hundred-car parking garage near Deseret Gymnasium. An estimated $150 million has been expended in the past twenty years by the church, local government, and businesses in "sprucing up" the downtown area of Salt Lake City.[37]

Zion's Securities has continued to acquire new properties that will be useful to the church in its building projects. On a site acquired adjacent to Temple Square a large new auditorium with thirty-five thousand seats was once planned for church and community use. Civic dialogue and deliberation resulted in the donation of this land to Salt Lake City and County to construct the Salt Palace and Performing Arts Center. The company acquired a thousand acres on Twenty-first South and Redwood Road, Salt Lake City, after World War II and developed plans for the construction of the Latter-day Saint Distribution Center and Beehive Clothing Mills. Zion's Securities owns the ZCMI building and lot in Salt Lake City, which was recently enlarged into the largest department store in the Mountain West. It also assisted in the location of a new ten-million-dollar federal office building, on First South and State, close to Temple Square. Further afield, the company also owns properties in Hawaii, Los Angeles, Wyoming, Florida, and in Price and Cedar City, Utah.

In January 1977 the First Presidency announced the formation of a sister corporation, Beneficial Development Corporation, to manage all development work formerly done by Zion's Securities and the church. Beneficial also serves as a vehicle for church mortage-loan funds. It operates through private developers throughout the West and concentrates on the acquisition and creation of industrial parks.

During the period of "creative adjustment" that followed the Supreme Court decision upholding the Edmunds-Tucker Act of 1887, the church sold the bulk of its business interests. After that it followed a conservative policy of investment and development until the 1930s. Among its income-earning properties are:[38]

Zion's Cooperative Mercantile Institution (ZCMI). This wholesale and retail firm was organized in 1868. The church (through Deseret Management) owns a controlling 30 percent of the stock (the remainder lies in private hands). With sixty million dollars in sales in 1976, the firm operates six ZCMI department stores in Utah.

Deseret National Bank, Zion's Savings Bank & Trust Company, Utah First National Bank, and Utah Savings & Trust. Deseret National began in 1871 as the Bank of Deseret and the following year obtained a charter as Deseret National. It was the first Mormon bank in the Great Basin and the leading bank in the territory until well into the twentieth century. The bank, which assisted the church and its members during sixty years of development, experienced difficulty during the depression of the 1930s and was eventually acquired by First Security Corporation—a bank holding company that operates a large number of banks in Utah and Idaho. Zion's Savings Bank & Trust Company was established in 1873 to take over the savings department of Deseret National. As with Deseret National, the original officers and directors were largely church officials, and the church owned roughly one-half of the stock. In 1957 Zion's Savings was merged with Utah First National and Utah Savings & Trust to form Zion's First National Bank, with the church continuing at that time to own approximately 50 percent of the enterprise (assets of $140 million). Both of the other banks in the combine were regarded as Mormon banks, and there was substantial church investment in each. With the stated intention of serving the intermountain community far more widely than its predecessors had done, the merged concern planned a series of branch banks. As Zion's First National moved along this road, however, church officials apparently came to feel that this new impetus would involve the church in a highly competitive commercial activity for which its leaders had a "personal distaste." Having received a favorable offer, the church sold its controlling interest in Zion's First National to a syndicate of persons friendly to the church.[39]

Utah-Idaho Sugar Company. Beet sugar manufacturing in the Mountain West was launched in 1889 with the formation of the church-directed Utah Sugar Company. The success of this company, and the profitability that followed the enactment of the Dingley Tariff of 1897, induced the company to erect factories at several locations in Utah and Idaho; in 1907 these were united under the Utah-Idaho Sugar Company, a company in which the church held most of the stock. In 1907 half of the stock was sold to Henry Havemeyer and the American Sugar Refining Company. In 1914, when the Antitrust Division of the Justice Department required American Sugar Refining to divest itself of its beet sugar interests, the church and a syndicate of Mormon businessmen acquired a controlling stock interest in Utah-Idaho and also Amalgamated Sugar Company. (The latter had been started by David Eccles and associates with the construction of a factory in Ogden, Utah, in 1898, followed by the construction of other factories in Utah, Idaho, and Oregon.) The church sold its interest in the Amalgamated Sugar Company to Marriner Eccles, Marriner Browning, and associates in 1930. Utah-Idaho (renamed U & I Company) had assets of about fifty million dollars in 1977. The church owns about half of the common stock and four-fifths of the preferred stock. Annual sales exceed two hundred million dollars.

Beneficial Life Insurance Company and Utah Home Fire Insurance Company. Wholly owned today by the Corporation of the President, Beneficial Life was first organized in 1905 with other initiators to provide low-cost and "safe" life insurance for Latter-day Saints and others. The company has written more than two billion dollars in policies. In recent years, although much smaller, it has developed an investment program that enables it to compete with Prudential, Metropolitan, and other national companies. Closely related to Beneficial is Utah Home Fire Insurance Company, organized by Heber J. Grant and others in 1886, which is Utah's largest domiciled casualty company. Grant, who had a genius for business, assisted in founding many successful enterprises in Mormon country.

Utah Hotel Corporation. This company was organized by the church and a group of Salt Lake City (non-Mormon) businessmen in 1909 for the purpose of constructing and operating a hotel near Temple Square. Opened in 1911, Hotel Utah was expected to provide "a wholesome atmosphere" for visitors to church headquarters. The company, owned by Deseret Management, operates the 530-room Hotel Utah, 189-room Temple Square Hotel, and 156-room Utah Motor Lodge—all of which adjoin Temple Square in Salt Lake City.

Beehive Clothing Mills. This enterprise has plants in Utah, England, and

Mexico, and is the exclusive manufacturer of articles of temple clothing for Latter-day Saints. The central Salt Lake City facility is a reconverted Remington Arms ammunition plant. The company is a wholly owned subsidiary of the Corporation of the President.[40]

In recent years the managements of these "church companies" have been enhanced by the addition of well-trained young Latter-day Saints who have graduated from such business schools as Harvard and Stanford.[41] Not surprisingly they have recognized the need for computer work and brought about the organization of Management Systems Corporation, which provides computing service and systems development for departments of the church, for church-owned companies, and for some commercial firms. The profits that all of these taxable enterprises yield have helped to provide a regular flow of funds for education, temples, and other church works.

While the church has only intermittently published data on revenues and expenditures, a study of its economic activities suggests that in the first half of the twentieth century it accumulated a considerable reserve that was invested conservatively in real estate, bonds, and savings deposits. Under the direction of David O. McKay, who became president in 1951, its current revenues and a substantial proportion of its accumulated reserve were expended on long-needed church facilities.

Despite its vigorous promotion of economic development, the church has never in this century approached economic control of the intermountain region. For example, it has no substantial block of stock in many of the area's most powerful enterprises—Union Pacific Railroad, First Security Corporation, Western Airlines, Utah Power & Light Company, Kennecott Copper Corporation, United States Steel Corporation, Consolidated Freightways, Mountain States Telephone and Telegraph Company, and others. Until recently the church had no portfolio of securities. It has historically invested funds but primarily as an owner-participant, calculated to enhance the welfare of its members.

In 1971 James Gollin published a study of Roman Catholic wealth in America.[42] He found that the combined assets of the Roman Catholic church were slightly less than those of American Telephone and Telegraph. But for those who saw Catholicism as a power-hungry tycoon (those critics whom *Time* labeled "the church-as-Fort Knox school"), Gollin pointed out that most Catholic assets were non–income producing and that the liquid assets were timidly invested. Despite the rumors of limitless wealth that have been stimulated by secrecy, the Catholic church is often unable to find funds for buildings or the beleaguered parochial schools. There are instructive comparisons here. Mormonism's wealth, too, is often thought of as enormous, and this impression may be strengthened by the policy of not releasing precise figures. Certainly substantially less than those of AT&T, Mormon resources are largely tied up in schools, churches, and programs that are a drain rather than assets that produce further income. One gathers that its liquid assets are being managed with responsibility and efficiency; there is a careful annual audit by a professional accounting firm, and a brief report is made at annual conferences. While the church now has some income from its investments, the basic cash flow still comes from its members in the form of tithes and other donations. The church is able to carry out its extensive program only because its members contribute regularly and liberally to its treasury.

15

{ "In the World"— }
Institutional Responses

We have great works to perform on this earth, and I suppose the whole program of the Church could be put in one of three categories: missionary work, temple work, and keeping Church members active and faithful. . . . The Prophet Joseph Smith said: "Brethren, shall we not go on in so great a cause? Go forward and not backward. Courage, brethren: and on, on to the victory! Let your hearts rejoice, and be exceedingly glad."

—Spencer W. Kimball (1977)

Arnold Toynbee saw the concept of "challenge and response" as one of the keys to understanding the rise and fall of civilizations. From its beginning the Mormon movement faced challenges to its survival—persecution, internal dissension and apostasy, repeated moves, pressure from outside economic and political forces, including the actions of federal and state governments. The church rode through the storms, maintained its separate identity and sense of mission, and entered the twentieth century stronger than ever before.

The challenges of the twentieth century were in part those confronted by other religious groups. On the intellectual level there were disturbing currents and crosscurrents. The revival of the "God is Dead" notion in the 1960s represented only the most dramatic aspect of skepticism and secularism that to some seemed to set the mood of the century. At the same time there were signs of vitality in the traditional Christian faiths—revivals, theological ferment, Vatican II, the ecumenical movement—and eventually a proliferation of alternative religions such as Zen Buddhism, transcendental meditation, Krishna Consciousness, and the Reunification Church of Sun Myung Moon.

How would young Mormons respond? Latter-day Saints in greater numbers than before were moving through the halls of institutions of higher learning. The rise of mass media, including radio and television, had long since made it impossible to seal them off from the larger world. (Such insulation had never been possible, but never had the bombardment with news, views, and values of the larger society been so relentless, so penetrating.) Socially there were challenges that some might regard as an even more serious threat: the "counterculture" of the 1960s and 1970s, drugs, pornographic movies, the whole shift to undisciplined life-styles.

It is not hard to find individual Mormons who are indifferent to their religion; there are dropouts and those who have gone into a position of infrequent involvement, and a few whose disillusionment has turned to bitterness, causing them to become active enemies of the church. But to determine the condition of any army it is not enough to interview scattered deserters and stragglers without ascertaining how representative they are—whether there are fresh recruits coming into the ranks—and the overall state of morale and combat readiness. In these terms the Mormon church has had a remarkable record in the generation since World War II. Unlike most American denominations, it has continued to grow in membership, and the level of activity or member involvement has never been so high. Attendance at the sacrament meeting—the week's most important worship service—has risen from a pre–World War II average of approximately 35 percent of total ward membership (including children) to an average of 48 percent in the 1970s. Sunday School attendance (adults as well as children) averages about the same.

In *Why Conservative Churches Are Growing* Dean M. Kelley, a director of the National Council of Churches, contrasted the gradual decline of "mainline" Protestant and Catholic churches in America with a steady growth of conservative churches in the 1960s. Of all churches, he found the Latter-day Saints had shown "the greatest rate of membership growth for any religious body of over a million members in this country"—an increase of 5.6 percent per year. Although he found much that liberal churches could learn from their conservative counterparts, particularly in addressing the questions of meaning in life and death, Kelley predicted that conservative strength would wane as the stream was "fished out" of conservative-oriented persons.[1]

However insightful Kelley's analysis of the past, his predictions about the future have not yet been vindicated, at least insofar as the Latter-day Saints are concerned. In 1977 Mormon missionaries baptized twice as many converts (140,000) as in 1968, and the 1977 membership (3.97 million) reflected a continuing increase at a rate exceeding 5 percent annually.

The following statistical summary gives the distribution of church membership as of December 31, 1977:

Mountain West (Utah, Idaho, Arizona, New Mexico, Montana, Wyoming, Colorado, Nevada)	1,457,357
Pacific Coast States (California, Oregon, Washington, Alaska)	558,062
Remainder of the United States	443,291
Canada	72,926
Total, United States and Canada	2,531,636
Mexico and Central America	244,505
Asia and the South Pacific Islands	229,951
South America	213,463

Great Britain, Scandinavia, and Europe	162,316
Africa	8,148
Total outside the United States and Canada	858,383
Address unknown and in transit	576,000
Total Membership, December 31, 1977	3,966,019

The most significant growth in the past generation, perhaps, has been in the number of members outside the United States. The forceful, internationally oriented leadership of David O. McKay (1951–1970) brought dramatic increases in Mormon proselyting efforts and effectiveness. The 1960s saw the development of missions in Italy, Spain, and South America and another explosive growth in the Polynesian Islands. In Samoa, Tonga, Fiji, and Tahiti, where young American missionaries had earlier worked mainly to assist the few native leaders in basic church organization and where most converts had come from the church schools, effective proselyting techniques and the use of the native missionaries had by the late 1960s produced such a high convert rate that approximately one-fourth of the population in some of these island communities were Mormons. Virtually the entire Mormon ward and stake ecclesiastical church organization, including provision of mission presidents and most of the missionaries, was in local hands. The 1960s saw a comparable development in the Asian countries, Japan, Korea, Hong Kong, Taiwan, the Philippines, and more recently Indonesia.

In the 1970s the most phenomenal success in Mormon proselyting and the development of native leadership occurred in South and Central America, particularly Mexico. After slow growth from a few thousand in the 1950s, Mormon populations tripled in the next decade and quadrupled in the 1970s. Indigenous church members have been called upon to head congregations, schools, and missions. Many young people of these countries have served as missionaries. In Mexico over twenty-eight stakes had been organized by 1977. It may seem to be a paradox that what many in recent times have thought of as a uniquely American church, the major one founded in the United States, should be one of the fastest-growing churches in Third World countries, especially at a low point in American popularity there.

Growth is just one aspect of the dynamics of Mormonism during the twentieth century. Like other people, Mormons have problems. Some of these are simply those of human beings living in the postmodern age; some are modified, reduced, or intensified by Mormonism; and some are even created by the religion. Although there are various helps and supports in the Mormon religion, both in theology and in programs, it would be inaccurate to imply that the Latter-day Saints have somehow been wafted above the stresses and strains of life. Bishops and other church officials who spend much of their time in counseling are acutely aware that "all is not well in Zion." Scholarly study of Mormon values and behavior—in effect a kind of self-examination by Mormon scholars—has made it possible to pinpoint several of the stress areas.[2] The following summary of current research furnishes examples.

The much-discussed "breakdown" of the family in society at large has had its impact within the church. Numbers of children born per family have decreased; age at marriage has risen; many mothers are working outside the home. If in all of these areas the Latter-day Saints have had a better record than the national average, as seems to be indicated by studies, they reflect the same trends with some kind of time lag or suppressor factor. As for divorces, those between parties married in the temples are few compared with national figures; but when all divorces involving Mormons are considered together, there seems to be very little advantage. Clearly divorce is, or has been, on the rise within the church, as elsewhere.

Estimates of the rise of drug use during the 1960s and 1970s were received with alarm by church authorities, who frequently reiterated the Word of Wisdom prohibitions against the use of tobacco and alcohol and, by implication, marijuana, LSD, and other drugs. There are to our knowledge no adequate figures indicating consumption of such products by Mormons. Practicing, church-attending Mormons must certainly be almost totally free of these problems. However, among teen-agers and college-age people the Mormon population is not totally immune. An interesting study by Carl D. Chambers in 1973 revealed that whereas Mormons were "under-represented" in the use of barbiturates, marijuana, and hashish—meaning that those who reported using these included a smaller percentage of Mormons than there were Mormons in the population at large—the Saints were "over-represented" in the use of tranquilizers and pep pills, among others.[3] Available figures require careful interpretation and perhaps qualification, but, as sociologist Glenn M. Vernon remarks, "it is clear that Utah Mormons are not unfamiliar with the use of both legal and illegal drugs."[4] In the case of alcoholic consumption, there is the interesting paradox that while most Mormons imbibe not at all, among those few who do drink there is evidently an unduly high proportion of alcoholics.

A difficult thing to measure is the hypertension and depression that are such common experiences of modern adults. Mormons have some reassuring teachings and institutional supports that should help them to achieve better mental health. But they are not sealed off from modern conditions, and the fact that their religion makes high demands with consequent feelings of discouragement or depression accompanying failure might well increase their susceptibility to mental anxiety. Different subpopulations—missionaries, adult singles, the aged—have different problems that must be isolated. Two indices—the consumption of tranquilizers and antidepressants and the incidence of suicide—lead Mormon investigators to conclude that the psychological problems of church members are not substantially different from those of the population at large.

A group in the church that experiences special frustrations is the adult singles, including those not yet married, the divorced of both sexes, and widows and widowers. With many church programs and activities designed for family participation, it can be unrewarding, to say the least, for those who live alone. With the increased incidence of divorce and the tendency of young Mormons, paralleling the society at large, to postpone marriage, adult singles form an increasingly significant group.

Studies of dropouts from the church are too few to permit analysis of the incidence and impact of such disaffection on Mormons. On the basis of general familiarity with several different wards we have lived in and from conversations with those familiar with foreign missions, we can say that the inflow of new members, both children born in the church and converts, is countered to some extent by an outflow of those who lapse into infrequent involvement or complete inactivity. Preliminary studies by sociologists Armand Mauss and Julie Wolfe suggest that the causes for disaffection are primarily social—some kind of disappointment with the group experience—rather than theological.[5] With respect to the church's most important service, the weekly sacrament meeting, approximately 20 to 30 percent of those in the middle-of-the-road American wards do not attend at all, or perhaps only once a year, and thus may be considered "disaffected." In congregations farther from the center, although there are exceptions, the disaffected nonattenders may constitute as much as 50 percent.

As indicated in the foregoing, most disaffection seems to arise from social dissatisfaction. Nevertheless, some Mormons, especially those new in the church or those of high school and college age, encounter what seem to be intellectual challenges to their faith. Whether this occurs more often with Mormons than with others we do not know, although there are specific truth claims and value positions—the Book of Mormon, other modern scriptures, opposition to birth control—that sometimes raise problems in the minds of young Mormons. Contributing to a sense of malaise in this area are the publications of some anti-Mormon writers and publishers.

These are not the only problems confronting Mormons in the last quarter of the twentieth century. Nor are they entirely new or unique, for many of them have parallels in other religious groups. It is the special configuration of them, with different emphases due to the Mormon group life, that is in a sense unique. Just as every religious person experiences certain tensions in applying his or her faith to concrete life situations, the Latter-day Saint undergoes crises of conscience in mediating the conflicting demands on time, heart, and resources. Thus the anguish of a Latter-day Saint woman who has fallen in love with an appropriate man who is not a member of her church. She wishes to have the priesthood bearer in her home, and yet she wants to marry only this man. Or the pain of a man who has been married for many years, is the father of a large family, and has been confronted by a wife he loves who insists on having her "freedom" to choose a life-style incompatible with Mormon standards. Or the distress of a Latter-day Saint parent who discovers that one of his children is about to give up the faith. On a lesser scale, a Mormon national golf champion, who has been taught all his life to keep the sabbath day holy, spends his professional life playing in tournaments that inevitably extend through Sunday. Or a prominent Mormon politician who believes that the use of intoxicating beverages is harmful yet finds himself, as governor of his state, under obligation to serve according to the wishes of his constituents.

Perhaps the most poignant tensions are experienced when professional and personal commitments clash, or seem to clash, with religious commitments. The believer in democratic freedoms who is indignant that church officials sometimes make "high-handed" decisions; the actor who would never take the name of God in vain but who must represent on stage an obscenity-spouting, completely villainous character; the business employee, a strong believer in honesty, who finds himself carrying out a superior's order that requires him to deceive his customers; the novelist who is instructed by her publishers to "introduce a little illicit sex" into a work that she believes is basically positive and heartwarming; or a bishop who must refuse to allow his own child to marry in the temple because of an unworthiness that only he is aware of—such soul struggles are part and parcel of the Mormon experience.

To face up to these problems Mormons have reacted on different levels and with different degrees of success. To appreciate what is being done in the church of the 1970s to enable it more adequately to meet the needs of its members, we shall examine developments in the organizational bureaucracy as well as in the life-style of a composite Mormon family.

To keep pace with the growth in membership and participation, church administration has increased to a size and complexity scarcely predictable at the turn of the century. In 1977 three thousand employees at church headquarters in Salt Lake City staffed twenty-six departments, such as the building department, which supervises construction of chapels and stake centers; translation, which makes church magazines and other literature available in seventeen languages; and welfare services, which provides training, motivation, and resources to help church members achieve "family preparedness."

All departments are responsible, through their managing directors and appropriate committees, to the First Presidency, which directly supervises church planning and correlation. The Quorum of the Twelve oversees all ecclesiastical affairs, including priesthood and auxiliary organizations (Relief Society, MIA, Primary), church education and curriculum, temples, genealogy, and missionary work. The presiding bishopric directs welfare services, translation and distribution, physical facilities, management data, and computerized membership records. As a result of church growth outside of the United States in recent years, particularly in Central and South America and East Asia, the members of the First Quorum of the Seventy have been assigned as full-time area supervisors to direct all church operations in various parts of the world. Within each area, regional representatives serve as line officers, under the direction of area supervisors, to stake presidents, bishops, and regional programs.

In addition to the central office building with its many departments, the church has created distribution centers for the shipping of forms and supplies, an educational network staffed by full- and part-time teachers and administrators, as well as hundreds of employees and consultants in welfare programs, public relations, and the many tax-paying business operations already surveyed in the previous chapter. The development has come gradually but at an accelerated rate after World War II. Joseph Anderson, the secretary to the First Presidency from 1922 to 1972, still remembered at age eighty-six the slower pace when a small staff of three or four people handled correspondence and filing in the presidency's office, when it was common for visitors to "drop in" for a chat with the president of the church, and when one could be personally acquainted with all its leaders and, through attendance at quarterly stake conferences, practically all those on the stake level as well.[6]

It may be helpful to borrow some terminology from the institutional history of medieval and early modern Europe. One of the important trends in twelfth- and thirteenth-century France was the professionalization and bureaucratization of the royal government. The former term describes the employment of full-time administrators to collect taxes, try disputes, and protect the interests of the king. The second term refers to the creation of different departments with special areas of responsibility, a trend that, once set in motion, led to subdivision and splitting off as further specialization proved necessary. In each of these departments or offices a corps of secretaries kept records and filed them away for future reference. Written reports were turned in. This dual process of professionalization and bureaucratization has occurred at different times in human history as different organizations and states went through the transition from an informal, hit-or-miss administration to one more stable.

If this same terminology describes an important side of recent Mormon history, it must be qualified. In the neutral sense (implying no value judgment) of expanding offices and departments, growing specialization, increased reliance on professionals, and a system of reports from local units whose number and complexity can be appreciated only by the clerks responsible for them, the Mormon church has gradually become bureaucratized at the center (with some new regionalization developing as well). Its resources have been mobilized in order to look after church needs with the efficiency characteristic of business organizations. This is an important fact, but to dwell on it without qualification would be seriously to distort the genius of Mormon organization. For at the top, above all departments of personnel, social services, membership records, media, motor pools, and the like, stand the "general authorities," the leaders who govern the church. Especially those considered to be "prophets, seers, and revelators"—the three members of the First Presidency, the Twelve Apostles, and the church patriarch*—are in the position of final authority. If bureaucracy should clash with personal leadership, the latter, in contrast with growing tendencies in government, would win. Actually such tension bears little relationship to actual practice, for the church bureaucracy is seen as an extension of the general authorities' control, not a rival to it; it is a means utilized to meet modern needs.

The fifteen men who stand at the top of the church are specifically the three members of the First Presidency and the Twelve Apostles; these function as two separate quorums or boards, the presidency having executive responsibility for the entire church and the apostles discussing policy matters and supervising directly or indirectly the various administrative departments. At times all fifteen of these leaders meet together, and if there are any differences of opinion, they are not allowed to become public knowledge. What is unusual about these men is their age and the manner of succession. It is in effect a process of cooptation; when vacancies occur, they are filled by the in-group. (As in all such matters the decisions are presented to a general church conference for "sustaining" vote, but this is *pro forma.*) Once selected as an apostle, one is at the bottom of the ladder; each time someone in this body is removed by death, those below move up one notch. Tenure is for life. In time, if one enjoys unusual longevity, the top of the Quorum of Apostles is reached, and it is this person, when the president of the church dies, who succeeds to the presidential office. Normally those who are called as new apostles are in their fifties and sixties; the older apostles are in their seventies, eighties, or even nineties. The president of the church—having survived a trial of survival—is inevitably advanced in years.

On the face of it, the governing councils of the church seem similar to the United States Supreme Court. Would not such a gerontocracy mean that decisions are made by men out of touch with present realities, having absorbed their thought patterns and values not merely one but two generations ago? It seems like a double generation gap. Is it realistic to expect men of such age to have the health and stamina to take on exacting responsibilities?

* An official responsible for giving special blessings to individual church members.

These are fair questions. In practice, however, the Mormon presidency and apostles have functioned remarkably well. Only in rare instances has health deteriorated to such a point that leadership has suffered, and then the others in the council provided the necessary cushion. One major advantage of the system of succession by survival is its orderliness. Struggles for the throne of power are noticeable only by their absence from Mormon history. To devout Mormons, of course, the explanation for their system of church government is simple: It was established by God, who has chosen this means of determining those who on earth will lead his church.

If the number of full-time administrators and secretaries is many times larger than it was a generation ago, ample room has been left for the tradition of voluntary church service. Even on the central level many people serve freely as advisors, in the preparation of instructional materials, and on the boards of directors for the church auxiliary organizations. However skilled, many of these people are essentially amateurs at their assigned tasks, although they include university professors, professional men and women, executives, and some retired persons. More important, Mormonism on the local level has remained what it was from the start—a lay organization. There is no professional clergy in the ward congregation or the stake, and the general authorities are lawyers, educators, engineers, journalists, and business executives drawn from various fields. Regions, stakes, missions, and wards are still do-it-yourself units with leaders called from the congregations to serve as bishops, stake presidents, counselors, and heads of local auxiliary organizations for terms that vary but often amount to about five years. Compared with the total number of church members whose assignments have significant administrative responsibility, the number of those staffing the educational system and the centralized departments remains small. The bureaucratization has been channeled and confined for specific purposes.

The participation of lay members is a vital characteristic of Mormonism. It refers not simply to attendance at meetings but to specific assignments or "callings" in one's ward or stake. In every ward, or at least in an average ward, something like two hundred positions are staffed by church members who earn a living following their own line of work or as homemakers:

Bishoprics and clerks	The bishop and two counselors, plus four clerks, responsible for all historical, financial, membership, and statistical records of the ward.
Priesthood quorums	Twenty-four in presidencies of six quorums or groups, plus "home teaching" assignments involving most active males above the age of fourteen, plus instructors for each of the quorums or groups. Also a priesthood organist and chorister.

Relief Society	A presidency of three, a secretary, four or more instructors in subject matter areas, organist and chorister, from one to several women responsible for a weekly nursery, and a corresponding additional staff in many wards holding separate Relief Society meetings in the evenings or Sundays. Plus "visiting teaching" assignments to most women who participate in the Relief Society.
Sunday School	A presidency of three, two secretaries, a coordinator for young children, two choristers, two accompanists, and a staff of fifteen to twenty teachers of adults and children. Also four librarians to serve these and other teachers.
Young Men and Young Women	A presidency of three and secretary for each, with assistants as needed, usually not more than four or five, plus a total of perhaps twenty-four young men and women as class presidents and secretaries. Also four sports directors and coaches, three or more Cub Scout leaders, and an average of ten or twelve persons serving on committees related to Cub Scout and Boy Scout units sponsored by the ward.
Primary Association	A presidency of three, a secretary, one or two choristers and accompanists, and a teaching staff of variable size, perhaps averaging twelve.
Unmarried adults	Usually four or more officers.
Recreation	Usually three persons on an Activities Committee and two or three sports directors.
Musical staff	Two or more music personnel: music director, music chairman, choir director, organist, choir accompanist, choir presidency. In addition, two or three dozen members of the ward choir.
Stake officers and teachers	An average of eighty persons divided among eight wards, for an average of about ten per ward.

In addition there are *ad hoc* assignments, stake missions, welfare assignments, and the like.

People called to these assignments are expected to be "worthy"—a word which in the Mormon vocabulary means that one pays tithes and offerings, attends meetings, endeavors to be honest in dealing with others, observes the Word of Wisdom, and adheres strictly to the moral code that allows sexual relations only within the bonds of matrimony. Of course there are times when these minimal standards of worthiness are not achieved. In such cases, after a searching personal interview, the individual is admonished to get his or her life "in order" before qualifying to serve in a church position. It might seem that such screening would be conducive to a strong sense of self-righteousness on the part of those devout Mormons who do qualify. In practice, in our experience, Mormons who serve as bishops, teachers, and the like, are quite aware that there are many challenges still remaining and that one cannot afford to rest on one's laurels. The screening procedure does assure, by and large, that Mormon officers—including those mentioned plus the twenty-five thousand missionaries—are people of rectitude and commitment.

There is in both the central and the local organizations a good deal of administrative scurrying: new programs, subdivisions of old programs, reshuffling of charts and flow diagrams, study committees and task forces. Although the stated objectives are different and although the claims to authority and ordinances that stretch across the eternities are far more sweeping, the Mormons in their own way seem to be behaving as educational administrators, government officials, or businessmen—in short, as twentieth-century people. George Bernard Shaw, in *Man and Superman,* observed that: "In hell, we drift; in heaven, we steer." The Mormons appear to be steering.

All these programs and the accompanying bureaucratic machinery are designed to serve the basic unit of the church, the family. To give a better sense of the tempo of Mormon life—how these various programs are actually experienced by people—it will be helpful to examine a composite family. We do not present this picture as the typical family, for it does not fairly represent single-parent families, adult singles, and that percentage of the population, probably more than one-fourth, depending on the area, who are "inactive" or disaffected. Yet there is something to be said, when attempting to understand a group, for examining those who fully represent its values. Even those who fall short in some respects will share many of the experiences of the deeply involved Latter-day Saint family.

To begin with, such a family is probably domiciled west of the Great Plains—in 1977 three-fifths of all Latter-day Saints lived in the western states or western Canada. Given the rapid growth of the church elsewhere, it may not be many years before most Mormons reside outside of the United States. From 1960 to 1973 church membership in the United States rose a total of 77 percent; outside the United States 350 percent.

Our composite family is likely to be urban—another significant change in the makeup of the Mormon profile. As late as 1920 nearly 80 percent of all Mormons resided in rural stakes; by 1977, 72 percent of the stakes were in metropolitan areas. Even if there is some fuzziness here, in that stakes centering in cities may well include outlying wards or families living in suburbs and on acreages, the general trend from farm to city, although coming slightly later, is unmistakably the same as that which has occurred nationally.

The "typical" Mormon family is young; half of Utah Mormons are under twenty-four, and if anything the median is lower in areas of new growth. There are considerably more children in the family than in America's families generally. The Mormon birthrate in 1977 of 31.66 births per thousand was more than twice as high as the national average. The father may be employed in virtually any occupation—from a top executive in a multinational corporation to a farmer in southern Utah. He is likely to be an elder in the church, and his sons over twelve years old will be deacons (ages twelve to fourteen), teachers (ages fourteen to sixteen), or priests (ages sixteen to nineteen). The mother of the family probably finds her main role in the home, although increasing numbers of Mormon women (about one-third) have sought gainful employment outside the home. Both mothers and daughters find many opportunities for participation, including teaching and supervising, in the ward programs.

Fathers and sons attend Sunday morning priesthood meetings—a brief preliminary meeting for all priesthood holders, followed by quorum class-work consisting of a doctrinal lesson and priesthood assignments. The young men are responsible for the collecting of "fast offerings" at members' homes on the monthly fast day; preparing, blessing, and distributing the sacrament (eucharist) to members at Sunday school and sacrament meeting; assisting the bishop in any other capacity he may request; and, with a senior companion, visiting members' homes at least once a month as a "home teaching" team. Home teachers represent the quorum presidency and bishop, looking after any spiritual or temporal needs of the families assigned to them.

Fathers, in addition to serving as home teachers, often hold another position in the ward or stake—as a member of the bishopric, stake presidency, stake high council, quorum presidency, or as an officer or teacher in any of several auxiliary organizations. The father's most important church assignment is his position as head of the family. In practice, we have observed, husband and wife usually function as co-leaders. They hold a Family Home Evening every Monday night. This is a regular activity that emphasizes participation by all members in education, discussion, and recreation. To assure that the experience will be fruitful, the church publishes a special manual each year with suggested topics, activities, games, and visual aids. To those who charge that family life must have come to a sorry state if such experiences have to be programmed, church leaders respond that many families are missing out entirely on such experiences amid the hectic demands of modern life and that the recommendations represent a minimum, not a maximum, of family interaction. Week after week the family spends an hour or so together in a relaxed atmosphere enjoying activities, discussing matters of common concern, and being instructed in principles of mental health and Christian living.

Although home life is emphasized as Mormons attempt to counteract the centrifugal forces that are detracting from it, many activities of the family center not in the home but in the ward meetinghouse, a kind of home away from home. It has often been remarked that the ward is an extended family, and the custom of addressing adult church members as "Brother Jones" or "Sister Martinez" reinforces the feeling. Mormon wards are "congregations," as we have noticed earlier, but they have always been much more than that. Their function is only partially fulfilled by holding weekly worship services and Sunday schools. Indeed, the Mormon ward, whether in Salt Lake City, Edinburgh, São Paulo, or Nukualofa, is typically a beehive of activity, with dozens of meetings held throughout the week. These range from circles of the adult women in the Relief Society, through the Primary classes for children up to age twelve, to the multifarious activities of the Young Men and Young Women for youths from twelve up through their teen-age years. This last organization, often meeting on a Tuesday or Wednesday evening for an hour and a half, would occupy the time of the teen-age members of our typical family in youth-run service projects, social activities, scouting and exploring, and, on occasion, trips and summer camps. "Why should the devil have all the good tunes?" a revivalist preacher is supposed to have asked. Through their weekday church programs Mormons have been working energetically to see to it that much of the leisure time of their people will be occupied in constructive church-sponsored activities.

In addition to the Sunday meetings and the auxiliary organizations, every Mormon ward has other social activities (dinners, dances, picnics, and the like) and welfare projects (in which the people join together at scheduled times to cultivate the crops or can the peanut butter or complete whatever enterprise is developed in this particular unit). In wards within a hundred miles of temples there are special "temple nights," when several adults join together in car pools to attend a session for performing baptisms, sealings, and other "work for the dead."

For young people of junior high and high school age there are seminary classes held daily during the school week. These follow courses of instruction in Bible, church history, and theology, but they also sponsor "fireside chats" and recreational dances. In some areas a released-time arrangement allows students to attend such classes in seminary buildings near their schools, but in other locations Mormon youngsters go to an early morning seminary class before the start of their regular school day. In parts of Europe, Asia, and South America even this has been impossible. Not to be deprived of a valuable learning experience, young people in those areas read the seminary materials on their own through a home study arrangement, often meeting weekly with a volunteer instructor for discussion and special help in an attempt to assure that their religious education will keep pace with their secular education.

All of these organizations and activities and programs mean that an "active" Mormon is just that—active. There is no encouragement for one to maintain a purely nominal connection. Just in terms of hours per week it will be informative to consider what this means for our composite Mormon family. A teen-age church member will spend something like the following each week:

Priesthood meeting (boys and men)	1 hour
Sunday School	1.5
Sacrament meeting	1.5
Young Men, Young Women	1.5
Seminary	5
Fireside, social, or other	2
Family Home Evening	1.5
	14 hours

These figures, which do not count travel time, vary slightly, depending on the week. Other family members may spend perhaps less time if they are not enrolled in weekday seminary classes, but it is common to have something close to ten hours occupied in church-sponsored meetings or activities each week. This is an average Mormon family with a desire to be full-fledged members but with no particular special assignments. Adults who serve in bishoprics, as Relief Society officers, and the like put in additional time that is hard to calculate, but it is probably accurate to say that for these special callings "church service time" each week ranges between twenty and forty hours.

Church demands on time occasionally seem onerous, even more than the financial expectations in tithing and other donations. There are complaints about "busy work" and excessive expectations of committed time. There may be a recurrent clash between role expectations: A father or mother's duty may pull in one direction, while an assignment in a church organization tugs in another. All of this is the inevitable static that results from the insistent but conflicting demands on every conscientious person's time and energies.

If our composite family contains members who are temperamentally introverts or "loners," people preferring quieter life-styles, the church programs may seem uncomfortable—or they may be looked upon as opportunities to emerge from a shell and may help to develop a more balanced personality. The scholarly and thoughtful members who espouse the life of the mind may find that the group activities go against their personal grain. Doubtless there is some tension here, but many are able to work out a satisfactory compromise that allows time for contemplation and study while also participating in many of the church programs. Some Mormons anxious to participate in community service find that the demands of the church on their time make participation in other activities extremely difficult, while others lead the pack, so to speak, in service clubs, hospital boards, and community drives. Again the challenge is to the individual to strike a balance, and church members are encouraged to contribute time and talent to their communities.

The expectations of the church go beyond the expenditure of time. They also require contributions of money. The composite Mormon family, if it is a convert family, will face adjustments in its budget. The most important financial obligation is tithing, the 10 percent of income that every member is supposed to pay. Even young children earning their first income by doing odd jobs are expected to give this percentage, thus developing the idea early that the biblical tithe is the Lord's way of financing his church and its service. The payment is voluntary, of course, but there are frequent reminders of the obligation, and at the end of every year the bishop of the ward holds a "tithing settlement." The family members are expected to meet with their bishop and discuss their particular situation, ideally reporting that they have paid a "full tithe" for the year and verifying the accuracy of their joint records. Such discussions are confidential, as are the amounts donated and the tithing status of all individuals.

Mormon tithing may appear to be a heavy price for membership, but payments for church programs do not stop there. The family will pay a "fast offering" once a month—a small amount that represents something equivalent to the cost of two family meals, which they do without during a brief, relatively painless fast in order to contribute to the needy. All such funds are expended locally. There is a "ward budget" donation intended to defray the costs of operating the ward, such as maintaining the chapel, paying utility bills, buying supplies for the auxiliaries, transportation to camps, and the like. Some wards have suggested 1 percent of income for their budgets, but each bishop has discretion as to how this money is raised, a major portion of which is reimbursed to the ward from central tithing funds, so that more affluent wards help those with lesser means. Church members can also be faced with an additional challenge if the ward is building a chapel, for a certain percentage of the construction costs—about 50 percent in the United States, sometimes less in areas that are less well established—must be raised by the local congregation. This usually results in various fund-raising projects as well as special building contributions. Ad hoc in nature, for the specific purpose of chapel buildings, these donations can stretch over two or three years. The family who lives in a ward where the chapel is already constructed probably contributes to the church something close to 11 or 12 percent of its income.

Mormons find their temporal, day-to-day existence very much influenced by the church. For many years they have been urged to develop a storage program that would provide at least one year's supply of the family's basic needs of food, clothing, and shelter. The goal is repeated at intervals every year, and local church members are offered specific help in the form of advice on storage. However, special prices for quantity buying through church organizations are discouraged out of respect for tax-paying vendors. It is improbable that most Mormon families have sufficient reserves for an entire year, but many have substantial quantities of canned fruit and vegetables, tins of flour and honey, and other commodities that could provide sustenance for several months in case of emergency. The practical reasons for this particular program, which Mormons accept as the will of the Lord, are a combination of sheer prudence, the experience of scarcity and near-starvation in pioneer times that led early church leaders to urge a storage program, the sufferings and hardships undergone more recently during the Great Depression, and the appeal during an inflationary trend of buying commodities a year or two prior to consumption.

The Mormon family is influenced by its religion not only in the food storage program but even at the table for meals. In 1834 Joseph Smith announced a revelation known as the Word of Wisdom, which enjoined the Saints to eat wholesome food and to avoid tobacco, alcoholic beverages, and "hot drinks," the last term later defined to mean tea and coffee, in order to achieve vigorous health ("to run and not be weary"). After several decades of fairly lax interpretation in frontier America, this health code was given renewed emphasis during times of religious revival. Beginning in the 1880s, it was the subject of an increasing educational campaign, and observance of the Word of Wisdom at least in its most obvious prohibitions became a prerequisite for appointment to leadership positions, service as missionaries, and entrance into the temples. The committed family was to have a healthy diet and an exercise program and was to practice "moderation in all things," although there are Mormons who are guilty of stressful living, overwork, and obesity. These infractions are recognized as unwise but do not disqualify church members from full participation. There is no flexibility of interpretation, however, in the requirement that they abstain from tea, coffee, alcohol, and tobacco—the four don'ts. (Mormons who do not comply with these parts of the health code are often referred to as jack-Mormons.) Abandoning consumption of these items can be a real challenge to converts; in France, where wine is the accepted mealtime beverage, Mormons must make do with unfermented fruit juices or mineral water.

The Word of Wisdom gives rise to interesting problems. One of the authors, doing his military service in counterintelligence, found that recruiting officers often delighted to ask young Mormons what they would do if in the performance of duty they had to go into a bar where abstinence from drink-

ing would call attention to oneself. There can also be moments of awkward-
ness in the ever-present "reception" and cocktail parties. On the surface it
may appear that the Mormons are confused on priorities, avoiding a cup of
tea or coffee rather than prosecuting weightier matters of the law. But the
health of Mormons does benefit from their code, as statisticians have demonstrated, and the correlation between lung cancer and the use of tobacco has
presented little problem to Mormons. Statistically, Mormons have a far lower
rate of cancer than the population generally.[7] The Word of Wisdom functions much like the dietary regulations of Orthodox Jews in providing external marks and symbols that to some degree set apart the faithful from the
larger community. And its positive observance may contribute to the family
budget amounts equivalent to the liquor and tobacco bills of other families.

Since no one is immune from the maladies and pressures of modernity, a
Mormon family might contain a member who is addicted to drugs, is a ho-
mosexual, becomes an unwed mother, or experiences marital friction and divorce. In the last century church leaders accepted the necessity of the most
competent professional medicine available. Several frontier doctors were early
converts, and Mormon men and women in the late nineteenth century were
urged to train as physicians. Now, however, members are not just left to cope
with psychological and emotional problems on their own or aided only by
whatever help that can be provided by well-meaning bishops and stake presidents, whose main occupations may be in fields as unrelated as construction
or retail sales; rather, Mormons are encouraged to seek professional counseling, and regional centers provide such services in some parts of the United
States and Canada. There have been some precautionary efforts to see to it
that the extremes of psychotherapy are not recommended, but not until recently were there procedures by which a bishop confronted with problems of
emotional disturbance and social disequilibrium could obtain professional
help from a church agency. To oversee these pastoral functions, a churchwide
Social Services Department was established in 1969; by 1977 it had agencies
or offices in sixteen states in the United States and at least one each in Australia, Canada, and New Zealand. In addition to counseling and psychiatric
therapy this department supervises adoptions as well as the program that
places Native American children in the homes of white Mormons. The 7,500
ward bishops and branch presidents have continued to serve in individual
counseling and interviewing; they remain the backbone of the system. Some
have natural aptitudes and spiritual sensitivity that enable them to do an im-
measurable amount of good for the individuals and families of their jurisdic-
tions. And each ward and stake is counseled to maintain a roster of the
physicians, nurses, psychiatrists, social workers, and other professionals in
each locality. The day has not yet arrived when orthodox Mormons will re-

gard a psychiatrist as their first source of help in times of distress. But professional services are available and acceptable when they are necessary or appropriate.

In attempting to find the right balance between skilled professionals and dedicated volunteers, one of the most successful blendings achieved by the Social Services Department is in the family-centered "home-teaching" program at the Utah State Prison. Each inmate who chooses to be involved is assigned a home-teaching family, which visits weekly, sharing an evening with the inmate and any members of his family who wish to participate. The program is designed to supplement Sunday and weekday services and religion classes normally held in the prison, and it helps create feelings of acceptance and understanding. In practice, it has been a process of mutual education as stereotypes on both sides are broken down.[8] Similar church programs using volunteer couples or families work with alcoholics and homosexuals.

One church activity that can hardly avoid touching the life of the composite Mormon family is the missionary program. If they are converts, of course, their membership probably resulted from meeting young missionaries and, after instruction, accepting baptism. But this program has equally profound repercussions on the families from which the missionaries come. If our composite family has four children, divided equally by sex, chances are very strong that both sons will serve two-year missions. Young women also act as missionaries, but because they often marry before "a call," there are proportionately fewer who do so. Departure usually occurs at age nineteen or twenty. During the two years of the young person's mission the home family is affected financially by the obligation of sending out a monthly payment (current average about $160) to support the missionary, culturally by receiving letters that describe experiences in Korea or Venezuela or, if the "call" is less exotic, Saskatchewan or Kansas, and spiritually by sacrificing and praying in an effort to share Mormonism with those called in Saint parlance "the honest in heart." Whether this family experience stretches over two years, four years, or, as in some remarkable instances, up to ten or twelve years, the results are powerful as commitment to the restored gospel is dramatized and deepened.

Although proselyting service is voluntary and the financing private, the system is a church program. The original "call" to go where he is most needed (one does not choose his own "field of labor"), the training of the outgoing "elders" (as they are called), supervision and regulation during the two years of service, assignment of companions (Mormon missionaries work in pairs), transfers from one city to another at intervals of several months— all this is initiated by the bishop in consultation with the family and is under the direction of a central church missionary committee which assigns each volunteer to a particular mission. Mature men and their wives are placed in charge in each mission of about 150 elders and sisters. Those called to non-English-speaking territories spend the first two months at the Language Training Mission in Provo, Utah, where intensive training is given in twenty-five languages. The instruction includes lectures on the history and culture of the peoples the missionaries are assigned to work with. This helps cushion the shock for the Idaho farm boy suddenly immersed in the culture of Thailand or Tahiti, or for the Japanese-American from Hawaii abruptly confronted with the modes of living and thinking of his relatives in Japan.

In 1974 President Spencer W. Kimball announced: "The question is frequently asked: Should every young man fill a mission? And the answer has been given by the Lord. It is 'Yes.' Every young man should fill a mission."[9] Although not "every" young Mormon responds, for reasons varying from lack of means to lack of enthusiasm and on rare occasions physical or mental disability, the number who serve has sharply increased, and by 1977 there were more than twenty-five thousand missionaries in the field. Even if the total number of missionaries remains stable rather than further expanding, a single decade will result in over a hundred thousand Saints returning from their proselyting experience to fill the ranks of leadership positions in the wards and stakes. These are the shock troops of Mormonism. The acceleration of the whole program is a crucial aspect of the church's institutional response to current challenges.

If the Mormon family lives within traveling distance of a temple, this church institution will have great significance in the family's life. Not standard meetinghouses for Sunday worship, Mormon temples are few. It is in these edifices that Mormons are married and participate in other sacred ceremonies for the living and the dead. There is a lengthy instructional "endowment" ordinance in which participants observe a series of dramatic renderings of episodes that illuminate the plan of Christian life and salvation. Covenants with respect to fundamental gospel principles are made at this time. As with the holy practices of other religions, the details are considered sacred and are not freely discussed.[10] It is for this reason that non-Mormons—and "nonvaliant" (nonobservant) Mormons—are not permitted in temples. When a new temple is completed, or an older one remodeled, it remains open to the public for a few weeks. Once the temple is dedicated or rededicated, however, only those worthy of "recommends"—certificates of worthiness from their bishops—may enter, and even then not just to pay a visit but to perform specific ordinances and ceremonies.

The Mormon family is affected by the temple in different ways. Parents return to the place of their marriage to renew their understanding of the Christian message and its universals and to do vicarious temple work for people of past generations. The young people in the family, as they reach the age of romantic interests and courtship, are encouraged to think in terms of the temple. They are expected to seek friends of the opposite sex who are church members and who also desire a temple marriage. When, after preliminary courtship and proposal, a marriage takes place, it is surrounded with much of the excitement characteristic of many American weddings, with bridal showers and receptions in honor of the bride and groom preceding and following the sacred event. But there is no equivalent in mainline Christianity to the ceremony itself. Family members of the principals and their special friends, if eligible for admission, are present in what is essentially a sacred and special family experience.

The church has no use for trial marriages or anything less than a lifetime commitment. The temple ceremony gives a symbolic, visual, and personal setting that leaves no room for doubt that this is intended as a once-only experience. Not all Mormon marriages take place in a temple; those who marry spouses of other faiths or those not eligible for the temple are married by civil authorities, the ward bishop, or the clergy of another faith. But without question temple marriage constitutes the ideal for devout Mormons.

For the composite Mormon family, then, the temple provides a focal point for certain momentous experiences, quite different from the pace and tone of the ward meetinghouse services. Those who attend a Mormon meeting, noticing large numbers of children and a certain amount of confusion or informality resulting from the lay participation, may conclude that the religion lacks ceremony or ritual and the kind of worship associated with liturgical traditions. In the temples, as far as their own perceptions are concerned, the Mormons have sacred space.

One of the activities for which Mormons are famous is genealogical research. It does not appear to be part of what is commonly regarded as religious living, but Mormons believe family ties, present, past, and future, to be eternal. People who have died without hearing the restored gospel can have ordinances performed for them vicariously in the temples. Such work cannot be performed en masse but must be done individually, a living person undergoing the experience as proxy for a specific dead person, males for males, females for females. (Incidentally, Mormons do not think that a departed soul will have to accept such vicarious activity; the free choice will still be his or hers.) Living Saints feel a strong responsibility for their ancestors. To identify them by name and date it is necessary to do genealogical research, which has become a mission of intense personal interest and service.

In 1894 the Mormons organized a society to promote genealogical research, and in recent decades they have utilized modern technology to microfilm parish registers and other vital statistics from around the world. Computer technology has facilitated the processing of these names. In Salt

Lake City a genealogical library with some three hundred microfilm readers is almost always filled to capacity by researchers, many of them non-Mormons. The more than one million reels of microfilm accumulated by 1977 are also accessible to researchers in other parts of the world, who can use them through one of the 225 "branch libraries." The success of Alex Haley's *Roots* has helped to arouse an interest in genealogical research among many people. Mormons see this interest in the past as part of a dimly perceived plan of God to turn the hearts of the children to the fathers and the hearts of the fathers to the children.[11]

The responsibility to do genealogical research is often called to the attention of Latter-day Saints in their wards, where classes and workshops are offered. A Mormon family probably has a "book of remembrance" containing the pedigree charts and family group sheets of several generations. Pictures, personal histories, and other documents help to give the Mormon family a pronounced sense of where it came from—its own "roots"—and each member a strong identity. But it is also true that genealogical research is not an enjoyable activity to all Mormons. Many see it as a chore that they are willing to put off. Efforts to arouse enthusiasm in wards often end with individual reluctance. At the same time the overall amount of research and genealogical activity sponsored by the church is impressive. Each member is also encouraged to keep a personal history.

Education has long been a kind of obsession among Mormons.[12] "A man is saved no faster than he gains knowledge," Joseph Smith said. Another aphorism of the founding Prophet announced, "The glory of God is intelligence." Although throughout most of the nineteenth century they were handicapped in translating the idea into practical programs, Mormons in this century have a rather impressive record in education. While precise church figures are unavailable, Utah (72 percent of its population being Mormons) of all the states in the last thirty years has usually had the highest proportion of its population in school, the highest proportion of high school graduates, the highest medial-level of school years completed, and has usually spent on education the greatest amount in relation to total personal income.[13]

Most Mormons receive all their formal education in public schools and universities that have no connection with the church, although the church does promote its educational goals institutionally. The church has not assumed the responsibility of providing schools for all of its members throughout the world, but it does encourage sound education, public or private. According to an official policy statement, "where other educational systems are nonexistent, seriously deficient, or inaccessible to our members, the Church may provide basic education for its members under carefully established criteria."[14] For this reason by 1977 there were Mormon schools, mainly elementary with some secondary and normal schools, in Mexico, South America, and the Polynesian Islands, with approximately eighteen thousand students. In addition, more than thirty thousand students attended church-sponsored colleges or universities.

Education is valued in the composite Mormon home, and at least some of the children will continue on for college training. There are Mormon families in which six or eight children have gone on to receive doctorates and achieve eminence in medicine or physics or some other professional field. Although they are in the minority, as a result of the accepted Mormon value system they have gone on to achieve unusual records. A composite family will send three of its four children to a university or a technical college, of whom one or two will probably graduate. In the United States virtually all normal Mormon children will have had a high school education, and Utah maintains nine state universities and colleges for its million-plus inhabitants, plus church-supported Brigham Young University, Latter-day Saint Business College, and the privately supported Westminster College.

Cultural activities of the Saints are often associated with the Mormon Tabernacle Choir. Less well known are the Mormon Youth Symphony and Chorus and the Promised Valley Playhouse, all in Salt Lake City, and annual pageants in Palmyra, New York; Manti, Utah; Oakland, California, and elsewhere. These provide opportunities for Mormons with musical or dramatic talent. The impact on the average church member lies in the cultural activities of wards and stakes, where it is not unusual, by the time adulthood is reached, for a member to have been in speech and talent contests and in the cast of several variety shows ("road shows"), to have sung in ward choirs and quartets (Handel's *Messiah* at Christmastime, for example), and to have been in the cast of *The Music Man,* historical pageants, one of the annual ward plays, or some other production in a stake event. Most of these have been sponsored by the local Young Men and Young Women (formerly Mutual Improvement Associations). Their quality is often less than excellent, but Mormons justify the effort in terms of the numbers of people involved who might otherwise not experience such participation.

Until recently, the General Board of the MIA conducted an annual June conference in Salt Lake City at which many thousands of young church members participated in gigantic drama, musical, and dance festivals. The dance festival, held in the University of Utah stadium, for example, was an impressive spectacle of color and rhythm as several thousand dancers performed different styles of folk and ballroom dance in unison.

In Relief Society meetings, as in Mutual (meetings of the Young Men and Young Women), adult women of the church for many years have given attention to literature and choral groups. More recently there has been an emphasis on studying the cultural traditions of different nationalities. Efforts are made to raise the level of "cultural refinement," although the degree of success depends almost entirely on the educational background of people attending as well as that of the teacher. There are individual women who find the program inadequate and who are frustrated both in what they consider to be rather unexciting travelogues and by the recalcitrance of the human material in the classes, while others are enthusiastic and excited by it. If measured against the yardstick not of some imaginary ideal but of their own individual development prior to church activity, most members would concede that the church experiences in music, drama, and art classes have considerably broadened their horizons.

Two other cultural stimuli deserve mention. First, the church magazines are a primary source of communication from the centers to hundreds of thousands of homes throughout the world. Although the primary purpose of these magazines is didactic, which sharply limits the kinds of poetry and art they encourage, they are well designed and, through contests in poetry, fiction, nonfiction, and photography, work steadily at raising the cultural standards of their readers.

The "cultural evenings" held in conjunction with area conferences and annual regional meetings each June are equally significant because they are a means of demonstrating to church members throughout the world that Mormonism encourages quality performances of music, drama, and art. Such presentations have been made recently in Japan, Korea, France, Germany, the Netherlands, Denmark, Finland, Mexico, and several South American countries. Calling upon the best talent in the area and carefully prepared several months ahead of time, these cultural evenings, involving a combination of music, pageant, and drama, have helped Mormons to perpetuate their culture. An outstanding cultural development of recent years was the establishment in 1963 of the Polynesian Cultural Center in Hawaii. Students at the Church College of Hawaii (now Brigham Young University–Hawaii Campus) representing nearly every group of Polynesian peoples, established under church sponsorship, living Tongan, Tahitian, Fijian, Samoan, Maori, and Hawaiian villages to preserve ancient arts, crafts, and ways in order to provide employment for Polynesian students attending the college and to give visiting tourists an authentic feeling for the native cultures. It continues to be a major tourist attraction in Hawaii.

It should be observed that among Mormons, art is seldom for its own sake. The most favored expressions of art, like the most favored educational pursuits, are those that are most useful in achieving ends other than mere self-expression or even personal expansion. A musical play, for example, that fosters cooperation, group interaction, and the involvement of otherwise inactive ward members will be promoted, whereas a one-person recital by an accomplished violinist, even though he is a ward member, will not. A creative writer will be praised more for a producible play or a poem that teaches a moral principle than for a publishable novel or a volume of confessional poetry. On the local level there is little incentive for excellence in the plastic arts beyond scenery for a dramatic production or posters advertising group activities. Fine paintings and sculptures are seldom found in ward buildings. Artistic endeavors which foster group feeling or aid in the inculcating of shared goals find easy approval over the solitary endeavors of a single talent, however valued one's efforts might be on the open market.

We have followed our composite Mormon family far enough to recognize that Mormonism is more than a Sunday religion. In time, in money, in energy, in innumerable specific decisions, membership in the Mormon church makes a difference. The response to these programs is largely a matter of individual attitude. Outside students of Mormonism, even some who are considering membership, sometimes recoil in disbelief at the relentless demands of the church. Those Mormons who drop out, and there are some each year in every ward and branch throughout the church, often find the demands simply more than they are willing to bear. But what are perceived as "demands" by some are perceived by others—by those Mormon families most fully committed to the cause—as opportunities. They see the involvement as providing numerous opportunities for growth—spiritually, socially, even physically and intellectually.

It is helpful to think again in terms of the modern malaise, the lack of roots, the identity crises of the young, the scarcity of meaningful personal friendships, the frequent moves that create instability, and all of the other characteristics of our time that have contributed to "future shock." By its activism, coupled with its lay character and the enlarged family feeling of the ward unit, Mormonism provides powerful compensating mechanisms. Its demands of time and resources assure that it will not be taken lightly. It is virtually impossible to invest the expected effort and resources without a genuine spiritual and psychological commitment. And the investment has an effect in producing the feeling of commitment. Another image may help in understanding how it is that Mormons can enter into obligations so readily and how such a religion, which can hardly be called easy, attracts surprising numbers of new converts each year. Peter Berger's book *The Sacred Canopy* treats, in a large context, the function of traditional religion in providing a context of meaning for its adherents.[15] Without question, Mormonism functions to provide such a canopy for most Latter-day Saints. They have goals and objectives on a local, manageable scale. They have a sense of being involved in something larger than themselves. They see themselves as moving toward eternal goals but with the assistance of the church programs and specific personal and family objectives as guideposts along the way.

16

{ Group Personality: The Unsponsored Sector }

Mormons are like artichokes. At first encounter you either like them or you don't. But those who have unfavorable first impressions, often find that once the outer layers are peeled away, both Mormons and artichokes are most likeable. In fact, most people who get to know Mormons become their friends. And a little objective research on Mormon beliefs reveals that, except for a few doctrinal differences, these people who call themselves Latter-day Saints are just like the rest of us . . . very human beings.

—Boston *Globe* (1967)

Mormons are not adequately summed up by looking at them in their Sunday best in the pews of their meetinghouses. We have noted that they have problems as well as strengths, that they are busily engaged in organizational programs at the central level, that on the level of everyday living an average family of "active" Mormons spends many hours each week in meetings, and that many areas of life are touched by their religion. But what kind of people are the Mormons? Is there something more definite that can be said about their group personality? And what, if anything, do they do outside of the official programs?

"Who is this new man, this American?" asked Crèvecoeur in the eighteenth century. His endeavor to describe his subject was one of the first to portray the national character, and the attempt has been made repeatedly since. Not surprisingly there have been many efforts, both unsystematic and systematic, to etch the Mormon group personality. "They stand facing the rest of the world like a herd of rather amiable musk oxen, horns out, in a protective ring, watchful but not belligerent—full of confidence but ready to be reasonable, and wanting to be liked." Thus wrote Wallace Stegner in 1964.[1] E. E. Ericksen, who was the first to produce an interpretative study of Mormon group life, wrote that to find the true meaning of Mormonism one must analyze its spiritual life, study the problems that have confronted the people, and determine the group sentiments derived from the struggle with these problems. "Group conflict and struggles have created and maintained the basic Mormon sentiments," Ericksen declared.[2] A more recent study by sociologist Thomas F. O'Dea compared the Mormons with other culture groups and emphasized their cohesiveness and cooperation.[3] "Mormondom," O'Dea wrote, "became a subculture with its own peculiar conceptions and values, its own self-consciousness, and its own culture area."[4] The theologian Martin Marty wrote in 1976: "So frugal, earnest, clean-living, moral, and upward-bound are most Mormons that theirs has come to be called the typical *Reader's Digest* religion."[5] Other terms that often recur in descriptions of the Mormon people by modern observers are conservative, industrious, literalist, optimistic, fundamentalist, and rural—each of which requires careful definition and probably qualification. But without question, the Mormons have displayed a strong spirit of group consciousness.

The most interesting recent analysis of the Mormon group personality was written by John L. Sorenson, a social anthropologist at Brigham Young University.[6] Mormons, he says:

Are pragmatists, accepting as good that which works to fulfill valued objectives. They deal with the world actively and creatively.

Are always learning. They believe life is for experience and growth—for advancement. They believe in continually striving for perfection, and they feel an intense pressure to achieve and find it difficult to relax.

Put great emphasis on primary groups—face-to-face relations. Leaders interview people regularly—when calling them to positions, when determining their worthiness to participate in temple ceremonies, and when receiving their declarations at tithing settlement.

Like to organize and do things as a group. They make good organization people, whether in large corporations or in local neighborhood clubs. Harking back to their past, in other words, they prefer to act cooperatively. Thus, they are strong in the performing arts where numbers of people are involved, but their institutional life has not given the same encouragement to the private arts: painting, sculpture, and creative literature. As a group, they also strive for autonomy—independence from other social groups.

Wish to be "well-rounded," avoiding overspecialization, which means, perhaps, superficiality in some areas of life.

Tend to obey authority, accepting statements of general church authorities even when mutually incompatible. They find it easy to develop heroes or role models among general authorities. The emphasis on authority and obedience accords with their desire for predictability and order.

Wish to be thought well of by each other, the authorities, and "the world."

Tend to see the rest of the world as always on the brink of disaster, but minimize their own weaknesses and failures.

We would add two other characteristics of the Mormons as a group: They put great emphasis on spirituality, having confidence in intuitive judgments ("the voice of the Spirit"); and they are a people of unexpected humor and resilience. While some observers think that Latter-day Saints take themselves too seriously, what they are really taking seriously is their life obligations. Those who know them best have discovered reservoirs of drollery and wit that help to explain their psychic survival.

Such characterizations of group personality are informative, but they should be regarded as efforts to discern tendencies rather than as a description of all Mormons. Essentially it is the same problem, on a lesser scale, as that of portraying a "national character." Some scholars are impatient with such generalizations, which fail to point up generational differences, sometimes confuse the norm with the reality, and, since they are inevitably selective, run the risk of omitting "countervailing" influences.[7] Such reservations aside, anyone familiar with Mormons will discern much truth in the Sorenson profile. It will be interesting to find out in what ways it will have to be modified as a result of accelerated change and internationalization of the church.

Despite the extensive demands of the church on the time and energies of the Latter-day Saints, not all of their activities entail church control or sponsorship. In fact, some of the most interesting achievements of Mormons are those made on their own initiative. Joseph Smith once explained that he taught his people correct principles and then left them to govern themselves. Mormons are encouraged by their leaders to look for opportunities to serve and, where possible, to make their contributions on an individual or family basis.

It is not surprising that the first of the individual contributions of Mormons to civilization was in the field of agriculture. The Mormons had been, by force of Great Basin geography, a rural people; they had to be good farmers to survive in that inhospitable region. In the process they developed a love for the soil, a sense of working with God to make the earth fruitful, a nearly religious preference for farm-village life. They earned a reputation as careful husbandmen and as tenacious practitioners of hardscrabble agriculture.[8]

When Mormon students went east in the 1890s to secular universities, it was natural that some of them should study science and that they should return to Zion to apply their learning in creative ways to agriculture. The first Mormon student to do so was John A. Widtsoe (1872-1952).[9] Born on the island of Fröya, off the coast of Norway, brought to Utah at the age of eleven by his widowed mother, Widtsoe attended school in Logan and graduated from Brigham Young College in 1891. President of Brigham Young College at the time was Joseph Marion Tanner, who encouraged Widtsoe and six other graduating students to accompany him to Harvard.[10] There Widtsoe majored in physical chemistry and wrote for the Harvard *Crimson* and *Advocate,* graduating *summa cum laude* in 1894.

At Harvard, confronted for the first time with eastern secular education, Widtsoe experienced a religious soul-searching. "Was Mormonism," he wrote,

> what it pretended to be? Did Joseph Smith tell the truth? I read, listened, compared, thought, prayed. It was a real search for truth. Out of it in time came the certain knowledge that the restored gospel is true and that Joseph Smith was indeed a Prophet, and restorer of the simple true gospel of Jesus Christ.[11]

Fortified with this "testimony" and with a strong belief in the capacity of science to solve problems, both intellectual and physical, Widtsoe returned to Logan, where he was engaged by the Agricultural College of Utah (later Utah State Agricultural College, now Utah State University) to teach chemistry and conduct research for the local agricultural experiment station. Employed six years after its founding (1888), Widtsoe was the first Mormon to enter the collegiate division of the faculty. In 1898 he married Leah Dunford, daughter by a previous marriage of Susa Young Gates. Leah had studied nutrition and "domestic science" at the University of Utah and the Pratt Institute in Brooklyn, New York. Earlier the same year he had been awarded a traveling graduate fellowship from Harvard to attend Göttingen University in Germany, from which he received the Ph.D. degree in biochemistry in 1899. Upon his return to Utah in 1900 Widtsoe became director of the Utah Agricultural Experiment Station and professor of chemistry at the agricultural college.

Ambitious, prodigiously industrious, and idealistic, Widtsoe launched the experiment station on a program of improving the agricultural potential of the Great Basin region. In particular, he set for himself and his colleagues three tasks: examining irrigation from a scientific point of view, studying the possibilities of dry-land farming, and conveying useful information to farmers and housewives in Utah. These tasks preoccupied Widtsoe while he was director of the experiment station (1900-1905), while he was head of the Department of Agriculture at Brigham Young University in Provo (1905-1907), and while he was president of the Utah State Agricultural College (1907-1916). He left the latter in 1916 to become president of the University of Utah for five years, after which he served as a member of the Quorum of the Twelve Apostles until his death in 1952.

Widtsoe shared with Brigham Young and others a conviction that "agriculture . . . is the beginning of economic, social, and political wisdom." Our business, he wrote, "was to conquer the desert in terms of processes based on scientific study."[12] It was eminently proper, he wrote, "that Utah, the pioneer irrigation state, should lead out in such work."[13] Under Widtsoe's direction the experiment station published a series of bulletins on irrigation science. The soils, climate, and waters of the state's arid land were analyzed; the best crops and livestock for the farms were recommended; the dairy, horticultural, and sugar beet businesses were encouraged; and thousands of acres never before farmed were reclaimed.[14] Widtsoe, who was a fine writer of clear expository prose, summarized these and other findings in a text, *Principles of Irrigation Practice* (New York, 1914), which enjoyed wide usage in the United States and in other nations. He is often regarded as the founder of irrigation science.[15]

In pursuit of his second goal, opening up to cultivation arid lands that could not be irrigated, Widtsoe set up dry-land farming experiments at several locations in Utah, published bulletins on the research, and later wrote a text, *Dry Farming: A System of Agriculture for Countries under a Low Rainfall* (New York, 1910), which became the standard treatment of the subject. So important was it regarded internationally that the work was immediately translated into French, Spanish, Hungarian, Russian, Japanese, Swedish, and Italian. The editor of the Italian edition commented:

> If it is true that faith works miracles, no other work can be more valuable than this by Widtsoe, because written by a man whose faith in the possible redemption of the desert is ardent and unlimited. This faith is breathed through every page of the work with suggestive power to impress and convince even the most skeptical. And since in the desert region of the United States dry farming has already yielded notable success, this proves the undoubted utility of the book which is presented as a guide to the farmer in the arid sections of Italy and its colonies.[16]

As described by Widtsoe, the technique of dry-land farming is based on the attempt to conserve moisture in the soil so that crops can pass through a rainless season without harm. The land is so tilled that moisture is carried over from year to year; rainfall, when it comes, is absorbed by the soil and there held until needed by the plants. The practices advocated by Widtsoe include deep plowing in the fall to store rainfall in the deep soils; proper fallowing so that water stored in the soil one year may be carried over to another year and thus give the crop the benefit of two years' rainfall; vigorous cultivation of the topsoil to prevent direct evaporation of water; proper manuring to minimize the amount of water taken by the plants; careful limitation of seeds in proportion to water so that the water will not be used by plants that will not survive; and suitable breeding to get plants that will yield well even under conditions of small water supply.[17]

By virtue of his book and his leadership in the dry-land farming movement, Widtsoe served as president of the International Dry-Farming Congress in 1912. In his presidential address he pointed out that "deserts"—arid and semiarid lands with less than twenty inches of rainfall per year—were the lands of greatest agricultural promise, and it was proper that Utah's Mormons, with long experience in farming such land, even without irrigation, should participate in the movement to reclaim them. "Brigham Young's problems in the valleys of Utah," he declared, "were world problems." As the result of dry-farming, he could dare to say, "The desert shall blossom as the rose."[18]

Widtsoe was a long-time member of Utah's Water Storage Board, was instrumental in securing approval of the Colorado River Compact, was a consultant on the reorganization of the United States Bureau of Reclamation, was irrigation advisor to the province of Alberta, Canada, and was a member of the irrigation study commission for the Canadian government. Throughout his life Widtsoe was a nourisher of idealized Mormon values concerning the land. He "taught the power of science to enhance the capability of the land to feed the peoples of the world and to raise farming to the status of a noble profession."[19]

In pursuit of the third goal set for the experiment station, that of educating farmers and housewives, Widtsoe started a series of "farmers' institutes," "farmers' roundups," and "housekeepers' conferences," in which farm and homemaking specialists from the agricultural college and experiment station gave lectures to rural families and responded to their questions and problems. Not that the local farmers and housewives always welcomed the advice they received. As Widtsoe tells it:

> Up in Heber, the leading citizen, examining my hands, looked heavenward and remarked, "Oh Lord, that the time should come that a man with such hands should teach us how to farm." Down in Richfield one of the farmers arose in the institute meeting to remark that he had helped build the bridges and kill the snakes in Sevier County, and that he knew more about farming in the county than I would ever know. He concluded his oration by inviting me to return to my hotel and take the first train out of Richfield and never to return. Five years later he was one of our most enthusiastic supporters. Dr. E. D. Ball and I held the well advertised first farmers' institute in Springville. Only two men came out. Nevertheless we practiced on them. After the meeting we discovered that one of the two was stone-deaf, who passed time by attending meetings, and the other was the janitor who had to be present. Eight years later when our agricultural train reached Springville, we were met by the mayor, city council with a brass band, and the meeting hall was crowded to capacity. It did not take long to convert the people of Utah.[20]

This beginning led to the stationing of agricultural and homemaking authorities in the various counties of the state under an arrangement that was later adopted nationally. Indeed, the first county farm agent in the United States was Luther Winsor, who served farmers in the Uinta Basin region of eastern Utah beginning in 1911. The first irrigation engineering graduate of Utah State Agricultural College, Winsor later was invited by the Shah of Persia (now Iran) to supervise the building of an irrigation network in that country and spent some five years there as director general of irrigation works.[21] "It gives one a thrill," Winsor wrote, "to be working over again the ground that was trod by the ancient prophets and to put water back into the ditches that have been dry so many long centuries."[22]

Leah Widtsoe, wife of John, had established a Department of Home Economics at Brigham Young University in 1897, one of the first such in the nation. A similar arrangement was made for a resident county home demonstration agent who had been trained at the college. Amy Lyman, one of Leah's students, was sent to Sanpete and Sevier valleys and was the first county home demonstration agent in the United States.[23]

Early Mormon county farm agents and graduates of Utah State Agricultural College were imbued with the desire to "magnify their callings." Some of them later attained national influence. Edgar B. Brossard, the eighth of twelve children born to French Canadian Mormon converts,[24] reared on a cattle ranch near Oxford, Idaho, and a graduate economist of the college, issued farm management studies that attracted national attention in the 1920s. As agent for the experiment station, he took business records of fifty farms in various localities in Utah and showed where they made money and where they lost. Said Brossard:

> We had had quite phenomenal success in Utah with the cooperation of the farmers. They were mostly Mormons, and the bishops of the areas gave us 100 percent cooperation in extending the use of the Church meetinghouses and encouraging the farmers to give us the data requested. There's nothing like the Church organization and cooperation. I'd go to the bishop and his counselors and explain our program. They'd call in the farmers, and we'd gather at the meetinghouse.[25]

Employed by the United States Tariff Commission to perform studies of farm costs, Brossard was appointed a member of the commission in 1925 and served until his retirement in 1959. During eight of those years, under presidents Hoover and Eisenhower, Brossard was chairman of the commission.

One of Widtsoe's students and a colleague of Brossard at the agricultural college was William M. Jardine, from a British convert family that settled at Cherry Creek, near Malad, Idaho. Jardine became a professor of agronomy at the college, later went to Kansas State College, where he became, in succession, professor of agronomy, director of the experiment station, and president. He served as secretary of agriculture in the administration of Calvin Coolidge, as Herbert Hoover's ambassador to Egypt, and as president of Wichita University.

Another of Brossard's students was Ezra Taft Benson, a native of Whitney, Idaho, not far from Oxford and Malad, who was a specialist in farm cooperatives with the Idaho Extension Service, then executive secretary of the National Council of Farmers' Cooperatives, and finally secretary of agriculture in the cabinet of Dwight D. Eisenhower. In 1978 Benson was president of the Quorum of the Twelve Apostles of the church and honorary director of the Ezra Taft Benson Agriculture and Food Institute established at Brigham Young University in 1975.

Still another student of Widtsoe and colleague of Brossard was Philip V. Cardon, grandson of Waldensian convert immigrants from Italy, who became a county farm agent, editor of a farm paper, and a professor at Utah State. Cardon was next principal agronomist in charge of forage crops and diseases from the Bureau of Plant Industry in the U.S. Department of Agriculture, administrator of the Agricultural Research Administration, and more recently was director general of the United Nations Food and Agriculture Organization.

An early student of Widtsoe's at the Logan college was Franklin S. Harris. Descended from a brother of Martin Harris, who mortgaged his farm to print the Book of Mormon, he acquired his early education in the Mormon colony at Colonia Juárez, Mexico, attended Brigham Young University and Utah State Agricultural College, graduating in 1907, and completed a Ph.D. at Cornell in soils and agronomy in 1911. He was induced by Widtsoe to return to Logan and served as a professor and later as director of the experiment station. Harris continued Widtsoe's work in agricultural research and published many articles, bulletins, and books on such subjects as irrigation, dry-farming, and sugar beet culture. Among his books were *Principles of Agronomy* (New York, 1915), a widely used textbook; *Sugar Beets in America* (New York, 1918); and *Soil Alkali* (New York, 1919). Harris became president of Brigham Young University in 1921 and under his administration the institution attained national accreditation for its teaching and research. He also served as president of Utah State University from 1945 to 1950. Under the joint influence of Widtsoe and Harris Latter-day Saint men became involved in international technical aid programs and rural sociology. Harris himself developed a program of training that produced graduates who went on to dominate the fields of soil physics and agronomy.

The significant participation of Latter-day Saints in international technical assistance programs began with the International Dry-Land Congress meeting at Lethbridge, Canada, in 1912, when Widtsoe met Mirza Ali Gholi Khan, a Persian diplomat attending the conference. They discussed the problems of farming large areas of arid lands, and a friendship developed. Widtsoe invited the young diplomat to give the baccalaureate address at the Utah college. Persian students began enrolling in the college to study agricultural methods being used in Utah and found not only geographic similarities but also cultural meeting points—Mormonism had much in common with Islam. This interchange has continued down to the present. A large share of the prominent administrators of Iran have been educated in Utah. In 1939 Riza Shah Pahlavi introduced a plan for the agricultural improvement of Iran, with Harris as general advisor. It was under the latter's direction that Luther Winsor directed the restoration of irrigation in Iran. Harris again spent a year in Iran in 1946, as the result of which a program of technical cooperation (the Point Four Program) was instituted in which Utah State University sent a staff of agricultural specialists, the University of Utah delegated public health specialists, and Brigham Young University provided a number of educators to improve university programs. The success of this program led to appointments of the same and other personnel to other countries. Three prominent Mormon educators, Dilworth Walker, Wesley P. Lloyd, and Grant Calder, supervised important projects in Burma; Harold Bentley did the same in Ethiopia; one contract currently involves Utah colleges with Bolivia; and Glen L. Taggart, now president of Utah State University and a rural sociologist, served as dean of international programs at Michigan State University and as vice-chancellor of the University of Nigeria.[26] Harris also directed the early stages of the American foreign aid programs in Greece, Turkey, and the Middle East after 1946.

Another influence of Widtsoe and Harris resulted in a Mormon infusion into the field of rural sociology. One of their early students, Lowry Nelson, a native of Ferron, Utah, became a county farm agent, editor of the *Utah Farmer,* and founding director of extension services at Brigham Young University. As professor of rural economics at BYU, Nelson began a series of studies of Mormon farm villages that attracted national attention.[27] Nelson received the Ph.D. in rural sociology from the University of Wisconsin in 1929 and later authored basic texts on the subject: *Rural Sociology* (New York, 1948), *American Farm Life* (Cambridge, Mass., 1954); and *Community Structure and Change* (New York, 1960). As a long-time professor at the University of Minnesota, Nelson taught many of those who became prominent in the field of rural sociology in the United States, including three Utahans he had originally taught at Brigham Young University: Nels Anderson, T. Lynn Smith, and Nathan T. Whetten. Each of these made significant contributions to the discipline.[28] Nelson himself served as founding editor of *Rural Sociology* (1936–1940), president of the Rural Sociological Society

(1944), and assistant director of the Division of Rural Rehabilitation of the Resettlement Administration (1935–1936). He was United States member of the Permanent Agricultural Committee of the International Labor Organization (1936–1951), and a consultant in many countries on rural programs.

Mormon scholars have made significant contributions in the field of soil physics and agronomy. Wilford Gardner, a historian of soil physics research who is at the University of Wisconsin, suggests that approximately half of the soil physicists in the English-speaking countries are Mormons or received their advanced degrees under Mormon professors. "Out of the ten soil physicists whose work is most frequently cited by others, eight are Mormons, and fourteen of the top twenty [are Mormons]."[29] Sixteen of the chairmen of the soil physics division of the Soil Science Society of America in the past forty years, according to Professor Gardner, have been Mormons, and he found a similar Mormon presence in the American Society of Agronomy and the American Society of Agricultural Engineers.

This paramount position stems from two students of Widtsoe and Harris, Willard Gardner and Thomas L. Martin. Born of early pioneers in Pine Valley, in southern Utah, Gardner taught for four years at the Murdock Academy in Beaver, Utah, completed a Ph.D. in physics at Berkeley, California, and returned to Utah State Agricultural College to launch the study of soil physics. His first wide recognition came in 1920 with the publication in *Soil Science* of a basic physical approach, utilizing mathematical analysis, to the problems related to the movement of water in soils. Many subsequent scholarly contributions followed the spirit of this early paper. Gardner's portrait hangs with those of five others in the Rothamstead Agricultural Experiment Station in England as one of the distinguished contributors to the field of soil science. "We must," Gardner said in typical Mormon language, "educate ourselves for the great mission that devolves upon us to multiply and replenish the earth and subdue it."[30] In 1948 Gardner was cited by the American Society of Agronomy as the "father of modern soil physics." His students include: L. A. Richards, of the U.S. Salinity Laboratory at Riverside, California, a grandson of Brigham Young's doctor and counselor Willard Richards, who shares with Gardner the title "most influential person in modern soil physics"; Don Kirkham, with a Ph.D. in physics from Columbia University, whose application of theoretical and mathematical physics to difficult drainage problems has attained international recognition; Orson W. Israelsen, of Hyrum, Utah, an internationally recognized authority on irrigation and drainage whose book *Irrigation Principles and Practices* (New York, 1932) has gone through several editions and has been translated into five languages and who has been an irrigation consultant in ten countries; Sylvan Wittwer, of Hurricane, Utah, now director of the Michigan State Agricultural Experiment Station, acknowledged by many to be a leading authority on plant nutrition and the preservation of vegetable root crops; and Dean Peterson, currently chief of the soil and water management division of the Department of State's Agency for International Development.[31]

Martin was a native of Lancashire, England, who emigrated to Utah at age fifteen, studied at Brigham Young University, and completed the Ph.D. at Cornell. Only five feet tall ("I have a pint-sized body with a giant-sized ambition"), Martin returned to BYU to devote the remainder of his life teaching agronomy. In subsequent years some 110 of his students went on to obtain a Ph.D. in soils and agronomy, and several of them have served as presidents of the American Society of Agronomy, which cited Martin in 1950 as "teacher of the year." At the time of Martin's death in 1958 seventy-five of these students held professorships at thirty-two universities. One of them, Rudger H. Walker, was chief of an international mission to Thailand (1947–1948), head of the U.S. Agricultural Mission in Iran (1958–1960), and on the board of the American University in Beirut, Lebanon (1954–1978). Another, Nyle C. Brady, son of Mississippi converts who settled in the Mormon colony in San Luis Valley, Colorado, served as dean of the College of Agriculture at Cornell, director of research for the U.S. Department of Agriculture, president of the Soil Science Society of America, author of a leading text on soils, and is currently director general of the International Rice Research Institute of Manila, the Philippines. Another, Daniel O. Robinson, served as director of agriculture at Arizona State University and advised the government of Morocco on agricultural development.

That Mormons have exerted a significant impact on several of the agricultural arts and sciences may be attributed in part to the strong social consciousness developed among those living under an irrigation canal. As Widtsoe explained:

> If the canal breaks or water is misused, the danger is for all. In the distribution of the water in the hot summer months when the flow is small and the need great, the neighbor and his rights loom large, and men must gird themselves with the golden rule. The intensive culture, which must prevail under irrigation, makes possible close settlements, often with the village as a center. Out of the desert, as the canals are dug, . . . come great results of successful experiments in intimate rural life; and out of the communities reared under irrigation . . . come men who, confident that it is best, can unflinchingly consider their neighbors' interests with their own; and who, therefore, can assume leadership in the advancing of a civilization based upon order and equal rights.[32]

Kusum Nair, an Indian writer and educator who benefited from a grant from the World Bank to make a study of agriculture in the United States, Japan, and India, devoted parts of two chapters to the Mormons in her prize-winning book *The Lonely Furrow*. One American, she wrote, told her that most Americans could not do irrigated farming. "It is much harder work [than other kinds of agriculture]." "An American," her informant went on, "can look big—six feet tall. But he *cannot* work hard. Now the orientals and Mormons can do that kind of work. They don't mind it. But not Americans. It's too hard. It's different. We don't understand it." The Mormons, he explained, "learnt to do it only because they had to." Mrs. Nair concludes her discussion of the Mormons, which is entitled "Spiritual Secularism," by expressing her delight that, as with farmers in India, the Mormons had succeeded in blending education and secular practice with religious belief and practice.[33]

While Mormonism is not synonymous with agrarianism and while only a minority of Mormons today live on farms, there has been a historical, if not doctrinal, association between Latter-day Saints and agriculture. Mormons continue to maintain a reverence for the biblical image of the sower going forth to sow. There is still in Mormon literature and folklore a mystical fire about the head of the husbandman. The culture continues to give the farmer status as a personage of particular and admired position, of unyielding traits of wholesomeness, who performs the most basic rites of society. The farmer remains, among Mormons, a symbol of their belief that man is exalted by serving as God's partner in dressing and redeeming the earth.

Mormons, of course, have achieved and made contributions in fields other than agriculture. A recent study of the social origins of American scientists and scholars concludes that, in relation to population, Utah was the most productive of all the states "for all fields [of learning] combined, in all time periods." Utah ranked first in biological and social sciences, second in education, third in physical sciences, and sixth in arts and professions. This ranking, the author declared, "seems clearly to be due to the influence of Mormon values." Values that Mormons share with other highly productive religious groups include, according to the author, a belief in a world of order, law, pattern, and meaning; a high valuation of learning; a restless, inquiring spirit; an optimism concerning man's ability to discover truth, accomplish things, and change the world; and seriousness of purpose, sense of mission, and willingness to share responsibility beyond the family.[34]

The increasing urbanization of Utah (one-third of the population of Utah now resides in the Salt Lake City metropolitan area), and the dispersion of Latter-day Saints throughout the nation, particularly in such urban centers as Los Angeles, Seattle, Phoenix, Denver, Chicago, New York, and Atlanta, has caused Mormons to become involved in various types of civic activity. For example, more Latter-day Saints have responded to what they consider a void of social programs intended to help the disadvantaged. Inauguration of the health and agricultural missionary programs has opened some outlets for idealists who wish to help church members in less well-developed areas, but on the whole those who wish to assist people in the larger American society resort to individual or family efforts, political parties, government-sponsored programs, professional associations, and other private or non–Latter-day Saint church-related organizations.[35] That members were not to confine their Christian humanitarianism to formally organized Mormon channels was made clear by a statement of the First Presidency in September of 1968:

> The growing world-wide responsibilities of the church make it inadvisable for the church to seek to respond to all the various and complex issues involved in the mounting problems of the many cities and communities in which members live. But this complexity does not absolve members as individuals from filling their responsibilities as citizens in their own communities.
>
> We urge our members to do their civic duty and to assume their responsibilities as individual citizens in seeking solutions to the problems which beset our cities and communities.
>
> With our wide ranging mission, so far as mankind is concerned, church members cannot ignore the many practical problems that require solution if our families are to live in an environment conducive to spirituality.
>
> Where solutions to these practical problems require cooperative action with those not of our faith, members should not be reticent in doing their part in joining and leading in those efforts where they can make an individual contribution to those causes which are consistent with the standards of the church.[36]

Some members have interpreted "their own community" very broadly. In 1967 thirty-one-year-old Cordell Andersen, who had been a missionary in Guatemala, packed his family into a camper and headed for Cobán. Within two years he had established Paradise Valley Plantation in order to work with the Pokonchi Indian families there. His program, the Foundation for Indian Development, has emphasized medical care, education, and general economic self-help. Andersen and his wife, Maria, are inspired by a quotation from Joseph Smith: "The nearer we get to our Heavenly Father the more we are disposed to look with compassion on perishing souls, feel that we want to take them upon our shoulders and cast their sins behind our backs."[37]

About the same time, in 1968, several American Mormons—Dr. Melvin A. Lyman and others—acting independently, although apparently with a *nihil obstat* from the church administration, established AYUDA ("help" or "assistance" in Spanish). Designed to provide voluntary assistance to both Mormons and non-Mormons in Latin America, particularly among Indians, this nonprofit organization opened a medical clinic in Cunen, a mountain village in Guatemala. Since then more than one hundred volunteers—doctors, nurses, educators, builders, and bankers—have donated from two weeks to twelve months of service. The clinic now also includes a dental clinic, a preschool, a secondary school, and a demonstration farm.[38]

In 1967 Stan Bronson, a Latter-day Saint serviceman stationed in Korea, wished to "do something significant" for the orphan children of that country. He devoted his spare time to playing his guitar and teaching them to sing. A group of children began to follow him around, and he arranged for them to sing on military bases and for service clubs. With the cooperation of fellow Latter-day Saint servicemen and the permission of the Korean government, he established the voluntarily staffed Tender Apples Foundation. Donations were solicited, and eventually the foundation established a home for thirty girls, ages ten to seventeen. The president of the Korean Mission Relief Society, Kun-ok Hwang, agreed to be their "mother," and the girls were placed in the home and earned their support by singing. They cut records and eventually became a well-known singing group in Korea. As each girl "graduates," a new one is accepted into the home and singing group.[39]

Other Mormons have utilized existing ward organizations for special programs. Members of the Alexandria Ward, who live in the Washington, D.C., metropolitan area, developed projects in response to the needs of their community and in "an attempt to apply the teachings of the church to the problems of daily living and to bring to bear the insights and strength of Mormon theology and organization upon their solution."[40] Although the general concept was stimulated by a stake leader's suggestion, it was developed and sustained by individual ward members. Voluntary participation was emphasized, and the formal church organization was utilized as a resource of information on opportunities. "Unlike work at the stake farm, the project is not termed a 'priesthood responsibility,' to avoid even subtle ecclesiastical suasion."[41] Care was taken to select and plan specific projects wisely. The first was with the Headstart Day Care Center, sponsored by Hopkins House, a settlement active in a number of welfare activities in Alexandria.[42] Approximately thirty-five Mormon families were involved in physical services at the center, teaching assistance, Saturday outings, and limited financial aid. A second project involved Sunday services for the elderly residents of the Woodbine Nursing and Convalescent Home. Another project, run on a stake basis, was the collection and delivery of seven truckloads of food to riot-torn areas.

The increasing tendency of Latter-day Saints born in the Mountain West to locate in urban areas outside that region, together with the influx into the church of thousands of converts in the Northeast, Southeast, and Midwest as well as in populated areas on the Pacific Coast, has caused a closer association of Latter-day Saints with blacks. The church's long-standing policy of withholding the priesthood from blacks "of African lineage," which had aroused controversy earlier, was a subject of renewed attention, particularly during the American civil rights movement of the 1960s.[43] Protest rallies were held in Salt Lake City and elsewhere, delegates from many civil rights groups sought to induce the church to change its policy, Brigham Young University athletic teams were picketed while on road trips, and at some contests anti-Mormon riots were staged.[44]

There were several thousand blacks who were faithful Mormons in the 1960s and early 1970s (exact statistics are unavailable because membership rolls do not list race). Although denied the priesthood, some of them did nonetheless officiate in church auxiliary organizations.[45] The First Presidency, in an official statement in 1969, declared: "Negroes [are] not yet to receive the priesthood, for reasons which we believe are known to God, but which He has not made fully known to man."[46] Some individual Mormons, emphasizing the generally equalitarian ethos of Mormonism, had concluded many years earlier that the church's stand was historically determined policy rather than divinely inspired revelation. In either case, the practice had its roots in the antiabolitionist atmosphere of Missouri, where the Mormons had settled in the 1830s. Blacks would be eligible to receive the priesthood, church members were assured by their president, when the Lord was willing.[47]

While there were individual members of the church who viewed the withholding of the priesthood as some kind of divine judgment on blacks, there was not, in practical terms, the bigotry that such a policy might be expected to have encouraged. In the Mormon scriptures there are passages reemphasizing the worth of all souls: "He [Jesus] inviteth them all to come unto him and partake of his goodness; and he denieth none that come unto him, black and white, bond and free, male and female . . . and all are alike unto God, both Jew and Gentile."[48] Statistical studies indicated that, compared with other Christian groups, Mormons did not have a higher degree of prejudice.[49] Perhaps this was because, with their own historical experience, the Mormons retained a heritage of concern for the underdog. Mormon leaders clearly stated that blacks should have full constitutional rights and urged members to "do their part as citizens to see that these rights are held inviolate. Each citizen must have equal opportunities and protection under the law with reference to civil rights."[50]

The formation in 1971 of the Genesis Group, an organization for black Mormons in the Salt Lake Valley, grew out of the efforts of three black members of the church.[51] Rather than wait for the development of an official program by the church administration, Ruffin Bridgeforth, Darius Gray, and Eugene Orr approached Gordon B. Hinckley of the Quorum of the Twelve Apostles, and he evidently carried to the First Presidency their petition for permission to meet as a group. The primary goal of the three men was the institution of an administratively autonomous group analogous to other branches in the Salt Lake Valley organized around ethnic rather than geographical boundaries; but they also hoped for several other, less direct consequences. One was the consideration and clarification of the question of priesthood ordination for worthy blacks. Another was the eradication of myths about and resentment toward blacks among church members. A third hoped-for result was a change in the church's missionary program so that blacks would be openly proselyted. A more direct consequence was the strengthening and reinforced fellowshipping of the one hundred or more blacks in the Salt Lake Valley who were already members of the church.

In October 1971 a committee of general authorities, including Hinckley, Thomas S. Monson, and Boyd K. Packer, met with the three black leaders and established the Genesis Group. Bridgeforth became its president, with Gray first counselor and Orr second counselor. The group operated its own independent Mutual Improvement Association (MIA), Primary, and Relief Society, but its members attended church sacrament meetings within the wards in which they lived. Officers and members were especially pleased when President Harold B. Lee gave a priesthood session conference address in April 1972 in which he emphasized the importance of civil rights.[52] Joseph Freeman, an active member of the Genesis Group, told *The New York Times*: "Many white people are hoping for a change, praying that the black will hold the priesthood, same as the blacks are. But for now, we're on the right train. Maybe we're not the engineer, but it's better than missing the train."[53]

For almost one hundred and fifty years Mormonism has been seen by its adherents as something more than a sect—as *the* Church of Jesus Christ on earth. This claim assured that, despite appearances to the contrary, the Church of Jesus Christ of Latter-day Saints could not be satisfied to see itself as a small ark of safety in a troubled world. The gospel, after all, was intended for all of God's children, and Mormons too accepted the fatherhood of God and the brotherhood of all men. In addition to this expansive self-definition—which certainly did not rest on an inferiority complex—Mormons exhibited a special sympathetic interest in such groups as the American Indians, Native Latin Americans, Polynesians, and Melanesians, all thought to be descendants of "Book of Mormon peoples" and thus in a sense blood brothers. Its exclusivist claims were thus counterbalanced by a universalist, all-encompassing outreach to "every nation, kindred, tongue, and people."

As related just above, however, there existed for many years a tension between the pretensions of universalism and the failure to attract members of African ancestry. In 1972 a friendly observer of Mormondom, Thomas O'Dea, contended that the way in which Mormon leaders would respond to the black issue was potentially diagnostic. "The profound turmoil over the problem of race, which the Mormon church experienced throughout the 1960s and still experiences in the new decade," he wrote, "may indeed prove to be the painful propaedeutic of the kind of transformation that would renew and reinvigorate the spirit of the original open and innovating Mormonism."[54]

On June 9, 1978, the church announced that the priesthood could thenceforth be given to all faithful, worthy males, without regard to race or color. Contained in a letter of the First Presidency addressed to all general and local officers of the church through the world, the document deserves quotation in full:

Dear Brethren:

As we have witnessed the expansion of the work of the Lord over the earth, we have been grateful that people of many nations have responded to the message of the restored gospel, and have joined the Church in ever-increasing numbers. This, in turn, has inspired us with a desire to extend to every worthy member of the Church all of the privileges and blessings which the gospel affords.

Aware of the promises made by the prophets and presidents of the Church who have preceded us that at some time, in God's eternal plan, all of our brethren who are worthy may receive the priesthood, and witnessing the faithfulness of those from whom the priesthood has been withheld, we have pleaded long and earnestly in behalf of these, our faithful brethren, spending many hours in the Upper Room of the Temple supplicating the Lord for divine guidance.

He has heard our prayers, and by revelation has confirmed that the long-promised day has come when every faithful, worthy man in the Church may receive the holy priesthood, with power to exercise its divine authority, and enjoy with his loved ones every blessing that flows therefrom, including the blessings of the temple. Accordingly, all worthy male members of the Church may be ordained to the priesthood without regard for race or color. Priesthood leaders are instructed to follow the policy of carefully interviewing all candidates for ordination to either the Aaronic or the Melchizedek Priesthood to insure that they meet the established standards for worthiness.

We declare with soberness that the Lord has now made known his will for the blessing of all his children throughout the earth who will hearken to the voice of his authorized servants, and prepare themselves to receive every blessing of the gospel.

Sincerely yours,

Spencer W. Kimball
N. Eldon Tanner
Marion G. Romney[55]

The announcement was received, almost universally, with elation; and wards, branches, and missions with black members eagerly began to interview worthy blacks in preparation for ordination. Observers found that the revelation had both real and symbolic meaning. It removed any existing "excuse" for discrimination and prejudice, improved the church's relationships with blacks, permitted all worthy members to participate in temple rites, opened the way for active missionary work in "central cities" and in Africa, and assured that local leadership, regardless of race and color, would be able to administer baptism, serve as missionaries, and, indeed, serve in all echelons and branches of the church's government. That the announcement was made as revelation—as the Lord making his will known to the leaders of his church—was, of course, particularly gratifying to faithful Latter-day Saints, who interpreted this as evidence that God continues to exercise direction in the affairs of the church.

It is perhaps appropriate that this long-awaited communication should have been conveyed by the presidency of Spencer W. Kimball. A long-time resident of Arizona and an apostle since 1943, Kimball has devoted much of his attention to Indians. From the beginning of his presidency in 1974 he has articulated the universality of Mormonism and has reiterated the importance of carrying the "restored gospel" to all people.[56]

A few individual efforts of Latter-day Saints have come as a direct response to administrative decisions by the institutional church. The initial stimulus for the formation of Cornerstone, a nonprofit organization interested in preserving historic and architecturally significant Mormon buildings, was the razing of the Coalville Tabernacle in 1971. A graceful structure of simplified Gothic design, the tabernacle was built between 1879 and 1889 forty miles northeast of Salt Lake City. The circumstances surrounding its destruction are still so emotionally charged that the actual chain of events is difficult to reconstruct. The needs of the Coalville congregation dictated a larger, more modern building, and after some discussion the tabernacle was razed.[57]

Destruction of the building, whose interior architectural integrity had been impaired by remodeling in 1944 but whose external aesthetic and historical significance remained, created a groundswell of concern among both Mormons and non-Mormons about the future of other historic church buildings. In December 1971 Cornerstone was founded by a group of young church members who sought to document the architectural and historical significance of churches and tabernacles and to consider alternate uses for them when they could no longer serve their original function. Church members were becoming more sensitive to the need for maintaining their physical heritage.[58] Already convinced that some of these tangible symbols of spiritual values constructed before the days of uniform church architecture ought to be preserved, the church in 1974 created the position of Church Curator, who has responsibility for the church's collection of art and artifacts and, with a broad-based committee, makes recommendations on historic buildings and sites.

The use of periodicals to express points of view and promote programs outside the framework of the official church has had a long history in Mormonism, going back to the *Utah Magazine* and *Woman's Exponent* in the 1860s and 1870s. This kind of expression experienced a new flurry of activity in the 1960s and 1970s.

Although the institutional church attempts to meet the needs of women members with an increasingly diversified Relief Society program, opportunities to serve in a variety of other functions, and emphasis upon the importance of traditional feminine roles, some women feel the need for further activities. *Exponent II*, "a modest but sincere newspaper" published quarterly by Mormon Sisters, Inc., of Arlington, Massachusetts, takes its name and nature from the *Woman's Exponent*, which was issued by leading Mormon women between 1872 and 1914. *Exponent II* attempts to provide spirited and open discussion of the problems of being a Mormon woman in the 1970s. "Poised on the dual platforms of Mormonism and feminism," it offers a platform for frank discussion of Mormon life-styles.[59] Its content is marked by openness, and its candid tone provides a refreshingly forthright recognition of problems and a discussion of possible solutions.

Exponent II is produced by a group that had existed informally for several years as the Boston Women's Group, which initially developed from a Cambridge (Mass.) Ward Relief Society project that created *A Beginner's Boston* (Cambridge, 1967; 2nd ed., 1970), a travel guide to the area that provides insights into New England's culture. Later they published *Mormon Sisters: Women in Early Utah* (Boston, 1976), a series of essays on the roles, personalities, and problems of early Mormon women.

The same need for sharing feelings and exploring attitudes with sympathetic people led to the organization of the Salt Lake City General Retrenchment Society in the spring of 1974. The original Retrenchment Society was a group of leading Mormon women who met semimonthly between 1870 and 1914. They "retrenched" from ignorance, studying physiology, politics, theology, and women's sphere of responsibilities. The Retrenchment Society of the 1970s decided to extend their private discussion and growing awareness of woman's roles in society through a lecture series cosponsored by the Utah Endowment for the Humanities. The lectures on the general topic "Utah Women: Roots and Realities" ranged from an analysis of women in the scriptural tradition to discussion of women in Utah minorities. Both *Exponent II* and the Retrenchment Society suggest the stresses upon traditional Mormon women's roles and the desire of many women to combine the spiritual benefits of the religion with the options and opportunities available for personal development and service.

An awareness of the importance of the roots of Mormonism and the need to examine them professionally led to the formation of the Mormon History Association in December 1965 in San Francisco. The group originally consisted primarily of professionally trained Mormon historians—members of both the Church of Jesus Christ of Latter-day Saints (LDS) and the Reorganized Church of Jesus Christ of Latter Day Saints (RLDS)—but the membership now includes many history buffs. The association functions in several important ways for those who desire to explore their own cultural heritage in historical research and writing as much as through participation in standard church programs. It publishes the *Journal of Mormon History,* holds an annual meeting at which a variety of papers on Mormon history are presented, sponsors programs at meetings of other professional historical associations, circulates a newsletter, and grants awards for the best book and best articles on Mormon history published each year.

Dialogue: A Journal of Mormon Thought, which began at Stanford University in 1966, has provided a forum for scholarly examination of virtually every topic that might interest Mormons. The statement of purpose in the first issue of the quarterly journal declares its aims as being:

> to express Mormon culture and examine the relevance of religion to secular life. It is edited by Mormons who wish to bring their faith into dialogue with human experience as a whole and to foster artistic and scholarly achievement based on their cultural heritage. The journal encourages a variety of viewpoints; although every effort is made to insure accurate scholarship and responsible judgment, the views expressed are those of the individual authors and are not necessarily those of the Mormon Church or of the editors.[60]

Although many consider the journal an expression of liberal Mormon thought, its intent is to "serve as a forum for the encounter of diverse opinions, not as a platform for the promulgation of one kind of opinion."[61] Special sections of the journal were designed to "foster a spirited exchange of views," including criticism and comment on contemporary events; reviews of important articles, books, records, films, and artistic events of special interest to Mormons; and critical surveys of current literature on Mormon themes.

Dialogue has provided aid and comfort to an independent yet loyal intellectual community in the church. It has also been helpful to young Mormons who question and apply aspects of their secular education to their religion. Above all, *Dialogue* has enabled Latter-day Saint men and women to articulate the reasons for their commitment to Mormonism and the culture it has produced, as well as the tensions (if any) that this creates in their profession.

Other publications have been subtly influenced by *Dialogue,* both graphically and editorially. *BYU Studies,* originally established in 1959 as "A Voice for the Community of LDS Scholars," was revitalized. The illustrations and format of the official church publications for youth, children, and adults became less conservative, and, in fact, several of the artists who worked with *Dialogue* became members of the staffs for these publications. And since 1976 *Sunstone*, a quarterly journal organized and operated by Latter-day Saint students and young adults, has attempted to deal with the modern problems of Mormonism in a less academic atmosphere than that supplied by *Dialogue*. Spearheaded by Mormon students attending the University of California at Berkeley, *Sunstone* has sought to

> provide an opportunity for young people and older amateurs to express their views and meet their peers in an atmosphere more compatible with their informal lifestyle and more conducive to their participation—an arena for lively discussion with high student, rather than professional, academic and literary standards. . . . *Sunstone* sees itself more as a companion than a competitor of *Dialogue*.[62]

The desire of Mormons to grow intellectually is reflected in diverse and sometimes subtle ways. Many members are involved in private study groups. The formation of literary, "polysophical," debating, and self-improvement societies by Mormons predates the settlement of the Great Basin. The general structure of such circles—a few persons or couples getting together on a regular basis for some kind of mutual intellectual and spiritual improvement and social fulfillment—has continued to the present. The fact that the groups have persisted during a time when official church programs have become more complex and demanding indicates that members feel a basic desire to associate with other Mormons on a self-determined rather than church-directed basis. These informal units study a book, article, or topic and then discuss their opinions, or they may rotate the responsibility for presenting a talk or paper of mutual interest. In some cases, parents gather to discuss problems of raising their children, pooling their knowledge and occasionally inviting a guest speaker.[63]

One of Joseph Smith's statements on the fundamental beliefs of the church declares that "if there is anything virtuous, lovely, or of good report or praiseworthy, we seek after these things."[64] This should leave ample room for Mormons to participate in music, dance, literature, painting, and sculpture. Some activity in these fields has been directly sponsored by the church: hymn writing, choral groups, operatic efforts, play writing and production, social dancing and pageantry, architecture for church buildings, sculpture for monuments, murals for temples. Such encouragement by the church continues, with wards, stakes, missions, and the church magazines offering an outlet. A Mormon Arts Festival, held at Brigham Young University since 1969, follows the tradition of fairs and festivals of a century past in stimulating university exposure to playwrights, painters, sculptors, and composers.[65] In general, it is fair to say that the Mormon literature and art that finds expression through official channels tends to be didactic (which is no criticism to those who see this as its prime function), is generally competent rather than great, and has answered rather well the needs and interests of the Mormon audience. There have been individual achievements under direct sponsorship that are outstanding (some of the murals painted for the temples, the architecture of some early buildings), and, with the higher educational levels of the twentieth century, the future is rich with possibilities.[66]

Church leaders have not had the resources to function like the Medici or the papacy of the Renaissance, so most noteworthy cultural achievements have fallen outside church programs—work Mormons produce on their own. Much of this—like artistic productions of Presbyterians, Methodists, or atheists—has no obvious connection with their religion. Knud and Sören Edsberg, Danish converts, father and son, are examples. The work of the former is realistic, mainly portraiture but also including landscapes and farm scenes, while the work of the latter is largely abstract.[67]

Among those artists who have dealt with Mormon themes have been the composer B. Cecil Gates, a grandson of Brigham Young, who in the early years of this century studied in Germany and composed cantatas and other choral works. LeRoy J. Robertson, whose *Trilogy* won the international Reichhold Award in 1947, composed, in addition to many hymns, several symphonic works, a violin concerto, and an ambitious Book of Mormon *Oratorio;* this last work is the most impressive yet in terms of its fusion of the Christian oratorio tradition with a Mormon theme.[68]

The various books of Richard L. Evans, religious essays based on "The Spoken Word" of the Mormon Tabernacle Choir broadcasts over CBS, have probably reached more individuals than the writings of any other Saint. Deliberately general in tone so as to appeal to a wide audience, they are nevertheless permeated with Mormon values and frequently quote from its scriptures.[69]

Two biographers of Mormon background have attained national recognition. Merlo Pusey, a newspaperman with the Washington *Post,* wrote a prizewinning life of Charles Evans Hughes and went on to prepare biographies of Eugene Meyer and the early Mormon leaders George A. Smith, John Henry Smith, and George Albert Smith. Fawn McKay Brodie, from Huntsville, Utah, published at the age of thirty her protopsychobiography of Joseph Smith and later wrote lives of Thaddeus Stevens, Sir Richard Burton, and Thomas Jefferson.

One area of scholarship in which the Mormons have made significant impact is folklore. Scholars who have made contributions in this area include Austin and Alta Fife, Hector Lee, Wayland Hand, Thomas Cheney, and William A. ("Bert") Wilson. While each of these scholars has done significant work on other regions of the United States and foreign countries (for example, Fife in French and Wilson in Finnish folklore), their work on the Saints has done much to establish Mormon folklore as a rich vein deserving study. One of the favorite subjects of the scholars has been J. Golden Kimball, often called the "Will Rogers of Mormondom." Son of Apostle Heber C. Kimball, a six-foot-three-inch beanpole of a man, once a mule skinner in the Bear Lake region, Kimball had a colorful vocabulary, which he used, even from the pulpit, in a shrill magpie voice. Beloved by Latter-day Saints as no other person but the Prophet, he died in 1938, at age 85, leaving a personalized legacy of unwearying dedication to Mormonism, liberally spiced with anecdotes, which, as they were told and retold, became part of the lore of the Latter-day Saints. He helped Mormons diminish their pretensions, pride, and self-deception, and reminded them that they must not take themselves too seriously.[70]

In the field of fiction perhaps the most important writer of Mormon background has been Vardis Fisher, whose series *Tetralogy* (1932–34) and *Testament of Man* (1947–1960) are recognized as major achievements. There are differences of opinion on Fisher's importance, perhaps, and it may be that the next generation will be in a better position to evaluate him. In any case, his Mormon upbringing had a powerful influence not only on *The Children of God* (1939), a novelistic, basically sympathetic retelling of the Mormon epic, but also on his other novels.[71]

Among writers concentrating on the Mormon experience, Virginia Sorensen, some of whose writings have appeared in *The New Yorker*, has published *A Little Lower than the Angels* (1942), *On This Star* (1946), *The Neighbors* (1947), *The Evening and the Morning* (1949), *Many Heavens* (1956), *The House Next Door* (1954), *Kingdom Come* (1960), and *Where Nothing Is Long Ago* (1963). One reviewer described her *Kingdom Come* as having "the amplitude of a book from the time of Dickens or Thackeray."[72] A historical novel that some consider the best on a Mormon subject is Maurine Whipple's *The Giant Joshua* (1941, 1976), dealing with the conflicts arising from the pioneering venture in southern Utah. Recently Herbert Harker has published *Turn Again Home* (1977), which weaves the experience of Mormons in Alberta, Canada, into a kind of "whodunit" with archetypal overtones.

Two short-story writers who have lately provided insights into the dilemmas of Mormon life are Douglas Thayer and Don Marshall, both professors at Brigham Young University. "I'm interested in writing about the righteous person struggling hard to live a righteous life," says Thayer. "His conflicts may be very subtle, but they're real. I don't want to write about people who are corrupt. All that incredible evil has been explored too much."[73] The result of this approach is the collection *Under the Cottonwoods* (1977), which provides valuable insights into the Mormon experience in a Utah town. Don Marshall's *The Rummage Sale* (1972) probed various aspects of typical Mormon experience, some of them rather uncomfortable. The work was a commercial success and led to *Frost in the Orchard* (1977). "Black writers and Jewish writers and Southern writers have all found world-wide audiences—why shouldn't we?" asks Marshall.[74]

From as long ago as Nauvoo in the 1840s, when Brigham Young played the role of the high priest in *Pizarro*, Mormons have been active in promoting drama. The Salt Lake Theatre's record of producing works of importance commencing in 1862, with high-quality acting and staging, probably compares favorably with any such group in the country. These traditions have continued into the twentieth century, with the Mutual Improvement Association stimulating productions on the local level for many years. In the writing of plays, however, it would be hard to argue that those emanating from Mormon playwrights up to the present generation are worth reading as literature, much less resurrecting as dramatic productions. A didactic strain continues to be strong in works produced down to the present. *Promised Valley*, a musical by Arnold Sundgaard and Crawford Gates in the vein of Rodgers and Hammerstein, appeared in 1947 and continues to be shown each summer. In the 1970s Doug Stewart's and Lex d'Azevedo's musical *Saturday's Warrior* combined a story based on the Mormon belief in a premortal existence with catchy lyrics and rock rhythms; the work was a popular success in the western United States.

Nevertheless, young Mormon playwrights are reaching out for new combinations, some of them exciting in their dramatic qualities as they utilize Mormon characters and scenes. Martin Kelly's *And They Shall Be Gathered* (1969) portrays the tensions in an Armenian family when a young couple joins the Mormon church. The portrayal is not black and white; good is found in the non-Mormons, who fail to understand why anyone would want to associate with this strange religion, and there are human failings in the Mormon characters. In 1971 audiences responded very favorably to Carol Lynn Pearson's *The Order Is Love* (music by Lex d'Azevedo), which has its setting in Orderville in southern Utah, home of the longest-lasting United Order experiment. Again, the tendency of the past generation of Saints to see the world in terms of a two-valued orientation, Mormons as good people, non-Mormons as bad, is discarded in favor of a more interesting combination showing the complexity of human nature in all its perversity in the Mormon communal experiment. Similarly, Robert Elliott's *Fires of the Mind* deals with Mormon missionaries in Taiwan in a cogent contrast of cultural values and personalities. Orson Scott Card, a young Mormon playwright, has produced *Father, Mother, Mother, and Mom* depicting life in a polygamous family.

Thomas Rogers reached out in *Huebener* to show dramatically the dilemma of clashing commitments when an idealistic young Mormon in Nazi Germany was executed for his resistance activity. Utilizing authentic incidents and dialogue, as in the one-man-show format that Hal Holbrook used in portraying Mark Twain, James Arrington wrote and produced *Here's Brother Brigham* in 1976, performing as Brigham Young before hundreds of appreciative audiences.[75]

A good deal of this dramatic creativity centers at Brigham Young University, but there are private groups and companies also producing new plays. As yet, no Mormon play has been successful on Broadway or before a general audience.[76] Nevertheless, there is creative ferment here that augurs well for the future.

Not many Mormon poets have attained national recognition, although Sarah Carmichael, in the pioneer period, attracted the attention of William Cullen Bryant, and some mistakenly thought that Orson F. Whitney's epic *Elias* (1904) was in a class with Milton's works. One of the most promising young writers, David Wright, died at a young age before his work reached maturity. A generation ago, *Poems* by a Mormon convert from Pennsylvania, Jon Beck Shank, was highly regarded by some critics. May Swenson, of Mormon background, has more recently been recognized in national poetry circles.

Unknown outside of a Latter-day Saint audience are a dozen other poets of genuine merit who often incorporate Mormon themes or references into their works. Perhaps the most respected Mormon poet has been Clinton F. Larson, who has published *The Mantle of the Prophet and Other Plays* (1966), *The Lord of Experience* (1967), and *Counterpoint* (1973). Other current poets include: Emma Lou Thayne, Carol Lynn Pearson, John Sterling Harris, Arthur Henry King, Clifton Holt Jolley, Linda Sillitoe, Mary Bradford, and others. Carol Lynn Pearson, whose several books of poetry are strongly interlaced with Mormon theology, wrote "Ritual."

> Why ritual?
> May I not receive
> Christ without burial
> By water?
> If I remember
> That He bled,
> If I believe
> What need for
> Sacramental bread?
>
> Only this I know:
> All cries out

> For form—
> No impulse
> Can rest
> Until somehow
> It is manifest.
> Even my spirit,
> Housed in heaven,
> Was not content
> Until it won
> Embodiment.[77]

This is unpretentious but understandably appealing to modern Mormons. Another example is "The Gathering" by Edward L. Hart:

> They came by thousands at a slow clip,
> All but those buried at Haun's Mill
> Or Florence or some place that the lip
> Of man had no name for yet to trip
> The tongue of the young, who wanted still
> To find home over the next hill
> Or lush pastures past each desert strip.
>
> They came over the mountains and around
> The Horn in ships and wagons, or dragged
> Handcarts over stony and frozen ground,
> Often opened and shoveled in a mound
> Upon woman and children or the man who lagged
> In his shafts only on the day he sagged
> In death on the crosspiece: Zion bound.[78]

In art, we have already noted that much work by Latter-day Saint artists is in the areas of landscape, portraiture, or abstraction. However important, it is not identifiably Mormon. Some artists, however, have been fertile in monumentalizing the Mormon past as part of their output, such as C. C. A. Christensen (1831–1912), whose paintings were exhibited at the Whitney Museum of American Art in 1970 and reproduced in color in *Art in America,* Torlief Knaphus (*The Handcart Pioneers,* 1926), Mahonri Young (*This Is the Place Monument,* 1947), and Minerva Teichert (1889–1976) (a series of drawings and paintings on Book of Mormon and Mormon history topics).[79] A noted illustrator whose paintings of Book of Mormon scenes have been widely reproduced is Arnold Friberg. Trevor Southey has produced several paintings that attempt to convey the meaning of the plan of salvation (ranging from premortal to postmortal existence in Mormon theology). And convert Gary Smith has been attracted to the powerful artistic potentiality of certain crucial moments in church history, especially those surrounding the martyrdom of Joseph Smith. As with music, literature, and poetry, Mormons have not yet arrived, nor are they at the forefront of the world's cultural attainment. But they have achieved in these areas probably better than they are usually given credit for.

Most individual responses of modern Mormons involve a kind of tie with the past. In some cases it is an examination and evaluation of models and precedents; in others, it is a seeking for the roots of the present in order to understand, and to a degree, even shape the future. Some individual responses are formalized into official church programs. Some are tolerated or ignored, others given an informal "blessing" by one or more church officials, in the spirit of former President Heber J. Grant's response to a young man eager to help the church: "Help the church?" said the Prophet. "Go and do the best you can in whatever you'd like to do—and do it well."

Identity crises are not new to Mormonism;[80] at least four have already been touched upon. The first, occurring between 1830 and 1838, had to do with the formulation of a general program for the "restoration" of the "true church" and the commitment of the Saints to gathering in the West. The second was one of leadership at the time of Joseph Smith's death in 1844; it was concluded by the assumption of the role of prophet and president by Brigham Young. The third crisis involved the struggle to preserve the integrity of the church and kingdom between 1847 and 1889, as increasing pressures forced an agonizing reappraisal of economic and political policies. The fourth, during the church's conflict with the federal government, was precipitated by the decision of the U.S. Supreme Court to uphold the Edmunds-Tucker Act of 1887. The Manifesto of 1890 and Utah's statehood in 1896 were signs of reconciliation, although some of the hostilities continued to linger on.

In recent years the church has found itself confronted with a fifth crisis of sizable proportions: the confrontation with modern skepticism and hedonism and the counterculture of youth. It has responded with programs and policies, marked by a growing professionalism and increasing internationalization. In addition to programs, a large sphere of individual activity remains; and Mormons—artists and writers, educators, journalists, musicians, and all kinds of ordinary people—have not hesitated to follow various paths as they work out the relationship of their religion to their individual needs.

In this general time of reappraisal there is, as with Lutherans, Episcopalians, and others, a continuing and in some ways healthy tension between what might be called conservatives and liberals within the church. In an imaginative use of Mormon symbolism, Richard Poll has suggested that these might be referred to as the "Iron Rod Saints" and the "Liahona

Saints."[81] Both terms come from the Book of Mormon. The Iron Rod was the word of God; persons who held on to it could follow the straight and narrow path to the fruitful tree of life. The Liahona was the compass that émigrés from Israel used to guide them on the way; but it did not fully mark the path, and the clarity of its directions varied with the circumstances of the user. As suggested by the symbolism, the Iron Rod Saint finds the answers to all his questions, both large and small, in scripture, the works of prophetic authority, official pronouncements, and the Holy Spirit. Revelation, both past and present, is the iron rod that will lead one to exaltation in the Kingdom. The Liahona Saint may be skeptical of the answers Iron Rod Saints think they have found in their sources. No human instrument, the Liahona Saint feels, is always capable of transmitting the word of God so clearly and comprehensively that it can be universally understood and easily appropriated. Individual human consideration is both necessary and desirable to identify the specific path any particular person must follow. Both kinds include "good" Latter-day Saints—deeply committed, living the standards, and active in their wards and stakes.

That both Iron Rod and Liahona Saints have been converted to Mormonism and have remained loyal and active is evidence of its vitality and vigor. Unlike fundamentalists in some other faiths, conservative Mormons include many highly educated individuals who emphasize strong reliance on the wording of scripture, the authoritative structure of church government, and a church-centered social system. Liberals emphasize the boldness and innovative character of the Restoration, faith in the essential goodness of man and his possibilities of eternal progression, and the church's commitment to education and the resulting emphasis on rationality. The checks and balances inherent in the two traditions and types of membership give Mormonism both stability and progressivism.

Has Mormonism, then, been able to meet the needs of its people in the contemporary world but at the same time retain its most basic values? While it may be argued that its complex organization, multiple programs, and paternalistic atmosphere attempt to shield its youth from modern realities, it may also be true that these very things help combat the social deterioration often wrought by current forces. Some may wonder whether what they see as a program-oriented institutional approach, coupled with inventive individual responses, can continue to resist the centrifugal forces of modernity. What they probably miss in their observation is the reality of the process Mormons know as "continuous revelation." Changes come frequently in methods, organization, and programs. But the goals remain—to produce sons and daughters of God who will strive to emulate His creativity, intelligence, and love. Despite its past travail and present challenges, Mormonism clearly remains a vibrant force in the lives of its members.

Appendix
Bibliographical Essay
Notes

Appendix

First Presidencies of the Church of Jesus Christ of Latter-day Saints, 1830–1978

The name of the president is given at the left, with his counselors listed under him. The dates in parentheses are dates for birth and death. Those after the comma refer to the years that were served in the position indicated.

JOSEPH SMITH (1805–1844), 1830–1844
 Oliver Cowdery (1806–1850), 1830–1838;
  Second elder, 1830–1834; Assistant president, 1834–1838
 Sidney Rigdon (1793–1876), 1833–1844
 Frederick G. Williams (1787–1842), 1832–1837
 Hyrum Smith (1800–1844), 1837–1844
 William Law (1809–1892), 1841–1844
 John C. Bennett (1804–18?), 1841–1842
 Amasa M. Lyman (1813–1877), 1843–1844

BRIGHAM YOUNG (1801–1877), 1847–1877
 Heber C. Kimball (1801–1868), 1847–1868
 Willard Richards (1804–1854), 1847–1854
 Jedediah M. Grant (1816–1856), 1854–1856
 Daniel H. Wells (1814–1891), 1857–1877
 George A. Smith (1817–1875), 1868–1875
 John W. Young (1844–1924), 1873–1877
 George Q. Cannon (1827–1901), 1873–1877
 Brigham Young, Jr. (1836–1903), 1873–1877
 Albert Carrington (1813–1889), 1873–1877

JOHN TAYLOR (1808–1887), 1880–1887
 George Q. Cannon (1827–1901), 1880–1887
 Joseph F. Smith (1838–1918), 1880–1887

WILFORD WOODRUFF (1807–1898), 1889–1898
 George Q. Cannon (1827–1901), 1889–1898
 Joseph F. Smith (1838–1918), 1889–1898

LORENZO SNOW (1814–1901), 1898–1901
 George Q. Cannon (1827–1901), 1898–1901
 Joseph F. Smith (1838–1918), 1898–1901

JOSEPH F. SMITH (1838–1918), 1901–1918
 John R. Winder (1821–1910), 1901–1910
 Anthon H. Lund (1844–1921), 1901–1918
 John Henry Smith (1848–1911), 1910–1911
 Charles W. Penrose (1832–1925), 1911–1918

HEBER J. GRANT (1856–1945), 1918–1945
  Anthon H. Lund (1844–1921), 1918–1921
  Charles W. Penrose (1832–1925), 1918–1925
  Anthony W. Ivins (1852–1934), 1921–1934
  Charles W. Nibley (1849–1931), 1925–1931
  J. Reuben Clark, Jr. (1871–1961), 1933–1945
  David O. McKay (1873–1970), 1934–1945

GEORGE ALBERT SMITH (1870–1951), 1945–1951
  J. Reuben Clark, Jr. (1871–1961), 1945–1951
  David O. McKay (1873–1970), 1945–1951

DAVID O. MCKAY (1873–1970), 1951–1970
  Stephen L. Richards (1879–1959), 1951–1959
  J. Reuben Clark, Jr. (1871–1961), 1951–1961
  Henry D. Moyle (1889–1963), 1961–1963
  Hugh B. Brown (1883–1975), 1961–1970
  N. Eldon Tanner (1898–), 1963–1970
  Joseph Fielding Smith (1876–1972), 1965–1970
  Thorpe B. Isaacson (1898–1970), 1965–1970
  Alvin R. Dyer (1903–1977), 1968–1970

JOSEPH FIELDING SMITH (1876–1972), 1970–1972
  Harold B. Lee (1899–1973), 1970–1972
  N. Eldon Tanner (1898–), 1970–1972

HAROLD B. LEE (1899–1973), 1972–1973
  N. Eldon Tanner (1898–), 1972–1973
  Marion G. Romney (1897–), 1972–1973

SPENCER W. KIMBALL (1895–), 1973–
  N. Eldon Tanner (1898–), 1973–
  Marion G. Romney (1897–), 1973–

Bibliographical Essay

The primary sources of Mormon history are largely in the archival collection of the Church of Jesus Christ of Latter-day Saints, housed in the east wing of the twenty-eight-story Church Office Building in Salt Lake City. They include:

1. Minute books and other records of the church and its many general, regional, and local units. There are perhaps as many as a million volumes of these records for the period 1830 to the present; they include data on the settlement and development of many localities.

2. Diaries of some three thousand members of the church, including general authorities, stake officers, and ward officers.

3. Papers of many general officers of the church and of many church-sponsored organizations. There are more than six thousand manuscript collections; one of the largest of these is the Papers of Brigham Young, which includes about 30,000 pages of outgoing and incoming correspondence, all properly identified.

4. Journal History of the Church, which is a day-by-day record of events, consisting of newspaper clippings, excerpts from diaries and letters, and other records. There are more than one thousand volumes in this massive compilation.

5. The Manuscript History of Brigham Young, a massive day-by-day compilation which includes forty-seven thick handwritten volumes with overall about 48,000 pages.

6. Ledgers and account books of the church and many of the enterprises and organizations it has sponsored.

7. Many records of Utah Territory during the period 1851–58, including legislative papers; official correspondence; minutes of legislative sessions; papers of the territorial militia, penitentiary, and library; census records, tax rolls, election returns; and many records of the State of Deseret.

8. Immigration records created in connection with the Perpetual Emigrating Fund and the immigration system operated by the Mormons, 1840–1887.

9. Many collections relating to the American Indian, including the papers generated during Brigham Young's two terms as Superintendent of Indian Affairs (1851–57) as well as the pre-territorial period, 1847–51, and the records kept by Indian farmers, missionaries, and church Indian agents.

10. Social records of the church, including marriage and divorce papers, educational records, and the papers of the Brigham Young family.

11. Church Historian's Office Record Group, which contains office journals for most of the years 1844 to the present.

12. All, or essentially all, the publications of the church from 1830 to the present, including books, periodicals, pamphlets, tracts, and letters of instruction.

All or nearly all of these manuscript materials are available to researchers, with the exception of certain minutes of presiding quorums which have not yet been released by those quorums. In addition, as might be expected, the archives contain some confidential material, such as minutes of ecclesiastical court trials and records of financial contributions, which are not available.

Housed in the west wing of the Church Office Building is the Genealogical Department of the church, which has collected and administers approximately one million microfilm rolls of church records, county courthouse records, state archives, national records, and foreign depositories in many parts of the world. These include probates, tax records, property holdings, land records, census records, vital statistics, and deeds. There is also a computerized collection of about thirty million names and related vital statistics, and several million family group records, an impressive collection of published local histories, and many thousands of family records. These records are as invaluable to demographers and social historians as to genealogists and family historians.

Additional manuscript collections are found in Special Collections, Brigham Young University Library, Provo, Utah; Library of the Utah State Historical Society, Salt Lake City; Western Americana Collection, University of Utah Library, Salt Lake City; Special Collections, Utah State University Library, Logan, Utah; Henry E. Huntington Library and Art Gallery, San Marino, California; University of California Library, Berkeley; Yale University Library, New Haven, Connecticut; New York Public Library, New York; and the Library of Congress, Washington, D.C. Guides to some of these collections have been published.

The almost inconceivable wealth of primary material chronicled by Mormon participants makes especially useful a recent work that introduces 2,894 valuable firsthand accounts: Davis Bitton, *Guide to Mormon Diaries and Autobiographies* (Provo, Utah: Brigham Young University Press, 1977). Two collections of primary material are William Mulder and A. Russell Mortensen, eds., *Among the Mormons: Historic Accounts by Contemporary Observers* (New York: Alfred A. Knopf, 1958); and Richard H. Cracroft and Neal E. Lambert, *A Believing People: Literature of the Latter-day Saints* (Provo, Utah: Brigham Young University Press, 1974).

Reference works of proven value prepared and published by the church and its Assistant Historian, Andrew Jenson, include *The Historical Record*, 9 vols. (Salt Lake City, 1882-1890); *Encyclopedic History of the Church* (Salt Lake City, 1941); *Church Chronology* (2nd ed., Salt Lake City, 1899); and *Latter-day Saint Biographical Encyclopedia*, 4 vols. (Salt Lake City, 1901-1936). A modern reference work updated annually is *Deseret News Church Almanac* (Salt Lake City, 1974-).

The list of church periodicals that have presented the "official" Mormon point of view, as well as occasional articles on aspects of Mormon history, is too long to be mentioned here, but of particular value for a general introduction are two Salt Lake City monthlies published by the church: *The Improvement Era* (1897-1970) and the *Ensign* (1971-). The Reorganized Church of Jesus Christ of Latter Day Saints, of Independence, Missouri, has published the monthly *Saints' Herald* (1860-).

Until recently the published literature on Mormon history tended to be classified under two headings: those that supported Mormonism and those that attacked it. All such works for the first century have been listed in Chad Flake, ed., *A Mormon Bibliography, 1830-1930: Books, Pamphlets, Periodicals, and Broadsides Relating to the First Century of Mormonism* (Salt Lake City: University of Utah Press, 1978). This indispensable and massive compilation also indicates libraries and archives in which the books and pamphlets are located.

Early Mormon accounts were Joseph Smith, "History of Joseph Smith," the first part of which was published in *The Times and Seasons* (Nauvoo, Ill.), 1842-1846; in the

Deseret News (Salt Lake City), 1851–1857; and in the *Latter-day Saints' Millennial Star* (Liverpool, Eng.), 1852–1862. It was republished by the church in 1902–1912 in six volumes, under the editorship of B. H. Roberts, as *History of the Church . . . Period I, by Joseph Smith* (Salt Lake City). Usually referred to as the "documentary" *History of the Church,* this is an indispensable collection of primary sources on early Mormonism, selected and edited from a Mormon point of view. A seventh volume in this series was published in Salt Lake City in 1932 as the "Apostolic Interregnum." There followed George A. Smith, *The Rise, Progress, and Travels of the Church* (Salt Lake City, 1869); Orson F. Whitney, *History of Utah,* 4 vols. (Salt Lake City, 1892–1904); B. H. Roberts, "History of the Mormon Church" in *Americana,* which appeared serially 1909–1915 and was later revised and brought up to date in *A Comprehensive History of the Church of Jesus Christ of Latter-day Saints: Century I,* 6 vols. (Salt Lake City, 1930); Joseph Fielding Smith, *Essentials in Church History* (Salt Lake City, 1922), which was originally written as a priesthood text and subsequently went through twenty-eight editions in a general trade edition; and a text used for many years in the seminary system (high school) of the church: William E. Berrett, *The Restored Church: A Brief History of the Growth and Doctrines of the Church* (Salt Lake City, 1961), now in its fifteenth edition.

Of the books intended primarily to attack Mormonism and its claims, the first was Eber D. Howe, *Mormonism Unvailed* (Painesville, Ohio, 1834), which contained the statements of a number of persons who claimed to have known Joseph Smith and his family and associates in western New York State. A second work in a similar polemical style was John C. Bennett, *The History of the Saints . . . ,* by an apostate insider (Boston, 1842). In the same tradition, although more moderate in tone, were John Hyde, *Mormonism: Its Leaders and Designs* (New York, 1857); T. B. H. Stenhouse, *The Rocky Mountain Saints* (New York, 1873); and William Alexander Linn, *The Story of the Mormons* (New York, 1902).

Two nineteenth-century attempts to provide a relatively impartial account of Mormon history were Edward W. Tullidge, *History of Salt Lake City and Its Founders* (Salt Lake City, ca. 1886); and H. H. Bancroft, *History of Utah, 1540–1886* (San Francisco, 1889). Both were written from primary-source material furnished by the Mormon church and its leaders, and both contain a liberal portion of Mormon history, including pre-Utah history, as well as conventional Utah accounts.

In this century, a number of doctoral dissertations and other studies that eventuated as books have been written by professional historians and social scientists. E. E. Ericksen, *The Psychological and Ethical Aspects of Mormon Group Life* (Chicago, 1923); Andrew Love Neff, *History of Utah, 1847–1869* (Salt Lake City, 1940), which includes Mormon history before the settlement of Utah; Nels Anderson, *Desert Saints: The Mormon Frontier in Utah* (Chicago, 1942); Thomas F. O'Dea, *The Mormons* (Chicago, 1957); Ray B. West, Jr., *Kingdom of the Saints: The Story of Brigham Young and the Mormons* (New York, 1957); Leonard J. Arrington, *Great Basin Kingdom: An Economic History of the Latter-day Saints, 1830–1900* (Cambridge, Mass., 1958); Glenn M. Vernon, *Sociology of Mormonism* (Salt Lake City, 1975); and Mark Leone, *The Mormons* (Cambridge, Mass., forthcoming).

In recent years a number of practicing Mormons have been trained as historians, and the literature of Mormon history displays a more professional character. A pair of college-level texts on Mormon history used in Brigham Young University religion classes are Ivan J. Barrett, *Joseph Smith and the Restoration: A History of the Church to 1846* (Provo, Utah, 1973), and Russell R. Rich, *Ensign to the Nations: A History of the Church from 1846 to the Present* (Provo, Utah, 1972).

By far the best survey history of the church now available is James B. Allen and Glen M. Leonard, *The Story of the Latter-day Saints* (Salt Lake City, 1976). This 722-page narrative, which balances recent scholarship with the "faithful history" typical of earlier Mormon treatments, is the first major volume that carries Mormon history from 1830 to the 1970s. *The Story of the Latter-day Saints* contains an exhaustive bibliography (62 pages) of books and articles on the Mormons and their history.

The principal works of recent Mormon scholarship are reviewed in Rodman W. Paul, "The Mormons as a Theme in Western Historical Writings," *Journal of American History*, 54 (December 1967): 511–23. Bibliographies include Thomas G. Alexander and James B. Allen, "The Mormons in the Mountain West: A Selected Bibliography," *Arizona and the West* 9 (Winter 1967): 365–84; and Leonard J. Arrington, "Scholarly Studies of Mormonism in the Twentieth Century," *Dialogue: A Journal of Mormon Thought* 1 (Spring 1966): 15–32. A recent compilation with many original articles on the Mormon Church and the Mormons in their Western setting is Howard R. Lamar, ed., *The Reader's Encyclopedia of the American West* (New York: Thomas Y. Crowell, 1977).

The products of the research and writing of recent scholars are found in the *Journal of Mormon History* (annually, 1974–), published by the Mormon History Association, head-quartered in Provo, Utah; *Brigham Young University Studies* (quarterly, 1959–), with a predominance of articles on Mormon history; *Dialogue: A Journal of Mormon Thought* (quarterly, 1966–), now published in Washington, D.C.; *Exponent II* (Boston), a quarterly newspaper concerning Mormon women, published by and for LDS women (1974–); *Task Papers in LDS History* (intermittently, 1975–), distributed by the LDS Church Historical Department in Salt Lake City; *Sunstone: A Journal of Mormon Scholarship, Issues, and Art* (quarterly, 1975–), published in Salt Lake City; *Ensign*, a monthly magazine published by the LDS church (1971–); and in such professional periodicals as *Journal of American History, Western Historical Quarterly, Pacific Historical Review, Utah Historical Quarterly, Arizona and the West*, and *Idaho Yesterdays*. Papers by behavioral scientists on the sociology of Mormonism have been published by the Association for the Study of Religion, under the editorship of Glenn M. Vernon, in an annual periodical (1974–) entitled *Measuring Mormonism*. Bibliographical surveys of the accumulating scholarly works on Mormonism have appeared from time to time in *BYU Studies, Dialogue,* and *Ensign*.

Notes

Major publications, manuscripts, and archives will be referred to in the notes by means of the following abbreviations or symbols:

BYU Studies	*Brigham Young University Studies,* published quarterly by Brigham Young University Press, Provo, Utah (1959–).
Church Archives	Archives of the Church of Jesus Christ of Latter-day Saints, Historical Department, 50 East North Temple Street, Salt Lake City, Utah.
Dialogue	*Dialogue: A Journal of Mormon Thought,* published at Stanford, California (1966–70), Los Angeles, California (1971–75), Washington, D.C. (1976–).
Doctrine and Covenants	*The Doctrine and Covenants of the Church of Jesus Christ of Latter-day Saints,* rev. ed. (Salt Lake City, 1923). The numbers that follow *Doctrine and Covenants* will stand for the section and verse numbers, as in the case of biblical citations. Readers should be aware that much of this publication appears also in the *Doctrine and Covenants of the Reorganized Church of Jesus Christ of Latter Day Saints* (Independence, Mo., 1935), with different sections and verses.
Ensign	*Ensign,* a monthly magazine published by the Church of Jesus Christ of Latter-day Saints (Salt Lake City, 1971–).
HC	*History of the Church of Jesus Christ of Latter-day Saints: History of Joseph Smith, the Prophet, by Himself and Apostolic Interregnum,* edited by B. H. Roberts, 7 vols., 2nd ed. rev. (Salt Lake City, 1957).
JD	*Journal of Discourses,* 26 vols. (Liverpool, Eng., 1854–1886).
JH	Journal History of the Church of Jesus Christ of Latter-day Saints, Church Archives, 1830–.
Roberts, *Comprehensive History*	B. H. Roberts, *A Comprehensive History of the Church of Jesus Christ of Latter-day Saints,* 6 vols. (1930; reprinted, Provo, Utah, 1965).

Chapter 1

[1] Whitney R. Cross, *The Burned-over District* (Ithaca, N.Y., 1950), pp. 3–13.

[2] Sources for the early history of the Smith family are: Lucy Mack Smith, *Biographical Sketches of Joseph Smith the Prophet and His Progenitors for Many Generations* (Liverpool, Eng., 1853); Donald Q. Cannon, "Topsfield, Massachusetts: Ancestral Home of the Prophet Joseph Smith," *BYU Studies* 14 (Autumn 1973): 56–76; Richard Anderson, *Joseph Smith's New England Heritage: Influences of Grandfathers Solomon Mack and Asael Smith* (Salt Lake City, 1971).

[3] Cross, *Burned-over District,* p. 139.

[4] Smith history from Lucy Mack Smith, *Biographical Sketches*; religious views on pp. 57, 48.

[5] Lucy Mack Smith, *Biographical Sketches,* p. 70.

[6] Ibid., pp. 62–66, 73.

[7] Quoted by Richard L. Anderson, "Circumstantial Confirmation of the First Vision through Reminiscences," *BYU Studies* 9 (Spring 1969): 379.

[8] Quoted by Elder Hugh B. Brown in an address at Brigham Young University, 8 March 1950.

[9] *HC* 1:5.

[10] *HC* 1:7.

[11] Rev. Wesley P. Walters, "New Light on Mormon Origins from the Palmyra Revival," *Dialogue* 4 (Spring 1969): 60–81.

[12] Milton V. Backman, Jr., *Joseph Smith's First Vision* (Salt Lake City, 1971).

[13] The different accounts of the First Vision are treated in Dean C. Jessee's "The Early Accounts of Joseph Smith's First Vision," *BYU Studies* 9 (Spring 1969): 275–96. James B. Allen compares eight accounts in "Eight Contemporary Accounts of Joseph Smith's First Vision—What Do We Learn from Them," *Improvement Era* 83 (April 1970): 4–13. Paul R. Cheesman, "An Analysis of the Accounts Relating Joseph Smith's Early Visions" (Master's thesis, Brigham Young University, 1965), enlarges upon the subject and includes a transcription of the earliest account.

[14] The account is in "Kirtland Letter Book, 1829–35," pp. 1–6, Church Archives. Our transcription is the same as in Cheesman, "Analysis of the Accounts," p. 128.

[15] Ibid., p. 129. See also Jessee, "The Early Accounts," p. 280.

[16] Accounts of the coming forth of the Book of Mormon are found in the Cheesman transcript of the 1831–32 history and in the 1838 official history as recorded in *The Pearl of Great Price,* rev. ed. (Salt Lake City, 1952), pp. 50–57.

[17] Exod. 28:30.

[18] Roberts, *Comprehensive History* 1:78, preserves this precise wording, thus indicating that the 1832 account was in use in the Church Historian's Office at that date, although a full transcript of it was not published until some forty years later.

[19] Lucy Mack Smith, *Biographical Sketches,* p. 83.

[20] Ibid., p. 88. Lucy Mack Smith gets the date wrong, placing her son's death in November 1824, but examination of the marker and other evidence puts the date as November 18, 1823.

[21] *HC* 1:17.

[22] Painesville, Ohio, 1834.

[23] Richard L. Anderson, "Joseph Smith's New York Reputation Reappraised," *BYU Studies* 10 (Spring 1970), pp. 285, 287–90.

[24] The trial is treated in Fawn M. Brodie, *No Man Knows My History: The Life of Joseph Smith, the Mormon Prophet* (New York, 1946), pp. 30, 31, and includes one possible transcript of the trial on pp. 405-7. Marvin S. Hill, "Joseph Smith and the 1825 Trial: New Evidence and New Difficulties," *BYU Studies* 12 (Winter 1972): 223-33, treats recently uncovered evidence concerning the trial, discusses the various conflicts and contradictions involved, and relates the subject to Joseph's mysticism and background. Wesley P. Walters, "Joseph Smith's Bainbridge, N.Y., Court Trials," *Westminster Theological Journal* 36 (Winter 1974): 123-55, presents the evidence through the eyes of one who is convinced Joseph Smith was a fraud.

[25] Lucy Mack Smith, *Biographical Sketches,* pp. 91-93.

[26] Anderson, "Joseph Smith's Reputation," p. 309.

[27] Ibid., pp. 301-30. Hugh Nibley uses this sequence as the basis for a theory of transference, noting that practically every exotic detail of the treasure digging can be found in press accounts predating any supposed Smith involvement. *The Myth Makers* (Salt Lake City, 1961), pp. 89-190.

[28] Anderson, "Joseph Smith's Reputation," pp. 296-97, 300.

[29] Harris's account is in *HC* 1:20. Anthon's letters may be found in Roberts, *Comprehensive History* 1:100-107.

[30] See Stanley B. Kimball, "The Anthon Transcript: People, Primary Sources, and Problems," *BYU Studies* 10 (Spring 1970): 325-52.

[31] See David Whitmer, *An Address to All Believers in Christ* (Richmond, Mo., 1887); Truman G. Madsen, "Guest Editor's Prologue," *BYU Studies* 10 (Spring 1970): 254.

[32] *Doctrine and Covenants,* sec. 9.

[33] Roberts, *Comprehensive History* 1:109-15.

[34] Lucy Mack Smith, *Biographical Sketches,* pp. 121 ff.

[35] *HC* 1:22-31.

[36] *HC* 1:32.

[37] More complex than it appears at first glance, the Book of Mormon also includes information about an earlier migration to the Western Hemisphere by the Jaredites and another migration in the sixth century B.C. by the Mulekites.

[38] *HC* 1:52-59.

[39] *HC* 1:18.

[40] Marvin S. Hill, "Brodie Revisited: A Reappraisal," *Dialogue* 7 (Winter 1972): 83-85, treats the reliability of the witnesses to the Book of Mormon, as does Richard L. Anderson in a series of articles appearing in the *Improvement Era* 81-83 (1968-1970).

[41] Persuasive refutations of the Spaulding-Rigdon theory are given in Brodie, *No Man Knows My History,* pp. 419-33; Lester E. Bush, Jr., "The Spalding Theory Then and Now," *Dialogue* 10 (Autumn 1977), 40-69.

[42] See, e.g., Brodie, *No Man Knows My History,* pp. 34-49, 69-73.

[43] Richard L. Bushman, "The Book of Mormon and the American Revolution," *BYU Studies* 17 (Autumn 1976): 3-20.

[44] Hugh Nibley, *Lehi in the Desert and the World of the Jaredites* (Salt Lake City, 1952); and the articles by Dee F. Green and John L. Sorenson published as part of a roundtable, "The Prospects for a New World Archaeology," *Dialogue* 4 (Summer 1969): 71-94.

[45] *HC* 1:39.

[46] *HC* 1:51.

[47] The story of the earliest converts is related in *HC* 1:44-51, the "Revelation on Church Government" in 1:64-70, and the actual organization of the church in 1:75-80. See also Laurence M. Yorgason, "Some Demographic Aspects of One Hundred Early

Mormon Converts, 1830–1837" (Master's thesis, Brigham Young University, 1974).

⁴⁸ Eber D. Howe, *Mormonism Unvailed* (Painesville, Ohio, 1834), p. 236; John C. Bennett, *The History of the Saints* (Boston/New York/Cincinnati, 1842), p. 175; Diary of Joseph Smith, 27 November 1832, Church Archives; Diary of John Smith, 29 July 1839, Church Archives; Joseph Smith to Emma Smith, 12 November 1838, Church Archives; *JD* 3:51.

⁴⁹ Erik Erikson, *Young Man Luther: A Study in Psychoanalysis and History* (New York, 1958), p. 67.

⁵⁰ Isaac Hale affidavit, in Howe, *Mormonism Unvailed,* p. 263.

⁵¹ *HC* 2:353–54.

⁵² Erikson, *Young Man Luther,* pp. 149, 150.

⁵³ A generation ago there appeared John Henry Evans, *Joseph Smith, An American Prophet* (New York, 1933), still useful in understanding Joseph Smith and the church he founded. Standard for some historians for many years was Brodie, *No Man Knows My History,* a readable anticipation of what is now called "psychobiography," with the limitations implied by the term. On the problems of a biographer writing on such a subject see Jan Shipps, "The Prophet Puzzle: Suggestions Leading Towards a More Comprehensive Interpretation of Joseph Smith," *Journal of Mormon History* 1(1974): 3–20. Worth examining, also, is T. L. Brink, "Joseph Smith: The Verdict of Depth Psychology," *Journal of Mormon History* 3(1976): 73–84. The most recent serious biography, which takes account of materials and scholarship unavailable to earlier scholars, is Donna Hill, *Joseph Smith, The First Mormon* (New York, 1977).

Chapter 2

¹ References to the field being "white to the harvest" are found in *Doctrine and Covenants* 4:4; 6:3; 11:3; 12:3; 14:3; 33:3, 7.

² *HC* 1:146.

³ References to numbers of members in the early years of the church are found in *HC* 1:146. See also *JH,* 31 December 1831.

⁴ On the numbers of members in Great Britain and hopes for emigration, see the early volumes of the *Latter-day Saints' Millennial Star* (Liverpool, Eng.), 1840–1970.

⁵ On the size of Nauvoo, the earlier estimates of 15,000 or more seem exaggerated. See David E. Miller and Della S. Miller, *Nauvoo: City of Joseph* (Santa Barbara, Calif., and Salt Lake City, 1974); and a forthcoming doctoral dissertation by James Kimball, University of Utah.

⁶ *Deseret News Church Almanac* (Salt Lake City, 1974), p. 205.

⁷ Ibid. This source has statistics for various states, countries, and missions.

⁸ Thomas F. O'Dea, "Mormonism and the Avoidance of Sectarian Stagnation: A Study of Church, Sect, and Incipient Nationality," *American Journal of Sociology* 60 (November 1954): 285–93.

⁹ *JD* 2:251–52.

¹⁰ Sydney E. Ahlstrom, *A Religious History of the American People* (New Haven, Conn., and London, 1972), pp. 357–58.

¹¹ Quoted in Milton V. Backman, Jr., *American Religions and the Rise of Mormonism* (Salt Lake City, 1965), p. 202.

¹² Quoted in Marvin S. Hill, "The Role of Christian Primitivism in the Origin and Development of the Mormon Kingdom, 1830–1844" (Ph.D. diss., University of Chicago, 1968), p. 155.

[13] *Papers of Benjamin Franklin,* ed. Leonard W. Labaree (New Haven, Conn., 1959), 1:102–3.

[14] "The continually progressive change to which the meaning of words is subject, the want of an universal language which renders translation necessary, the errors to which translations are again subject, the mistakes of copyists and printers, together with the possibility of willful alteration, are of themselves evidences that the human language, whether in speech or in print, cannot be the vehicle of the word of God." Thomas Paine, "The Age of Reason," in *Selected Works of Thomas Paine,* ed. Howard Fast (New York, 1943), p. 297.

[15] Ahlstrom, *Religious History of the American People,* p. 475.

[16] Hill, "Role of Christian Primitivism," p. 9.

[17] Ibid., p. 10.

[18] Ahlstrom, *Religious History of the American People,* p. 450.

[19] Ibid., p. 494.

[20] Especially useful is Eric Rohmann, "Words of Comfort, Gifts of Love: Spirit Manifestations among the Shakers, 1837–1845" (Senior paper, Antioch College, 1971).

[21] Lucy [Mack] Smith, *Biographical Sketches of Joseph Smith the Prophet and His Progenitors for Many Generations,* p. 37.

[22] Ibid., pp. 53–54.

[23] Hill, "Role of Christian Primitivism," pp. 56–57.

[24] Ibid., p. 57.

[25] Ibid., pp. 57–58.

[26] Ibid., pp. 58–60.

[27] Laurence M. Yorgason, "Some Demographic Aspects of One Hundred Early Mormon Converts, 1830–1837" (Master's thesis, Brigham Young University, 1974).

[28] D. Michael Quinn, "Organizational Development and Social Origins of the Mormon Hierarchy, 1832–1932" (Master's thesis, University of Utah, 1973). Cf. S. George Ellsworth, "A History of Mormon Missions in the United States and Canada, 1830–1860" (Ph.D. diss., University of California, Berkeley, 1951), pp. 343–94.

[29] Orson Spencer, *Letters Exhibiting the Most Prominent Doctrines of the Church of Jesus Christ of Latter-day Saints* (Liverpool, England, 1848), pp. 8–9.

[30] Quoted in *Latter-day Saints' Messenger and Advocate* 1 (February 1835): 77. See also Gordon I. Irving, "Mormonism and the Bible," *BYU Studies* 13 (Summer 1973), 473–88.

[31] *Latter-day Saints' Messenger and Advocate* 2 (March 1836): 276.

[32] Irving, "Mormonism and the Bible," p. 45.

[33] Ibid., pp. 55–57, 63–64.

[34] "What we may call *the principle of selective emphasis* has accounted for the most extensive proliferation of American religious groups." A. Leland Jamison, in James Ward Smith and A. Leland Jamison, *Religion in American Life,* 4 vols. (Princeton, N.J., 1961), 1:179–80.

[35] *HC* 4:541.

[36] Joseph Smith's "inspired revision" of the Bible is published by the Reorganized Church of Jesus Christ of Latter Day Saints, Independence, Mo. Two of many studies of the changes and their significance and how the "translation" was accomplished are Reed C. Durham, Jr., "A History of Joseph Smith's Revision of the Bible" (Ph.D. diss., Brigham Young University, 1965); and Robert J. Matthews, *"A Plainer Translation": Joseph Smith's Translation of the Bible* (Provo, Utah, 1975).

[37] An excellent review of the literature on the subject is Lester E. Bush, Jr., "The Spalding Theory Then and Now," *Dialogue* 10 (Autumn 1977): 40–69.

[38] Painesville (Ohio) *Telegraph,* 15 March 1831, as cited in Hill, "Role of Christian Primitivism," p. 101.

[39] Spencer, *Letters,* pp. 10–11.

[40] *Book of Mormon* (Palmyra, N.Y., 1830), Book of Helaman, pp. 439–40.

[41] Ibid., Second Book of Nephi, p. 65.

[42] Thomas F. O'Dea, *The Mormons* (Chicago, 1957), p. 28. For recognition of compromise and ambivalence, see Hill, "Role of Christian Primitivism," pp. 102–4.

[43] On the Book of Mormon's role in providing an epic historical past for America, see especially Peter Meinhold, "Die Anfänge des amerikanischen Geschichtsbewusssteins," *Saeculum* 5(1954): 65–86.

[44] A comparison of the contents of the Book of Mormon with the context of thought about national origins as expressed just before 1830 is made in Richard L. Bushman, "The Book of Mormon and the American Revolution," *BYU Studies* 17 (Autumn 1976): 3–20.

[45] Recent studies of the witnesses, emphasizing their veracity and the consistency of their testimony, are by Richard Lloyd Anderson in the *Improvement Era* 71–73 (1968–1970), passim.

[46] As early as 1833 Mormons were claiming external evidence. After reporting on the high civilization of ancient America described in Elias Boudinot's *Star in the West* (Trenton, N.J., 1816), the official newspaper editorialized: "The facts . . . [are] not only proof of their skill, but [are] good proof, to those that want evidence, that the book of Mormon is true." *The Evening and the Morning Star* (Independence, Mo.), June 1833. Cf. chap. 1, n. 43.

[47] The revelations are for the most part printed in *HC.* They were first published in book form in *A Book of Commandments* (Zion [Independence, Mo.], 1833) and then, revised, in the *Doctrine and Covenants* (Kirtland, Ohio, 1835), later editions making editorial changes and adding new documents. See Melvin J. Petersen, "A Study of the Nature of and the Significance of the Changes in the Revelations as Found in a Comparison of the *Book of Commandments* and Subsequent Editions of the *Doctrine and Covenants*" (Master's thesis, Brigham Young University, 1955).

[48] Lowell L. Bennion, *The Religion of the Latter-day Saints* (Salt Lake City, 1940). See also Parley P. Pratt, *Key to Theology* (London, 1855), for an early interpretation of Mormon cosmology.

[49] Nephi L. Morris, *Prophecies of Joseph Smith and Their Fulfillment* (Salt Lake City, 1920).

[50] See the early issues (1832–1834) of *The Evening and the Morning Star.*

[51] Parley P. Pratt, *A Letter to the Queen of England, Touching the Signs of the Times and the Political Destiny of the World* (Manchester, Eng., 1841), p. 2.

[52] Richard Lloyd Anderson, "Joseph Smith and the Millenarian Time Table." *BYU Studies* 3 (Spring–Summer 1961): 55–66.

[53] "Articles of Faith," no. 10. Early church periodicals of the 1830s and 1840s invariably contained a column entitled "Signs of the Times." William I. Appleby compiled an elaborate journal along these lines and published a lengthy poem on the same subject.

[54] Louis G. Reinwand, "An Interpretive Study of Mormon Millennialism During the Nineteenth Century" (Master's thesis, Brigham Young University, 1971).

[55] S. A. Davis, "The Glad Tidings," in *Latter-day Saints' Messenger and Advocate* 3 (1837): 489–91.

[56] *Deseret News Weekly,* 8 December 1869.

[57] See Mircea Eliade, *Myth and Reality* (New York, 1968); also C. G. Jung, *Modern Man in Search of a Soul* (New York, 1933); Joseph Campbell, *The Hero with a Thousand*

Faces (New York and Cleveland, 1956); and George Santayana, *The Life of Reason: Reason in Religion* (New York, 1936).

[58] Mario S. De Pillis, "The Quest for Religious Authority and the Rise of Mormonism," *Dialogue* 1 (Fall 1966): 68–88.

[59] Ibid., p. 77.

[60] See, e.g., *Autobiography of Parley Parker Pratt* (Salt Lake City, 1938).

[61] *HC* 2:233; 4:577 ff.

[62] Katherine Hanson Shirts's thoughtful but untitled and unpublished paper in our possession was prepared during her term as a research fellow for the Historical Department of the Church in 1973.

[63] J. B. Turner, *Mormonism in All Ages; of the Rise, Progress, and Causes of Mormonism; with the Biography of Its Author and Founder, Joseph Smith, Junior* (New York, 1842), pp. 229–31.

[64] Robert N. Hullinger, "Joseph Smith, Defender of the Faith," *Concordia Theological Monthly* 42 (February 1971): 72–87.

[65] Spencer, *Letters,* p. 11.

[66] Good studies of leadership patterns among the early Mormons are nonexistent. But for suggestions, see A. Karl Larson, *Erastus Snow* (Salt Lake City, 1972); Leonard J. Arrington, *Charles C. Rich* (Provo, Utah, 1974); and Jonathan R. T. Hughes, *The Vital Few* (New York, 1966), chapter on Brigham Young. The authoritarianism of the church, often mentioned, is a complex phenomenon, with important qualifications.

[67] Erich Fromm, *Escape from Freedom* (New York, 1941). A very illuminating essay is Marvin S. Hill, "Quest for Refuge: An Hypothesis as to the Social Origins and Nature of the Mormon Political Kingdom," *Journal of Mormon History* 2 (1975): 3–20.

[68] Eric Hoffer, *The True Believer* (New York, 1951); Richard Crossman, ed., *The God That Failed* (New York, 1950).

[69] Ahlstrom, *Religious History of the American People,* p. 483.

Chapter 3

[1] *HC* 1:261–65.

[2] *HC* 1:390–93.

[3] Roberts, *Comprehensive History* 2:474–75.

[4] *HC* 1:19.

[5] Max H. Parkin, "The Nature and Cause of Internal and External Conflict of the Mormons in Ohio between 1830 and 1838" (Master's thesis, Brigham Young University, 1966), pp. 52, 58–62, 88.

[6] "Manifesto of the Mob," *HC* 1:375–76.

[7] "Propositions of the Mob," *HC* 1:397–98.

[8] Alphonso Wetmore, comp., *Gazeteer of the State of Missouri* (St. Louis, 1837), pp. 93–95.

[9] See Dallin H. Oaks and Marvin S. Hill, *Carthage Conspiracy: The Trial of the Accused Assassins of Joseph Smith* (Urbana, Ill., 1975).

[10] Nancy Towle saw "nothing indecorous" in the Mormons as a people, but her feeling about their public religious "performances" was pronounced: "I viewed the whole with the utmost indignation and disgust: and as a mere profanation and sacrilege of all religious things." William Mulder and A. Russell Mortensen, eds., *Among the Mormons: Historic Accounts by Contemporary Observers* (New York, 1958), p. 61.

[11] See chap. 1.

[12] *HC* 1:375.

[13] *HC* 1:396.

[14] Wetmore, *Gazeteer,* pp. 94–96.

[15] Richard L. Bushman, "New Jerusalem, U.S.A." (Honor's thesis, Harvard University, 1955), pp. 86–90. For a comprehensive study of Mormon involvement with the Indians, providing some explanation of gentile fears, see Lawrence G. Coates, "A History of Indian Education by the Mormons, 1830–1900" (Ed.D. diss., Ball State University, 1969). See also chap. 8.

[16] *Missouri Republican* (St. Louis), 20 December 1833, as cited in Bushman, "New Jerusalem, U.S.A.," p. 86.

[17] Bushman, "New Jerusalem, U.S.A.," pp. 86–90.

[18] An interesting example is a meeting of Joseph Smith with three Potawatomi Indian chiefs in April 1843. They had grievances against the U.S. government and thought Smith had political and military powers that would enable him to help them. According to Wilford Woodruff, who was present, Smith declined because his "hands were tied by the United States." *HC* 5:480; 6:402–03. On the other hand, Brigadier General Henry King, the interpreter, wrote to Iowa governor John Chambers: "It seems evident, from all that I can learn, from the leading men among the *Mormons* and from various other sources that a grand conspiracy is about to be entered into between the *Mormons and Indians* to destroy all white settlements on the frontier." Coates, "History of Indian Education," pp. 55–56.

[19] *HC* 1:375, 397.

[20] *HC* 1:397.

[21] Wetmore, *Gazeteer,* p. 93.

[22] *HC* 2:450.

[23] Bushman, "New Jerusalem, U.S.A." pp. 82, 86.

[24] Ibid., p. 91.

[25] Warren Jennings, "The City in the Garden: Social Conflict in Jackson County, Missouri," in F. Mark McKiernan, Alma R. Blair, and Paul M. Edwards, eds., *The Restoration Movement: Essays in Mormon History* (Lawrence, Kan., 1973), p. 105; Parkin, "Nature and Cause of Conflict," pp. 200–25.

[26] Parkin, "Nature and Cause of Conflict," pp. 200–25; Robert Kent Fielding, "The Growth of the Mormon Church in Kirtland, Ohio" (Ph.D. diss., Indiana University, 1957), chaps. 7–8; Robert Bruce Flanders, *Nauvoo: Kingdom on the Mississippi* (Urbana, Ill., 1965), chap. 5.

[27] Parkin, "Nature and Cause of Conflict," p. 223.

[28] Painesville (Ohio) *Telegraph,* 31 January 1834; Parkin, "Nature and Cause of Conflict," 205.

[29] E. D. Howe, *Autobiography and Recollections of a Pioneer Printer* (Painesville, Ohio, 1878), p. 44.

[30] *HC* 1:397.

[31] Leland H. Gentry, "A History of the Latter-day Saints in Northern Missouri from 1836 to 1839" (Ph.D. diss., Brigham Young University, 1965), pp. 250–51.

[32] Kenneth W. Godfrey, "Causes of Mormon Non-Mormon Conflict in Hancock County, Illinois, 1839–1846" (Ph.D. diss., Brigham Young University, 1967), chap. 5.

[33] Ibid., pp. 48–50.

[34] Ibid., pp. 50–51.

[35] Ibid., p. 54.

[36] Thomas L. Ford, *History of Illinois* (Chicago, 1854), p. 319.

[37] William Harris, *Mormonism Portrayed; Its Errors and Absurdities* (Warsaw, Ill., 1841), p. 15.

[38] Roberts, *Comprehensive History* 5:490.

[39] Klaus Hansen, "The Political Kingdom of God as a Cause for Mormon-Gentile Conflict," *BYU Studies* 2 (Spring–Summer 1960): 241–60.

[40] J. Keith Melville, "Brigham Young on Politics and Priesthood," *BYU Studies* 10 (Summer 1970): 489.

[41] Jean B. White, "Utah State Elections, 1895–1899" (Ph.D. diss., University of Utah, 1968).

[42] Jennings, "City in the Garden," p. 110.

[43] *JD* 14:120.

[44] Gentry, "History of the Latter-day Saints," chap. 9; F. Mark McKiernan, "Mormonism on the Defensive: Far West," in McKiernan, Blair, and Edwards, eds., *Restoration Movement*, pp. 121–40.

[45] The leading student of the Danites has concluded that Sidney Rigdon may have given support to this determined group, particularly at the beginning; see Leland H. Gentry, "The Danite Band of 1838," *BYU Studies* 14 (Summer 1974): 421–50. Joseph Smith declared that he was unaware of the extent of the group's "frauds and secret abominations and evil works of darkness" until the matter came to light in the courts. Although the Danites have persisted as a theme in Western literature, there is no hard evidence of their continuation after the departure from Nauvoo. Most historians now suppose that the actions once attributed to the Danites were probably those of individuals or of Mormon security forces—deputy sheriffs, territorial militia, minutemen.

[46] Samuel W. Taylor, *Nightfall at Nauvoo* (New York, 1971); Godfrey, "Causes of Mormon Non-Mormon Conflict," chap. 10; *Warsaw* (Ill.) *Signal*, 1844–1845, passim.

[47] *Warsaw* (Ill.) *Signal*, 15 January 1845.

[48] Godfrey, "Causes of Mormon Non-Mormon Conflict," p. 79. The most important treatment is Mervin B. Hogan, "Mormonism and Freemasonry: The Illinois Episode," *Little Masonic Library* 2 (1977): 267–326. Appended to this article is a list of Hogan's other writings, a substantial scholarly output, on the subject of Mormonism and Masonry.

[49] See, e.g., Ford, *History of Illinois*, pp. 251–369.

[50] From the literature on crowds, the following are cited as examples: George Rudé, *The Crowd in History: A Study of Popular Disturbances in France and England, 1730–1848* (New York, 1964); E. J. Hobsbawm, *Primitive Rebels: Studies in Archaic Forms of Social Movement in the 19th and 20th Centuries* (Manchester, Eng., 1959); Charles Tilly and James Rule, *Measuring Political Upheaval* (Princeton, N.J., 1965); Neil J. Smelser, *Theory of Collective Behavior* (New York, 1971); and Elias Canetti, *Crowds and Power* (New York, 1966).

[51] Roberts, *Comprehensive History* 1:321–23; see also petition to Governor Daniel Dunklin in *HC* 1:414.

[52] Ford, *History of Illinois*, p. 406.

[53] Roberts, *Comprehensive History* 1:323.

[54] Ibid., 1:343–46; *HC* 1:410–15, 480.

[55] J. B. Turner, *Mormonism in All Ages; of the Rise, Progress, and Causes of Mormonism; with the Biography of Its Author and Founder, Joseph Smith, Junior* (New York, 1842), pp. 57–58.

[56] Godfrey, "Causes of Mormon Non-Mormon Conflict," pp. 170–73.

[57] *HC* 1:415; cf. the statement that "the officers of the county, both civil and military, were accomplices in these unparalleled outrages," in "Petition to the President," *HC* 1:489.

[58] Roberts, *Comprehensive History* 1:341–42.

[59] Oaks and Hill, *Carthage Conspiracy*, especially chap. 2.

⁶⁰ Gentry, "History of the Latter-day Saints," chaps. 10–13.

⁶¹ Roberts, *Comprehensive History* 2:274–87.

⁶² Ibid., 1:265–67; *HC* 1:354–55; Parkin, "Nature and Cause of Conflict," pp. 89–133.

⁶³ Gentry, "History of the Latter-day Saints," pp. 102–72, 511–17.

⁶⁴ Roberts, *Comprehensive History* 2:221–33.

⁶⁵ John Hay, "The Mormon Prophet's Tragedy," *Atlantic Monthly,* December 1869, pp. 669–78; reprinted in Keith Huntress, *Murder of an American Prophet* (San Francisco, 1960), p. 185.

⁶⁶ Ibid.

⁶⁷ The concept of guilt-free aggression, with the dehumanizing of the victims as one of the conditions for it, is developed in Nevitt Sanford and Craig Comstock, eds., *Sanctions for Evil* (San Francisco, 1971). The way in which referring to the Jews as "lice" and "vermin" facilitated their persecution in Nazi Germany is discussed in Haig Bosmajian, *The Language of Oppression* (Washington, D.C., 1974).

⁶⁸ William Jarman, *Uncle Sam's Abscess, or Hell Upon Earth* (Exeter, Eng., 1884).

⁶⁹ The standard features of vigilantism are treated analytically by Richard Maxwell Brown, "The American Vigilante Tradition," in Hugh Davis Graham and Ted Robert Gurr, eds., *The History of Violence in America: Historical and Comparative Perspectives* (New York, 1969), from which the quoted phrases in this paragraph are taken. See also Richard Slotkin, *Regeneration through Violence: The Mythology of the American Frontier, 1600–1860* (Middletown, Conn., 1973).

⁷⁰ In addition to the works by Bushman, Parkin, Gentry, and Godfrey, already cited, see Warren Jennings, "Zion Is Fled: The Expulsion of the Mormons from Jackson County, Missouri" (Ph.D. diss., University of Florida, 1962).

⁷¹ Marvin S. Hill, "Religion in Nauvoo," *Utah Historical Quarterly* 44 (1976): 170–80. Denials that the persecution was for religion are frequent in the Warsaw (Ill.) *Signal.*

⁷² "Scattered through the country, they might have lived in peace, like other religious sects, but they insisted upon their right to congregate in one great city." Ford, *History of Illinois,* p. 251.

⁷³ *JD* 1:144.

⁷⁴ Edward Partridge to parents and friends, 22 October 1834, printed in *Woman's Exponent* 12 (1 August 1883): 36.

Chapter 4

¹ New York *Sun,* 4 September 1843, quoted in Robert Bruce Flanders, *Nauvoo, Kingdom on the Mississippi* (Urbana, Ill., 1965), p. 278.

² *Doctrine and Covenants,* 28:2, 6.

³ George A. Smith, Sermon, 10 January 1858, in *JD* 7:111–17.

⁴ *JD* 7:114; *Latter-day Saints' Millennial Star* (Liverpool, Eng.) 25(1863): 487.

⁵ Leland H. Gentry, "The Danite Band of 1838," *BYU Studies* 14 (Summer 1974): 421–50; Ivan J. Barrett, *Joseph Smith and the Restoration,* rev. ed. (Provo, Utah, 1973), pp. 369–71, 383–85; William Mulder and A. Russell Mortensen, eds., *Among the Mormons: Historic Accounts by Contemporary Observers* (New York, 1958), pp. 93–94.

⁶ Robert Flanders, "The Succession Crisis in Mormon History: Dilemmas of a Radical Kingdom and a Realized Eschatology" (n.d., unpublished manuscript in possession of the authors).

⁷ *HC* 3:250–54.

⁸ *Doctrine and Covenants,* sec. 14:3.

⁹ James B. Allen and Malcolm R. Thorp, "The Mission of the Twelve to England, 1840–41: Mormon Apostles and the Working Classes," *BYU Studies* 15 (Summer 1975): 499–526; and James B. Allen and Thomas G. Alexander, eds., *Manchester Mormons: The Journal of William Clayton, 1840 to 1842* (Santa Barbara, Calif., and Salt Lake City, 1974). For the early baptism and emigration figures, see *Latter-day Saints' Millennial Star 1* (1840–41): 20, 302.

¹⁰ David E. and Della S. Miller, *Nauvoo: The City of Joseph* (Santa Barbara, Calif., and Salt Lake City, 1974).

¹¹ For a discussion of polygamy in Nauvoo, see Flanders, *Nauvoo,* pp. 261–71; and Danel W. Bachman, "A Study of the Mormon Practice of Plural Marriage before the Death of Joseph Smith" (Master's thesis, Purdue University, 1975).

¹² Jan Shipps, "From Satyr to Saint: American Attitudes toward the Mormons, 1860–1960" (Paper delivered at the 1973 Annual Meeting of the Organization of American Historians).

¹³ Quoted in Mulder and Mortensen, *Among the Mormons,* pp. 126–27.

¹⁴ Klaus J. Hansen, *Quest for Empire: the Political Kingdom of God and the Council of Fifty in Mormon History* (East Lansing, Mich., 1967), pp. 60–61.

¹⁵ Flanders, *Nauvoo,* p. 88.

¹⁶ Brigham Young in *JD* 8:38.

¹⁷ Dean Jessee, "Howard Coray's Recollections of Joseph Smith," *BYU Studies* 17 (Spring 1977):344–45.

¹⁸ Josiah Quincy, *Figures of the Past* (Boston, 1883), p. 400.

¹⁹ *HC* 6:367.

²⁰ Warren Jennings, "Thomas Sharp" (Paper delivered to the Mormon History Association Convention, Independence, Mo., 14 April 1972).

²¹ *Doctrine and Covenants,* 124:16–17.

²² Robert B. Flanders, "The Kingdom of God in Illinois: Politics in Utopia," *Dialogue* 5 (Spring 1970):26–36.

²³ *HC* 6:305, 311–12.

²⁴ *HC* 6:314–15.

²⁵ Emmeline B. Wells, "Joseph Smith, the Prophet," *Young Woman's Journal* 16 (December 1905): 555.

²⁶ Donna Hill, *Joseph Smith: The First Mormon* (New York, 1977), p. 7.

²⁷ Angus M. Cannon, "Joseph Smith, the Prophet," *Young Woman's Journal* 17 (December 1906): 546.

²⁸ Quincy, p. 381.

²⁹ *HC* 5:498.

³⁰ *JD* 3:51.

³¹ Joseph Smith Journal, 15 May 1843, Church Archives.

³² *Autobiography of Parley Parker Pratt* (Salt Lake City, 1938), pp. 230–32.

³³ *Doctrine and Covenants,* 121:36; 41:36.

³⁴ Richard L. Bushman, as quoted in *Church News,* 9 August 1975, p. 13.

³⁵ Joseph Smith to Emma Smith, 12 November 1838, quoted in Heman C. Smith, *History of the Church of Jesus Christ of Latter-day Saints,* 4 vols. (Lamoni, Iowa, 1897), 2:290–91.

³⁶ Joseph Smith to Emma Smith, 21 March 1839, Church Archives (punctuation introduced).

³⁷ For primary sources on the events surrounding the martyrdom, see *HC* 6:416–631; and Keith Huntress, *Murder of an American Prophet* (San Francisco, 1960). The most

important scholarly study is Dallin H. Oaks and Marvin S. Hill, *Carthage Conspiracy: The Trial of the Accused Assassins of Joseph Smith* (Urbana, Ill., 1975).

[38]   *HC* 6:442.

[39]   Dallin H. Oaks, "The Suppression of the *Nauvoo Expositor*," *Utah Law Review* 9 (1965): 862–903.

[40]   Warsaw (Ill.) *Signal*, 19 June 1844, quoted in Oaks and Hill, *Carthage Conspiracy*, p. 15.

[41]   *HC* 6:537.

[42]   *HC* 6:540.

[43]   *HC* 6:546.

[44]   *HC* 6:549.

[45]   *HC* 6:555.

[46]   *HC* 6:565.

[47]   *HC* 6:594–5.

[48]   *HC* 6:605.

[49]   Brigham Young to Vilate Young, 11 August 1844, Church Archives (punctuation introduced).

Chapter 5

[1]   A detailed survey of this issue is D. Michael Quinn, "The Mormon Succession Crisis of 1844," *BYU Studies* 16 (Winter 1976): 187–233. See also Reed C. Durham, Jr., and Steven H. Heath, *Succession in the Church* (Salt Lake City, 1970).

[2]   Minutes of a Special Meeting in Nauvoo, 8 August 1844, p. 1, Brigham Young Papers, Church Archives. See also *HC* 7:231–42.

[3]   Mormon scholars point to the leadership role that the *Doctrine and Covenants* (the church's constitution, as it were) assigns to the Quorum of the Twelve Apostles. See sec. 107, given March 28, 1835; also "The Government of God" in *Times and Seasons* (Nauvoo, Ill.) 3 (1842):855–58. Obviously the revelations played an important role in the discussions that followed the assassination of Joseph and Hyrum Smith, but the letters and diaries of the time show that church members were not as certain of proper succession procedures as the church is today.

[4]   Brigham Young's feelings were further expressed as follows: "I do not care who leads the church even though it were Ann Lee; but one thing I must know, and that is what God says about it. . . . My private feelings would be to let the affairs of men and women alone, only go and preach and baptize them into the kingdom of God." Minutes of a Special Meeting, p. 9.

[5]   Journal of George Laub, 4 March 1846, Church Archives.

[6]   *Deseret News*, 12 March 1892.

[7]   *JH*, 9 August 1844.

[8]   Diary of Brigham Young, 1837–1845, Church Archives.

[9]   *JD* 8:37.

[10]   Ibid.

[11]   *JD* 8:38.

[12]   Minutes of Young Family Meeting, Nauvoo, Ill. 18 January 1845, Brigham Young Papers, Church Archives.

[13]   *JD* 14:197–98.

[14]   "History of Brigham Young," *Deseret News*, 3 February 1858.

[15]   *JD* 3:91.

[16]   *JD* 8:38.

17   *JD* 1:90.

18   "History of Brigham Young," *Deseret News,* 10 February 1858.

19   Fawn M. Brodie, *No Man Knows My History: The Life of Joseph Smith, the Mormon Prophet* (New York, 1946) pp. 126–7.

20   *JD* 8:173.

21   *HC* 5:412.

22   *Latter-day Saints' Millennial Star* 5 (1843): 100.

23   Diary of Brigham Young, 1 September 1844, Church Archives.

24   Even the vast majority of those away from Nauvoo supported Brigham Young and the Twelve. This includes the Mississippi Saints, mentioned later, the Saints in Great Britain, and those in New York and New England.

25   Russell R. Rich, *Those Who Would Be Leaders* (*Offshoots of Mormonism*) and *Little Known Schisms of the Restoration* (Provo, Utah, 1967); F. Mark McKiernan, *The Voice of One Crying in the Wilderness: Sidney Rigdon, Religious Reformer, 1793–1876* (Lawrence, Kans., 1971); and for continuing efforts to make good Rigdon's claims down to the 1870s, see the Stephen Post Papers, Church Archives and Archives of the Reorganized Church of Jesus Christ of Latter Day Saints, Independence, Mo.

26   A stimulating article is Klaus Hansen, "The Making of King Strang: A Re-examination," *Michigan History* 46(1962): 201–19. See also O. W. Riegel, *Crown of Glory: The Life of James J. Strang, Moses of the Mormons* (New Haven, Conn., 1935); Milo M. Quaife, *The Kingdom of St. James: A Narrative of the Mormons* (New Haven, Conn., 1930); *The Diary of James J. Strang,* transcribed, deciphered, and annotated by Mark A. Strang (Lansing, Mich., 1961). Recent studies have been made by Myron Sorensen, Salt Lake City.

27   Details on sects from Rich, *Those Who Would Be Leaders,* pp. 11–37. See also Dale L. Morgan, "A Bibliography of the Churches of the Dispersion," *Western Humanities Review* 7 (Winter, Spring, Summer 1953).

28   Rich, *Those Who Would Be Leaders,* pp. 49–51.

29   Quoted in Inez Smith Davis, *The Story of the Church* (Independence, Mo., 1964), p. 391. See also Joseph Smith and Heman C. Smith, *History of the Church of Jesus Christ of Latter Day Saints,* 4 vols. (Lamoni, Iowa, 1900), especially vol. 3. See also F. Henry Edwards, *The History of the Reorganized Church of Jesus Christ of Latter Day Saints,* 8 vols. (Independence, Mo., 1969–76) vols. 5–8.

30   Davis, *Story of the Church,* p. 393.

31   Ibid. See also A. R. Blair, "Reorganized Church of Jesus Christ of Latter Day Saints: Moderate Mormonism," in F. Mark McKiernan, Alma R. Blair, and Paul M. Edwards, eds. *The Restoration Movement, Essays in Mormon History* (Lawrence, Kans., 1973), pp. 212–13.

32   Davis, *Story of the Church,* p. 404.

33   Blair, "Moderate Mormonism," pp. 217–18.

34   Ibid., pp. 219–24.

35   Robert Flanders, "The Succession Crisis in Mormon History: Dilemmas of a Radical Kingdom and a Realized Eschatology" (unpublished paper in possession of the authors).

36   Among the dissenters from the Utah church, the only serious rival to the Reorganization movement was the Church of Christ, Temple Lot, which coexisted on friendly terms with the Reorganization for a number of years. This faction, led by Granville Hedrick, quietly purchased most of the Independence, Mo., temple site and located their headquarters there. Late in the century a squabble over the ownership of the temple lot drove a wedge between the two groups, with the Hedrickites retaining the site.

[37] Ivan J. Barrett, *Joseph Smith and the Restoration* (rev. ed., Provo, Utah, 1973), p. 633.

[38] Ibid., pp. 632–33.

[39] Hyrum L. Andrus, "Joseph Smith and the West," *BYU Studies* 2 (Spring–Summer 1960):136–39.

[40] *HC* 5:85, entry for 6 August 1842; see also Roberts, *Comprehensive History* 2:181–82.

[41] Manuscript History of Brigham Young, 30 September 1845, p. 125, Church Archives. See also Hubert Howe Bancroft, *History of Utah* (San Francisco, 1890), p. 214 *n*.

[42] Robert Bruce Flanders, *Nauvoo: Kingdom on the Mississippi* (Urbana, Ill., 1965), pp. 337–41.

[43] The Mormon migration is discussed in Andrew Love Neff, *History of Utah, 1847 to 1869* (Salt Lake City, 1940); Roberts, *Comprehensive History,* vol. 3; James B. Allen and Glen M. Leonard, *The Story of the Latter-day Saints* (Salt Lake City, 1976), pp. 217–56; Preston Nibley, *Exodus to Greatness: The Story of the Mormon Migration* (Salt Lake City, 1947); Bernard DeVoto, *The Year of Decision: 1846* (Boston, 1946); and especially Milton R. Hunter, *Brigham Young the Colonizer* (Salt Lake City, 1940). Some of the color and drama of the trek is captured in Wallace R. Stegner, *The Gathering of Zion: The Story of the Mormon Trail* (New York, 1964).

[44] Manuscript History of Brigham Young, 3 March 1847, p. 65, Church Archives.

[45] Ibid., 13 September 1845, p. 25, Church Archives.

[46] William Mulder and A. Russell Mortensen, eds., *Among the Mormons: Historic Accounts by Contemporary Observers* (New York, 1958), p. 175.

[47] T. Edgar Lyon, "Uncommon Aspects of the Mormon Migration" (Speech delivered to LDS Student Association, Salt Lake City, 14 October 1965).

[48] Russell R. Rich, *Ensign to the Nations* (Provo, Utah, 1972), pp. 14–15; David M. Potter, *Trail to California: The Overland Journal of Vincent Geiger and Wakeman Bryarly* (New Haven, Conn., 1945), pp. 7–40.

[49] Roberts, *Comprehensive History* 3:67. On the Battalion, see also John R. Yurtinus, "A Ram in the Thicket: The Mormon Battalion in the Mexican War" (Ph.D. diss., Brigham Young University, 1975).

[50] Papers of Thomas Bullock, 28 July 1847, Church Archives.

[51] Ibid., 30 July 1847.

[52] Thomas L. Kane Papers, letter of July 11, 1850, Church Archives.

[53] Roberts, *Comprehensive History* 3:131, 136.

[54] The revelation, which is recorded in several contemporary diaries, is published in *Doctrine and Covenants,* section 136.

[55] Richard H. Jackson, "Myth and Reality: Environmental Perceptions of the Mormons, 1840–1865: An Historical Geosophy" (Ph.D. diss., Clark University, 1970), chaps. 2–3.

[56] Diary of Wilford Woodruff, 4 May 1847, Church Archives.

[57] Manuscript History of Brigham Young, 23 July 1847, p. 99, Church Archives.

[58] Erastus Snow Sermon, 14 September 1873, *JD* 16:207. See also Roberts, *Comprehensive History* 3:160–230; and Rich, *Ensign,* pp. 97–146.

[59] Potter, *Trail to California,* p. 40.

[60] "Camp Journal Kept by Thomas Bullock of the Journeyings of the Camp of Israel from Winter Quarters, to the Great Salt Lake City—in the year 1848, May 29, 1848," Church Archives.

[61] Quoted in Mulder and Mortensen, *Among the Mormons,* p. 214.

[62] *Hymns, Church of Jesus Christ of Latter-day Saints* (Salt Lake City, 1948), no. 13.

[63] William Clayton's Journal (published by the Clayton Family Association, Salt

Lake City: 1921), p. 326, entry for 28 July 1847; Journal of Wilford Woodruff, 25 July 1847; C. Edward Jacob, ed., *The Record of Norton Jacob* (Salt Lake City, 1949), pp. 71–74.

⁶⁴ "Journal of Priddy Meeks," *Utah Historical Quarterly* 10 (April 1942): 164.

⁶⁵ Thomas L. Kane, *The Mormons* (Philadelphia, 1850), p. 66.

⁶⁶ William G. Hartley, "Mormons, Crickets, and Gulls: A New Look at an Old Story," *Utah Historical Quarterly* 38 (Summer 1970): 224–39.

⁶⁷ R. G. Cleland and Juanita Brooks, eds., *A Mormon Chronicle: The Diaries of John D. Lee*, 2 vols. (San Marino, Calif., 1955), 1:88.

⁶⁸ Quoted in Orson F. Whitney, *Life of Heber C. Kimball* (Salt Lake City, 1888), pp. 389–90.

⁶⁹ Milton R. Hunter, *Brigham Young the Colonizer* (Salt Lake City, 1940).

Chapter 6

¹ Erastus Snow, "From Nauvoo to Salt Lake in the Van of the Pioneers," *Improvement Era* 15 (1912): 551, entry for 8 August 1847.

² Frank E. Manuel, "Pansophia, A Seventeenth-Century Dream of Science," in *Freedom from History and Other Untimely Essays* (New York, 1971), pp. 89–113, especially p. 92; see also Henry Nash Smith, *Virgin Land: The American West as Symbol and Myth* (Cambridge, Mass., 1950).

³ In 1964, after the opening of large parcels of new lands in the twentieth century through U.S. Bureau of Reclamation projects, the irrigated lands in Utah represented only about 2 percent of the state's total land area. Farming lands, which included dry land and privately owned grazing acreage, were about 24 percent of the total area. See "Selected Statistics of Farms and Ranches in Utah by County, 1964," in Philip R. Kunz and Merlin D. Brinkerhof, *Utah in Numbers: Comparisons, Trends and Descriptions* (Provo, Utah, 1969), table 210, p. 293.

⁴ Ibid., table 247, p. 332. The average annual rainfall of all reporting stations between 1930 and 1960 was 10.36 inches.

⁵ In 1964, lumber production in Utah was substantially less than that of neighboring states, except for Nevada. Utah's total of about 70 million board feet compares with 411 million in Arizona and 1,656 million in Idaho. Ibid., table 186, p. 268.

⁶ By 1965, Utah would rank second among the United States in copper and gold production, third in lead and silver, and fourth in iron ore. Ibid., table 172, p. 248.

⁷ Ibid., table 247, p. 332.

⁸ A useful map of the location of Indian tribes in areas settled by Mormons can be found in Catherine S. Fowler and Don D. Fowler, "Notes on the History of the Southern Paiutes and Western Shoshonis," *Utah Historical Quarterly* 39 (Spring 1971): 99; see also Floyd A. O'Neil, "The Reluctant Suzerainty: The Uintah and Ouray Reservations," *Utah Historical Quarterly* 39 (Spring 1971): 130–44, especially 130.

⁹ Fowler and Fowler, "Southern Paiutes and Western Shoshonis," pp. 98–105.

¹⁰ O'Neil, "Uintah and Ouray Reservations," p. 130.

¹¹ Wilford Woodruff reported the distance traveled to be 1,200 miles. Journal of Wilford Woodruff, 24 July 1847, Church Archives. The present-day highway distance from Salt Lake City to Omaha is more direct—almost exactly 1,000 miles.

¹² The pioneer company left Mormon encampments near the Missouri on April 16, 1847. Their advance party arrived in the Salt Lake Valley sixty-six days later, on July 21. The Pilgrim voyage from England to Cape Cod in 1620 took exactly the same amount of

time—sixty-six days. Overland transportation in both periods was, of course, significantly more expensive than transportation by water routes.

[13] "Come, Come Ye Saints," *Hymns* (Salt Lake City, 1948), no. 13.

[14] "Eleventh General Epistle of the Presidency," 10 April 1854, *Deseret News,* 13 April 1854. Also in James R. Clark, ed., *Messages of the First Presidency,* 6 vols. (Salt Lake City, 1965–1975), 2:126–43.

[15] *JD* 4:32. Sermon 17 August 1856.

[16] *Official Report of the Irrigation Congress . . . 1891* (Salt Lake City, 1891), p. 43.

[17] These implements and methods are described in Joel Shoemaker, "Cooperative Irrigation," in Utah Irrigation Commission, *Irrigation in Utah* (Salt Lake City, 1895), p. 73.

[18] Leonard J. Arrington and Dean L. May, "A Different Mode of Life: Irrigation and Society in Nineteenth Century Utah," in James H. Shideler, ed., *Agriculture in the Development of the Far West* (Washington, D.C., 1975), pp. 3–20.

[19] A detailed account of the initial laying out of the city is in Leonard J. Arrington, *Great Basin Kingdom: An Economic History of the Latter-day Saints, 1830–1900* (Cambridge, Mass., 1958), pp. 45–57. See also Journal of Wilford Woodruff, 28 July 1847, Church Archives.

[20] The original bowery was built the day after the settlers arrived in the valley and was 40 by 28 feet, according to Roberts, *Comprehensive History* 3:285. Mary Reynolds in "Boweries on the Temple Block," typescript, Church Archives, has discussed the use and history of the several successive boweries used for public meetings in Salt Lake City. A description of the "old tabernacle" is in *Deseret News,* 17 April 1852. The present tabernacle was formally dedicated in 1875. *Deseret News,* 9 October and 20 October 1875, reported the dedication proceedings. The roof of the 250-by-150-foot building is supported by a set of wooden arches of lattice-truss construction, each spanning 150 feet and fastened together with wooden pegs and rawhide thongs.

[21] Aldous Huxley, *Tomorrow and Tomorrow and Tomorrow and Other Essays* (New York, 1956), pp. 235–51.

[22] James E. Talmage, *The House of the Lord* (Salt Lake City, 1962); Arrington, *Great Basin Kingdom,* pp. 111–12, 214–15, 339–40, 401.

[23] *JH,* 9 November and 20 November 1847 and 6 March 1848.

[24] The Twelve to Orson Pratt, *JH,* 9 March 1849; also Brigham Young in *JH,* 27 October 1850.

[25] Besides the section pertaining to these colonies in Milton R. Hunter, *Brigham Young the Colonizer* (Salt Lake City, 1940), pp. 315–41, see Ralph Kent Rich, "The Idea Behind the San Bernardino Colony" (B.A. thesis, University of Utah, 1966); Alton B. Poulsen, "The Mormon Outpost of San Bernardino, California" (Master's thesis, University of Utah, 1947); Joseph Snow Wood, "The Mormon Settlement in San Bernardino, 1851–1857" (Ph.D. diss., University of Utah, 1968); George William Beattie and Helen Pruitt Beattie, *Heritage of the Valley: San Bernardino's First Century* (Pasadena, Calif., 1939); Leonard J. Arrington, *Charles C. Rich: Mormon General and Western Frontiersman* (Provo, Utah, 1974), pp. 137–214; and a chapter in Robert V. Hine, *California Utopian Colonies* (San Marino, Calif., 1953). There has been much less study of other early outlying colonies. Fred R. Gowans and Eugene E. Campbell, *Fort Supply: Brigham Young's Green River Experiment* (Provo, Utah, 1976), provides useful material on one colony. The best interpretation is Eugene E. Campbell, "Brigham Young's Outer Cordon: A Reappraisal," *Utah Historical Quarterly* 41 (Summer 1973): 221–53.

[26] D. N. Meinig, "The Mormon Culture Region: Strategies and Patterns in the Geography of the American West," *Annals of the Association of American Geographers* 55

(June 1965): 191–220. See also Richard Sherlock, "Mormon Migration and Settlement after 1875," *Journal of Mormon History* 2 (1975): 53–68.

²⁷ Besides relevant sections of the major works cited, see Harold Judson Flower, Jr., "Mormon Colonization of the San Luis Valley, Colorado, 1878–1900" (Master's thesis, Brigham Young University, 1966); also David Williams Lantis, "The San Luis Valley, Colorado: Sequent Rural Occupance in an Intermountain Basin" (Ph.D. diss., Ohio State University, 1950).

²⁸ David E. Miller, *Hole-in-the-Rock: An Epic in the Colonization of the Great American West* (Salt Lake City, 1966), is the standard account of this episode.

²⁹ Useful information on Canadian colonization is in Melvin S. Tagg, "A History of the Church of Jesus Christ of Latter-day Saints in Canada, 1830–1963" (Master's thesis, Brigham Young University, 1963); and D. A. Koch, "Mormon Colonization in Canada" (degree and date unknown, Concordia Theological Seminary, St. Louis, Mo.). The standard work on Big Horn Basin colonization is Charles Lindsay, *The Big Horn Basin* (Lincoln, Nebr., 1930). See also Sherlock, "Mormon Migration and Settlement."

³⁰ See under the relevant dates in the Journal of George A. Smith, Church Archives.

³¹ Remarks of 28 July 1847, reported C. Edward Jacob, ed., *The Record of Norton Jacob* (Salt Lake City, 1949).

³² *JH,* 8 April 1849.

³³ James Linforth, ed., *Route from Liverpool to Great Salt Lake Valley* (Liverpool, Eng., 1855), pp. 16–17.

³⁴ *Latter-day Saints' Millennial Star* 2 (15 August 1849): 246–49; and 12 (1 May 1850): 141.

³⁵ *JH,* 26 January 1852; Brigham Young, Sermon, 7 April 1861, in *Deseret News,* 22 May 1861.

³⁶ *Salt Lake Tribune,* 14 August 1898; *Deseret News,* 3 October 1860, 7 April 1861, 28 April 1876.

³⁷ See Fred G. Taylor, *A Saga of Sugar* (Salt Lake City, 1944); also Phillip De La-Mare, "Deseret Manufacturing Company," Church Archives.

³⁸ Leonard J. Arrington, *Beet Sugar in the West: A History of the Utah-Idaho Sugar Company* (Seattle and London, 1966).

³⁹ Arrington, *Great Basin Kingdom,* p. 219. Ivan J. Barrett, "History of the Cotton Mission and Cotton Culture in Utah" (Master's thesis, Brigham Young University, 1947), provides a useful overview of the cotton industry in southern Utah.

⁴⁰ See Leonard J. Arrington, "Planning an Iron Industry for Utah, 1851–58," *Huntington Library Quarterly* 21 (May 1958): 237–60.

⁴¹ As reported in company records in the Southern Utah State College Library, Cedar City, Utah.

⁴² "Minute Book of the Deseret Iron Company," Southern Utah State College Library.

⁴³ *Deseret News,* 2 May 1855; Journal of Isaac C. Haight, April, 1855, p. 80, Ms., Church Archives. *Latter-day Saints' Millennial Star* 18 (26 January 1856): 60.

⁴⁴ Brigham Young, Sermon, 27 May 1855, in *JD* 2:282.

⁴⁵ Journal of Isaac C. Haight, 1857–1858, pp. 94–116, Church Archives.

⁴⁶ Kunz and Brinkerhof, *Utah in Numbers,* table 172, p. 248.

⁴⁷ See Leonard J. Arrington, "The Deseret Telegraph—A Church-Owned Public Utility," *Journal of Economic History* 11 (Spring 1951): 117–39.

⁴⁸ *Deseret News,* 11 January 1870, has a detailed account of the dedication proceedings.

⁴⁹ Robert L. Wrigley, Jr., "Utah and Northern Railway Co.: A Brief History," *Oregon*

Historical Quarterly 48 (September 1947): 245–53; Merrill D. Beal, "The Story of the Utah Northern Railroad," *Idaho Yesterdays* 1 (Spring 1957): 3–10, (Summer 1957): 16–23; and Leonard J. Arrington, "Railroad Building and Cooperatives, 1869–1879," in Joel E. Ricks, ed., *The History of a Valley: Cache Valley, Utah-Idaho* (Logan, Utah, 1956), pp. 172–86.

⁵⁰ See Leonard J. Arrington's treatment of the Utah Southern Railroad in *Great Basin Kingdom*, pp. 277–82; *Territorial Enquirer* (Provo, Utah), 8 March 1879.

⁵¹ See Leonard J. Arrington, Feramorz Y. Fox, and Dean L. May, *Building the City of God: Community and Cooperation among the Mormons* (Salt Lake City, 1976), chaps. 5–6.

⁵² Leonard J. Arrington, "Taxable Income in Utah, 1862–1872," *Utah Historical Quarterly* 24 (January 1956): 21–47; D. Michael Quinn, "The Mormon Hierarchy, 1821–1932: An American Elite" (Ph.D. diss., Yale University, 1976), pp. 81–157.

Chapter 7

¹ *Doctrine and Covenants* 29:7–8.

² *Doctrine and Covenants* 133:7, 12.

³ *Hymns* (Salt Lake City, 1948), no. 344.

⁴ For indication that other immigrants to America had motives similar to those of the Mormons, see Louis B. Wright, *The Cultural Life of the American Colonies, 1607–1763* (New York, 1957), pp. 45, 73–74.

⁵ *Latter-day Saints' Millennial Star* (Liverpool, Eng.) 16 (1852): 763.

⁶ James B. Allen and Malcolm R. Thorp, "The Mission of the Twelve to England, 1840–41: Mormon Apostles and the Working Classes," *BYU Studies* 15 (Summer 1975): 499–526; P. A. M. Taylor, *Expectations Westward: The Mormons and the Emigration of Their British Converts in the Nineteenth Century* (Edinburgh and London, 1965).

⁷ *Latter-day Saints' Millennial Star* 8 (15 October 1846): 90.

⁸ Ibid., 7 (1 May 1846): 139.

⁹ Ibid., 8 (15 October 1846): 90.

¹⁰ Taylor, *Expectations Westward*, p. 27.

¹¹ Quoted in Leonard J. Arrington, *Great Basin Kingdom: An Economic History of the Latter-day Saints, 1830–1900* (Cambridge, Mass., 1958), p. 97. All data on the Perpetual Emigrating Fund are taken from pp. 97–108. See also Gustive O. Larson, *Prelude to the Kingdom: Mormon Desert Conquest. A Chapter in American Cooperative Experience* (Francestown, N. H., 1947).

¹² Charles Dickens, *The Uncommercial Traveller*, Vol. VI of *The Works of Charles Dickens* (10 vols., New York, n.d.), pp. 635–38.

¹³ *Parliamentary Papers*, 1854, vol. 13, esp. Qq. 4985, 5016, 5049–54, 5073, 5076–79, 5085, 5167–83, as cited by P. A. M. Taylor, *Expectations Westward*, p. 173.

¹⁴ Brigham Young, Sermon, 3 October 1852, in *Deseret News*, 11 May 1854.

¹⁵ A detailed account of the 1856 handcart immigration is found in LeRoy R. and Ann W. Hafen, *Handcarts to Zion, 1856–1860* (Glendale, Calif., 1960), pp. 53–141. The Hafens place the total number of deaths in the Willie and Martin companies at between 197 and 217. Cf. Wallace Stegner, *The Gathering of Zion* (New York, 1964), "Ordeal by Handcarts" pp. 221–48.

¹⁶ Brigham Young, Sermon, 30 November 1856, in *Deseret News*, 10 December 1856.

¹⁷ Diary and Autobiography of Mary Goble Pay, typescript, pp. 6–7, Church Archives.

¹⁸ Larson, *Prelude to the Kingdom*, pp. 215, 235–36.

[19] *Latter-day Saints' Millennial Star* 26 (17 December 1864): 813.

[20] William Hepworth Dixon, *New America* (Philadelphia, 1867), p. 177.

[21] *Deseret News*, 13 April 1854.

[22] Larson, *Prelude to the Kingdom*, p. 239.

[23] Taylor, *Expectations Westward,* pp. 154-55.

[24] Larson, *Prelude to the Kingdom*, p. 240.

[25] William Mulder, *Homeward to Zion* (Minneapolis, 1957), pp. 114-15.

[26] *New York Times*, 17 September 1879.

[27] Douglas Alder, "The German-Speaking Immigration to Utah, 1850-1950" (Master's thesis, University of Utah, 1959), pp. 25-26. See also Stanley B. Kimball, "The Mormons in the Habsburg Lands, 1841-1914," *Austrian History Yearbook* 9-10 (1973-74): 143-65.

[28] Arrington, *Great Basin Kingdom,* pp. 361, 366-67.

[29] Alder, "German-Speaking Immigration," p. 27.

[30] Ibid., pp. 28-32; and Brad Morris, "Internationalization of the Church," 1972 (unpublished manuscript in possession of the authors), pp. 48-53.

[31] *New York Times,* 1 June 1890.

[32] Quoted by Morris, "Internationalization," p. 31.

[33] Ibid., p. 56.

[34] Mulder, *Homeward to Zion*, pp. 72, 87.

[35] Ibid., p. 195.

[36] Cindy Rice, "Spring City: A Look at a Nineteenth-century Mormon Village," *Utah Historical Quarterly* 43 (Summer 1975): 262-63.

[37] Mulder, *Homeward to Zion*, pp. 250-53.

[38] See Douglas F. Tobler, "Karl G. Maeser's German Background, 1828-1856: The Making of Zion's Teacher," *BYU Studies* 17 (Winter 1977): 155-175.

[39] Ibid., pp. xi-xii.

Chapter 8

[1] 1 Ne. 12:22-23; 2 Ne. 5:24.

[2] 1 Ne. 22:8. A treatment of Mormon theology with respect to the Indian is Dean L. Larsen, *You and the Destiny of the Indian* (Salt Lake City, 1966). See also Ake V. Strom, "Red Indian Elements in Early Mormonism," *Temenos* 5 (1969): 120-68.

[3] An account of these travels is in Parley Parker Pratt, *Autobiography* (Salt Lake City, 1966), pp. 47-57.

[4] Sidney Rigdon, Joseph Smith, Jr., et al., in Kirtland, Ohio, to John Thornton et al., in Liberty, Missouri, 25 July 1836. Quoted in *Latter-day Saints' Messenger and Advocate* 2 (August 1836): 357.

[5] Joseph Smith to the Potawatomi Indians, 28 August 1843, Joseph Smith Papers, Church Archives. For Smith's account of this event, see *HC* 5:365, 480.

[6] Henry King to John Chambers, 14 July 1843, *Letters Received by the Office of Indian Affairs, 1824-81, Iowa Superintendency, 1838-49* (Washington, D.C.: National Archives Microfilm). See a full, documented account in Lawrence G. Coates, "A History of Indian Education by the Mormons, 1830-1900" (Ed.D. diss., Ball State University, 1969), pp. 52-55.

[7] *Proclamation of the Twelve Apostles of the Church of Jesus Christ of Latter-day Saints* (New York, 1845). Dated 6 April 1845, this "proclamation" was written by the Mormon poet, missionary, and theologian Parley P. Pratt.

[8]   Andrew Love Neff, *History of Utah, 1847 to 1869* (Salt Lake City, 1940), p. 369.

[9]   Leland H. Creer, *Utah and the Nation* (Seattle, 1929), p. 174.

[10] Manuscript History of Brigham Young, 12 June 1849, p. 90. Church Archives.

[11] *Deseret News*, 14 December 1854. See also Dale L. Morgan, "The Administration of Indian Affairs in Utah, 1851–1858," *Pacific Historical Review* 17 (November 1948): 383–409.

[12] Brigham Young, Sermon, 28 July 1866, in *JD* 11:263; Creer, *Utah and the Nation*, p. 167.

[13] Quoted in Juanita Brooks, "Indian Relations on the Mormon Frontier," *Utah Historical Quarterly* 12 (January–April 1944): 19.

[14] Solomon Kimball, "Our Pioneer Boys," *Improvement Era* 11 (July 1908): 668–80.

[15] Leonard J. Arrington, "How the Saints Fed the Indians," *Improvement Era* 57 (November 1954): 801; idem, "The Mormon Tithing House: A Frontier Business Institution," *Business History Review* 28 (March 1954): 24–58.

[16] William Halls, letter to *Deseret News*, 16 August 1866.

[17] Leonard J. Arrington, *From Quaker to Latter-day Saint: Bishop Edwin D. Woolley* (Salt Lake City, 1976), pp. 337–38, 355; "Indian Women of the West," ed. Kate Carter, *Heart Throbs of the West*, 12 vols. (Salt Lake City, 1936–1951), 1:110; Susa Young Gates, "Relief Society Beginnings in Utah," *The Relief Society Magazine* 9 (April 1922): 185. Also Emmeline B. Wells, "History of the Relief Society," *Woman's Exponent* 32 (June 1903): 6. The minutes of several of these Indian Relief Society organizations are in Church Archives.

[18] A Mormon description of this trade is found in the preamble to "An Act for the Further Relief of Indian Slaves and Prisoners," as passed by the Utah territorial legislature in 1852: "They are carried from place to place packed upon horses or mules lariated out to subsist upon roots or starve, and are frequently bound by thongs made of rawhide until their hands and feet become swollen, mutilated, inflamed with pain and wounded; and when with suffering, cold, hunger and abuse, they fall sick, so as to become troublesome, are frequently slain by their masters to get rid of them." *Laws of Utah* (Salt Lake City, 1852), pp. 93–94.

[19] Daniel W. Jones, *Forty Years among the Indians* (Salt Lake City, 1890), p. 51.

[20] *Memoirs of John R. Young, Utah Pioneer 1847* (Salt Lake City, 1920), p. 62. Sally became famous for her excellent cooking. On one occasion, when she was serving a group of chieftains at Brigham Young's table, the Pahvant chief, Kanosh, fell in love with her and tried to buy her from Brigham Young. Young would not sell her, but said she was free to accept Kanosh's offer if she wished. She refused, but Kanosh was persistent, and ultimately she did accept his proposal. He built her a "white man's house" and allowed her to follow "white man's ways." Later Kanosh married another Indian woman, this time a tradition-oriented female, who hated Sally and her white customs. One day when Kanosh was away, she killed Sally and buried her in a shallow grave. When Kanosh returned and found Sally gone, he suspected what had happened and angrily hunted until he found her grave. "In his grief he seized the murderess, and would have burned her at the stake, but white men interfered. In due time the Indian woman confessed her guilt, and in accordance with the Indian concept of justice, offered to expiate her crime by starving herself to death. The offer was accepted, and on a lone hill in sight of the village, a wick-i-up was constructed of dry timber. Taking a jug of water, the woman silently walked toward her living grave. Like the rejected swan, alone, unloved, in low tones she sang her own sad requiem, until her voice was hushed in death. One night when the evening beacon fire was not seen by the villagers, a runner was dispatched to fire the wick-i-up, and retribution was complete." Ibid., p. 63. See also "Indian

Women of the West," in Carter, *Heart Throbs of the West*, 1:108–26, 157–64; Susa Young Gates, *The Life Story of Brigham Young* (New York, 1931), pp. 134–45; Elizabeth D. Kane, *Twelve Mormon Homes Visited in Succession on a Journey through Utah to Arizona* (Philadelphia, 1874), pp. 13–15.

[21] *Deseret News*, 28 June 1851.

[22] Juanita Brooks, "Indian Relations," p. 7; *Deseret News*, 10 January 1852.

[23] Juanita Brooks, *Dudley Leavitt: Pioneer to Southern Utah* (Salt Lake City, 1942), p. 58.

[24] The best studies are in Brooks, "Indian Relations," pp. 27–48; and "Indian Women of the West," pp. 108–26, 157–64.

[25] Daniel H. Wells to "Dear Brothe[r]s [and Sisters]," 19 April 1850, Daniel H. Wells Collection, Church Archives. See also the account in Neff, *History of Utah*, p. 161.

[26] Roberts, *Comprehensive History* 3:464.

[27] Neff, *History of Utah*, p. 375.

[28] *JH*, 25 July 1853.

[29] Several handwritten accounts are in Church Archives.

[30] The Mormons followed the policy of giving rifles and bullets to the Indians so that the latter could shoot their own game and not have to steal from the Mormons.

[31] This much-abbreviated account is based primarily on S. N. Carvalho, *Incidents of Travel and Adventure in the Far West* (New York, 1857), pp. 188–93. See also Brigham Young, Sermon, 3 December 1854, in *JD* 2:143.

[32] Neff, *History of Utah*, pp. 382–86.

[33] The Mormons never had formal restrictions against intermarriage with the Indians, and some of the pioneer mission leaders were advised to encourage it. The instructions of Orson Hyde to the Green River Mission on this point were remembered by James S. Brown as follows: "We were to identify our interests with theirs, even to marrying among them, if we would be permitted to take the young daughters of the chief and leading men, and have them dressed like civilized people, and educated." Brown tells of a conference with Chief Washakie of the Shoshoni nation. The chief agreed with all of the objectives of the missionaries, but when the suggestion of Brigham Young that some of the missionaries take Indian women for wives was mentioned, one old and wise Indian counselor said, "No, for we have not got daughters enough for our own men, and we cannot afford to give our daughters to the white man, but we are willing to give him an Indian girl for a white girl. I cannot see why a white man wants an Indian girl. They are dirty, ugly, stubborn and cross, and it is a strange idea for white men to want such wives. But I can see why an Indian wants a white woman." Chief Washakie "said the white men might look around, and if any one of us found a girl that would go with him, it would be all right, but the Indians must have the same privilege among the white women." With this the council ended. James S. Brown, *Giant of the Lord: Life of a Pioneer* (Salt Lake City, 1902), pp. 320, 334.

[34] Instructions from Salt Lake, March 19, 1875, in "Indians" file, Church Archives.

[35] James A. Little, *Jacob Hamblin* (Salt Lake City, 1881), pp. 21–22.

[36] Ibid., p. 22.

[37] Ibid., pp. 23–24.

[38] Juanita Brooks, "Jacob Hamblin: Apostle to the Lamanites," *Pacific Spectator* 2 (Summer 1948): 330. Cf. Charles S. Peterson, "Jacob Hamblin, Apostle to the Lamanites, and the Indian Mission," *Journal of Mormon History* 2 (1975): 21–34.

[39] Ibid., pp. 320, 323.

[40] Juanita Brooks, "Jacob Hamblin; 'Apostle to the Indians,'" *Improvement Era* 47 (April 1944): 253–54.

[41] This was particularly true after the lamentable Mountain Meadows Massacre, described in chap. 9. See also Juanita Brooks, *The Mountain Meadows Massacre* (Stanford, Calif., 1950).

[42] Daniel Jones, *Forty Years among the Indians*, p. 372.

[43] The best summary is Neff, *History of Utah*, pp. 398–409.

[44] Ibid.

[45] Ibid., p. 406.

[46] Ibid., p. 407.

[47] Lawrence G. Coates, "Mormons and Social Change among the Shoshoni, 1853–1900," *Idaho Yesterdays* 16 (Winter 1972): 2–11.

[48] The Catawba nation, still Mormon, was assimilated by the 1950s and therefore disorganized. See Douglas Summers Brown, *The Catawba Indians: The People of the River* (Columbia, S.C., 1966), pp. 340–47 et passim; and Charles A. Callis, "Among the Catawbas," *Improvement Era* 39 (August 1963): 473.

[49] On the climate of opinion, see Dennis L. Lythgoe, "The Changing Image of Mormonism in Periodical Literature" (Ph.D. diss., University of Utah, 1969).

[50] St. Paul, Minn., dispatch in *Deseret Evening News*, 7 November 1890; "Probably a Mormon Trick," *New York Times*, 8 November 1890; and James Mooney, "The Ghostdance Religion and the Sioux Outbreak of 1890," Part Two of the *Fourteenth Annual Report of the Bureau of Ethnology to the Secretary of the Smithsonian Institution* (Washington, D.C., 1896).

[51] Lawrence Coates, "The Mormons, the Ghost Dance Craze, and the Massacre at Wounded Knee" (Paper delivered at Western History Association Convention, Rapid City, S.D., 3 October 1974, typescript in possession of the authors). This interpretation is based on inferences drawn from many letters sent by missionaries to church officials and letters sent by Mormon leaders to missionaries during the last decade of the nineteenth century.

[52] The authors, both raised in southern Idaho, can attest to the fact that there, reservation Indians were often treated with the same disdain by both Mormon and non-Mormon whites.

[53] This follows by nine years the 1934 passage of the Wheeler-Howard and Johnson-O'Malley Acts, which repudiated the severalty policy, promoted community ownership and control, decentralized the administration of Indian policy, increased appropriations for Indian education, and encouraged the Secretary of the Interior to enter into contracts with states and private institutions "for the education, medical attention, agricultural assistance, and social welfare [of the Indian]." S. Lyman Tyler, *Indian Affairs: A Study of the Changes in Policy of the United States toward Indians* (Provo, Utah, 1964), p. 66.

[54] See especially Coates, "History of Indian Education."

[55] "This Mission President Is a 'Cowboy's Cowboy,'" *Deseret News*, 10 May 1969.

[56] To critics of the placement program who contended that it alienated Indian children from their parents and culture, Arthur Allison, a Navaho "graduate" of the program and a business major at Brigham Young University, replied: "The only hope many of my people have is alienation from conditions that have contributed to their poverty . . . lack of education, illiteracy, alcoholism—all the problems that wreck lives. . . . I do not believe the program encourages the student to lose love for his real parents, only for those things in his culture which ought not to be preserved. This is constructive alienation." Paul H. Schneiter, "BYU: Giving the Indian a Place in the Sun," *Deseret News,* 24 January 1970.

Chapter 9

[1]   Parley P. Pratt to "All the Saints," 9 July 1846, in Roberts, *Comprehensive History* 3:94-95, 415.

[2]   Dale L. Morgan, "The State of Deseret," *Utah Historical Quarterly* 8 (April-July-October 1940): 65-239.

[3]   Norman F. Furniss, *The Mormon Conflict, 1850-1859* (New Haven, 1960), p. 10.

[4]   Ibid., p. 55.

[5]   Philip G. Auchampaugh, *Robert Tyler, Southern Rights Champion* (Duluth, Minn., 1934), p. 180.

[6]   Juanita Brooks, *The Mountain Meadows Massacre* (Stanford, Calif., 1950); Juanita Brooks, *John Doyle Lee: Zealot, Pioneer Builder, Scapegoat* (Glendale, Calif., 1961).

[7]   Juanita Brooks, ed., *On the Mormon Frontier: The Diary of Hosea Stout*, 2 vols. (Salt Lake City, 1964), 2:654.

[8]   Eckles to Cass, 9 July 1858, Record Group 107, National Archives, Washington, D.C., as cited in Alan E. Haynes, "The Federal Government and Its Policies Regarding the Frontier Era of Utah Territory, 1850-1877" (Ph.D. diss., Catholic University of America, 1968), p. 115.

[9]   Attorney General Black to Eckles, 17 May 1859, as cited in Haynes, p. 116.

[10]   Stenhouse to Young, 7 June 1863, Brigham Young Correspondence, Church Archives; also Preston Nibley, *Brigham Young: The Man and His Work* (Salt Lake City, 1937), p. 369.

[11]   *Doctrine and Covenants* 87:1.

[12]   *JD* 9:7.

[13]   Ibid.

[14]   Gustive O. Larson, "The Mormon Reformation," *Utah Historical Quarterly* 26 (January 1958): 56.

[15]   *Deseret News*, 30 April 1862.

[16]   Minutes of the State of Deseret are in Church Archives.

[17]   Haynes, "Federal Government," pp. 149-50.

[18]   *Deseret News*, 4 March 1863.

[19]   Robert Dwyer, *The Gentile Comes to Utah* (Washington, D.C., 1941), p. 27.

[20]   Ibid., pp. 19, 25-26.

[21]   *JD* 12: 290.

[22]   Samuel Bowles, *Our New West* (Hartford, Conn., 1869), p. 260.

[23]   The best treatment of the Godbeites is Ronald W. Walker, "The Godbeite Protest in the Making of Modern Utah" (Ph.D. diss., University of Utah, 1977).

[24]   McKean to Judge Louis Dent, brother-in-law of Ulysses S. Grant, quoted in Edward W. Tullidge, *Life of Brigham Young; or, Utah, and Her Founders* (New York, 1876), pp. 420-21.

[25]   Dwyer, *Gentile Comes to Utah*, p. 151.

[26]   Salt Lake City *Tribune*, 11 November 1877.

[27]   Davis Bitton, "Polygamy Defended: A Study of 19th Century Polemic" (Paper delivered at the Western History Association Convention, Reno, Nev., 13 October 1970).

[28]   Salt Lake City *Tribune*, 14 December 1884.

[29]   *Anti-Polygamy Standard* (Salt Lake City) 1 (April 1880): 1.

[30]   Charles A. Cannon, "The Awesome Power of Sex: The Polemical Campaign against Mormon Polygamy," *Pacific Historical Review* 53 (February 1974): 61-82.

[31]   *Reynolds v. United States*, 98 U.S. 145.

32   *JD* 23:65–67.

33   Journal of John M. Whitaker, 130 ct. 1886, Church Archives.

34   Salt Lake City *Tribune*, 28 July 1887.

35   Orson F. Whitney, *History of Utah*, 4 vols. (Salt Lake City, 1892–1904), 3:547–48.

36   The economic aspects of this legislation are covered in Leonard J. Arrington, *Great Basin Kingdom: An Economic History of the Latter-day Saints, 1830–1900* (Cambridge, Mass., 1958), pp. 353–79. The standard reference on the political consequences is Gustive O. Larson, *The "Americanization" of Utah for Statehood* (San Marino, Calif., 1971).

37   *The Late Corporation of the Church of Jesus Christ of Latter-day Saints v. United States,* 140 U.S. 665.

38   Diary of Wilford Woodruff, 25 September 1890, Church Archives; "Official Declaration," *Doctrine and Covenants*, after sec. 136.

39   Wilford Woodruff, Sermon, 6 October 1890, in *Latter-day Saints' Millennial Star* (Liverpool, England) 52 (24 November 1890): 739.

Chapter 10

1   The Autumn 1976 issue of *Dialogue: A Journal of Mormon Thought* contains a number of articles dealing with sexuality and Mormon culture.

2   Some basis for the idea of a "one and only" based on a covenant in the spirit world prior to birth is found in "The Origin and Destiny of Women," an editorial by Apostle John Taylor in the church's New York newspaper, *The Mormon*, 29 August 1857.

3   *Young Woman's Journal* 5 (December, 1893): 147–48.

4   Hugh B. Brown, *You and Your Marriage* (Salt Lake City, 1960), p. 18.

5   D. Michael Quinn, "The Mormon Hierarchy, 1832–1932: An American Elite" (Ph.D. diss., Yale University, 1976).

6   Kimball Young, *Isn't One Wife Enough?* (New York, 1954), chap. 5.

7   *Doctrine and Covenants* 29:47.

8   A few of the many sermons are in *JD* 4:73; 7:205; 10:224–25; 14:285–88; 20:7.

9   Diary of Daniel Wood, passim, Church Archives.

10   *JD* 10:361.

11   3 Ne. 17:21–24.

12   Joseph Smith to Emma Smith, 12 November 1838; Brigham Young to Mary Ann Young, 12 June 1844; and Albert Carrington to Calvin Carrington, 10 February 1869; Church Archives (original of Carrington letter in possession of Myra Bird, Salt Lake City).

13   Davis Bitton, "The Mormon Child: Growing Up on the Mormon Frontier," paper presented at the conference on Childhood in American Life, Indianapolis, Indiana, 31 March 1978.

14   Diary of Orson Hyde, 16 September 1832, Church Archives.

15   Barbara Welter, "The Cult of True Womanhood, 1820–1860," *American Quarterly* 18 (Summer 1966): 151–74; Claudia Bushman, ed., *Mormon Sisters: Women in Early Utah* (Boston, 1976). See also chap. 7, this volume.

16   In many ways the definitive treatment of Mormon polygamy is Young, *Isn't One Wife Enough?* On the social origins of Mormon polygamy, see Lawrence Foster, "Between Two Worlds: The Origins of Shaker Celibacy, Oneida Community Complex Marriage, and Mormon Polygamy" (Ph.D. diss., University of Chicago, 1976). The institutional development of early polygamy is presented in Danel W. Bachman, "A Study of the Mormon Practice of Plural Marriage before the Death of Joseph Smith" (Master's

thesis, Indiana-Purdue University, 1975). See Davis Bitton, "Mormon Polygamy: A Review Article," *Journal of Mormon History* 4 (1977): 101–8.

[17] Jac. 2:28–30.

[18] William W. Phelps to Brigham Young, 12 August 1861, original in vault and typescript in Joseph Smith Papers, Church Archives.

[19] Udney Hay Jacob, *An Extract from a Manuscript Entitled the Peacemaker, or the Doctrines of the Millennium: Being a Treatise on Religion and Jurisprudence* (Nauvoo, Ill., 1842). Discussed in Lawrence Foster, "A Little-known Defence of Polygamy from the Mormon Press in 1842," *Dialogue* 9 (Winter 1974): 21–34.

[20] Summaries of the Mormon theology developed in the Nauvoo period dealing with sealings, work for the dead, and the eternal family are found in Richard D. Poll, "The Twin Relic: A Study of Mormon Polygamy and the Campaign by the Government of the United States for Its Abolition, 1852–1890" (Master's thesis, Texas Christian University, 1939), chap. 2; Young, *Isn't One Wife Enough?*, chap. 2; and Hubert Howe Bancroft, *History of Utah* (San Francisco, 1889), pp. 388–95.

[21] Mal. 4:6.

[22] Charles A. Shook, *The True Origin of Mormon Polygamy* (Cincinnati, 1914). Shook was reared in a family belonging to the Reorganized Church of Jesus Christ of Latter Day Saints, but he later apostatized.

[23] *JD* 3:266.

[24] Thomas Edgar Lyon, "Orson Pratt—Early Mormon Leader" (Master's thesis, University of Chicago, 1932), pp. 34–44.

[25] Lyman O. Littlefield, ed., *Reminiscences of Latter-day Saints* (Salt Lake City, 1888), pp. 46–48.

[26] Fawn M. Brodie, *No Man Knows My History: The Life of Joseph Smith, the Mormon Prophet* (New York, 1945), Appendix C.

[27] *United States Circuit Court (8th Circuit) . . . The Reorganized Church of Jesus Christ of Latter Day Saints, complainant vs., the Church of Christ at Independence, Missouri . . .* (Lamoni, Iowa, 1893), pp. 364, 367, 394. This is usually referred to as the Temple Lot Case.

[28] Affidavit of Melissa Willes, 4 August 1893, in Raymond T. Bailey, "Emma Hale, Wife of the Prophet Joseph Smith" (Master's thesis, Brigham Young University, 1952), pp. 98–100.

[29] For estimates of fluctuating numbers involved in polygamy, see Stanley S. Ivins, "Notes on Mormon Polygamy," *Western Humanities Review* 10 (Summer 1956): 229–39.

[30] All Western populations seem to have had a certain percentage of unmarried adult females, although the sex distribution in Utah was very close to fifty-fifty. Among Mormons, or at least those practicing their religion, females were undoubtedly in the majority. This subject awaits precise study.

[31] The decision in the *Reynolds* case is in *Reynolds v. United States*, 98 U.S. 145. See the critical review by George Q. Cannon, *A Review of the Decision of the Supreme Court of the United States* (Salt Lake City, 1879). By 1886 there was some modification of the Mormon position on these issues. Before the Supreme Court, George Ticknor Curtis said, "Of course I do not stand here to contend that a man's religious belief operates to prevent the legislative power from prohibiting conduct which that power deems injurious to the welfare of society. The Mormons once made that contention, at least up to a certain point; but I am not asked to make that contention now, and I could not make it if I were." George Ticknor Curtis and Franklin S. Richards, *Pleas for Religious Liberty* (Washington, D.C., 1886), p. 25. Other Mormons continued to insist on the religious exemption and to condemn the failure or malice of the Congress and the Court in not recognizing their constitutional rights.

[32]   Gustive O. Larson, *The "Americanization" of Utah for Statehood* (San Marino, Calif., 1971), p. 49.

[33]   *To the Last Frontier: Autobiography of Lucy Hannah White Flake,* ed. Roberta Flake Clayton, multilith copy, Church Archives.

[34]   Nels Anderson, *Desert Saints: The Mormon Frontier in Utah* (Chicago, 1942), pp. 402-3.

[35]   Andrew Karl Larson, *Erastus Snow* (Salt Lake City, 1971), pp. 747-48.

[36]   George Tanner, son of an Arizona polygamist, remembered with sorrow that his half-brothers and half-sisters suffered from many slights, and he felt it important to try to reestablish some equity by listing the children in exact order of birth. George S. Tanner, oral history interview, August 24, 1972, typescript, Church Archives.

[37]   "Autobiography of Olive Andelin Potter," typescript, Brigham Young University Library.

[38]   Juliaetta B. Jensen, *Little Gold Pieces* (Salt Lake City, 1948), pp. 54-63.

[39]   Annie Clark Tanner, *A Mormon Mother* (Salt Lake City, 1969).

[40]   Susan Terry, "In Answer to Some Facts," *Woman's Exponent* 10 (1 April 1882): 168.

[41]   *JD* 20:275-6.

[42]   Gordon Irving, "The Law of Adoption: One Phase of the Development of the Mormon Concept of Salvation, 1830-1900," *BYU Studies* 14 (Spring 1974): 291-314.

Chapter 11

[1]   Elizabeth Ann Whitney, "A Leaf from an Autobiography," *Woman's Exponent* 7 (1 September 1878): 51.

[2]   *Doctrine and Covenants,* 59:9-12; 88:118-20.

[3]   *Doctrine and Covenants,* sec. 20 and 61.

[4]   Joseph Sudweeks, *Discontinued LDS Periodicals* (Provo, Utah, 1955); Loy O. Banks, "Latter Day Saint Journalism" (Master's thesis, University of Missouri, 1948).

[5]   *Doctrine and Covenants,* 29:34-35; 41:9; 72:8; et passim.

[6]   Ernst Kantorowicz, *The King's Two Bodies: A Study of Medieval Political Theology* (Princeton, N.J., 1957).

[7]   "Minutes of Bishops Meetings, Salt Lake City, 1852-1880," 7 April 1855, p. 106, Church Archives.

[8]   Sec. 20 of the *Doctrine and Covenants,* dated April 1830, is often referred to as the first Mormon constitution. For tracing changes in early Mormon organization, this section should be compared with the *Book of Commandments* (Independence, Mo., 1833).

[9]   "Minutes of Bishops Meetings with Presiding Bishop, 1851-1862," 18 July 1861, Church Archives.

[10]   William G. Hartley, "Ordained and Acting Teachers in the Lesser Priesthood, 1851-1883," *BYU Studies* 16 (Spring, 1976): 379.

[11]   "Minutes of Bishops Meetings," 24 June 1851, 12 December 1855, 11 March 1856, et passim.

[12]   Early Mormon leaders were often versatile, following several different vocations, and hence difficult to categorize.

[13]   Glen M. Leonard, "A History of Farmington, Utah, to 1890" (Master's thesis, University of Utah, 1966), p. 45.

[14]   "Salt Lake Thirteenth Ward, Economic Record, 1857," Church Archives.

[15]   Leonard J. Arrington, *Great Basin Kingdom: An Economic History of the Latter-day Saints, 1830-1900* (Cambridge, Mass., 1958), pp. 137, 353, 400-01, 504.

[16] "Minutes of Bishops Meetings," 3 April 1856.

[17] Ibid., 6 March 1856.

[18] Ibid., 25 February 1852.

[19] Leonard, "History of Farmington," pp. 113-15.

[20] *Deseret News*, 20 July 1850.

[21] Calvin S. Smith, "Public School Land Policies of the State of Utah" (Ph.D. diss., University of Chicago, 1928).

[22] "Minutes of Bishops Meetings," 14 February 1854.

[23] Roberts, *Comprehensive History* 4:100-120.

[24] "Minutes of Bishops Meetings," 23 September 1856.

[25] Ibid., 7 October, 21 October, 10 November 1856. Also Howard Clair Searle, "The Mormon Reformation of 1856-1857" (Master's thesis, Brigham Young University, 1956).

[26] Matthias F. Cowley, *Wilford Woodruff* (Salt Lake City, 1909), p. 375.

[27] William G. Hartley, "The Priesthood Reorganization of 1877: Brigham Young's Last Achievement," forthcoming in *BYU Studies*.

[28] The organization of the Primary is described in Aurelia Spencer Rogers, *Life Sketches . . . and History of Primary Work* (Salt Lake City, 1898), pp. 205-332.

[29] *Improvement Era* (May 1912): 830-31.

[30] Ibid., 15 (August 1912): 847.

[31] *History of Relief Society, 1842-1966* (Salt Lake City, 1966), pp. 104-5.

[32] Amy Brown Lyman, "Conservation," *Relief Society Magazine* 4 (September 1917): 566-67.

[33] "Provo First Ward Deacons Quorum Minutes Book, 1903-1904," 2 April 1903, Church Archives.

[34] "Ogden First Ward and Second Ward Deacons Quorum Minutes, 1906-1907," 14 December 1908; "Logan First Ward Aaronic Priesthood Minutes, 1905-1910"; "Provo First Ward Minutes, 1903-1904," Church Archives.

[35] "Cardston, Alberta, Canada, Ward Lesser Priesthood Minutes 1897-1909," 15 February 1909, Church Archives.

[36] William G. Hartley, "The Priesthood Reform Movement, 1908-1922," *BYU Studies* 13 (Winter 1973): 137-56.

[37] Presiding Bishopric's Office Circular No. 3," 14 June 1918, Church Archives.

[38] See special issue on architecture, *Utah Historical Quarterly* 43 (Summer 1975).

[39] Thomas F. O'Dea, *The Mormons* (Chicago, 1957), pp. 115-16; Rodman W. Paul, "The Mormons as a Theme in Western Historical Writing," *Journal of American History* 54 (December 1967): 519-21; Dean L. May, "The Mormons," in *Harvard Encyclopedia of American Ethnic Groups* (forthcoming).

[40] See the charming essay by Wayne C. Booth, "Farkism and Hyperyorkism," in his *Now Don't Try to Reason with Me* (Chicago, 1970), pp. 267-71. Other sources of local folklore include Virginia Sorensen, *Where Nothing Is Long Ago: Memories of a Mormon Childhood* (New York, 1963); Juanita Brooks, "The Water's In!", *Harper's Magazine* 175 (1941): 608-613.

[41] Versions of this story are found in Thomas E. Cheney, ed., *Lore of Faith and Folly* (Salt Lake City, 1971), pp. 31-35; and Austin and Alta Fife, *Saints of Sage and Saddle: Folklore among the Mormons* (Bloomington, Ind., 1956), pp. 272-73.

[42] Ezra J. Poulsen, *Joseph C. Rich: Versatile Pioneer on the Mormon Frontier* (Salt Lake City, 1958), p. 201.

[43] As told by the bishop of Orderville, Utah, Ward to Leonard Arrington, 25 July 1975.

[44] Grace Johnson, *Brodders and Sisters* (Manti, Utah, 1973), p. 8.

[45] Journal of Abraham A. Kimball, p. 203. Church Archives.

[46] For what follows, see Leonard J. Arrington and Dean L. May, "Cedar City: The Building of a Community" (Paper delivered at the 125th Anniversary Celebration of the Settlement of Cedar City, 11 November 1976), Church Archives. See also Gerald Sherratt, "A History of the College of Southern Utah, 1897 to 1947" (Master's thesis, Utah State University, 1954).

[47] Davis Bitton, " 'These Licentious Days': Dancing among the Mormons," *Sunstone* 2 (Spring 1977): 16–27.

[48] Because of the rich cultural offerings and lively civic involvement, many persons who grew up in Mormon wards achieved national prominence. In addition to other persons mentioned elsewhere in this work, the following are suggestive: John Moses Browning, inventor of the Winchester repeating rifle, the automatic pistol, the Browning automatic, the machine-gun rifle, the antiaircraft gun, from Ogden, Utah, wards; Gutzon and Solon Borglum, sculptors of the Mount Rushmore figures and of statues in Boston Common, Philadelphia, and Washington, D.C., from Saint Charles, Idaho, and Ogden, Utah, wards; Susa Young Gates, officer of the National Woman Suffrage Association and the International Congress of Women, from Salt Lake Eighteenth Ward; Bicknell Young, nephew of Brigham Young, who eventually abandoned Mormonism in favor of Christian Science, replaced Mary Baker Eddy as head of the First North "Mother Church" in Boston, and was thus titular head of that faith, from Salt Lake Eleventh Ward; Richard W. Young, graduate of West Point, head of a brigade in Cuba, member of the Supreme Court of the Philippines, from Salt Lake Seventeenth Ward; Arthur Shepherd, assistant director of the Cleveland Symphony Orchestra, and major American composer, from Salt Lake Eleventh Ward; W. H. and E. O. Wattis, key organizers of the six companies that built Boulder (Hoover) Dam, from Uinta Ward in Weber Valley, Utah; David M. Kennedy, secretary of the treasury in the administration of Richard Nixon, from Randolph Ward in Utah.

Chapter 12

[1] These early activities of Nauvoo women are recounted by Sarah M. Kimball in an autobiographical sketch published in Augusta Joyce Crocheron, *Representative Women of Deseret* (Salt Lake City, 1884), p. 26.

[2] These excerpts are taken from "Minutes of the Female Relief Society of Nauvoo," 17 March and 28 April 1842, Church Archives. Spelling and punctuation have been standardized.

[3] Ibid., 28 April 1842, 16 June and 7 July 1843.

[4] Ibid., 28 April 1842.

[5] Quoted in Robert Bruce Flanders, *Nauvoo: Kingdom on the Mississippi* (Urbana, Ill., 1965), p. 267.

[6] Crocheron, *Women of Deseret*, p. 26. This was Sarah M. Granger, who married Hiram Kimball, and not the Sarah M. Whitney Kimball who was a plural wife of both Joseph Smith and Heber C. Kimball.

[7] Eliza R. Snow, *Sketch of My Life*, p. 13, microfilm of holograph, Church Archives. The original is in the Bancroft Library, University of California at Berkeley.

[8] "Last Testimony of Sister Emma," *Saints' Advocate* 2 (October 1879): 50–51.

[9] "Minutes of General Women's Meeting, 17 July 1880," in R. S. Reports, *Woman's Exponent* 9 (1 September 1880): 54–55.

[10] Journal of Patty Sessions, 12 March 1846, Church Archives.

[11] "Journal of Mary Ann Weston Maughan," in Kate B. Carter, comp., *Our Pioneer Heritage*, 20 vols. (Salt Lake City, 1958–1977), 2:377.

[12] "Autobiography of Bathsheba W. Smith," typescript, p. 15, Church Archives.

[13] Journal of Jean Rio Baker, 28 April 1851, photocopy of typescript, Church Archives.

[14] Journal of Angelina Farley, 22 September 1850, microfilm of holograph, Church Archives.

[15] Journal of Eliza Marie Partridge Lyman, 17 October 1848, Church Archives.

[16] Lucinda Lee Dalton, *Autobiography*, microfilm of holograph, Church Archives. Original in Bancroft Library.

[17] Heber C. Kimball Sermon, 30 August 1857, in *JD* 5:163.

[18] Heber C. Kimball Sermon, 21 July 1857, in *JD* 5:29; Brigham Young Sermon, 15 June 1862, in *JD* 9:308.

[19] Journal of Martha Spence Heywood, 27 April 1856, typescript, Church Archives. For a discussion of women's involvement in the early Polysophical Society, see Maureen Ursenbach, "Three Women and the Life of the Mind," *Utah Historical Quarterly* 43 (Winter 1975): 26–40.

[20] Some early interpretations of doctrines regarding woman's place are discussed in Jill C. Mulvay, "Eliza R. Snow and the Woman Question," *BYU Studies* 16 (Winter 1976): 258–64.

[21] *New York Daily Tribune*, 20 August 1859, as quoted in William Mulder and A. Russell Mortensen, *Among the Mormons: Historic Accounts by Contemporary Observers* (New York, 1958), pp. 327–28.

[22] "Great Indignation Meeting," *Deseret News Weekly*, 19 January 1870.

[23] *Woman's Exponent* 14 (15 June 1885): 14.

[24] "The Women of Utah Represented at the International Council of Women, Washington, D.C.," *Woman's Exponent* 16 (1 April 1888): 165.

[25] Brigham Young Sermon, 31 August 1875, in *JD* 18:77.

[26] Brigham Young Sermon, 18 July 1869, in *JD* 13:61.

[27] Quoted in Leonard J. Arrington, "Blessed Damozels: Women in Mormon History," *Dialogue* 6 (Summer 1971): 25; E. R. Snow to Mrs. L. G. Richards, *Woman's Exponent* 3 (15 April 1875): 173; Leonard J. Arrington, "The Economic Role of Pioneer Mormon Women," *Western Humanities Review* 9 (Spring 1955): 145–64.

[28] Annie Wells Cannon, "Women in Education," *Woman's Exponent* 17 (1 June 1888): 2. The written laws included only masculine terminology and were interpreted to exclude women. See Jill C. Mulvay, "The Two Miss Cooks: Pioneer Professionals for Utah Schools," *Utah Historical Quarterly* 43 (Fall 1975): 401.

[29] L. L. Greene Richards, "Woman, 'Rise," *Young Woman's Journal* 4 (February 1893): 201.

[30] Interview published in the *San Francisco Examiner*, 8 November 1896, reprinted in the Salt Lake City *Herald*, 11 November 1896, as quoted in Jean Bickmore White, "Gentle Persuaders: Utah's First Women Legislators," *Utah Historical Quarterly* 38 (Winter 1970): 45.

[31] *Dictated Sketch of the Life of Mary Isabella Horne*, 1884, microfilm of manuscript, Church Archives. Original in Bancroft Library.

[32] "Fifteenth Ward, Riverside Stake Relief Society Minutes, 1868 to 1873," 19 February 1870, Church Archives.

[33] See Ronald W. Walker, "The Stenhouses and the Making of Mormon Image," *Journal of Mormon History* 1 (1974): 51–72.

[34] "Ethics for Young Girls," *Young Woman's Journal* 16 (April 1905): 205.

[35] Susa Young Gates and Leah D. Widtsoe, *Women of the "Mormon" Church* (Salt Lake City, 1926), p. 5. See also Carolyn W. D. Person, "Susa Young Gates," in Claudia L. Bushman, ed., *Mormon Sisters* (Cambridge, Mass., 1976), pp. 199–223.

[36] "General Conference of Relief Society," *Relief Society Magazine* 8 (December 1921): 704.

[37] An account of social-work assignments made to church auxiliaries is recorded in "Primary General Board Minutes," vol. 6, 1918–1920, 7 May 1920, typescript, Church Archives.

[38] Gates and Widtsoe, *Women of the "Mormon" Church*, p. 29.

[39] J. Reuben Clark, Jr., "The Present Duty of Relief Society," *Relief Society Magazine* 23 (May 1936): 274.

[40] Marba C. Josephson, "Woman's Place in the Forward March of the Church," *Improvement Era* 50 (July 1947): 452.

[41] Spencer W. Kimball, "Women, Wonderful Women!" *Relief Society Magazine* 45 (January 1958): 8.

[42] Eleanor Knowles, comp., *Gospel Insights from the Sermons and Stories of William J. Critchlow, Jr.* (Salt Lake City, 1969), p. 108.

[43] N Eldon Tanner, "No Greater Honor: The Woman's Role," *Ensign* 4 (January 1974): 7. This talk was republished by the church as a pamphlet entitled *The Role of Womanhood*, which was translated into several languages and circulated churchwide.

[44] Belle S. Spafford, "The Mormon Women," in *Selected Addresses from the 1974 Relief Society General Conference* (Salt Lake City, 1975), pp. 32–33.

[45] Claudia Lauper Bushman, "Women in Dialogue: An Introduction," *Dialogue* 4 (Summer 1971): 6.

[46] Claudia L. Bushman, "Exponent Is Born," *Exponent II* 1 (July 1974): 2.

[47] Elouise Bell, "Feminism at BYU," *Exponent II* 2 (March 1976): 10.

[48] Barbara B. Smith, "New Lamps for Old," *Ensign* 6 (April 1976): 67–69.

[49] "Kanab Relief Society Minutes, 13 February 1881," *Woman's Exponent* 9 (1 April 1881): 166.

[50] John A. Widtsoe, "The 'Mormon' Woman," *Relief Society Magazine* 30 (June–July 1943): 372.

[51] Tanner, "No Greater Honor," p. 10.

[52] "A Woman's Preparation," *Ensign* 7 (March 1977): 59.

[53] "Cedar Fort Retrenchment Association Minutes, 21 April 1875," in "R. S. Reports," *Woman's Exponent* 4 (1 June 1875): 2.

[54] Widtsoe, "The 'Mormon' Woman," p. 372.

Chapter 13

[1] *Doctrine and Covenants*, 124:49.

[2] Roberts, *Comprehensive History* 6:363–74; Davis Bitton, "The B. H. Roberts Case of 1898–1900," *Utah Historical Quarterly* 25 (January 1957): 27–46.

[3] Roberts, *Comprehensive History* 6:390–99.

[4] See Donald Bruce Gilchrist, "An Examination of the Problems of the L.D.S. Church Influence in Utah Politics, 1890–1916" (Ph.D. diss., University of Utah, 1967). Gilchrist incorrectly concludes that there was no separation of the church from state politics from 1890 to 1916. For a recent study showing how this has changed, see Douglas S. Foxley, "Mormon Myth or Monopoly: A Contemporary Study to Determine the Perceived Influence of the Mormon Church on Utah Politics" (Master's thesis, Utah State University, 1973).

⁵ This overlooks the fact that a leading business and financial leader, Apostle Heber J. Grant, was an ardent Democrat. See Roberts, *Comprehensive History* 6:329–36; Edward Leo Lyman, "Isaac Trumbo and the Politics of Utah Statehood," *Utah Historical Quarterly* 41 (Spring 1973): 128–49; see the statement of Wilford Woodruff that the church did not claim the right to direct voting but did claim the right to counsel its members against corruption in politics, *Deseret News*, 29 September 1894.

⁶ Roberts, *Comprehensive History* 6:329–36.

⁷ Ibid., 6:403–408. The speech is in *Congressional Record*, 58 Cong., vol. 39, pt. 4, pp. 3608–13.

⁸ Frank J. Cannon and Harvey J. O'Higgins, *Under the Prophet in Utah: The National Menace of a Political Priestcraft* (Boston, 1911). Also Frank H. Jonas, "Utah: The Different State," in Frank H. Jonas, ed., *Politics in the American West* (Salt Lake City, 1969), p. 329.

⁹ Salt Lake City *Tribune*, 9 January 1903.

¹⁰ See Milton R. Merrill, "Reed Smoot, Apostle in Politics" (Ph.D. diss., Columbia University, 1950).

¹¹ *Improvement Era* (October 1912): 1120–21.

¹² Bruce T. Dyer, "A Study of the Forces Leading to the Adoption of Prohibition in Utah in 1917" (Master's thesis, Brigham Young University, 1958), p. 11; Larry E. Nelson, "Utah Goes Dry," *Utah Historical Quarterly* 41 (Fall 1973): 358–72.

¹³ S. George Ellsworth, ed., "Simon Bamberger: Governor of Utah," *Western States Jewish Historical Quarterly* 5 (July 1973): 231–42.

¹⁴ Dean E. Mann, "Mormon Attitudes toward the Political Role of Church Leaders," *Dialogue* 2 (Summer 1967): 32–48.

¹⁵ Roberts, *Comprehensive History* 6:352.

¹⁶ *Conference Reports* (Salt Lake City, 1880–   ), October 1899, p. 24.

¹⁷ Ibid., April 1901, p. 70.

¹⁸ House of Representatives, *Hearings Held Before the Special Committee on the Investigation of the American Sugar Refining Company and Others*, 27 June 1911 (Washington, D.C., 1911), p. 1041; Alfred Henry Lewis, "The Viper's Trail of Gold," *Cosmopolitan*, May 1911, pp. 825–26.

¹⁹ Journal of Anthon H. Lund, 4 February 1904, Church Archives.

²⁰ "Hearings," p. 1041.

²¹ More favorable attitudes toward the Mormons began to develop during World War I. See Dennis L. Lythgoe, "The Changing Image of Mormonism in Periodical Literature" (Ph.D. diss., University of Utah, 1969); Jan Shipps, "From Satyr to Saint." The last of the old-style muckraking books was Cannon and O'Higgins, *Under the Prophet in Utah*. One of the first with some appreciation for Mormon values was Ruth and Reginald Kauffman, *The Latter Day Saints: A Study of the Mormons in the Light of Economic Conditions* (London, 1912).

²² *An Epistle to the Church of Jesus Christ of Latter-day Saints* (Salt Lake City, 1886).

²³ Leonard J. Arrington, *Great Basin Kingdom: An Economic History of the Latter-day Saints, 1830–1900* (Cambridge, Mass., 1958), p. 361.

²⁴ First Presidency to the Presidents of Stakes and Bishops of Wards, 25 October 1890, Church Archives.

²⁵ D. Michael Quinn, "Utah's Educational Innovation: L.D.S. Religion Classes, 1890–1929," *Utah Historical Quarterly* 43 (Fall 1975): 379–89.

²⁶ M. Lynn Bennion, *Mormonism and Education* (Salt Lake City, 1939), pp. 177–78.

²⁷ Leonard J. Arrington, "The Latter-day Saints and Public Education," *Southwestern Journal of Social Education* 7 (Spring-Summer 1977): 9–25.

[28]   Leonard J. Arrington, "The Founding of the L.D.S. Institutes of Religion," *Dialogue* 2 (Summer 1967): 137–47.

[29]   *Improvement Era* 6 (December 1902): 150–51.

[30]   Ibid.

[31]   Ibid. See also William G. Hartley, "The Priesthood Reform Movement, 1908–1922," *BYU Studies* 13 (Winter 1973): 137–56.

[32]   See Brigham H. Roberts, "The Life of B. H. Roberts," typescript, Church Archives; Robert H. Malan, *B. H. Roberts: A Biography* (Salt Lake City, 1966); Davis Bitton, "B. H. Roberts as an Historian," *Dialogue* 3 (Winter 1968): 25–44; Leonard J. Arrington, "The Intellectual Tradition of Mormon Utah," *Proceedings of the Utah Academy of Sciences, Arts and Letters* 45 (1968): 1–20.

[33]   *The Gospel* (1888), *The Mormon Doctrine of Deity* (1903), *Defense of the Faith and the Saints* (2 vols., 1907, 1912), *Joseph Smith the Prophet-Teacher* (1908), *A New Witness for God* (1909, 1912), and three important study manuals for the Seventies Course in Theology: *The Doctrine of Deity* (1910), *The Atonement* (1911), and *Divine Immanence and the Holy Ghost* (1912). In addition to the multivolume histories cited, Roberts also wrote the *Life of John Taylor* (1888), *The Missouri Persecutions* (1900), *The Rise and Fall of Nauvoo* (1900), and *The Mormon Battalion* (1916). All these works were published in New York City.

[34]   *Conference Reports*, April 1902, pp. 14–16.

[35]   Truman G. Madsen, "The Meaning of Christ—the Truth, The Way, The Life: An Analysis of B. H. Roberts' Unpublished Masterwork," *BYU Studies* 15 (Spring 1975): 259–92.

[36]   Sterling M. McMurrin, "Introduction," in B. H. Roberts, *Joseph Smith the Prophet-Teacher* (Princeton, 1967), introduction unpaged.

[37]   *Improvement Era* 9 (July 1906): 713.

[38]   Ralph W. Chamberlin, *Life and Philosophy of William W. Chamberlin* (Salt Lake City, 1925); and Ephraim E. Ericksen, "William H. Chamberlin: Pioneer Mormon Philosopher," *Western Humanities Review* 8 (Autumn 1954): 277–85.

[39]   The 1911 BYU controversy is discussed and documented in Ernest L. Wilkinson, *Brigham Young University: The First Hundred Years*, 4 vols. (Provo, Utah, 1975–76), 1: 409–33; and Richard Sherlock, "A Turbulent Spectrum: Mormon Reactions to the Darwinist Legacy," *Journal of Mormon History* 5 (1978): 33–59; Duane E. Jeffrey, "Seers, Savants, and Evolution: The Uncomfortable Interface," *Dialogue* 8 (Autumn–Winter 1973): 41–75.

[40]   Quoted in Wilkinson, *Brigham Young University* 1:419.

[41]   Although attendance at Chamberlin's religion and philosophy classes remained high, the administration denied him permission to teach any religion classes in 1913, his name and courses were omitted from the 1914–15 catalogue, and in 1916 he was informed that he was being transferred to the Department of Education. Chamberlin resigned, spent a year of study at Harvard, then taught philosophy through the University of Utah Extension (1917–1920) and Utah State Agricultural College Extension (1920–1921). Chamberlin, *Life and Philosophy*, pp. 209, 211, 270.

[42]   For a review of the modernist-fundamentalist controversy, see Sydney Ahlstrom, *A Religious History of the American People* (New Haven, 1972), pp. 763–824, 839–41, plus bibliography.

[43]   Joseph F. Smith, "Philosophy and the Church Schools," *Juvenile Instructor* 46 (April 1911): 209.

[44]   The institutionalization of prophecy has been a key factor in the strength and unity of Mormonism. Antinomian tendencies in Joseph Smith's day were minimized by

suggesting that every member was entitled to revelation, but only as it pertained to his or her own sphere of responsibility. Thus, the prophet-president was the only one author-ized by God to receive revelation or to declare doctrine for the entire church.

[45] Excommunication from the church is a serious matter among Mormons and is essentially a function of local leaders. The principal considerations are whether the per-son has apostatized—by vociferous opposition or simple withdrawal—or whether he has committed some grievous sin, such as adultery; in the latter case, excommunication is carried out as the first step on the path of forgiveness, rehabilitation, and restoration of full membership. The procedure is as follows: A charge is usually made by the local bishop or a home teacher, and the accused is notified in writing of the charge and of the date of a hearing. The hearing is conducted by the stake president, meeting with his counselors and the stake high council. The president asks the high council to draw num-bers. Those with even numbers are asked to speak for the accused and to make sure that his rights are respected. After the charge is read, the accused is asked to explain or defend himself; he may bring in witnesses to testify on his behalf. The stake president may also invite others who know of the case to testify, and the accused has the right to rebut their testimony. After all testimony has been heard, the accused leaves the room, and the high council discusses the case. The president may then retire for a moment of prayer and possibly discussion with his counselors. He then returns and renders a judgment that he believes to be just and fair, and asks the high council members to sustain this judgment. If they do, the accused is once more brought into the meeting and stands while the judgment is rendered. Where there are obvious signs of repentance on the part of the accused, this will be given full consideration in the judgment that is pronounced. Ex-communications are rare; one of the authors served as a high councilor for twelve years and in that period participated in only one excommunication proceeding. In that case, the accused was disfellowshipped (that is, his priesthood rights were taken away) but was not severed from the church.

[46] See Davis Bitton, "Anti-intellectualism in Mormon History," *Dialogue* 1 (Au-tumn 1966): 111–34, with an accompanying reply by James B. Allen (pp. 134–40). Shortly after the BYU affair E. E. Ericksen, Ph.D. student in philosophy at the Univer-sity of Chicago, was visited by Superintendent Cummings and told that "the philosophy I was being taught at the University of Chicago was not the kind that was wanted by my Church," and "that should I be given a position in the Church school system I would be in for trouble as were the BYU professors." Ericksen transferred to economics, but later passed his exams in both philosophy and economics. Scott G. Kenney, "The Religious Life and Thought of E. E. Ericksen," 1975 (unpublished paper in the possession of the authors), p. 10.

[47] *Conference Reports,* April 1903, p. 3.

[48] 2 Ne. 9:28–29.

Chapter 14

[1] "The Marriott Story: Mixing Mormon Principles with the Best of Sears, P&G, and IBM," *Forbes,* February 1971, pp. 16–24; "Mormon Mystery," *Time,* 11 July 1977, p. 69.

[2] For the nineteenth-century background, see Leonard J. Arrington, *Great Basin Kingdom: An Economic History of the Latter-day Saints, 1830–1900* (Cambridge, Mass., 1958); and David James Croft, "The Private Business Activities of Brigham Young, 1847–1887," *Journal of the West* 16 (October 1977); 36–51. For the twentieth-century background, see Bill Beecham and David Briscoe, "Mormon Money & How It's Made,"

Utah Holiday, 22 March 1976, pp. 4–11; and Wallace Turner, *The Mormon Establishment* (Boston, 1966), especially pp. 102–36.

³   While there is no equivalent report for more recent years, some idea may be gleaned from the fact that in 1978 the church had approximately two and one-half times as many members, almost four times as many missionaries, and almost three times as many wards and stakes. And of course the general price level has risen substantially.

⁴   In what follows, we have benefited from Chris Rigby, "The Building Program of the L.D.S. Church," 1972 (typescript, in possession of the authors). See also Peter L. Goss, "The Architectural History of Utah," and Allen D. Roberts, "Religious Architecture of the LDS Church: Influences and Changes Since 1847," in *Utah Historical Quarterly* 43 (Summer 1975): 208–39, 301–27; and Ebbie LaVar Davis, "Form-Function Relationships in the Development of LDS Church Architecture" (Master's thesis, Brigham Young University, 1970).

⁵   Eugene E. Campbell, "The Logan Tabernacle," in Joel E. Ricks, ed., Everett L. Cooley, assoc. ed., *The History of a Valley: Cache Valley, Utah-Idaho* (Logan, Utah, 1956), pp. 286–88.

⁶   Leonard J. Arrington and Melvin A. Larkin, "The Logan Tabernacle and Temple," *Utah Historical Quarterly* 41 (Summer, 1973): 301–14.

⁷   Interview with Charles Ursenbach, 9 July 1978.

⁸   Carl Fritz Johansson Oral History, interviews with Carl-Eric Johansson, 1973, Oral History Program, Church Archives.

⁹   John M. Russon Oral History, interviews with Richard L. Jensen, 1975, Oral History Program, Church Archives.

¹⁰   Richard L. Jensen, " 'Bell-Snickered' Builders," "Church Section," *Deseret News,* 1 April 1978.

¹¹   George Mortimer Oral History, interviews with William G. Hartley, 1975, Oral History Program, Church Archives.

¹²   "Round Table: The Coalville Tabernacle," in *Dialogue* 5 (Winter 1970): 41–65.

¹³   Mark Leone, "Why the Coalville Tabernacle Had to Be Razed: Principles Governing Mormon Architecture," *Dialogue* 8 (Summer 1973): 38.

¹⁴   Phil Robinson, *"Sinners and Saints": A Tour across the States, and round Them, with Three Months among the Mormons* (Boston, 1883), p. 139.

¹⁵   Mark P. Leone, "The New Mormon Temple in Washington, D.C.," in *Historical Archaeology and the Importance of Material Things,* Leland Ferguson, ed. (n.p.: The Society for Historical Archaeology, 1977), pp. 43–61.

¹⁶   A recent, thoughtful commentary is Paul Swenson, "Nostrums in the Newsroom," *Dialogue* 10 (Spring 1977): 46–57. Excellent histories are Wendell J. Ashton, *Voice in the West: Biography of a Pioneer Newspaper* (New York, 1950); and Monte R. McLaws, *Spokesman for the Kingdom: Early Mormon Journalism and the Deseret News, 1830–1898* (Provo, Utah, 1977).

¹⁷   Deseret Book Company, *Deseret Book Company, 1866–1976* (Salt Lake City, 1976).

¹⁸   See Herbert F. Murray, "A Half Century of Broadcasting in the Church," *Ensign* 2 (August 1972): 48–51; Fred C. Esplin, "The Church as Broadcaster," *Dialogue* 10 (Spring 1977): 25–45.

¹⁹   See Leonard J. Arrington, "History of the LDS Church Hospital System," 1970 (typescript in possession of the authors).

²⁰   Leonard J. Arrington, "Economy in the Modern Era," in Joel Ricks, ed., *The History of a Valley: Cache Valley, Utah-Idaho* (Salt Lake City, 1956), pp. 242–44. See also Richard Daines, "History of the Church Welfare Program," 1972 (typescript in possession of the authors); Leonard J. Arrington and Wayne Hinton, "Origin of the Wel-

fare Plan of the Church of Jesus Christ of Latter-Day Saints," *BYU Studies* 2 (Winter 1964): 67; and Leonard J. Arrington, Feramorz Y. Fox, and Dean L. May, *Building the City of God: Community and Cooperation among the Mormons* (Salt Lake City, 1976), pp. 337–58.

[21] *Deseret News,* 7 August 1931; Paul C. Child to Spencer W. Kimball, 12 June 1971, typescript, Church Archives.

[22] Child to Kimball, 12 June 1971; Leonard J. Arrington, "Harold B. Lee," in Preston Nibley, *The Presidents of the Church* (Salt Lake City, 1974), pp. 427–57.

[23] *Deseret News,* 4 January 1935.

[24] Quoted in *Church Welfare, A Discussion* (Salt Lake City, 1939), p. 8.

[25] "Church Section," *Deseret News,* 17 August 1937.

[26] "Address of Melvin J. Ballard," *Conference Reports,* October 1935, p. 50.

[27] Arrington and Hinton, "Origin of the Welfare Plan," p. 67.

[28] Ibid., p. 78.

[29] Heber J. Grant, *Conference Reports,* October 1936, p. 3.

[30] *What Is the "Mormon Security Program"?* (Independence, Mo., 1938), pp. 9–10.

[31] *Deseret News,* 9 June 1936.

[32] See William G. Hartley, "War and Peace and Dutch Potatoes," *Ensign* 8 (July 1978): 19–23.

[33] Peter Gillins, "Church Helps Rejuvenate City," *Church News,* 25 February 1978, p. 7.

[34] Bruce D. Blumell, "The Latter-day Saint Response to the Teton, Idaho, Flood, 1976," *Task Papers in LDS History,* no. 16, December 1976, Church Archives.

[35] *Salt Lake Tribune,* 26 March 1961; Annual Reports of LDS Church Welfare Plan, Church Archives.

[36] Graham H. Doxey, quoted in the *Salt Lake Tribune,* 14 May 1961.

[37] Gillins, "Church Helps Rejuvenate City."

[38] Among other articles, see Ronald J. Ostrow, "Mormon Merchants," *Wall Street Journal,* 20 December 1956; "Change Comes to Zion's Empire," *Business Week,* 23 November 1957, pp. 108–16; four releases to the Associated Press on the expansion and activities of the Mormon church by Dwight L. Jones, 29 June, 30 June, 1 July, 2 July 1959; Louis Cassels, "Church to Keep Holdings in the Business Field," UPI, Logan, Utah, *Herald Journal,* 12 May 1960; "Business-like Saints," *The Economist* (London), 20 January 1963, p. 228; Bill Beecham and David Briscoe, "Mormon Money & How It's Made," *Utah Holiday,* 22 March 1976, pp. 4–11; and Jeffrey Kaye, "An Invisible Empire: Mormon Money in California," *New West,* May 8, 1978, pp. 36–41. Perhaps it should be added that, so far as the authors can determine, church business enterprises have no tax advantage over other business enterprises.

[39] Cassels, "Church to Keep Holdings."

[40] Of the various enterprises mentioned in the text, those owned by Deseret Management Corporation are the following: Beneficial Development Company, Bonneville International Corporation, Deseret Book Company, Utah Deseret Farms of California, Deseret Farms of Florida, Deseret Farms of Texas, Inc., and Elberta Farm Corporation.

[41] Randall Hatch, "The Mormon Church: Managing the Lord's Work," *MBA,* June 1977, pp. 33–37.

[42] James Gollin, *Worldly Goods* (New York, 1971). Also James Gollin, "God's Mammon," *Time,* 8 November 1971, p. 93. Gollin calculates the combined assets of U.S. dioceses and religious orders at $34.2 billion. No similar estimate has been made of the assets of the Mormon church, though it surely would not represent one-tenth of the figure Gollin gives for the American Catholic church.

Chapter 15

This chapter is necessarily based on our own observations and reading about Mormonism in this century. Sources include many articles in the *Ensign* and the *New Era;* *BYU Studies, Dialogue,* and *Sunstone;* master's theses and doctoral dissertations; and books published by church administrators and scholars.

General appraisals of the Mormon church in the twentieth century, in addition to those in the general histories, include: James B. Allen and Richard O. Cowan, *Mormonism in the Twentieth Century* (Provo, Utah, 1967); and James B. Allen, "The Mormon Search for Community in the Modern World," in F. Mark McKiernan, Alma R. Blair, and Paul M. Edwards, eds., *The Restoration Movement: Essays in Mormon History* (Lawrence, Kans., 1973), pp. 307–40.

On specific topics, we suggest: Douglas D. Alder and H. George Fredrickson, "Mormonism and the Mormon Ward," 1976, typescript, Church Archives, a valuable study of types of wards in existence in the 1970s and their various characteristics and activities; Ronald W. Walker and D. Michael Quinn, " 'Virtuous, Lovely, or of Good Report': How the Church Has Fostered the Arts," *Ensign* 7 (July 1977): 81–93; Joan H. Iverson, "The Tabernacle Choir," *Improvement Era* 58 (August 1955): 564–65, 591; and the annual *Deseret News Church Almanac* (Salt Lake City, 1974–   ).

¹ Dean M. Kelley, *Why Conservative Churches Are Growing: A Study in Sociology of Religion* (New York, 1972), p. 54.

² A particularly valuable review of such studies is Glenn M. Vernon, *Sociology of Mormonism* (Salt Lake City, 1975). Our own impressionistic summary, which follows, comes partly from a reading of this book.

³ Carl D. Chambers *et al., The Incidence and Prevalence of Drug Use and Alcoholic Beverage Consumption in the State of Utah* (Washington, D.C., 1973).

⁴ Vernon, *Sociology of Mormonism,* p. 158.

⁵ Julie C. Wolfe and Armand L. Mauss, "Dimensions of Religious Defection: A Study of Inactivity among Mormons" (forthcoming).

⁶ See Joseph Anderson, *Prophets I Have Known* (Salt Lake City, 1973); also Joseph Anderson, oral history interview, typescript, Church Archives.

⁷ See John A. Widtsoe and Leah D. Widtsoe, *The Word of Wisdom: A Modern Interpretation,* 2nd ed. (Salt Lake City, 1938); Leonard J. Arrington, "An Economic Interpretation of the Word of Wisdom," *BYU Studies* 1 (Winter 1959): 37–49; idem, "Have the Saints Always Given as Much Emphasis to the Word of Wisdom as They Do Today?" *Ensign* 7 (April 1977): 32–33; Joseph L. Lyon *et al.,* "Cancer Incidence in Mormons and Non-Mormons in Utah, 1966–1970," *New England Journal of Medicine* 194 (January 1976): 129–33; idem, "Low Cancer Incidence in Mortality in Utah," *Cancer* 39 (June 1977): 2608–18.

⁸ The programs, methods, and purposes are described in Lawrence E. Cummins, "How Love Scales Prison Walls," *Ensign* 3 (February 1973): 5–11.

⁹ *Ensign* 4 (October 1974): 8.

¹⁰ For information on temples, see James E. Talmage, *The House of the Lord* (Salt Lake City, 1968).

¹¹ Mal. 4:6.

¹² A descriptive and interpretative discussion of church educational programs is found in Leonard J. Arrington, "The Latter-day Saints and Public Education," *Southwestern Journal of Social Education* 7 (Spring–Summer 1977): 9–25.

¹³ A number of studies have suggested high achievement among Utahans. Education

studies show high achievements in education, and a recent study of business leaders shows both Utah and Mormon culture ranking high as producers of executives of large corporations. Most of these studies conclude by saying that Mormon culture and its values account for the high proportion of superior people. See Mark W. Cannon, "Mormons in the Executive Suite," *Dialogue* 3 (Autumn 1968): 97–108; R. H. Knapp and H. B. Goodrich, *Origins of American Scientists* (Chicago, 1952).

[14] Church Educational System, 1974–75 Church Schools Annual Report (Salt Lake City [1975]), p. 1.

[15] Peter Berger, *The Sacred Canopy* (New York, 1967).

Chapter 16

[1] Wallace Stegner, *The Gathering of Zion: The Story of the Mormon Trail* (New York, 1964), p. 300.

[2] E. E. Ericksen, *The Psychological and Ethical Aspects of Mormon Group Life* (Chicago, 1922), p. 9.

[3] O'Dea's basic study was summarized in *The Mormons* (Chicago, 1957).

[4] Thomas F. O'Dea, "Mormonism and the Avoidance of Sectarian Stagnation: A Study of Church, Sect, and Incipient Nationality," *American Journal of Sociology* 60 (November 1954): 292.

[5] Martin E. Marty, ed., *Our Faiths* (New York, 1976), p. 219.

[6] John L. Sorenson, "Toward a Characterization of Mormon Personality," 1974 (typescript).

[7] Walter P. Metzger, "Generalization about National Character: An Analytical Essay," in Louis Gottschalk, ed., *Generalization in the Writing of History* (Chicago and London, 1963).

[8] Morris Garnsey, a non-Mormon economist at the University of Colorado, declared: "The Mormon culture has made a magnificent positive contribution to the life of the Mountain West. Its emphasis upon conservation and husbandry is of particular importance in the economic sphere." *America's New Frontier: The Mountain West* (New York, 1950), p. 54.

[9] The first "Mormon boys" to receive the Ph.D. in residence were Widtsoe and Joseph F. Merrill. With a degree in engineering, Merrill later became, in succession, dean of the College of Mines and Engineering at the University of Utah, church commissioner of education, and member of the Quorum of the Twelve.

[10] A native of Payson, Utah, Tanner graduated from Brigham Young Academy in Provo in 1878, taught there for a period, and then was made president of Brigham Young College in Logan in 1888. After three years he went with Widtsoe and others to Harvard, where he studied law. In 1896 Tanner was made president of the Agricultural College of Utah (now Utah State University) and served four years. In 1900, because of strong feelings on the part of some members of the Board of Trustees about the propriety of a polygamist serving as president of the college, Tanner resigned. He served briefly as deputy state superintendent of schools and in 1901 became superintendent of church schools, serving until 1906. Joel E. Ricks, *The Utah State Agricultural College: A History of Fifty Years, 1888-1938* (Logan, Utah, 1938), pp. 53–57; and Andrew Jenson, *Latter-day Saint Biographical Encyclopedia,* 4 vols. (Salt Lake City, 1901–36) 1:710.

[11] *In a Sunlit Land: The Autobiography of John A. Widtsoe* (Salt Lake City, 1952), p. 37.

[12] Ibid., pp. 73–74.

[13] Utah Agricultural Experiment Station, *Bulletin No. 75* (Logan, Utah, 1902), p. 2.

Although it is true that the ancient art of irrigation may have lacked a "scientific" basis, the system of the Nabateans and others in the Middle East several hundred years before Christ was far more sophisticated than anything erected by the Mormons in the nineteenth century. See, e.g., Philip C. Hammond, *The Nabateans: Their History, Culture, and Archaeology* (Lund, Sweden, 1974), pp. 52–53.

[14] John A. Widtsoe, "The Utah Agricultural College," *Improvement Era* 16 (July 1913): 953–56.

[15] Widtsoe shares with F. H. King of the University of Wisconsin the honor of founding irrigation science. Neither King nor Widtsoe was aware of the other's work at the outset, and King's research was not recognized nationally as soon as Widtsoe's. See Wilford R. Gardner, "Mormon Contributions to Irrigation Science," 1975 (typescript).

[16] "Editorial," *Improvement Era* 21 (September 1918): 1020.

[17] John A. Widtsoe, "The Conquest of Drouth," *Improvement Era* 16 (February 1913): 287–89. This reprints Widtsoe's presidential address to the International Dry-Farming Congress, Lethbridge, Alberta, Canada, March 1912.

[18] John A. Widtsoe, "The International Dry-Farming Congress," *Improvement Era* 15 (May 1912): 609–14.

[19] Dale C. LeCheminant, "John A. Widtsoe: Rational Apologist" (Ph.D. diss., University of Utah, 1977), pp. 163, 171. Also Widtsoe, *Federal Reclamation by Irrigation* (Washington, 1924); *Success in Irrigation Projects* (Washington, 1928); *How the Desert was Tamed* (Salt Lake City, 1948); and countless articles in agricultural and church periodicals.

[20] *In a Sunlit Land*, p. 79.

[21] See, e.g., Luther M. Winsor, "From Sagebrush to Sand Dunes," *Improvement Era* 48 (June 1945): 340–41, 373–74; and "The Thirsty Farms of Iran," *Improvement Era* 63 (July 1960): 506 ff.; (August 1960): 574 ff. Also Marian Crawford, "Mr. White Beard," *Deseret News*, 7 May 1950.

[22] Winsor, "Sagebrush to Sand Dunes," p. 374. It should be acknowledged that New York State claims to have appointed the first county farm agent, but Widtsoe insisted, to the end, that Utah was first. Widtsoe, *In a Sunlit Land*, p. 115.

[23] Widtsoe, *In a Sunlit Land*, p. 115. Dr. and Mrs. Widtsoe persuaded Senator Reed Smoot to induce Congress to approve a bill they had written providing for a national program of training women in home economics for service as county home demonstration agents. The bill was eventually passed as the Parnell Act. A noted scholar and writer in her own right, Mrs. Widtsoe coauthored with her mother, Susa Young Gates, *The Life Story of Brigham Young* (New York, 1931); *Women of the "Mormon" Church* (Salt Lake City, 1926); and *The Prince of Ur* (Salt Lake City, 1945); and coauthored with her husband *The Word of Wisdom: A Modern Interpretation* (Salt Lake City, 1938). She also founded the Utah Women's League of Voters and was its first president.

[24] Brossard's father's family had been in the Montreal region since 1630. His mother was "a Mormon girl" who helped convert his father. Edgar B. Brossard, oral history interview, 14 February 1973, p. 3, Church Archives.

[25] Edgar Brossard, oral history interview, 21 February 1973, p. 28.

[26] See *Half a Century of Friendship between Iran and Utah* (Logan, Utah, 1962); *Bolivia and Utah State University: A Decade of Contracts* (Logan, Utah, 1975).

[27] Lowry Nelson, *A Social Survey of Escalante, Utah* (Provo, Utah, 1925); *The Utah Farm Village of Ephraim* (Provo, Utah, 1928); *Social and Economic Aspects of American Fork, Utah* (Provo, Utah, 1933); *The Mormon Village: A Study in Social Origins* (Provo, Utah, 1939); and "The Mormon Settlements in Alberta," in C. A. Dawson, *Group Settlement: Ethnic Communities in Western Canada* (Toronto, 1936). These and other studies

have been evaluated and updated in his book *The Mormon Village: A Pattern and Technique of Land Settlement* (Salt Lake City, 1952).

²⁸ See Nelson, *Rural Sociology: Its Origin and Growth in the United States* (Minneapolis, 1969); and Nelson, *Eighty: One Man's Way There, A Memoir* (Provo, Utah, 1973).

²⁹ Gardner, "Mormon Contributions to Irrigation Science," p. 4.

³⁰ Willard Gardner, "Subduing the Earth," *Improvement Era* 20 (December 1920): 151.

³¹ W. R. Gardner, "The Impact of L. A. Richards upon the Field of Soil Water Physics," *Soil Science* 113 (1972): 232-37; Orson W. Israelsen, *Forty Years of Sound and Forty Years of Silence: An Autobiography* (Salt Lake City, 1968).

³² John A. Widtsoe, *The Principles of Irrigation Practice* (New York, 1914), p. 476.

³³ Kusum Nair, *The Lonely Furrow: Farming in the United States, Japan, and India* (Ann Arbor, Mich., 1969), pp. 37-38. Nair's italics.

³⁴ Kenneth R. Hardy, "Social Origins of American Scientists and Scholars," *Science* 185 (9 August 1974): 497-506. See also E. L. Thorndike, "The Production, Retention, and Attraction of American Men of Science," *Science* 92 (16 August 1940): 137-41; E. L. Thorndike, "Origin of Superior Men," *Scientific Monthly* 56 (May 1943): 424-33; and A. W. Astin, "Productivity of Undergraduate Institutions," *Science* 136 (1962): 129.

³⁵ For a discussion of this problem, see Gary B. Hansen, "Wanted: Additional Outlets for Idealism," *Dialogue* 5 (Autumn 1970): 26-37.

³⁶ *Deseret News,* 7 September 1968.

³⁷ Barbara Tietjen Jacobs, "Awakening Guatemala," *Ensign* 1 (July 1971): 24-30; Elizabeth Shaw, "Alone in a Valley: Cordell Andersen's Private Peace Corps," *Sunstone* 1 (Spring 1976): 45-52; newsletters of the Foundation for Indian Development and sermons of Cordell M. Andersen on file with the Church Archives.

³⁸ The description of this organization is based upon James B. Allen, "The Mormon Search for Community in the Modern World," in F. Mark McKiernan, Alma R. Blair, Paul M. Edwards, eds., *The Restoration Movement* (Lawrence, Kansas, 1973), 333; and Don C. Woodward, "Ayuda—A Story of People Who Really Care," *Deseret News,* 9 July 1977.

³⁹ "Music Grows Tender Apples," *New Era* (Salt Lake City), October 1975, p. 43. For earlier efforts of LDS servicemen to help Korean orphans, see "Church Section," *Deseret News,* 30 January 1954.

⁴⁰ William O. Robinson, "Mormons in the Urban Community," *Dialogue* 3 (Autumn 1968): 45. This article describes projects, procedures, and philosophy in detail.

⁴¹ Ibid.

⁴² Belle Cluff, "Reflections at Hopkins House," *Dialogue* 3 (Autumn 1968): 48-51.

⁴³ See Wallace Turner, *The Mormon Establishment* (Boston, 1966), pp. 218-66; and Thomas F. O'Dea, "Sources of Strain in Mormon History Reconsidered," in Marvin S. Hill and James B. Allen, eds., *Mormonism and American Culture* (New York, 1972), pp. 147-67.

⁴⁴ G. Homer Durham, "The Racial Revolution in America," *Improvement Era* 71 (October 1968): 93-95; and Brian Walton, "A University's Dilemma: BYU and Blacks," *Dialogue* 6 (Spring 1971): 31-36.

⁴⁵ Perhaps the most thoughtful study of the issue is by Lester E. Bush, Jr., "Mormonism's Negro Doctrine: An Historical Overview," *Dialogue* 8 (Spring 1973): 11-68. In the same issue of *Dialogue,* Gordon C. Thomasson, Hugh Nibley, and Eugene England provide other points of view, as do responses by readers in subsequent issues. Books on the subject include John L. Lund, *The Church and the Negro* (n.p., 1967); and Stephen Taggart, *Mormonism's Negro Policy: Social and Historical Origins* (Salt Lake City,

1970). For other responses that suggest the nature of the controversy and some of its implications, see David L. Brewer, "The Mormons," in *The Religious Situation: 1968*, Donald R. Cutler, ed. (Boston, 1968), pp. 518–54; and Lowell Bennion, "Commentary" on David L. Brewer, "The Mormons" in the same volume, pp. 843–55; Armand Mauss, "Mormonism and the Negro: Faith, Folklore and Civil Rights," *Dialogue* 2 (Winter 1967): 19–40; Wynetta Willis Martin, *Black Mormon Tells Her Story* (Salt Lake City, 1972); and Alan Gerald Cherry, *It's You and Me, Lord* (Provo, Utah, 1970).

[46] Statement of 15 December 1969, in "Church Section," *Deseret News*, 10 January 1970.

[47] Spencer W. Kimball interview in *U.S. News and World Report*, 19 December 1977, p. 61.

[48] 2 Ne. 26:33.

[49] Armand L. Mauss, "Moderation in All Things: Political and Social Outlooks of Modern Urban Mormons," *Dialogue* 7 (Spring 1972): 57–70. Mauss's studies have been conducted along the lines established by Charles Y. Clock and Rodney Stark, *Christian Beliefs and Anti-Semitism* (New York, 1966), which he also uses as a basis for comparison. Mauss's other study on the subject is "Mormonism and Secular Attitudes toward Negroes," *Pacific Sociological Review* 9 (Fall 1966): 91–99.

[50] First Presidency Statement of 15 December 1969, in "Church Section," *Deseret News*, 10 January 1970.

[51] For information on the group, see "Church Section," *Deseret News*, 23 October 1971; and *The New York Times*, 6 April 1972. Much of the following is based on Wayne Swensen, "The Genesis Group: The Beginning or the End," Senior seminar paper, Brigham Young University, 1972.

[52] *Ensign* 2 (July 1972): 203.

[53] "Black Group Clings to Mormon Church Despite Restriction," *The New York Times*, 30 April 1978.

[54] Thomas F. O'Dea, "Sources of Strain in Mormon History Reconsidered," in Marvin S. Hill and James B. Allen, eds., *Mormonism and American Culture* (New York, 1972), p. 167.

[55] *Deseret News*, June 9, 1978. The full text of the announcement also appeared in *The New York Times*, June 10, 1978, and was followed by additional comment in the next day's edition. There was also comment in the *Deseret News* and Salt Lake City *Tribune* for several days after the announcement.

[56] A good biography of Kimball is Edward L. Kimball and Andrew E. Kimball, Jr., *Spencer W. Kimball: Twelfth President of The Church of Jesus Christ of Latter-day Saints* (Salt Lake City, 1977).

[57] Thomas Wood (text) and Douglas Hill (photographs), "The Coalville Tabernacle: A Photographic Essay," *Dialogue* 2 (Summer 1967): 63–74; Mark Leone, "Why the Coalville Tabernacle Had to Be Razed: Principles Governing Mormon Architecture," *Dialogue* 7 (Summer 1973): 30–39; and Edward Geary and Paul G. Salisbury, "Roundtable on the Coalville Tabernacle," *Dialogue* 5 (Winter 1970): 41–58.

[58] See the special section on Mormon architecture in *Dialogue* 3 (Spring 1968): 17–28; Fred Buchanan, "Cornerstone: Meeting Place of Past and Future," *Dialogue* 8 (Summer 1973): 106–7; and Douglas Hill, "Early Mormon Churches in Utah—A Photographic Essay," *Dialogue* 1 (Autumn 1966): 13–19.

[59] Claudia L. Bushman, "*Exponent II* Is Born," *Exponent II*, July 1974.

[60] "Statement of Purpose," *Dialogue* 1 (Spring 1966): inside front cover.

[61] G. Wesley Johnson, "Editorial Preface," *Dialogue* 1 (Spring 1966): 6. For other statements on *Dialogue*'s purposes and progress, see Eugene England, "The Possibility of Dialogue—A Personal View," *Dialogue* 1 (Spring 1966): 8–11; Garth L. Mangum, "A

Progress Report on *Dialogue*," *Dialogue* 3 (Autumn 1970): 38–40; Robert A. Rees, "The Possibilities of *Dialogue*," *Dialogue* 4 (Autumn 1974): 4–5; and "An Interview with Eugene England," *The Carpenter: Reflections on Mormon Life* (Madison, Wis.), Spring 1970, pp. 9–23.

[62] Scott Kenney, "Letter to the Editor," *Dialogue* 9 (Summer 1974): 5.

[63] This tradition of a kind of extracurricular church has a long history in Mormonism. Davis Bitton, "Study Groups in Pioneer Utah," 1973 (typescript in possession of the authors). To our knowledge no one has made a systematic study of those operating at present, but from our personal knowledge we are aware of several hundred such groups.

[64] *The Pearl of Great Price*, rev. ed. (Salt Lake City, 1952), the last of thirteen Articles of Faith.

[65] See Lorin Wheelwright, ed., *Mormon Arts,* vol. 1 (Provo, Utah, 1972).

[66] See Jill C. Mulvay, "Three Mormon Women in the Cultural Arts," *Sunstone* 1 (Spring 1976): 29–39; Allen Roberts, "Utah's Unknown Pioneer Architects: Their Lives and Works," *Sunstone* 1 (Spring 1976): 67–85; Allen Roberts, "More of Utah's Unknown Pioneer Architects: Their Lives and Works," *Sunstone* 1 (Fall 1976): 42–56; Paul L. Anderson, "William Harrison Folsom: Pioneer Architect," *Utah Historical Quarterly* 43 (Summer 1975): 240–59; Peter L. Goss, "The Architectural History of Utah," *Utah Historical Quarterly* 43 (Summer 1975): 208–39; James L. Haseltine, "Mormons and the Visual Arts," *Dialogue* 1 (Summer 1966): 17–29; idem, *100 Years of Utah Painting* (Salt Lake City, 1965); and *Ensign* 7 (July 1977), special issue on the arts.

[67] Doyle L. Green, "The Edsbergs: Father and Son," *Ensign* 5 (October 1975): 42–47.

[68] See evaluation by music critic Lowell Durham in *Dialogue* 3 (Summer 1968): 19–40.

[69] Some of the many books by Richard L. Evans, all brought out by a national publisher, are: *Unto the Hills* (1940); *This Day . . . and Always* (1942); *The Spoken Word* (1945); *At the Same Hour* (1949); *Tonic for Our Times* (1952); *From the Cross Roads* (1955); *The Everlasting Things* (1957); *From Within These Walls* (1959); *May Peace Be with You* (1961); *Faith in the Future* (1963).

[70] Examples of Mormon treatment of their folklore are Hector Lee, *The Three Nephites: The Substance and Significance of the Legend in Folklore* (Albuquerque, N.M., 1949); Austin and Alta Fife, *Saints of Sage and Saddle: Folklore among the Mormons* (Bloomington, Ind., 1956); Thomas E. Cheney, ed., *Lore of Faith and Folly* (Salt Lake City, 1971); and William A. Wilson, "The Study of Mormon Folklore," *Utah Historical Quarterly* 44 (Fall 1976): 317–28. Works on J. Golden Kimball include S. Claude Richards, *J. Golden Kimball: The Story of a Unique Personality* (Salt Lake City, 1966); Thomas E. Cheney, *The Golden Legacy: A Folk History of J. Golden Kimball* (Santa Barbara, Calif., and Salt Lake City, 1973); and "The Golden Legend," in the Fife volume, pp. 304–15. A more recent female personality who has generated considerable folklore is Jessie Evans Smith, wife of President Joseph Fielding Smith. See Linda W. Harris, "The Legend of Jessie Evans Smith," *Utah Historical Quarterly* 44 (Fall 1976): 351–64. Works by non-Mormons that have treated Mormon folklore include Wallace Stegner, *Mormon Country* (New York, 1942); Richard M. Dorson, "Utah Mormons," in his *Buying the Wind: Regional Folklore in the United States* (Chicago and London, 1964), pp. 497–535; and Jan Brunvand, *A Guide for Collectors of Folklore in Utah* (Salt Lake City, 1971).

[71] Joseph M. Flora, "Vardis Fisher and the Mormons," *Dialogue* 4 (Autumn 1969): 48–55. A revisionist article that corrects some earlier assumptions is Leonard J. Arrington and Jon Haupt, "The Mormon Heritage of Vardis Fisher," *BYU Studies* 18 (Fall 1977): 27–47.

[72] Review by Chad Walsh in *Saturday Review*, 16 April 1960. A comprehensive study

is Mary Lythgoe, "Virginia Sorensen: An Introduction" (Master's thesis, University of Utah, 1956).

[73] Quoted in Kathleen Lubeck, "Two Mormon Writers: Translating the Peculiar Culture into Words," *BYU Today*, April 1977, pp. 4-6.

[74] Ibid.

[75] For a survey of current Mormon drama, see Frederick Bliss and P. Q. Gump, "Mormon Shakespeares: A Study of Contemporary Mormon Theatre," *Sunstone* 1 (Spring 1976): 54-66.

[76] An unsuccessful effort to produce a Mormon comedy was a 1968 play by Don C. Liljenquist, *Woman Is My Idea*, reviewed by C. Lowell Lees in *Dialogue* 4 (1969): 109-11. Earlier, in the 1920s, Joseph J. Cannon's *Wild Pigeons* essayed a Broadway opening.

[77] *Dialogue* 1 (Summer 1966): 100, with the permission of the publisher and author. See also Carol Lynn Pearson, *Beginnings* (1968), *The Search* (1970), and *Growing Season* (1976) (all publ. Provo, Utah). See also selections of other Mormon poets in Richard H. Cracroft and Neal E. Lambert, comps., *A Believing People: Literature of the Latter-day Saints* (Provo, Utah, 1974), pp. 249-328.

[78] Edward L. Hart, *Improvement Era* 67 (July 1964): 574, with the permission of the publisher and author.

[79] Wayne K. Hinton, "A Biographical History of Mahonri M. Young, A Western American Artist" (Ph.D. diss., Brigham Young University, 1974); Richard Oman and Susan Oman, "A Passion for Painting: Minerva Kohlhepp Teichert," *Ensign* 6 (December 1976): 52-58.

[80] A more extensive treatment of what follows is Leonard J. Arrington, "Crisis in Identity: Mormon Responses in the Nineteenth and Twentieth Centuries," in James Allen and Marvin Hill, eds., *Mormonism and American Culture* (New York, 1972), pp. 168-84. Used by permission.

[81] Richard D. Poll, "What the Church Means to People Like Me," *Dialogue* 2 (Winter 1967): 107-17. In another context, Father Eugene Kennedy of the Roman Catholic Church suggests the terms "extrinsic" religionists, who rely on rules, rituals, and dogmas, and seek authoritative answers to all their questions, and "intrinsic" religionists, who constantly raise questions, are willing to undergo a life of risk, and emphasize the humanness in man and society. See *Newsweek*, 4 October 1971, p. 88.

Index

Index

A Note About the Authors

Leonard J. Arrington was born in Twin Falls, Idaho, in 1917. Educated at the Universities of Idaho and North Carolina, he is the author of several books on the history of the Mormons and the American West, among them *Great Basin Kingdom: An Economic History of the Latter-day Saints, 1830–1900* (1958). He is also a regular contributor to many scholarly journals, and has received a number of awards. Mr. Arrington has taught at North Carolina State, UCLA, and Utah State University, and since 1972 has been both Director of the History Division of the Church of Jesus Christ of Latter-day Saints and the Lemuel Redd Professor of Western History at Brigham Young University.

Davis Bitton was born in Blackfoot, Idaho, in 1930. He has degrees from Brigham Young and Princeton Universities, and has taught at the University of Texas and the University of California at Santa Barbara. At present he is Professor of History at the University of Utah. Mr. Bitton is the author of *The French Nobility in Crisis, 1560–1640* (1969), as well as three other books and numerous articles for historical and Mormon journals.

Both Mr. Arrington and Mr. Bitton are residents of Salt Lake City, Utah.